Solving the Simpson
Murder Mystery

Y0-EKP-020

Christopher Springer

New evidence exposes the **real** killer

Solving the Simpson Murder Mystery

The O.J. book which dares to explain it all

Springer USA, Inc.

Special thanks to Charlene

who has been my

"Simpson case Encyclopedia"

Christopher Springer

75% of all Americans polled believe O.J. murdered Nicole and Ron.

This book is written for *"the other 25%"* **who can think** and, therefore, trust O.J. – more than they trust the perjuring Mark Fuhrman and Philip Vannatter!

Notice!

Any statement regarding some-one's actions, motives, guilt, or innocence, as set forth anywhere in my book – even when not specifically so stated in each case – represents my personal theory or opinion, only – and not proven facts.

All persons mentioned anywhere in my book should, therefore, throughout this book – as well as in reality – be considered innocent of any crime or act of professional misconduct suggested anywhere in my book, unless confessing to same, or until proven guilty of same in a court of law.

Christopher Springer

CONTENTS

Clarifying a matter of "speech"

A few people who read the manuscript to this book before its printing, pointed out a problem they had with a particular part of my "speech," before they grew accustomed to it. They suggested that I clarify this in an introductory notice, which I hereby do.

The book you are about to read makes countless references to statements and claims by investigators, prosecutors, plaintiffs and others, regarding the evidence and O.J.'s presumed guilt. Much of what they said was **factually incorrect**, although it is **actually correct** that they did say it, claim it, think it, argue it – or whatever.

I felt a need to emphasize it – whenever I could – if such statements, claims, thoughts, arguments etc. – in **my** opinion and/or in reality – were **factually** false, although the statements, arguments, etc. were **actually** made.

Perhaps, an example will best illustrate this. Referring to the book dispute between Vannatter and Lange on one side, and Fuhrman on the other, I write somewhere in chapter 29:

> *"... Both parties were invited on national TV to talk about all the evidence against O.J., that someone had missed or bungled – but which* "clearly proved" *that O.J. **were** guilty!"*

Of course, normally, we would say *"... the evidence which clearly proved that O.J. **was** guilty!"*

I use **were** instead of **was** to emphasize that although **Vannatter and Fuhrman** actually claimed that this evidence proved O.J. guilty – in **my** opinion O.J. is innocent, and this so-called evidence **factually** does **not** prove O.J. guilty.

My readers will find this use of I/he/she/it **were** instead of I/he/she/it **was** quite a few places. Chances are you won't even notice it. I just want you to be aware that it is **deliberate**, to emphasize that I **disagree** with the content of the statement or the claim that is being made.

Christopher Springer

CHAPTER 1

Only In America!

Nicole's and Ron's murderer, the **real** murderer, purposely planted some evidence which pointed straight to O.J. – like the Rockingham glove and the blood in the Bronco. This evidence should convince the investigators, immediately, that O.J. were guilty.

However, the murderer also planted a lot of other – **neutral** – evidence, which can best be described as *"a sloppy mess."* This evidence, in its pristine state, as it appeared at the crime scenes, did not implicate anyone – not O.J., and not the murderer. It simply served as **"bait"** for the investigators.

Mostly, this evidence was made up of Nicole's blood, purposely planted and spread "everywhere." In addition there were the Bundy glove and the knit cap.

If the investigators were convinced that O.J. were guilty, they could use this **neutral** evidence – tamper with it, replace it, or plant blood, hairs and fibers on it – to make O.J. appear **more** guilty! That was the murderer's plan, and it was a "clever" one!

Detective Vannatter took the "bait" and **immediately** replaced some of Nicole's blood swatches from Bundy with false O.J. blood swatches – in the crime lab. The murderer could not have done that – he did not have access to O.J.'s blood. Only an investigator could have done it! So, from that moment on, the investigators could never, later, come after the **real** killer – without exposing their own evidence "fabrication." Hence, even if they, later, realized that O.J. was innocent, **the investigators had to continue pursuing him with ever more falsely fabricated evidence –** thereby protecting the **real** killer – in order to protect **themselves**!

What was the murderer's motives? Obviously, he wanted to harm both Nicole and O.J. His motive was hate – racial hate for the successful African-American O.J., and hate for the white woman who had once had the audacity to choose this man over any from her own race. Later another motive took over – the challenge of the crime. Proving that his plan was near perfect, and daring to carry it out, became an irresistible challenge for the murderer.

What murderer would know enough about the LAPD to be able to figure out such a diabolic murder scheme? There is a saying: *"It takes one – to know one"*!

The case against O.J. Simpson should never even have been brought before the court. Rarely ever have I seen a murder more obviously "set up" to frame an innocent man, than the murder of Nicole Brown Simpson. **All the evidence** cried out,

"Frame up – set-up – conspiracy!"

This book will prove it. Every gravel of the so-called *"mountain of evidence"* appeared to have been fabricated, planted, or tampered with.

A confirmed racist, Los Angeles Police Department (LAPD) detective, Mark Fuhrman, admitted on audio tape that LAPD officers frequently planted evidence, fabricated evidence, or did whatever was necessary to convict suspects. He also stated on tape that he got so enraged when observing racially mixed couples, that if he spotted such a couple, for instance riding together in a car, he would pull them over and cite the driver. And if the driver had not broken any laws, so there was no reason to cite him or her, Detective Fuhrman would make up something! As an example, he mentioned asking for the driver's license, tearing up the license, and subsequently, citing the driver for driving without a license!

According to Detective Fuhrman, every African American, the members of the NAACP and of the ACLU ought to be bombed or burned to death. According to Fuhrman, *"They are the cancer of society"*!

However, even as much as he hated African Americans, he hated, even more, white women having relationships with African

Americans. According to Detective Fuhrman it was *against the Law of Nature for a white woman to be in a relationship with a black man.*

There is a real motive for wanting to murder Nicole Brown Simpson – and framing her African-American ex-husband!

On the now infamous *"Fuhrman Tapes,"* Detective Fuhrman, admitted to having beaten four innocent suspects to within an eyelash of killing them. And he went on to brag about being so clever at framing innocent suspects with false evidence and lying about it on the witness stand, that he and his LAPD colleagues could easily **commit murder and get away with it!** This "psycho" allegedly "found" the second murder glove behind O.J.'s house. Detective Fuhrman was later convicted of perjury in the Simpson case.

The lead investigator, Detective Philip Vannatter, broke every rule in the book in terms of mishandling O.J.'s blood vial.

Detective Vannatter spent one and a half hours in his office, alone with O.J.'s fresh blood vial. Yet, until this was exposed in court by O.J.'s attorney, Vannatter lied on the witness stand about even bringing O.J.'s blood vial to his office.

Subsequently, 1.5 ml of the blood in O.J.'s vial ended up missing – before any lab technician even opened the vial to analyze O.J.'s blood! Later, O.J.'s blood showed up where there evidently was no blood earlier. Some of this blood even contained the blood preservative EDTA – proving that the blood could not have come from O.J.'s body directly, but must have been planted from his blood vial!

Detective Vannatter was exposed lying so many times that both the court and the media lost track of it! Even Judge Ito characterized Detective Vannatter as having a *"reckless disregard for the truth"*!

Unfortunately, when Detective Fuhrman was the only one present, how do we **prove** that he actually planted the glove behind O.J.'s house, where he said he "found" it?

When nobody was watching what Detective Vannatter was doing with O.J.'s blood vial in his office, how do we **prove** that the lead investigator fabricated false blood evidence against O.J.?

Of course, we can't. But even if we cannot **prove** it, there had to be a frame up, a set-up, and a conspiracy. Although there was an apparent *"mountain of evidence,"* there was something suspicious, something contradictory, something inconsistent, something flawed, or plainly and simply, something **"wrong"** with every single piece of evidence in the Simpson case.

Besides, the murder scene revealed clear evidence and absolute proof that O.J. was framed.

As of the day I am writing this, I am the only person who has discovered, or at least explained, what constitutes this absolute proof that O.J. was framed, and that he, therefore, is innocent.

Possibly, the detectives, the criminalists, the hired experts, the prosecutors, or the attorneys for the plaintiffs, might have discovered this revealing evidence, too. But if they did, they kept it secret, as part of the conspiracy to convict O.J., thereby covering up their own, or their colleagues' mishandling of the Simpson case.

As I bring my readers through this book, I shall demonstrate clearly what is wrong with every piece of evidence in this case. I shall demonstrate that all of it must have been fabricated, planted, or tampered with – although I can not in each case point with absolute certainty to the individual perpetrators – or specifically which method, of many, they might have used.

I shall, however, explain how it, most likely, was done. Although I can not prove specifically how each piece of evidence was fabricated, I shall do the second best thing:

I shall prove that O.J. Simpson did not murder Nicole Brown Simpson and Ronald Lyle Goldman.

Of course, that, irrefutably, proves that **all** the evidence against Mr. Simpson must have been fabricated.

Is it possible that dozens of investigators, forensic experts and prosecutors could have overlooked this? Is it possible that thousands of media reporters and legal analysts could have been so totally blind? I don't think so. There had to be a conspiracy. Otherwise, all of these people must have been carrying their head in a handbag! Yet, they could fool the entire world? How? – And why?

By the time the plaintiffs rested their case, midway through the civil trial, about 75% of the American people were convinced that O.J. were guilty of double homicide. Only about 15% believed he was innocent.

How is it possible to deceive, totally, more than 150 million people in the most technologically advanced, informed and educated country in the world? For someone who claims to have solved the Simpson case, **that** question is more intriguing than the murder mystery itself.

What created the Simpson controversy is not befitting a people who claims to constitute the greatest democracy of the world; nor is it befitting the country that most ardently criticize other countries for human rights violations.

As a society, do we dare to face the consequences and hold the culprits responsible, or will this worst scandal in our nation's jurisprudence be covered up and swept under the rug?

There are many reasons why O.J. became the victim in this case. As I point them out, it is time for the people of the United States of America to do some soul searching.

First and foremost, the Simpson case was created by a totally incompetent Los Angeles Police Department. Not only did the LAPD harbor such rogue officers as Detectives Fuhrman and Vannatter. The entire atmosphere of the LAPD was one in which such officers could be protected by the rest of the organization. And an officer like Vannatter could even be promoted and rise to the rank of senior homicide investigator.

Finding a suspect and obtaining a conviction seemed much more important than finding the **right** suspect, and obtaining a **just** conviction. Fabrication of false evidence, "testi-lying," and cover-ups seemed so rampant within the LAPD that not even the honest officers found it worthwhile to react.

First of all, this was possible because **nobody polices the police!** Even **if** a decent officer reacted to what went on, where was he going to take his complaint? To the LAPD itself, naturally!

But even the DA's office was part of the problem. With a highly politicized DA's office, several failed prosecutions, and District Attorney Gil Garcetti running for office – he simply had to win the Simpson case.

Besides, crime is such a serious problem in Los Angeles, that people accepted police misconduct – as the least of two evils.

The brunt of the Simpson scandal rests with the media, though. U.S. media is not famous for restraint and objectivity. Several European countries would not even have allowed the media to cover the case before the trial. Influenced by deliberate "leaks" from both the LAPD and the DA's office, U.S. reporters, though, would gladly step over corpses to "solve" the Simpson case, even before the police had arrested Mr. Simpson.

Every day, we can witness corrupt police departments all over the U.S., because no powerful organization entrusted to police itself has ever resisted corruption.

We see the same among top executives in major corporations. While smaller stockholders suffer the hazards of a volatile stock market, a few executives – with the power to do it – can get together behind closed doors in a board room and grant each other stock options and bonuses worth tens of millions of dollars. Politicians are not much different, accepting millions in contributions from lobbyists for special interest groups, in return for tax breaks and other benefits for wealthy multinational corporations.

The media represent, perhaps, the most powerful institution in the U.S. Yet, the media act and behave as if they were totally above the law. Nobody polices the media either – nobody but the media themselves.

Rather early, it must have become evident to most reporters that O.J. was innocent, and that the media had made a terrible mistake in prejudging him. Instead of correcting themselves, the media, too, covered up and started the worst character assassination imaginable – to protect their own image of infallibility.

The media didn't even allow O.J. to defend himself against the media's attacks. And while the TV media offered free air time for organizations and individuals to raise money to attack and sue O.J., he was not even allowed to **purchase** air time to promote his video to present his side of the case and support his family and pay his legal expenses.

But O.J. was fighting even tougher odds. In the wake of the Kennedy Smith acquittal, Anita Hill's adversities during the Clarence Thomas senate hearings, the Mike Tyson rape case, and an increase in domestic violence – powerful women's organizations were just waiting for a victim they could identify with. Nicole Brown Simpson was that victim. And O.J. became the defenseless villain they could attack to further their cause.

Various women's organizations staged candle light vigils and demonstrations as much attacking O.J., as honoring Nicole's memory.

The race issue! No question about it. The Simpson case was racially motivated, right from day one. In spite of what we like to believe, the U.S. is still seething with racism.

We saw it in the Rodney King case. We see it in the epidemic of racial murders of young black motorists, committed by white police officers. We see it in the spread of neo-nazi and white supremacist organizations across the nation, and in the burning of churches belonging to black congregations.

The atrocities that occurred during our, not too distant, age of slavery, was not simply the acts of a few ruthless, immoral criminals. Rather it was the "law of the land" and the **convictions** of an entire southern population, that Africans were an inferior race that could be enslaved, sold, exploited, abused, flogged, abducted, raped and murdered. White children believed that. White women believed that. The media believed that. Politicians believed that. The justice system, then, believed that.

Unless slavery and racism were concepts deeply embedded in

the spirit of the American people, such atrocities could never have flourished as they did. Today, racism is checked by criminal laws and threat of punishment. But deep inside the souls of countless white people lies the evil seed ready to surface. When put to the test, most whites **will** believe that O.J. is, at least, *a little bit more guilty — because **he** is **black**, and **Nicole and Ron** were **white***.

Otherwise, how can we explain that 75% of all blacks thought O.J. was innocent towards the end of the criminal case, while 75% of all whites thought he were guilty?

In explaining the odds O.J. was fighting I want to return to the media. Even if the media were protecting themselves and covering up their serious misjudgment, how could they persuade 150 million Americans to go along with them, if the evidence so clearly demonstrated that the media were wrong and O.J. was innocent?

The answer lies in the very format of modern day American journalism. Look at the leaders in TV news broadcasting. Each day's entire world and national news is presented in less than 20 minutes of actual newscasts. Major events are condensed to 5-15 second "sound bytes."

Perhaps the most important persons in the news staffs are the ones who condense a major news story to a 10 second sound byte that can persuade the audience to stay with the network through the next **commercial**.

Even the programs designed to discuss certain topics in more depth, quickly deteriorate into shouting matches where nobody is allowed to speak uninterruptedly for more than a few seconds, and none of the participants are making the faintest effort to listen to their opponent's arguments.

This explains better than anything why U.S. media could persuade 150 million Americans to believe O.J. murdered Nicole and Ron.

Take the knit cap that was found at the Bundy murder scene!

"Hairs on Cap Tie O.J. to Murder Scene!"

That was a typical headline from newspapers, or a typical five second sound byte from TV newscasts. This was all that most of the public saw and heard – or understood – about that cap. Add to it the gloves and the blood – O.J. is guilty!

If a reporter or a journalist wanted to raise a question about the cap, he would be told by his producer or editor to do it in 15 seconds or in three lines. The media don't want people to think. The media prefer to present the news in short headlines or sound bytes the public can swallow without thinking!

So, few ever raised questions like this:

Why would an African-American murderer wear a dark, knit ski cap in Los Angeles at 10:30 pm in the middle of June?

The cap didn't disguise the murderer. To the contrary, it was certain to **draw attention to** the murderer should he run into someone on his way to or from the murder scene. Hence, the cap could not possibly have been worn as a **disguise**.

I assume nobody suggests the ski cap was worn to keep the murderer's ears warm in the middle of the summer! I like to hear anyone suggest another purpose of the cap, adversary to O.J.

It is true that there were twelve hairs on the cap, similar to O.J.'s. But the very presence of the cap suggested that those hairs were planted by the investigators – since there was no logical explanation for the presence of the cap. Besides, there were six black, "treated" hairs on the cap – none of them were O.J.'s!

There were also two caucasian hairs on the cap. Those hairs were dyed – they were originally light brown. They were never identified as belonging to anyone associated with the case. How can that be reconciled with O.J. being the murderer? The only purpose of the cap, as far as I can see, is that

the cap was deliberately brought along, to be left by the murderer, thereby giving the police investigators the **opportunity** to plant O.J.'s hairs on it.

Fifteen seconds sound bytes, or newspaper headlines never got around to discussing such possibilities. It was the same with every piece of evidence in the Simpson case. In 15 seconds sound bytes and in newspaper headlines the evidence seemed overwhelming against O.J. But for anyone with the brains to put two and two together, all the evidence actually exonerated O.J. Here are a few more such **"news flowers"**:

"Bloody Murder Glove Found behind O.J.'s House!"

The inference was, of course, that O.J. were guilty. But what was the glove doing there? Who put it there? What murderer would remove one bloody murder glove at the murder scene and leave it there, but bring the other bloody glove to his home and dispose of it behind his own house before leaving for Chicago? And especially – if O.J. were guilty – why would O.J. do that, if he obviously knew how to get rid of the murder weapon, the bloody clothes, and the bloody shoes?

And why was no blood found near the Rockingham glove, when there **allegedly** were a trail of blood from the bodies of the victims at Bundy, and all the way into O.J.'s foyer at Rockingham? Why was the blood on that glove still wet, and why were there no insects or debris on the Rockingham glove when Detective Fuhrman, allegedly, "found" the glove – almost seven and a half hours after O.J. had left for Chicago?

L et us, just for a minute, assume that O.J. were the killer, and that he lost his left glove at Bundy, without noticing it – how incredible that may seem – and that he, therefore, left Bundy with only one glove! If not before, then, at the latest, when he were driving back to Rockingham, with both hands – one gloved and one bare – on the steering wheel just inches from his face, O.J. must have realized that he had lost one glove at Bundy.

At that moment, he **must** have realized that since his **left** glove were at **Bundy**, the worst possible thing he could do would be to leave the bloody **right** glove at **his house**. Anything but that! Throw it out the car window – or whatever. But for all the gold in Africa – don't leave that other glove at Rockingham.

[Don't forget that we are still **hypothesizing**!]

Give O.J. some credit! Using the sharp murder knife, couldn't he have cut the glove into two strips, and flushed them down his toilet? Or couldn't he have put the strips in a plastic bag, stuck the bag in his pocket, and brought the strips with him onboard the plane to Chicago? There, on the plane he could have flushed the other murder glove down the airplane's toilet – in two flushes. Then, half of the later labelled **"Rockingham glove"** would have landed somewhere in the Rocky Mountains, and the other somewhere in Utah!

Uh-uh! Knowing that the **left** glove was lost at Bundy – according to his adversaries – O.J. decided to throw away the **right** glove behind **his house**! Give me a break!

Like the cap, the bloody murder gloves were obviously part of the real murderer's elaborate scheme to frame O.J.

Typically, in his book, *"Murder in Brentwood,"* former LAPD Detective Mark Fuhrman is spreading the "news" that the morning after the murders, he saw *"O.J.'s dark blue/black sweat suit"* in O.J.'s washing machine at Rockingham.

There has been a lot of media hype about this imaginary – supposedly bloody – dark sweat suit, which O.J. **allegedly** should have worn when he were over at Bundy killing Nicole and Ron!

Uncritically, during Fuhrman's **book promoting interviews**, the media let Mark Fuhrman "inform" us that he "saw" this sweat suit in O.J.'s washing machine the morning after the murders. Allegedly, he and one of the police officers at Rockingham, Brad Roberts, looked at the sweat suit together, and Brad Roberts then showed it to two of the detectives from the LAPD's Robbery/Homicide division, only hours after the murders.

WOW! That sure is incriminating to O.J.! So that's what he did with his bloody sweat suit! He put it in his washing machine – before he left for Chicago! Now we know –

Mark Fuhrman and the media told us!

The LAPD searched everywhere for that imaginary sweat suit. They checked every sewer drain from Bundy to Rockingham – and even farther. No sweat suit. Then they searched all over O.J.'s Rockingham estate. They also considered that O.J. might have put the sweat suit in a bag and dumped it in a waste can at the airport. Hence, they searched all over the L.A. airport. Negative! So, they searched the O'Hare airport in Chicago, as well as the hotel O.J. stayed in. Negative! Then, Prosecutor Marcia Clark suggested that O.J. had brought the bag with the bloody sweat suit back to Los Angeles and given it to his attorney friend, Robert Kardashian!

All for nothing! The bloody sweat suit was in O.J.'s washing machine! What a smart hiding place! No wonder Detective Vannatter & Co. didn't think about checking there! Only Fuhrman thought about that – but he didn't tell anyone about what he found – until it was time to write a book!

Evidently, O.J. knew how to get rid of the bloody knife and the bloody shoes. But I guess – even with the LAPD in hot pursuit – O.J. didn't want to throw away his sweat suit – at least, not until he had washed it!

On their TV shows, how can Larry King, Tom Brokaw, Geraldo Rivera, and Charles Grodin, with straight faces, sit and listen to Mark Fuhrman explain to the American People where *"O.J.'s dark sweat suit"* was – and not even question him about his remarkable discovery?

Are my readers beginning to understand how the U.S. media brain washed those 75% of us who don't think? Here is another typical newspaper headline or TV sound byte:

"Victims' Bloods Found In O.J.'s Bronco!"

Again, the inference was, of course, that O.J. were guilty. But how could Detective Fuhrman claim to have seen those faint blood stains against the light brown interior of the Bronco, at five o'clock in the morning, simultaneously denying that he opened the Bronco's door?

And why was some of the blood in the Bronco **not** there on the day after the murders, but showed up in the Bronco several weeks later? Next:

"Nicole's Blood Found on O.J.'s Sock!"

Same inference. But why was that blood not there when the socks were examined – twice – shortly after they were collected into evidence? There were written lab reports to that effect. News reporters didn't bother with such details!

And why was there EDTA in Nicole's blood on that sock, but not in the fabric of the sock itself? And why was the concentration of EDTA in the blood on the sock **exactly the same** as the concentration of EDTA in the blood on **swatches prepared as reference samples** from Nicole's blood on her dress? Had someone transferred some of the blood from Nicole's dress onto one of O.J.'s socks?

The plaintiffs and their "experts" in the civil trial "explained" that the blood on the sock could not have come from the EDTA vial of Nicole's blood that the police received from the coroner, because Nicole's blood in the vial contained a much higher concentration of EDTA than the blood on O.J.'s sock. **The blood on the sock must have come from the same source as the blood on the dress – namely, from Nicole's body, directly – they argued!**

Besides, they argued, **had** Nicole's blood on O.J.'s sock come from the EDTA vial, it should have been more **contaminated**, because that blood stayed moist longer than blood which, for instance, had been smeared onto a piece of clothing! This conclusion – in itself – is plausible. We all know that bacterial growth is furthered by moisture and warmth, and the blood inside Nicole's body – from which her EDTA vial was prepared – definitely stayed moist and warm longer than blood she might have smeared on O.J.'s sock.

The "scientists" pointed out that the degree of contamination in the blood on O.J.'s sock, was in the same range as the degree of contamination in Nicole's blood on her dress.

What a series of arguments! Not one news reporter or talk show host understood that the contamination and the concentration of EDTA in Nicole's blood **on the swatches prepared from Nicole's dress**, were almost exactly identical to the contamination and the concentration of EDTA in Nicole's blood **on O.J.'s sock**, because

> the criminalists, who – weeks after the murders, in the LAPD's crime lab – prepared **wet swatches** from the blood on Nicole's dress, had simultaneously **moistened O.J.'s sock** and pressed it against the same bloody section of Nicole's dress – in the exact same manner he transferred the blood onto the wet swatches he prepared as reference samples from Nicole's dress?

EDTA is an anti-coagulant chemical. If Nicole's blood (in her body) had an EDTA concentration close to the one in the blood on her dress, or on O.J.'s sock – **Nicole would have bled to death in her sleep**, long before any murderer could have gotten to her. This lethal concentration of EDTA can be explained as having come from detergent residues in the fabric of Nicole's dress.

Nicole's wet blood on her dress absorbed some of this detergent EDTA on the night of her murder. Later, when the criminalists in the LAPD's crime lab, moistened the blood on the dress, and transferred it to their wet swatches, they got this same EDTA concentration in the blood on their swatches.

> However, if a "smart ass" among the criminalists, **simultaneously**, also moistened O.J.'s sock and pressed it against the same blood spot on Nicole's dress – the EDTA concentration (and contamination) in Nicole's blood on O.J.'s sock would, of course, be almost exactly the same as the EDTA concentration (and contamination) in Nicole's blood on her dress! **We certainly didn't need a Ph.d. in biochemistry to understand that – or what?**

Because the media never analyzed the evidence – only threw it out for their audiences in short newspaper headlines and TV sound bytes – they made O.J. appear as guilty as sin, while in fact every piece of evidence in this case clearly supported the theory that he was being framed – not only by the murderer, but also by the investigators! Those were some of the adverse odds O.J. had to contend with.

I**t is time to set things straight, and solve this murder mystery! It doesn't take a "rocket scientist" to do it. Just someone with everyday common sense – like you or me!**

If my readers will allow me, I shall take all of you on a tour of the Simpson case. I guarantee that you will be in for quite a revelation! But be patient! Although I, as the only one at this time, have discovered evidence which can clearly be characterized as **"Perry Mason" evidence, or "the smoking gun" evidence,** there are several issues we need to discuss first, so you may have the background knowledge necessary to understand this particular revealing evidence, as well as all the rest of the evidence, and all that went on in this case.

Furthermore, my goal is not simply to prove that O.J. was framed. I shall prove **how** he was framed – and **why.** I shall explain where every piece of evidence came from – or might have come from – and how it was – or could have been – fabricated or planted.

Most of all, however, I assume my readers want to know the answers to the questions:

Who murdered Nicole and Ron – if O.J. didn't?
Why were they murdered?
How were they murdered?
And, how did the murderer escape justice?

So allow me to walk you through this murder mystery from the beginning! That way you will better understand the real evidence in the case, once we get around to it.

CHAPTER 2

"Cockroaches"

O.J.'s adversaries argued that the concept of **reasonable doubt** in the criminal trial put the prosecution at a disadvantage. The true test of O.J.'s guilt or innocence would be reflected through the outcome of the civil case, where a (9 to 3) majority of the jurors decided – by a **preponderance** of the evidence – whether it is more likely than not that O.J., **rather than someone else**, killed Nicole and Ron.

> I know this is the **law**, but it is still absolutely outrageous! **It is a law the U.S. does not share with any other civilized, or uncivilized country in the world!**

First of all, where and when is this ordeal going to end? Imagine O.J., who was found innocent by a **unanimous** jury of mixed ethnic background, both genders, and all ages! In spite of being found innocent, O.J. would later risk losing all his assets to the families of the two people whose murders he had no part in – in a **second** trial, where his adversaries did not even have to prove, beyond a reasonable doubt, that he be the murderer!

Of course, we all know that O.J. lost the civil trial. But hypothetically, had O.J. prevailed by a margin of 5 to 7, for instance, the plaintiffs could have appealed that verdict, I assume, and started all over again. Even if the verdict were 12 to 0 – unanimously in O.J.'s favor – he would have had no recourse against the plaintiffs, in terms of recovering his legal costs! I am baffled by the U.S. justice system, and by legislators who have passed such laws!

Secondly, if there is, at least, some circumstantial evidence against a defendant, like a construed motive and some physical evidence (which the real murderer could have planted, or the investigators could have fabricated) – then the **preponderance**

of the evidence requires that

> **the defendant** – who in most cases have no resources and no investigative training – **must solve a murder mystery which the police have failed to solve,**

. . . by demonstrating and convincing the jurors that, in spite of this evidence, it is more likely that **someone else**, rather than the defendant, is the murderer!

Again, this is an outrageous law, which throughout the rest of the world has made the U.S. justice system the laughing stock among international legal scholars.

The mere notion of someone – with or without resources and investigative training – **having to prove his innocence,** is unheard of in any other civilized country!

How do you prove a **"negative"**?
How do you prove that you did **not** do something?

Let me give you an example (and there will be many of them throughout this book):

> A **bird** flies in through an open dining room window, while a young boy is home alone, in the adjacent living room, sitting on the couch, with his basketball in his lap, and watching TV.
>
> In the dining room, the panic stricken bird flaps around. The bird knocks a crystal vase off the dining table. The vase falls to the floor and shatters. Then the bird escapes through the open window.
>
> The boy hears the noise and enters the dining room after the bird has escaped. He shuts the window. Then he tosses his basketball over towards a corner of the dining room and begins to pick up the broken pieces.
>
> In the meantime, the boy's mother returned from shopping and entered the kitchen through the garage, just as the vase hit the floor. She put her groceries on the kitchen counter and

locked the garage door before walking towards the dining room.

The boy's basketball is still bouncing when she enters! With an expression leaving little doubt as to what she is thinking, she looks at the ball and then at her son's hands, holding some of the shattered pieces of what was once an expensive crystal vase.

The boy knows what his mother is thinking and starts crying.

> _"Mom! I didn't do it ... It was already broken ... I wasn't playing with the ball ... "_

His mother isn't listening.

The ball rebounded softly off the wall, and it comes rolling back ... slowly ... from the corner and out towards the middle of the room. The boy shivers for a second as the ball comes to a halt, resting against his mother's right ankle.

> _"Your father gave me that vase – full of roses – when he proposed to me! It was my most precious possession! ... You know what I've said about playing with your basketball indoors ... As if breaking the vase wasn't enough – have you started lying to your mother now?"_

The boy, who knows nothing about the bird, obviously, appears to be guilty – beyond **any** doubt! How in heavens name can the boy **prove** that **he** did **not** break the vase?

- How can you **prove** that you did **not** run a stop sign driving home from work yesterday – if you know you didn't, but a police officer claims you did?
- If you live alone, how can you **prove** you did **not** eat dinner last Wednesday?
- If someone slashed your neighbor's tires last night, while you were home alone sleeping, and nobody saw who did it, how can you **prove** that **you** did **not** do it?

You can often prove that someone is guilty – prove that they **did** something. But (without an alibi or witnesses) to prove a **"negative"** – to prove that you did **not** do something – is often impossible. You can only claim that you did not do it!

That is why every civilized country in the world requires that the prosecution, **in a criminal trial,** prove the defendant's guilt – **beyond a reasonable doubt.** And the law does not require that the defendant – in a criminal trial – **proves his innocence,** or even tries to explain how **he** believes the crime occurred.

Only in the U.S. can you be found **not guilty** of murder, by a unanimous jury of your peers, and then later be found responsible for the victim's death, anyway – because you are unable to prove that **someone else,** more likely than yourself, committed the murder!

> I certainly hope and pray that nobody is murdered in your back yard while you are home alone, sleeping – with a cut on your finger!

The evidence in the Simpson case simply does not support a guilty verdict! Whatever evidence there is – some way or another – every single piece of it is flawed. I won't say that every piece of evidence is fabricated, or absolutely unreliable, or worthless. What I am saying though, is that there are minor or major flaws with every single piece of evidence amassed against O.J.:

- Why was the blood on the Rockingham glove wet more than 7 hours after O.J. had left for Chicago?
- Why didn't the gloves fit O.J.?
- Why was there "no blood apparent" on the socks when they were first examined? Then, six weeks after the murders, Nicole's blood was detected on one of the socks!
- Why was there EDTA in the blood on the socks?
- Two of the three blood drops on the Bundy gate didn't show up on photographs taken shortly after the murders.
  Yet, they showed up 3 weeks later – containing EDTA! Why?

- LAPD Detective Mark Fuhrman denied having opened the door to O.J.'s Bronco on the morning of June 13, 1994. Yet, the blood spots Fuhrman reportedly saw on the Bronco's doorsill, could hardly be seen, unless the door was opened. Did Fuhrman open the Bronco's door and smear blood from the Rockingham glove inside? Or did someone smear those blood spots on the doorsill later, to corroborate Fuhrman's false testimony?

- Some of the blood spots that were found in the Bronco three weeks after the murders, and six weeks after the murders, were not there on the day after the murders! Why?

- Why would someone wear a knit ski cap for disguise – or to keep his ears warm – in the middle of June?

- Where did the unidentified hairs on that cap come from?

- Caucasian, blond, light brown hairs were found on both the knit cap and on the Rockingham glove! Why didn't the investigators try harder to identify those hairs?

- Were those hairs from the same Caucasian person? If so, how could this person's hairs end up on **both** the **cap** and the **murder glove** unless this person was directly involved in the murders?

- Why didn't Ron scream for help?

- How could O.J. have been bleeding profusely at the murder scene, then stopped bleeding outside the rear gate at Bundy and not bleed a single drop in the Bronco (except for a minuscule smear that might have been planted), then started again in his driveway, but stopped when he – allegedly – went behind his house where the glove was "found," but started again in his foyer, but stopped again before he went upstairs to his bedroom?

- Did O.J. have a "faucet" on the cut on his finger, so he could shut the bleeding off, or turn it on, at will?

- Why did the police nurse place O.J.'s blood vial in an unauthorized, unsealed envelope, before handing it over to the lead investigator, Detective Philip Vannatter – who had no business even touching O.J.'s blood vial?

- Why did Detective Vannatter lie under oath, saying that he drove, with the vial, directly from the nurse's office to Rockingham, when, in fact, he went to his office instead, where he spent almost 90 minutes, alone, with O.J.'s blood vial – doing nothing, allegedly, but drink a cup of coffee?

- During those 90 minutes, alone in his office with O.J.'s blood vial, did he fabricate false blood swatches with O.J.'s blood – which could later replace the **real** blood evidence swatches collected at the crime scenes?

- What happened to the 1.5 ml of blood that undoubtedly disappeared from O.J.'s blood vial between the time Vannatter received the vial from the nurse, and the first time someone else opened it?

- Why were there wet blood transfers (that should not have been there) on the blood bindels Ms. Andrea Mazzola, allegedly, prepared from the five blood drops alongside the bloody shoeprints at Bundy – causing the renown criminalist, Dr. Henry Lee, to exclaim, *"Something is wrong!"*?

- When Ms. Mazzola's blood evidence bindels were opened up to be analyzed at the FBI's crime lab, why were her initials missing from some of those blood evidence bindels, when she testified under oath that she put her initials on **all** the **real** evidence bindels she prepared from Bundy?
  Were her bindels replaced by someone in the LAPD's crime lab, before the blood evidence was sent out to the FBI's crime lab to be analyzed?

- How could a whole bunch of fibers from the Bronco's carpet – **allegedly** – be transferred from O.J. to Ron's shirt? Did O.J. roll on the floor of his Bronco, driving to Bundy?

- How could another fiber from the Bronco's carpet end up on the knit cap, if O.J. allegedly wore it on his head? Was he doing headstands, too, in the Bronco?

- Why did the bloody shoeprints leading away from the murder scene "turn around" and head back to the victims bodies? And why were there no blood drops next to this first set of bloody shoeprints leading away from the murder scene?

- If O.J. – allegedly – left his blood everywhere, in particular in his own house, it would be no more incriminating if his bloody fingerprints were also found in his house. Yet, in spite of all the blood that was found everywhere, and in spite of O.J. allegedly losing one glove at Bundy and one behind his house – why wasn't a single bloody fingerprint from O.J. found at any of the crime scenes?
- If a cut on O.J.'s finger, allegedly, bled all the way from the victims' bodies and into his foyer, and O.J., allegedly, climbed the fence behind his house – why wasn't there any blood on the fence, or on the ground behind his house?
- Where are the murderer's bloody clothes, bloody shoes, and bloody knife?

The list of unanswered questions could continue for pages! As I stated,

there is, indeed, something flawed or suspect tied to every single piece of evidence in the Simpson case.

CHAPTER 3

A "Legal Lynching" And The Bill Of Rights

Incited by the media, millions of Americans are so enraged with O.J. that they would gladly kill him, if they knew they could get away with it! Of course, they can't. So instead, people like former Prosecutor Darden, who had his shot at O.J. in court, but missed, and talk show hosts Charles Grodin and Geraldo Rivera, repeatedly called O.J. a *"murderer"* on national TV, hoping that they could influence the jury in the civil trial to "lynch" O.J. for them!

Every day outside the Santa Monica courthouse there were hordes of people shouting, *"Murderer – **Murderer – MURDERER!**

Had this been 1897 instead of 1997, O.J., most likely, would have been lynched by an angry white mob! O.J. was found ***"not guilty"*** in the criminal trial – not by a black juror holdout, not by a slim **black majority,** but **unanimously**, 12 – 0, by a jury of **whites,** blacks and Hispanics alike, of both genders and all ages!

In spite of that, O.J. was returned to the courtroom in what can only be described as a **"legal lynching"** of a black man by a white majority community!

The **white** lynch mob hauled the acquitted **Negro** back into their own local *"Star Chamber"* courtroom.

They assigned the case to the most prejudiced, biased, and unfair judge in their jurisdiction – Judge Hiroshi Fujisaki!

The first thing Judge Hiroshi Fujisaki did was to lock the door to his "star chamber" by excluding TV cameras in "his" court room. (By the way, I used to think that the courts belong to us – the people!)

It is true that O.J.'s attorney did not request TV cameras in the courtroom. But the **decision** not to allow TV cameras, was Judge Fujisaki's.

The judge did not want the public – African Americans in particular – to observe how he intended to exercise his **"star chamber justice"**! He didn't even allow reporters to take photographs in the "star chamber" or bring tape recorders!

Only a handful of reporters were allowed in. Through these hand picked representatives of the extremely biased and anti-O.J. media, the rest of the world would get their **interpretation** of Judge Fujisaki's **"legal lynching"**!

Those who oppose cameras in the courtrooms may disagree with me. But I think **it is the public's Constitutional right to have TV cameras in the courtrooms whenever anyone requests to put them there** – at least in criminal cases, but also in civil cases.

The Sixth Amendment to the United States Constitution, included in the Bill of Rights, reads:

> *"In all criminal prosecutions, the accused shall enjoy the right to a speedy **and public** trial by an impartial jury ..."*

In 1791, when the Bill of Rights was ratified, a "public trial" **meant to the underwriters** that

> **anyone who wished to attend a trial, to ensure himself that the trial was fair, impartial, and Constitutional, had a right to attend the trial.**

The Sixth Amendment did not in any way restrict the public's right to attend the trials, neither by gender, race, wealth, intellect, or other demographics; nor did the Sixth Amendment limit people's right to follow public trials as best they could through enhancements such as hearing aids or eyeglasses if necessary; nor did the Sixth Amendment limit the rights of people who could not personally attend a trial, to follow that trial through the media – by limiting the media's right to cover the trial on behalf of people who were otherwise prevented from learning about it.

Of course, in 1791 primitive means of communication limited the public's access to trials to those living close to the courthouse. But it was the **intentions** of the underwriters of the Sixth Amendement, that **all** trials in U.S. courthouses should be open to **all** citizen of the United States, whether he or she lived around the corner from the courthouse, or in the outer limits of the Union!

The First Amendment to the Constitution reads:

> *"Congress shall make **no law** ... abridging the freedom of speech, or of the press ..."*

In 1791, *"freedom of speech"* meant for someone to stand on a street corner and express his opinion! The underwriters of the Bill of Rights could not possibly foresee the technical revolution that were to take place over the next 200 years. But there can be no misunderstanding what their **intentions** were:

If you had a weak voice, your message might only reach a few. If you had a stronger voice, your message would carry farther. If you had access to a bullhorn or to the local press, you could express your free speech to an even larger audience. The intention behind the First Amendment was clearly that the citizens of the United States should have the right to spread their opinions to whomever they chose, not only in person, but by whatever mechanical and technical means the underwriters foresaw at that time.

Mass media in 1791 meant a local newspaper, or a book publisher. The U.S. Supreme Court, however, has interpreted the "intentions" of the First Amendment to cover whatever mechanical or technical means later appearing and being able to carry the freedom of speech. Hence, with time, the First Amendment was interpreted to include radio and television.

Had the underwriters of the Bill of Rights lived in 1996, there can be no doubt that they had included also the *"Internet"* – and added:

> *"... and any other, future means of transmitting words, sounds, and images"*!

This has been the position of the U.S. Supreme Court with respect to the First Amendment. Only lately have people become overly interested in what goes on in our courtrooms. Hence, the Supreme Court has not ruled on the **Sixth** Amendment in accordance with the **First** Amendment, or in accordance with the **intentions** of the underwriters of the Bill of Rights.

There can be no doubt, however, that the underwriters of the Bill of Rights **intended** for all U.S. citizens to be able to follow **in their entirety** any trial in a U.S. court of law, to ensure themselves that the law is followed and applied with fairness.

In 1791, just as for the First Amendment, the underwriters only envisioned citizens appearing in person in the local courtroom. But the **intentions** of the underwriters were clearly that

> **any trial** should be open to **any citizen,** by **whatever means available** – just as they intended for free speech to be exercised by whatever means available.

The U.S. Supreme Court may be a little slow in reacting. But I am convinced that it is my own, and my readers' Constitutional right, as set forth in the Bill of Rights, to attend any trial, criminal or common law (civil trial) that is otherwise open to members of the public,

- in person,
- via the printed press,
- via video or audio recordings,
- via telephone transmission,
- via radio transmission,
- via television transmission,
- via data transmission, and/or
- via any other present or future technical, mechanical, electronic, or other, means of communication.

The Seventh Amendment does not specifically mention public trials in Suits at Common Law **(civil trials)**. But again, we must interpret the **intentions** of the underwriters of the entire Bill of Rights.

It is in keeping with the intentions of the underwriters of the Bill of Rights, that

> **the public shall have the unrestricted right to oversee that no citizen of the United States is unlawfully convicted – or corruptly acquitted – neither by a corrupt or prejudiced jury, by a corrupt or prejudiced judge, or against our laws.**

No judge shall have the power to set aside this principle. The very intentions of the underwriters of the Bill of Rights were to ensure that **no biased judge or biased jury should be given the opportunity to abuse their powers to – <u>in secrecy</u> – wrongfully convict, or acquit, a defendant.**

In my opinion, prosecutors, plaintiffs, or defendants, should not even have the right to recommend or demand the presence or absence of TV cameras in the courtroom. The concept of **"public trials"** is not only a right held by **defendants and plaintiffs. It is a right held by the public!**

> The right to attend trials, in person or **through any medium,** is not a right granted U.S. citizens through the Bill of Rights for their **entertainment purposes,** but a **democratic necessity** in order to safeguard the public against corruption or abuse of power by appointed or elected officials.
>
> **The protection of the public against abuse of power by authorities, and the rights of all Americans to keep a watchful eye on all elected or appointed officials, is perhaps the most important and unmistakable principle of the entire Constitution of the United States.**

The underwriters of the Bill of Rights recognized that *"power corrupts"!* Hence, they **intended** for the entire nation – **the public** – to be the watchdogs of our authorities, and of our judicial system and our judges, in particular.

For a judge to restrict this right of the public to oversee that he, in particular, is administering the law fairly and impartially – as intended by the underwriters of the Bill of Rights – **is so outrageously unconstitutional** that Thomas Jefferson and his colleagues must be turning in their graves over Judge Hiroshi Fujisaki's rulings.

Jefferson & Co. must, likewise, be flipping in their graves over the United States Supreme Court's reluctance to declare that TV cameras in all courtrooms is not just a privilege, but the constitutional right of every American who wants the TV cameras to be there.

Judge Fujisaki's rulings were so bad that I can't even find an example to illustrate it.

Here is the highest, most fundamental law of our nation, the Bill of Rights, telling every judge in the country (in essence):

*We, the underwriters of the Bill of Rights, guarantee the **entire** public the right to observe that all judges preside over their courtrooms fairly and in accordance with the law.*

Along comes Judge Hiroshi Fujisaki and says (in essence):

*I don't give a hoot about the Constitution and the Bill of Rights! This is **my** courtroom! **I decide whom I will admit!** I will allow in a handful observers who agree with me, but the rest of **the public** – stay the heck out of my courtroom!*

Judge Hiroshi Fujisaki was stepping on everyone's constitutional rights when he disallowed cameras in the courtroom! This wasn't feudal Japan anno 1796 – it was the United States anno 1996!

Judge Fujisaki may argue that the public's right to attend trials in person or through the media, is limited to **criminal trials.** The Seventh Amendment does **not** specify **public trials** in suits at common law **(civil suits).**

However, the Seventh Amendment does not give judges the

right to exclude the public either! The Seventh Amendment mentions the *"value in controversy … [exceeding] … "twenty dollars,"* as the measure by which a suit is considered serious enough to be tried by a jury. That demonstrates the state of mind of the underwriters of the Bill of Rights.

It isn't that the underwriters intended to keep civil trials closed to the public; the underwriters simply didn't foresee that anyone would be interested in attending such trials. And they certainly didn't prohibit anyone from attending!

It was surely not the intentions of the underwriters of the Bill of Rights to make provisions for the public to oversee that a defendant was not wrongfully or unlawfully convicted by a partial judge or jury **in a criminal trial only – but leave it to a judge to oversee himself in suits at common law (civil suits).**

Since civil suits are usually about **financial** settlements there is even **more reason to demand cameras in civil courts.**

In a criminal trial, the judge may care less whether or not a criminal defendant spends a few years in prison. Few would be interested in bribing the judge to ensure a conviction; and the criminal defendant rarely have the means to bribe a judge, anyway, to ensure an acquittal.

However, in civil suits, where the outcome of the trial is strictly about money, oftentimes about tens of millions of dollars, there is a much greater risk that one of the parties might try to bribe the judge – and a much greater temptation for a judge to accept a bribe, or to skew a trial to obtain a verdict that may be financially advantageous to the judge.

If therefore, the **intentions** of the underwriters of the Bill of Rights were for the public to oversee our elected or appointed officials – and our judges in particular – then, the intentions of the underwriters, had they lived today, would surely have been, not only to **allow** TV news cameras also in civil courtrooms, but to make TV news cameras **compulsory** in every U.S. courtroom!

My readers may wonder why I spend so much time on the Bill of Rights and the absence of cameras in the courtroom. Is it that important? Yes! First of all, the absence of TV cameras in the courtroom allowed Judge Fujisaki to skew the case against O.J. But perhaps equally important, the absence of cameras in the courtroom robbed O.J. of the best defense he had during the criminal trail!

Where do my readers believe much of the information about police misconduct, tampering with evidence, sloppy evidence handling procedures, Mark Fuhrman's racism and the Fuhrman tapes, Kathleen Bell and her meeting with Fuhrman, etc. originated? Much of it came from the public who followed the case on TV.

When Judge Fujisaki disallowed cameras in the courtroom, he took away one of O.J.'s best defense weapons, namely the watchful eyes of 200 million TV viewers.

Let's turn to something else! Many of my readers are perhaps not aware of it, but reasonably educated men and women know that the Japanese are perhaps the most **racially intolerant** people in the world.

We can see it in the ancient history of the closed Japanese feudal society; we saw it in World War II; we see it in the present day demographic make-up of the Japanese society (which consists of less than 1% of non-Japanese ethnic background!); and we see it in the way Japanese officials treat foreigners – whether the issue is fair and open markets, or foreign tourists waiting in one or two endless lines at the passport check-ins, at the international arrivals in Japanese airports – while a dozen or more passport check-ins **reserved for Japanese citizens, only**, have no waiting lines at all.

I know, because during my first and only visit to Japan, a frequent business traveller warned me about this as our plane approached the airport. Still I did not quite believe it could be as bad as he said. But my fellow passenger was right. I waited in such a line, which didn't move for more than one hour, before I decided to drop Tokyo! I turned around, on the spot, went back to the transit hall, and booked the first flight out of Japan – to Hawaii instead!

Most other countries treat foreign visitors as their guests and try to accommodate them as well as possible. To the Japanese, for-eigners are, rather, seen as adversaries, competitors, and intruders.

Judge Hiroshi Fujisaki did not disappoint the racist lynch mob! O.J. is black. So was one of the jurors – **exactly one** – until she, too, was dismissed by Judge Fujisaki! The rest of the twelve member jury constituted 9 whites and two of mixed Hispanic or Asian origin.

During jury selection, if a prospective **black** juror answered he believed O.J. **might be innocent** – Judge Fujisaki **dismissed** the prospective juror for that reason!

If a prospective **white** juror answered that he believed O.J. **were guilty,** Judge Fujisaki **kept** the juror!

When there was no **other** reason to keep a prospective black juror off the jury, the counsels for the plaintiffs used "the exemption rules" to remove black jurors. Each side were allowed six exemptions for no reason. The plaintiffs used all six, and removed six prospective black jurors without cause! Yet, they had the nerve to tell us, after the trial, that race played no part in their civil case!

Next, Judge Fujisaki precluded the defense from even mentioning Detective Mark Fuhrman, whom most unbiased people believe planted the murder glove behind O.J.'s house, and possibly also smeared blood from that glove in O.J.'s Bronco. At least, Detective Fuhrman had the opportunity to do it!

I know I am about to step over the line here, but it is necessary in this case, in the name of fairness to a black man in the hands of a white lynch mob, as well as to his children!

Detective Fuhrman is a confirmed **neo-nazi** and a **convicted perjurer** who collects **nazi World War II** medals as a hobby, and who **was convicted of perjury during his sworn testimony** against O.J. in the criminal trial, and who was **instrumental in casting suspicion on O.J.** in the first place.

Many of my readers may be too young to remember World War II and how our enemies, **Nazi Germany** and **Japan – side by side –** fought the U.S. and her Allied forces on two different fronts 55 years ago, and which evil racist philosophy **both** of those enemies **would** have imposed on the rest of the world – had they succeeded in **enslaving** us all.

Born in a country occupied by Hitler's nazi soldiers, his SS troops, and his Gestapo, for five years during the Second World War, I found it **more offensive** that the **Japanese-**American Judge, Hiroshi Fujisaki, protected the **neo-Nazi** sympathizer, former LAPD Detective Mark Fuhrman, from being questioned by the counsels for the African-American defendant – than the fact that Defense Attorney Johnnie Cochran compared Mark Fuhrman to a "Hitler sprout" who had not yet risen to power.

Next, Judge Fujisaki decided, unilaterally, that the defense could not argue that the LAPD investigators had planted or fabricated certain pieces of evidence. That **was** the defense!

Judge Fujisaki's ruling was like telling a Samurai warrior to go out and fight till the end – but leave his sword behind before he enters the battle field! **With a judge like Hiroshi Fujisaki, what do we need jurors for?**

Then, Judge Fujisaki allowed Mr. Petrocelli, the counsel for the plaintiffs to state to the jury that O.J. took a lie detector (polygraph) test and failed it with a score of minus 22 – adding that such a score indicated *"extreme deception"*!

First of all, polygraph tests are not even admissible as evidence in California. Secondly, there is no proof that O.J. even took a polygraph test! Even if he did, we don't know the content of any questions.

For all we – or the counsel, or Judge Fujisaki, knew, O.J. could have been **instructed to lie,** about his children's birthdays or the latest baseball scores, simply to demonstrate to O.J. or his attorney how the polygraph worked!

Were that the case, a score of minus 22 would indicate that O.J. was an extremely poor liar. Hence, if he can state with conviction that he did **not** murder Nicole and Ron – there is every reason to believe him!

Instead, the jurors were misled to believe O.J. had taken a complete polygraph test and demonstrated "extreme deception" when claiming his innocence, and that the **alleged** polygraph test, therefore, had proven that he were guilty!

For Judge Fujisaki to allow the counsel to state circumstances surrounding the issue of a polygraph test in this manner, was such a gross and bias decision that many legal scholars claimed never to have seen or heard anything like it in their entire legal careers.

A law professor stated on national TV that if one of his first year law students had suggested a ruling like Judge Fujisaki's, the student would have flunked the professor's course outright! That's how badly Judge Fujisaki skewed the trial in O.J.'s disfavor.

As if that wasn't enough, Judge Fujisaki returned a couple of days later instructing the jury to **forget** about the counsel's mentioning of the polygraph test and his mentioning of O.J. allegedly having failed the polygraph test with a score of *"minus 22"* which indicated *"extreme deception"*! If the jurors didn't remember it from the first time, when the counsel mentioned it, they surely remembered it now when Judge Fujisake repeated it!

Judge Fujisaki's attempt to "repair" the damage of his awful earlier ruling, made the damage even worse! But perhaps that was his intention! It was as if someone in the third row, secretly, had brought a chimpanzee to the courtroom, some of the jurors hadn't noticed it yet, and Judge Fujisaki had told the jurors:

"Don't look at the chimpanzee in the third row!"

People I have spoken to, seriously raised the question if Judge Fujisaki, perhaps, was bribed, or if the District Attorney's office, which strongly supported the plaintiffs, had some compromising information about the judge, and had threatened to publicize it unless Judge Fujisaki secured a verdict against O.J. in the civil trial.

It is necessary to dwell on the issue of the alleged polygraph test a little longer. A former FBI agent, John Douglas, specializes in creating murder profiles. Allegedly, he was the model for the main character of the acclaimed movie, *"Silence of the Lamb."*

Mr. Douglas was hired by Mr. and Mrs. John Ramsey, the parents of the slain Colorado girl, JonBenet Ramsey. January 30, 1997, Mr. Douglas appeared on the TV talk show *"Rivera Live."* He informed the audience that he had advised **Mr. and Mrs. Ramsey** against submitting to a polygraph test. With authority Mr. Douglas explained to the audience **why** he advised against a polygraph test.

So shortly after the murder of their daughter, the parents (and in other cases, people close to a murder victim) might – although innocent – be so occupied by feelings of responsibility that it might be adversely reflected in their responses to polygraph tests.

For example, a female murder victim – someone's girlfriend – might have called her boyfriend shortly before she was murdered, and suggested that they go out together. The boyfriend, perhaps, declined, saying it was too late. Then the girl was murdered. Although totally innocent, the boyfriend is struck by guilt – because if he had accepted to go out with his girlfriend, she would not have been murdered.

If the boyfriend had submitted to a polygraph test shortly after his girlfriend's murder, his **misguided** feeling of responsibility for her death, might be misinterpreted by a polygraphers as true evidence of guilt.

What does this have to do with O.J. Simpson and his **alleged** polygraph test?

Well, according to Mr. Douglas, **he was also consulted by counsel for the plaintiffs, Mr. Daniel Petrocelli, on behalf of the plaintiffs in the Simpson civil case.**

In particular, **Mr. Petrocelli consulted Mr. Douglas to get his advice on whether or not to challenge O.J., publicly, to a new polygraph test.**

Mr. Douglas, former FBI agent, specialist on murder profiles and polygraph tests, explained on *"Rivera Live"* that **he advised**

the plaintiffs against challenging O.J. to a "stipulated" polygraph test (admissible as evidence by a **"stipulation"** in advance from both sides).

Mr. Douglas told the audience on *"Rivera Live"* what he had explained to Mr. Petrocelli, during **17 hours of consultation**, namely that with time, a murderer might rationalize his crime, justify it in his mind, and actually believe that he is innocent. Therefore, even if O.J. were guilty, and even if he, allegedly, failed a polygraph test a couple of days after the murders – he might very well pass a polygraph test during the civil trial.

It says something about Fred Goldman's attorney in the civil case, Mr. Petrocelli, that he wanted O.J. to submit to a polygraph test, because he hoped it could help his client's case. But Mr. Petrocelli – and I assume Fred Goldman was fully aware of what was going on – did not dare, simply, to suggest to O.J.:

"Would you submit to a stipulated polygraph test today?"

Mr. Petrocelli dared not suggest this, although he was tempted by the concept, unless he was absolutely certain the outcome would be in his favor! So he consulted an expert on murder profiles and polygraph tests first. And when the expert suggested that O.J. might pass a polygraph test, and even told Mr. Petrocelli that **the polygraph test O.J. allegedly might have failed, was unreliable** – the counsel for the plaintifs chickened out! What a jerk! What a coward! What a cheat! And **what revealing evidence of Mr. Petrocelli's own doubts regarding O.J.'s alleged guilt!**

But Mr. Petrocelli (and Mr. Douglas) are worse than that, even. Being consulted for 17 hours and specifically on the issue of O.J.'s alleged polygraph test – there can be no doubt that Mr. Douglas informed Mr. Petrocelli about the fact that polygraph tests taken by a close friend or relative of a murder victim, shortly after the murder, might very likely reflect **a false sense of guilt,** on behalf of that friend or relative.

Typically, O.J. – although 100% innocent – might have felt extremely guilty and responsible for Nicole's death, by virtue of having rejected her attempt of a reconciliation, resulting in their divorce and Nicole's moving to Bundy. O.J. might have felt that if he had still been married to Nicole, she would, most likely, not have been murdered – because she would then have been living with O.J. at Rockingham.

This is very likely the reason O.J., allegedly, failed the polygraph test – **if he took one – and if he failed it**.

This same feeling of guilt – although he was innocent – could also explain O.J.'s audio taped response to Detective Lange during the Bronco chase and alleged suicide attempt, where O.J. is heard saying:

> *"All I did was love her! ... I am the only one who deserves to be hurt!"*

O.J.'s statement to Detective Lange was no reflection of guilt – merely an expression of O.J.'s misguided sense of being, somehow, responsible, since he had divorced Nicole, so he was no longer there to protect her when the murderer struck. This is emphasized also in the so-called "suicide note" he wrote shortly before embarking on the Bronco ride. Quote:

> *"First, everyone understand, I had nothing to do with Nicole's murder. I loved her, always have, always will. If we had a problem, it's because I loved her so much.*
>
> *... I've had a good life. I'm proud of how I lived. My mama taught me to do unto others – I treated people the way I wanted to be treated. I've always tried to be up and helpful. So why is this happening? I am sorry for the Goldman family. I know how much it hurts.*
>
> *... Don't feel sorry for me. I've had a great life, great friends. Please think of the real O.J. and not this lost person. Thanks for making my life special. I hope I helped yours.*

> *Peace and love, O.J."*

Clearly, both the letter and the conversation with Detective Lange reflected a person who was, and knew he was, totally innocent of Nicole's murder, but who still felt responsible for her death – not because of something he had done, but rather, because of something he had failed to do – namely keep their marriage together.

Being such an expert on murder profiles and polygraph tests that Mr. Petrocelli consulted him on this issue, John Douglas **must** have explained to Mr. Petrocelli, that O.J.'s response to the alleged polygraph test might very well be a reflection of such an irrational sense of responsibility for Nicole's death, and that his response two years later, therefore, might be quite different.

Consequently, Mr. Douglas advised the counsel for the plaintiffs against challenging O.J. to a new polygraph test – the reason being that O.J. would, most likely, pass a second polygraph test today!

So this "tricky" lawyer, Mr. Petrocelli, and his client, Fred Goldman, chickened out of challenging O.J. to a stipulated, second polygraph test! Instead, Mr. Petrocelli presented the jury with the **alleged** result of the **alleged** early polygraph test, **which Mr. Petrocelli's own polygraph consultant, John Douglas, must have told him was totally unreliable**, because of the near proximity in time between the murders and the alleged test – combined with the warm feelings O.J. had for Nicole even after their divorce.

> **This example demonstrates the integrity – or rather, the lack of integrity – amongst O.J.'s adversaries. People who use such tactics – I would not hesitate to call them "charlatans." But that is my personal opinion.**

I hope, for my assessment of Fred Goldman's integrity, that he did not sit in on his attorney's consultations with Mr. Douglas, and that Mr. Petrocelli did not inform his client about these consultations – although I doubt it.

While discussing the fairness and integrity of the counsels for the plaintiffs, another issue is worth mentioning.

Three days into the jury deliberations in the civil case, the Los Angeles District Attorney's office which had prosecuted O.J., informed Judge Fujisaki that the only African-American on the jury had lied on her jury questionnaire, hiding the fact that her daughter was the personal secretary for a high ranking official at the LA's District Attorney's office who prosecuted O.J. in the criminal trial.

One of the questions the potential jurors were required to answer truthfully, was whether they were related to someone employed by the Los Angeles DA's office, the Los Angeles Police Department (LAPD), or the FBI – all of which had investigated and/or prosecuted Mr. Simpson. Failure by this juror to disclose that her daughter worked for the DA's office was synonymous with **perjury.**

This matter is certainly worthy of some comments. However, I underline that all my information regarding this issue comes from what I saw and heard via the media. There was a lot of speculation going on, and much of the information I received might be incorrect. Anyway, here follow some reflections I believe alert and independent observers ought to have made.

Many whites – even white police officers – believe strongly that O.J. is innocent, just as many blacks believe strongly that he is guilty. The fact that the dismissed juror was black, did not imply that she was pro-O.J. – nor that she was anti-O.J. – simply by virtue of being black.

To make an educated guess as to which way she might be leaning, we should rather look to her daughter, who also lives in L.A. (indicating that mother and daughter probably have a normal, warm relationship). The daughter worked closely with one of the DA's who prosecuted O.J., and still had a vested interest in seeing the plaintiffs prevail in their civil suits.

It is only natural to assume that the mother is proud of her daughter and the position she holds, and hence, that the mother also holds the DA's office in high regard, and therefore, sympathized with the plaintiffs. Similarly, had the daughter worked for Johnnie Cochran's law firm, we could expect her mother to be influenced by her daughter's viewpoints and sympathize with the defense.

This African-American juror made a false statement on her questionnaire, denying that she had relatives (her daughter) employed by the Los Angeles DA's office. Had she disclosed her daughter's position, she would probably never have been accepted as a juror. Apparently, she had a motive for lying, in order to get on the jury.

If she lied about her ties to the DA's office, **she might as well have lied about her opinion of the case!** According to the news media, this juror expressed some doubt that O.J. were guilty. Since she lied about her ties to the DA's office, she might as well have lied about her doubting O.J. were guilty.

Let me try to analyze what might have been going on here!

If this juror wanted to get on the jury for some suspect reason which we don't have to discuss yet, then **she had to make herself acceptable to both sides!**

I find it inconceivable that the DA's office did not know that the mother of the secretary of one of their highest ranking officials was among the potential jurors selected for the Simpson jury. An obvious first question to the **secretary** must have been:

"How does your mother feel about O.J.?"

As closely as the DA's office and the LAPD worked with the plaintiffs in the civil case, I take it for granted that this information quickly reached the counsels for the plaintiffs.

Suppose the daughter revealed that her mother was pro-Simpson. In addition, she was black. They would have every reason **not** to accept her as a juror. When she, therefore, was **the only black juror the counsels for the plaintiffs accepted,** we should suspect that something, obviously, was going on here! The counsels for the plaintiffs won't tell us what went on. Naturally, the DA's office is silent. So we can only speculate.

Possibly, the plaintiffs were informed by the DA's office that this juror – in spite of being black – was **anti-O.J.!**

They were also informed that this juror's daughter worked for the DA's office, which could be as valuable as **having a spy camera in the jury room!** Regardless of the juror's sentiment in the case, keeping her on could provide the DA's office, and hence, the plaintiffs, with a day-to-day update on the sentiment of the entire jury. This could be essential in purposely causing a mistrial, for instance, if the sentiment of the jury was pro-O.J.!

Consequently, the juror was accepted by the plaintiffs in spite of being black, and in spite of indicating during questioning that she might be pro-O.J. (however, even her doubt regarding O.J.'s guilt might be a deception). After all, knowing that this juror's daughter worked for the DA's office, the plaintiffs could easily get her kicked off any time they wanted to.

She may have been advised by her daughter to conceal her ties to the DA's office, and to express a "somewhat" **pro-Simpson** view, in order to be accepted by the **defense.**

If in addition, the plaintiffs **knew, through the jurors daughter, via the DA's office,** that she **factually** was **anti-O.J.** – then she was likely to be accepted also by the **plaintiffs!**

Let's also look at this from a statistical point of view. The plaintiffs had six exemptions (without cause) and used all six. In each case they kicked out a potential **black** juror. This dismissed juror was the seventh, and last, black juror. Looking at this from a purely statistical point of view, there is an 85.7% chance that this juror **should** have been excluded by the plaintiffs during jury selection, because of her race and her "somewhat" pro-Simpson stand – but she wasn't!

Even if the plaintiffs didn't know about this juror's ties to the DA's office at the time of jury selection, **it is inconceivable that the DA's office** (and hence the counsels for the plaintiffs) **did not learn about these ties until three days into the jury deliberations – it is absolutely inconceivable!**

Of course, the counsels for the plaintiffs as well as District Attorney Gil Garcetti may deny this. But I trust my readers have enough common sense to realize what was going on here.

The DA's office (and hence the counsels for the plaintiffs) must have known about this juror for a long time. Yet, they did not report it to Judge Fujisaki until three days into jury deliberation.

If this assumption is correct, it meant that the plaintiffs had some kind of advantage by keeping this juror on the jury.

It could be that she was in fact anti-O.J., in spite of her response to questions during jury selections. Of course, the plaintiffs would be interested in keeping an anti-O.J. juror. In particular, if that juror was black, and hence, gave the jury as a whole the appearance of being, at least, somewhat racially mixed.

Here is yet another point. Usually, expelled jurors are hunted down by the media within minutes. They are offered large fees for appearing on TV and providing inside information.

However, in this particular case, the plaintiffs – and I assume the juror herself – had a vested interest in preventing any information about her dismissal from reaching the public.

Unless this expelled juror and the plaintiffs (and the DA) were on the same side in this, I would have expected this juror to have appeared on TV within minutes of her dismissal. The fact that she is nowhere to be found for months, is "strange" – to say the least. It indicates that she was on the side of the plaintiffs.

> Is this yet another example of the media's anti-O.J. bias, that they aren't interested in digging up anything that could jeopardize the plaintiffs verdict in the civil trial?

I doubt very much that the media had taken on such an indifferent attitude if the verdict had been **for** O.J., and one of the jurors, for instance, had lied about her ties to Johnnie Cochran's law firm!

There is even another explanation why this juror, surprisingly, has never spoken to the media. Her false statement on her jury questionnaire is comparable to **perjury**. The DA's office, therefore, holds a grip on this former juror. The best reason I can come up with, as to why she has never spoken to the media, is that the

DA's office has threatened to prosecute her for perjury – unless she keeps her mouth shut. Someone from the media ought to find this woman and get her story!

Is there also a contradiction here? If this juror was allied with the plaintiffs (and with the DA's office) – why did they decide to expose her, causing her dismissal from the jury?

First of all, only one of the remaining alternate jurors were black – most of them were white. So if the DA's office (and the plaintiffs) exposed her, she was likely to be replaced by an equally pro-plaintiffs alternate juror.

Secondly, **why did the plaintiffs, apparently, object to the dismissal of the juror,** if they (or the DA's office) were the ones who exposed her?

That could have been pure "theatrics"! The counsels for the plaintiffs knew that once this juror's ties to the DA's office were exposed, there was **no way on this earth** that Judge Fujisaki would keep her on the jury and risk a reversible error.

By objecting, Mr. Petrocelli made it appear that he had no prior knowledge about the dismissed juror's ties to the DA's office.

But here comes the third question! If the DA's office, (and the counsels for the plaintiffs) knew about this juror's ties to the DA's office, and still kept quiet for 5 months, because they found it advantageous to the plaintiffs to keep her on the jury – why did they suddenly reverse themselves and expose her ties, three days into the jury deliberations?

The answer to that question **could** be that the juror might have become convinced that O.J. was innocent – as a result of the trial – and this fact reached Mr. Petrocelli, via the juror's daughter and the DA's office. Were that the case, Mr. Petrocelli, naturally, would want her off the jury immediately. Having the information necessary to expel her, he might have decided (together with the DA's office) to do just that!

However, for the **real** answer to this question I think we have to look beyond the Simpson case! The big news story **the day**

before this juror's ties to the DA's office were disclosed to Judge Fujisaki, was **"the FBI crime lab scandal"**!

Here Defense Counsel Robert Baker had been arguing on behalf of O.J. that the scientific test results and the testimonies, not only from the LAPD's lab and criminalists, but **even from the FBI's lab** and criminalists, were **highly unreliable**, to say the least.

On the other hand, we had Mr. Petrocelli holding up the FBI's crime lab as the standard bearers for integrity and reliability!

What happened, then, the day before the DA's office informed Judge Fujisaki about the African-American juror's daughter?

> **In a major investigative report released by the Inspector General of the Justice Department, the FBI's crime lab and their scientists were blasted, as incompetent, biased, unreliable, lying, slanting test results in favor of prosecutors, etc., etc.!**
>
> **Some of the very same FBI people who played a central role in the prosecution's (and the plaintiffs') case against O.J. – both as scientists, criminalists, and expert witnesses – were severely reprimanded, demoted, or fired!**

This must have been **a tremendous blow to the plaintiffs!** Suddenly they saw their most important arguments floating in the gutter.

> Their greatest concern must have been how **to keep this information from reaching the jurors!**

What did they do? They called a meeting – **"damage control"** is the name for it. They consulted with their allies in the DA's office, who, of course, for five months must have been fully aware of the African-American juror's ties to the DA's office. Then they came up with the following solution:

After having keep it secret for five months, the DA's office informed Judge Fujisaki that on her jury questionnaire the African-American juror had concealed her close ties to the DA's office

Naturally, Judge Fujisaki immediately dismissed the juror. That was expected.

Then the counsel for the plaintiffs argued strongly for **sequestration of the jury** during the remainder of their deliberations!

According to Mr. Petrocelli, the purpose of the sequestration should be to prevent the jury from being influenced by **whatever the dismissed juror might say in media interviews.** But that was not Mr. Petrocelli's **real** motive for demanding the jury sequestered.

Typically, this dismissed juror is **the only Simpson juror** – dismissed or not – who has never spoken a word in public about the case, and whom **the media has never been interested in talking to!**

I think Mr. Petrocelli's **real** motive for demanding the jury **sequestered** was to **keep the jurors from learning about the full scope of the FBI scandal** – as well as reading about, or watching **and listening to, legal analysts in the media discussing, the ramifications of the FBI scandal, as it pertained to the Simpson case** which the jurors were deliberating.

The dismissed juror was more valuable to the plaintiffs if her dismissal could **cause the sequestration of the jury before the full scope of the FBI scandal reached them** – than she was by keeping her on the jury to better the chances of securing a verdict for the plaintiffs.

There is also another plausible explanation for the circumstances surrounding this dismissed African-American juror. Most likely, this black juror was on the side of the plaintiffs – and they knew it, through her daugther and the DA's office – so they kept her on as long as they could.

After three days of jury deliberations, she could report back to the DA's office and the plaintiffs, that the jurors were unanimously in favor of the plaintiffs. So now, the plaintiffs didn't need her on the jury any longer.

The plaintiffs were more concerned that this juror's ties to the DA's office – and her failure to disclose that on her jury questionnaire – should not jeopardize the inevitably pro-plaintiffs verdict. Hence, the DA's office exposed the juror, in time for the plaintiffs to have her replaced by an alternate – thereby securing the pro-plaintiffs verdict they knew the jury had already reached, and also preventing this juror from becoming an issue on appeal.

The exposure of the last black juror, and her subsequent predictable, instant dismissal was simply **damage control** by the plaintiffs (and by their allies in the DA's office, who also had a vested interest in seeing O.J. lose the civil case).

I want my readers to take notice of the following **"word of wisdom"**:

> When people do something **strange or unexpected – yet deliberate** – there is usually **a specific motive** behind it, or reason for it.

That's how I feel about this story of the last dismissed juror, too. The counsels for the plaintiffs, and the District Attorney must have had their motives and reasons for handling the matter of the dismissed African-American juror the way they handled it. The only reason or motive I could see, was cheating and deception.

Back to Judge Fujisaki's courtroom during the civil trial. No sooner had we put the polygraph issue behind us, before Judge Fujisaki made his next outrageous ruling. A telephone operator at a women's shelter was allowed to testify that another woman, identifying herself as "Nicole," had called the shelter and told the operator that her (the caller's) husband had said he would kill the caller if he saw her with another man.

There were serious discrepancies in the operators' testimony. Her alleged report from the telephone conversation had countless shortcomings. The report was partially written long after the conversation allegedly took place. The date of the conversation was recorded by the operator as 5/17. Later, when it became evident that the operator was not at work, in the shelter, on 5/17, someone else, using a different pen, crossed out the date 5/17, and wrote 6/17 instead – a date the operator was working!

The operator's testimony was also total "hearsay" and, based on that alone, it should not have been admitted. On top of that, this operator's testimony was **"double hearsay" – if such a thing exists!** Not only did the operator testify to what the caller had told her. She testified to what the **caller** had told the **operator** that the **caller's husband** had told the **caller!**

The caller might have been O.J.'s ex-wife – or not. Regardless, this testimony was so far from being admissible under California law as a testimony could be. Of fairness to both sides in a law suit or in a criminal trial, the courts operate under the guidelines of certain procedural laws. It is not for a judge to break those laws whenever he finds it expedient to do so to further his own opinion in a case he is presiding over.

Already before the plaintiffs had rested their case, it had become evident, even to some of the most anti-O.J. legal analysts on TV, that Judge Hiroshi Fujisaki had rendered several of the worst decisions in our nation's jurisprudence – all in favor of the plaintiffs.

Law professors, judges, former prosecutors and attorneys both for and against O.J. openly agreed that Judge Fujisaki – long before the trial started – had made up his mind that O.J. were guilty, that in the judge's opinion O.J. had gotten away with murder in the criminal trial, and that he wasn't going to get away with murder in Judge Hiroshi Fujisaki's courtroom.

Seventy-five percent of the plaintiffs' case was not a presentation of evidence. It was merely a "smear campaign" against O.J.

A witness testified that he saw O.J. slap Nicole in 1986. With the prevalent anti-O.J. sentiment, we don't know if this witness simply overheard an argument between O.J. and Nicole, and decided to lie about it in an effort to harm O.J.'s case, testifying that O.J. slapped Nicole on that occasion – if there even were an occasion. Nobody can impeach his testimony today, anyway.

Countless witnesses have testified that Nicole, allegedly, feared O.J., and that he consistently hit her. Yet, evident from letters she wrote to O.J., Nicole was the one begging O.J. to come back to her!

During Nicole's and O.J.'s divorce proceedings in 1992, and on the infamous 911 tape from October 25, 1993, as well as on a secret audio tape made by a police officer responding to one of Nicole's 911 calls, Nicole was repeatedly asked if O.J. had hit her. Clearly, without any hesitation, Nicole answered, *"No!"* On the secret audio tape she even added,

"He hasn't hit me since New Years Day in 1989"!

Was this a murder trial, or a trial about domestic disturbance? The victim herself, Nicole, declared – on three different records – that O.J., in spite of their stormy relationship, had not beaten her – not even once – during the 5 1/2 years leading up to her murder?

Isn't it time to ask ourselves what was going on in this case?

CHAPTER 4

The Media

There is no way O.J. could have murdered Nicole and Ron. Joseph Bosco, the author of "A Problem Of Evidence" (William Morrow & Co.; N.Y., 1996), explains in his book, that the evidence simply wasn't there.

Up until the civil case, every jury – "mock" or real – that had "tried" the case, either in a grand jury hearing, in the criminal trial, in a "mock" trial organized by the attorneys for either side, or on a TV talk show – failed to render a guilty verdict!

Donald Freed and Raymond P. Briggs, the authors of "Killing Time" (MACMILLAN, N.Y.; 1996), proved with high tech tests and computer analyses that there is no way O.J. could have murdered Nicole and Ron within the time frame constructed by the investigators and the prosecutors. O.J. could not possibly have committed these murders.

None of the three authors, however, explained where all this suspect evidence came from, and who **did** murder Nicole and Ron – if O.J. didn't ...

Based on the evidence, I will – from a different perspective than the three authors' – prove that O.J. did not kill Nicole and Ron. But I will also take the next two steps that no one, to my knowledge, have taken yet. I will explain:

- who, in my opinion, actually murdered Nicole and Ron;
- why he did it;
- how he did it;
- how he got away with it; and
- where all the falsely planted and fabricated evidence came from.

Surely, more tragic crimes have been committed, than the murders of Nicole Brown Simpson and Ronald L. Goldman. And contrary to O.J., many people have suffered the ultimate injustice of not only having been charged with, but convicted of, and executed for, crimes they did not commit.

Yet, the murder case against O.J. Simpson was one of the worst travesties of justice in the history of the U.S. Because this case demonstrated, better than any other case, that when influential members of our law enforcement, and justice systems, join forces and climb aboard the (mis-)"Carriage of Justice," no one is safe – not even from the threat of execution!

When corrupt investigators and prosecutors persuade a jury to send an innocent man to his execution – it's usually the end of that story. Why spend resources on proving that the defendant was wrongfully convicted, when the man is already dead and can not be brought back to life?

In the Simpson case we could all witness the corrupt investigators and prejudiced prosecutors, work the white lynch mob. Because O.J. was rich and famous he escaped their lynching tree. However, nobody should doubt that if O.J. had not been O.J., he would have been on death row today – awaiting execution!

A corrupt justice system would have murdered O.J. before the very eyes of his children – while a crazy mob of ignorants would have danced and chanted as the lethal gas would have consumed Sydney's and Justin's father!

More frightening, however – and more surprising – is the fact that these evil and misguided forces were able to persuade almost the entire media to join them.

We are used to looking at the media as the watchdogs against injustice in our society. Instead, we see in the continued Simpson saga, that the media are the driving forces in this crusade to convict and punish an innocent man. This surely, does not speak highly of the morals and the intelligence of those who control our media.

Perhaps those who control our media are racist, even. Not when the issue is a **principle** and the spotlight is on them –

but deep inside – when the life of **one black man**, only, is at stake.

I have tried, in vain – at least two hundred times – to present parts of my information to "anyone" in the media. As soon as they realize I believe O.J. is innocent, they cut off the conversation and flatly refuse to talk to me.

Let's "hypothesize" a little! Suppose someone by chance had shot a video of the murders, but been afraid to intervene. Ashamed because he had not come to Nicole's and Ron's rescue, the man hid the tape somewhere among a stack of home movies, rather than bring it to the police. Then, accidentally, he died before he could hand the tape over to the authorities. Eventually, without checking the contents, the man's relatives sold all his home movies – including the tape of the murders – during a large garage sale. I bought it – still hypothetically speaking!

I honestly believe that even if I had come across such a videotape actually covering the murders of Nicole and Ron – showing clearly the face of the murderer, and he is not O.J. – the media would still not even want to review the tape!

People have been wrongfully sentenced to death in this country, you know! Police make mistakes, prosecutors make mistakes, jurors make mistakes – and the media make mistakes.

Yet, there is **a total media boycott** of everyone with information favorable to O.J. I haven't seen anything like this – not even during Senator Joseph McCarthy's anti-communist crusade in the fifties!

I shall bring forth much more compelling evidence of O.J.'s innocence than the short list of questions I mentioned in chapter 2 ["Cockroaches"]. But isn't this list by itself more than enough to suggest that O.J. is being framed?

Rarely have I seen a more obvious example of a crime, set up to frame an innocent man, than in the case of the murders of Nicole and Ron. I will prove it in the following chapters. I hope the media not only become deeply embarrassed upon learning what I shall tell them, but that they take lesson from it!

CHAPTER 5

"The First" And *"The Fifth"*

L et me take the bull by the horn, and state right away that I believe Detective Mark Fuhrman, formerly of the LAPD, not only planted the second murder glove behind O.J.'s house, but that

Detective Mark Fuhrman carefully planned and executed the murder of Nicole Brown Simpson, and subsequently also murdered Ron Goldman when he, unexpectedly, showed up at the murder scene!

My readers only need to tune their TV sets to the evening news, or open their newspapers, to realize that it wouldn't be the first time a white police officer had murdered someone for racist reasons.

(If Detective Fuhrman did not personally murder Nicole and Ron, I believe he is in some way responsible, perhaps as a member of a racist, white supremacist, or neo-nazi group).

In my book I will outline a theory which explains:

- why Fuhrman might have decided to murder Nicole,
- how Fuhrman, over several years, in minute details, could have perfected his plan to murder Nicole and frame O.J.,
- how Fuhrman could have executed his gruesome plan,
- how Fuhrman could have fabricated and planted the initial crucial pieces of evidence against O.J. – not simply to frame O.J. directly, but more importantly, to "set up" the LAPD investigators to continue and complete the fabrication and planting of false evidence against O.J., and finally,
- how the investigators, probably, took Fuhrman's "bait" and swallowed it – bait, hook, line, and fishing rod!

These are bold statements, but I believe I have convincing arguments to support them. Naturally, Detectives Fuhrman and Vannatter will not be pleased when they, presumably, read my book. I emphasize, therefore, as I did at the opening of my book:

> What I write on the following pages, are **not** proven facts, but only my theories and opinions about the murders of Nicole and Ron, and the subsequent investigation.

What I present is an alternative murder theory consistent with O.J.'s innocence.

> **<u>Even though I don't always repeat it, what I express or argue throughout this book, are my THEORIES and OPINIONS, only – and NOT proven facts.</u>**
> **My readers must make up their own minds, as to the validity of my arguments, and draw their own conclusions as to Mark Fuhrman's guilt or innocence, as well as the possible guilt or innocence of others mentioned in my book.**
> Detective Mark Fuhrman, as well as others mentioned in my book, should be considered innocent of any specific crime or act of professional misconduct, until proven guilty of same in a court of law, or until they confess.

The First Amendment of the Constitution guarantees me the right to express my opinion regarding the murders of Nicole Brown Simpson and Ron Goldman. Were it not for this right to free exchange of ideas and opinions, not only would our democracy falter, but in particular, many crimes would remain unsolved, because people would be afraid to express their theories and present their information, under the threat of being sued or prosecuted.

Based on his, alleged, discovery of the second murder glove behind O.J.'s house, Detective Fuhrman, more than anyone, is the person responsible for the serious accusations directed against O.J. Simpson. Yet, when asked, under oath on the witness stand, if he brought that glove to O.J.'s house and planted it there,

Detective Fuhrman pleaded his Fifth Amendment privilege and refused to answer the defense attorney's question.

Asked if he lied during his testimony, and whether he had fabricated false evidence in criminal cases, Detective Fuhrman also pleaded his Fifth Amendment privilege.

Scholars may argue what the legal implications of Fuhrman's Fifth Amendment privilege are. But to most ordinary citizens the implications are clear:

> Mark Fuhrman, when asked if he planted the glove behind O.J.'s house, pleaded his Fifth Amendment privilege to refuse to answer on the grounds that his answer might incriminate him.
>
> To most ordinary people this means one of two things – which are, in reality, one and the same. If Fuhrman did **not** plant the glove, he could have answered "no," and had nothing to fear because of this answer.
>
> However, Detective Fuhrman **did** plant the glove (again, my theory and opinion), and accordingly he refused to answer, because if he answered "yes," he would be subject to serious charges for having planted false evidence in a murder case, and if he answered "no," and it was later uncovered that he was lying, he would be subject to perjury charges as well!
>
> Besides, had Fuhrman admitted that he planted the Rockingham glove, he would implicate himself strongly as a possible murder suspect! Because he could hardly have picked up that glove at Bundy after he arrived there at 2:10 am. Hence, if he planted it, he must have brought it with him to Bundy, and on to Rockingham. That makes him, at least, part of a murder conspiracy.

Later, when subpoenaed by the defense to testify in the civil trial, Fuhrman hid by moving from California to Idaho, and refused to come forward.

So, Mark Fuhrman refused to answer the defense attorney's question. That was his Constitutional privilege. But in refusing to answer, he certainly opened up for speculations that he, indeed, planted that glove.

If Detective Fuhrman, as a sworn witness in a criminal trial, can assert **his Fifth Amendment** privilege not to answer the defense attorney's question as to whether or not he brought the bloody murder glove to the spot where he alleged that he found it – then I, certainly, should be allowed to assert **my First Amendment** privilege to free speech, and to express my theory as to why Detective Fuhrman refused to answer.

If Detective Fuhrman wants to face me and challenge my words in a forum like "Larry King Live" or "Rivera Live" – or in a court of law – I welcome him! First, he must, however, stop hiding behind his Fifth Amendment privilege. I doubt that he dares.

CHAPTER 6

Experts And Amateurs

Before I start analyzing the Simpson case, there are some other topics I need to say a few words about. Many of my readers, I am sure, may wonder:

> "Who is this Christopher Springer, claiming that he has solved the Simpson case? We don't see any Ph. D.'s, no professorships, and no prior books or awards. He doesn't seem to be an expert on anything in particular, and certainly not an expert on homicide investigations."

You are exactly right! I am no expert in any particular field or science that may seem to apply to this case. I do have something else, however, which is much more important: **I have a fair knowledge of many different fields!**

My background covers some police work as a military police sergeant, a short military career, some teaching experience, some college background in psychology, physical education, biochemistry, anatomy, physiology, mathematics, statistics, and philosophy.

A central part of the Simpson case is the struggle between Ron and the murderer. My experience as a former competitive boxer and fencer helps me understand what was, and was not, possible in terms of the struggle between Ron and a murderer armed with a knife.

Nicole and O.J. were divorced. Domestic violence, allegedly, played a role in this murder mystery. My personal experience from a broken marriage, as well as from a happy one, allows me to understand this domestic violence issue better than many people.

For a layman, I believe I have a better than average knowledge of the law, more life experience than most people, and, hopefully, quite a bit of common sense.

For 10 years I supported myself as a professional poker player, winning major poker tournaments both in the States and overseas. At poker tables all over the world, and as a teacher, I have learned to tell, almost as well as a polygraph, when people are bluffing or "cheating." That sure came in handy in the Simpson case!

I also have three U.S. patents to my credit. As an inventor I am used to looking at old problems from new angles, logically analyzing the problems, never accepting that a problem cannot be solved. I am able to come up with solutions to problems others have failed to solve. My unique inventions are being marketed from Japan and Australia to North and South America, and throughout Europe.

Last, but not least, I believe I have the ability to communicate my ideas in simple, logical terms, and in a plain and straight-forward language that most people can understand. At least, that is the impression I am left with after having discussed the Simpson case and my theories with quite a few people.

Although I do not qualify as an expert in any of the fields above, I have a good working knowledge of each of them. That gives me an advantage vis-a-vis the investigators, the lawyers, the prosecutors, and the so-called "experts" in the Simpson case.

The Simpson case is so complex. Rather than repeat all of the above, let me say that it covers all of the fields I mentioned – and then some!

Being an expert on fingerprints doesn't get you far in terms of solving the Simpson case. Nor does being an expert on DNA, or on domestic violence.

On the other hand, you don't have to be an expert investigator from the LAPD to realize that, either O.J. murdered Nicole and Ron, in which case **he** left the five blood drops at Bundy – or O.J. did **not** murder Nicole and Ron, in which case someone else – either the **real murderer**, or the **investigators** – fabricated that blood evidence.

To find out the truth about those blood drops it doesn't help you much to be an expert on DNA with a Ph.D. in biochemistry.

The important question isn't, *"Whose blood is on the swatches?"* but *"Where did the blood on the swatches come from?"*

Doctors Irwin Golden, Lakshmanan Sathyavagiswaran, and Werner Spitz may be excellent pathologists. But based on my life experience I believe I am better qualified to answer how the murderer attacked and killed Nicole and Ron. Watching Dr. Sathyavagiswaran and Prosecutor Brian Kelberg demonstrate to the jury in the criminal case how they believe O.J. killed Ron, was like watching my mother teach John Rambo how to fight!

Dr. Spitz' demonstration in the civil trial wasn't much better.

Five different medical examiners have studied the bodies of Nicole and Ron, either directly (Dr. Golden) or indirectly through Dr. Golden's autopsy reports and autopsy photographs.

These "expert" medical examiners have Ph.d.'s and credentials as long as a roll of toilet paper. Some of them charged $50,000 or more for their "expert" opinions!

Yet, every one of the medical examiners missed several extremely significant clues from the autopsies, that hold the keys to solving this murder mystery!

How is that possible? It is possible, because – although, perhaps, excellent forensic pathologists – they don't possess the **broad background of experience** necessary to tie the results of the autopsies to other clues in the case, or to real life experiences.

In chapter 30 (***Medical Examiners – Bought And Paid***) I shall return to the medical examiners and their possibly significant blunders.

If you can understand, logically, why O.J. could not have lost the Bundy glove, even if he were the murderer – then, of course, you can also understand why the murderer must, purposely, have planted both gloves.

Understanding that both gloves must have been deliberately planted by the murderer, you can readily understand that O.J. must be innocent – because he could not have planted the Rockingham glove, since the blood on it was wet – and undisturbed by debris and insects – almost 7 1/2 hours after O.J. left for Chicago.

Unless you have the ability to draw logical conclusions like that, through several steps of deductions and implications, it is not going to help you anything – in terms of solving the Simpson case – to be a lawyer or a prosecutor, a criminalist or a detective, a psychiatrist or a biochemist, or a judge or a battered wife.

This is where my broad background is important. I know more psychology than most of the DNA experts. I believe I know more about how knives are used for fighting, than any of the prosecutors or medical examiners. As a former police sergeant, I know more about police work than most biochemists or experts on domestic violence. Although I am a novice compared to the chemists from the FBI's lab and Cellmark Diagnostics lab – I probably know more chemistry and biochemistry than Prosecutor Darden or counsel for the plaintiffs, Mr. Petrocelli.

What is important in solving a complicated case like the Simpson case is the ability, not only to reason up and down a narrow field of a specialized science, but to reason **across** from one field of science to another – so that you can discover and understand the truth **behind** each piece of evidence and how it **ties in** with the rest of the case.

Things aren't always what they seem to be at first glance, or when viewed isolated from the rest of the case. My little story about the boy and the shattered vase, explained that – I hope!

Since you bought my book, you are probably a person who doesn't accept things, out of hand, just because you heard it on TV or read it in a newspaper. You probably bought my book because you feel that there are a lot of unanswered questions in the Simpson case.

You want answers backed up by reasonable arguments – not just the media propaganda you have been served in this case, and emotional outbursts which makes little or no sense. Hence, I feel confident that we will be able to communicate!

To understand the real significance of much of the evidence in this case, you often need a broad background and a lifetime of experience, so you can view each piece of evidence from different angles, and consider all its possible sources of origin.

Just as important as having knowledge, is the ability to **apply** that knowledge in a logical, practical manner.

You may be an Einstein in physics. But unless you also have a practical mind, you may not even know how to turn on your stove and prepare an omelet, and although someone may be a Nobel Prize laureate for medicine, he may be completely helpless if he gets lost in the wilderness.

Science has reached so far today that to be on the cutting edge in any particular field, you pretty much have to give up everything else and equip yourself with "blinkers" and "tunnel vision."

In solving the Simpson murder mystery we need experts in a variety of fields and sciences. But more important than to have a team of narrow minded experts, is it to have **one** person with a broad background, and good working knowledge of an entire spectrum of sciences. In other words, a person who can understand **all** the experts and piece together their specialized results to form a logical, comprehensive theory that embodies **everything – all the evidence** – and not only scattered pieces here and there.

Normally, the ones to paint the total, complete picture should be the prosecutors. But when the prosecutors become so biased and prejudiced that they fail to interpret the evidence objectively, their case suffers and they are left stumbling around in darkness.

The various pieces of this murder mystery fit together so perfectly! But one would never discover that just by being a hair and fiber expert, a DNA expert, a shoe expert, a medical examiner, or a prosecutor.

To uncover the entire picture, you don't have to be an expert on anything in particular. But you need an extremely broad background from many different fields and sciences, combined with plenty of life experience, and a good portion of common sense.

That is why, based on my broad background, I believe I am as qualified to solve the Simpson case for you as any expert.

In this book I shall try to guide you through many series of logical deductions and implications on our road to "Solving The Simpson Murder Mystery."

Normally, a criminal investigator in the Simpson case would have an advantage over "armchair detectives" like you and me. His advantage is his knowledge of the evidence and the facts of case, and his access to that knowledge when he needs it.

However, in the Simpson case we all, basically, have access to the same information! There is such a multitude of information in this case all of it public:

- some 70,000 (?) pages of court transcripts from the criminal trial,
- thousands of pages of depositions,
- enough books to fill a bookshelf,
- truck loads of newspaper and tabloid articles, and
- thousands of hours of TV programs filled with explanations and analyses.

In our age of advanced communications, anyone who owns a PC, a telephone and a TV set can access every bit as much information about the Simpson case as lead investigator Philip Vannatter. It isn't a matter of having access to that information, but a matter of applying that information correctly.

Many theories, facts, or pieces of evidence apply to different aspects of the case. Consequently, my readers will find many facts, points, and arguments repeated in my book – several times, even!

Certain clues may prove that evidence was fabricated. One of these clues may also – together with other clues – prove that O.J. is innocent. To make each point clear and complete, I would have to mention such a clue in connection with both points.

Let me give you an example, but be aware that I leave out many details in this example. So don't be too critical, at this stage!

The murder gloves were much too small for O.J.'s hands. They didn't fit. The gloves simply didn't appear to be his! This helps to prove that O.J. is innocent. Naturally, I will mention the tight gloves in that context.

But the tight fit of the gloves also – together with several other clues – proves that O.J., even if he were the murderer, could not have lost the Bundy glove in a struggle with Ron.

Consequently, O.J.'s left finger could not have been cut in a struggle with Ron, either. That, together with some other clues, proves that O.J. could not have bled at Bundy – even if he were the murderer! Hence, the blood drops at Bundy could not have come from O.J. directly. They must, therefore, have been fabricated.

Naturally, I will mention the tight fit of the gloves also in that context.

Finally, if the blood drops at Bundy must have been fabricated, they must have come from O.J.'s blood vial. That puts many of Detective Vannatter's dubious actions – as well as the 1.5 ml of blood that were missing from O.J.'s blood vial – in a different light. Peripherally, I will mention the gloves in this context as well.

I will discuss all the clues I believe pertain to each topic. Hence some of these clues will be redundant at times, but this redundancy is sometimes necessary to present the full picture.

The fact that a certain clue, or piece of evidence, serves to exonerate O.J. directly, and at the same time – in a different context – serves to prove that a police officer must have murdered Nicole and Ron, and – in yet another context – serves to prove that the prosecutors must have known this, but covered it up, etc., etc., just goes to corroborate my overall theory since certain clues and pieces of evidence, apparently, tie all of it together.

Let me round off this chapter by making a reservation. The tremendous amount of information available in this case – from a multitude of sources – increases the risk of misinformation.

Everybody seems to be quoting everybody else. Mistakes appear, and are passed on from reporters to authors, to lawyers, to newspapers, to TV, to prosecutors and investigators, and back to TV and newspapers!

I have heard and read so much nonsense that I cannot even begin to list it – from so many involved in this case, including Prosecutor Darden and his colleagues, Detectives Lange and Vannatter, not to forget Detectiev Fuhrman, and from O.J.'s attorneys, as well as from TV talk show hosts Geraldo Rivera and Charles Grodin, and countless of their colleagues.

Don't forget, either, that some of this **misinformation is even taken directly from the official court transcripts**! *"How is that possible?"* you may ask! Actually, it is not so strange, once you think about it.

There was Detective Philip Vannatter on the witness stand, under oath, saying **he left the police nurse's office, downtown, at 2:30 to drive straight to Rockingham, where he arrived around 3:30 pm.** Of course, every word he spoke was taken down by the court's stenographers – exactly as he spoke them. Hence, if you read that page of the court transcripts – that's what you'll think happened!

Then this testimony is being used by reporters in their articles and TV programs. This again is being quoted by others who hold opinions about the Simpson case.

However, **five days** and **"580 pages later,"** O.J.'s attorney revealed that Vannatter was lying. He didn't leave for Rockingham at 2:30. Vannatter lied – to conceal that he had spent 90 minutes alone in his office, with O.J.'s blood vial in his possession. The time log from Rockingham showed that he didn't arrive at Rockingham until around a quarter to five!

Likewise, when an expert witness for the prosecution testified that there were no EDTA in Nicole's blood on O.J.'s sock, that ended up in the court transcripts, too.

Six weeks later, a defense expert disputed the prosecution's claim, and documented that there **was** EDTA in that blood!

Take your pick!

When all this information and misinformation were tossed around and thrown back and forth between everyone associated with the Simpson case, we are bound to see a lot of factual errors.

It does not make it any easier that much of the misinformation is deliberate! Hence, I make no claim that my book is perfect. Not by a long shot!

I have tried to double check the information I present as the "facts of the case." But I would, actually, be surprised if my readers were not able to find numerous factual errors in this book.

None of these errors, however, have any significance with respect to my over all theory. Whether there were ten of O.J.'s hairs on the knit cap, or twenty, is not that important. What is important is the fact that there were many hairs from several other – unidentified – people, on that cap. And even more important is the question of what the cap was doing at Bundy in the first place. It certainly didn't make sense, that O.J. should have tried to make himself invisible, in a dark knit ski cap – in the middle of June!

So, read my book correctly! Use it to find out who murdered Nicole and Ron, and why O.J. got the blame! **But don't use my book as a "Simpson Case Encyclopedia"!**

CHAPTER 7

Why O.J. Lost The Civil Trial

O.J. did not murder Nicole and Ron. Yet, he lost the civil trial. There were several reasons for this. I doubt O.J could have prevailed in Judge Fujisaki's courtroom – regardless of which defense attorney had represented him. Judge Fujisaki skewed the trial so terribly against O.J. that nothing Mr. Baker did, or could have done, would have made any difference. Besides, Judge Fujisaki didn't allow Mr. Baker to do much anyway!

Under those circumstances, it was extremely difficult for Mr. Baker – and not inspiring at all! If you know you are going to lose – ultimately – because the judge has already made up his mind, to see to it that you lose – regardless – then it is tough to put up your best fight, trying to convince yourself that you have a shot at winning.

So, in the same chapter, where I will criticize Mr. Baker, let me also defend him. Maybe he gave O.J. his best defense.

Partly, because the civil trial was so immensely unfair to O.J., I decided to complete this book and publish it – to have on record my reasons for believing that O.J. is innocent, and that Nicole's and Ron's murderer is still at large.

Judge Fujisaki was greatly responsible for the outcome of the civil trial by skewing the civil trial in O.J.'s disfavor.

The media were equally responsible for this mis-"Carriage of Justice." I have dealt with that already.

Of course, the jurors who reached this outrageous verdict, were the ones mostly responsible for the outcome. How they could come to this decision – even considering Judge Fujisaki's rulings and the media's pressure – is unbelievable.

From what I have seen of the civil trial jurors after their verdict, they did not appear to be very intelligent – in spite of the media's attempt to portray them as such.

Many of their arguments and explanations seemed rather short sighted, and the over all impression I was left with, was that these jurors did not understand much of what went on in this case. Apparently, they had made up their minds long before the trial started, that O.J. were guilty – and they should see to it that he was found liable for the murders of Nicole and Ron. Allow me to mention a couple of things:

> After the last African-American juror was dismissed, the jury was admonished by the judge to start their deliberations from scratch. They didn't do that. They had already deliberated for three days. Yet, it took only eleven hours of actual deliberations – after they reconvened – before they had their verdict ready.

> By the way, much of those eleven hours, must have been spent on administrative matters, too, and on reaching a dollar amount for the compensatory damages (the 8.5 million dollars – whereever they got that figure from). Yet, the jurors claimed they conscientiously deliberated over *"all the evidence"*! That is not credible. After all, the case lasted almost five months.

> The alternate juror who replaced the only African-American juror confirmed that the other eleven jurors did not bother to restart their deliberations. They just informed him about their earlier deliberations and conclusions and expected him to accept that.

> Following the criminal jury's acquittal of O.J., **those** jurors were harshly criticized for deliberating for only **four** hours. The critics, basically the media, suggested that the jurors should have deliberated for at least one week! However, those same critics found the civil jurors' **eleven** hours of deliberation – including administrative and financial matters – more than adequate. That is disingenuous, to say the least.

> At the jurors' press conference they were asked what they thought about the three thumps on Kato's wall, which Kato

interpreted as an "earthquake"! One of the jurors "explained" that they had all discussed several possible explanations, and decided on what they believed to be the most plausible one. The conclusion of these *"intelligent," "conscientious," "hard deliberating,"* jurors was that O.J. had walked behind his house **to change clothes**!

Besides the fact that the ground was covered with leaves, and none of the leaves were disturbed, why would O.J. – assuming he **were** the murderer, of course – possibly, go behind his house to change clothes? Why couldn't he, just as well, have slipped out of his shoes, and changed in his foyer, or in his bathroom?

Disregard that question! So here is O.J. – barefoot and without clothes – walking up to his front door! Answer this instead: Didn't the jurors hear the limo driver, Allan Park, testify that he saw O.J. enter his house wearing a dark outfit?

At their press conference the jurors told us, *"Behind his house O.J. put his bloody clothes in a bag – to be disposed of later. That's when he lost the glove"* – allegedly! Then he walked away, headbutting his air-conditioning unit – as if he didn't know that it was there!

However, here are the real "gems" of the jurors' marvellous deliberation logic. In spite of hitting the air-conditioning unit so tremendously hard that Kato believed he experienced an *"earthquake"* – O.J. had no marks on his body (his head in particular) from that impact!

And top this! After having banged against the air-conditioning unit with such force, O.J. must, evidently – according to these jurors – have enjoyed the encounter so much that he did it again – **twice!**

It is frightening to imagine that such a jury – under slightly different circumstances – might have sent O.J. to the gas chamber!

Finally, how do we reconcile the logic of these jurors with Mark Fuhrman's and Brad Roberts' claim – that they, allegedly, saw O.J.'s dark sweat suit in his washing machine a few hours after the murders?

Didn't O.J. dispose of a bag with the murder clothes, after all?

These jurors were **not intelligent**! And they were **not credible**!

O.J. himself must bear much of the responsibility for his demise. His deposition statement regarding the Bruno Magli shoes, and his absolute refusal to admit that he once wore the shoes he was depicted wearing on more than 30 photographs, hurt his credibility.

Given the hostile atmosphere he found himself in, leading up to the trial, I can understand **why** O.J. would say he never owned or wore those *"ugly ass shoes."* However, when the photographs surfaced, he should have admitted that he lied – but explained **why** he felt compelled to lie, namely to save his children, whom he was fighting for, at that time, in the custody trial.

In my opinion, O.J. should also have admitted that he might have hit Nicole in 1989. He should have said:

> *"In 1989, in the heat of our scuffle, neither of us knew what we were doing. So, although I do not recall **hitting** her, **I may, still, have hit Nicole on that occasion.** However, I deeply regretted whatever I did to her. I pleaded "no contest" to a charge of battery.*
>
> *Then – on my own initiative – I pledged, never again to lay a hand on Nicole in anger. I backed up my pledge with a letter that would have negated our prenuptial agreement, and hence, would have cost me **five million dollars** – had I broken that pledge. But I kept my pledge to Nicole.*
>
> *During the last five and one half years, leading up to her murder, I never hit her or beat her – not even once. Nicole herself confirmed that – on three different occasions: To the 911 dispatcher in 1993 – to the LAPD officer who responded to her 911 call – and to the court during our divorce proceedings in 1992.*

*Nicole **"used"** the 911 calls for **moral support** – not because she was **hurt or threatened**!*

*I did **not** kill Nicole! I never beat her during the five and one half years leading up to her murder. I loved her – even after our divorce!"*

Mr. Petrocelli would of course have hammered away:

*"Ah! So you admit it! You **did** hit her! You hit her, and **hit her, and HIT HER** – until June 12, 1994, when you finally murdered her!"*

In response, O.J. would have had to keep his composure and answer:

*"I did **not** hit Nicole, and I did **not** physically hurt her, after 1989 – not even once! Repeating your accusation doesn't change those facts. And I did not kill Nicole! I loved her, and cared **about** her – and **for** her!"*

Had I been O.J.'s defense counsel I would have asked O.J. to comment on the accusations from witnesses who claimed he hit Nicole – and expected O.J. to reply:

*"I am not proud of what transpired between Nicole and me in 1989 – I am ashamed of it! I have told you already that I **may** have hit Nicole that day. I took responsibility for what happened, although **Nicole herself** told her friends that **she** was to blame!*

*However, something important happened on that occasion. **It shocked me to see what I had done to Nicole!** I knew it was terribly wrong to let our differences turn physical – regardless of what Nicole might have said or done. That's why I promised Nicole – and myself – never again to lay a hand on her in anger. I backed up my promise with a five million dollar pledge. **I kept that pledge!***

*Even when Nicole hit **me** – smack in my face, in front of one of our friends – I did not hit her back! As you heard during Al Cowling's testimony, I just* **'looked stupid'!**

As you enter the court house, you can hear the mob chanting: 'Murderer – **Murderer – MURDERER!'** *But I did **not** murder Ron – and the mother of my children!*

Some people will go to any length to hurt me – because they **think** *I killed Nicole and Ron. Some people who think I murdered them, would gladly commit perury in order to hurt me. Sadly, Nicole is not here to rebut their testimonies!*

*I don't ask you to believe **me**! But I ask you not to believe **them**, either! I ask you to believe **Nicole**! Nicole **is** speaking to you from her grave! Listen to the **entire** 911 tape! Listen to the secret tape made by the LAPD officer! And read the transcripts from our divorce proceedings! On all three occasions, Nicole set the record straight, for people who suggested that I beat her. These are Nicole's words – not mine:*

'O.J. never beat me after that incident on New Year's Day in 1989!'

*So even if you don't believe **me** – please, believe **Nicole**! If **you** respect her as much as **I** respect her!"*

Also Defense Counsel Robert Baker is responsible for losing this case for O.J. That is not to say that Robert Baker is a bad lawyer – he was just **not the right kind** of lawyer for O.J.

I realized that before the civil trial even started. And I tried to help both O.J. and Mr. Baker, by offering my assistance, throughout the trial, until I realized that Mr. Baker was not going to listen to what I might say. I sent Mr. Baker at least two dozen faxes and one hundred pages of important information which could help O.J.'s defense. To the best of my knowledge, he never used any of it. He didn't even acknowledge that he received it!

Throughout the civil trial I communicated with several other people – authors, investigative reporters, and ordinary citizens –

who also tried to get in touch with Mr. Baker, to offer assistance. Their experiences in trying to communicate with Mr. Baker were surprisingly and frustratingly similar to mine.

I want my readers to understand that this chapter was **not** written **after** the trial, as a kind of *"I told you so!"* or "20/20 hindsight." In many of my faxes to Mr. Baker, I pleaded with him to let me help him solve this murder mystery. I told him I didn't want any money, I didn't want to be in the spotlights, I was willing to carry my own expenses and travel to Los Angeles to assist him. I simply wanted to help O.J., by helping Mr. Baker.

Months before the civil trial, I wrote to Mr. Baker explaining that in the criminal trial, O.J.'s attorneys did not need to **solve** the crime or come up with **an alternative suspect**. Finding **reasonable doubt** was sufficient. They did that – by a wide margin!

However, in the civil trial, in terms of a **"preponderance of the evidence,"** Mr. Baker **could not** simply rely on *"contamination, sloppy police work, and conspiracy."* He actually had to **solve the murder mystery** – and I could do that for him!

Mr. Baker didn't even send me a fax note or give me a call to thank me for my willingness to help. He didn't even ask his secretary to acknowledge that he had received any of my faxes. Perhaps he didn't even read them!

Finally, when the thirty additional photographs of O.J wearing Bruno Magli shoes appeared over the Christmas holiday, I decided to write **one last fax** to Mr. Baker. But because he never responded to my earlier faxes I called his secretary first and explained the situation to her, urging her to bring my information to Mr. Baker's attention. Here is a transcript of the fax:

Chris Springer

(Address, phone, and fax number deleted)

January 3, 1997

F A X   L E T T E R

(This fax letter consists of 2 pages, inclusive)

TO: Robert Baker, Attorney

ATTN: Ms. (name deleted), Secretary

RE: The Bloody Bruno Magli Shoeprints And The Photographs!

Dear Ms. (name deleted):

It would be great if O.J. and Mr. Baker were in complete control of the issue of the bloody Bruno Magli shoeprints, the Bruno Magli photographs that seem to be popping up several places now, and O.J.s statement in his deposition that he never wore those *"ugly ass shoes."*

These photographs must worry them today. So why dont they give me a call? I can defuse this entire issue!

There is conclusive physical evidence in this case to turn the present problem of the Bruno Magli shoes to the advantage of the defense. Actually, the bloody Bruno Magli shoeprints and the Bruno Magli photographs are keys to proving that O.J. did **not** murder Nicole and Ron! The real physical evidence lies hidden in the Bundy murder scene. No one else has discovered it - but it was there. I have found it, and I will share it with the defense.

The problem is that I am, possibly, the only person (besides the real murderer) who has discovered this evidence, and the significance of it - and O.J. and Mr. Baker arent talking to me. However, I am only going to share this evidence with Mr. Baker or with O.J., personally!

If the Bruno Magli photographs are as much of a problem as everyone seems to think today, then what can O.J. and Mr.

Baker possibly lose, by hearing what I have to say? I am confident that I can turn this entire case around - in O.J.s favor.

I hope and pray that Mr. Baker has something - up his sleeve. But for someone watching the case unfold via TV, it seems like the defense is getting deeper and deeper into trouble. If so, will you please talk to Mr. Baker for me, Ms. (name deleted), and see if you can persuade him to contact me - for Sydney's and Justin's sake, at least!

Sincerely,

Chris Springer [end of fax]

Finally, Mr. Baker responded. I travelled to Santa Monica, California at my own expense and met with him and his son, Phil, in their office.

They seemed elated about the information and evidence I brought them. Apparently, they found my theory credible, and they told me that they would discuss it with the forensic pathologist, Dr. Baden, their medical examiner.

However, to my astonishment, Mr. Baker never introduced my information in court. After the trial I asked Phil Baker why they never introduced my information. He replied that they had discussed my theory, and – although reasonable – it was speculative and difficult to establish. With a judge like Fujisaki, there was little chance of introducing my information.

With the case winding down after the middle of January, it was too late, suddenly, to introduce completely new evidence and theories, or recall witnesses who had already been dismissed. So they did not even try!

That's incredible. I think the real reason was that they had already fumbled the football by waiting too long before they contacted me. Had Mr. Baker been in touch with me before, and throughout, this trial, we could have prepared for the introduction of this particular evidence already from the outset, both in the cross examination of the plaintiffs' medical examiner, Dr. Spitz, in the direct testimony of Dr. Baden, and by consulting expert witnesses on the specific issues I brought up.

I even suggested that Mr. Baker use me as an "expert witness" in this particular matter. By virtue of having discovered this evidence, and having understood its significance, I certainly ought to be qualified as an expert on the matter. And if I can explain this matter to my readers (which you must judge for yourself when you reach that part of my book), **I ought to be able to explain it to the jurors!**

Again, Mr. Baker didn't respond!

The particular evidence I am referring to – although important – was just one of at least a couple of dozen points I gave Mr. Baker, and which he didn't use. Perhaps he didn't even read my faxes?

Mr. Baker's major mistake was that he didn't present **an alternative murder theory!** The reason was that he didn't have any. That's what I offered to provide.

As did the prosecutors in the criminal trial, the plaintiffs presented a **"plausible"** theory of O.J. being the murderer, and they backed it up with "a mountain of evidence"!

Just like in the criminal trial, the defense (Mr. Baker) went after the evidence, claiming contamination, sloppy police work, and conspiracy to frame O.J. It was doomed to fail! I told Mr. Baker this, but he refused to listen.

What Mr. Baker didn't seem to realize, and what I want my readers to understand is this:

"Preponderance of the evidence" – in the eyes of the jurors – didn't mean that it was sufficient for Mr. Baker to point out that there were flaws in much of the evidence, or even in **most**

of the evidence.

"Preponderance of the evidence" meant that Mr. Baker had to prove – by this "preponderance," or "greater portion," of the evidence – that it was more likely than not that **someone else** – rather than **O.J.** – had murdered Nicole and Ron!

Contradictory perhaps, but in reality it wasn't sufficient to prove that O.J. – **most likely** – did **not** murder Nicole and Ron. **"Someone,"** obviously, did murder Nicole and Ron. Consequently, Mr. Baker, **in reality,** had to prove that this **"someone"** – more likely than O.J. – is the murderer!

Mr. Baker, literally, had to **solve** the murder mystery, which the police had failed to solve. It was just like I have explained earlier in my book, where I talk about "proving your innocence."

How could Mr. Baker expect to do that – hence, how could he even **hope** to win this case – when he didn't have an alternative suspect, and no alternative murder theory?

L ook at it this way: The jury in the civil case should consider the evidence, and decide whether that evidence pointed to O.J. – or to **"Mr. X"**!

The first thing Mr. Baker should have done was to introduce **Mr. X** – point to an alternative, **actual suspect**! Secondly, Mr. Baker should have presented a defense theory as to **how Mr. X**, allegedly, committed the murders, consistent with – and this is where it should come in – the preponderance of the evidence!

In other words, Mr. Baker should demonstrate that **more of the evidence before the jury fit Mr. X** and the murder theory of the defense, **than fit O.J.** and the murder theory of the plaintiffs!

Mr. Baker, as I said earlier, fumbled the football. The reason was that Mr. Baker was the **wrong kind** of lawyer for the Simpson case. The civil case was **not a litigation case** (in the strictest sense), although O.J. was sued by the plaintiffs for monetary damages.

Just like in the criminal case, this was still **an unsolved murder mystery.** If O.J. lost, there would be a settlement to be litigated – and Mr. Baker, unquestionably, is an excellent litigator. But a "litigator," unfortunately, was not what O.J. needed. He needed – just like in the criminal case – **a criminal defense lawyer**. Or more than that, perhaps, O.J. needed a supportive **prosecutor** in his corner!

O.J. needed a **"prosecutor"** on his side, who could **"prosecute" Mr. X** in Judge Fujisaki's courtroom! O.J. needed a "prosecutor" who could paint a picture of Mr. X – fictional or real – and then show

- that this Mr. X, had both **motive** and **opportunity**,
- that Mr. X, preferably, had **no alibi**,
- that **the MO fit** Mr. X, and
- that a **preponderance** of the evidence fit Mr. X – as well as, or better than it fit O.J.

"Litigator" Robert Baker simply isn't that kind of an attorney. In the cases Mr. Baker ordinarily handles, I suppose, the jurors usually know exactly what happened – the crime has already been solved! Allow me to give my readers another of my examples:

Let's say that Mr. Simpson, accidentally, had run over his ex-wife with his Bronco, and he was sued for wrongful death, by Nicole's parents. **That** would have been a case for Mr. Baker!

The facts of the matter were clear. The real issue, to be litigated, was the degree of responsibility – if any – held by Mr. Simpson, and other parties involved.

Let us assume that Nicole had come running out into the street, without looking. So O.J. didn't have time to stop. Let us assume that Nicole had been drinking – a little. Let us assume that O.J., too, had been drinking, but just a little, so that legally speaking he was not DUI.

Let us assume that O.J. were driving slightly faster than the posted speed limit.

Let us also assume that the brakes on his Ford Bronco were defective.

Let us assume that the defect was due, in part, to a faulty brake construction by Ford Motor Company, on this particular model.

Let us also assume that O.J.'s Bronco had been in for service earlier that same day, and that the mechanic didn't notice that the brakes were defective, because he forgot to check them – as he should have done, according to the service manual.

Let us also assume that O.J. had a $5,000,000 liability insurance policy. However, he is being sued for $10,000,000.

And let us, finally, assume that even Nicole had her own personal $3,000,000 accident insurance – in addition to her $5,000,000 life insurance!

Let me stop there! If those were the circumstances, I trust my readers realize O.J. would need a good **litigation** lawyer – like Mr. Baker!

In such a case I think O.J. would be very well served by having Mr. Baker in his corner. The main difference between such a fictional civil suit, and the real civil suit against O.J. is that in the fictional example, all the circumstances are known. We know what happened. We know that O.J. drove the Bronco – too fast, and that he had been drinking. We know that Nicole didn't watch where she was running. We know the mechanic didn't check the brakes – as he should have – etc., etc.

We know who and what caused the tragedy. But the jury had to assess the degrees of responsibility between Nicole herself, O.J. personally, Ford Motor Company, the mechanic personally, as well as the firm he worked for – and last, but not least – the degree of responsibility of the half a dozen or so insurance companies representing the individuals and the corporations above.

In the real civil case against O.J., Mr. Baker and the plaintiffs didn't even know who murdered Nicole and Ron. A litigator like Mr. Baker is not the best counsel to solve that puzzle.

Had O.J. been found guilty in the criminal trial, and had the plaintiffs sued for $15,000,000, while O.J. had been worth $25,000,000, and he even had a $10,000,000 insurance policy possibly covering crimes or accidents he might cause when under extreme mental stress – again, Mr. Baker would, probably, have been the right man.

However, the plaintiffs in the real civil case sued O.J. for $50,000,000! And O.J. was almost broke after three years of legal battles. You don't need to be a famous litigator to realize that if O.J. was found liable, the plaintiffs would clean him out, for everything he owns and much of what he will ever earn in the future.

If you are broke, and you are found liable, does it matter if the verdict is for $18,000,000 or $34,000,000?

Mr. Baker may be "the best" when it comes to litigating with tough corporate counsels for major corporations and giants in the insurance industry. But he was not the right attorney for O.J. during the civil case.

L et me return to the so-called "mountain of evidence" against O.J. by presenting yet another of my examples:

- Fuhrman is a racist. Maybe he planted **some** of the blood in the Bronco.
  OK! Let's throw out some of the blood from the Bronco – but also keep some of it.
- Maybe Fuhrman also found the Rockingham glove at Bundy, and that he planted it behind O.J.'s house.
  OK! Let's throw out the Rockingham glove, but keep the Bundy glove.
- Vannatter is lying, and there was EDTA in the blood drops on the rear gate at Bundy.
  OK! Let's throw out two of the three blood drops from the gate.
- The LAPD kept the cap and a sample of the Bronco carpet

in the same open box in their crime lab.

OK! Let's throw out the carpet fiber on the cap – and just keep the carpet fibers on Ron's shirt, since the shirt, at least, was not kept in the box together with the carpet.

– However, what about the five blood drops next to the bloody shoeprints? They were collected before Vannatter received O.J.'s blood sample. [Although those five blood drops were not tested for EDTA, most people believe those five blood drops were tested for EDTA and proven not to contain EDTA].

OK! EDTA test or not – let's keep those blood drops.

Continuing like this, the "mountain" of evidence is gradually reduced to a good size **"hilltop" of evidence.**

This "hilltop of evidence" contains only the evidence which indisputably – for those who don't know better – points to O.J.! None of this "hilltop of evidence" points to anyone else.

So now the counsel for the plaintiffs addresses the jury during closing arguments:

> *"We have generously conceded to disregard all the evidence that could possibly have been contaminated or tampered with. Hence, the* **'mountain of evidence'** *has been reduced to a large* **'hilltop of evidence.'** *All of this hilltop of evidence, therefore, points to O.J.* **– and none of it points to anyone else. And this evidence is irrefutable!**
>
> *So, by a* 'preponderance of the evidence,' *who murdered Nicole and Ron? Did a* **'phantom'** *murder them? Did they, perhaps, commit* **suicide**"? *Or did* **O.J.** *murder Nicole and Ron?*

What I have explained above is the weakness of having a litigation lawyer as your defense counsel, **when you are innocent** – and have been found innocent – but **the plaintiffs still accuse you of murder!**

I tried to communicate this to Mr. Baker. I told him in many of my fax letters that he needed to claim, first of all, that **"someone else" – the real murderer** – killed Nicole and Ron. Secondly, Mr. Baker had to show that the evidence in the case was more consistent with this **real** murderer having killed Nicole and Ron, than with O.J. having done it.

If he did that, there wouldn't even be a litigation part of the civil case, because the verdict would be for O.J.

I explained to Mr. Baker that I had a totally different theory about the murders, than what had been expressed by the prosecutors, the plaintiffs, and the media, and that my theory reconciled **all the evidence in the case.** I informed Mr. Baker that my theory proves that O.J. is innocent, and that someone else – the real murderer – killed Nicole and Ron.

I proceeded to inform Mr. Baker I could prove that almost all the evidence against O.J. was either planted, fabricated, or simply misinterpreted. Finally, I asked Mr. Baker repeatedly – for O.J.'s sake – to set aside just a few minutes, so I could, at least, **begin to explain to him** what really happened at 875 South Bundy Drive, on June 12, 1994, between 10:00 and 11:00 pm.

As I said, Mr. Baker didn't even ask his secretary to acknowledge the fax letters I sent him. Possibly, he didn't even read them!

I think Mr. Baker made a blunder by concentrating on the timeline. I wrote to Mr. Baker about this, and explained why this was a serious mistake – and completely unnecessary. I explained why, in my opinion, the timeline strategy could backfire, **because Dr. Baden's original timeline could never hold up in court** – and it didn't!

That's when I wrote yet another of my fax letters to Mr. Baker. I reminded him about what I had written earlier. I was not gloating because Dr. Baden's timeline theory had just been destroyed under cross examination. I just felt sorry for O.J. Again, I offered to help Mr. Baker.

I informed him about my book manuscript, and said I was willing to hand it over to him, if he wanted it. But I was not simply going to mail a hard copy of it to his office and have it thrown around until someone else ended up publishing my information and theories.

All my information was his, for free, if he wanted it. If not, I told him, I would keep it to myself, until I published it.

No response! That's when I decided to add this chapter to my book. I tell my readers about this, and I inform you about my disappointment with Mr. Baker, so my readers shall know that this chapter does not represent 20/20 hindsight – which we all know is perfect! Had Mr. Baker taken my advice and accepted my assistance already before the trial started, O.J. might have prevailed also in the civil case, although, with a judge like Mr. Fujisaki, it might, perhaps, not have made any difference.

CHAPTER 8

The Book

At the time when Nicole and Ron were murdered, I was the owner of a small import/distribution business. I worked out of a home office in a corner of my living room. I could watch the TV set from my desk.

There were days when I had nothing to do. A fulfillment company handled the warehousing and shipping for my firm. I had to be present when clients called, but even when I had to prepare orders to be faxed to the fulfillment company, I could still choose the time of day to do it. That gave me an excellent opportunity to arrange my schedule as I pleased, and watch every phase of the Simpson case as it progressed.

Like so many people I was consumed by the case and had followed it closely throughout the pre-trial stages. There were many things I could not reconcile with O.J. being the murderer. But writing a book about the Simpson case was the farthest thing from my mind.

Soon I started to distrust the prosecutors and their witnesses. They presented one thing after the other, which in my opinion, had to be positively false. At first I called, wrote, or faxed the news media about these inconsistencies, trusting that the media would appreciate my calling their attention to them.

Quickly, it became evident that the media were only interested in things which portrayed O.J. in a negative manner. For someone like me trying to reach O.J. or his attorneys, personally, was futile. Eventually, writing a book, seemed like the only way for my information and theories to reach the public.

First, my manuscript comprised about 120 pages. OK, so it was going to be a rather "small book" – proving that O.J. was innocent, and that Mark Fuhrman, probably, murdered Nicole and

Ron, and framed O.J.!

However, as the trial progressed, more and more evidence proved that my theory was correct. I had to keep adding pages. Soon the manuscript reached 150 pages! But each time I thought my theory was complete, new evidence popped up in support of it.

Then – along came *"The Fuhrman Tapes"*! If the photographs of O.J. wearing Bruno Magli shoes was the deciding factor in the civil trial, *"The Fuhrman Tapes,"* surely, must have been the deciding factor in the criminal trial.

Shortly after the *"Not guilty"* verdict, my manuscript comprised some 200 pages. But it didn't end there. Even after the criminal trial, information kept pouring out from everywhere. Again my manuscript grew. The result of it all was my first book about the case, titled *"If O.J. Didn't . . ."*

However, the civil trial followed, and more information kept pouring out. There exists infinitely much more information about this case, than what my first book covered. So, one day I decided to write the present follow up. Quickly the manuscript grew to over 600 pages. But at some point, I simply had to stop. I think this book proves for all purposes that my theory is correct, and that O.J. is innocent. By adding another 500 pages to prove the same thing, I felt I would be "beating a dead horse."

Besides, much of the information in this case is totally irrelevant. What does Faye Resnick's personal problems, Nicole's and O.J.'s partying in the eighties, O.J. being cornered in traffic years ago, Nicole losing her keys shortly before her murder, someone in Los Angeles being robbed at knife point a few years ago, and things like that have to do with the question of who murdered Nicole and Ron?

If someone other than O.J murdered Nicole and Ron and tried to frame O.J., then, obviously, this person knew enough about Nicole and O.J. that he could have acquired a pair of Italian shoes, to frame O.J.! So what does it even matter, whether O.J. owned a pair of Bruno Magli shoes or not? Enough is enough!

CHAPTER 9

Distortions And Lies, Right Off The Bat!

I believe in justice and in the judicial process. I expected to see the prosecution present the facts of the case, fairly and honestly – not only what pointed to O.J. being guilty, but also what pointed to his innocence. Then it should be up to the jury to weigh the evidence and come up with a just verdict.

In her opening statement, Prosecutor Marcia Clark mapped out the road she was going to follow:

> *O.J. was an abusive husband, who had beaten Nicole throughout their marriage. This abuse gradually escalated and led to the inevitable tragedy when O.J. finally committed **"the ultimate abuse"** by killing Nicole.*

From what I knew about the case when the criminal trial started, I couldn't possibly see that there was such a history of continued abuse. And I certainly didn't see how one episode of **alleged** physical abuse in 1989 could serve as the prediction of a murder which took place five and a half years later?

But what did I know? I had to wait and see. A principle of mine is that regardless of what anyone says or does, I always think the best of people, until they, themselves, give me reason to change my opinion. The defense and the prosecution had, so far, painted two totally different, and irreconcilably pictures of O.J. Simpson. Now, I wanted to study the artists – "up close and personal" – before I made up my mind as to which artist was the "naturalist" and who was the "surrealist," or rather, who was the **"artist"** – and who was the **"con-artist"**!

January 31, 1994. The prosecution called their first witnesses, 911 dispatcher, Sharon Gilbert, and then former LAPD officer, today LAPD detective, John Edwards. Suddenly I saw what Marcia Clark had been building up to. Swiftly and dramatically, like a wet rag being thrown in my face, Prosecutor Marcia Clark and Detective John Edwards wiped away all my illusions about a fair trial. This was **war**! The **truth** didn't matter – only **winning** mattered!

According to Detective Edwards he had responded to Nicole's 911 call in 1989 and arrived at Simpson's Rockingham estate. Allegedly, Nicole had come storming out of the house wearing nothing but a bra and sweat pants. She threw herself into Officer Edwards' arms and, according to his testimony exclaimed:

"He is going to kill me! . . . He is going to kill me!"

This statement suited Prosecutor Clark's theory perfectly. It pointed to the future – to June 12, 1994! But after a lifetime at poker tables all over the world, and years of teaching, I can tell when people are bluffing or cheating! I didn't buy Detective Edwards' testimony for a second. He was tailoring his testimony to suit Marcia Clark's opening statement.

My real wake-up call came a few seconds later, when it dawned on me, that **Detective Edwards didn't do this on his own!** How could he remember the exact words Nicole had spoken 6 years earlier? Obviously, Prosecutor Marcia Clark and Detective Edwards had concocted his testimony.

Ms. Clark had instructed Detective Edwards exactly what **she** wanted Nicole to have said!

Normally, if a prosecutor asked Detective Edwards what Nicole had told him, that would be "hearsay" and not permitted as evidence, unless Nicole could corroborate it through **her** testimony. But Nicole was dead.

That was, in a way, a draw-back for Prosecutor Clark. Nicole could not corroborate what she might, or might not, have told

Officer Edwards. However, Prosecutor Marcia Clark knew how to turn a disadvantage into an advantage.

Since Nicole could not verify Detective Edwards' testimony, **she could not refute it either!** Detective Edwards could quote Nicole any which way he wanted – **if Prosecutor Clark could find a way for his "hearsay" testimony to be admitted.**

There is an **exemption** to the "hearsay rule" if the "hearsay" statement has been spoken impulsively and in a state of serious emotion, like if your son came storming into your living room exclaiming:

> *"The Johnsons' house is on fire!"*

You would be allowed to testify to that, even though your son might not be present to corroborate what you claim he said.

If Marcia Clark could agree with Detective Edwards (who was the only witness) to create a scenario of drama, emotions, and spontaneous outbursts by Nicole, then, Detective Edwards could pretty much quote Nicole as having said anything he wanted her to have said – or rather, anything Prosecutor Marcia Clark wanted the jury to **believe** that Nicole had said!

So, the two of them agreed to pretend that Nicole had come storming out of the house, half naked, screaming, *"He is going to kill me! He is going to kill me!"* – before throwing herself into Officer Edwards' arms.

How can I be so sure of this? First of all, Nicole did **not** come storming out of her house. She had been hiding in the bushes for quite some time. Most likely, she just just stood up and walked over to the gate when she saw Officer Edwards' patrol car. However, for Officer Edwards' "hearsay testimony" to be admitted, he and Prosecutor Clark had to concoct a story of urgency and spontaneity. Hence – according to Officer Edwards – Nicole did not walk over towards the gate – she came *"storming out of the house"*!

Next, Detective Edwards didn't leave any room for interpretations or nuances with respect to **the exact words** Nicole allegedly spoke:

> (**Future** tense) *"He is **going to** kill me!"*

Let us try to put ourselves in Nicole's place back then, and accept Detective Edwards' testimony that Nicole came storming out of the house. **Allegedly,** Nicole believed that O.J. wanted to kill her. She had, allegedly, been beaten by her husband. Desperately she called 911. Officer Edwards arrived and buzzed the intercom, demanding to speak to the woman who had called 911 (to assure himself *"that she was alive, and not kept hostage"*).

Someone answered that the matter had been resolved and Officer Edwards, therefore, could leave, but Officer Edwards was persistent. Someone might be preventing Nicole from talking to the police.

Let's **assume** that the **alleged** beating continued, or the threat was still emminent when Officer Edwards arrived, and now O.J. was trying to get rid of the police officer who responded to Nicole's 911 call – still hypothetically speaking.

If so, Nicole must have been scared stiff by the thought of the officer leaving the scene without rescuing her. So, allegedly, she made a desperate dash to freedom. That's when she, allegedly, came storming out of the house and towards Officer Edwards.

This was what Prosecutor Clark and Detective Edwards wanted the jury to believe, at least.

Again, **assuming** that this was correct, put yourself in Nicole's situation! In one dramatic sentence she should have been trying to convey the situation to the police officer. Of course she would have been totally consumed by her, alleged, **recent** dramatic experience – she should have been!

So, what she should have told Officer Edwards – **if we can believe him at all** – was this:

> *"He beat me up! . . . . He beat me up!"* or: *"Help me! . . . The guy is crazy!"*

That's what **you** would have said! Right! That's what **I** would have said! That's what **anyone** would have said. And that's what **Nicole** must have said – **if we can believe Detective Edwards at all!**

Nicole must have been totally consumed by her present ordeal at that exact moment. She must have wanted to tell Officer Edwards in a few words **what had just happened to her.**

She couldn't have brushed that aside, and instead have begun to **"philosophize"** about what O.J. might or might not do to her a week or a month later, or 5-6 years down the line!

I don't for a second believe that Nicole exclaimed:

"He is GOING TO kill me!"

If Nicole said anything like that to Officer Edwards, she probably said:

He beat me up!" or *"He's crazy!"* or *"Help me!"*

"He beat me up!" referred to what, allegedly, had already happened, something of the **past.** It didn't point to the **future.** It didn't point to **June 12, 1994.** But Prosecutor Marcia Clark decided that

"He is GOING TO kill me,"

. . . just fit the prosecution's theory better!

Nicole is dead. Nobody can ask her what she said – the exact words. So the prosecution and Detective Edwards were **"free-rolling"!** He could have testified to anything! He could even have testified that Nicole had predicted the exact date of her murder, and the way it would happen! The defense would have no way of refuting it.

You may argue that if O.J. had beaten her, it didn't really make much difference whether Nicole said one thing or another. However, it did make a difference. Because it showed again and again,

> **the prosecution was tailoring the evidence, the witnesses, and the facts, to suit their own theory. And when the facts didn't fit their theory, they skewed the facts in an effort too make them fit!**

I know there are still those who simply cannot make themselves believe that a police officer would lie under oath when testifying in a murder case. So I watched the videotape of Detective Edwards' testimony, to listen to the tone of his voice and look at his demeanor as he uttered the words, *"He is going to kill me!"* I found something interesting.

According to Detective Edwards, Nicole, allegedly in fear of being killed (by O.J.), had come storming out the house and was leaning over the post for the hydraulic gate opener – **inside** the gate. But according to Detective Edwards, rather than getting herself to safety – on the **outside** of the gate – he and Nicole carried on a "lengthy" conversation – **on opposite sides of the gate!**

> *"He is going to kill me! He is going to kill me!"*
> *"Who is going to kill you?"*
> *"O.J.!"*
> *"O.J. – who?"*
> *"O.J.! . . . He is going to kill me!"*
> *"You mean 'O.J.' – the football player?"*
> *"Yes – he is going to kill me! He is going to kill me!"*

It sounded almost as if Nicole had to **qualify herself** before Officer Edwards would allow her to get out! According to Detective Edwards, Nicole finally exited, threw herself into his arms and repeated twice: *"He is going to kill me! He is going to kill me!"*

I was amazed that Detective Edwards during his testimony didn't also throw in, *". . . with a knife . . . on June 12, 1994"*!

When asking Detective Edwards what further happened, the prosecutor got in a few more "punches." This is how Prosecutor Clark continued the examination of Detective Edwards (in essence):

> *"So then, after Nicole had screamed,* **'He is going to kill me! He is going to kill me!'** *she exited the gate, threw herself into your arms, and repeated,* **'He is going to kill me! He is going to kill me!'** *– what happened next?"*

Detective Edwards replied:

> *"Well ... after she had screamed* **'He is going to kill me! He is going to kill me!'** *she exited, threw herself into my arms and repeated,* **'He is going to kill me! He is going to kill me!'** *Then she ..."*
>   ... Bla ... bla ... bla ...

Seriously, I think the prosecution presented the jury with, *"He is going to kill me!"* – I would guess – 20-30 times in about 5 minutes! It was almost embarrassing to watch!

I wish my readers could have watch the rest of Detective Edwards' testimony, too. With a demeanor as if he were trying to recall in his mind the episode many years earlier, he went on to describe Nicole's bruised face.

First, he described a cut on her **lip** – by pointing to his own **cheek bone!** Then, he went on to describe Nicole's bruised cheek bone by touching his own **left** cheek bone. He put his hand down and paused, so as to emphasize the details of that injury, before he said:

> *"On her **right** cheek bone, I believe it was"*!

All in all, to put it mildly, Detective Edwards' testimony was not too credible. *"Poorly rehearsed."* is perhaps a nice way of describing it! *"Concocted"* may be a better description.

Little surprise that **Officer Edwards was one of the LAPD officers specifically mentioned in the Christopher Commission Report. And Detective Fuhrman, by the way,**

missed this dubious "honor" by one single police brutality claim – he had five, but needed at least six!

The Report was commissioned by the city of Los Angeles, in direct response to the Rodney King beating, and allegations of racism, beatings, vicious brutality, evidence fabrication, and perjury by countless LAPD officers!

And here they were again – in the Simpson case! Both Fuhrman and Edwards had been to Simpson's house earlier, investigating alleged domestic abuse. Fuhrman is right smack in the middle of things and suspected – by me, at least – of actually being the murderer! And Edwards is testifying on behalf of the prosecution – obviously skewing his testimony to make the defendant, O.J., appear guilty – which, of course, is helping his colleague, Fuhrman, if he, indeed, is the murderer!

According to Prosecutor Christopher Darden – that day in 1989, **O.J.'s fuse was lit.** The fuse kept burning, shorter and shorter – until one day in June, 1994, when the fuse had burnt up and the time bomb exploded! That was when O.J., allegedly, murdered Nicole and Ron.

It was a nice allegory – if it had been true! But Mr. Darden's theory was absurd. Darden and the rest of the prosecution team argued:

"Once a wife beater – always a wife beater!"

Based on this fascinating, and perhaps, in many cases, true statement, they **hypothesized** that O.J. beat Nicole regularly, until he eventually killed her.

The first, **and only**, incident of alleged beating which the prosecutors could present even the slightest evidence of, occurred on New Years Day, 1989. The only reason for this is that **O.J. pleaded "no contest"** to a misdemeanor charge of spousal battery.

By virtue of his "no contest" plea, O.J. was **statutorily** found guilty of spousal battery, and sentenced to some community service. But my readers should realize that O.J. did not admit to the charges. He simply pleaded "no contest" to spare Nicole's and his marriage from the media's spotlight.

Nicole, later, admitted to friends that she was drunk, and that she was as much to blame for that incident as O.J.

It is definitely worth noticing that O.J., after that incident, voluntarily wrote Nicole an appologetic letter, in which he stated that if he **ever again** laid a hand on her in anger, their prenuptial agreement should be declared null and void.

That was quite an admission! During Nicole's and O.J.'s divorce, based on their prenuptial agreement, I believe I have heard that O.J. – instead of alimony – paid off Nicole according to their divorce settlement, with **one lump sum** of about $500,000 to $1,000,000.

O.J.'s estate was worth almost eleven million dollars! Without the prenuptial agreement, if O.J. had hit Nicole after January 1989, Nicole could file for divorce, and walk away with close to **five and a half** million dollars!

Wow! In other words, a slap on the cheek after 1989 could cost O.J. **close to five million dollars!**

Is it at all plausible that O.J. would agree to something like that – voluntarily – on his own initiative – in writing – unless he felt, sincerely, that he would never even be **tempted** to harm Nicole again?

And is it at all plausible that O.J. – after having given Nicole such a document – would slap her around at the cost of **five million dollars?**

Furthermore, five million dollars was quite a temptation for any young woman, especially if she was getting a divorce. Yet, during their divorce proceedings in 1992, Nicole did not claim that O.J. had beaten her. Not even once!

So whom are we going to listen to in this case? Prosecutors Darden and Clark? Geraldo Rivera? Charles Grodin? The rest of the media? Nicole's sister, Denise, and her family, out to destroy O.J.? The counsels for the plaintiffs?

Why not listen to Nicole herself? The court records from her and O.J.'s divorce proceedings are available, I assume!

Nicole is not *"talking to us from her grave,"* the way Prosecutor Marcia Clark so dramatically described it to us during her closing arguments! Nicole is talking to us from the divorce proceedings in 1992!

There she was assisted by her divorce attorney who was trying to help her walk away with the best possible divorce settlement. She would have gotten five million dollars, if O.J. had beaten her after January 1989. So, (in essence) she told the court:

> *We had our differences and our squabbles, for which I am to blame, as much as O.J., but **he never beat me** (after New Year's Day 1989)!*

What's going on in the media? They ran an **excerpt** of the tape from Nicole's 911 call on October 25, 1993. We have all probably heard it so many times – even presented with graphics, on TV – that we know the excerpt by heart.

Based on the **excerpt** it sounded as if O.J. were beating the hell out of Nicole – because she sounded so desperate and fearful!

> **The fact is that O.J. was not even in the room Nicole was calling from!** That's usually when the media **"cut and paste"** the tape!

Later in the tape, O.J. did go upstairs, and he and Nicole were together in the same room. There was no beating going on, and Nicole didn't try to run away. Nor did she sound even the least bit afraid of O.J.

The dispatcher asked Nicole if O.J. had beaten her and she flatly denied it! Nicole was asked if she needed the assistance of a paramedic – **because that is how she sounded in <u>the media's</u>**

edited excerpt from the opening of the tape!

Again, Nicole said "no" (*"Uh-uh"*). Again, she confirmed that O.J. had not beaten her, and the continuation of the 911 tape confirmed that he didn't do it later either.

On the tape, **Nicole even admitted that the whole episode was her fault**, because of her association with some prostitutes, and that she regretted having called 911 – even before O.J. entered the room. But the media never bothered to present such details:

Nicole: *"And it's all my fault ... and now, what am I going to do? Get the police in this, and the whole thing? It's all my fault! I started this before! Oh, brother...!"*

The LAPD's 911 dispatcher obviously got the picture after a while!

Dispatcher: *"OK. So basically, you guys have just been arguing?"*

In spite of all this, the media managed to edit and reproduce that tape to make it sound and look as if O.J. just walked straight through the French doors and beat the hell out of Nicole!

It's astonishing, what a clever audio editor and a TV producer with the right studio equipment can do in terms of distorting the truth!

I bet they could change the Pope's Christmas blessings from the Vatican to make him look and sound like a black rapper inciting the killing of white police officers in New York!

Today, with their modern digitalized equipment, the media can distort the truth in any way they want – whether it be audio tapes, videotapes, or photographs. Never in the history of mankind have the media been more biased and unfair towards a human being, than against O.J. Simpson.

During the 911 episode in 1993, one of the officers who responded to the 911 call had a **secret tape recorder**. That could be interesting evidence, so why didn't Prosecutors Clark or Darden introduce the tape in court? Because the tape totally shattered the prosecution's ***"burning fuse"*** theory.

On the tape, the officer asks Nicole if O.J. had beaten her. Clearly, Nicole's voice is heard responding to the officer's question:

No! He hasn't beaten me since New Year's Day 1989.

Eight times before, Nicole had called 911. Yet, when asked by the dispatcher during the 1993 episode, if O.J. had hit her in connection with these 911 episodes, she denied that. During their divorce proceedings – when she must have been pretty turned off by her husband – not even for the sum of five million dollars could she claim that O.J. had beaten her, except that one time in 1989.

That makes me wonder! What could make a wife call 911 on eight occasions – without having been physically harmed on any one of those occasions?

I recognize a pattern here! I believe Nicole was using the 911 calls as a weapon against O.J. – just like children call on their parents during scuffles between siblings. I know something about that, and I think it is relevant. Let me get personal:

I have two sisters and a brother. As kids, normally, we were the best of friends. But we could also be the worst of friends, fighting over toys, "goodies" and snacks, shared and revealed secrets, etc. – just like most siblings do.

My scuffles were usually with my older siblings. We could wrestle over toys or other pieces of "property," but we never fought each other physically. Often, my siblings would start a squabble by taking my toys, and if I couldn't take them back, I would instead take some of their much better toys – and refuse to trade. Sometimes I might even break their toys – accidentally, of course!

Then, one day, they figured out something smart. They gave me back my toys, making me look like the only villain! Then they called on our parents and said I had taken **their** toys. That worked – every time!

Soon, I was portrayed as the "trouble maker" in the family. And from then on, whenever my siblings felt I was getting the upper hand, they either threatened to call on our parents, or they even made good on their threats.

One of our parents would come running, and regardless of who, or what, had started the scuffle, my parents would always take my siblings' side and tell me:

> *"You know, Chris – you are usually the one who starts trouble around this house! You got your football back! So, give your brother back his truck, and don't ever take your sisters diary again! Now, go to your room . . . and stay there – till I tell you that you can come out!"*

Our parent would leave, I would head for my room, while my brother an sister were making "faces" at me, whispering:

> *"We told you so ... We told you so ..."*

Nicole once called 911. She learned, just like my siblings, that it worked! The police weren't interested in long explanations and stuff. They automatically **sided with the person who called 911** – in particular since she was a woman.

Nicole caught on quickly! Just like my siblings had learned that they could gain back the upper hand by calling on, or threatening to call on, our parents – Nicole realized that she could gain back the upper hand against O.J. by calling, or threatening to call, 911!

Now, Nicole was a strong willed person. She was also pretty strong, physically, for a woman – and fit. She was not easy to push around. She was pretty evenly matched with O.J., since O.J. did not use his physical advantage (except perhaps that one time in 1989). But there were occasions when she and O.J. had their squabbles, and she felt she couldn't handle it.

Although Nicole later, on several occasions, told her friends that she was to blame for most of those rows – in the heat of the battle, she would not give in to O.J. So, as a last resort, she called 911.

Calling 911 is serious – something that should be limited to situations of severe danger, like children trapped in a burning building, seriously injured auto accident victims, assaulted people, witnesses to a robbery, etc. 911 shouldn't be used as a replacement for family counselors – where there is no violence or physical abuse.

Calling 911 is something you do when your life is in jeopardy! Yet, **eight times Nicole called 911.** Each time the police responded. Each time they asked the obligatory question: *Has your husband hit you?* And each time Nicole told them: *No, he hasn't hit me!*

Nicole used – or I would even say "abused" – the 911 emergency system for moral support and as a weapon against O.J. – where she instead should have called a marriage counselor, or a **divorce attorney**! Nicole called 911, just like children siblings often call on their parents for support during arguments.

There is strong evidence to support O.J.'s claim that he never beat her – not even once – in spite of eight 911 calls from Nicole!

Nicole herself is the first to state this, both on the secret audiotape the police made, to the dispatcher on the 911 tape in 1993, and during her and O.J.'s divorce proceedings in 1992!

Yet, the prosecution were trying to use the 911 tape from 1993, and the fact that Nicole and O.J. divorced in 1992, as evidence that O.J. murdered Nicole in 1994! I mean, this is so "way out" that I begin to worry about the mental state of these prosecutors!

Besides, I am getting personally insulted, if Marcia Clark and Christopher Darden think I am likely to believe something that absurd!

Hypothetically speaking – had there **not** been any squabbles and **no** 911 calls, **then** I could possibly consider that O.J. **might** be a man who kept his emotions and his rage hidden inside. **Then,** perhaps, in 1994, something caused all of this built up rage to explode. And because there was no established pattern or precedence for how O.J. might react when he got upset – we could, perhaps, hypothetically, speculate that he might have reacted with murder.

However – in reality – quite the opposite was the case! Nicole and O.J. had heated arguments and outbursts when they indeed "let it all hang out"! They yelled and screamed and told each other exactly how they felt. O.J. – no less than Nicole – kept nothing inside! And as we know, Nicole even called 911 – eight times!

In other words, we **know** exactly how O.J. reacted when he was in his wildest emotional state: He shouted! He slammed doors! Allegedly, he even banged up on Nicole's Mercedes!

However, in spite of his occasional anger – **during the five and a half years leading up to the murders – O.J. never physically harmed Nicole. Not even once!**

Obviously, Prosecutors Marcia Clark and Christopher Darden were presenting us with a totally false picture of O.J. With their deceptions and trickery they managed to turn the entire media and the majority of the American people, against O.J.

One photograph of Nicole, frequently reproduced in the media, was a picture of Nicole's face, where her face had deliberately been made up to make her face look battered – in preparation for a movie she appeared in with O.J., or something like that. Both the prosecutors and the media knew the history behind this particular photo. Yet, they used it indiscriminately as evidence of O.J.'s alleged physical abuse of Nicole!

As the title of this chapter stated, it was

"Distortions And Lies, Right Off The Bat ..."

CHAPTER 10

No Motive

Let us review the prosecution's arguments regarding O.J.'s alleged motive. They argued that O.J. was a wife beater who had beaten Nicole repeatedly, and that the murder of Nicole was simply a continuation and escalation of O.J.'s physical abuse of her.

To support their theory of "physical abuse leading to murder" the prosecution argued as follows:

Thirty percent of all men who murdered their women, had previously abused their women.

Since O.J., allegedly, had abused Nicole physically, he must have murdered her.

The claim was absolutely false! But besides, it lacked, so totally, any kind of logic, that it was almost embarrassing to hear a prosecutor, or a reporter, present it. To better illustrate the argument's warped sense of logic, let me present a comparable argument:

Most millionaires started out with two empty hands.

Accordingly, if you have two empty hands, you'll probably end up as a millionaire.

The prosecutors were completely screwing up the premise and the conclusion of their so-called "physical abuse leading to murder" theory. There is another statistic that better applies to the Simpson case, but it didn't suit the theory of the prosecutors, so they didn't mention it:

Less than 1/10 of one percent of all men who physically abuse
their wives or girlfriends, proceed to murder these women.
Accordingly, even if O.J. had abused Nicole physically, there
is less than one chance in one thousand that he killed her!

To support their theory of physical abuse leading to murder, the
prosecution presented audio tapes from two episodes, 9 and
5 1/2 years old, respectively, when Nicole had called 911 during
her and O.J.'s arguments.

The way the 911 tape from October 25, 1993 was edited and
presented by the media, one clearly got the impression that O.J.
physically abused Nicole during that episode. However, by reading a transcript of the **entire** tape, a totally different picture evolves.

O.J. vehemently denied that he ever hit Nicole – in particular
during that 911 episode. On the 911 tape from 1993 we can clearly
hear the dispatcher ask Nicole if O.J. had hit her. Just as clearly,
Nicole answered, *"No"*! To assure herself that Nicole was
unharmed, the dispatcher followed up by asking Nicole if she
needed *"any paramedics or anything."* Again, Nicole's answer
was **"no"** (*"Uh-uh"*)!

Actually, according to O.J., he and Nicole had argued earlier
that day, but settled their differences. O.J. was on his way home,
but Nicole called him back again! When he came back to Nicole's
house (then on Gretna Green), Nicole had already called the cops!

This seems plausible, if we listen to the 911 tape.

Nicole: [To the 911 dispatcher] *Could you get somebody over here
now, to . . . Gretna Green. **He's back.** Please!*

It was almost as if Nicole had staged the whole thing! Remember,
she was trying to change their divorce settlement at that time.
If Nicole could establish physical abuse, and their prenuptial agreement, consequently, were overturned, she stood to gain almost five
million dollars!

Basically the entire 911 episode was a "shouting match"
between Nicole and O.J. over trivial matters. This is evident from

the dispatcher's follow-up question:

Dispatcher: *"OK. You just want him to leave?"*

A little later, after more shouting and screaming over trivial matters, like a phone book, the dispatcher, again, asked Nicole:

Dispatcher: *"OK. So basically, you guys have just been argu-ing?"*

To anyone unbiased, it should be evident that these episodes of so-called "domestic violence," which the prosecution (and the media) repeatedly referred to, where nothing more than heated arguments – exactly what Nicole confirmed over and over again in the above mentioned 911 tape, and which the dispatcher also clearly understood.

Towards the end of the 911 tape the dispatcher asked an interesting question. With clear reference to what had just occurred – an argument escalating into a shouting match, without any kind of physical abuse, followed by, or preceded by, Nicole calling 911 – the dispatcher asked Nicole the following:

Dispatcher: *"Has this happened before, or no?"*

Nicole: *"Many times!"*

This last exchange is interesting! Rather than indicating that O.J. had hit Nicole repeatedly, the exchange demonstrated the direct opposite, namely that

> O.J. did **not** hit Nicole, even during their heated arguments when Nicole called 911.

The dispatcher clearly referred to the episode she had just witnessed over the phone, and characterized by saying:

"OK. So basically, you guys have just been arguing."

In this episode there was never any physical abuse or violence – just loud arguments over trivial matters. Nicole confirmed that, and the dispatcher, obviously, understood this.

With **clear reference to this particular kind of disputes** between Nicole and O.J., the dispatcher asked Nicole:

*"Has **this** happened before, or no?"*

Nicole did **not** qualify her answer by claiming or suggesting that on **earlier** occasions when she and O.J. had their heated arguments, then O.J. **also** hit her. Instead, without hesitation, Nicole answered:

"Many times"!

This last exchange between Nicole and the dispatcher should make it crystal clear that **also Nicole's earlier 911 calls were nothing but heated arguments** – without any physical abuse by O.J.

The way the now infamous 911 tape from 1993 has been played out by the media is a striking example of how a certain episode – when "cleverly" edited by the media – can be presented to the public as evidence of the direct opposite of what that episode really represented!

Those in the media, responsible for such distortion of the truth, ought to be held accountable, and lose their jobs. But that won't happen because the entire media is just as biased and self-serving as they accuse everyone else of being.

We see the same phenomenon of distortion of the truth, **camaraderie, codes of silence, and cover-ups**, whether the issue is Watergate, Whitewater, the CIA, politicians in general, the police (the LAPD in particular), sexual misconduct in the Navy, as well as in the Army.

Any organization expected to police itself has failed to do so, and will continue to fail to do so.

By repeating it over and over again, the edited version of the 911 tape is being used by the media to further create a totally skewed impression of O.J.'s personality and behavior, as well as of Nicole's role as a victim of physical abuse, rather than an even partner in repeated trivial quarrels between two evenly matched spouses.

O.J. denied having hit Nicole. According to O.J., she hit him, however, while he just covered his face and his groin, letting Nicole hit him. I believe many couples may recognize this pattern:

> A couple get into a heated argument. The woman, actually, is the one who turns physical and starts hitting her man – trusting that he will not hit her back, since she is a woman!
>
> The man accepting that he should never hit a woman, simply covers his face and his groin and allows the woman to hit him – because it doesn't really hurt that much for a strong man to be hit by a woman.

This pattern is supported by what we know about Nicole's hot temper. O.J. claimed this, and Nicole admitted to friends and relatives that she indeed did hit O.J. during their arguments. And a neighbor of the Simpsons' testified that Nicole had actually struck her housemaid in the face, during a dispute over some household matter.

A.C. Cowlings, who was as much a friend of Nicole's, as of O.J.'s, testified that he never saw O.J. hit Nicole. However, he did see Nicole hit O.J., once. When asked what O.J. did in response, A.C. Cowlings answered:

"Looked stupid!"

Think about that! Here is a man who during an argument with his wife is struck in the face by his wife – and he does **nothing** to retaliate! In spite of such restraint the entire nation labels him a "wife beater"! Were is the public's sense of fairness and reality?

Or is it just the media that is out of whack?

During the 1985 and 1993 episodes, O.J. had, arguably, cracked the windshield of Nicole's Mercedes with a baseball bat, and broken a French door in their house, respectively. The prosecutor referred to these incidents as proof of O.J.'s violence and lack of self control.

O.J. vehemently denied having smashed the windshield of the Mercedes, and the prosecutors could not prove that he had done that. Allegedly, the windshield received a crack. But O.J. had bought the car, and maintained it. He paid for the damage. And Nicole continued to drive the car as it was, and didn't repair the windshield for many weeks! So it couldn't have been too serious.

The one who brought up this allegation was actually Detective Mark Fuhrman, who had responded to Nicole's 911 call back in 1985. But Fuhrman didn't write any report on the alleged broken windshield until 4 years later!

Regarding the broken French door in 1993, **O.J. didn't break that door. It was already broken, by O.J.'s children.**

Even if we accept that these episodes **might** have occurred, I believe they prove exactly the opposite of physical abuse! Obviously O.J. and Nicole were in the middle of intense arguments, screaming and shouting at each other.

Precisely, as Nicole told the 911 dispatcher in 1993, O.J. did **not** hit her during these intense arguments. When words had no effect, O.J. still had enough self control and discipline to realize, that it was unacceptable for him to even contemplate hitting his wife (or any woman).

So, as a last resource, and to make a "statement," maybe O.J. instead grabbed a baseball bat and cracked the windshield of Nicole's Mercedes, and on another occasion, kicked the French door in their house – although I doubt it!

O.J. knew he would have to pay for the cracked car window and the broken door. Therefore, if he broke them, what he, allegedly, was doing when he and Nicole could no longer communicate, was to **hurt himself – instead of Nicole!**

I would call that a socially, fully acceptable, controlled response to his anger. Wouldn't we all wish that angry men, during arguments with their women, threw their floppy disks out the window, kicked their pick-up trucks, or broke their fishing poles, in anger – rather than punched their women in the nose! I fail to understand how O.J.'s reactions can be criticized even if he **did** break the French door and the window – as long as he did not beat up on Nicole!

Another point is worth mentioning. The episodes with the Mercedes and with the French door has been played over and over by the media – "a million times" – as two of the worst examples of O.J.'s violent temper. I have just put those episodes in their proper perspective. Remember also, though, that **these episodes – the worst the media, the prosecutors, and the plaintiffs could dig up from O.J.'s past – happened almost nine years apart**!

If that is the worst O.J.'s adversaries can say about him – *"he cracked his wife's car window **nine years ago"** –* I suggest they shut up! How many of my readers can say, honestly, that the most violent thing they have done the last nine years, is break your own window, or slam a French door (or a screen door) so it cracks?

Alternatively, the prosecutors argued that O.J. was so unbearably jealous of Nicole that he killed her, because he couldn't stand the thought of Nicole in the arms of another man. Again, this is perhaps even more absurd than the physical violence motive.

According to the prosecution, O.J. was so jealous that he stalked Nicole one night, after they were separated and she had moved to her house on Gretna Green. **That was a lie!** O.J. had stopped by Nicole's house on his way home one night, to talk to Nicole about **something Nicole herself had wanted to discuss with O.J.**

It was late, so rather than ringing the doorbell, possibly waking up Nicole and the children if they were asleep, O.J. instead peeked through the living room window first, to see if Nicole was still up.

When one of her neighbors, later, reported seeing O.J. walking around Nicole's house, Nicole herself cleared up that misunderstanding, telling the neighbor that she had specifically asked O.J. to come over.

Anyway, O.J. was over by Nicole's house one night. Out of consideration for Nicole and the children, in case they were asleep, O.J. peeked through the window before ringing her doorbell.

There on the couch he saw Nicole – who was still his wife, legally speaking – having oral sex with a lover, **while O.J.'s two children were in their rooms upstairs**!

(The man in question, Mr. Keith Zlomsowitch, has admitted that Nicole performed oral sex on him on that occasion).

What if O.J.'s children, Sydney, age 8, and Justin, age 5, had woken up, from thirst or from a bad dream, and had wandered downstairs, quietly, for a glass of milk, or to be comforted by their mother – and had found their mother in such a compromising situation, with a man who wasn't even their father?!

What kind of man is this Keith Zlomsowitch, who didn't care if he had exposed himself to O.J.'s young children in this manner?

Anyway, O.J. didn't lose his temper and break down the door. Nor did he burst in on them and beat the shit out of the man – which I am certain most of my readers feel he deserved!

Instead, O.J. discretely rang the door bell to make them stop and think about what they were doing. Then he left quietly. Nicole and Mr. Zlomsowitch didn't even know that he had seen them!

Only the following afternoon did he talk to them about the episode. *"I saw you last night,"* he said.

However, O.J. wasn't angry, and he didn't beat up any of them. He simply asked them to be more discrete, and not make out where his young children might walk in on them!

I often wondered what Mr. Zlomsowitch was doing on the plaintiffs' witness list. And why did the plaintiffs ask for Mr. Zlomsowitch's deposition statement? Whenever his name came up I told whomever I discussed the case with, that such an immoral person could never be called to testify for the plaintiffs! I could have wagered a million dollars on that! Besides, O.J.'s restraint in connection with that episode, spoke greatly in his favour.

Isn't it clear now, that the only reason the plaintiffs took Mr. Zlomsowitch's deposition statement, was to have him declare that O.J., allegedly, "stalked" him and Nicole on that particular night.

Then the plaintiffs could leak Mr. Zlomsowitch's ridiculous "stalking" claim to the media, pretending that this man – this sex maniac – was going to testify that O.J. was a "stalker." When Mr. Zlomsowitch had served his purpose of presenting O.J. as a "stalker" in the eyes of the public, **thereby tainting the jury pool,** Mr. Zlomsowitch would be stricken from the plaintiffs witness list!

I would like to ask the counsel for the plaintiffs, Mr. Petrocelli:

> *"Why didn't the plaintiffs call Mr. Zlomsowitch as a witness?"*

Regardless of what Mr. Petrocelli may answer – if he has an answer – my follow-up question to Mr. Petrocelli would be:

> *"It was no secret what Keith Zlomsowitch was going to say during his deposition. Besides, Mr. Zlomsowitch was **the plaintiffs own witness.** Consequently, if Mr. Zlomsowitch wasn't going to testify in the civil trial – **what was the purpose of getting a deposition statement from him?"***

I have already answered that question above. Can Mr. Petrocelli provide a different – reasonable – answer?

I often hear members of the media scornfully mention Ms. Rosa Lopez who, without being called as a defense witness, gave a court-room deposition regarding O.J.'s Ford Bronco being parked at Rockingham on the night of the murders.

When the media bring up Ms. Rosa Lopez' name with scorn, why don't they discuss Mr. Keith Zlomsowitch in the same context?

On another occasion, Nicole told O.J. that she had an affair with O.J.'s long time friend, the football star Marcus Allen.

Did O.J. hit Marcus Allen, or get mad at him? No! Instead, O.J. forgave his friend.

Later, when Marcus Allen got married, O.J. proved his sincerity by opening up his home to his friend, and hosting the wedding reception at Rockingham. O.J. was entertaining the newlyweds in his home, realizing that the groom once had an affair with O.J.'s own wife! WOW! How can anyone even **suggest** that this man is abnormally jealous?

In this context it didn't matter that Marcus Allen denied that he and Nicole had an affair, as long as Nicole had told O.J. about it – and O.J., evidently, believed it. During his deposition, Marcus Allen denied that the alleged affair took place. But he admitted that O.J. had discussed the matter with him. According to Marcus Allen, he had repeatedly tried to talk to Nicole about the matter, trying to clear it up, but Nicole had refused to discuss the matter.

O.J.'s recount of the matter seems, therefore, to be fully corroborated by Marcus Allen, although the alleged affair, perhaps, never took place.

For as much as Nicole was concerned, she either had the affair with Marcus Allen – or she made up the story – **trying to make O.J. jealous!** O.J. evidently believed the affair took place. However, although he didn't approve of his wife's conduct, he didn't beat her! Apparently, O.J. didn't even get jealous (more than we should expect), since he hosted Mr. and Mrs. Allen's wedding recepion at Rockingham.

As a last resource, the prosecution presented yet another variation of **"the jealousy motive."** The prosecution argued that the day before the murders of Nicole and Ron, O.J.'s girlfriend, Paula Barbieri, had left a message on O.J.'s answering machine, to the effect that their relationship was over. O.J. denied that he retrieved the message before leaving for Chicago on the night of the murders.

Anyway, the prosecution argued that this message made O.J. so upset that he grabbed a pair of gloves, a knit ski cap for disguise, and a knife.

Then, allegedly, he entered his Bronco, raced over to Nicole's home at Bundy, and rang her door bell. As soon as she opened the door and came outside, O.J. knocked her down, slit her throat and stabbed her to death. Then Ron Goldman showed up, unexpectedly, so O.J. killed him too.

Of all the prosecution's many motive-theories, this is perhaps the **most ridiculous** one! Yet, **this** is the theory they eventually stuck with.

If O.J. got upset because Paula had broken up with him, why should he kill **Nicole** – if he were upset with **Paula**?

After a couple's divorce, if the ex-husband's new girlfriend breaks off **their** new relationship, the ex-husband tends to be disappointed over his new girlfriend and their present, broken relationship.

Consequently, he is likely to reminisce more favorably about his ex-wife, and the relationship **they** once had, rather than wanting to kill his **ex-wife** – over something his **new girlfriend** may have said or done!

This latest motive-theory from the prosecution reminds me of a satiric poem by a renown 19th century Danish poet, Ludvig Holdberg.

In his poem, titled **"The Blacksmith And The Baker,"** Holdberg writes about a small Danish town where the judge finds the town's blacksmith guilty of murdering a townsman. But the judge sentences the town's baker to hang for the murder, instead of the blacksmith!

The lesson Mr. Holdberg wanted to communicate to his readers, was that we should always be prepared for death, because death may strike when we least expect it.

Anyway, in the poem, the judge explains that someone has to pay for the crime. Since the town has two bakers, but only one blacksmith, the judge sends one of the bakers to the gallows, instead of the blacksmith!

The prosecution must have felt the same way:

O.J. got upset when Paula broke off their relationship. O.J. decided that someone had to pay for his anger. Paula was out of town – so he killed Nicole instead!

If it weren't for the serious nature of this case, one might tend to laugh of the prosecution's many ridiculous arguments and theories. As if this wasn't enough, take the following:

O.J. Simpson was one of the most charismatic persons in the U.S. He was a successful football star who, after completing his football career, had made an equally successful transition to the corporate world.

He came from a loving, Christian family and believed deeply in God. O.J. had two wonderful children with Nicole, and – in spite of her partying lifestyle – he adored her for the loving way she helped raise their children, even after he and Nicole separated.

O.J. was wealthy. He had some marvelous sponsor contracts with major corporations. He served on the board of executives of several corporations. His work included starring in major feature movies, travelling to exotic destinations, representing, and playing golf – one of his greatest passions.

O.J. lived in one of the most fashionable and exclusive residential communities in the U.S. He owned a beautiful estate. In his garden were the swimming pool, the jacuzzi, the private tennis court, his golf practice tee, and his children's playground. In his garage were his Ford Bronco, his Ferrari – and his Bentley!

In addition, O.J. was extremely handsome, and amicable. Women adored him, and he could pick and chose among them, if he wanted to.

About a year before the murder of Nicole, she and O.J. went through an orderly divorce. According to their prenuptial agreement, O.J. kept all of his assets, including his Rockingham estate. He bought Nicole out of their divorce settlement with a lump sum, and only paid child support – no alimony!

Hence, if any man on the surface of the earth seemed to have everything any man could wish for – it was O.J.! So why can anyone believe that he would risk giving up everything, to be executed, or to spend the rest of his life in prison, just for the "satisfaction" of killing Nicole? The mere notion is absolutely absurd!

To counter such arguments, some suggested that O.J. were under the influence of drugs on the night of the murders. Negative! The police received O.J.'s blood vial only hours after the murders. If there were even the slightest trace of drugs or alcohol in his body, the blood analyses would have picked it up, and the prosecution and the media would have feasted on it! But O.J. was absolutely clean! Close friends, and even present enemies, of O.J. (Ron Shipp) confirmed that they never saw O.J. use drugs!

So then the prosecution argued that O.J. were so upset because of Paula, or that he were so jealous this particular evening, that he didn't think about the consequences. He just raced over to Bundy to kill Nicole in a violent rage.

Again this is absurd, and the evidence proves it. Suppose O.J. were the murderer! Allegedly, he put on a dark, knit ski cap (which was later found at the murder scene), and a dark sweat suit. Then he put on a pair of gloves (also found at the crime scenes).

If O.J. were the murderer, why would he, allegedly, put on those items? According to the prosecution, **to disguise himself, and to avoid leaving fingerprints or other clues at the murder scene, of course.**

But if so, that means O.J. **were** considering the consequences of getting caught! He **were**, in other words, thinking about having to give up all he had worked so hard for, spending the rest of his life in prison, or being executed, never being able to play with his children and take part in their lives, never playing golf, depriving his children of their beloved mother, causing his own mother unbearable sorrow, and dozens of things like that.

Again, assuming O.J. were the murderer, if he didn't have thoughts like that, but simply didn't care what happened to him or anyone else, as long as he got to kill Nicole, then **why would he bother to disguise himself, or to wear gloves?**

Those alleged items of disguise prove that **if** O.J. **were** the murderer, then he were also contemplating what he stood to lose if he got caught. Would he, in that case, have elected to give up all that he had in life, just for a sudden urge to kill his children's mother – whom he still had loving feelings for?

It is in my opinion so utterly and outrageously ridiculous to suggest that O.J. could have killed Nicole, that it is absurd to even discuss it! But since O.J. was charged and prosecuted, and since most people – spearheaded by the media – still argue that he is guilty, I must discuss it. It should, however, be clear, from what I have written above, that

> **even if O.J. were the murderer – he had no apparent motive what-so-ever!**

CHAPTER 11

A *"Mountain Of Evidence"*

Whether O.J. had a motive to kill Nicole, or not, is a matter of opinion. The prosecutors said he had a motive, I say he didn't. So let us for the time being put aside the issue of motive, and look at the evidence instead.

Leading away from the Bundy murder scene were bloody shoeprints from size 12 Bruno Magli shoes. This is the size O.J. wears. The Bruno Magli shoes are not a pair of shoes you and I would wear. After all, they retail for $160! They are, however, typically, a kind of shoes that the, then, wealthy O.J. would wear. Besides, he liked Italian shoes and, allegedly, owned two-three dozen pairs.

During the course of the civil trial, eventually, some 30 photographs surfaced, depicting O.J. wearing Bruno Magli shoes.

Next to the bloody Bruno Magli shoeprints at the Bundy murder scene the investigators discovered five blood drops. The blood drops were marked, photographed, recorded and collected, before O.J. had even returned from Chicago, and hence, long before the LAPD received a reference sample of O.J.'s blood in an EDTA vial.

Seven weeks later the blood swatches containing the blood from the five blood drops were sent to Cellmark Diagnostics Lab or to the FBI's crime lab in Washington DC, for DNA analyses. Several weeks later the DNA analyses were ready. It was O.J.'s blood – with a probability of one hundred and seventy million to one (or something like that)!

No question about it! O.J., apparently, must have bled at the murder scene on the night of the murders! This assumption was further strengthened when the investigators recovered three drops of blood on the rear gate at Bundy, and this blood, also, was found to contain O.J.'s DNA.

One bloody murder glove was found at Bundy, next to Ron's body. It is an expensive glove, bought at Bloomingdale's – again, typically a glove O.J. could be expected to own. It was theorized and alleged that Ron must have fought with O.J. before dying, and that O.J. had lost the left glove during the struggle.

It was further theorized that after the murders, O.J. didn't notice that he had lost the left glove, or he didn't care, or he didn't find it in the darkness, so it was left at Bundy. Its mate was not immediately found.

Monday June 13, 1994, at about 6:15 am, on the morning after the murders, Detective Mark Fuhrman found the right mate to the Bundy glove, behind O.J.'s house at Rockingham. According to Detective Vannatter, who carefully touched the glove, it was *"sticky and moist"* from the blood that covered it.

Later the investigators uncovered the victims' bloods, as well as O.J.'s, inside his Ford Bronco. The investigators also uncovered blood drops in O.J.'s driveway at Rockingham and three drops of blood inside his front door. All these blood drops were later analyzed and found to be O.J.'s blood.

The blood drops inside the door were observed by O.J.'s house guest, Kato Kaelin, before Kato left the house on the morning after the murders. When Kato observed the three blood drops, O.J. was still on an airplane between Chicago and Los Angeles, and the police had, therefore, not yet received his blood sample.

Later in the day, the investigators received an EDTA vial of O.J.'s blood. The defense suggested that some of this blood was planted at the various crime scenes, to make it appear that O.J. were guilty. But much of the blood evidence was collected before the police obtained O.J.'s blood sample, and the blood in the vial contained EDTA, a chemical which prevented the blood from coagulating and from getting contaminated. The EDTA is already present inside all EDTA vials as they come from the pharmaceutical manufacturer, and hence, present in the EDTA vials already before blood enters the vials.

If blood had been planted from O.J.'s vial, it should have

contained EDTA. The EDTA would show up in subsequent blood analyses, proving that the blood had come from the vial, instead of from O.J.'s body directly. Except for two of the blood drops on the rear gate at Bundy, the presence of EDTA was not established in any part of the blood evidence I have mentioned above. It seems, therefore,

- that no part of this blood, attributed to O.J., could have been planted or fabricated by the investigators, and
- that O.J., on the night of the murders, must have bled at the murder scene, as well as in his Bronco, in his driveway, and in his foyer.

A dark knit ski cap was found near the victims at Bundy. It was immediately assumed that O.J. had worn the cap to disguise himself, but lost it in a struggle with Ron. The cap was examined in the LAPD's crime lab. On the cap the lab technicians found several hair fragments similar to O.J.'s hairs. (Hairs can not be absolutely identified, but only be described as "similar" to a certain person's hair).

Examining Ron's bloody clothes, the criminalists found fibers from a carpet identical to that in O.J.'s Bronco, on Ron's shirt. Again, they found a fiber matching the Bronco's carpet on the knit cap!

The investigators also collected a pair of socks, found in O.J.'s bedroom. The socks, later, turned out to have blood on them. The blood was DNA analyzed. The blood was Nicole's. Apparently, she had grabbed O.J.'s ankle as she fell or lay on the ground.

Eventually, O.J. returned to Los Angeles, around noon on the day following the murders. By that time he had a small cut on his left middle finger knuckle. This cut could, of course, explain why O.J.'s blood was found "everywhere."

O.J. could not account for the time of the murders, other than to say he was at home, alone, getting ready to go to the airport to fly to Chicago on a business trip.

Add to that O.J.'s and Nicole's stormy relationship, their

divorce, and O.J.'s alleged history of physical abuse, and

it seemed that there had never been a more solid murder case in the history of the U.S. criminal justice system, for as much as physical and circumstantial evidence were concerned.

Although there were speculations concerning evidence tampering, the five blood drops next to the bloody shoe prints at Bundy could – seemingly – not possibly have been planted, since they were collected before the investigators had retrieved a vial of O.J.'s blood.

Apparently, O.J. must have been bleeding at the murder scene on the night of the murders.

O.J. himself could not give any credible explanation as to how his blood could have been found at the murder scene.

In the eyes of District Attorney Gil Garcetti, the prosecutors, the investigators, the media, and the majority of the American people, **this blood evidence – alone – was more than enough to convict O.J.**

Faced with this **"mountain of evidence"** which I have mentioned above, most people may think I am crazy to even begin to question O.J.'s guilt. Maybe there was something "fishy" about the socks, and maybe an over-eager investigator planted some carpet fibers from the Bronco on Ron's shirt.

However, the evidence was, apparently, so overwhelming, that even if Judge Ito had thrown out most of it, the rest would build a case stronger than any prosecutor had ever had to work with ...

(... **if** the evidence was trustworthy!)

CHAPTER 12

The Contradictory Evidence

S o, how can I even suggest that O.J is innocent, and that all this *"mountain of evidence"* is worthless? Do I suggest that several dozen investigators and criminalists at Bundy could have conspired to plant O.J's blood next to the bloody shoeprints – when they didn't even have his blood at the time the five blood drops were collected? For all they knew, O.J. might have been in Europe, or on Hawaii, at the time of the murders!

Do I suggest that the lead investigators would have dared to start asking everybody else if they would agree to plant blood evidence in order to nail O.J.? Do I suggest that a police officer – when he came to Bundy to investigate – had brought along a knit cap with O.J.'s hairs in it? The mere notion of evidence planting or evidence fabrication, or of a conspiracy, seemed so far-fetched.

Yet, I shall prove to you in this book, that O.J. is totally innocent. Nothing of the so-called *"mountain of evidence"* is real. Someone else murdered Nicole and Ron, for totally different reasons than O.J. allegedly had. **And the evidence proves it!**

It is my belief that Detective Mark Fuhrman is the murderer. He planted some of the evidence.

But more importantly:

Detective Fuhrman created a crime scene that "set up" his rogue colleagues within the LAPD, and immediately snared them into believing O.J. were as guilty as sin!

Once the investigators believed that – already a few hours after the murders, or more precisely, the very moment Fuhrman presented them with the bloody Rockingham glove – they used the physical evidence of the crime scenes, which Fuhrman conveniently had created, and started fabricating all the rest of the false evidence against O.J.

As you will learn, it didn't take a major conspiracy to do it. Contrary to what O.J.'s adversaries argue, it only required that a few people in key positions **"looked the other way"** when they learned about it. The rest Detective Vannatter could take care of – all by himself. Maybe he had some assistance, but not necessarily.

To begin with, Vannatter felt real good about the evidence he created against O.J. Everyone was already convinced O.J. were guilty, because of O.J.'s alleged history of domestic abuse (which Detective Fuhrman also, conveniently, had told them about); and because of the bloody gloves that Detective Fuhrman had planted, and which the investigators observed within hours – one at Bundy and one behind O.J.'s house .

Because they were convinced that O.J. were guilty, Vannatter felt that tampering with the actual evidence, or fabricating additional evidence, to make sure O.J. were convicted, was not really criminal, or immoral. It was, rather, like

> *"giving Justice a helping hand"!*

The LAPD investigators were used to doing that!

If we begin to view the evidence from this perspective, you will see that absolutely **every piece of evidence in the case can be explained by this theory.**

On the other hand, if we consider **the prosecution's theory** of O.J. being the killer – although many pieces of evidence may be **construed** to point to O.J.'s guilt – there are other pieces of evidence that can **not possibly be reconciled** with their theory. Accordingly, **there must be something wrong with the prosecution's theory. So O.J. must be innocent.**

What first caught my attention and suspicion in this case was the obvious "set-up" represented by the gloves. It simply didn't make sense that a murderer should be so concerned about not leaving any clues for the investigators, that he wore gloves – and, allegedly, even a knit ski cap for disguise – but at the same time it didn't bother him that he created the bloodiest mess of a murder scene that most of the investigators had ever seen – and that he even brought some of this bloody mess right to his own doorsteps!

There was an inconsistency here, or a contradiction. And inconsistencies and contradictions make me suspicious that things aren't what they seem to be!

How can a murderer, so concerned about not leaving finger-prints that he wears gloves, drop one murder glove at the murder scene, and not even pick it up again? And how can this murderer bring the other glove to his home, and dispose of it behind his own house, where it could and would be found – **if he allegedly knew how to dispose of his bloody clothes, bloody shoes and bloody knife, so perfectly that the investigators never could find those items?!**

New inconsistencies in other words. Did someone purposely plant one glove at Bundy and one behind O.J.'s house, in order to make it **appear** that O.J. were the murderer?

The dark, knit ski cap. Would a black murderer wear a dark knit cap – for disguise – in Los Angeles in the middle of June?

When you disguise yourself, the most important rule to observe is to try to **"blend in."** And you definitely don't want to wear anything that makes people take a second look at you if you are spotted. Wearing a knit ski cap in Los Angeles in the middle of June, represented **the absolute opposite of a disguise**! And certainly, the prosecutors couldn't argue that O.J. wore the knit ski cap in the middle of the summer – to keep his ears warm!

New inconsistencies, in other words. So what was the real purpose of the knit ski cap? If the gloves were purposely planted by the murderer in order to frame O.J. and convince the investigators that he were guilty, then perhaps the cap served a similar purpose.

Perhaps the cap was never worn by the murderer as a disguise. Perhaps, instead, the cap was merely brought along and purposely left behind by the **real** murderer, **as "bait" for the investigators** – who were already "set up" with the gloves, to believe O.J. were guilty – so that the investigators should **plant O.J.'s hairs on the cap,** and thereby tie O.J. to the murder scene also by means of his hairs!

A police investigator would have no difficulty in providing some of O.J.'s hairs. All he needed to do was to enter O.J.'s jail cell, while O.J. was in court during the pre-trial hearings. Allegedly searching the cell for illegal drugs, the investigator could pick a few dozen hairs from O.J.'s pillowcase. Or simpler than that even, the investigators could remove all the hairs they wanted, from O.J.'s hair brush in his bathroom at Rockingham.

There is an interesting point here. If the real murderer, indeed, tried to frame O.J. like this, by "setting up" the investigators, then the real murderer apparently had some good inside information about **"the LAPD's more dubious investigative procedures."** The real murderer might, therefore, very well be an LAPD officer himself – in particular, a homicide detective! This was one of the things that initially triggered my interest in Detective Fuhrman.

There might be another explanation for the cap, also. Perhaps it **was** used as a disguise – however, not by an African-American murderer, but by **a Caucasian!**

An African American, like O.J., could not disguise his looks with such a dark knit cap. In the darkness, the top of his head would not appear much different with the cap, than without it. And his face would look the same from a block away! Like Defense Attorney Johnnie Cochran said when he put the knit cap on his head during closing arguments.

*If O.J. put on such a knit cap, from a block away, **he is still O.J.** – with a knit cap on!*

A white person, however – much more so than an African American – can disguise himself, by wearing a dark knit cap.

Without a cap, an African American's hair can be described by a witness as African-American hair – period!

With or without a dark knit ski cap, we can pretty well guess what an African American's hair look like – underneath that cap.

A Caucasian murderer, however, can benefit much better from disguising his hair in a knit ski cap. With the ski cap on, any Caucasian murderer becomes a murderer with a dark knit ski cap on his head. However, without the cap, a Caucasian murderer may be described by a witness as having *"long, short, straight, wavy, curly, red, white, brown, gray, dark blond, medium blond, or light blond hair"* – in addition to a long list of **combinations** of those same attributes!

Suddenly, things started to add up and make sense! Was the murderer a white person? Or were there several persons involved? Was O.J. framed?

Was there perhaps a similar explanation behind the outrageously bloody murder scene? Even if O.J. had wanted to kill Nicole, it seemed so unlikely that he would have chosen a knife as the murder weapon.

Allegedly slitting Nicole's throat, in cold blood, and getting his ex-wife's warm blood – the blood of the mother of his children – splattered all over himself, and sensing how her body shivered, as he sliced through her skin, flesh, muscles, tendons, veins, and arteries, until the blade of the knife hit the vertebra of her spine – seems so overly disgusting and repulsive that I simply refuse to believe that O.J. could have chosen a knife as his murder weapon – even if he had wanted to kill Nicole.

If O.J. had killed Nicole like that, he would have puked and fainted, rather than fought and overpowered Ron a few seconds later.

Yet another inconsistency in other words. So, could the murderer's choice of murder weapon, and the overly gruesome MO ("Modus Operandi" – i.e. the way the murders were committed) have been yet another piece of the murderer's plan to frame O.J.?

If the murderer's plan was to frame O.J., then the murderer, obviously, must have known O.J. Accordingly, he might also have been familiar with O.J.'s preference for Italian shoes.

Hence, the murderer might have purchased a pair of Italian Bruno Magli shoes, particularly for the purpose of planting bloody Bruno Magli shoeprints pointing to O.J.

If the murderer wanted to leave shoeprints from Bruno Magli shoes on the dry, tiled walkway at Bundy, then he needed to **amplify** those shoeprints in some way. Perhaps the cold-blooded murderer planned to kill Nicole by slitting her throat, just so as **to create a pool of blood.** Then, wearing his Bruno Magli shoes, **he could step in this pool of blood, thereby leaving behind clearly identifiable bloody shoeprints – pointing to O.J.**

That could explain the murderer's **choice of murder weapon.** But there is more to this. The normal way of killing someone with a knife, is to stab the victim. But that would not create the bloody mess the murderer needed. If the victim is stabbed in the heart, for instance, the heart is quickly paralyzed and stops beating. Furthermore, most of the bleeding would be internally. There would only be a trickle of blood on Nicole's dress.

In order to create a sizable puddle of blood, which the murderer could step in, he sliced Nicole's throat. That way he kept her alive for perhaps 30 seconds while Nicole's heart was pumping and her blood gushing out through the severed arteries in her neck.

Before Nicole's heart stopped beating the murderer stabbed her repeatedly, to make the murder look like the rage of a jealous ex-husband, rather than a well planned and deliberate "arterial phlebotomy." Or perhaps the murderer decided, at some point, that he had all the blood he needed, so he just tried to kill Nicole as quickly as possible at that point.

Yet another theory may be that the unconscious Nicole, as she bled onto the tiled patio, started to move, reflexively. This could have upset or scared the murderer, or made him so **uncomfortable** that he rammed the knife into Nicole's neck tree or four times, frantically, to kill her as quickly as possible at that point.

Perhaps the murderer wanted to create a bloody mess. And perhaps he purposely stepped in the blood with his distinctly identifiable Bruno Magli shoes, size 12, in order to point to O.J. also by means of his shoes.

Does that make sense? As a matter of fact – it does! **I shall, actually, prove, later, that this is exactly what the murderer did!** However, bear with me for a while, so I can present things in order!

The murderer knew that O.J. wore expensive Italian shoes, size 12. So the murderer simply bought a pair of Bruno Magli shoes, size 12. (By the way, size 12 is probably Detective Fuhrman's shoe size as well).

If the murderer bought a pair of Bruno Magli shoes, it didn't matter if O.J. ever owned a pair of Bruno Magli shoes. They were his "kind" of shoes!

Later, if O.J. produced a pair of clean Bruno Magli shoes, the prosecutors would triumph, arguing that since O.J. had **one** pair, he might as well have had **two** pairs, used one pair during the murders, and disposed of the shoes afterwards.

And if O.J. did **not** have any pair of Bruno Magli shoes, the prosecutors would still triumph, saying that O.J. didn't have "his" Bruno Magli shoes **anymore** – because he threw them away after the murders.

The murderer would frame O.J. regardless of whether O.J. ever owned a pair of Bruno Magli shoes, or not. O.J. would be put in a "catch 22" situation. The question of where *"O.J.'s Bruno Magli shoes"* were, was the kind of **"trick question" that does not have any correct answer.** Therefore, the prosecutors should never have been allowed to make the Bruno Magli shoes an issue, unless they could prove conclusively that **the particular pair** of Bruno Magli shoes that had created the bloody shoeprints at Bundy, **belonged to O.J.** and was **worn by O.J.** at Bundy during the murders of Nicole and Ron.

The defense might just as well have asked Prosecutor Darden

where **"his"** Bruno Magli shoes were, suggesting that **he** were the murderer who had left the bloody shoeprints! If Darden could not come up with **"his"** Bruno Magli shoes, it might be because he disposed of them after the murders!

Somewhat the same argument goes for the gloves. The $55.00 gloves, bought at Bloomingdale's, pointed to O.J. If O.J. had produced a pair of such gloves, the prosecutors would argue that he might as well have had another pair. And when O.J. didn't come up with a pair of those gloves, the prosecutors argued, the reason was that O.J. had lost the gloves – one at Bundy, and the other behind his house!

There is a photo – published in the National Enquirer – allegedly showing O.J. wearing Bruno Magli shoes. The counsels for the plaintiffs (in the civil case) argued, of course, that the photo is real, while O.J. and his attorneys argued that the photo is doctored.

There is no way an expert can prove conclusively that the photo is not doctored. Modern photographic technology has come so far today, that fabricating such a photo is "chicken feed."

The photo, therefore, means next to nothing! In my opinion, the photo is **real**! O.J. lied when he said he never wore those *"ugly ass shoes."* But he didn't lie because he were guilty! He lied becuase he was afraid of losing his children – if the public (and the jury) found out that he had, indeed, owned a pair of Bruno Magli's.

To conclude something objectively regarding the photo it is **useless to study the technical quality** of the photo. Instead, you have to study the **circumstances surrounding the photo** and the person behind it.

The photographer took the photo of O.J. at a football game about eight months before the murders. Allegedly, the photo was taken with a strong zoom lens from across the football field. Yet, it came out so clearly that the pattern underneath O.J.'s shoes were clearly visible. Maybe!

But how about this! **"Every"** American had heard about the bloody Bruno Magli shoeprints the murderer left behind. Any person who had ever taken photographs of O.J. Simpson would, naturally, check all such photographs to see if they accidentally might have caught O.J. on film, wearing Bruno Magli shoes.

Being a professional, the photographer is, of course, constantly on the lookout for opportunities to sell his photographs. Part of his job is to keep in mind, possibly, every photograph he has on file, so he can sell them whenever the opportunity is there.

A professional photographer does not, simply, throw all his photos in one big drawer! Part of being a professional photographer is to keep all photos organized in easily accessible files, according to names, places, objects, times, subjects, or other categories, so that he can easily find the photographs he needs, when an opportunity to sell them presents itself.

If this particular photographer is even just the least bit organized in his work, he would have a file on O.J., or on football players, containing every photograph he ever took of O.J., or at football games.

For the photographer to suggest that he never looked through his O.J. file during the entire criminal trial, but then – **after** the trial was over – he suddenly looked through his O.J. photos and found this photo of O.J. wearing Bruno Magli's – is not believable at all.

The photographer discovered the O.J. photo **before** the trial was over, but he didn't sell it to the National Enquirer until **after** the criminal trial!

When he allegedly found this photograph, he didn't turn it over to the police. Instead, he sold it to the National Enquirer! But he didn't sell it directly. He gave it to a friend, so that the friend could sell it for him.

To top this, the National Enquirer refused the photo the first time it was offered to them!

Those are the circumstances we should look at to decide whether we believe the photo is a fake or not.

The photo in itself could be fake or real. There is no way to tell, technically speaking. Instead, we must try to find the most likely explanation for the circumstances surrounding the photo.

I immediately think of a good reason why the photographer

did what he did. He had the photo he took of O.J. at the football game. Perhaps, he doctored the photo to make it appear that O.J. wore Bruno Magli shoes. Nobody could tell the difference. His plan was to sell it, to make money off it.

However, the photographer could not do that during the criminal trial, because if the prosecution subpoenaed the photo as evidence, and the photographer did not immediately admit that the photo was a fake, then he could be sentenced to many years in prison for fabricating false evidence in a murder case – if the photo was later proven to be doctored.

One way that could occur, would be if someone else came up with a photo of O.J. **not** wearing Bruno Magli shoes at that football game.

Hence, to be able to sell the photo without risk, should someone prove that it was a fake, the photographer waited until **after** the criminal trial before he presented the photo. The photo could no longer be used as evidence against O.J. in a criminal trial. So, at that stage the photographer could not be charged with fabricating false evidence if the photo was proven to be a fake. That makes sense.

So now he approached the tabloids. If the photo was a fake, the photographer could still be sued for fraud, if he himself sold the photo to the National Enquirer. Since he was the alleged photographer, he would have to answer directly **"yes"** or **"no"** to the National Enquirer's question, whether the photo was doctored or not.

The National Enquirer initially rejected the photo! That was certainly strange, considering that they purchased and published that same photo from someone else, later.

Could it be that the photographer was evasive towards the National Enquirer regarding the photo's authenticity? Could it be that the photographer refused to give a written statement to the tabloid that the photo was not doctored? Could it be that the photographer refused to sign an agreement to cover for the National Enquirer, if the photo was a fake and the National Enquirer should later be sued – for instance by O.J. if he were held liable based, in part, on the photo?

That sounds likely to me. Otherwise, why would the National Enquirer refuse the photo from the photographer, but purchase the same photo later, from someone else?

So what did the photographer do after the National Enquirer refused his photo? He made a deal with a friend, to let the **friend** sell the photo!

The photographer could argue: *"I didn't sell the photo, my friend sold it!"*

His friend could argue: *"I didn't make the photo, the photographer did!"*

Do you see! You can **not** do things like that when you deal with district attorneys and prosecutors in a murder case! But once the criminal phase is over, you can deal with a **tabloid newspaper** that way!

Hence, perhaps, the photographer made an agreement with his friend saying that his friend could sell the photo – for whatever it is worth – and keep half the proceeds. That way **the photographer** was off the hook, and **got his share of the money.**

The friend, on the other hand, made an agreement with the National Enquirer that they could publish the photo, but that the seller, "the friend," could not vouch for the authenticity of the photo, since he didn't shoot the photo. That way **"the friend"** was off the hook, and **got his share of the money.**

The National Enquirer purchased the photo. They took it to a photography "expert" who said that he could not detect any sign of doctoring, and believed the photo is real. Nobody can sue the "expert" for stating what he "believed," or for not seeing that the photo is a fake. Therefore, **"the expert"** was off the hook, and **got his share of the money.**

The National Enquirer published the photo and boosted the sale of the newspaper because of the photo. In connection with the photo they published a statement from the "expert" saying that he believes the photo is real. That way, the **National Enquirer** was off the hook, and **got their "lion's share" of the money generated by the, possibly, fake photo.**

This way the media can build up an image of O.J. being guilty, and make money in the process. Simultaneously, the responsibility for this despicable act is eliminated.

Towards the end of the civil trial about thirty additional photographs surfaced, depicting O.J. wearing Bruno Magli shoes. Apparently these photographs are authentic, since one of them was published in the *"Buffalo Report"* 8 months before the murders. However, there are many unanswered questions even in connection with those 30 photos.

I shall deal with this issue later. In doing so, I shall prove that **these photos – even if they are authentic – tend to exonerate O.J. rather than incriminate him!**

Assuming that O.J. were the murderer, it seems that everything he could possibly drop, lose, deposit, or in any other manner leave behind at the crime scenes – the left glove at Bundy, the right glove behind his house, the knit cap at Bundy, the bloody shoeprints at Bundy, his blood drops next to the shoeprints, the victims' bloods in the Bronco, and the Bronco fibers on the knit cap and on Ron's shirt, etc. – were, indeed, left behind, and conveniently recovered by the investigators, so as to point O.J. out as the murderer.

Wouldn't we suspect that such a "sloppy" and careless murderer had also left behind, somewhere, his bloody shoes, his bloody clothes, and his bloody knife? Yet, these items were never recovered!

And wouldn't we suspect that such a sloppy murderer, who allegedly had lost his left glove in a struggle with Ron – without noticing it, and dropped the other bloody glove behind his house – would leave behind bloody fingerprints everywhere?

Yet, not a single fingerprint tying O.J. to the murders was found at any of the crime scenes (Bundy, the Bronco, and Rockingham). His bare left hand, allegedly dripped three drops of blood on the rear gate at Bundy and smeared his and the victims' blood everywhere inside the Bronco. Yet, his bloody hand, obviously, didn't touch any of the Bundy gates, or the Bronco's steering wheel, or the Rockingham gate, or his door knob, etc., since O.J. did not leave his bloody fingerprints anywhere.

These facts are significant by themselves. But they are significant also in a somewhat indirect way. Here is why:

> The real killer, who was framing O.J. and setting up the investigators, could plant the gloves, the cap, and the bloody shoeprints. He could make it appear that O.J. had left this trail of evidence. But **he could not plant O.J.'s fingerprints.**
>
> So, while the entire trail of evidence pointed to a murderer so sloppy that it appeared he didn't care about anything – **mysteriously this sloppy murderer with bloody hands did not leave one single fingerprint anywhere!** Not at Bundy, not on the Bundy gates, not in the Bronco, and not in O.J.'s house.

Doesn't this suggest to my readers that someone was framing O.J. by planting all the evidence that **could** be falsely fabricated, but **none of the evidence that only O.J. could have left behind** – if he were the murderer?

The real murderer could not plant the clothes, the shoes, or the knife, either – for obvious reasons. Those were items O.J., allegedly, would have carried with him into his house, and the real murderer didn't have access to the interior of O.J.'s house – at least not right after the murders. Nor could he plant those items outside O.J.'s house, or at Bundy – because no murderer would take off his shoes or pants out in the open, leave them there, and walk around outdoors, barefoot and without pants!

With respect to those items the real murderer could not use them to frame O.J., **so he carried them home and disposed of them himself.**

Furthermore, there was an added risk that hairs or fibers from the real murderer's body, car, or home, could be on those items. So the real murderer did not dare to plant them. **That's why those items were never recovered, although the gloves, the blood, hairs, and fibers were found "everywhere"!**

Much of the same argument goes for the murder knife. The real murderer was not likely to "lose" the knife anywhere. So it would be too suspicious if the real murderer also planted the knife somewhere in O.J.'s surroundings. Furthermore, the knife was probably a specialized, extremely sharp knife. It would have to be, in order to slice Nicole's neck cleanly into her spine. If so, the knife might have certain characteristics that could tie it to the real murderer, rather than to O.J. So the real murderer chose to bring the knife home with him, as well.

Are my readers beginning to understand that the mere presence and absence of the items I have discussed above, point to a murderer with good knowledge of criminal investigations and with close ties to the LAPD? All these clues indicate that they were deliberately planted in order to frame O.J. and "set up" the police investigators.

It was simply too perfect from an investigator's point of view – if O.J. were the murderer, and he had left all of those clues behind.

This feeling is strengthened by **the total absence of the four clues that could have been crucial for O.J. – if he were the murderer – namely the shoes, the clothes, the knife, and his bloody fingerprints.**

If O.J. was **not** the murderer, then the **real murderer** could have disposed of, or hidden, the clothes, the shoes, and the knife, anywhere on the surface of the earth. That's why they were never found.

Had O.J. disposed of them, however, it is totally unbelievable that the investigators have not yet found them. The prosecutors' talk about a missing bag, and things like that, is sheer bull-shit. If these items had ever been in O.J.'s possession on the night of the murders, the investigators – with all their manpower and resources – would have found them rather quickly.

Eventually, I will point to dozens of other discrepancies in the evidence against O.J. But this must do for now.

CHAPTER 13

The Glove Evidence

It is time to give some real substance to our theory. We need to look at the evidence and indeed **prove** that O.J. could not have left it, because he is not the murderer. The first items we will examine are the gloves – because **the gloves are two of the keys to solving this murder mystery.**

So far, neither of the attorneys, nor any of the legal analysts on TV, or anyone in the media, seem to understand the real significance of the gloves. It came as no surprise to me that the gloves did not fit O.J. when he tried them on in the courtroom. It wasn't even close. Those were not O.J.'s gloves!

The real significance of the gloves, though, is the following:

1. The Bundy glove was not accidentally dropped at the murder scene, or pulled off the murderer's hand by Ron.
2. Not just the Rockingham glove, but **both** gloves, were removed by the murderer himself, **after** Nicole and Ron were dead. Consequently, both gloves were **deliberately** planted **by the murderer.**
3. Furthermore, the Rockingham glove was deliberately planted
   – not by an investigator who was trying to **boost his case**
   – not by a **racist** investigator who wanted to frame the black hero, O.J., but
   – by the murderer himself, with the purpose of **framing O.J. for two murders O.J. did not commit, so that O.J. should end up in the gas chamber or in prison for life, and the murderer himself could go free.**

Isn't it obvious? If O.J. were the murderer, calmly planning to kill his ex-wife, Nicole, and using gloves so as to avoid leaving any evidence pointing to himself, why should he **deliberately** take off one bloody murder glove, and **purposely** leave it next to the victims, and then just as **purposely** bring the other bloody glove to his home and dispose of it behind his own house before leaving for Chicago?

Anyone who doesn't see the outrageous contradiction in such a behavior, leaves me speechless! But I think my readers agree with me. I hear the objections from O.J.'s adversaries, though:

*"O.J. could have **lost** the Bundy glove at the murder scene."*

Did O.J. also **lose** the Rockingham glove behind his house, without noticing it? Be real!

How can we prove that the murderer, himself, **deliberately** planted **both** gloves, by removing **one glove** at the murder scene, and bringing **the other glove** to Rockingham? We don't have to prove that!

Prosecutor Christopher Darden proved it for us!

Displaying all their best efforts the prosecution demonstrated beyond any doubt whatsoever, that the gloves fit O.J. so snugly that he could hardly put them on or remove them during the prosecution's glove demonstration in court.

What the prosecutors **"explained,"** however, after displaying this apparent **"grande fiasco,"** was that **the gloves were supposed to stretch and fit that snugly!**

What else **could** they say? But let us agree with their "glove expert" in his assessment that the gloves fit the way they were supposed to fit, or rather – the only way those gloves **could** fit O.J.

When the defense tried to argue that the gloves could not be O.J.'s because they didn't fit, the prosecution went out of their way to argue, both on redirect and on rebuttal, that the snug fit was the way those gloves were supposed to fit, and indeed did fit his hands.

Most of my readers, I assume, saw on TV how tightly those gloves fit O.J.'s hands. Maybe O.J. acted a little bit. But the **leather** certainly couldn't **"act."** In "close-up" on TV we could all see how O.J. had to stretch the leather to the limit to try to pull the gloves on.

Much fuss has been made about the latex gloves O.J. was required to wear in the courtroom, underneath the murder gloves. Those latex gloves might have made it a little harder to get the gloves on and off, because of the friction. But the important point, which most people seem to forget, regarding the murder gloves, is **how tightly they fit – once they were on O.J.'s hands.**

The key to the glove evidence is not how difficult it would have been **for O.J.** to put those gloves **on his hands**, but how difficult it would have been for **Ron** to pull them **off O.J.'s hands!**

It should be clear to anyone, that such tight fitting, stretching gloves don't simply slide off your hands when you let your arms down! Nor can you shake them off. You have to struggle extensively with both hands, not only to put them on, but even more so to get them off again!

Consequently, even if O.J. were the murderer, he did not **lose** the Bundy glove.

L et us try to find out if **Ron could have pulled the glove off** the murderer's hand during an **alleged** struggle.

My readers have to think **"hypothetically"** now. If the murderer had **small** hands – like a child or a woman – then, of course, Ron might, **hypothetically**, have pulled the glove off the murderer's hand. However, were that the case, then O.J., obviously, is not the murderer – because O.J. has **extremely large** hands.

When considering the possibility that Ron might have pulled the glove off the murderer's hand, my readers have to imagine that the murderer had **exactly as large hands as O.J.** Why? Because **if the murderer has smaller hands than O.J. – then O.J. could not be the murderer!**

Prosecutors Marcia Clark and Christopher Darden may not understand that. But I am sure my readers have no trouble understanding it!

Even if someone got a good grip inside the opening of one glove, it could not simply be ripped off!

I challenge any member of the former prosecution team, any 'Simpson book' author, any legal analyst on any Simpson program on TV, and (with all due respect) Ron's father, to try to pull such a glove off my hand during a mock struggle with me – within the timeframe generally accepted for the struggle between Ron and the murderer.

I am certain it is impossible! Hence, I will wager $10,000 in a bet against any of the above mentioned persons who can do it.

I have written to "Rivera Live" and offered to wager $10,000 against Geraldo Rivera (which he may give to his favorite charity, if he wins) – if he can pull such a glove off my hand during a "mock" struggle with me!

Of course, Mr. Rivera has made so many millions of dollars off the Simpson case that $10,000 may seem like nothing to him. Be that as it may, he has, at least, not accepted my challenge as this book manuscript is going to the editor.

It is impossible, as you probably have found out if you tried it. But let us assume – **hypothetically** – that Ron **did** grab the opening of the glove and ripped it off the murderer's hand. If so, the glove should have been pulled almost completely **inside out**, and the lining should be smeared with Ron's blood. Neither was the case.

Since the glove was **not turned inside out** – not even a little bit – and since there were smears of Ron's blood on the Bundy glove, it is pretty obvious to anyone with an open mind that **the glove was removed the "normal" way** – by someone pulling repeatedly on each of the glove's fingertips until it came loose. That's the way people normally remove a tight fitting glove.

This is consistent with a scenario where the murderer had already cut Ron's neck and stabbed him to death with the knife in his right hand. Naturally, the murderer's right hand glove was covered with Ron's blood at this point.

Assuming the murderer wanted to remove **one** of his gloves,

only, at Bundy – and bring the other glove to O.J.'s house – **the murderer could not readily remove the right glove,** because he was holding the knife in his right hand!

However, **he could remove the left glove,** using the **thumb and index finger** of his right hand, without dropping the knife.

So, with the bloody, gloved right thumb and index finger he pulled repeatedly on each of the fingertips of the left glove, until the glove came off. That is why the **left** glove was deposited at Bundy, and why there were **smears of Ron's blood** on it.

Removing a tight fitting glove from **someone elses** hand – the "normal" way, by repeatedly pulling on each of the fingertips – is an **intricate task** that requires **good eyesight, near perfect eye-arm-hand-finger coordination – and the full cooperation of the person wearing that glove!**

It is **outright impossible** that Ron could have done that – **after his neck was cut,** and he, therefore, was **blinded by tears, and in a state of panic, shock, and excruciating pain.**

Don't forget, either, the fact that Ron and the murderer were in a middle of a life and death struggle, where Ron had to use **both his hands** to protect himself from the murderer's **right** hand, which was wielding the deadly knife and stabbing him repeatedly!

Let me now explain why Ron – if he tried to pull the glove off the murderer's hand – must have done so **after his neck was cut – which is unthinkable!**

Obviously – if the murderer had cut or stabbed Ron any-where on his body before his neck was cut, Ron would have screamed so you could have heard it for half a mile. Don't tell me that the murderer could have inflicted such pain on Ron without Ron screaming, both in pain and as a call for help!

The only reason why Ron did **not** scream for help as he was repeatedly stabbed and cut, was that **the very first injury** to Ron's body **must have been the three-four inches long, deep stabbing and cutting wound on the left side of his neck,** near his larynx.

Although Ron's larynx was intact, the trauma to his neck was probably so massive and so close to his larynx that its function was

paralyzed, preventing Ron from articulating any sound.

Physically and physiologically, according to a medical examiner, Ron might, perhaps, have been able to scream. But **psychologically and neurologically**, Ron could not utter a sound, due to the large gash in his neck.

Had the first injury to Ron's body been in an area well away from his throat, I am certain Ron would have screamed so loud that he would have awakened the entire neighborhood.

Let me give my readers an example to illustrate how the paralysis of Ron's larynx functioned. It is a bit grotesque, but so was the murder of Ron.

To write your name on a wall, with a felt pen, you hold the pen between your thumb, index finger, and middle finger. You don't use the ring finger and little finger at all. They don't even touch the wall. OK?

Suppose you were ready to write your name, and someone suddenly and quickly chopped off your ring finger and little finger. The perpetrator didn't touch your thumb, index finger, or middle finger. However, the pain and shock would be so immense that there is no way you could write your name, even if you were offered a billion dollars to do it!

You wouldn't even be able to move your thumb, index finger, and middle finger for the next half hour! The pain from the cut ring finger and little finger would be so intense that it would totally "occupy" all the nerves in your hand and arm, and preclude any nerve impulses from your brain from reaching the muscles of your other fingers, so as to direct your thumb, index finger and middle finger to move in a well coordinated pattern necessary to write your name.

Look at the nerves in your arm, forwarding nerve impulses from your brain to your fingers, as a telephone cable. Normally this telephone cable (the nerves) in your arm has the capacity to carry all the messages you want to send, both ways. You can sense the pen being cold, at the same time as your brain sends nerve impulses to your finger muscles in your lover arm, instructing them to move your fingers so as to write your signature on the wall.

At the same time, if you have a small wound on your little finger, and it hurts a little bit, it can pick up another "telephone line" (nerve) and inform your brain about that, so your brain can tell some other finger muscles to move your little finger out to the side to protect the wound.

When a severe injury occurs, however, like cutting off of two fingers completely, the pain receptors near that wound fire nerve signals rampantly! It's like in the "old days" when everyone in the U.S. tried to call their families on Christmas Day. You got a busy signal. Or you simply didn't get a dial tone.

That's comparable to what happens if two of your fingers were cut off. The pain impulses occupy all the "telephone lines" (nerves) in your arm. There is no way nerve impulses from your three other fingers holding the pen can reach your brain, to be interpreted, so the brain can transmit additional impulses to the finger muscles in your arm, and make them move the fingers holding the pen, in a well defined and coordinated pattern needed to write your signature on the wall. All the lines are busy!

Exactly the same happened to Ron's neck. Although his vocal chords were intact, as well as the intricate set of muscles that create voice, the huge gash in his neck **paralyzed his entire neck,** and not just the immediate area that was directly cut. All the telephone lines (nerves) in the front half of his neck, to and from his brain, were occupied, sending messages of pain, and instructions to his neck to try to close and protect the huge gash. There simply weren't any open lines (nerves) for **"voice mail"** messages! That's why he was unable to scream – even if he had wanted to.

Back to the glove. If Ron had even just **tried** to remove the murderer's left glove, he must have done so with a huge 3-4 inch long, deep cut in his neck. The pain must have been unbearable. Just **trying** to move his head or scream must have hurt even more. His eyes must have been filled with tears that totally impaired his vision. Think about it, if you have ever been punched in the nose, how tears instantly stream from your eyes and impair your vision.

The pain Ron experienced must have been several times as severe. How could Ron, at all, have had perfect eye-arm-hand-finger coordination at that stage, enabling him to meticulously search out, and pull, repeatedly, on each of the fingertips of the murderer's left glove, until it came loose? I mean, to even suggest that, is totally absurd. And is it even imaginable, that **the murderer** would have let Ron do that?

Don't forget, either, that the murderer wasn't standing still. He was repeatedly stabbing and cutting Ron in the face, in the neck, in the head, on his arms, and all over his body. How can the prosecutors even suggest that Ron would have "fiddled around" with the murderer's **left** hand, when the murderer's **right** hand clearly represented the constant, deadly threat and fatal disaster?

O.J.'s adversaries can, of course, place themselves in total denial, and simply say that they still believe Ron removed the left glove during a struggle with O.J. There is nothing anyone can meet such an *"argument"* with – when basic, common sense does not work!

If the former prosecutors, investigators, and the plaintiffs, as well as others of O.J.'s adversaries, want to state that two plus two equal thirteen – then let them! I can not argue with people like that! But I hope, and assume, that I am addressing normally intelli-gent human beings, and not dilettantes!

The obvious conclusion – the only conclusion – is that the murderer himself removed the Bundy glove – after Nicole and Ron were dead. There can be absolutely no doubt about that!

In other words, whoever the murderer is, he **himself** must **slowly and deliberately – after the murders –** have removed the Bundy glove at the murder scene and **purposely** have left it there!

From people who talk before they think, I have heard the

argument that O.J. could have killed Nicole and removed the Bundy glove **before** Ron showed up. O.J. could have tossed the glove away before attacking Ron. Why is that impossible?

Well, had that happened, there would not have been **smears of Ron's blood on that glove.** There might, perceivably, have been a blood drop or two on it – but not **smears** of Ron's blood! However, it is highly unlikely that there would even be a blood drop on the glove if it was removed before Ron showed up, because the glove was found underneath some shrubbery, where a splatter of blood was not likely to reach it.

Can we, please, put this point behind us now?

The murderer kept the Bundy glove on until after Nicole and Ron were dead!

After Nicole and Ron were dead, the murderer had all the time in the world to remove the left glove, slowly and deliberately. He was not disturbed. How do we know that?

Well, the murderer came to Bundy to kill Nicole, which he did. Ron showed up, so the murderer killed Ron too. Hence there were **two victims** and **no eyewitnesses.**

Naturally, if a fourth person had showed up to disturb the murderer, the murderer would have attacked that person too, and we would have had **three** victims – or **two** victims and **one eye-witness!**

What I have explained in this chapter, so far, is the key to understanding the significance of the murder gloves, which again, is crucial in terms of solving this murder mystery. Let us look at some of the implications we can draw from this glove analysis – so far:

First of all, since the murderer must have **removed the left (Bundy) glove himself** – after the murders – O.J. could not have cut his left finger during a struggle with Ron – **even if O.J. were the murderer.**

The reason for this is that **the Bundy glove was not torn, nor was there any corresponding cut in the glove. For O.J.'s left finger to be cut while he was wearing the glove, the glove must have been cut, too.**

Nor could O.J. have had **a prior cut on his finger** which opened up and began to bleed during an alleged struggle with Ron, because then O.J.'s blood should have been found inside the glove, and in particular, **inside that finger of the glove** – and it wasn't.

Finally, the minuscule cuts on O.J.'s left fingers were the only lacerations to his skin – on his entire body.

But even if O.J. had showed up the next day with only three fingers on his left hand, he couldn't have lost the other two fingers at Bundy on the night of the murders! My readers, and all other intelligent people should realize that

> **O.J. could not have bled at Bundy – even if he were the murderer!**
>
> Consequently, **if the five blood** drops that were found next to the bloody shoeprints at Bundy, allegedly **came from O.J., then they must have been fabricated!**

There isn't any longer a question of **whether** the five blood drops were fabricated or not. The only valid questions to ask, are – **how** were the five blood drops at Bundy fabricated – **who** fabricated them – and **why**?

How could those five blood drops have been planted, so cleverly that it seems impossible to believe they were planted? I will answer that question later. However, the **implications** of this revelation is even more important:

> Obviously, if the murderer, or the investigators – so **"cleverly"** – fabricated those five blood drops next to the bloody shoeprints, they could easily have fabricated **every** piece of evidence in this case!

When this dawned on me, I suddenly saw the Simpson case in a totally different light. I trust my readers, too, are beginning to understand what we are facing in this case.

Suddenly, my task, as I perceived it, was no longer to question **whether or not** certain pieces of evidence had been fabricated. **All of it must have been fabricated**, either by the murderer, or by the investigators. My task now, was to figure out – **how – by whom – and why!**

Let me, however, stay with the glove evidence for a while. The gloves are so crucial to understanding this murder mystery.

Since the murderer, regardless of who he is, removed the left (Bundy) glove himself, **after** Nicole and Ron were dead, and he dropped that glove on the ground next to Ron's body – **and left it there** – he must have done that **on purpose!**

But if the murderer then did **not** take off the other (right) glove, at the same time, **to leave it together with the left glove**, but instead brought the right glove to O.J.'s house at Rockingham, the murderer must, again, have done that, too, **on purpose!**

This proves – without any doubt – that **the murderer himself was the one who purposely wanted to establish a direct connection between the Bundy murder scene and O.J.'s Rockingham home,** by planting one glove next to Ron's body, and planting the other glove behind O.J.'s house. There was absolutely **nothing coincidental or accidental** about it!

Understanding this, **we can now draw the following important conclusions:**

- Both gloves were deliberately deposited where they were found.
- Hence, whoever deposited the Rockingham glove, also deposited the Bundy glove.
- Consequently, whoever deposited **either** glove **is** the murderer!
- And **inversely**, whoever did **not** deposit one of the gloves, could **not possibly** be the murderer!

- O.J. could **not** have deposited the Rockingham glove, because – according to Detective Vannatter, who carefully touched it when he first saw it – **the blood on that glove was still** *"sticky and moist,"* almost **eight hours** after the murders!
- **So, O.J. could not possibly be the murderer!**

Even O.J.'s adversaries can not make a 180 degree turn now, and start to "babble" about O.J.'s blood being found at Bundy, and about domestic violence, and a *"mountain of evidence"*! Together, we have proven, logically, step by step, that

- **O.J could not be the murderer**, and
- **O.J. could not have bled at the murder scene** – even if he were the murderer!

DON'T EVER FORGET THAT!

As we have already proven, the blood evidence at Bundy, wrongfully attributed to O.J., **must** have been fabricated – whether we like the idea, or not. There is no way around that fact.

The logical question, therefore, isn't **whether or not** the so-called *"mountain of evidence"* was fabricated, but **how** it was fabricated, **who** did it, and **why.**

I told my readers the glove evidence was crucial to solving this murder mystery. So far the glove evidence has revealed two extremely important facts:

1. The murderer must have planted **both** gloves – deliberately. Since O.J. could not have deposited the Rockingham glove – **O.J. could not have murdered Nicole and Ron.**
2. Even if O.J. were the murderer (which he isn't), the glove evidence proves that the murderer kept the gloves on until **after** Nicole and Ron were dead.
    There was no tear or cut on the fingers of the left glove,

nor was there any trace of O.J.'s blood inside the left glove. Consequently, even if O.J. were the murderer, **he could not have bled at Bundy on the night of the murders.**
Therefore, **the blood evidence at Bundy – attributed to O.J. – must have been planted or fabricated!**

Now we are getting somewhere! Since O.J. is not the murderer, we have a murderer on the loose! First we have to nail him. Then we have to explain where all the **"mountain of evidence"** came from. Obviously, it didn't come from O.J.!

I have presented my readers with the first **solid proof** that the investigators and prosecutors fabricated false evidence against O.J. There will be much more, and much stronger, evidence of that in the chapters to come. But we all have to start somewhere.

Possibly, my book will also be read by some of O.J.'s adversaries. They, obviously, are in total denial, and refuse to accept the fact that the police – all over the country – oftentimes condoned by prosecutors and district attorneys, fabricate false evidence against innocent, as well as guilty suspects – every day! The only real problem with this is that **we just catch them one out of one hundred thousand times that they do this!**

Let me give you an example from the Simpson case – and in particular, from the glove evidence, since that is the chapter we are in.

The investigators, the prosecutors, the district attorney, most of the media, legal analysts on TV talk shows, and most of the public interested in the case, have argued that **if** the gloves didn't fit O.J., it might have been because O.J. were required to wear latex gloves, and because the murder gloves had **shrunk**, from being wet with blood.

That is plain "bull"! The latex gloves were so thin, that they meant nothing in this context. **And the murder gloves didn't shrink, either!**

The gloves were made from **leather** – animal "skin"! Skin may get stiffer when it dries up after having become wet. **But it**

doesn't shrink. How would our pets – and people – look, if skin shrunk after getting wet?

Can you imagine? Your Golden Retriever runs out in the rain one morning, and comes back in the late afternoon sunshine – looking like a Cocker Spaniel!

Would you take a shower every day, if your skin shrunk when it got wet? Well, were that the case, I guess you would, and most cosmetic surgeons would be out of work. Seriously, though – skin doesn't shrink!

A piece of woolen **cloth** may shrink, however. But it doesn't shrink because the woolen hairs get **smaller.** The cloth shrinks because the hairs get more **curly** when they get wet.

Back to the Simpson case. The gloves didn't shrink. That argument was a blatant lie, concocted by the prosecutors in an attempt to "explain" why the murder gloves didn't fit O.J.!

The fact of the matter is quite the opposite! The gloves actually got bigger!

Yes, it's true! During the civil trial, one of the criminalists, **a sworn LAPD officer working for the investigators and the prosecutors,** testified that she was given the task of **measuring – accurately –** the murder gloves, soon after they were brought into evidence. **She also measured the gloves shortly before O.J. was asked to try them on** in the courtroom during the criminal trial.

The gloves had actually "grown" 1/4 of an inch while they were in the custody of the LAPD and the prosecutors!

Now, reasonably intelligent people understand that the gloves didn't actually "grow" while they were kept in two unsealed paper bags inside an open cardboard box in the LAPD's crime lab, or later in the prosecutors' office. More correctly, we could say, instead, that

the gloves had "gotten bigger" while in the LAPD's and the DA's custody!

The people responsible for this "miracle," as well as O.J.'s other adversaries, may linger in their state of total denial.

The rest of us, of course, realize that "miracles" like that simply don't happen! Someone from the LAPD or from the DA's office removed the gloves from their bags, inserted some object inside them, blocked them out, and stretched them, to make them 1/4 inch bigger.

When they were reasonably satisfied with this **corruption of the evidence,** Prosecutor Christopher Darden requested that O.J. Simpson be required to try the gloves on for size – in front of the jury!

Still the gloves didn't fit – not even by a long shot!

I trust my readers understand from this example, that

the investigators – and even the prosecutors – in the Simpson case, had no qualms about corrupting the evidence – or fabricating false evidence – against O.J.

Even after the "fiasco" with the glove demonstration the prosecutors and their glove "expert" continued their attempt to corrupt the glove evidence, in an effort to undo the damage of the devastating glove demonstration. While the lawyers were at a side-bar, and Prosecutor Darden tried to get a ruling from Judge Ito – that O.J. should be instructed to try on the gloves again, this time without the latex gloves – the prosecution's glove "expert" where shamelessly trying to block out the gloves even further, by inserting an object into the fingers of the glove!

After several desperate, failed attempts, O.J.'s defense attorneys finally managed to stop this corruption of the most important piece of evidence in the case! The incident was caught on video by the camera in the courtroom. Do my readers understand, now, why

I argue for TV cameras in all courtrooms?

By the way, this glove "expert" who tried to expand the gloves even further, wrote in his report to the prosecution that he hoped to be *"invited to the prosecution's victory party after the criminal trial"*! Unbiased? What do **you** think?!

Above, I mentioned an open cardboard box wherein the gloves were kept, inside plain, unsealed paper bags. However, there were other pieces of evidence in that same box!

In another unsealed paper bag was the knit cap that was collected at the murder scene. And believe it or not – the box also contained an unsealed, unwrapped roll of carpet – taken from O.J.'s Bronco!

It is my contention that the hairs similar to O.J.'s that allegedly were found on the knit cap, must have been collected by investigators, from the pillowcase in O.J.'s jail cell, or from his hair brush in his bathroom, and planted on and in the knit cap, to frame O.J.

Otherwise, how could anyone suggest that the murderer, regardless of who he is, could have worn this cap during the murders? He certainly didn't wear it as **a disguise – to "blend in"** – and definitely not to keep his ears warm in L.A. in the middle of the summer! So what was the murderer's purpose for the cap, unless it was to give the investigators the **opportunity** to plant O.J.'s hairs on it, in order to frame O.J.?

Eventually, the prosecutors claimed that a hair, similar to O.J.'s was also found on one of the gloves, and a fiber from a Bronco carpet was found on the knit cap, as well as on one of the gloves.

For **six weeks,** we had all those items thrown together, **unsealed**, in the same open cardboard box in the LAPD's evidence room, inside their crime lab's locked door.

As explained above, someone from the LAPD took the gloves out of that box, blocked them out and stretched them, in order to make O.J. appear **"1/4 inch guiltier"**!

We can prove that, because we have the measurements for the gloves, taken by one of the LAPD's own criminalists shortly after the murders. And we could compare those measurements to the measurements that same criminalist recorded when she measured the gloves shortly before O.J. was requested to try on the gloves in front of the jury!

Before requesting that O.J. try on the gloves, if somebody, obviously, corrupted the glove evidence in this manner – in order to frame O.J. and make him appear guilty – wouldn't we be justified in assuming that the same person, or another person with the LAPD, also stuck his hands inside that cardboard box and planted a carpet fiber on the cap, and a hair from the cap on one of the gloves?

O.J.'s problem is that this evidence tampering is almost impossible to expose. Everything takes place behind closed doors inside the LAPD's crime lab, or in the prosecutors' office. If they deny it, there is, normally, no way O.J.'s attorneys can prove it. Therfore, according to procedural laws (lack of **foundation**), O.J.'s attorneys were not even allowed to **suggest** that the investigators or the prosecutors corrupted the evidence or fabricated evidence.

Still, we have proven, already, that the crucial blood drops at Bundy **must** have been fabricated. And we have proven that the gloves **must** have been tampered with, to make O.J. appear guilty. There can't be any doubt about that.

Realizing how difficult it is, under normal circumstances, to prove that investigators have tampered with the evidence, these two examples are probably just the tip of a huge and dangerous **"iceberg of evidence corruption."**

If the investigators and prosecutors have the right man – the guilty perpetrator – there should, of course, be no need to fabricate, or tamper with, even the slightest little piece of evidence. Had I sat on the jury – in either of the trials – I would have acquitted O.J. immediately. The jurors shouldn't even be interested in additional evidence, as soon as one tiny, little piece of evidence is proven, undoubtedly, to have been fabricated by one of the LAPD investigators!

In a restaurant you observe **one** chef pluck his nose while preparing food – and he doesn't wash his hands! Even though there were other chefs in that restaurant, whom you had not seen pluck **their** noses – you wouldn't eat in that restaurant, would you?

I guess Prosecutors Marcia Clark and Christopher Darden would, though!

CHAPTER 14

Detective Mark Fuhrman

Remember what we know now! Whoever deposited the Rockingham glove, also deposited the Bundy glove. This person is, therefore, the murderer or part of a murder conspiracy. O.J. could not have deposited the Rockingham glove. Therefore, he could not have deposited the Bundy glove, either. Consequently he is not the murderer! The all important five blood drops at Bundy **must** have been fabricated.

> **Regardless** of what so-called "evidence" pops up during the rest of this case – **O.J. is not the murderer**. We have reached that conclusion from our discussion of the glove evidence. **I asked you not to forget that, remember?**

However, there is such overwhelming evidence that O.J. is innocent, that we shall reach that same conclusion from **several different angles.** One of them will be presented in this chapter.

Detective Mark Fuhrman alleged that he found the Rockingham glove behind O.J.'s house at about 6:15 on the morning after the murders. He went back into O.J.'s house to inform his colleagues, the other detectives – the lead investigators, Philip Vannatter and Tom Lange, as well as Detctive Ronald Phillips – of his discovery.

One at the time Fuhrman led the other detectives outside to show them the glove behind O.J.'s house. Detective Vannatter stooped down and touched the glove. He must have gotten wet blood on his finger, since he later testified that the blood on the glove was *"sticky and moist"*!

Later, both Detective Vannatter and Fuhrman tried to work their way out of this extremely important observation and testimony, by saying that none of them actually touched the glove. The glove just, *"looked moist"*! However, Vannatter's earlier statement was on record – crystal clear: The glove was *"sticky and moist"*!

Of course, an object can **look** *"moist,"* but still be **dry**, if the surface is shiny, or consists of a substance that has the same visual appearance in both a moist and a dry state – like, for instance, a bowl of newly made jello in your refrigerator! Just by looking at it, you cannot tell whether or not the jello is ready (firm) or still liquid. Hence, you could mistakenly say that the jello looks moist, although it is firm.

However, there is no way anyone can just **look** at an **apparently moist** object and conclude that the object is **"sticky"**! To conclude that an object is **"sticky,"** you have to **touch** it!

There can be no doubt that Detective Vannatter – characterizing the glove as being *"sticky and moist"* – must have touched it carefully, and gotten blood on his fingertip.

Of course, the lead homicide detective does not "ram" his finger into what appears to be a bloody murder glove. A homicide detective knows the importance of not compromising vital evidence in a murder investigation! Consequently, Detective Vannatter must have just "tapped" the glove, extremely **carefully**. Still, he must have gotten "sticky and wet" blood on his fingertip. Hence, the blood on the glove hadn't even begun to form a semi-dry outer crust.

The detective noticed that the blood on the glove was *"sticky and moist"* some time between 6:15 and 6:30. In other words,

the blood on the glove was completely moist almost eight hours after the murders, and seven and a half hours after O.J. left for the airport to fly to Chicago!

The weather at Rockingham that night was mild and relatively dry. That means that the temperature was clearly above the dew point.

Consequently, had the glove been deposited behind the house by O.J. – in other words, before O.J. left for Chicago – the blood on the glove would have been "bone dry" by the time Detective Fuhrman allegedly "found" it!

There is the second conclusive evidence and proof that O.J. is innocent, and that someone was trying to frame him – with the gloves, but also with all the other evidence, as you shall learn in the coming chapters.

Let me explain something about the drying process of blood – although most of my readers probably know this.

Water "evaporates" and disappears as it "dries." This drying process can be greatly slowed or hastened according to such factors as the humidity of the air, and the temperature. A characteristic trait about a water spot in the process of drying up, is that the water which remains at any given time, is completely liquid and wet, until the moment it evaporates and disappears.

Blood, on the other hand, does not "evaporate" and disappear as it dries. Blood **remains** as it dries. It only changes consistency, gradually, from liquid to firm matter, in a process called "coagulation." This is a completely different chemical phenomenon, compared to the evaporation of water.

When exposed to the free oxygen in the air, blood coagulates, which means that the liquid blood hardens. It is this phenomenon we can observe when the blood from a wound forms a dry crust.

This coagulation process occurs rather quickly, sometimes in a matter of minutes, other times in a matter of an hour, or even a couple of hours. But unless there was rain or mist in the air, or the atmosphere was extremely humid – temperature well below the dew point – **the blood on the Rockingham glove would have been bone dry by the time Detective Fuhrman allegedly found it** – if it were deposited behind O.J.'s house before O.J. left for Chicago.

Those of my readers who live in an area where the temperature is around minimum 60 F during the night, and where the temperature is also forecast to be above the dew point on a given night, can conduct their own experiment – using an old leather glove and fresh animal blood. The blood should not be watered down, and not be coagulated.

Dip the glove in the blood around 10:30 pm (about the time of the murders) and wipe off excessive dripping blood on a piece of cloth. We can assume that this was the appearance of the Rockingham glove, since it did not drip a single drop of Ron's or Nicole's blood (only minuscule smears in the Bronco) between the murder scene and Rockingham. Leave the glove outdoors before going to bed. Take a look at the glove around 6:15 the next morning (about the time when the detective observed that the glove was "sticky and moist").

This should convince anyone that O.J. did not kill Nicole and Ron! Several people have actually performed a drying experiment of a bloody glove under almost the exact same conditions that existed behind O.J.'s house on the night of the murders. According to these experiments, the Rockingham glove would have been bone dry around 3:00 am if the glove were deposited by O.J. (or someone) at 10:40-42 pm – the time Kato heard the thumps on his wall!

There is only one explanation why the blood on the glove was still "sticky and moist" when Detective Vannatter touched it. The glove must have been kept in an **air tight** container – like a **plastic bag** or similar – for **most** of the seven and a half hours before Detective Fuhrman allegedly "found" the glove.

However, even inside a plastic bag there is oxygen, both in the air inside the bag, and in the glove material itself. You have a somewhat similar situation or environment as when you put a water proof, plastic band-aid on a bleeding wound. Even under the water proof plastic band-aid the blood coagulates, the bleeding stops, and a hard crust is formed.

Therefore, even if the Rockingham glove was kept in a plastic bag, the blood on it would coagulate (dry), although not as quickly as out in the open.

What we can conclude from this, is that since coagulation takes place even inside a plastic bag or some other air-tight container, and the blood on the glove was "sticky and moist" more than 7 1/2 hours after the murders,

the glove must have been kept inside a plastic bag or some other air-tight container, **up until only a short time**

before Detective Fuhrman allegedly found the glove.

Another point is the absence of insects on and around that bloody glove. If that wet and bloody glove had been on the ground for more than seven and a half hours it should have been covered with insects when Detective Fuhrman found it. I am not just talking about flying insects that would disappear when someone approached the glove, but crawling insects, most of all – especially, since the scent of blood tend to attract insects.

Unquestionably, someone must have placed that glove on the ground, behind O.J.'s house, just a short while before Detective Fuhrman found it.

It is highly unlikely that the murderer – unless he is Mark Fuhrman – **would have dared to trespass onto O.J.'s property, or the neighbor's property, with the murder glove in a plastic bag in his pocket, in an effort to plant the glove behind O.J.'s house, many hours after the murders, and at a time when two (later three) police cars** (one "black&white") **were parked outside O.J.'s estate.**

Should the murderer – assuming he is not Detective Fuhrman – be spotted, arrested for trespassing or as a possible burglar suspect, and subsequently be searched, the police would find the bloody murder glove in his pocket! The murderer would be nailed, on the spot, for the murders of Nicole and Ron!

In other words, if the murderer were someone other than Detective Fuhrman, he would never have dared to plant the bloody murder glove behind O.J.'s house shortly before Fuhrman, allegedly, found that glove. There is only one reasonable conclusion to be drawn from this:

Detective Mark Fuhrman planted the Rockingham glove.

According to our discussion of the glove evidence, **Detective Fuhrman is, therefore, the murderer.**

We shall now reach that same conclusion in a totally different way. Many people (besides myself) have also suspected that Detective Fuhrman planted the Rockingham glove. However, these other people speculated that Fuhrman planted the glove in order to harm O.J. because O.J. was an African American. They failed to draw the more obvious conclusion, namely that

Fuhrman planted the glove, also in order to cover up a double homicide he himself might have committed!

It is suspicious that Detective Fuhrman, who is an admitted racist, and who was no longer assigned to the Simpson case, should find this most crucial piece of evidence!

Sure, Fuhrman had just spoken with Kato Kaelin. Kato said he heard some severe **"thumps"** on his wall, at a time corresponding to shortly after the time the murders took place at Bundy. So Fuhrman wanted to investigate, allegedly, what could have caused those thumps behind O.J.'s house.

However, it was suspicious that Fuhrman was the one who spoke to Kato in the first place – and alone. Secondly, it was suspicious that Fuhrman didn't relay this information to Vannatter, the lead investigator, and let Vannatter decide whether or not Fuhrman, or anyone else, should go behind O.J.'s house to investigate. It was as if Fuhrman himself had to make certain that he got the opportunity to go behind O.J.'s house **alone**!

It is also suspicious that the blood on the glove was sticky and moist when Fuhrman found it. But even more suspicious is the fact that if this glove had been deposited by O.J. before he left for Chicago, and not by Fuhrman, there should have been blood in and around the area where the glove was found, since O.J., allegedly, were dripping blood "everywhere."

Yet, there was no trace of blood on the ground, or on any of the leaves on the ground, where Fuhrman "found" the glove.

These facts have made many people conclude that Fuhrman – somehow – brought the glove to Rockingham and planted it behind

O.J.'s house – at the same time as he, allegedly, found it.

What these people, as well as the former prosecutors, counsels for the plaintiffs, and most of O.J.'s adversaries, fail to understand, however, is

how Fuhrman could have come into possession of the Rockingham glove.

Fuhrman himself is the first to point out that he arrived at Bundy around 2:10 am. At that time there were already 17 other police officers at the murder scene. They had already searched the entire area and found only one glove.

Everyone – including Fuhrman – argued that it was highly unlikely – or impossible, rather – that Fuhrman as the eighteenth officer at the murder scene, could just get out of his car, walk around for a while, and stumble upon a second murder glove at Bundy – which none of the other officers had seen!

I agree completely. But I want to add: Even **if** Fuhrman had found the second glove at Bundy, he could not have picked it up at that time, in order to bring it to Rockingham and thereby frame O.J.

Why not? Well, if Fuhrman had picked up that second glove at Bundy (hypothetically speaking), concealed it, brought it to Rockingham, and alleged that he found it behind O.J.'s house – some of the other officers at Bundy might protest, saying that it was impossible for that glove to be found at Rockingham, because they had already seen it at Bundy!

Suddenly, Detective Fuhrman could have been accused of planting evidence in a capital murder case, for which he could have been sentenced to life in prison (if found guilty).

Some people, with whom I have discussed my theory, argued that if any of the other officers had seen the second glove at Bundy, Fuhrman would have known about that.

Possibly! But if Fuhrman was innocent, he wouldn't have risked his life and future on such an assumption – just for the pleasure of trying to frame O.J.!

Remember also that most of the 17 other officers at Bundy were just ordinary police officers, who were assigned to the murder scene simply to seal off the area, direct traffic, and keep unauthorized people away. They could, conceivably, have spotted the second glove – if it was there – and said nothing, because they were not investigators, but ordinary police officers, who simply assumed, automatically, that the detectives on the scene had already detected the glove and reported it.

Conclusion: There was no second glove at Bundy. Detective Fuhrman did not find the second murder glove when he arrived at Bundy, about 2:10 am, to investigate the murders. If Fuhrman, indeed, planted the Rockingham glove – and the appearance of that glove strongly suggested that he did –

. . . the only other possible explanation is that when Fuhrman arrived at Bundy, about 2:10 am, he already had the second murder glove in his possession – for instance hidden in a plastic bag inside one of his socks – because he had actually murdered Nicole and Ron earlier that night!

It is time to take a closer look at Detective Mark Fuhrman!

CHAPTER 15

"The Fuhrman Tapes"

Don't be fooled by Mark Fuhrman! He is an extreme racist and possibly a vicious psychopath, something that will become more evident as you read this chapter. However this monster is so smooth when he wants to be, that he fooled us all during his testimony against O.J., where he politely and smilingly, even cracking a joke once in a while, answered Defense Attorney F. Lee Bailey's questions,

> *"Yes, Sir"; "No, Sir"; "That's what I'm saying, Sir"; "The name, Kathleen Bell does not . . . he-he . . .* [Bailey: *". . . ring a bell?"*] *. . . he-he . . . yes!"*

. . . while he in fact was committing perjury, and calling Ms. Kathleen Bell and other defense witnesses, *"liars"*, when they testified that Fuhrman addressed black people as *"niggers"* and advocated genocide against people of the African race.

In front of 100 million TV viewers, most of whom found Detective Fuhrman, "charming, honest, polite, sincere," and other adjectives like that, this perjuring racist smiled while he was lying through his teeth. Following his conviction for perjury October 3, 1996, Fuhrman was interviewed on ABC's *"20/20."*

With shiny eyes, Fuhrman **"explained"** to the American people, during this interview, that he had **forgotten** about *"The Fuhrman Tapes"* which he made together with an aspiring screenplay writer, Ms. Laura Hart McKinny, and wherein he was heard using the word "nigger" more than 40 times! It was, after all, almost 10 years ago, he said.

Again, Fuhrman was lying to the American people. **The last *"Fuhrman Tapes"* were made shortly after the murders!** Ms. McKinny testified that she and Fuhrman even discussed the

Simpson case shortly before the trial, and that Fuhrman, on that occasion had claimed he was a key player in the investigation, due to his finding the Rockingham glove.

Against such irrefutable evidence, how could Detective Fuhrman, with tears in his eyes, **"explain"** during his interview on *"20/20,"* that he had forgotten about *"The Fuhrman Tapes"* he made with Ms. McKinny. How could he **"explain"** that this was the reason he didn't *"remember"* – during F. Lee Bailey's cross examination – that he ever used the **"N-word"**!

Mark Fuhrman is lying through his teeth every time he opens his mouth in public! Even when he appears to be on the brink of crying, this "psycho" is so smooth and calculating, that he would have fooled his own mother. My readers – **don't be fooled by Mark Fuhrman again!**

Remember what F. Lee Bailey asked Fuhrman during cross examination, regarding his use of the "N-word":

Bailey: Would you remember, Detective Fuhrman, if you had used the language that we have just reviewed?
Fuhrman: *Yes*
Bailey: That is important enough language to you, that it would impress itself on your memory – as did the meeting with the Simpson's in '85 – is that correct?
Fuhrman: *Yes, Sir!*

I have already expressed my "Fuhrman theory" in an earlier book. I assume my theory had reached Fuhrman ahead of his interview on *"20/20."* If Fuhrman murdered Nicole and Ron, he knows that I am on to him, and so are others – investigative reporters and private investigators! He is fighting for his life. So don't be fooled, again and again, by this dangerous psycho!

If Fuhrman thinks someone is about to crack this case, he would gladly move to Harlem, NY – or like a politician, kiss African-American babies on TV – if he thought it would further his cause. But he was, and remains, a racist.

Detective Mark Fuhrman investigated an incident of alleged

domestic abuse at Nicole's and O.J. Simpson's residence in 1985. Fuhrman was at that time an extreme racist who hated black people like O.J. But as much as Fuhrman hated black people, **he hated, even more, white women who dated, or were married to black men.**

Fuhrman's prejudice towards black people – and in particular towards interracial couples – had not changed one bit between 1985 and the time of the murders! If, anything, such relationships made Fuhrman even more crazy as the years passed.

Prosecutor Darden, himself an African American, had interviewed Detective Fuhrman prior to his testimony in the criminal trial against O.J. After the interview, Darden realized that Fuhrman was just as much of a racist, as he had ever been, and that

interracial couples – like Nicole and O.J. – in particular, still upset Fuhrman more than anything!

At one point during a break in the direct examination of Fuhrman, Prosecutor Darden decided to put Fuhrman to the test.

Darden refused to examine Fuhrman, because of Fuhrman's obvious racism. So, Prosecutor Marcia Clark was examining Fuhrman. Let me quote from former Prosecutor Christopher Darden's book, *"In Contempt"* (Harper Collins/Regan Books, N.Y., 1996):

[Quote] When the time came, of course, Marcia did as I had asked and set off on one of her detailed, structured direct examinations. Later, as Fuhrman sat leaning against the jury box during a recess, I whispered to Marcia, *"Follow my lead."* I put my arm around her shoulder and pulled her head to rest on my chest, and we walked in Fuhrman's direction. His face turned bright red and he stared at us.

"What are you doing having that guy hanging all over you like a cheap suit?" Fuhrman asked Marcia after I'd left. I took it very seriously, perhaps Mark Fuhrman hadn't changed after all. [End of quote].

Fuhrman responded to Nicole's 911 call in 1985 and entered O.J. Simpson's residence to investigate. Accordingly, from that day, Detective Fuhrman knew the Simpsons – and they knew him!

Observing the obviously successful and wealthy African-American O.J., and his estate in the fashionable and exclusive upper Brentwood community, with its swimming pool and jacuzzi, the private tennis court, the golf practice tee, O.J.'s expensive cars (his Mercedes, Ferrari, and Bentley), the luxurious home, etc., greatly upset the racist Detective Fuhrman who made, perhaps, $15,000 a year at that time, and had to put up with being called *"Pig!"* on every street corner.

As if that wasn't enough imagine Fuhrman's fury when Nicole exited, perhaps wearing a revealing outfit, and it dawned on Fuhrman that this stunning, young, blonde woman was sharing bedroom with her husband, the African-American O.J.!

Although Fuhrman was able to hide his emotions and put on a casual, professional appearance – just as he did during his perjuring testimony in court, and in the interview on *"20/20"* – the meeting with the Simpson's in 1985 greatly upset him. He immediately despised both of them and decided to harm them – if he could.

Somewhere along the line he decided to kill Nicole and O.J. But one day he got an even better idea:

If Fuhrman killed them both, the police might, perhaps, look for a racist murderer who hated interracial couples, and Fuhrman might become a suspect, since that description fit him, and he also knew the Simpsons.

So, Fuhrman decided, instead, to kill the white Nicole, only, and frame O.J. for her murder!

Having investigated the alleged incident of domestic violence, Fuhrman knew that O.J. would immediately become the prime suspect if Nicole was murdered.

On the now infamous *"Fuhrman Tapes,"* from the transcripts of which I shall quote shortly, Fuhrman brags about how he was framing suspects with fabricated evidence, so cleverly that no one could expose him. Specifically, he also brags about being equally clever at lying during his testimonies.

He is so good at this, he says, that nobody could expose him. This was even more so, since his colleagues within the LAPD would also lie to support him, should his actions or his testimonies be scrutinized.

At one point on the tapes, Fuhrman even brags about being so clever at framing innocent people and lying when testifying about it, that he *"could have murdered people and got away with it"*!

In his psychopathic mind, Fuhrman believed that murdering Nicole, and framing O.J. would be something to be proud of!

Indirectly, on *"The Fuhrman Tapes,"* this guy actually confessed to the murders of Nicole and Ron – over and over again. All the evidence in the Simpson case pointed to Fuhrman! Yet, nobody realized it, or took him seriously.

Through his *"Fuhrman Tapes"* Mark Fuhrman is crying out to be caught! [Or perhaps he realizes his mental problems, and is crying out for help]!

It is absolutely incredible how the investigators – and the media – could overlook Mark Fuhrman as a **murder suspect**, and instead accuse O.J. Simpson!

B eing a homicide detective, Mark Fuhrman believed he knew how to murder Nicole without leaving any evidence pointing to himself. He also believed he knew how to frame O.J.

But more importantly, Fuhrman believed he knew how to **"set up"** the LAPD investigators and convince them right away that O.J. were guilty, so that **the investigators would continue to fabricate such false evidence against O.J. which Fuhrman could not fabricate himself.**

That is **one of the major points** of this murder mystery!

In the years that followed, the idea of killing Nicole and framing O.J. for the murder became an **obsession** with Fuhrman. He planned the murder in minute details. In his mind he tried to think about every little detail that might go wrong and eliminate any little flaw in his plan. It was like a challenge – a "title fight": **Detective Mark Fuhrman against the rest of the world!**

Before I continue with Fuhrman's plan for murdering Nicole, it is time to let Detective Fuhrman speak for himself through his testimony in the Simpson trial, and through *"The Fuhrman Tapes,"* on which he is being interviewed by Ms. Laura Hart McKinny. Then my readers can judge for themselves how far-fetched – or how sound – my theory is, that Mark Fuhrman – and not O.J. – murdered Nicole and Ron.

My readers may want to put a "book mark" on this page! Go back and review the following excerpts after reading my detailed description on how I believe Detective Fuhrman carried out the murders of Nicole and Ron!

I start by repeating part of Defense Attorney F. Lee Bailey's cross examination of Detective Fuhrman, regarding Fuhrman's alleged use of the word "nigger."

Bailey: Would you remember, Detective Fuhrman, if you had used the language that we have just reviewed?
Fuhrman: *Yes.*
Bailey: That is important enough language to you, that it would impress itself on your memory – as did the meeting with the Simpson's in '85 – is that correct?
Fuhrman: *Yes, Sir!*

Perhaps Defense Attorney Bailey is a bit "clever" with his **"compound question"** here. Nevertheless, Detective Fuhrman clearly admits that the meeting with the Simpson's in 1985 was more than a routine call to investigate an incident of domestic violence or disturbance. According to Fuhrman's testimony, the meeting with the Simpson's in 1985 **"impressed itself on Detective Fuhrman's memory"**!

O n *"The Fuhrman Tapes"* Fuhrman talks about a man who had shot four police officers, killing two of them. He had served his sentence and now attended UCLA.

Fuhrman: *If I had arrested the son of a bitch, I would have killed him. If I ever see the son of a bitch and we're alone, I would kill him.*

McKinny: How can you get away with that?

Fuhrman: *If there's nobody except him and me, dead men tell no tales! See, he killed two policemen. I have an obligation. If I have the opportunity, I should kill him. And that's all there is to it.*

McKinny: Say you were working with a partner who saw you do that?

Fuhrman: *Can't do that. You gotta have a partner that's like your brother.*

Fuhrman talked a lot about killing people. Some of it clearly supports my theory, that murdering Nicole, the **risk** involved, the **challenge** of it, the **intensity** of it, became an **obsession** with Fuhrman. **It was something he eventually had to do**, simply to prove to himself that he **could** do it – **and get away with it**! Take this excerpt, for instance:

Fuhrman: *I don't want [people] to think I'm a coward. So sometimes that'll stimulate me to do what I have to do. I like it because there is something that is on the line . . . and I like working under pressure.*

. . . And you look around and say, most of these pukes couldn't do it. It's control, power, whatever you call it.

McKinny: What [annoys] you when you hear liberals talk?

Fuhrman: "Don't you shoot to wound 'em?"

No, we shoot to kill 'em! Now, the Department says we shoot to *stop, not to kill, which is horseshit! The only way you can stop somebody is to kill the son of a bitch. And **what's the big deal?** If you've got a reason to shoot somebody, you've got a reason to kill him!*

Here is another excerpt:

Fuhrman: *Where would this country be if every time a sheriff went out with a posse to find someone who just robbed and killed a bunch of people, and he stopped to talk to them first – to make sure they had guns? . . . **We still should be shooting people in the back!** It's just that you have to hire people who are capable of doing it!*

Here is yet another excerpt. It shows a little bit of Fuhrman's disrespect for women. **The last quote makes me think of how I believe Detective Fuhrman grabbed Nicole by her hair from behind and cut her neck, and how he later snuck up on Ron from behind, cut his neck, and stabbed him to death.**

Fuhrman: *If you did things that they teach you in the Academy, you'd never get a fucking thing done. I'll split up the people, that's fine. You split up two suspects and say, "Where are you from? What's [your] name?" That's great, but if he doesn't tell you, you give him a shot in the stomach with your stick and say: "Listen boy, I'm talking to you, and you better give me some attention, or I'm gonna fucking drop you like a bad habit!"*
Now, can you tell me a female [officer] you see doing that?
McKinny: No.
Fuhrman: *Those are field interrogation techniques for assholes!*
McKinny: Well, where did you learn those field interrogation techniques, if you didn't learn them in the Academy?
Fuhrman: *Well, probably [when I was] 8 years old. You learn that when somebody pushes. If you can't beat them face on, you sneak up behind them and just grab them by the hair*

and keep punchin'em until they go down.

Isn't this exactly how we picture the murderer surprised Nicole, grabbed her by her hair and cut and stabbed her *until she went down,* and shortly thereafter surprised Ron more or less the same way, cutting him down **from behind**!

Remember, I didn't make up the quotes above. **They were Fuhrman's words,** describing how he liked to attack people from behind and hit them till they *"go down"*! Fuhrman said this, during the years before Nicole and Ron were murdered exactly like that!

Here is more. Below, Fuhrman is talking about police officers who are not willing to break the rules and lie. They got "morals."

McKinny: What do you mean, he's got morals?

Fuhrman: *He doesn't know how to be a policeman.* [Whispers] "I can't lie . . ." *Oh* [he] *makes me fucking sick to my guts. You know, you do what you have to do to put these fucking assholes in jail. If you don't, you fucking get out of the fucking game!*

About the NAACP and the ACLU Fuhrman had this to say:

Fuhrman: *The NAACP, the ACLU should be bombed, and everybody should be killed in it.*

Here is more of Detective Fuhrman's interrogation techniques, from his own mouth:

Fuhrman: *When I was working gang, we used to get a murder. And you'd know which gang did it, but they wouldn't talk. So, I would go pick up three or four gang members and bring them to the station. I take one in the basement and beat the shit out of him, without even asking him a question. Bring him up and sit him down. He is bleeding, face is all puffed up, got hurt.*
Next guy, take him downstairs. "OK. Who shot him?" *That's*

how you get information!

Many of my readers may not know this, but those were the "gentler," moderate interrogation techniques of Hitler's secret police – the **GESTAPO** – during World War II! I know, because I was born in a country occupied by the Nazi's during the war.

Detective Mark Fuhrman has ties to a **neo-nazi** organization, and his hobby was to collect **Nazi World War II medals!** Such medals were symbols of, and rewards for, Nazi soldiers' atrocities during the war! Perhaps Defense Attorney Johnnie Cochran wasn't so far off when he said that

> *Mark Fuhrman might have developed into a modern day* "Hitler" – ***had he had Hitler's power!*** *We have to stop people like Fuhrman **before** they develop into* **"Hitler's"**!

Fuhrman goes on to talk about Internal Affairs investigations against him for alleged brutality. What he describes, again, brings my thoughts to the Bundy murder scene. I wonder what my readers think.

The most striking characteristic about the MO in the Simpson murder case was the extremely bloody murder scene. Pay particular attention, therefore, to Fuhrman's fascination with blood! My readers may also recall the prosecution suggested that Nicole had been **tortured**! So read what Fuhrman says!

Fuhrman: *I had 66 allegations of brutality: AEW under color of authority; assault and battery under color of authority;* ***torture*** *. . . all kinds of stuff!*
Two guys, well there was four guys. Two of my buddies were shot and ambushed. Both alive, and I was the first unit on the scene. Four suspects ran into an apartment project's second story apartment. We kicked the door down. We grabbed a girl that lived there, one of their girlfriends. Grabbed her by the hair and stuck a gun to her head, and

used her as a barricade ...

Notice, again, how Fuhrman describes grabbing a woman by her hair, from behind! That's how Nicole was attacked and killed!

Fuhrman: [Cont.] *Walked up and told them:* "I've got this girl. I'll blow her fucking brains out, if you come out with a gun!" *Held her like this ... **threw the bitch down the stairs** ... deadbolted the door.* "Let's play, boys!"

Again, notice Fuhrman's total disrespect for women. The young woman certainly hadn't done anything wrong. Still, Fuhrman treats her as an object he can just kill and throw away! He calls her a *"bitch"* and throws her down the stairs!

Maybe Fuhrman's total disrespect for the life of the girl was caused by her relationship to the Latino boys/men he so dispised. Did Fuhrman harbour a similar disrespect for the life of Nicole, who was married to O.J. – a man of a race Fuhrman despised even more, namely African Americans.

Is it too much to ask O.J.'s critics, including his former prosecutors and the plaintiffs, who based their entire cases against O.J. on his alleged abuse of Nicole, to please take a closer look at this psychopathic monster, named Mark Fuhrman!

During his interview on *"20/20,"* Fuhrman tried to diminish the effect of *"The Fuhrman Tapes,"* saying that those tapes do not depict anything real. He was just trying to contribute to a screenplay. Almost with tears in his eyes he told the interviewer that what was on the tapes had no basis in reality.

OK! So let us read some more from the tapes. We are still in the same episode.

McKinny: Can we use that in the story [the screenplay]?
Fuhrman: [No!] *It hasn't been 7 years. Statute of limitations!*

Fuhrman's comment here is interesting. It shows that **he is not making up stories. Fuhrman is correctly relating what actually happened! That's why he won't let Ms. McKinny use this episode in her screenplay – yet!** Fuhrman is concerned about the 7 years statute of limitation, because the episode was still under investigation by the Internal Affairs.

> **Why should Fuhrman be concerned about the statute of limitations, if the things he described were just stories he made up for a screenplay?**

Again, **don't let Mark Fuhrman fool you**! And some day, when the LAPD come out with a "report" whitewashing Fuhrman, and claiming that he was just lying and exaggerating – then don't let that report fool you either!

Remember this whenever you see Mark Fuhrman, tears in his eyes, tell a TV reporter or an interviewer that he is *"sorry,"* and that he never meant what he said on the Fuhrman Tapes – it was just his misguided attempt to write a screenplay!

By the way, the four men were innocent. They filed complaints with the LAPD, their injuries were documented by the hospital where they were treated. One of the men died from his injuries! I don't care if the LAPD detectives managed to cover it up and protect each other through their **"code of silence."** It is still murder! And Fuhrman was one of the perpetrators!

On another occasion Fuhrman was accused of shooting a suspect who was already apprehended, and for planting a knife as evidence. The case was scheduled to go to trial just before Fuhrman was scheduled to testify against O.J. So the City of Los Angeles settled the case, paying the plaintiffs $100,000 – to avoid the embarrassment of this ongoing lawsuit while Fuhrman testified in the Simpson case.

Anyway, let's continue with the episode with the four Latinos.

Fuhrman: *I have 300 and something pages Internal Affairs investigation just on that one incident. I got several other* *ones. I must have about 3,000 or 4,000 pages of Internal Affairs investigations out there.*

Don't you wonder? According to the LAPD, the Los Angeles DA's office, and the California Attorney general, this monster of a policeman has been thoroughly investigated and found to be

> ***". . . a good detective who has done nothing criminal during his 20 years with the LAPD"!***

Here is how former LAPD Chief Daryl Gates characterized Mark Fuhrman on *"Larry King Live,"* february 1997:

> ***". . . a hell of a fine police officer"!***

It makes you wonder what the LAPD's **"not so fine"** police officers were like, or what?

Afterwards, Mr. Larry King shook Mark Fuhrman's hand and wished him good luck in Idaho – where Fuhrman lives a few miles from the headquarters of a white supremacist organization!

According to the LAPD, District Attorney Gil Garcetti, and the Attorney General, there is nothing to indicate that Fuhrman ever planted evidence in the Simpson case, or that he even had the opportunity to do it! According to the same sources, Fuhrman even loves African Americans and other minorities, and he is not a racist!

I honestly don't know whether to laugh or cry when I hear something like that reported on the *"Larry King Live"* or *"Rivera Live"* show! It is deeply tragic and disturbing that the American justice system, has sunk so low. And it is just as disturbing that the media are no longer capable, or willing to stand up for justice in this country!

<u>Fuhrman:</u> [Still talking about the four young men in the apartment] *Anyway . . . we basically **tortured** them.*

Here is that word again. Fuhrman must have enjoyed **torturing** people. **Did he enjoy torturing Nicole and Ron as well?** And notice Fuhrman's fascination with blood – regardless of whether this next segment is fact or fiction!

Fuhrman: [Cont.]*There were four policemen, four guys. We broke 'em. Numerous bones in each of them.*

Their faces were just mush.

*They had pictures on the walls . . . there was **blood all the way to the ceiling,** with fingermarks like they were trying to crawl out of the room.*

*[Internal Affairs] showed us pictures of the room. It was unbelievable. There was **blood everywhere**. All the walls, all the furniture, all the floor. It was just **everywhere**. These guys, they had to shave so much hair off. One guy, they shaved it all of. Like 70 stitches to his head. You know, **knees cracked** . . .! Oh, it was just . . .*

We had 'em begging that they'd never be gang members again . . . begging us!

So with 66 allegations, I had a demonstration in front of Hollenbeck [police] station chanting my name. Captain had to take them into roll call, and that's where the Internal Affairs investigation started.

*It lasted 18 months. I was on a photo lineup, suspect lineup. I was picked out by 12 people. So I was **pretty proud of that**! I was the last one interviewed. The prime suspect is always the last one interviewed. They didn't get any of our unit – 38 guys – they didn't get one day!*

The custodian – the jailer of the sheriff's department got five days, since he beat one of the guys at the very end.

*Immediately after we beat those guys, we went downstairs to the garden hose in the back of the place. We washed our hands. We had **blood all over our legs, everything**. With a dark uniform, you know, in the dark, you can't see it. But when you get in the light and it looks like somebody took red paint and painted all over you . . . ! We had to clean*

our badges with water, **_there was blood all over them_** _..._
The chiefs and everything were coming down because two
officers were shot. "Where are the suspects?"

"I think some of the officers over here got them. They took
them to the station."

Somehow nobody arrested them! We handcuffed them and
threw them down two flights of stairs, you know. That's how
they came! "Look out! Here comes one! Oh, my God, look
out, he's falling!"

... But anyway, the point is ... well, they know I did it.
They know damn well I did it. There is nothing they could
do, but I could!

Most of those guys worked the 77th [Street division]
together. We were tight! I mean **_we could have murdered_**
people and got away with it! _We were tight._ **_We all knew_**
what to say. _We didn't have to call each other at home, and_
say, "Okay." _We all knew what to say._

... Most good police officers understand, that they would
love _to take certain people ..._ _and_ **_just take them to the_**
alley and blow their brains out!

When I tell my readers that I will explain in this book how all the
physical evidence and all the circumstantial evidence in the Simpson
case are **consistent** with Detective Mark Fuhrman having murdered Nicole and Ron – is anyone going to tell me, after having
read what Fuhrman says, thinks, and does, that this man could not
have murdered Nicole and Ron?

Does anyone, instead, find it more likely that the congenial,
religious, amicable, considerate, emotionally balanced, always
friendly and smiling O.J., killed Nicole – whom he still loved and
had deep affection for – just because he had some heated arguments with her in 1985, 1989, and 1993, when he, allegedly, beat
up on a Mercedes and a French door, rather than beating up on
Nicole?

Don't my readers, just like I, have flashbacks to the bloody
murder scene at Bundy, when they read Fuhrman's vivid descrip-

tions of beatings, murder, **torture**, blood everywhere, sneak attacks from behind, *"punching till they go down,"* **grabbing a young woman's hair from behind,** beating people to **"mush"**?

We should all read Fuhrman's words again! I have reversed the "italics" so it reads easier:

Fuhrman: I had 66 allegations of brutality... **TORTURE**, all kinds of stuff!

We grabbed a girl that lived there, one of their girlfriends. **Grabbed her by the hair** and stuck a gun to her head, and used her as a barricade. . . . Walked up and told them: *"I've got this girl. I'll blow her fucking brains out, if you come out with a gun!"*

Held her like this . . . **threw the bitch down the stairs . . .** We broke 'em. Numerous bones in each of them. Their faces were just mush. They had pictures on the walls . . . there was **blood all the way to the ceiling, with finger-marks like they were trying to crawl out of the room.**

[Internal Affairs] showed us pictures of the room. It was unbelievable. There was **blood everywhere**. All the **walls,** all the **furniture,** all the **floor**. It was just **everywhere**.

These guys, they had to shave so much hair off. One guy, they shaved it all off. Like **70 stitches to his head**.

You know, **knees cracked** . . .! Oh, it was just . . .

We had **blood all over our legs**, everything. With a dark uniform, you know, **in the dark, you can't see it**. But when you get **in the light and it looks like somebody took red paint and painted all over you**! We had to clean our badges with water, **there was blood all over them . . .**

Isn't the Bundy murder scene right up Detective Fuhrman's alley? One of the hardest things to reconcile with O.J. as a suspect in the murders of Nicole and Ron, is the use of a knife, and the extremely gruesome and bloody M.O. It takes an extremely violent, sadistically ruthless person to commit such a vicious crime.

The murders of Nicole and Ron do not reflect the actions

of a jealous husband. Murder based on jealousy is "a crime of **passion**." A jealous husband might, spontaneously, kill his cheating wife in the heat of the moment, when he catches her in her lover's arms.

If the only weapon available in the house at that moment is a knife, the husband may grab it. But jealous husbands would almost never **plan** to murder their wives with a **knife**. And rarely would a jealous husband, who kills his wife, torture the woman he, obviously, loves so dearly that he can't stand to see her in the arms of another man!

Nicole's murder bears no sign of being "a crime of passion." Her murder was a typical **hate crime**! It was typically the crime of a psychopath who hated her and murdered her for some insane reason that ordinary people can hardly comprehend.

The gruesome, murder of Nicole was typically the act of a racist psychopath, like Detective Fuhrman, who believed it to be – in his words, **_"against nature"_** for a white woman to have a relationship with a black man; and who in addition hated blacks so intensely that he felt – if he had the power to do it – he would be justified in gathering all _"niggers"_ and burn, or bomb, them to death!

The gruesome MO and, typically, the use of a knife, ties in with Detective Fuhrman in yet another way. Fuhrman is a former U.S. Marine who served in Vietnam. The Special Forces of the U.S. Marines were trained in the use of knives. On recognizance patrols, if they surprised, or were surprised by, an enemy sentry, it would routinely be necessary to kill the enemy sentry silently – with a knife, rather than a gun, so his unit should not be alarmed.

Between hours of battle, Marines would frequently sharpen and polish their knives. Sometimes their own lives could depend on the ease and swiftness with which they could slit through the throat of an enemy sentry. Often the Marines would take pride in having the sharpest knife in their unit. They would demonstrate this by slicing a hair or a piece of paper in mid air.

How does this connect with the murders at Bundy? No question about it – the person who slit Nicole's throat must have had some prior experience or training in the use of a knife to kill people. In addition, the knife that slit Nicole's neck – clean into her spine – must have been extraordinarily sharp.

The murder knife was not a knife O.J., on the spur of the moment, could have grabbed in his kitchen drawer. Had this been any ordinary kitchen knife, or even a new hunting knife, it would still not have cut Nicole's neck all the way into her vertebra in one single, clean cut.

The murder knife might perceivably have been sharpened and used by a commando or a Marine – like Mark Fuhrman – who knew how to handle such an ugly weapon, and who knew how to sharpen it like a straight razor.

Dr. Irwin Golden who performed the autopsies on Nicole and Ron, suggested that there might have been two killers, because some of the knife wounds might have been inflicted with a double edged knife, while most of the wounds seemed to have been inflicted with a single edged knife. During the civil trial, the medical examiner for the plaintiffs, Dr. Werner Spitz suggested that some of the knife wounds seemed to have been inflicted with a **serrated** knife.

However, the rest of the evidence at the murder scene suggetsed that there was only one murderer – and hence, only one knife. How is that possible? **There is a simple explanation.** The murderer used **a commando knife**, like the ones used by some Marines. These knives are, first of all, extremely sharp. Besides they are designed as a combination of a **single edged** knife and a **double edged** knife. And one edge is even **partly serrated**!

One side of the knife has a sharp edge, which ends in a serrated section of about two inches – near the handle. The other side of the knife has a sharp edge, too – but only for about two inches from the tip. From there on it is single edged.

There you have it! One murderer! One knife – a commando knife! Partly single edged! Partly double edged! And partly serrated! A typical knife the Vietnam veteran, former U.S. Marine Mark Fuhrman, might own. But hardly at all, a knife O.J. would whip up on the spur of a moment – in response to a "Dear

John" message from Paula Barbieri on his answering machine!

Some who refuse to listen to reason, and still maintain that O.J. is the murderer, argue that Detective Fuhrman was never convicted of the actions he describes on the tapes, and that he, therefore, might be making up these "stories."

First of all, the four men Fuhrman and his LAPD buddies almost beat to death (one died), the charges filed by his victims, the Internal Affairs investigations, his concern about the statute of limitations, the case the City of Los Angeles settled for Fuhrman just before he was scheduled to testify, etc. all prove that he is talking about **real events**.

However, does it make any difference – if what he is talking about on the tapes are just his **fantasies**?

Even if a man has not committed such atrocities, what kind of personality does he harbor if he can even fantasize about it and idolize it?

"The Fuhrman Tapes," however, is not the only proof of Mark Fuhrman's psychopathic, violent, racist personality. On the following pages, I shall put *"The Fuhrman Tapes"* into a wider context, showing that these tapes did not reflect Fuhrman's misguided attempt to write a screenplay – as he claims today. This **was** Fuhrman!

Before I continue, however, I want my readers to be aware of the fact that the prosecutors and **the DA's office – Prosecutor Marcia Clark in particular – knew everything I am going to reveal about Mark Fuhrman.** Still, the prosecutor embraced Detective Fuhrman, and tried to protected him from any kind of negative exposure – even after he was caught perjuring himself.

Please keep this in mind as you continue to read – because one of my central claims regarding this case is that **the investigators, the prosecutors and the DA's office knew, all along, that Mark Fuhrman had murdered Nicole and Ron.**

The L.A. District Attorney's office sent an investigator to Eatonville, WA, where Fuhrman used to live, to gather some background information on him before the trial. The investigator learned that Fuhrman and his younger brother had been notoriously infamous for terrorizing one of the African-American teenagers in Eatonville. The Fuhrman brothers were known as the towns most racist bullies.

Next: All along, Prosecutor Marcia Clark must have known that Fuhrman had five serious complaints for police brutality filed against him. That was in his official personnel file, I guess. This means that Fuhrman was just one complaint shy of being included among the one hundred most infamous problem cops in the LAPD – mentioned in the Christopher Commission Report.

Prosecutor Clark also knew about Detective Fuhrman's attempts to retire from the LAPD with disability pension. The associated medical reports also included information about his personal background. I cannot quote the entire reports – it would take up too much space. I shall instead quote short passages to explain what kind of person Mark Fuhrman really is. My readers may have some idea by now, based on "The Fuhrman Tapes." Take the following as a supplement.

August 8, 1981, Mark Fuhrman was placed on medical leave by a psychiatrist, **Dr. Gottlieb,** MD, and continued to see Dr. Gottlieb as a patient.

According to Fuhrman himself, Dr. Gottlieb treated him for depression and anxiety, as well as an *"explosive personality."* Fuhrman felt under a great deal of pressure, and was unable to deal with the stress. He felt he might *"explode and hurt some-one."*

December 16, 1981 another psychiatrist, **Dr. John Hochman**, MD, examined Fuhrman and wrote a report on his findings.

November 30, 1982, **Dr. Ronald R. Kroeger**, MD, wrote a report on Mark Fuhrman for Workers' Compensation Division in Los Angeles. In his report, Dr. Kroeger makes many refereces to Dr. Gottliebs report, and also quotes Mark Fuhrman. Here is a bouquet of quotes from Fuhrman's psychiatric reports:

Gottlieb: [Fuhrman] is **preoccupied with violence.**

Kroeger: [Fuhrman] has been seeing Dr. Gottlieb twice weekly for psychotherapy, *"working on violence and depression."*

Fuhrman: I never had any regrets over any damage i did to people (broken limbs, etc.) I never had any second thoughts over what I did in Vietnam. I loved it, and never had any "flash-backs."

March 15, 1980 my second wife left me. She had been cheating on me. It was best I didn't find out till afterwards. **I would have killed both of them!**

Gottlieb: In no way can [Fuhrman] be assigned to duty in any part of the Police Department. The evidence is in the patient's dreams of violent feelings. He needs to continue psycho-therapy on a twice a week basis.

Kreuger: I would agree with the assessment of the psychologicals (Dr. Geary) that [Fuhrman] is narcissistic, self indulgent and somewhat emotionally unstable. The narcissism would go along with his preoccupation with violence.

If [Fuhrman] returns to police work his casual attitude towards violence will have to be evaluated by his superiors.

Fuhrman: I recall one time I was on duty, that a man spit on me. I broke the man's elbows and his knees, and then reached for my gun. I realized I had a problem and sought psychiat-ric help.

Hochman: One is led to the conclusion that the high incidence of **psychopathology** by the many elevated scales is an exag-geration.

The psychiatric reports on Fuhrman go on like this for pages and pages. I cannot quote it all, but I think it is important to include from Dr. Hochman's report something about Mark Fuhrman's family history.

Hochman: [Fuhrman's] father worked as a truck driver and a car-penter. The patient describes him as an *"insensitive and irrespon-sible bull shitter,"* who *"doesn't mind hurting people that are close* *to him."* When the patient was 7 years old, his parents divorced. His father moved to Spokane. The patient would see his father once a month, but they did not get along with each other. His father is now 56 years old [in 1981]. The patient has not seen him for nine years. [End of quotes].

Like his colleagues, Dr. Gottlieb recognized that Fuhrman, perhaps, was "faking it." But Dr. Gottlieb also recognized Fuhrman's clear signs of psychopathology. If Fuhrman was "faking it" – that in itself was a clear sign of severe psychological problems. Most importantly, Dr. Gottlieb understood that a man of Fuhrman's personality was totally unsuited to be a police officer.

Of all the doctors who examined Fuhrman around 1980-82 Dr. Gottlieb was the only one who strongly warned about putting Fuhrman back on police duty.

The other doctors saw Fuhrman more as a cheater, who faked psychopathology in an effort to retire from work with disability benefits, when he in fact was physically healthy and able to work!

Hence, these doctors who were more concerned with the finances of the City of Los Angeles, than with Fuhrman's dangerous psyche, recommended that he be denied disability benefits.

How little these doctors understood! Typically, the person who perhaps best understood Fuhrman and his psychopathology was not a doctor at all, but **the author, Joseph Bosco.**

Mr. Bosco also saw right through another "cheater", Prosecutor Marcia Clark. As I have mentioned earlier, and will return to several times throughout my book – the prosecutors knew, rather early, that O.J. was innocent, and that Mark Fuhrman, most likely, had murdered Nicole and Ron, and set up the investigators.

Joseph Bosco's words can hardly be improved on, so I take the liberty to quote him from his book, *"A problem of Evidence"* (page 210-211). Quote:

"All the folks who still say Mark Fuhrman wasn't smart enough to get away with planting the glove need to reread [these psychiatric reports] and note how artful, and really quite clever, a cheater Fuhrman is. His attempts at deceiving psychiatrists demonstrate he'd done his homework on psychopathology. He not only knew the right symptoms and current psycobabble buzzwords, he knew enough to fake responses in a Rorschach test to indicate severe pathology, which isn't easy to do. Unless you are a psychopath. Since he did not exhibit any noticeable "affect" to accompany his verbalization, these doctors decided he was just a neurotic bad actor with a personality disorder, a liar who should be forced to return to police duty! One doctor, who saw Fuhrman during his drawn-out disability claim, did suggest in passing that it might be a good idea to keep him away "from guns" when he returned to the force. Good idea, just a little naive. There isn't a position in the LAPD for a regular police officer restricted permanently from carrying a firearm.

It is ironic, if nothing else, that Fuhrman's saying, *"I would have killed both of them,"* regarding his second wife's infidelity, is not wholly dissimilar to what Fuhrman and his partners are accusing O.J. Simpson of doing.

It is notable that Fuhrman bragged about excessive violence and bigotry in mid-1981, almost four years before he repeated himself to Laura Hart McKinny [*The Fuhrman Tapes*]. When do we start to believe he's not just boasting or exaggerating?

All of the foregoing Marcia Clark must have known about Mark Fuhrman before she, a sworn officer of the State, a defender of its Constitution, called him to the stand. She sweetly emphatized with him over the injury done to his good name by the defense, and then, in the name of the People of California, she vouched for his absolute truthfulness before the Simpson jury and the nation. She put a man who allegedly celebrated Hitler's birthday on the witness stand to commit perjury. [End of quote].

I couldn't have said it better. So I didn't even try! I hope Mr. Bosco forgives me for the above quote.

Only one thing puzzles me. Why did no one, including Joseph Bosco, see past Fuhrman's psychiatric problems, his racism, his hatred for inter-racial couples, his violence, his evidence fabrication and his perjury, to the clear evidence of him having planted the glove behind O.J.'s house – and from there to the logical conclusion that he actually might have murdered Nicole and Ron?

The picture of Mark Fuhrman is not complete unless I also mention MAW (Men Against Women) and WASP (White Anglo-Saxon Police). These are two underground organizations that sprung up within the LAPD to counter the effects of the new "politically corret" hiring policies of the LAPD. The new policies of hiring more minorities and women upset countless racist, sexist bigots within the LAPD.

The two secret organizations grew out of a desire by certain LAPD officers to obstruct the new hiring policies, and also harass and resist minority and female officers who were hired. It was the secret organization MAW (Men against Women) which Ms. Laura Hart MacKinny wanted to write a screenplay about, when she met up with Detective Fuhrman in the mid 80's and produced *"The Fuhrman Tapes."*

The first meeting between Ms. McKinny and Fuhrman has been described as **accidental**, but it wouldn't surprise me if Ms. McKinny, who obviously had some background information about MAW, was cunning enough to frequent a hang-out where she expected, or hoped, that she would meet up with Detective Fuhrman, who is said to have been the "Grand Marshal" of MAW.

Fuhrman's statements on the tapes he and Ms. McKinny produced were not an attempt by Fuhrman to contribute to the screenplay. The screenplay was Ms. McKinney's project. Rather, I think Fuhrman enjoyed airing his racist, sexist, opinions and brag about his tough, violent behavior.

Today, when these statements have come back to haunt him, Fuhrman is trying to excuse himslef, by saying he was just contributing to a screenplay.

> *"By the way,"* he adds, *"the **hero** of the screenplay, is a 90 lbs, 5' 5" minority female cop! So how can I be accused of being a racist, sexist bigot?"*

That is typical Mark Fuhrman. There seems to be evidence that Fuhrman was the "hooded" Grand Marshal of the MAW, and that he presided over weekly "tribunals" in the organization, when the organization discussed ways of obstructing the integration of minorities and women into the LAPD, and planned actions of intimidation and harassment of minority and female officers already in the force.

Typically, the smooth talker this psychopath is, Fuhrman tries to tell the American people that he was creating a screenplay in which the heroine was a 90 lbs., 5'5" tall, female officer of minority background – exactly the kind of officers Fuhrman and MAW opposed. Hence, he can't be the racist, sexist bigot he is accused of being. However, what Fuhrman claims about this today, is just nonsense. The characters of the screenplay was Ms. McKinny's creation. Fuhrman had no influence over that. He would have hated the screenplay had Ms. McKinny finished it. Fuhrman just could not resist mouthing off against minorities and women – whenever, and to whomever!

Let me round off this chapter about Mark Fuhrman's personality by quoting some passages from Dr. Robert D. Hare's book, ***"Without Conscience"*** (Simon and Schuster, 1994).

Dr. Hare discusses criminal psychopaths. He lists the Key Symptoms of Psychopathy this way:

<u>**Emotional/Interpersonal**</u>	<u>**Social Deviance**</u>
glib and superficial	impulsive
egocentric and grandiose	poor behavior controls
lack of remorse or guilt	need for excitement
lack of emphaty	lack of responsibility

Emotional/Interpersonal	Social Deviance (cont.)
deceitful and manipulative	early behavior problems
shallow emotions	adult antisocial behavior

I must warn my readers that the mere presence of one or more of these symptoms does not characterize a person as psychopathic. Many pefectly healthy people can display one or more of these sypmtoms.

On the other hand, if a person is a psychopath, he will have one or more of these symptoms – probably several of them.

Following are some symptoms of psychopathic behavior, taken from Dr. Hare's book. When reading this, keep in mind Mark Fuhrman's background, *"The Fuhrman Tapes,"* his book, his TV appearances, his failed polygraph test (which I will return to in a later chapter), and everything else you may know about Fuhrman after having observed him and his lies on TV over the last 3 years. Quote:

Psychopaths are often witty and articulate. They can be amusing and entertaining conversationalists, ready with a quick and clever comeback, and can tell unlikely but convincing stories that cast themselves in a good light. They are often very likable and charming. To some people, however, they seem too slick and smooth.

Psychopaths may . . . tell stories that seem unlikely in light of what is known about them. [Yet, they have] a smooth lack of concern at being found out.

I, I, I ... Psychopaths have a narcissistic and grossly inflated view of their self-worth and importance, and see themselves as the center of the universe, as superior beings who are justified in living according to their own rules.

Psychopaths often come accross as arrogant, shameless braggarts – selfassured, opinionated, domineering, and cocky. They love to have power and control over others. They appear charismatic and "electrifying " to some people.

Psychopaths show a stunning lack of concern for the devestating effects their actions have on others.

Psychopaths sometimes verbalize remorse, but then contradict temselves in words and actions.

Psychopaths' lack of remorse or guilt is associated with a remarkable ability to rationalize their behavior and to shrug off personal responsibility for actions that cause shock and disappointment to family, friends, associates and others who have played by the rules. Usually they have handy excuses for their behavior, and in some cases they deny that it happened at all.

Lying, deceiving, and manipulation are natural talents for psychopaths.

With their powers in gear and focused on themselves, psychopaths appear amazingly unfazed by the possibility – or even by the certainty – of being found out. When caught in a lie or challenged with the truth, they are seldom perplexed or embarrassed – they simply change their stories or attempt to rework the facts so that they appear to be consistent with the lie. [End of quotes].

Those of my readers who have continued to follow the Simpson saga, and in particular the discussion surrounding Mark Fuhrman, his testimony, his perjury conviction, his book, his polygraph test, his TV appearances etc., must think that the key symptoms for psychopathy and the examples quoted above, where taken straight out of a psychiatric case file for Mark Fuhrman.

I trust my readers have understood what kind of a person Mark Fuhrman really is. Strangely, when I first started out investigating Mark Fuhrman as a murder suspect, I despised the man for what he did. Because there was no doubt in my mind that he murdered Nicole and Ron, and framed O.J.

However, the more I learn about him, and the more certain I become that he, indeed, committed this heinous crime – the more **I feel sorry for the guy**. Even if Mark Fuhrman murdered Nicole and Ron, he does not belong in **prison** – he belongs in a

hospital! Because Mark Fuhrman is **a sick human being**!

It is tempting to stay with this topic for a while. However, I must move on, on my road to solving the Simpson case.

CHAPTER 16

A Conspiracy

What you have just read (from *"The Fuhrman Tapes"* transcripts) are the words from Fuhrman's own mouth. It is chilling to learn about the mind set of this racist, brutal deviant. Such a person could not exist in a racist vacuum within the LAPD for 19 years. Fuhrman must have socialized with other LAPD officers who shared his violent and racist attitude and beliefs.

With the public release of the full *"Fuhrman Tapes"* we are learning about Fuhrman's involvement with others of his kind within the LAPD. Gradually, the public is becoming aware of such secret underground organizations as MAW and WASP.

It is not at all far fetched to assume that other LAPD officers share Fuhrman's racist beliefs and attitudes. As I am working on this manuscript, in late 1996, there seems to be, almost, an epidemic of black males murdered by white police officers. I will return to this later.

Such racists police officers tend to find each other, as if there were secret "vibes" between them. It is, however, not much of a mystery how such people get together.

Perhaps one night, after some major arrests, Fuhrman shared a couple of beers with some of his colleagues in a local bar frequented by police officers. Referring to the day's happenings, Fuhrman turned to one of his colleagues:

> *Those damn niggers ought to have their heads cut off – every one of them. All they do is push drugs, commit crimes, fuck around, and live on welfare!*

Now, perhaps his colleague replied:

> *How can you say a thing like that! Most African Americans*

are decent, hard working, honest people. But look at how many young African Americans live. ... No home ... no job ... no family ... no education ... and drugs everywhere! Most young blacks never had a decent chance in life!

If so, Fuhrman quickly moderated his racist statement, saying that he only referred to the really serious criminals among blacks, and he didn't literally mean to cut their heads of, it was just a matter of speech. Then Fuhrman went and sat down with some of his other colleagues instead.

However, if his colleague agreed with him, and perhaps fired off some additional racial slurs of his own, Fuhrman knew he had found a **"buddy"**! They began to hang out together, watch the ball games, have a few beers, and exchange ideas.

I think Fuhrman had an accomplice, or perhaps several. They all shared Fuhrman's extreme racist ideas and attitude. One day when Fuhrman knew he could trust them, he related to two of his buddies what he wanted to do:

I want to kill this white bitch, Nicole Brown Simpson, and this nigger, O.J., she is screwing!

His buddies laughed and said that it was an "excellent" idea!

We ought to kill all white bitches who screw around with niggers. And we ought to kill their nigger boyfriends as well!

That's when Fuhrman revealed his plan for murdering Nicole, but not O.J. Instead, he wanted to frame O.J. for the murder of Nicole. That way, if O.J. were convicted, he would be murdered anyway, only that the State of California would do it, on behalf of Fuhrman and his buddies. Fuhrman laughed as he spoke!

His buddies called Fuhrman *"a genius."* They had another beer. **A conspiracy was formed!**

Fuhrman explained about the domestic violence episode he investigated at Rockingham. He continued:

I could go back and visit Nicole, one day when O.J. is away at a football game – I think she likes me! She would recognize me. I could pretend I was following up on the domestic violence incident, and ask how she and O.J. are getting along lately. She might invite me in. Then I could find out what kind of shoes O.J. wears. Perhaps I could pick up a cap or some other items I could plant near her body after I kill her.

Eventually Nicole and O.J. separated, and she moved away from Rockingham. But that didn't change Fuhrman's sinister plan. Actually, it made things simpler. It would have been harder to kill Nicole, and frame O.J., if they were living together. Because Fuhrman would have to kill Nicole when O.J. was not there. But if O.J. was not there, he might have an alibi.

Maybe this was the reason why Fuhrman waited as long as till 1994 before he killed Nicole and framed O.J. It was simply too difficult to kill Nicole and frame O.J. while Nicole and O.J. were living together.

Fuhrman visited Nicole several times. There are indications to that effect.

Fuhrman definitely gave his colleagues the impression that he had an intimate relationship with Nicole up until the end of her life. His colleagues openly joked about it, saying, ***"Fuhrman is Nicole's cop."*** Fuhrman also told them, **before** the murders, **correctly,** that he had seen **"Nicole's boobs job,"** which he could hardly have done, unless he knew her intimately.

Eventually, Fuhrman found out that O.J. had two-three dozen pairs of Italian shoes, and that his shoe size was 12. While visiting Nicole, Fuhrman could also have seen a pair of Isotoner Aris gloves in a hallway closet. So now he purchased a pair of Bruno Magli shoes and a pair of Aris gloves.

As I explained earlier, it didn't matter if O.J. had a pair of Bruno Magli shoes or not, or a pair of Aris gloves. If Fuhrman planted those gloves, and bloody shoeprints from his Bruno Magli shoes size 12, O.J. would be **damned if he did, and damned if he didn't** come up with such shoes and gloves!

The more Fuhrman and his buddies talked about the murder, and the more they believed they had a perfect plan – the more this plan became an obsession with them. Murdering Nicole and framing O.J. became a challenge they could not resist!

They believed they had the perfect plan for the perfect murder. Being homicide detectives they knew better than anyone how they could get away with murder, and how to set up the murder to look like O.J. did it.

For years they talked about it. Occasionally, one of them would think about something they had overlooked

– for instance, **what to do if a neighbor arrived unexpectedly**.

They discussed the problem and solved it. Fuhrman would simply pull his gun, hold up his police badge, and pretend he was investigating the murder of Nicole. Then he would treat the neighbor as a possible suspect, order him up against a wall or a fence, so as to search him for a weapon – and then quickly kill the neighbor too.

The more perfect their plan, the harder it was to resist the temptation of committing **the perfect murder**, and get rid of Nicole and her *"nigger husband"* at the same time.

Let me discuss a theory with my readers. My readers must judge for themselves, first of all, if the theory has any merit, and secondly, if it applies to Detective Fuhrman.

People with a tendency for certain criminal or asocial behavior often seek out occupations where they may have the opportunity to live out their otherwise unacceptable criminal or asocial behavior in a guarded environment, or in an acceptable manner – without the risk of being exposed and prosecuted or persecuted.

- Let's say someone is a pedophile. He becomes a boy scout leader, or perhaps a pediatrician.
- Someone is a voyeur. He becomes a gynecologist.

- Someone is an exhibitionist. She becomes a nightclub dancer.
- Someone is addicted to gossip. He/she becomes a psychiatrist.
- Someone is a hair fetishist. He becomes a hair dresser.

I agree! My examples were, perhaps, not particularly well chosen. But I think my readers get the idea. Don't start to wonder if your gynecologist is a voyeur, or your hairdresser is a fetishist, though!

What I do suggest, however, is that many psychopathic, potential serial killers probably work as law enforcement officers or soldiers, thereby having a "license to kill," as part of their job.

I am not talking about **"one time"** murderers who kill someone for profit, or because of a dispute or other specific motives. I am talking about "serial killers" or "random killers," who kill simply because it gives them pleasure to do it.

In particular, I am talking about potential murderers who feel that this urge is so strong that they are likely to give in to it. Some of these people may realize that if they follow their urge, they are likely to get caught – sooner or later – in which case their own lives are over.

I suggest that one of the reasons why outrageous war crimes, massacres, and other atrocities so often follow in the wake of battle, is that the military harbors countless such psychopaths, who have joined the military mainly for the opportunity to torture and kill people with little risk of getting punished. Some of the atrocities committed by U.S. soldiers in Vietnam were simply too horrible to be mentioned.

However, today our armed forces are rarely involved in wars. Rather than to wait, perhaps for decades, for the opportunity to go to war and satisfy their lust to kill, many potential serial killers, who would otherwise have joined the military, they now join police forces around the country instead.

There they are given a badge, a gun, and a license to kill people who commit crimes and resist arrest.

Whoever follows police docu-dramas on TV can clearly see that some of these police officers, who kick down doors and swarm into suspects' homes with their guns drawn, are totally out of control.

There is one clear indication that certain people have joined the police force simply for the opportunity to kill someone without the risk of a murder conviction:

Most police officers go through their entire careers without ever firing a shot at a suspect. Some never even draw their guns throughout a 20 year career as a police officer, and they are never accused of police brutality or misconduct. Still they do their job to perfection. If you use your head, you rarely have to use your gun!

On the other hand, there are a few police officers who repeatedly are accused of police brutality, and who not only fire at suspects as soon as they find an opportunity to do so, but who *"shoot to kill"* – as Fuhrman recommends on his tapes. Some of these police officers have killed several suspects over short periods of time.

This indicates to me that there are certain police officers out there, who indeed have joined the police forces – in particular in big cities like Los Angeles – just for the opportunity to kill someone. They are nothing but random killers, with an insatiable urge to commit murder. Rather than risking a conviction as a civilian, they join the LAPD, and get a license to murder people without serious consequences – and they make a decent living at the same time.

Remember Fuhrman's own words:

> *"Now, the department says we shoot to stop, not to kill, which is horseshit! The only way you can stop somebody is to kill the son of a bitch. And what's the big deal? If you've got a reason to shoot somebody, you've got a reason to kill him!"*

I have a question: Are there indications that Detective Fuhrman is such a person? Is he perhaps a potential random killer, with this insatiable urge to murder someone, not for a specific reason like profit, to cover up a rape, or as revenge for some earlier dispute, for instance – but simply for the pleasure of killing someone, seemingly without any motive? Was Fuhrman hiding behind his badge?

Of course, everything I quoted from *"The Fuhrman Tapes"* indicates that. But there is one more significant indication pointing in the same direction.

Fuhrman joined the U.S. Marines and spent some time in Saigon as the Veitnam war was coming to an end. Fuhrman could see combat if he wanted to. But he could probably also avoid it if he wanted. Typically, Fuhrman didn't join a communications unit or supply unit, but the Marines – the one unit where he had the best chances of experiencing real, front line combat, and look the enemy in the eye when he killed him.

One should perhaps expect that a Vietnam veteran, like Fuhrman, had seen and experienced enough killings in Vietnam, and that he was happy to escape the brutality of the war when he returned home.

Not Fuhrman! He wanted more! So rather than settling down in his home state, he went looking for another line of work where he could continue to satisfy his lust for blood. He moved to Los Angeles and joined the LAPD, which was already notoriously infamous for their police brutality.

I don't think Mark Fuhrman joined the Marine Corps because he was a patriot, and later joined the LAPD because he wanted to serve his community.

I think Fuhrman picked the one military unit where his chances of killing people were the best.

And when the war ended and, hence, his opportunity to kill people without repercussions no longer existed – Fuhrman quit the Marines and joined the LAPD which was already notoriously infamous for police brutality and violence.

Protected by his newly earned LAPD badge, Fuhrman could continue to satisfy his lust for blood without the risk of being charged with assault or murder.

Fuhrman's psychopathic nature manifested itself in the episodes he describes on *"The Fuhrman tapes."* Clearly, he almost killed four people – allegedly "in the line of duty"! His murderous instincts were still in him. One day he decided that Nicole was going to be his victim.

Nicole's murder was racially motivated. Fuhrman hated interracial couples – they made him furious. But if it hadn't been Nicole, it would have been someone else, for the same or for another reason.

If anyone can even **suggest** that O.J. had a motive for killing Nicole, please take a look at **Mark Fuhrman's motives** – and **his** background! This **"psycho"** has been on a straight course to murder for over 20 years! It is a mystery that he waited as long as till June 12, 1994!

CHAPTER 17

Rogue Cops

It is nothing new that police officers kill people for racist reasons – or just for the heck of it.

I assume my readers recall how five white police officers killed a young black man in a predominantly white, and by many described as a racist district of Pittsburgh in the fall of 1995.

The young man had no police record, he was unarmed and not under the influence. He was simply, with the owner's permission, driving the Jaguar belonging to his cousin, a Pittsburgh Steelers football star.

Upon seeing the black man in the Jaguar, the police immediately suspected the driver of having stolen the car, or being a drug dealer. They stopped him, commanded him out of the car, provoked him, jumped him, and sat on him for as long as twenty minutes – until they had choked him to death!

During the ensuing coroner's grand jury hearing the five white police officers testified that the "suspect" had resisted arrest. Give me a break! Were they saying that five strong police officers sitting on a suspect, could not simply have handcuffed him, strapped his legs, and gotten up again in 30 seconds?

The police officers gave the same – almost defiant – testimony (in essence):

I only held the suspects legs. I had my back to my colleagues and didn't see what any of them were doing behind my back.

Five white police officers killing an innocent black man in a predominantly white, racist community. Five identical testimonies:

None of the police officers did a thing or saw a thing!

Nevertheless, the coroner's autopsy report concluded that the victim choked to death as the result of prolonged, extreme pressure to his abdomen, chest, and neck!

Later, one of the officers turned state witness. As a result three of the other officers were charged with murder!

Unless such officers are potential murderers on the lookout for an opportunity to kill someone, they would never let a minor traffic incident like this one, escalate into murder!

In the fall of 1996 the first of the three officers were prosecuted. An all white jury were picked from a district in the eastern part of Pennsylvania. They acquitted the white police officer!

Was this a racially motivated jury nullification? Was it "pay back" for the acquittal of O.J.?

Where is the white majority protesting this verdict?

During the beating of Rodney King, they were allegedly some 25 LAPD officers standing around, watching, cheering, and not seeing a thing!

Reports from New Orleans, released on national TV during the fall of 1995, exposed that the NOPD for decades had been run like a criminal mafia, committing theft, burglary, robbery, extortion, protection rackets, drug dealing, bank robbery – and even murder!

Whenever a rookie police officer protested what was going on, it was made clear to him that if he didn't *"adjust to the system,"* he might end up *"accidentally"* shot during a drug bust, or something like that. Any complaints were, of course, investigated by the NOPD themselves, and filed away as unfounded.

In Philadelphia a major federal investigation of the PPD revealed that the PPD was run more or less like the NOPD. It is suspected that thousands of innocent people may have been accused, convicted, and sent to prison, based on false evidence concocted by PPD officers.

Police Chief Williams, head of the LAPD during the Simpson case, was recruited from the PPD after the Rodney King incident. Before he moved to Los Angeles he must have witnessed what went on in Philadelphia over the last 10-15 years – and done nothing to stop it? How could he be expected to clean up the LAPD?

In the fall of 1996 a New York police officer was acquitted of murder after killing a young man in a choke-hold. The young man was playing football with some friends. Their ball hit the police officer's car. Shortly thereafter the police officer killed the young football player.

Just a week or so later, an African American was stopped at a street corner in St. Petersburg, Florida. He was ordered out of his car. The car rolled a foot or so forward. The police officer fired three shots at the driver and killed him! A few days later, the majority white grand jury refused to indict the police officer.

Los Angeles, February 28, 1997: A special LAPD task force, the Special Investigations Section – often referred to as **"The Death Squad"**– had been surveilling a group of suspected robbers for months. That day, the robbers appeared to be preparing a new robbery. But rather than arrest them before they could hurt anyone, "The Death Squad" deliberately allowed the **heavily armed** robbers to commit their crime. In doing so, the police exposed ordinary citizens to deadly danger.

There was no way to know whether or not the armed robbers might kill their victims after having robbed them! Still, the police calmly waited outside the bar where the robbery took place – instead of preventing the robbery to proceed in the first place. Once the robbers had made their escape, "The Death Squad" pursued them and opened fire, killing two of the robbers.

The police may say whatever they want to say. Many observers say the police could have prevented this crime from ever taking place. The police responded by saying that unless they allowed the robbery to take place, they could not get the robbers convicted.

That is bull! With today's modern technology, the SIS could have used electronic/audio/visual surveillance, wiretap etc. and caught these robbers on tape, as they were planning their robbery. After all there is something called **"conspiracy to commit a crime"**!

Add to that illegal weapons possession, carrying concealed weapons, purchasing stolen goods, auto theft (I assume they didn't commit armed robbery using their own private autos), carrying firearms/stolen goods accross state lines (if the stolen weapons were purchased out of state), etc., etc. – and I am sure the police with the help of the DA's office could have come up with sufficient charges to put these robbers behind bars for 50 years!

Undoubtedly, the robbers were criminals. But in my opinion, this "Death Squad" had decided that on February 28, 1997, they wanted to satisfy their lust for blood and killings! "The Death Squad" didn't act like police officers. They **executed** those robbers. They followed them, knowing that a confrontation would result in an exchange of fire. The SIS squad wanted to kill someone that day. So they allowed the robbers to commit the robbery first. That gave the SIS squad their "license to kill"!

As I have claimed earlier in my book, some members of the SIS – just like Detective Mark Fuhrman of the "regular" LAPD – are nothing but random killers who have found a safe haven within the police, and a "licence to kill" people – with their police uniforms, police guns, and police badges!

Is that the kind of law enforcement American citizens want? What when law abiding citizens – even children – some day get caught in the cross fire?

Sure enough, the robbers were armed and dangerous criminals. Our streets are that much safer now that two of them are dead. I cannot say I regret that! However, that is not the issue I discuss in my book. What I am trying to explain is that there are police officers within the LAPD who enjoy killing people, and who use their uniforms, their police weapons, and their police badges as a licence to kill. When police officers like that exist – what is to say that some of them – like Detective Mark Fuhrman – would not plan and commit a "straight" murder?

What is wrong with police departments in this country? The cases I have mentioned are just the tip of a terrible iceberg that may never be fully exposed. I don't believe there exists in the U.S. any other occupation whose members, percentage wise, commit even close to as many crimes, serious crimes in particular, and murders specifically – as U.S. police officers. Hardly a day goes by when we cannot read about it in the newspapers or watch it on TV.

Reports of police corruption, police brutality, abuse of power, abuse of office, giving false testimony, planting false evidence against innocent people, and even murder by police officers, have become part of everyday life in our country. I would frankly suggest that the average young, black citizen runs a greater risk of being assaulted or murdered if stopped by police on a deserted road, than when walking through a gang infested Los Angeles neighborhood after dark!

It is time for people to wake up and not only face this reality, but do something about it. It is incredible but true, that we sometimes need protection from rogue cops, more than we need protection from criminals.

Of course, the rogue police officers are a minority in most police departments. But as long as the many decent, honest, hard-working police officers across the country refuse – or are afraid – to stand up and take steps to get rid of their rogue colleagues, **they are all part of the problem.**

Even people in general are responsible for the present situation, and it will get worse before it gets better! I think many whites are already so afraid of crime that they condone this kind of behavior by the police. And jurors, for the same reason, consistently acquit rogue police officers accused of crimes or misconduct. They may be making a grave mistake.

If we don't stop this epidemic of white police officers murdering African Americans in particular, but generally, anyone they find an excuse to kill – just to be acquitted by majority white juries – then African Americans may one day start an armed revolution – in self defense! No one should tolerate what is going on today within police departments all over our country.

Whites would be better off facing up to, and eradicating, the problem today – even if it means getting rid of a bunch of unfit police officers – rather than waiting for the other alternative.

CHAPTER 18

Mark Fuhrman's Motives

As I have explained earlier, O.J had absolutely no motive for killing Nicole. Detective Mark Fuhrman, however, had plenty of motives for killing Nicole and framing O.J. Detective Fuhrman's motives for killing Nicole and framing O.J. were complex.

First of all, Fuhrman hated both Nicole and O.J. – from the day he first saw them – because O.J. was black and successful, and because Nicole who was white, was married to the African-American O.J. That was his initial, primary motive

Secondly, as I explained earlier, Fuhrman may be a potential serial killer, or random killer, who simply decided to kill **"someone."** Nicole's number was up. But if it hadn't been Nicole, it would have been someone else.

Furthermore, Fuhrman told a police psychologist (back in 1981) that he felt he wasn't getting the recognition he believed he deserved, from his peers and his superiors. Nor was he getting the promotions he felt he deserved. He dreamt about making the "big bust" (solve a major, high profile crime), which would give him respect and promotion.

Of course, by murdering Nicole and subsequently planting –and "finding" – the Rockingham glove, Detective Fuhrman would be in the media's spotlight and receive credit for having solved the Simpson case!

It is worth noticing that this pattern of creating a crime or an accident, and then, "apparently," solving that crime, or being first on the scene of the accident to assist in the rescue operation – thereby being perceived as a "hero" – is such a common "fantasy" or daydream among law enforcement officers and rescue personnel, that it is recognized by psychologists and criminal investigators as a particular **"commit and solve"** or **"cause and rescue" syndrome**!

I believe Mr. Jewell was a true hero, and totally innocent of the Atlanta bombing during the Olympics. It was, however, this commonly known "cause and rescue" (or "commit and solve") syndrome which immediately led the FBI to suspect Mr. Jewell. That's how common this syndrome is!

The person who is first at the scene of an accident – and therefore, often an apparent hero – he is almost immediately also a prime suspect, in terms of having caused the accident (unless another cause, or another obvious suspect appears rather quickly).

Although only a small percentage of people with such fantasies actually carry them out, most law enforcement officers and most rescue personnel admittedly have had dreams of this nature.

Apparently, "solving" the murder (that he himself committed) would give Fuhrman the recognition he so desperately sought. That might have been another of Fuhrman's motives.

Again, it is worth noticing that Fuhrman in an interview (or a "prep" session) before his testimony admitted that he collected German Nazi medals from World War II, as a hobby. Being the racist he unquestionably is, and evidently also harboring neo-Nazi sympathies, Fuhrman must have felt that blacks and other minorities (as well as white women who had interracial relationships with black men) were inferior to Fuhrman's own, pure, white (Aryan) race.

The "best," or the ultimate, way for Fuhrman to prove this insane ideology to himself and his buddies, was to commit the murder of Nicole and the framing of O.J. – and get away with it! In doing so he demonstrated – to himself, at least – that the white race was superior to the African-American race. This could have been yet another of his motives.

Psychopathic serial killers like to brag about their "feats." The reason is that they believe they are superior to the rest of us. But they can't talk about their "feats" to anyone – openly. If they did, they would be exposed and caught. Instead, they often announce their upcoming murders, or they commit their murders according to certain characteristic MO's. They may, for instance, always kill on the same day of the week, or they may leave a certain message or a clue at the murder scenes. It is their way of bragging.

Fuhrman believed himself to be superior. In Vietnam he had probably killed several enemy soldiers, and liked it. He didn't have to prove his superiority to himself, as much as he needed to prove it to others. Obviously, **if** Fuhrman operated alone, he couldn't reap this reward of respect for his self-perceived superiority, by confessing or bragging in public about the murder of Nicole. But if he had some accomplices, they could brag about their crime together.

I find it likely, therefore, that Detective Fuhrman had one or more accomplices in the murders of Nicole and Ron. They could help him in the planning and the execution of the murder of Nicole and the framing of O.J., and they could assist Fuhrman in creating a fabricated alibi.

The last, but perhaps strongest motive for murdering Nicole and framing O.J., and the motive specifically responsible for pushing Fuhrman (and his accomplices) "over the edge," may be explained as follows:

The idea of killing Nicole and framing O.J. may have started as pure **"beer talk."** *Guys! I really want to kill this bitch, Nicole, and her nigger husband!*

From there it evolved into a **"mental game."** *Guys! I have thought about this. I'm sure I could do it, and get away with it!*

Next, perhaps it escalated into some sort of **"competition"** between Fuhrman and his buddies. *This is how I could have done it, without getting caught. How would you have done it – if you were to do it?*

Then it grew into a **"team project,"** and a form of entertainment. *Let's see if we can come up with a perfect plan, for the perfect murder! You know, really think about everything – so nobody could catch us – if we did it!*

The accomplices contributed ideas, criticized each others suggestions, and improved **"the plan,"** until it appeared to be **"perfect."** That's when **the dangerous game changed to a desire to actually carry it out.** *The plan is perfect. No one could catch us. Let's prove it by doing it!*

Eventually, they simply **had** to murder Nicole and frame O.J. It was the only way they could prove that their plan really was as perfect as they believed it was. In other words – that they were **as smart and clever or powerful – as they thought they were! It was the only challenge left!**

Fuhrman had killed before, in Vietnam. He agreed to do it! It was a murder

> based on **a psychopath's desire to kill**
> based on **racism and hate,**
> based on **a need for recognition,**
> based on **pride,**
> based on **a need to demonstrate superiority,**

– all of which eventually turned into **an irresistible challenge.**

CHAPTER 19

Mark Fuhrman's "Alibi"

At the time of the criminal trial, Detective Mark Fuhrman was never required to provide an alibi for the night of the murders, because he was never a murder suspect.

According to Fuhrman himself, however, **he attended a "Protective League" seminar at the La Quinta resort near Palm Desert, CA, because he was a delegate in the Protective League.** Palm Desert is about a 2 1/2 hours drive from Detective Fuhrman's former home in Thousand Oaks, Los Angeles, and a bit shorter distance from Brentwood, where both Nicole and O.J. lived. Brentwood, again, is about 15 minutes from Fuhrman's L.A. home.

Let me quote a passage from Detective Fuhrman's **direct** testimony during the criminal trial. Prosecutor Marcia Clark questioned Fuhrman about the night of the murders [the **"highlighting"** is done by me].

Ms. Clark: On the evening of June 12, 1994, at approximately 8:00 **pm**, where were you?

Fuhrman: *At approximately 8:00 pm, I was in – east of Palm Desert, in La Quinta Resort, at a Protective League seminar.*

Ms. Clark: Was that a police officers' function, Sir?

Fuhrman: *Yes. I am a delegate in the Protective League – or was at that time.*

Ms. Clark: Okay. And what time did you leave?

Fuhrman: *I believe I left somewhere around **8:00 o'clock, just as the barbecue was starting.***

Ms. Clark: And you left – when you left, you drove where?

Fuhrman: *I drove to my home.*

Ms. Clark: Remember what time you got home, Sir?

Fuhrman: *About – **about 10:30.***

Ms. Clark: And was anyone home when you got there?

Fuhrman: *My wife.*

Ms. Clark: What time did you go to bed?

Fuhrman: *I believe about **11:00**, maybe **a little later**.*

Ms. Clark: Did you receive a call at some point that night?

Fuhrman: *Yes, I did.*

Ms. Clark: After you went to bed?

Fuhrman: *Excuse me? – Yes I did.*

Ms. Clark: And what time did you get that call?

Fuhrman: *At 1:05 in the morning.*

Ms. Clark: Did it wake you up?

Fuhrman: *Yes.*

Ms. Clark: And what were you told in that call?

Fuhrman: *I was told by my supervisor, **the homicide coordinator,** Detective Ron Phillips, that we had a double homicide, and it was at 875 South Bundy, and that I would meet him at the station, and we would get a vehicle with a homicide kit and go out to the scene from there.*

Ms. Clark: Were you told anything about the identity of either victim?

Fuhrman: *Yes. Detective Phillips said that the female victim might be the ex-wife of O.J. Simpson.*[End of Quote].

Fuhrman, allegedly, came home about 10:30 pm, went to bed a little after 11:00 pm, and was awakened, about 1:05 am, by a call from his supervisor, Detective Ronald Phillips. Together they drove to the murder scene at Bundy.

That is Fuhrman's alibi. As a matter of fact, as Fuhrman's "alibi" appears, it is not much different from O.J.'s – except for Fuhrman's wife possibly supporting his alibi – should that ever become necessary!

After Detective Phillips had called Fuhrman, they agreed to meet at a police station in West Los Angeles, where they picked up a police car with a homicide kit. Eventually **they arrived at Bundy about 2:10 am.**

There are several things that bother me regarding

Detective Mark Fuhrman's alibi.

As close as I recall it, Detective Phillips testified that before Fuhrman left for the seminar that weekend, he had said (in essence):

> *If something comes up Sunday night, then **don't call me until after one o'clock, because I won't be home until then!***

Detective Phillips complied, so although the watch commander, Sgt. David Rossi was notified about the murders at **11:50 pm** – nobody called Detective Fuhrman until **1:05 am.**

At 12:10 am, Sgt. Rossi called Sgt. Robert Riski, who was in a patrol car. Sgt. Riske drove to the murder scene where he arrived at about 12:17.

According to Detective Phillips, Sgt. Rossi did not call him until 12:55 am. Allegedly, Phillips, in turn, called someone else first, and **then** Detective Fuhrman at 1:05 am.

None of this makes any sense to me. I doubt that this is what happened at all. In the case of a double homicide, of course, time is essential. The police stand a much better chance of catching the killer if they can get to the murder scene immediately. For all they know, the murderer could have lost his ID at the murder scene, or an eyewitness could perhaps identify the murderer.

Sgt. Rossi, and Detective Phillips couldn't know what they would find at the murder scene. Perhaps the murderer was on his way to the Mexican border or to the airport, already! Besides, what could be more important that night than a double homicide?

Of course, the watch commander, can get dispatched through to Sgt. Riske's patrol car immediately. Sgt. Riske should have been on his way to Bundy within one minute.

Yet, Sgt. Rossi, allegedly, did not call anyone who could respond to the murder scene, for 20 minutes. Do you believe that!

Next problem: Detective Phillips, the homicide coordinator on stand by duty that night, should be notified immediately – also within a minute or two, or perhaps three, at the most! Yet, according to Detective Phillips, he was not notified until 12:55 am – one hour and five minutes after Sgt. Rossi was notified of the murders! What is going on here?

Phillips then, knowing that Detective Fuhrman would not be home until after 1:00 am, called some other detectives first. Then, at 1:05 am, he called Fuhrman at home.

By the time of the criminal trial, I think both the investigators, the prosecutors and the rest of the DA's office knew that Fuhrman was the murderer. I shall soon pick Fuhrman's alibi apart, and justify that Prosecutor Marcia Clark knew that Fuhrman was committing perjury with respect to the alibi Ms. Clark helped him concoct during his testimony.

Somehow, the first priority was to protect Detective Fuhrman! They all knew he was the murderer, but they could not allow the scandal to become public. Hence, to explain why Detective Phillips, allegedly, did not call Fuhrman until 1:05am, I think the LAPD on orders from the prosecutors, "fixed" the telephone records to make it appear that Sgt. Rossi – rather than Phillips or Fuhrman – was the one who messed up and didn't call Phillips or Fuhrman until one full hour after Rossi was notified about the murders.

There are some indications that "something" went on during those first 65 minutes. The prosecutors blacked out several phone calls on the official phone records. Did Sgt. Rossi, or Detective Phillips call Fuhrman much earlier, but learn that he was not home?

After eventually calling Fuhrman at home, Detective Phillips called **another number**. Phillips himself said he just dialed the "wrong number." Yet, the prosecution would never release that "wrong number." Why not?

Could it be that Phillips called Fuhrman at home before 1:05 am, but nobody answered, because Fuhrman was out, disposing of the murder clothes and shoes – or planting evidence at Rockingham? So then Phillips had to call Fuhrman on his mobil phone?

Of course by the time we got around to the trial, the investigators and the prosecutors had to hide the fact that Fuhrman was not at home on the night of the murders. So the prosecution blacked out phone calls that could expose this?

Considering that Fuhrman, allegedly, came home about **10:30** pm, the murders were reported at **11:50** pm, and the first police officers arrived at Bundy at **12:17** am – **I find it strange that Fuhrman didn't call his supervisor, Detective Phillips – as well as his watch commander, Sgt. Rossi – as soon as he got home, to inform them that he got home earlier than expected,** and was back on **stand-by duty.**

Did Fuhrman want to emphasize that he would be out of town until **after 1:00** am, because he actually had decided to murder Nicole at **10:30** pm and fabricate a false alibi?

Did Fuhrman instruct his supervisor not to call him until after 1:00 am, because he didn't want anyone to call him and find out that he wasn't home until, say 11:40 pm – although he allegedly left the seminar at La Quinta around **8:00 pm**?

Did detective Fuhrman "anticipate" that *"something"* **would** come up that night, and which he eventually would have to investigate? Or did Fuhrman, perhaps, **know** that something would come up?

Did Fuhrman know that he was going to kill Nicole that night? Is that why he didn't want to be called at home before one o'clock?

Suppose Fuhrman **is** the murderer! He wanted to establish a false alibi (in case he should ever become a suspect) – if necessary **using his wife's testimony that he came home at 10:30 – while he in fact were out murdering Nicole and Ron, and trying to plant one of the murder gloves on O.J.'s property, or getting rid of his bloody shoes, clothes, and knife – and didn't come home until, say 11:40 pm.**

Again, **suppose** Fuhrman is the murderer. **What if the bodies of Nicole and Ron had been discovered** by a neighbor – just **minutes** after the murders – say **about 11:00 pm**? If so, **normally**, the police would have been alerted, someone would have called the homicide coordinator, Detective Phillips, and Phillips would have called Fuhrman **at 11:05, while Fuhrman, perhaps, was still on his way home from O.J.'s Rockingham estate** [where he tried to plant the glove] or from some other place where he had dumped the clothes, the shoes, and the knife!

Someone had to answer the phone, so Mrs. Fuhrman would pick it up. Phillips would ask for Fuhrman, and Mrs. Fuhrman would have to inform Phillips that her husband wasn't home from La Quinta yet!

However, the other seminar participants would later testify to when Fuhrman left the seminar. So Fuhrman **should** have been home **before 10:30 even! Fuhrman's alibi goes down the drain!**

However, **if no one calls Fuhrman,** and Mrs. Fuhrman agrees to back up Fuhrman's alibi, **Fuhrman can claim that he got home at 10:30 pm** – even if he didn't come home until **11:40!**

It doesn't make sense that Fuhrman should tell Phillips – and perhaps Sgt. Rossi – **not** to call him **at all**, until after 1:00 am.

And it doesn't make sense, either, that his instruction to Phillips and Rossi, about not calling him, was so **"strict"** that neither of them even **tried** to call Fuhrman, just to check if Fuhrman, perhaps, **might** have gotten home **earlier than expected!**

Let's assume, hypothetically, that something **very important** came up – like someone detonating a bomb – and causing multiple casualties – in an apartment building in Fuhrman's police district, or perhaps even in the police station itself – at, say about 11:55 pm!

What's wrong with Phillips – or Sgt. Rossi – calling Fuhrman, say about midnight, just in case Fuhrman happened to walk in the door exactly at that time?

Or why couldn't Phillips – or Rossi – have called at 12:05 am, **just to leave a message** with Mrs. Fuhrman, that Fuhrman should call Phillips – or the watch commander – as soon as he got home from La Quinta? That way Fuhrman wouldn't have to be woken up again at 1:05 am, either!

Detective Phillips, **the homicide coordinator,** or Sgt. Rossi, the watch commander – or both of them – were sitting on their "behinds" **– waiting for 75 minutes –** before any of them even **tried** to give Detective Fuhrman a call! If we can believe them.

What if Fuhrman had gotten **"indisposed"** at La Quinta, so that someone would have had to substitute for him? Things like that happen, you know. If so – because Rossi or Phillips **did not even try** to call Fuhrman – the police would have wasted more than an hour of valuable investigation time!

Fuhrman's and Phillips' **"story"** doesn't make sense – **not by a long shot!** There is **something wrong** with Detective Fuhrman's so-called **"alibi"** (– and you shall soon learn what it is)!

Do you see? There is something "fishy" about Fuhrman's instruction to Phillips (and perhaps, also to Sgt. Rossi):

If something comes up tonight, then don't call me until after 1:00 am, because I won't be home until then!

And there is something just as "fishy" about the fact that Detective Phillips – and Sgt. Rossi – **did not even try** to call Fuhrman before 1:05 am – just to check if he, perhaps, had come home earlier than expected! After all, they had **a celebrity double homicide** on their hands!

Allow me to gloat – just a little! Back in 1995, I did not know what alibi Detective Fuhrman, eventually, would come up with during his direct testimony in the criminal trial – or if he would even come up with an alibi. He was, after all, not a murder suspect, so he did not need to present an alibi if no one questioned him about it. I was too busy the day Fuhrman testified, so I did not even watch his testimony. I totally missed it – something that will become evident when you read my quote below.

However, I felt, so certain about my theory of Detective Mark Fuhrman being directly involved in the murders of Nicole and Ron, that I wrote, **already then**, in **my first book**, titled

"If O.J. Didn't ..." (Chapter 15, *"Framing O.J."*; page 95). Quote:

> "Regardless of what alibi Fuhrman may come up with, he was out prior to one o'clock on the night of the murders. What time he left his home, where he went, what he did, and who saw him during that night, ought to be subject to scrutiny, just as O.J.'s alibi was.
>
> **Alibis may be manufactured!** So even if Detective Fuhrman arguably spoke in front of 1,500 people at an out-of-state churchgoers' convention, between 10:30 and 11:00 o'clock on the night of June 12, 1994, his alibi ought to be checked and rechecked, together with whoever supported it." [End of quote].

As you have just learned – although there was no need for him to do it – Fuhrman **did** present an alibi during his direct testimony for Prosecutor Marcia Clark, March 10, 1995.

Substitute *"1,500 people at an out-of state churchgoers' convention"* (as I prophesized in my first book) with *"a couple of hundred people at an out-of-town police officers' convention"* (at La Quinta) – and I predicted Mark Fuhrman's actions – or his false alibi, rather – almost as if I were psychic! That will become evident once you read on.

There is more, regarding Fuhrman's alibi. First of all, if it took Fuhrman from 8:00 to 10:30 pm to drive from La Quinta to his home in Los Angeles, and assuming he was driving at the legal speed limit, **55 mi/hr** in 1994, **he could have been at Bundy as early as 9:30** pm, if he had put a portable flashing red light on the roof of his car and gone 90 mi/hr instead!

90 mi/hr is not fast at all for a police car with a flashing red light. Many ordinary motorists, even, go 90 mi/hr on the same interstates today.

Regardless of when he actually got home, **Fuhrman could have had plenty of time to murder Nicole and Ron around 10:30**

pm. He could even have had time to stop by Nicole's home around 9:30-10:00 pm to make sure she was home, and that she would be alone later that night!

One more thing. Isn't it **"convenient"** that the only person who could corroborate, or destroy, Fuhrman's alibi, was **Mrs. Fuhrman – who could never be subpoenaed to testify against her husband, if she refused to?!**

Nothing wrong said about Mrs. Fuhrman. I never met her, and know nothing about her. I am just philosophizing **at this point.**

It takes a special kind of woman to be married to a man like Fuhrman. Go back to your "book mark" (if you left one), where I discussed *"The Fuhrman Tapes"*!

Here is a man who uses the foulest of language – despises women in general – is the Grand Marshal of MAW (Men Against Women) – is a racist – advocates genocide – hates interracial couples – is a brutal sadist – didn't hesitate to grab a young girl by her hair – put a gun to her head – called her a bitch – threatened to kill her – and threw her down the stairs, just because she happened to live in the same building as four suspects! And he is a neo-Nazi who celebrates Hitler's birthday as a holiday!

I would guess that Fuhrman's wife either shares her husband's Nazi philosophies, his hatred for blacks and for interracial couples, and that she **loves him very much** – or that she is **totally dominated by her husband**, to the point where she dares not oppose him or have an opinion of her own. Accordingly, I don't rule out the possibility that Fuhrman's wife would be willing to support a false alibi for her husband – if necessary.

Let's go back to the seminar! It didn't make sense that Fuhrman, as a **delegate**, left before the rest of the participants. Furthermore, it was a **weekend seminar**. So for two days they had discussed all the "boring stuff." Then – according to Fuhrman – about 8:00 pm on Sunday night, the "serious" part of the seminar was over. It was time to relax, socialize, have some fun, and get something good to eat from the **barbecue.**

But what did Fuhrman do? He said – if we can believe him:

The heck with hamburgers and chicken legs! I am out of here!

Then he jumped in his car, and headed for Los Angeles! Did that make sense? Of course not! But now listen to this!

Fuhrman used the barbecue as a "time clock" for **when** – and an excuse for **why** – he left the seminar at 8:00 pm, in time to reach Los Angeles and his home at 10:30 pm.

However, the "barbecue" was <u>not</u> on Sunday – as Fuhrman testified to! It was on Saturday!

Furthermore, on the night of the murders – when Detective Fuhrman allegedly left the seminar to drive to Los Angeles at **8:00** pm – **there was not, even, any seminar!**

Steven Worth, co-author – with Carl Jaspers – of the book, ***"Blood Oath"*** [Rainbow Books, Inc.; Highland City, FL] have researched Fuhrman's so-called "alibi" for the time of the murders. According to Mr. Worth, three participants at that seminar have confirmed that the itinerary for the seminar on Saturday, June 11, and Sunday, June 12, was as follows.

<u>Saturday June 11:</u> The seminar lasted till 3-4:00 pm. Then there was an afternoon break. At seven o'clock in the evening there was a reception at the tennis court, and at eight o'clock in the evening there was a barbecue dinner.

<u>Sunday June 12:</u> The seminar had a morning session from 8:00 am, till 11:00 am – which marked **the end of the seminar. The paricipants at the seminar checked out from the hotel before noon. There was no seminar – and certainly no barbecue – Sunday evening!**

- Why did Fuhrman lie about the barbecue?
- Did Fuhrman "move" the barbecue to Sunday, in order to

make it more "edible" that he left La Quinta at 8:00 pm on the night of the murders?

– Did Fuhrman lie about the barbecue to cover up the fact that he wasn't in La Quinta **at all** on the evening of the murders?

Could Fuhrman have **confused** the two seminar days – Saturday and Sunday? Did he perhaps drive home after the barbecue on Saturday night – and just get his days mixed up during his testimony, thinking that the barbecue was on Sunday.

No chance! First of all, if he had any doubts, he should have checked with the organizers of the seminar, to make sure he was telling the truth during his sworn testimony. And if **he** didn't think of doing that, **Prosecutor Clark** should have thought about it when she prepared Fuhrman for his testimony!

Besides, if Fuhrman drove home after the barbecue (on Saturday) he must have planned to **get up again at 4:30 am on Sunday**, to drive back for the morning session of the seminar on Sunday!

Fuhrman may – perceivably – have forgotten that the barbecue was on Saturday instead of Sunday. But he would **not** have forgotten it, if he drove home Saturday night, **requiring him to get up at 4:30 am Sunday morning** – to drive back to La Quinta for the Sunday morning session from 8-11:00 am.

By the way it sounds correct that the seminar ended after the morning session at 11:00 **am** on Sunday. That is normal for such weekend seminars. It gives the delegates time to check out before noon, so they don't have to pay for an extra night at the hotel.

It is hard to prove today, about three years after the murders, whether Furman's **"alternative"** alibi holds up or not. But I can say this:

> In my opinion, **Fuhrman has less of an alibi than O.J.!**
> Besides, Fuhrman lied about his alibi in court!

I shall return to Fuhrman's busted alibi later in this chapter. But first, it is time to say something about Prosecutor Marcia Clark.

I have earlier claimed that both the investigators and the prosecutors knew that O.J. was innocent, and that Mark Fuhrman, most likely, is the killer. However – for various reasons – they had to cover it up. My allegation will be corroborated later. But here is an "aperitif."

As a prosecutor, sometimes, you don't know what to expect from a **hostile** witness. But **"the first rule in the book,"** for a prosecutor about to examine his or her **own** witness, is that you **prepare your own witness** – so that **you never risk asking a question you don't know the answer to.**

Indisputably, Prosecutor Clark must have gone over her questions with Detective Fuhrman in advance. The questions and answers clearly indicated that she had.

With all the suspect "baggage" Fuhrman carried at that time – being accused of having planted the Rockingham glove and the blood in the Bronco, being accused of racism and of having used the "N-word," etc. – Prosecutor Clark **must** have checked out Fuhrman's information about the seminar.

Imagine the scandal, if Fuhrman, for instance, **hypothetically**, had lied about even being at the seminar, to cover up that he were having an affair – and **that** had surfaced later!

Obviously, Prosecutor Marcia Clark **must** have checked out Fuhrman's answers. Hence, the prosecutor **must** have known that Detective Fuhrman lied! All it took for Prosecutor Clark to establish that, was a phone call to someone in the "Protective League." As I said then, and will repeat on several occasions in my book:

> **At the time of the trial, the prosecution knew that O.J. was innocent – and that Fuhrman was lying about almost everything. They must have known!**

However – forget for a while the fact that Fuhrman **was** lying! Far more interesting is the question: **Why** was Fuhrman lying?

Remember, at that time, **Fuhrman was only suspected of having planted the Rockingham glove behind O.J.'s house,**

at 6:15 am! He certainly didn't need a false alibi for the time of the murders, around 10:35-10:45 pm (and perhaps, for a subsequent trip to Rockingham, in an effort to plant the glove, and then home, by around 11:15 pm) – **to prove that he didn't plant the glove behind O.J.'s house eight hours later!**

Fuhrman only needed a false alibi for 10:30-11:15 pm– if he actually is the killer, and he didn't want anyone, to even begin, to suspect him!

Let us, therefore, continue to scrutinize Detective Fuhrman's alibi, as well as public statements he and his wife have made.

On *"Rivera Live,"* sometime after the preliminary hearings in 1994, someone accused Detective Fuhrman of having planted the Rockingham glove behind O.J.'s house. I didn't watch that particular program, but one of my sources have informed me that Mrs. Fuhrman, subsequently, called up Geraldo Rivera. Mr. Rivera, at that time, actually answered his phone, personally!

According to my source, Geraldo recounted the conversation on his program the next day. Allegedly, Mrs. Fuhrman sounded very nervous and had said (in essence):

> *Mark* [Fuhrman] *could not have planted the Rockingham glove behind O.J. Simpson's house – because he was in bed with me at the time of the murders!*

Think about that for a second! First of all, the murders took place at **10:35-10:40** pm. According to Detective Fuhrman's sworn testimony (to Prosecutor Clark), Fuhrman got home at 10:30 pm and **did not go to bed until** *"about 11:00 pm – maybe a little later"*!

> **So Mark Fuhrman could <u>not</u> have been in bed with his wife at the time of the murders – if Fuhrman is telling the truth! Either Mr. Fuhrman, or Mrs. Fuhrman, was lying!**

That is the first problem! But now it gets more **serious**! Fuhrman was never accused of having planted the glove *about* *the time of the murders.* Fuhrman was being accused of having planted the glove about **6:15 am** – when he said he "found" it. That is **almost eight hours after the murders!**

So, what did Mrs. Fuhrman mean when she called up Geraldo Rivera and said [in essence]:

> *Mark [Fuhrman] could not have planted the Rockingham glove behind O.J. Simpson's house – because **he was in bed with me at the time of the murders!?***

My observant readers have, of course, understood that Mrs. Fuhrman, who is the only one to corroborate her husband's **"10:30 alibi"** – was lying to protect her husband! **Mark Fuhrman was not in bed with Mrs. Fuhrman** at the time of the murders – as Mrs. Fuhrman claimed.

Of course, Mrs. Fuhrman was trying to protect her husband from the accusation that he planted the Rockingham glove behind O.J.'s house. But the protection "alibi" she gave her husband **did not cover the time when Mark Fuhrman was accused of having planted that glove?**

Detective Fuhrman was being accused of having planted the glove around **6:15 am** – while Mrs. Fuhrman tried to cover for him by saying that he was in bed with her at **10:35 pm. And even that was an obvious lie – according to Fuhrman's own sworn direct testimony to Marcia Clark! What is going on here?**

I think I know what is going on! **Mrs. Fuhrman knew that her husband murdered Nicole and Ron! And she knew that her husband planted the glove behind O.J.'s house, in order to frame O.J.!**

Mrs. Fuhrman was afraid of losing her husband, should he be exposed! So she tried to protect him by giving him a false alibi.

However, **Mrs. Fuhrman didn't know all the details** – only that the murders were committed around **10:35-10:45 pm** and that her husband planted the glove behind O.J.'s house, shortly thereafter.

She didn't know – at that time – that her husband did **not** plant the glove at **10:40-10:42** – when Kato heard the three loud, heavy "thumps" on his wall – but that her husband **returned to Rockingham the following morning,** together with the investigators – **and planted the glove then!**

Mrs. Fuhrman thought that her husband committed the murders at around 10:30-10:40 pm, and that he planted the glove shortly thereafter. So when Detective Fuhrman was being accused of having brought the second glove from Bundy to Rockingham, and planted it behind O.J.'s house – **Mrs. Fuhrman panicked!**

That's when she called up Geraldo Rivera personally, and – apparently **very nervously** – claimed that her husband could not have brought the glove from Bundy and planted it behind O.J.'s house, *". . . because he was in bed with me at the time of the murders"*!

Obviously, that was a lie! Shortly, I shall prove that Mrs. Fuhrman not only lied about **the exact time** she and her husband, allegedly, were in bed together, but that her statement **wasn't even close** to the truth! Mark Fuhrman – if we can believe him, at all – didn't **come home** until **11:15-11:30** that night, at the earliest! [But bear with me on that!]

Normally I wouldn't have accused Mrs. Fuhrman of lying, or of knowing about the murders. But her statement is obviously false. She made her statement to protect her husband with a false alibi. **Later, Mark Fuhrman changed his story** in a way that made Mrs. Fuhrman's statement **even more incorrect.**

Hence, if I am wrong about this, then Mr. and Mrs. Fuhrman should blame themselves. **Let me, anyway, remind my readers that I am just expressing my opinions and theories in this book.** It is impossible to know, for sure, all the facts. I have to **speculate** to try to make some sense out of all the strange things that happened in this case.

What am I leading up to here? Well, **a mysterious phone call** was made by a woman, to an LAPD dispatcher, at around 10:30 to 10:45 pm on the night of the murders. The woman identified herself as **calling from Channel 4 News.** Investigations revealed that **no one** from Channel 4 made that call!

That is not strange – obviously the woman didn't want to disclose her identity – so she was **not** from Channel 4. What is strange, however, is that the woman asked if the police were *"sitting on two dead bodies in West L.A."*!

> **Wow! This phone call occurred, in other words, just <u>before</u>, or at the exact same time as the murders took place at Bundy! And the bodies of Nicole and Ron were not to be discovered for another hour and a quarter, approximately!**

My readers didn't know about this? Well, if so, the reason is probably that this mysterious phone call has confused everyone who learned about it, to such an extent that they simply refuse to speculate over it. When people try to explain this – they get a "headache"! Who made that call? Did the caller know that two people were being murdered – or just about to be murdered – in West L.A.? Was a **woman** involved in the murders.

My readers' guesses are as good as mine, I am sure. **But there has to be an explanation! Here is what I think!**

Remember what I suggested earlier? **Mrs. Fuhrman knew** that her husband and some accomplices, were out to murder Nicole that night. It seems logical to conclude that, from Mrs. Fuhrman's own phone call to Mr. Rivera, during which call, she gives her husband a false alibi for the time of the murders – **when he doesn't, yet, need one!**

Mrs. Fuhrman was not directly involved. She had just picked up bits and pieces. But her husband had informed her that she had to cover for him, by supporting his false alibi.

Mrs. Fuhrman had heard the names of **both** Nicole **and** O.J. mentioned. But she didn't know, **at that time**, that **only Nicole** was to be **killed**, while **O.J.**, instead, was to be **framed** for the murder.

Mrs. Fuhrman thought both Nicole and O.J. were to be

murdered.

Mrs. Fuhrman either shared her husband's racist attitudes and loved her husband enough to go along with him, and protect him – or she feared her husband strongly enough that she dared not oppose him or expose him.

Mrs. Fuhrman knew the murders were to take place around **10:30 pm, because that is the time she had been told by her husband to confirm that he came home!**

So, here was Mrs. Fuhrman, sitting at home, alone, anxiously and nervously awaiting her husband's arrival! The time was 10:25.

"Have they done it yet?" she wondered. Of course, she was worried that something might have gone wrong. Perhaps her husband had been arrested. Perhaps he would be convicted and sentenced to death!

Mrs. Fuhrman jumped a little at the sound of the clock on the wall, as it struck 10:30 pm. A little later the clock showed 10:35. Anxiously, Mrs. Fuhrman looked at the door. The clock showed 10:37.

If the bodies had been **discovered** – but her husband was not yet back – it could mean that **something had gone wrong**, and that he had been **arrested**. However, if the bodies had not yet been discovered, her husband might be "just around the corner."

Mrs. Fuhrman could not stand the uncertainty any longer. **She had to know!** Determined, she picked up the phone and called a local LAPD station in West L.A.

She could not introduce herself as *"Mrs. Fuhrman,"* of course! But at the same time, she had to give the dispatcher a **plausible** reason for her strange inquiry. So, introducing herself as **a news reporter from Channel 4**, she asked if the police were

"sitting on two dead bodies in west L.A."

The dispatcher denied that. Mrs. Fuhrman hung up. Now she could relax a bit. Nothing had gone wrong – so far, at least!

Too far out!? Possibly! **But if you think so, why don't you try to come up with a better explanation, as to why a woman, wrongfully identifying herself as calling from Cannel 4 News, could call up the LAPD in West Los Andgeles, at the <u>exact</u> time when Nicole and Ron were being murdered – <u>but their bodies had not yet been discovered</u>, and ask if the police were** *"sitting on two dead bodies in west L.A."*!

However, this was just a digression. Since this phone call is, perhaps, the greatest unsolved mystery of this entire murder case, I thought I should try to put my spin on it.

In conjunction with Mrs. Fuhrman's attempts to give her husband an obviously false alibi for that exact time – the time of the murders – I don't think my theory about the mysterious phone call is so far fetched, after all! It is, at least, better than anything else I have heard suggested, so far!

Back to what we **do** know! Do you think you have heard it all, now? Think again! Here come Fuhrman's real problems:

Shortly after the murders, I was the only person who had put all the pieces together in this murder mystery, and explained how all the pieces of the puzzle fit my theory of Fuhrman being the murderer (in my first book).

No one else believed that at first. But gradually, more and more people started to take my theory seriously – in particular those who supported O.J. and believed in his innocence. **By the end of 1996** several independent **private investigators** were looking into **the theory that Fuhrman actually murdered Nicole and Ron.**

While Fuhrman had been cocky before – he suddenly became nervous. His book, which he promptly decided to write, was a clear example of **"damage control"**! He started to appear on countless TV and radio talk shows, trying to rehabilitate himself, and explain away the few mistakes he had made – and which I had discovered. He **appeared** confident. **But that is how he appeared, also when he perjured himself during the criminal trial.**

I had understood how Fuhrman could have **aborted a first attempt** to plant the glove at O.J.'s house – falling against the wall – and instead planted the glove the following morning. **Or, perhaps the thumps on Kato's wall were deliberately caused by an accomplice.** Perhaps an accomplice thumped the wall, just to make it **appear** that O.J. lost the glove before he left for Chicago. Perhaps Fuhrman's plan, all along, was to plant the glove the following morning, when he arrived to investigate the murders.

Hence, to me, the thumps on Kato's wall at around 10:40-10:42 pm did not represent the time when the glove was planted. I explained that in my first book, *"If O.J. Didn't ..."*

Fuhrman could have had **one accomplice** at Rockingham, thumping on the wall with a baseball bat – over the fence from inside the neighbor's property – as soon as Fuhrman called him on a cellular phone and said that Nicole was killed.

Another accomplice could have substituted for Fuhrman some place far away, using Fuhrman's credit card to give Fuhrman a false alibi. Meanwhile, Fuhrman himself could have committed the murder of Nicole (and Ron). The plan was for Fuhrman to plant the glove the following morning, but make people **believe** it was planted shortly after the murders.

As more and more private investigators read my book (I assume) and seriously started to look into my early theory, Fuhrman grew increasingly more nervous. By the time **his** book surfaced, he could feel private investigators clawing at his heels.

One key point in this murder mystery is that the thumps on Kato's wall were caused by the murderer (or one of his accomplices) – **but that was not the time when the glove was planted!** Fuhrman planted the glove the next morning.

However, Fuhrman could not have found the Rockingham glove at Bundy, when he came there to investigate the murders at 2:10 am. If Fuhrman planted the glove behind O.J.'s house around 6:15 am – then he must have brought the glove with him to Bundy, and on to Rockingham that morning. And if he **brought the glove with**

him to Bundy at 2:10 am – **then he is the killer!**

So, around the end of February 1997, Fuhrman was seen and heard on radio and TV talk shows, almost every day, calling everyones attention to the "thumps" on Kato's wall at around 10:40-10:42 pm, and **suggesting strongly, that those thumps were caused by the murderer – O.J. – depositing or losing the Rockingham glove behind his house, before leaving for Chicago.** Are you still with me? O.K.

Today, Fuhrman has to get people away from the notion that **he** planted the glove at 6:15 am, because that makes him part of the murder plot. Instead, today, Fuhrman must convince people that the glove was deposited around 10:42 pm. **Fuhrman suddenly needed a better alibi for the time of the murders.** Yes? But didn't he have an alibi? No!

As long as people only suspected Fuhrman of having planted the glove at 6:15 am the morning after the murders, Fuhrman was not too concerned about his alibi for the actual time of the murders. As long as his wife corroborated that he came home at 10:30 pm, that was O.K.

However, by February 1997, Mark Fuhrman sensed the heat was building. Several investigators had long since found out that he lied about the **barbecue**, that there was not even a **seminar** on the evening of the murders, that **his wife had lied** about him being in bed with her at the time of the murders, etc., etc. Investigators began realizing that Fuhrman, probably, was the murderer.

So Fuhrman began emphasizing that the glove must tie in with the thumps on Kato's wall. At first, I didn't understand why he was pushing that issue so vehemently. But then, in **February, 1997** on the *"O'Reilly Hour"* (Fox TV), Fuhrman **"shot himself in the foot"** – because he had to, sooner or later!

[I have to rely on one of my sources, since I didn't watch the program]. When challenged about the Rockingham glove, Fuhrman again emphasized that the glove must have been deposited – **by the murderer** – in connection with the thumps on Kato's wall. **Then he finally said it!** [In essence]:

I know where I was at 10:40 pm! I was pumping gas in Pomona! [40-50 minutes from Bundy!]. *But O.J. cannot tell us where he was – because he was behind his house, where he lost the murder glove!*

My immediate response to my "source" as we were talking on the phone, was that Fuhrman must sense his **"La Quinta/barbecue alibi"** was falling apart and that private investigators were on to him. He needed a better alibi for the time of the murders. But **he could not indicate that he considered himself a murder suspect in need of an alibi** – so he could not come right out and present it. He had to introduce his new alibi indirectly, pretending he was simply attacking O.J.'s alibi, instead.

As soon as my "source" informed me about Fuhrman's new **"pumping gas in Pomona alibi,"** I told her that Fuhrman's objective, probably, was not simply to attack O.J.'s alibi – as he pretended – but to introduce his own **Pomona alibi,** indirectly. Hence, he must have a way of **corroborating** this new alibi, which he so cleverly tried to introduce.

"Most likely," I told my source, *"Fuhrman must have in his possession a credit card receipt from Pomona, showing both the date, June 12, 1994, and the time, approximately 10:40 pm! I think he will tell us that himself – not yet, but shortly"*!

Right on! Some time later (February 28, 1997), on *"Talk Back Live"* (CNN), Fuhrman, again, repeated the same statement in the context of attacking O.J.'s alibi!

Apparently, Fuhrman was just accusing O.J. of not having an alibi for the time when the thumps on Kato's wall occurred – which, according to Fuhrman, coincided with the Rockingham glove being lost (by O.J.).

Then – **"casually,"** in the same sentence – he added, that he himself, for instance, knew exactly where **he** was at that time, because **he had used his "Gold American Express" credit card** to pump gas in Pomona, at the time Kato heard the thumps on his wall!

Today, apparently, Fuhrman wants us to believe that he can

prove that he stopped for gas in Pomona, on his way from La Quinta to his home, on the night of the murders.

But this is where things are starting to fall apart for Fuhrman. **If Fuhrman was pumping gas in Pomona at 10:40 – he could not have been home until 11:15 -11:30 pm!**

If so, not only did he **lie under oath** in his direct testimony for Prosecutor Clark, when **he said he got home around 10:30 pm**. **His wife must also have lied when she said that Fuhrman was in bed with her at the time of the murders!**

Fuhrman was clever, too, though – or tried to be! He did not want to mention **directly** that he had **a "credit card alibi" for the time of the murders**. So he didn't bring this up until the end of February, 1997. Furthermore – when he eventually brought up his **"Pomona alibi"** – he introduced it through the **"back door"** – by using it, **indirectly,** to attack **O.J.** in connection with the glove behind O.J.'s house.

> **Why didn't Fuhrman come forward with his c/c receipt from Pomona during his testimony in the criminal trial? Why did he instead lie about getting home at 10:30 pm** and going to bed at a little past 11:00 pm?

Because no one asked him about it! Fuhrman was **not a murder suspect** at that time. After the murders he didn't want to **volunteer** the information about pumping gas in Pomona at 10:45. He didn't want to "explain" that he had a *"credit card alibi" for the time of the murders* – **as long as no one accused him of being the murderer.**

The **"trick"** about letting **someone else** use your credit card at an **automated** credit card machine, like a gas pump, is as old as such gas pumps! Therefore, this is **not** an "alibi" **you** bring up **yourself**! You just keep it – in case **someone else** asks you:

> *"Where were you at 10:30 on the night of the murders?"*!

Everyone speculated about Fuhrman having planted the Rockingham glove – at 6:15 am. But no one could explain how he could have done it – because there were already seventeen officers at Bundy when Fuhrman arrived there to investigate, around 2:10 am, and neither of them had seen a second murder glove.

Had Fuhrman come forward and said: *"By the way, I have a credit card receipt showing that I was in Pomona, pumping gas – when Nicole and Ron were killed* [. . . so I could not have murdered them!]" – then, someone might have asked: *"Why the heck is he telling us that?"* Someone might have figured out that **a guy pumping gas** in Pomona – **using Fuhrman's credit card** – didn't mean that **Fuhrman himself** was in Pomona at 10:40!

The next conclusion would not be far behind – namely that if someone used Fuhrman's credit card, to give Fuhrman a false alibi for the time of the murders, then Fuhrman might actually be the killer. If so, that could explain how he could have planted the Rockingham glove – why the blood on that glove was still wet when he showed it to Detective Vannatter, eight hours after the murders, etc., etc.

This was exactly what I pointed out in my first book, *"If O.J. Didn't ..."* (chapter 17, *"More Pieces That Fit The Puzzle,"* page 107). [Discussing Fuhrman's perjury regarding his use of the N-word]. Quote:

> So why did he lie? What was he so afraid of?
>
> Obviously, Detective Fuhrman was afraid that admitting to having used racial slurs, might have opened up a Pandora's box to his true character, and possibly given someone the idea that he not only planted the glove because he was a racist and wanted to harm O.J. – but that he actually murdered Nicole and Ron, and framed O.J. for the murders.
>
> It seems obvious that **Fuhrman planted the glove!** That does not mean that Fuhrman found the second glove at Bundy when he arrived between 2 and 3 o'clock in the morning. He could have had it all along, because he might actually have murdered Nicole and Ron! [End of quote].

Suddenly the entire murder plot could have started to unravel. Therefore, during his testimony, **Fuhrman said nothing about pumping gas in Pomona** and, hence, that **his only alibi** for the time of the murders, was **a credit card receipt someone else could have provided.**

It was safer – and less conspicuous – to "move" the La Quinta barbecue from Saturday to Sunday, and just – casually – mention that he drove straight home from La Quinta, got home at 10:30 – and have his wife corroborate his alibi.

Since he couldn't use his "Pomona alibi," Fuhrman had to state that he came home, at least, **a little before the murders took place.** However, towards the end of 1996, Fuhrman sensed that private investigators were on to him. He sensed that the La Quinta story was unravelling. **By late February, 1997, he needed a better alibi** for his timeline, than simply **the non-existing barbecue in La Quinta – and his, obviously, "lying" wife!**

So, **out of necessity**, he dug out **the old credit card receipt** from Pomona, which one of his accomplices had actually provided on the night of the murders – as an alibi for Fuhrman – in case Fuhrman should become an **immediate** murder suspect after he "found" the Rockingham glove, back in 1994!

Sure enough, Fuhrman's new *"pumping gas in Pomona"* alibi directly contradicted his sworn testimony in the criminal trial. Actually, this exposed a new case of **perjury** by Fuhrman, which no one was aware of until now. So why would Fuhrman risk that?

Well, it wasn't really an **added** risk. Just as I predicted and suggested in *"If O.J. Didn't ...,"* Fuhrman's "alibi" about the Protective League seminar was false. Investigators had taken my advice and revealed that. It was just a matter of time, before that "secret" would explode in Fuhrman's face. So **he had to think further ahead**, and introduce his new **"Pomona alibi"** before his **"La Quinta barbecue alibi"** got publicly busted.

Was Mark Fuhrman's **"perfect murder"** plot beginning to fall apart around the winter of 1997?

Is this why Fuhrman **first** told Larry King, **cockily**, on

February 26, that he would be willing to debate **"anyone"** on *"Larry King Live"* – but **later** changed his mind when he heard that his opponent would be **Pat McKenna** [one of O.J.'s private investigators]?

No question about it – Fuhrman's alibi for the time of the murder is not trustworthy. It is "manufactured"! Even more suspect, however, is the fact that Fuhrman has been pushing a manufactured alibi in the first place.

Why should Fuhrman have to manufacture a false alibi for the time of the murders – if he is not the murderer?

CHAPTER 20

Mark Fuhrman's Failed Polygraph Test

During one of Mark Fuhrman's book promoting interviews on *"Larry King Live,"* late February 1997, F. Lee Bailey challenged Fuhrman to take a polygraph test on the question of the Rockingham glove. If Fuhrman would submit to – **and pass** – a controlled polygraph test on the question:

"Did you plant the bloody glove behind Mr. Simpson's house,"

then F. Lee Bailey would publicly appologize to Fuhrman – and we could, forever, put the question of the Rockingham glove behind us, for as much as Fuhrman was concerned. Said Mr. Bailey.

Fuhrman declined. On national TV Fuhrman squirmed like a worm, when Mr. Bailey repeated his challenge.

Remember what I just wrote – Fuhrman sensed that private investigators and investigative reporters were clawing at his heels, and that they had long since begun to suspect him of being the killer, although they have not yet made that accusation. Bailey's challenge was televised world wide, though, so later, Fuhrman probably felt he had to take the test – hoping he could beat the polygraph.

However, Fuhrman did not take the test with the polygraph expert F. Lee Bailey had suggested – the LAPD's own polygraph expert. Instead, Fuhrman searched and found his own expert, Mr. Paul Minor. The test was conducted on March 17, 1997.

March 21, Mr. Minor and Mark Fuhrman appeared on *"Larry King Live"* to present the world with the result of Fuhrman's polygraph test. **What a spectacle!**

During the test, Mr. Minor had asked Mark Fuhrman if he planted the bloody glove behind O.J.'s house. Fuhrman had answered *"No"* – and flunked – outright – on his answer!

It was clear to everyone watching the polygraph sheet in close-ups on the TV screen that Fuhrman and Mr. Minor lied. Fuhrman had clearly flunked on the question of the planting of the glove. Paul Minor pointed to the question on the polygraph sheet and to Fuhrman's physiological reactions as he answered *"No."* Even an amateur could see that Fuhrman was lying.

F. Lee Bailey was brought into the discussion on TV. He had watched the presentation of the polygraph sheet, on conference call with two other renown polygraph experts, who both declared that Fuhrman flunked when he answered *"No"* to the question about the Rockingham glove.

Yet, here they were, Mark Fuhrman and Paul Minor, on *"Larry King Live"* – claiming that Fuhrman passed!

Fuhrman and Minor might as well have held up a picture of a **bull** and claimed it was a picture of a **cat**! And if people protested and said the picture was surely that of a **bull**, the two would argue:

> *"No–no! It may **look to you** as a picture of a **bull** – but **it is, indeed,** a picture* of a *cat!*

The things that went on – and still go on – in this case are just too incredible! Regardless of their credentials and their reputation, people who believe O.J. is guilty will go to any length to promote that misconception.

The Simpson case has become a "national psychosis" bringing otherwise calm, reputable and respected professionals in affect, and turning such – otherwise honest – people into liars and cheaters.

In particular on the side of O.J.'s adversaries the Simpson case has brought out the worst in people – on a national scale. These people don't even care if they are caught

lying on national TV.

It is like a "war syndrome"! It is like O.J. Simpson were a national enemy, and that everything anyone can do to bring down this enemy, is fair and legal – just like torture and sabotage during a war!

Mr. Bailey requested that Mr. Minor should send the poly-graph sheet to **The American Polygraph Association**, to which Mr. Minor himself belonged, and ask the APA to appoint a panel of their polygraph experts to review Fuhrman's polygraph test sheet and decide whether or not, in their opinion, Fuhrman passed or flunked.

Mr. Minor flatly refused to have his opinion "second guessed" by the APA. Obviously the man was wrong. Obviously Mark Fuhrman had flunked the test on the question of the Rockingham glove.

Mr. Minor's excuses for not allowing the APA to review his "interpretation" of Fuhrman's polygraph test were:

1. Mr. Minor didn't want the polygraph test to *"make a circus of the Simpson case."*

The best way to prevent the polygraph test from turning into a circus, would, of course, be to let the APA review the results of Fuhrman's test, and issue its authoritative opinion – rather than to have the opposing parties continue to dispute each other.

2. Mr. Minor claimed that the test sheet was Fuhrman's **private property**, and having them publicly evaluated by the APA would violate Fuhrman's **right to privacy**.

Oh my! Here were Fuhrman himself, and his polygraph "expert," Mr. Minor, going on **world wide television** (*"Larry King Live"*) in promotion of Fuhrman's book, and showing the world every detail of the test sheet in close-up, and claiming that Fuhrman passed. And then – according to Mr. Minor – it would violate

Fuhrman's **right to privacy**, if they also let a panel of experts appointed by the APA review the actual test sheet! How embarrasing!

I am sure those of my readers who watched the two men on *"Larry King Live"* were convinced that Fuhrman flunked the test, and that he, therefore, probably **did** plant the Rockingham glove. But let me explain to those who didn't watch the show, what the rest of us saw. Unfortunately, since Mr. Minor refused to make the test sheet available to the public for review, I have to rely on describing it, rather than reproducing it in my book.

–   First of all, Mr. Minor admitted that he had gone over all the questions with Fuhrman, before the test, so Fuhrman knew what he would be asked.

How can you get a correct, **uncontrolled** reaction from Fuhrman, if you "rehearse" the questions with him before the test? There are even rumors that **Mark Fuhrman wrote the questions himself!**

–   After some initial adjustments and some "neutral" questions, Fuhrman's heart rate stabilized. Then he was asked if he had been involved in the Simpson case. Fuhrman's heartbeat increased.

Mr. Minor claimed the question was a so-called "control question." But was it? The word **"involved"** is a charged word. To a man accused of having planted the murder glove behind O.J.'s house, the question implied more than the fact that Fuhrman once investigated the murder case. The question could more readily be perceived by Fuhrman as an **accusation**. So, although he answered truthfully, *"Yes"* (he had been **"involved"** in the Simpson case), the polygraph clearly showed a "nervous reaction" where there ought not have been one.

Eventually Fuhrman's physiological reactions stabilized again. He was asked several questions about other debated pieces of evidence, such as the knife box Fuhrman claimed he found in O.J.'s bathroom, the sweat suit in O.J.'s washing machine, etc. There was little change in Fuhrman's physiological reaction to those questions.

Then came the critical question: ***"Did you plant the bloody murder gloove behind Mr. Simpson's house?"***

Fuhrman's heartbeat went through the ceiling! How anyone, Mr. Minor in particular, could claim that Fuhrman's reaction were consistent with the truth – is beyond any **normal** human being's perception of the the test sheet.

As a matter of fact, Fuhrman's heartbeat went so wild that **Mr. Minor immediately had to adjust Fuhrmans heart rate graph down,** manually – several notches – to prevent the heart rate graph from interfering with the galvanic skin response graph higher up on the same test sheet!

It was all there in close-up on the TV screen (on *"Larry King Live"*). Still, Mr. Minor had the **audacity** to claim that Fuhrman **passed** that question and were telling the truth! Have O.J.'s adversaries no shame at all?

This is how Mr. Minor **"explained"** Fuhrman's hyper-nervous reaction to the question of his planting the Rockingham glove:

Fuhrman's increased heart rate was not due to his response to the question, at all!

According to Mr. Minor, Fuhrman's increased heart rate was caused by some adjustment in his posture or position. He justified that by claiming that the jump in the graph actually started a couple of seconds before the question about the glove was raised.

I fail to understand how Mr. Minor's next statement could be anything but a "slip." By the way, I am surprised that Mr. Bailey did not catch it immediately and confronted Mr. Minor with his "statement." Anyway, the following was how Mr. Minor **underscored** his claim that Fuhrman's increased heart rate started a couple of seconds before the question was actually raised:

> *"You can see Fuhrman's reaction starts here – a couple of seconds earlier – in **anticipation** of the question"!*

Now, this is getting serious! How in heavens name could Fuhrman's heart rate jump – **in anticipation of a question that was not yet asked?**

Fuhrman was asked 17 questions about his involvement in the Simpson case. One of them was the question about the glove. In addition, Fuhrman was asked certain other questions about his home state, date of birth, and things like that – to relax him. When Fuhrman's heart rate started to increase rapidly, and eventually "shot through the ceiling" – that happened **in anticipation of the "glove question,"** according to Mr. Minor!

As I said – it had to be a "slip" by Mr. Minor. But it was an important one. My immediate reaction was this:

– Did Mr. Minor **accidentally** reveal that Fuhrman had **the list of questions in front of him**, so that he knew when critical questions would be asked?

Mr. Minor was beginning to remind me more and more of Detective Vannatter!

Be that as it may. Mr. Minor's next outreagous claim came just seconds later. While Fuhrman's heart rate was still at the its highest, Mr. Minor **re-introduced the glove question.** Mr. Minor realized that Fuhrman's reaction to the question, the first time, exposed him as a liar. So Mr. Minor asked Fuhrman the same question again, a few seconds later.

In front of a national TV audience Mr. Minor pointed to Fuhrman's physiological response the second time he answered, and to the fact that there was less increase in his heart rate the second time. *"So Fuhrman was telling the truth"!*

But when Fuhrman's heart rate had already shot through the ceiling, because he was lying about not planting the murder glove, and Mr. Minor asked him – again – while Fuhrman's heart was still beating like an air hammer – how could we expect any change in his heart rate at that point?

Besides, "the **piff** had already gone out of the soda bottle." It was like you opened a soda bottle and heard the "piff." If you put the cap back on and opened it again five seconds later, the piff was gone.

The same way with Fuhrman. **The first time Mr. Minor asked him if he planted the glove, we got Fuhrman's true reaction – his heart rate hit the ceiling!**

Fuhrman's heart rate jumped above the allotted paper space on the test sheet, so Mr. Minor had to adjust the heart rate graph down several notches. **Asking Fuhrman the same question a few seconds later was not likely to create an even wilder response.**

There could be no question in any sincere person's mind – if they looked at the test sheets:

Fuhrman flunked the polygraph test on the question of the glove behind O.J.'s house! Only one logical conclusion can be drawn from Fuhrman's response to the glove question, namely that **Fuhrman lied** and that he, therefore, **did plant the glove behind O.J.'s house.**

As we have discussed earlier, however, Fuhrman could not have picked up that glove at the time he came to Bundy to investgate the murders (at 2:10 am). **Fuhrman himself is the first person to explain that – both in his book, and on TV.**

If Fuhrman planted the glove behind O.J.'s house about 6:00-6:15 am, **Fuhrman must have brought that glove with him to Bundy** when he arrived there about 2:10 am. He could only have done that if he was actively involved in the murders of Nicole earlier that night.

Now, Mark Fuhrman has proven that – even with his polygraph tests.

CHAPTER 21

Did The Prosecutors Know?

Several times, I shall return to the suggestion that both the investigators and the prosecutors knew, rather early during the investigation, that O.J. was innocent, and that an LAPD officer – most likely Detective Fuhrman – had murdered Nicole and Ron. I also suggest that the prosecutors must have known that, at least, some – but probably all – of the evidence against O.J. was fabricated. I have already tied this suggestion to Fuhrman's alibi.

Prosecutor Marcia Clark knew about the allegations against Fuhrman for racism and for having planted the Rockingham glove.

She must also have known about Detective Fuhrman's 3-4,000 pages of Internal Affairs investigations, the 5 allegations against Fuhrman for police brutality, and Fuhrman's psychiatric case history! My readers shouldn't even question that. Such stuff is **elementary** for a prosecutor preparing a central witness for his testimony in a high profile murder case.

When it became more and more evident that Fuhrman had lied about blood spots he allegedly saw on O.J.'s Bronco on the night of the murders, Ms. Clark was instrumental in sending Criminalist Fung back to examine the Bronco for a **third** time, to look for those alleged blood spots. Of course, this third time, Fung found some blood spots that he hadn't seen on two previous examinations of the Bronco – exactly where Ms. Clark had told him to look!

Long before Prosecutor Clark conducted her direct examination of Mark Fuhrman, Ms. Rosa Lopez had been on the witness stand, outside the presence of the jury, and told how Detective Fuhrman had withheld her important information about O.J.'s Bronco being parked at Rockingham between 10:15 and 10:30 pm on the night of the murders. I return to this in a later chapter.

When Prosecutor Clark presented her first draft of the prosecutions case against O.J., in a meeting with all the "top brass" associated with the Simpson case – District Attorney Gil Garcetti's highest ranking assistant, Assistant District Attorney Peter Bozanich raised serious objections with regards to the murder glove that Fuhrman allegedly had "found" behind O.J.'s house. Mr. Bozanich allegedly said:

> ***"There is something wrong with that glove! What is it doing there? It doesn't make any sense!"*** *("Killing Time,"* by Donald Freed and Raymond P. Briggs; Macmillan – page 250)

I will return to some of these events later.

In preparation for his testimony, Prosecutor Clark **must** have discussed with Fuhrman what he was doing prior to being called to the murder scene – because a prosecutor does not ask one of his, or her, own witnesses, during the trial, a question she doesn't know the answer to! It is **the first rule** in the prosecutor's book on *"examining witnesses"*!

During her examination of Fuhrman, Ms. Clark asked Fuhrman about the Protective League seminar, when he left, etc. Hence, she must have asked Fuhrman those same questions during preparations for his testimony. That's logic – and **it is elementary for a prosecutor.**

Detective Fuhrman carried so much questionable "baggage" that I find it absolutely unthinkable, that Prosecutor Marcia Clark, before her direct examination of Fuhrman during the criminal trial, did not "cover her back" by checking out every detail of Fuhrman's story about the weekend seminar at La Quinta, and the time of the barbecue which was Fuhrman's "time factor," or "clock," for when he left La Quinta.

It is unthinkable that Marcia Clark had not checked out Fuhrman's story with some of the other participants at the seminar or with the president of the Protective League.

Therefore, **Prosecutor Marcia Clark**, most likely, **knew**

that Fuhrman lied about his "alibi"! Otherwise she is **a despicably poor prosecutor**!

If Prosecutor Marcia Clark knew, the other prosecutors knew it too! Even District Attorney Gil Garcetti must have known!

Why? Because Prosecutor Marcia Clark – if she knew that Detective Fuhrman lied about his alibi – would never have **dared** to "cover" for Fuhrman and let him lie on the witness stand, unless she had cleared it with District Attorney Gil Garcetti, and received his *"go ahead!"*

If Gil Garcetti, Marcia Clark, and the rest of the prosecution team – knowingly – allowed Fuhrman to present a false alibi for the time of the murders, they must have been part of a conspiracy to cover up the fact that Detective Fuhrman had murdered Nicole and Ron.

Fuhrman didn't need a false alibi from, say 10:30 to 11:15 pm to cover up the fact that he planted the Rockingham glove around 6:00 am the next morning!

The only reason Fuhrman needed a false alibi from 10:30 to 11:15 pm would be if he is the murderer!

Consequently, if the prosecutors and District Attorney Garcetti knew that Fuhrman presented a false alibi in court, they must also have known that Fuhrman is the murderer!

That is pretty serious, I would say!

Do my readers begin to understand, now, how **everyone** – from Detectives Lange and Vannatter, Criminalists Fung and Mazzola, to Prosecutors Clark and Darden, and all the way to District Attorney Gil Garcetti – **got sucked into Detective Fuhrman's "lethal web"**?

Fuhrman had set-up the investigators with certain pieces of

evidence. The investigators, Detective Vannatter in particular, had swallowed Fuhrman's bait. Vannatter, as I shall justify later, replaced some of the blood swatches from Bundy, with false blood swatches containing O.J.'s blood – taken from his blood vial. From that moment there was no turning back.

Vanatter had found a method of circumventing the EDTA in O.J.'s blood vial. Hence, it appeared that the false blood swatches with O.J.'s DNA could not have been fabricated, and that O.J., therefore, were guilty. Vannater was confident!

Later, both Detective Vannatter and the prosecutors understood that Fuhrman was the murderer, and that he had **set them up** by planting some of the evidence against O.J.

However, by that time it was too late to go after Fuhrman. **If they went after Fuhrman, at that point, there was no way of explaining how O.J.'s blood, apparently, was found at the murder scene – other than to admit that the police had fabricated it!**

Detective Vannatter knew that, but he also knew that the prosecutors had been instrumental in fabricating some of the false evidence against O.J. – or that they, at least, had **condoned** that the **investigators** had fabricated false evidence.

So Vannatter would not allow the prosecutors to take him down, without bringing the prosecutors down with him. Hence, they were all guilty in fabricating all the false evidence against O.J. And they were all dependent upon each other to cover it up.

Their only way out of the mess was to continue – more than ever – to go after O.J. **Only by prosecuting O.J., could they assure themselves that their terrible secret – remained a secret!**

None of them could expose what was going on? Already after a few days, Vannatter knew – and after a week or so the prosecutors also knew – that Fuhrman was the murderer, but they couldn't do anything about it, other than cover it up and continue to pursue O.J. If any of them squealed, they could all go to prison for 10 to 20 years!

Their **"code of silence"** which got them caught in a web of lies and cover ups, also protected them. Even if some honest, idealistic, rookie LAPD officer learned what was going on – he could not report it.

First of all, **would he be willing to send to prison all his colleagues** – who had tampered with the evidence, covered it up, or known about it, but said nothing – **just to save the reputation of an African American**? No way! This is the LAPD! The officer would never work again – anywhere!

Secondly, where was this rookie officer going to take his complaint? To his superior officer, of course. But how could the rookie officer trust that his superior didn't already know about the cover up, and was part of it?

Thirdly, even if the superior officer was **not** part of the conspiracy and the cover up, he would have to hand over the complaining officer's report to the LAPD's own investigators. **The culprits would end up investigating themselves!**

Conveniently, they would file away the complaint as "unfounded." **Nothing** would be accomplished by the rookie officer's report – except that he would have jeopardized his entire career! The word would spread that this **"rat"** was unreliable. He would never work again in any police department in the United States! He might even be beaten to death, or shot, during a drug raid, by vengeful, rogue colleagues!

During a drug raid, **they would send the "rat" through the door first.** As soon as the shooting started, **the honest police officer would find himself under fire.** His own partners, however, would wait before they followed the "rat" through the door – wait just long enough for the drug dealers to shoot him. Then they would enter and make the arrests. The death of the honest cop would be ruled an accident – for as much as his colleagues were concerned. Nobody could prove that his colleagues had deliberately waited 20 seconds before they followed him through the door.

Any subsequent LAPD officer who learned about Fuhrman,

the conspiracy, and the cover up, immediately realized that he simply couldn't do anything about it. So, he would have to lay the matter to rest.

Even if an honest investigation were conducted, it would be almost impossible to prove who, in particular, was responsible for each piece of fabricated evidence, who covered it up, and who simply knew about it without saying anything.

The gloves, the knit cap, and a roll of carpet from O.J.'s Bronco was kept unsealed in a large, open cardboard box! The cap and the gloves were in unsealed regular brown paper bags. And the carpet piece was rolled up and held together with a piece of brown packaging tape. It wasn't even wrapped!

Of course, half a dozen different criminalists would have brought out that box, analyzing and performing tests on the various pieces of evidence in it. The glove expert, a blood analyst, a hair expert, an expert on carpet fibers, and an expert on shoeprints (for the carpet). And while the box was out in the crime lab, any number of other criminalists, hypothetically, had accsess to it as well – during a lunch break or overnight.

Any one of them could have planted carpet fibers on the cap and on Ron's shirt (which was stored equally nonchalantly). Any one of them could have planted **hairs** on the cap and on one of the gloves – even if that person was only supposed to examine the **carpet**.

Hence, even if a court recognized that **one of them** had planted hair and fiber evidence, a jury could not convict any one of them, when they didn't know for sure who had done it. The rogue LAPD officers had a fail-safe system of protecting themselves.

Maybe that was why they didn't store the Simpson evidence more securely! By storing the evidence so nonchalantly that **several** individuals, hypothetically, could have tampered with it, **it became impossible to go after anyone in particular.**

Being a police officer, who had **sworn to uphold the law**, once an LAPD officer learned that something was seriously wrong with the Simpson case, and he did not, **immediately,** do something about it – he, too, committed a felony – and he, too, immediately, **became part of that same conspiracy**!

If he didn't report it immediately, **it became harder and harder to do it later**. For each day that passed, and he didn't report it, he committed another felony! It was an evil flame which consumed everyone who got near it!

B ut even **judges** are part of, and perpetuate, this atrocious problem. **How can police officers and prosecutors be discouraged from such despicably criminal practices when Judge Hiroshi Fujisaki in the Simpson civil trial, prohibited O.J. and his attorneys from even mentioning police conspiracy and fabrication of evidence?**

Unquestionably, someone fabricated most of the evidence against O.J. Imagine the message Judge Fujisaki was sending to those rogue investigators!

> *"This is not a case about police misconduct or a police conspiracy! The police is not on trial in this case!"*

That was basically what Judge Fujisaki told O.J.'s defense attorneys! Then he followed it up by sustaining virtually every objection the counsels for the plaintiffs raised. As soon as O.J.'s attorneys started to expose that a police witness lied during his testimony, and that evidence had been falsely manufactured or tampered with – the counsels for the plaintiffs shouted,

> *"Objection! Beyond the scope!"*

And Judge Fujisaki immediately followed up:

> *"Sustained – sustained – sustained ...!"*

Such a deplorable attitude by this pathetic judge encourages rogue police officers all over the country to murder innocent African Americans, fabricate false evidence whenever they feel like it, lie when testifying, and cover up for each other!

Worse than that, however, is the message Judge Fujisaki and judges like him are sending to every decent, honest, hard working, law abiding police officer – namely that judges will readily take the side of rogue police officers who abuse their powers and commit serious crimes under color of authority.

With such attitudes dominant among judges everywhere, how would any decent, honest police officer **even dare to report a rogue colleague?**

The predominant attitude of judges, who on a broad scale abuse their powers to protect police officers who commit crimes – is perhaps the most important reason why such officers are so hard to get rid of. **That is yet another reason to demand TV cameras in all U.S. courtrooms.**

Our law enforcement system has long since become a national disgrace. It is so corrupt that it may even be beyond repair!

Some of my readers, and in particular the **former Simpson investigators and prosecutors, will vehemently argue that they did nothing wrong, and that prosecutors and investigators simply don't do things like that. Well – do I have news for you!**

Thursday, December 13, 1996, the major national news story was this (Don Terry; *New York Times*, December 13, 1996):

"Ex-Prosecutors and Deputies in Death Row Case Are Charged With Framing Defendant"

Here is the story behind the headline:

In 1983 a ten year-old girl was kidnapped in her DuPage, Illinois, home, raped, and murdered. Her body was found a few days later.

Three men, two Hispanics and one white, were charged with the murders. The case against the white man ended in a hung jury, and he was released.

The two Hispanic men, Hernandez and Cruz – 19 years old at the time – were convicted and sentenced to death! They appealed.

In a second trial both men were convicted again. Hernandez was sentenced to 80 years in prison! Cruz was sentenced to death – for the second time!

Cruz spent the next eight years on death row, fighting for his life. Normally, he should have been put to death a long time ago.

The case against Cruz and Hernandez is a chilling example of a deliberate mis-"Carriage of Justice"!

I assume there must have been **some kind of evidence** against Cruz and Hernandez. Perhaps some hairs and fibers – which the investigators might have planted. Perhaps both defendants lacked an alibi. Perhaps witnesses had observed men who fit their descriptions, near the girl's house.

I don't really know, but there must have been some kind of "loose" evidence – planted or not – just like in the case against O.J. Simpson. Otherwise, two subsequent, unanimous juries could not have sent the young men to death row! Here is **"the rest of the story"**:

The evidence could not have been very reliable – since both men, ultimately and indisputably, were found to be innocent.

To strengthen their case three sheriff''s deputies and investigators, concocted a false story that Mr. Cruz, allegedly, had told the investigators about a **dream**. In recounting this dream to the investigators, Cruz – **according to the investigators** – had described details about the murder of the young girl, which only the real murderer could have known.

Many months had passed since the murder, and since the arrest of Cruz and Hernandez. Of course, if their story was correct, the investigators could not have failed to make a concurrent report of such an important piece of evidence.

Yet, there was no concurrent record of this alleged "dream confession." The three investigators simply showed up at the prosecutor's office one day, and told the prosecutor that they had *"forgotten"* about Cruz' "dream" – but now they remembered it!

Cruz denied having had such a dream. Consequently, he also denied having mentioned such a dream to any investigator. In my opinion, the investigators' story was so outrageous that no prosecutor on the surface of the earth could argue that he believed such nonsense! Yet, the prosecutors presented the "dream" as evidence against Cruz and Hernandez.

The three deputies testified under oath that their account was correct. Furthermore, during the trial, a fourth deputy corroborated their testimony by testifying that the three investigators had told this fourth deputy about the dream confession, shortly after it allegedly took place.

As my readers will understand, shortly, the "dream" was the strongest – and, in fact, the only – "real" evidence against Cruz and Hernandez! Here is why:

Of course the ten year old girl was not promiscuous! Semen recovered from the victim must, therefore, have been from the rapist/murderer. The semen matched neither of the defendants, Cruz and Hernandez – nor did it match the third, released, white defendant. Obviously someone else must have raped and murdered the child.

I haven't read anything to the effect of the following. But **my immediate reaction** was that this kidnapping/rape/murder must have been **the act of <u>one</u> man, only.**

Why? Well, a gang of hoodlums could perceivably attack and rape a woman getting lost in a gang infested neighborhood, or getting drunk at a rowdy party. However,

-   to break into the home of a **ten year-old girl**, while her parents were at work, and the girl was home from school, alone, with the flu,
-   kidnap the girl,
-   rape her, and
-   murder her,

. . . is such an outrageously heinous and perverted crime that it is **unthinkable** that **two** – not to mention **three** – men could have **agreed** on something that atrocious – and carried it out! How could **any** man dare to even mention such a thought – to anyone, but himself?

This crime **must** have been committed by **one** man only – a person so deviate and perverted that, hopefully, there are only a handful of them in the entire country! And then, to suggest that there were **three such monsters living in DuPage, Illinois, at the same time,** simply defies all logic!

Can my readers imagine Cruz saying to Hernandez and Buckley (the third defendant):

> *"Let's abduct this ten year old girl! Then we force her to have intercourse with us! – Afterwards, we murder her!"*

And then, Hernandez and Buckley should, allegedly, have answered:

> *"Yes! Good idea – just what we were thinking, too!"*

It is so horrible to even consider that there are people who could do something like that. Obviously, there was such a man in DuPage that dark day in 1983.

However, for the prosecutors to suggest that there were **three** such men in DuPage who had that same heinous thought that day – and dared to share it with each other, defies, at least, **my** logic!

As if this wasn't enough, another man, Dugan, confessed to his lawyer – already eleven years ago, in 1985 – that **he** had kidnapped, raped, and murdered the young girl in DuPage.

Dugan had been arrested, charged, and, later, convicted of raping and murdering a **seven year-old girl** and a 27 year-old woman, and he is presently serving a life sentence for these crimes.

The semen recovered from the ten year-old DuPage girl implicated Dugan.

The investigators and prosecutors in the Cruz-Hernandez case knew about Dugan's confession, but they kept this information secret, so Cruz' and Hernandez' defense attorneys – and the jurors – should not learn about it!

There you have it! The above is a short overview of the DuPage/ Cruz-Hernandez case.

I discussed this case in such detail, because I believe the prosecutors **must** have known that Cruz, Hernandez, and Buckley were innocent! I wanted my readers to know the facts, so you can make up your own minds about the DuPage case.

I am shocked that investigators and prosecutors, under such circumstances, can do their utmost to convict and execute two young men whom they **must** have known were innocent! And I am even more surprised that twelve jurors – unanimously – could convict Cruz and Hernandez – twice even!

It is spine-chilling to realize that both men could have been executed, as I sit here and write this, and that it took 12 years, most of them on death row, for Cruz and Hernandez to win their righteous freedom.

Last year, in a third trial, both Cruz and Hernandes were acquitted and released, after a sheriff's deputy admitted that he had lied about Cruz' alleged **"dream confession"** when he testified against Cruz and Hernandez.

In setting Mr. Cruz free **after a 12 year nightmare on death row**, the **judge**, Ronald Mehling, proclaimed that the state's case against Cruz was built on *"lies, mistakes and sloppy police work"*!

Have we heard those words before? It makes us think about the Simpson case. Right?

Since the mid 1970's almost 70 people have been released from death row nationwide, for lack of evidence – or more frequently, for conclusive evidence of their innocence!

Those are almost 70 innocent people whom investigators, prosecutors, dozens of unanimous 12-member juries, and judges, were willing – and trying their best – **to murder, in the name of Justice!**

Violent crimes scare the hell out of our communities these

days. But still, we need to raise, rather than lower, the threshold for finding people guilty in this country!

People may hide behind the law, or behind the Bible. It is still murder – in the first degree – when someone is sent to his execution based on

- – false evidence,
- – perjured testimonies from rogue cops or racist witnesses,
- – political ambitions of prosecutors and judges, and
- – prejudiced juries!

Referring to the DuPage case, at the time of their indictments:

- – The four sheriff's deputies who concocted the dream confession, are still **law enforcement officers**.
- – One of the former prosecutors is now a DuPage County **judge**!
- – Another of the former prosecutors is **assistant United States Attorney** in Chicago!
- – The third former prosecutor is, I believe, a **civil attorney**.

December 12, 1996, all seven men involved in the DuPage case on the investigative and prosecutorial side, were **indicted and charged** with *"conspiracy and obstruction of justice."*

I remind my readers that, until found guilty in a court of law, **all seven men are to be presumed innocent.**

If found guilty by a unanimous jury of their peers, I am sure the judge will impose proper sentences.

If acquitted, or released as a result of a hung jury, the seven men shall continue to be presumed innocent.

That is not to say that they didn't commit the crimes they were charged with. But in the absence of a guilty verdict we, the public, should treat them as being innocent, and allow them to go on with their lives.

So often have investigators and prosecutors in the Simpson case, as well as the media, argued that police officers and

266 • Solving The Simpson Murder Mystery

prosecutors could never conspire to frame an innocent man. Let me rephrase such a statement and say that it is, at least, hard to **prove** that they do it.

However, it happened in a heinous, high profile murder case in "upper class" DuPage County, Illinois, where there was a lot of pressure on the investigators to solve the crime, and pressure on the prosecutors to obtain a conviction.

Realizing that their case was weak and that their prime suspects might be acquitted, the police investigators conspired to fabricate false evidence, and lied under oath on the witness stand!

And the prosecutors, whom I refuse to believe were unaware of what was going on, welcomed the falsely fabricated evidence. Simultaneously, they withheld from the defense solid evidence of the defendants innocence, so the prosecutors could earn the convictions of two innocent men and send them to death row!

Hence, DuPage County residents, could, again, sleep in peace, and the prosecutors could be re-elected or promoted!

Do my readers see the parallels to the Simpson case? I hope so!

According to the attorney for one of the former prosecutors, he still *"believed the police witnesses had been telling the truth about the 'dream,' and he still believed them." "Now, we are making martyrs of murderers and indicting prosecutors who were trying to protect the public,"* the prosecutor's attorney declared.

He is in total denial, and is actually, still, calling Cruz and Hernandez "murderers"! Even when caught with their pants down, these officers of law and justice are in total denial of the fact that they nearly murdered two innocent young men, by trying to get them executed – based on false evidence and perjured testimony – for crimes the young men had not committed.

Following the indictments, what did the parents of the

murdered girl say to reporters, after being presented with solid evidence of the defendants' innocence – backed up by the indictments of the seven men responsible for this travesty of justice?

"Somehow, we still think Cruz and Hernandez are guilty"!

I understand them, and empathize with them! I really do! Having lost their child so tragically, they need **"closure"** – any kind of closure! And they want **"someone"** to pay for the crime against their daughter! I just don't think it should have been Cruz and Hernandez.

Does the story sound familiar? The DuPage case has so many similarities with the Simpson case that I simply had to include a résumé of the case.

The similarities are so striking that I don't even list them, side by side. **I trust my informed readers are already busy drawing parallels like crazy.**

Unfortunately, the DuPage case and the Simpson case represent an all too familiar story!

There is no way the Simpson case will be solved – in the sense that the guilty ones are charged and convicted – unless a federal investigation commission, with unlimited mandate both to grant immunities and to prosecute, cleans up both the LAPD and the Los Angeles D.A.'s office from top to bottom.

Only then might decent police officers dare to step forward and tell what they know about the former investigators and the prosecutors in the Simpson case.

And when the commission is finished in L.A., it ought to move on and do the same in most of our other major police departments.

Here is an interesting question: How could District Attorney Gil Garcetti, Prosecutors Marcia Clark and Christopher Darden, Detectives Lange and Vannatter – who, I maintain, knew that O.J. was innocent and that Fuhrman was the murderer – demonstrate publicly such **"sincere"** anger and disgust vis-a-vis O.J.?

If they knew that Vannatter had fabricated most of the evidence against O.J., and perhaps Fuhrman had even taunted them by admitting to the murders, because he knew it was too late for them to come after him – why could they be so angry with O.J., and actually **appear to believe** that he were guilty of the murders?

This has to do with psychology. Let me use District Attorney Gil Garcetti as an example.

At first Garcetti is angry with Fuhrman. But then he realizes that he can't touch Fuhrman, because Fuhrman has framed O.J. and set up the investigators so perfectly. Garcetti should have told the truth immediately and gone after both Fuhrman, the investigators, and his prosecutors. But pride, political ambitions, and loyalty to his friends and colleagues kept him from doing that. Instead he became part of the conspiracy.

Since he didn't go after the culprits right away – he could never do it later on. Take today, for instance. Assuming Gil Garcetti knew – how could he tell anyone about it today? How could he do that, and justify that he didn't do it sooner? Do my readers see, that from the day Gil Garcetti knew – and didn't do anything about it – he became part of the conspiracy, and could never, later, switch side.

From that point on, telling the truth about O.J.'s innocence and Fuhrman's guilt actually threatened Garcettis own career and future. It got on his nerves. Garcetti got frustrated and angry at **the entire situation.**

So in this next stage, Garcetti was not angry at Fuhrman personally, but more at the entire complex situation, including Fuhrman, Vannatter, Marcia Clark – and O.J. Yes, Garcetti even got angry at O.J. – because if it weren't for O.J., Garcetti wouldn't have been in this situation.

A period followed, where Garcetti filtered out **those he could not – or did not want to – blame or retaliate against.** Those were first of all his closest colleagues in this conspiracy, namely Marcia Clark and Christopher Darden.

He was still angry at Detective Vannatter who got all of them involved in the mess, even more so at Fuhrman who was the real villain, and he was also more and more angry at O.J., because he began to see O.J. as the **"real"** cause of the trouble, in spite of the fact that O.J. is totally innocent, both in the murders, in the evidence fabrication, and in the conspiracy and the cover-ups.

Eventually, Garcetti also got to terms with Vannatter. After all, it wasn't Vannatter's fault that Fuhrman killed Nicole and Ron, and "set up" Vannatter.

Gradually, Fuhrman and O.J. were the only two Garcetti, subconsciously, saw as responsible for Garcetti's troubles! All the others – in spite of their horrible crimes against O.J. – had subconsciously been filtered out from Garcetti's anger.

So then, at last, Garcetti's sub-conscious psyche had to choose between Fuhrman and O.J. **Consciously**, Garcetti knew O.J. was innocent, and that Fuhrman was the villain.

However, you see, Garcetti's **sub-conscious** psyche wasn't trying to decide which one was the bad guy and which one was the good guy. Garcetti's psyche was searching for the person who was responsible for the uproar in Garcetti's life. Garcetti's sub-conscious psyche was after the person – Fuhrman or O.J., it didn't matter – who most threatened Garcetti's existence.

It wasn't Garcetti's conscious mind, his intelligence, that ultimately decided that he hated O.J. It was Garcetti's sub-conscious mind which told him, for his peace of mind's sake, that he had to get rid of one of the two men – Fuhrman or O.J.!

Garcetti's sub-conscious psyche knows **no morality**. It only seeked gratification and **harmony**. So, when Garcetti couldn't go after Fuhrman, his sub-conscious psyche ordered Garcetti to attack O.J. instead!

Sub-consciously, Garcetti began to see O.J. as the only source of the threat to his safety, security, career, and future. **O.J. – the victim – had become Garcetti's villain!**

From there on, Garcetti more or less disregarded all the other

real culprits in this drama, and concentrated on portraying O.J. as the bad guy, in every way he could.

At some stage, Garcetti might even have begun to **believe** that O.J. **is** the murderer. Perhaps Fuhrman wasn't guilty, anyway! Perhaps **O.J.** did it ! Perhaps Vannatter simply framed a guilty man!

Garcetti got more and more angry with O.J. The others faded away. In his conscious mind, he **thought** he was angry with O.J. because he believed O.J. were guilty. In reality, Garcetti was angry with O.J. because his sub-conscious psyche had told him that attacking O.J. was the only way Garcetti could protect himself – from the situation he had been mixed up in.

The human mind is a strange, and sometimes scary piece of "mechanics"! How can we, otherwise, explain that presumably intelligent men like Gil Garcetti, and the investigators and prosecutors in DuPage, would, willfully, send innocent men to their executions?

CHAPTER 22

Christopher Darden And His Book

On TV talk shows like *"Larry King Live," "Rivera Live,"* and *"The Charles Grodin Show,"* Prosecutor Christopher Darden has been an outspoken critic of O.J. since his acquittal in the criminal trial. Darden has repeatedly called O.J., *"a murderer,"* on national television, in spite of the jury's unanimous *"Not guilty"* verdict.

Prosecutor Darden has another dubious reputation. He was notorious for antagonizing witnesses with insinuations and innuendos during his cross examinations.

Ms. Rosa Lopez, the housemaid of O.J.'s neighbor, provided O.J. with a strong alibi – namely that his Bronco never left Rockingham during the time of the murders. Darden cross examined Ms. Lopes so unfairly that I was ashamed watching him on TV. Prosecutor Darden tried to make Ms. Lopez out to be a liar, by cross examining her on totally irrelevant personal matters.

Of course, simply by virtue of prosecuting O.J. – who could not possibly have killed Nicole and Ron – Prosecutor Christopher Darden himself was the real liar in that mini-drama.

How can a, presumably, well educated man, like Christopher Darden – who must have known better – prosecute, and later persistently persecute an innocent man and call him a murderer – after the defendant's acquittal – unless the persecutor is lying?

The only other explanation is **lack of judgement**, on behalf of Mr. Darden. Let me, therefore, say a few words in regards to Mr. Darden's book about the Simpson case, *"In Contempt"* (Harper Collins/Regan Books, 1996).

By criticizing Christopher Darden's book I am leaving myself open to criticism. So be it! That's to be expected anyway.

The entire premise for Christopher Darden's book and his

opinion of the Simpson case is faulty – namely that O.J., in spite of his acquittal, is guilty. So his entire book is more or less nonsense.

Critics of O.J. and of myself may think otherwise and praise Christopher Darden's book. But I maintain that **you can not write a book proving that the earth is flat, and expect to be taken seriously by those who know better.**

Mr. Darden's book smells of "sour grapes." He is bitter because he lost the case of the century. In particular, he is bitter, because he has been seen by many as the prosecutor mostly responsible for O.J.'s acquittal, due, in large, to the infamous glove demonstration he orchestrated in the courtroom. Besides, maybe Prosecutor Darden's attitude turned some jurors off!

Mr. Darden is obviously wrong about O.J. Luckily he didn't persuade the jurors to go along with him. I am not going to criticize Mr. Darden's entire book. I am only going to criticize part of one chapter, for which Mr. Darden has reaped **most** literary praise – **just to demonstrate how totally wrong he is, in his book, as he was in the courtroom!** I am referring to Mr. Darden's description of how Nicole met her murderer.

Of course, Christopher Darden was not present. I assume he is not psychic. **Mr. Darden is just fantasizing!** I quote from his book:

> "As I stepped on the elevator, I thought about Ron and Nicole and was filled with images that continue to haunt me. I still could see exactly how it happened, in fact I see it still, much more vividly than I like, much more often than I want to. And every time I see it, I want to confront him, tell him that I can see inside his heart and that I know what happened.
>
> Through the window, you watched Nicole put away the dishes, didn't you? She finished and then she lit some candles and you watch her the way you had watched her so many times before, on dry runs. She stopped suddenly and looked out the window, but she couldn't see you, because it was dark

outside and well lit inside. All she could see was her own reflection and, for just a moment, you both stood staring at the same thing: her frightened face. She reached into her kitchen drawer and grabbed a long kitchen knife, her knuckles white around the handle. You were impressed. You knew how afraid she must be to grab a knife. Nicole had told you how frightened she was of knives, that it was her worst fear that one day she would be killed with a knife. And she went back to lighting candles.

Candles! That really got you, didn't it? That was your ritual, something that let you know she was ready to be taken. It infuriated you that she might be lighting candles for someone else. You moved along the bushes outside the window, watching her, the way you had watched her before. Was there a voice pulling you? Pushing you? Or was it just matter-of-fact, slow and measured?

How long were you planning to do it? When did it stop being a daydream and become a challenge – *"Can I get away with this?"* Maybe you didn't even know when you got there that night. Maybe it was like other missions, and just watching her like this made you feel better. Maybe it felt like a dream to you, standing out there, all in black, in quiet rubber-soled shoes, with dark gloves over your hands, and a cap on.

You watched her walk out of her kitchen and you shadowed her outside, onto the walkway, past the windows to the front steps. There you rang the door bell and you knew she had to come outside, because the intercom was broken. But she didn't come out, did she? Instead she took the knife again and peered out the window.

The Akita came over and sniffed you. He cocked his head in recognition. You watched her set the knife back on the counter, blade out (strange with the children home). And then she came running out to the gate and you filled with rage.

Whomever she was expecting, she knew him well enough to answer the door barefooted, in the skimpy black dress she'd worn at the recital. You were furious. Your wife, the mother of your children, was wearing that dress and expecting a man to come over while the kids were asleep. Was it more than you could take?

You came out of the shadows so quickly, so smoothly, you must've surprised yourself a little. You hit her with your fist and with the knife handle, right on the crown of her head. Then you grabbed her by her arm and drove the knife deep into her neck, four times." [End of quote].

If Christopher Darden is haunted by images of O.J. and Nicole, filled with sexual overtones like he describes in his book, I strongly suggest that there is something mentally wrong with Mr. Darden. There was nothing in the situation suggesting that sex or jealousy was a factor in the murders of Nicole and Ron.

What is so fundamentally wrong with Mr. Darden's description? Everything! But let me be more specific. First of all, if O.J. were there, as Mr. Darden describes it,

"all in black, in quiet, rubber-soled shoes, with dark gloves over your hands, and a cap on" – and let me add – *"with a razor sharp knife in your hand,"*

. . . then O.J. weren't daydreaming or stalking, or just looking!

If this is a correct description – **and O.J. had a plane to catch, remember** – then he were there for one purpose only, namely

to kill Nicole as quickly as possibly, and get the hell out of there!

All this fantasizing, contemplating, looking, shadowing, dreaming, and thinking, which Mr. Darden describes – only happened in Mr. Darden's own head. Maybe the former prosecutor could benefit from a few visits with the psychologist, Dr. Jennifer Ameli, whom Nicole allegedly was consulting prior to her murder.

Again, if Christopher Darden is right, and Nicole indeed was awaiting her lover – why would she grab a knife in fear?

And even more strange, if Mr. Darden is correct, and Nicole was so scared that she grabbed a knife to defend herself from some imaginary danger outside, which she couldn't see through the window – why would she put the knife down, before running out into that scary darkness when the buzzer rang?

I must ask – **where is Christoper Darden's sense of logic? Exactly! That's what was missing throughout the prosecution's case. The prosecution's theory lacked completely even the slightest sense of logic. And this, obviously, carried over into Mr. Darden's book.**

Next, I criticize Mr. Darden's theory, that Nicole's lighting candles was a sexual ritual indicating that she was *"ready to be taken"*! My ninety four year old grandmother lit some candles the other day – for heavens sake! What's wrong with you, Mr. Darden?

Even the fact that Nicole had been so busy the entire evening that she hadn't had time to change clothes, is construed by Mr. Darden in a sexual direction! According to Mr. Darden, Nicole wore her **"sexy black dress,"** in expectation of a lover.

Nicole's dress was not "sexy" to tempt a male lover! It was the dress she had worn during her daughter's, Sydney's, dance recital at school that day; and later, to dinner, together with her parents – Sydney's **grandparents**! Christopher Darden's insinuation is ludicrous. Again, what's wrong with you, Mr. Darden?

Furthermore, Mr. Darden's interpretation of Nicole's behavior indicates that he must know next to nothing about female psychology!

Not that I know that much about it either, although I majored in psychology. But I know something about **women!** If Mr. Darden's book is representative of his knowledge about women, then I stake my reputation against his in this field. My female readers must be the judges with respect to this. If I am wrong, you tell me, and I shall accept that! Now let me explain:

Nicole's and O.J.'s, then 9 year old, daughter, Sydney, had a dance recital at her school that afternoon. This was a big event, not only for Sydney, but also for her family, socially. Nicole's entire family were there, together with countless of their friends, and neighbors.

Bachelors like Mr. Darden, and even many fathers, think everything takes care of itself in a home with children. Fathers only have to come home from work, sit down and eat, play with the children for a while, and then turn on the evening news.

By some magic, the beds are always made, and dirty clothes find their own way to the washing machine and from there back into everyone's closets!

Mr. Darden may think that all Nicole had to do – just like O.J. – was to show up at Sydney's dance recital and applaud.

My female readers, however, especially mothers, readily understand that such an event takes a lot of planning and preparation.

They know how Sydney must have been all exited that entire morning – getting ready – dressing up – rehearsing at home in front of a mirror – grabbing some breakfast or a snack – talking to her girlfriends on the phone – while Nicole scrambled to sew the last stitches in Sydney's outfit – cleared the breakfast table – collected Sydney's breakfast plate from the couch – and her milk glass from the table by the telephone – made sure that Sydney's younger brother, Justin, did not feel left out and neglected – and that he was getting properly dressed as well – tucked his shirt back in after he had been somersaulting on Nicole's bed – wiped the chocolate milk from his lips and nose – did the dishes – picked up some toys – re-tied Justin's shoelaces – yelled at Sydney to get off the phone, in case her grandmother called etc., etc.

Mr. Darden may not understand this. But mothers know that I could have gone on and on, for ever. Amidst it all, Nicole must get ready herself.

Then there was the recital. Afterwards, the reception, or

gathering of friends and family outside the school – everyone neatly dressed and celebrating. O.J. was there too – happy proud, smiling, hugging and being hugged by his children, by Nicole, and by members of her family. Later, there was the dinner with Nicole's family and some friends at the Mezzaluna Restaurant. And after that, it was over to *"Ben and Jerry's"* for some ice cream for the kids.

Bam–bam–bam–bam ... one thing after the other, the entire day!

Finally, Nicole and the children were home, alone. But Nicole's duties were not over. Now she needed to spend some quality time with her children. And then it was time to get the children to bed. It was **9:30 pm**. But Nicole could not relax yet. She had to pick up after the children, put away the dishes, etc. etc.

At last, Nicole was alone and able to relax and think about herself for a change. It was **10:20**. She knew what she had been looking forward to the last couple of hours:

> fill her bathtub with warm water, light some candles by the tub, get out of the tight black dress she had worn the entire day, lower herself into the warm clean water and close her eyes ...!

She wasn't *"ready to be taken,"* as prosecutor Darden wrote! That is typical male chauvinistic, stereotype thinking! No woman wants to *"be taken"* in the condition she must have been in at that moment!

The bachelor, Christopher Darden, may fantasize about women in this manner, believing that all a woman is thinking about is to *"be taken"* by a man, as soon as the children are tucked away! But he shouldn't suggest that O.J. who had lived with Nicole for 16-17 years, knew that little about his own ex-wife!

If Nicole had expected her **lover** at that moment, and she was *"ready to be taken,"* as Christopher Darden fantasizes about, then she must have planned for the two of them to just rip each other's clothes off and jump straight into the bathtub! Otherwise the water would soon cool off.

Ladies! Tell me! Is it likely, as Mr. Darden so confidently suggests, that Nicole would have been ready for an intimate bath with her lover – without any hugging, caressing, and intimate foreplay first?

OK. So maybe she planned to make out for a few minutes on the sofa in the living room, before the two of them went skinny dipping!

Again, I have to ask my female readers for advice.

Nicole was wearing the same tight dress she had worn all day, and presumably the same underwear. It had been a long and strenuous summer day. She had perspired, as anyone would have done. She had not showered the entire day, obviously.

Would Nicole **even have contemplated** getting intimate with a lover in her condition, before she had taken a bath – **by herself** – brushed her teeth, changed into clean fresh clothes or a gown, and put on some perfume?

I doubt it. But I am a man. Maybe Mr. Darden is right! I'll let my female readers decide whether they believe Nicole was waiting for her lover, as Mr. Darden suggests, or **she was getting ready to unwind after a hectic day, with a warm bath – all by herself.**

Here is what I believe was on Nicole's mind. She probably skipped out of her shoes the minute she and the children got home, to give her feet some rest.

After the children were put to bed and she had picked up after them and put away the dishes, she filled her bathtub with water, shut the faucet, and lit the candles by the side of the bathtub. She was ready to get out of her dress and into the bathtub. But she hadn't started to undress yet. The reason was that she was expecting Ron to stop by to drop off her mother's eyeglasses.

Nicole's mother had forgotten her eyeglasses at the Mezzaluna

Restaurant earlier that evening. Nicole had called the restaurant. They had found the eyeglasses, and Ron Goldman, a waiter, had been kind enough to offer to drop them off at Nicole's home at around 10:30.

But Ron was not Nicole's lover. Ron's friend testified that Ron and he had already made plans to go out that night. So even **if** Ron and Nicole had been lovers, Ron would probably have told Nicole over the phone, that he couldn't stay that evening.

The knife on the kitchen counter had nothing to do with Nicole's imagined fear, as Mr. Darden suggests. It just happened to be there. If Nicole pulled out a knife in fear, why would she leave it on the kitchen counter and come running out to open the gate?

This is just a wild guess, but perhaps she had just removed her cup of ice cream from the freezer. Then she brought out the knife to cut open the ice cream cup, so she could put the ice cram in a bowl with some fruit salad, and enjoy it while she relaxed in the bathtub. But the murderer called before she had time to do it.

Anyway, Nicole was looking forward to her bath, all by herself. She was just waiting for Ron to drop off the eyeglasses. When the murderer rang the buzzer by the gate, Nicole was convinced it was Ron.

Specifically, because Nicole did **not** want a visit by Ron – since she was anxious to take a bath by herself – she decided to run down and meet Ron by the gate. Down there it was much easier for her not to invite Ron in, but just thank him for bringing the glasses over, and excuse herself.

Had Nicole let Ron through the gate and met him by her door, it would be more difficult not to show her appreciation by inviting him in for a cup of coffee or something.

Tragically, it wasn't Ron who rang the buzzer by the gate. It was the murderer. He had no idea that Ron was just a block or two away. The murderer attacked Nicole and killed her, as I shall describe it in a later chapter. **Then** Ron showed up, so the murderer had to kill him, too.

Nicole's appearance and actions during the final minutes of her life did not suggest **anything** of what Christopher Darden fantasizes about in his book! His fantasy about Nicole's final minutes is nonsense. That makes his theory about O.J nonsense, too.

Doesn't Christopher Darden know better? Or perhaps he does – because he, too, has been sucked into this conspiracy and the cover-up, through his loyalty to his colleagues? Perhaps that is what he eludes to in the title of his book – ***"In Contempt"***!

CHAPTER 23

The Time Of Death

Although I have not yet described the murders, in details, it is appropriate at this point to say something about **the time of death**, since I have just discussed **Nicole's last minutes in the former chapter.**

An important clue in solving a murder case is the time of death. Often the exact time of death can not be established. Investigators should, however, always do their utmost to establish the time of death as accurately as possible. Knowing the accurate time of death can break or uphold a suspects alibi.

Of course, by **not** establishing an accurate time of death, the investigators can sometimes include as suspects people who would have been excluded if the time of death had been accurately determined.

Realizing today, how the LAPD investigators – and possibly even the prosecutors – in the Simpson case, cheated, lied, perjured themselves, tampered with the evidence, planted evidence, fabricated false evidence, tried to deceive everyone with false theories and phony demonstrations, etc. – I would not be the least bit surprised if the investigators also, **deliberately,** neglected to determine the exact time of Nicole's and Ron's deaths.

By keeping the "window of opportunity" as wide as possible, they could destroy O.J.'s chances of establishing an alibi.

Everything indicated that the murders occurred between 10:30 and 10:50 pm, but I am just making a point. Suppose, for instance, that the time of death could have been established accurately to between 10:45 and 11:00. That would have made it impossible for

O.J. to get back to Rockingham, shower, get dressed, get rid of the knife, the shoes, and the clothes, and be outside again by the time the limo driver saw him at 10:55.

So, rather than establishing the time of death as accurately as possible – thereby, perhaps, providing O.J. with an alibi – the investigators **purposely** left open a **wider** window of opportunity, by saying that the death could have occurred some time between 10:00 and 11:00. As a result, even if O.J. had an alibi, the investigators would render it worthless!

In the Simpson case, determining the exact time of death could have been essential. O.J. didn't have a solid alibi for the time of the murders, other than saying he was home alone, getting ready to go to Chicago. A witness who heard Ron and the murderer argue, set the time to between 10:35 and 10:40 pm.

As it turned out, O.J.'s **real** "window of opportunity" is cut so narrow that he really didn't have time to commit the murders. It is astonishing that the jurors in the civil case did not take this into consideration.

One of Nicole's neighbors, Robert Heidstra was a central witness for the plaintiffs in the civil trial. He testified that he heard the murderer and Ron "argue" (*"Hey – hey – hey"*) at about 10:35-10:40 pm. He saw what is presumed to be the murderer's white sports utility car, speed away from the murder scene at around 10:40 to 10:45.

There is – at least – a **5 minutes** drive from Bundy to Rockingham. At Rockingham, O.J. – if he were the murderer – would have needed **another minute** to park his car, get out, open his gate, and walk behind his house, where he allegedly dropped the right murder glove at the same time as he thumped on Kato's wall.

Consequently, under no circumstances – even if he were the murderer – could O.J. have gotten back to Rockingham and thumped on Kato's wall until **10:46 to 10:51 at the earliest**.

However, there is **irrefutable** testimony and physical evidence (phone records) that Kato Kaelin heard the heavy thumps on his wall sometime between **10:40 and 10:42!** You see, Kato was talking to his friend on the phone when he heard the thumps.

Consequently, there is no way O.J. could have murdered Nicole and Ron in time to return to the back of his house by the time Kato heard the thumps on his wall. Hence, O.J. could not have murdered Nicole and Ron.

There is yet another irrefutable proof that O.J. is innocent. How many times must I prove this, before people begin to understand that O.J. is innocent, and that someone tried to frame him?

How could the jurors in the civil case not understand this? A second grader can add 6 minutes to the time 10:40 and realize that it would bring us past 10:42! The counsels for the plaintiffs realized that too! **So they put pressure on Kato and made him change his testimony from the criminal trial and the pretrial hearings**. Hence, in the civil trial, Kato claimed the thumps he heard might have occurred between 10:45 and 10:50! That's how the plaintiffs cheated! There was no doubt about Kato's original testimony during the criminal trial. And his phone records supported his original testimony. The thumps occurred between 10:40 and 10:42!

Another possibility is, of course, that O.J. did not cause those thumps on his wall. But then, these jurors should be able to explain what, or who, cased the thumps on Kato's wall, since O.J. could not have murdered Nicole and Ron at the time Robert Heidstra heard the *"Hey – hey – hey"* – and later saw a white car speed away. Not if he was behind his house, thumping on Kato's wall at the time Kato's phone record showed that the thumps occurred.

The investigators couldn't know how narrow O.J.'s window of opportunity really was, when they first came to Bundy to investigate the murders. There were so many things the investigators could have done to establish the time of death. When they didn't do any of them, it must have been **deliberate**. Let's look at some of the things they could have done, but didn't do.

First of all the investigators didn't allow the medical

examiner to examine the bodies until some 11 hours after the murders!

The coroner was notified rather early, but was told, specifically, to stay away until the investigators, Detective Vannatter & Co., called and said that the coroner could come to the murder scene and examine the bodies! That was a blatant breach of the investigators and the coroner's specific instructions!

It is just incredible! At the time the coroner arrived, all she could say was that the time of death occurred between 9:45 pm, when Nicole called Mezzaluna Restaurant, and 11:50 pm, when her body was discovered!

We didn't even need a coroner to determine that! In spite of this, the medical examiner, Dr. Lakshmanan Sathyavagiswaran, later, had the nerve to tell the jury, during his testimony, that even if he had lived across the street, and had been called to the murder scene right after the bodies were discovered, he could not have determined the time of death with any more accuracy.

If the medical examiner had been called immediately, and he had inserted a thermometer into the liver of, say Nicole, he would have gotten a specific reading of her body temperature at that time.

What the medical examiner was trying to tell the jury, was that the body temperature drops rather slowly, and since he couldn't know Nicole's exact body temperature when she was killed, he couldn't have said how long she had been dead when he, hypothetically, might have measured her liver temperature.

The medical examiner is not honest. He knows better! He knows that you don't simply insert a thermometer into the liver of a deceased, get a reading, and pull the thermometer out again. That's what he tried to feed the jury!

Rather, you take several temperature readings at fixed intervals. You plot the readings in a graph. Based on a number of readings, at different times, you can reconstruct a complete graph and a function of Nicole's gradual loss of body temperature.

The body temperature drops faster shortly after the time of death, than later. Additional factors, such as the temperature of the atmosphere, Nicole's bodyweight, the rate of temperature loss at the time of the first temperature reading etc., enable scientists to determine fairly accurately at what time Nicole's body temperature was at its estimated highest – in other words, at what time she was killed.

I don't say the estimate would be accurate to within five minutes, but it would have been a heck of a lot better than to arrive eleven hours later and say that she died between the time someone last spoke to her, and the time her dead body was found! What kind of mockery is that?

There was water in the bathtub when the police arrived. But the plug was leaking, so the tub gradually emptied.

It was obvious – to me at least – that Nicole was just about ready to take a bath. She wouldn't have lit the candles by the bathtub, and shut the faucet unless the tub was full and she was ready to enter. The only thing Nicole was waiting for was for Ron to drop off her mother's eyeglasses. But she probably expected him any moment. That's why she started to fill the tub. That's when the murderer called instead.

Accordingly, Nicole had probably shut the faucet only seconds, or minutes, before she was killed. By checking the sidewalls in the tub, forensic experts could probably have determined how full the tub had been. Therefore, if someone had marked off the water level at a certain time, the investigators could have refilled the tub and checked how long it would take for the water level to drop down to the "mark." That way they would have a fairly accurate clock for when the tub was full. That would, most likely, have been just seconds or minutes before Nicole was killed.

There were lit candles by the side of the tub. Most likely, Nicole didn't light those candles until she shut off the faucet and was ready to take her bath.

Assuming the candles were new, the investigators could have extinguished the candles at a certain time.

Then they could have purchased identical candles, placed them on one side of a double armed scale. On the other side of the scale they could put Nicole's partly burned out candles. The investigators could have lit the new candles, and checked the time when the scale tipped (which would indicate that the new candles had burnt as long as Nicole's old ones).

Similar experiments could have been performed with the melting ice cream that was found in a cup on the kitchen counter.

The ice cream was purchased about 8:30 pm. The children, of course, ate their ice creams right away. But Nicole probably wanted to wait, and eat hers after the children were in bed, and she were relaxing in her bathtub. So she put her ice cream cup in the freezer, and took it out just as she was getting ready for her bath – in other words minutes before she was killed.

The ice cream was still not fully melted by the time the first LAPD officers arrived at the murder scene. This could have been another important clue, which could have indicated a later, rather than an earlier time of death.

A melting experiment with such a cup of ice cream being removed from Nicole's freezer, might have provided another clue to the time of death – again, possibly, giving O.J. an alibi!

Nicole's stomach content was not saved.

Since we know what time Nicole had her last meal, her stomach contents could have provided another clue for estimating the time of death. The more digested her last meal was, the later the time of death. Again, this clue could have supported O.J.'s alibi.

There were so many clues that could have aided the investigators in determining the time of death. Neither clue was very accurate. But because the investigators could have used so many different clues in this case, the accuracy of each single clue was less important.

Yet, **the investigators "blew" every single one of the clues** that could have determined a more accurate time of death!

Knowing that the investigators also broke every other rule in the book, and obviously tried to frame O.J. with, at least, some, falsely fabricated evidence, I am tempted to believe that the failure to determine the time of death as accurately as possible was deliberate.

Isn't such a determination essential to solving a murder mystery? And if so, why would the investigators **not** try to determine the time of death as accurately as possible.

Here we need to **distinguish between** murder investigations **where the police have a strong suspect**, and murder investigations **where the police have no clues as to the identity of the murderer**.

Suppose someone had found a decapitated body alongside a deserted road, and no identification was immediately possible. In that case, determining the time of death, as accurately as possible, could be one of the few leads the police had **in their search for a suspect!** In such a case **they would do all they could to establish as accurately as possible the time of death.**

However, the police immediately suspected O.J. of having murdered Nicole. They weren't stumbling around in the darkness searching for a suspect. Rather, their objective was, from the very first minute, to gather evidence against, and secure a conviction of O.J.

In that situation, a narrow time-frame – a smaller window of opportunity – could only benefit O.J. That was the situation at Bundy on the morning of June 13. That is why **the police had a definite motive for not determining the exact time of death.**

Obviously, they had the right idea in this respect, since the timeline turned out to be one of O.J.'s best arguments, and the defense and the prosecutors/plaintiffs eventually ended up bickering over one or two minutes one way or the other.

Do you now see the significance of determining the time of death as accurately as possible – or not doing it?

The investigators' disregard for this important evidence, reflected their intentions and supports my theory that they also fabricated false evidence against O.J., and kept certain evidence out – if that evidence was beneficial to O.J. – and that they lied when testifying about it.

CHAPTER 24

The "Execution" of Nicole

Naturally, what I describe in this book is a **theory** only. Nobody, except the murderer himself, knows exactly what happened at 875 South Bundy Drive on June 12, 1994 between 10:30 and 10:45 pm.

Other people like myself, can only speculate. That is what the prosecutors did when they presented their criminal case against O.J. That's what the counsels for the plaintiffs did when they presented their civil suit against O.J. And that's what O.J. and his defense attorneys have been doing in their efforts to rebut their opponents' accusations.

In an effort to solve the Simpson murder mystery, we must all **"speculate"** and **"hypothesize."** The credibility of our various speculations and hypotheses will ultimately decide the public's final verdict. But even that final verdict, if it comes, may not represent the truth.

I believe my theory represents the truth. But I cannot be 100% sure. However, **I think it makes a heck of a lot more sense than anything I have heard from either the prosecutors or the counsels for the plaintiffs** in the continued O.J. Simpson Saga.

Since a man's (and his children's) **life, reputation, welfare, and future are at stake, I feel that I have an obligation to express the theory that follows.**

As I mentioned earlier, Detective Fuhrman might have had an ongoing relationship with Nicole, visiting her from time to time. That is how he learned about O.J.'s preference for Italian shoes, and his owning a pair of Isotoner Aris gloves.

Nicole may have given Fuhrman a pair of Isotoner Aris gloves

– the murder gloves – which she perhaps had bought and kept as a present for friends whenever she, suddenly or unexpectedly, needed it, and not for any particular occasion. Or Fuhrman himself might have purchased both the shoes and the gloves for the purpose of framing O.J.

Hence, the bloody shoe prints are not at all as incriminating to O.J. as his adversaries claim – even if it should turn out that O.J. owned a pair of Bruno Magli shoes.

There was nothing unusual about Fuhrman having a relationship with Nicole, in spite of hating her strongly enough to kill her. Fuhrman's mind is that of a racist. So let us look back on our country's dark period of slavery.

Plantation owners from the South might have despised their black slaves, whipped and flogged them, and called them "niggers" during the day. Yet, the slave owners would frequently use their female slaves as mistresses for the night. Aside from the sexual satisfaction, such relationships reassured the slave owners of their own power and superiority over their slaves, and instilled in their slaves that they were at the mercy of their slave masters.

We may see a contradiction in a relationship between Fuhrman and his victim, but Fuhrman wouldn't, since this, for him, was **not** a normal relationship based on love, equality, and mutual respect. Rather, his alleged relationship with Nicole was that of a racist neo-Nazi.

We saw the same throughout the Nazis' reign of terror in Europe during World War II. In their death camps the Nazis liquidated 6 million Jews. Yet they didn't hesitate to send thousands of young Jewish women and girls to military brothels. There nazi officers and soldiers could enjoy sexual encounters with these young women who otherwise, in the nazis' opinion, weren't even worthy of a life! The Japanese military forces were hardly any less terrifying in their domains during the war.

It is said that rape is as much a demonstration of power, as it is a demonstration of sexuality. Hence, if Fuhrman hated Nicole and O.J., having a relationship with Nicole, if possible, might be one way for him to reassure himself of his own superiority, and maintain his disdain and hatred for interracial couples.

If Nicole and Fuhrman had an ongoing relationship, Nicole might have told Fuhrman about O.J.'s upcoming business trip to Chicago. The trip was scheduled 5 weeks in advance, and "everybody" seemed to know that O.J. was going to Chicago on a late flight on June 12.

This might have been the opportunity Fuhrman had been waiting for. Sunday night, June 12, 1994, at 10:30 pm, was the ideal time for the murder of Nicole.

Fuhrman made the necessary arrangements in preparation for the murders. He sharpened and polished the knife he would use. Then he gathered his accessories – the Aris gloves, the Bruno Magli shoes, a dark blue-black coverall, a weapons belt, the knife, a pair of latex gloves, and a plastic bag with a knit ski cap. He put everything in a box and placed the box in the back of his car.

Fuhrman might have made arrangements with Nicole to see her Sunday night. Fuhrman might have called Nicole, or stopped by her home shortly before the murders, checking to see if she was home, assuring himself that O.J.'s plans had not changed, making certain that Nicole did not expect any visitors, and, of course, having Nicole agreeing to Fuhrman coming back later – after the children, assumably, were asleep, and Nicole had finished her bath – perhaps around 11:15 pm.

A witness, a neighbor of Nicole's reported that Nicole embraced a man outside her home at about 10:00 pm on the night of the murders. This man has never been identified. He could have been Fuhrman.

If this "mystery man" was Fuhrman, he might have suggested that he come back around 11:15. Nicole's response to that might have been that she was not expecting anybody and would be home alone (except for the children, of course, but they were already in bed).

It is true that Nicole expected Ron Goldman to stop by and deliver her mother's eyeglasses around 10:30. **But Nicole had no intention of inviting Ron in.** So he would not be around when

Nicole expected Fuhrman to come back. Therefore, she saw no reason to mention him to Fuhrman.

Fuhrman, however, **couldn't** wait till 11:15. **He had to time the murder of Nicole to shortly before O.J.'s departure to the airport.** The reason he stopped by Nicole, or called her, was just to reassure himself that she was alone, and that she didn't expect anyone that evening.

Nor did Fuhrman have to wait until 11:15, because he already knew that the children were in bed, and that Nicole was alone. And Fuhrman **thought,** at least, that he knew Nicole wasn't expecting any visitors. So instead of waiting until 11:15, he drove to a secluded area not far from Nicole's home. There he parked and changed into his murder outfit.

First he put on the dark coverall and the pair of Bruno Magli shoes. He strapped on his belt with his gun on the right side, his razor sharp knife sheathed on his left side, and his police badge in his belt. He stuck the plastic bag with the knit cap in his right pocket. Then he put on the pair of latex gloves, to avoid shedding hairs or fibers from his hands inside the Isotoner Aris gloves which he put on next. Again, he drove over to Nicole's home.

The time was 10:33. Fuhrman parked his car behind Nicole's condominium, in the alley, near Dorothy, a block away. Then he **walked around the block** to the front (east) gate at Bundy Drive.

There was a narrow, concrete, tiled walkway that led from the rear (west) gate by the alley behind Nicole's condo, to Bundy Drive in front of the building. The walkway led past the entrance to Nicole's apartment, onwards to four concrete, tiled steps leading down to a small 3 ft x 3 1/2 ft tiled "patio" directly inside the front (east) gate at Bundy Drive.

Fuhrman approached the front gate from the outside. The gate was warped from the latest earthquake. Sometimes when visitors called, Nicole had to go out and open the gate from the inside. Fuhrman knew this. So his plan was to ring the buzzer by the gate, but not enter if and when Nicole buzzed the electric gate opener.

Hence, Nicole would have to come down to the gate to help open it from the inside. The gate was almost hidden by the excessive foliage, so she couldn't see from her condo who was at the gate.

Fuhrman wanted Nicole to come down to the gate, so he could kill her there, instead of inside her condo where the children might wake up if there was a scream or a short struggle or some other noise when he killed Nicole.

Fuhrman wanted Nicole to come down to the gate, so he could knock her unconscious – **from behind, with his gun** – after she had opened the gate and turned around to lead the way back up the steps – rather than attack her while **facing** her in her doorway.

> **In my opinion, what I am about to explain, is an extremely important point, and one of the many keys to proving that O.J. did not kill Nicole in a jealous rage, as the prosecutors and plaintiffs argued.**

What you are about to learn through the next few chapters, holds the very key to solving this murder mystery.

To the best of my knowledge, I am the only one who has understood the significance of what you are about to learn – or if the investigators understood it, they concealed it, in order to frame O.J.!

Fuhrman had thought about everything! **Nothing related to this murder was left to chance!**

With Nicole standing in her doorway, Fuhrman might not be able knock her unconscious by surprise with a blow to her head –the most effective way – namely sideways on her chin.

Because of the door frame, and with Nicole standing **inside** the door opening, and Fuhrman on the **outside**, he could not get any **"leverage"** for a blow to her head, there by the door. Nicole might even dodge the blow, and scream for help.

However, if Nicole had to come down to the gate, Fuhrman could, by surprise, strike her from behind after she had opened the gate and turned around to lead the way back up the steps.

Fuhrman removed the knit cap from the plastic bag and put the bag back in his pocket. He unbuttoned his revolver's safety strap, and pulled out the gun. Then he wrapped the knit cap around the revolver's handle.

According to his plan, Fuhrman rang the gate's buzzer, and waited for Nicole.

Nicole, meanwhile, did not expect Fuhrman – yet. She was sure the caller were Ron (dropping off the eyeglasses Nicole's mother had forgotten at the Mezzaluna Restaurant).

Nicole had already filled her bathtub with water and lighted the candles by the side of the tub. She still had her black dress on, since she was waiting for Ron to stop by. But she had kicked off her shoes as soon as she returned home with the children.

If Nicole and Fuhrman had **not** made arrangements to meet, say at 11:15, Nicole simply wanted to accept the glasses from Ron as quickly as possible, and get back inside to her long awaited bath.

And if Nicole and Fuhrman **had** agreed to meet, say at 11:15, Nicole still just wanted to receive the glasses from Ron, and get back inside as quickly as possible, so she could take her bath and be ready by the time she expected Fuhrman.

Hence, under no circumstances did she intend to invite Ron in. However, since Ron definitely was doing Nicole a favor by dropping off the eyeglasses, it was a bit impolite – or difficult, at least – for Nicole **not** to say:

"I really appreciate this, Ron ... Would you like to come in – for a cup of coffee ... or is it too late ...?"

To make it easier for her **not** to invite Ron in – in spite of the kindness he demonstrated by bringing the eyeglasses over – Nicole had already decided to run out and meet Ron by the gate, as soon as he rang the buzzer – rather than buzzing the gate open and meeting him by her door. There by the gate she could more easily say:

> *"Thank you! I really appreciate this. By the way, excuse me*
> *for meeting you out here – barefoot and all. But it has been*
> *such a hectic day, and I am so tired. I was just about to take a*
> *bath – the faucet is still running! ... I'll see you at the*
> *Mezzaluna some day soon."*

The thing about the faucet would be a "white lie." But it would allow Nicole to give Ron a quick hug – exactly long enough to show her affection and appreciation, but yet, short enough to tell Ron, if he caught on to it, that this was not the time for a visit!

So here is the situation:

> **Fuhrman** had no idea that Ron was just two blocks away. He looked up and down Bundy Drive. There was no one in sight. Quickly he walked the few steps up from the sidewalk to the gate. He kept the gun – handle wrapped in the knit cap – behind his back, rang the buzzer by the gate and waited for Nicole to come down to open the gate. There he intended to strike her down from behind, with a blow from the handle of his gun, padded in the knit cap.
>
> As Nicole lay on the ground, Fuhrman would pull her head back, by her hair, and cut her neck, to create a pool of blood which he could step in, in order to leave bloody Bruno Magli shoeprints – **pointing to O.J.!** This was part of Fuhrman's **"master-plan"**!

> **Nicole** on the other hand, did not expect Fuhrman **yet** – or perhaps not at all that evening. Nicole expected Ron to drop off her mother's eyeglasses. She did not want to feel obligated to invite Ron in, so she had already decided to run down to the gate, to meet Ron there.

Ron was two blocks away. He had no idea what was about to happen to him.

So then Nicole, assuming the caller was Ron, ran down towards the gate to meet Ron – **barefoot** and in her **black dress**. But Ron was not there. Instead, Fuhrman was waiting for her!

Nicole knew Fuhrman, of course. Nicole skipped down the four steps to the small tiled "patio" inside the gate.

Perhaps she had a date with Fuhrman later that night. If so, she would still let him in, even though he came much earlier than expected.

And if she didn't have a date with Fuhrman, she surely recognized him. If Fuhrman, being a detective, told Nicole there was something important and urgent he had to talk to her about, she would, naturally, let him in and lead the way back towards the steps.

Nicole recognized Fuhrman and opened the gate. Nicole said, *"Hi,"* and turned around to lead the way up the steps.

With one long quick step Fuhrman was right behind Nicole, He didn't bother to close the gate.

With the butt end of his gun's handle, padded by the knit cap, he hit Nicole hard, on the upper right side of her head, knocking her unconscious.

As Nicole's knees buckled, Fuhrman grabbed her around her waist and **put her down gently, in the direction she was heading, with her neck over the first step.**

Fuhrman tossed the knit cap underneath some shrubbery in the **alcove, or "niche," adjacent to the north edge of the "patio,"** put the gun back in its holster, and took out his knife.

Five to ten seconds – that is all it took from the moment Fuhrman struck Nicole unconscious, and till **he pulled Nicole's head back by her hair and slit her throat from behind, cutting her neck all the way into the body of her third cervical vertebrae.**

Even though Nicole was **unconscious** and her neck was cut, **her heart continued pumping** blood for up to 20-30 seconds, until the interrupted blood flow, and hence the lack of oxygen, to her brain, caused her to black out and quickly die. As long as her heart continued to beat, her blood would be gushing out through the transected arteries in the gaping wound across her neck.

Fuhrman cut Nicole's neck so severely for two reasons. He was making sure she died. But more importantly, Fuhrman wanted Nicole's blood to flood the **patio**.

Nicole's neck was cut all the way to, and even a little bit into, the bony tissue of the body (frontal part) of her 3rd cervical vertebra. Under any other circumstances this would seem like an **extreme "overkill"!** It was excessive in terms of murdering Nicole. But it was also excessive in terms of simply transecting Nicole's common carotid arteries (the main arteries to the head).

However, this excessive, gaping wound made sense when we view it in relationship to my theory that

> Fuhrman **purposely wanted to spill as much of Nicole's blood as possible** – for the purpose of stepping in this puddle of blood, thereby **deliberately creating bloody Bruno Magli shoeprints**, as well as other blood evidence.

Not only did Fuhrman intend to cut Nicole's common carotid arteries. He also wanted to make sure that the blood gushing from the transected arteries did not end up inside Nicole's body – in her oral cavity, in her windpipe and lungs, and down her throat. Nor did he want Nicole's blood to run down her body and be absorbed by her dress.

Fuhrman wanted Nicole's blood to **"gush out"** from her severed arteries, **as from a faucet,** directly onto the patio! That is probably why he knocked her unconscious, grabbed her hair, bent her head back, and cut her neck way past the common carotid arteries – all the way to her vertebrae – so that he, **unrestricted by tendons and contracted muscles** – could bend her head back, far enough to expose the transected arteries, and allow the blood to gush out, more or less uninterruptedly, onto the **tiled "patio"**.

At some point Fuhrman decided he had enough blood on the patio. Or perhaps Nicole appeared to regain consciousness, causing her to move, and this disturbed Fuhrman. Or perhaps he wanted to disguise his motive for cutting Nicole's neck so severely. He wanted her murder to appear to have been committed in a jealous rage. So he stabbed and cut her repeatedly just before she died. Regardless of the reason, as if in panic he rammed the knife deeply into Nicole's neck several times. The loss of blood finally killed her.

I know it sounds gruesome, and it was gruesome! But what I have explained is a much more logical explanation than those of the prosecutors or the plaintiffs, as to why someone would cut Nicole's neck in this extremely excessive, but at the same time deliberate manner.

> Nicole's neck wasn't cut so severely simply **to kill her!** Nicole's neck was cut so severly **in order to fill the patio with her blood – so the murderer could frame O.J. with bloody Bruno Magli shoeprints!**
>
> Everything indicated that – and **I will later prove it beyond any doubt whatsoever.**

Whom do my readers find most likely to have killed Nicole in such a deliberately gruesome manner?

> The father of Nicole's children – trying to frame himself?
>
> Or the racist describing himself through *"The Fuhrman Tapes,"* and wanting to harm an inter-racial couple, and frame Nicole's African-American ex-husband?

I asked you to keep a bookmark at my quotes from *"The Fuhrman Tapes."* If you don't remember the quotes, I urge you to go back and review them before you answer the question above!

CHAPTER 25

Questions Unanswered

Nicole's head was near severed. Not even an insane murderer would have cut Nicole's neck like that, **unless there was a particular reason for it**! Regardless of O.J.'s feelings for Nicole, there is no way he would, or could, have cut Nicole's neck in such an extreme, grotesque manner – even if he had wanted to kill her!

Suppose a murderer just wanted to kill a woman with a knife – to cover up a rape, or to rob her. So he rams his knife into the woman's neck or heart, and she dies.

This is the MO of a murderer with no particular plan, except to kill his victim.

Next, suppose the murderer hates the woman, intensely! He is overly jealous and acts in a rage, and in addition he is under the influence of drugs. OK. So he confronts his victim, shouts at her, to let her know how much he hates her, and that he is going to kill her. He swipes at her with his knife, and eventually cuts her and stabs her, repeatedly, all over her body.

This is the MO of a murderer in an extremely vicious and, perhaps, jealous rage.

Finally, suppose the woman's neck and body were not stabbed, slashed, and cut, in a vicious, violent, **unorganized,** manner, but instead, her neck was cut in **one single, fairly clean, obviously deliberate, cut**! The cut went all the way into one of her vertebrae – the woman's head was **almost severed,** but not quite! She also had some other cuts, but they did not demonstrate the typically unorganized rage I mentioned in the second example.

This last MO does **not** reflect a murderer **out of control,** acting under the influence of drugs, or in a violent, jealous rage. Had that been the disposition of the murderer, and he had **almost** severed the woman's head, he would probably have gone "all the way" – or at least held her by her hair and cut her neck all the way around. In addition, the murderer would have stabbed and slashed the victim, viciously, all over her body.

Rather, this last M.O. which reflected the murder of Nicole, pointed to **a murderer in full control, acting exactly according to a deliberate plan.**

Whatever other wounds Nicole suffered – in addition to the major neck wound – were probably just the murderer's **deliberate** attempt to **cover up** the **real** purpose of that major neck wound.

The excessive manner in which Nicole's neck was cut, is consistent with my theory that the cutting of Nicole's neck was not just a way of killing her, but part of Fuhrman's deliberate "arterial phlebotomy" (draining of blood). He needed to cut most of Nicole's muscles tendons and organs in the front of her neck to be able to force her head back, open up the wound, and let the blood flow freely from her transected arteries onto the tiled patio.

Fuhrman wasn't merely out to kill Nicole. He was simultaneously, purposely setting up the investigators to believe O.J. were the perpetrator, by leaving bloody shoeprints from Bruno Magli shoes.

The manner in which Nicole was murdered, clearly suggested that this was not simply a killing. **It was a killing performed in a particular manner, as part of a deliberate plan to create a bloody murder scene.**

My readers know how hard it is to cut a **fresh** fish, or a chicken, or a raw steak, even with a fairly sharp kitchen knife. You have to cut several times, sometimes "sawing" back and forth! So even a brand new hunting knife could not have cut Nicole's neck, all the way into her vertebra, in one clean cut! **The murderer's knife must have been almost as sharp as a surgeon's scalpel!**

This again points to a perpetrator who must have planned and prepared for the murder in the most minute details, knowing exactly what he wanted to do, from the moment he parked his car in the alley, and till he had finally planted the second murder glove behind O.J.'s house.

The murderer deliberately made the crime scenes appear messy, sloppy, and **"nonchalant."** But nothing the murderer did was nonchalant! Everything about the murders supports my theory.

Just take a little detail like this: The murderer, obviously approached Nicole by ringing the buzzer by the front (Bundy Drive) gate. But he had already parked his car in the alley behind the house! So although he approached by the Bundy gate, and killed Nicole there, he had **already planned** to exit the murder scene in the opposite direction – through the rear gate! And some say this was a killing committed impulsively, by O.J. – in a jealous rage!

The murderer didn't wear a knit ski cap in the middle of the summer – to disguise himself, or to keep his ears warm – only to "lose" the cap at the murder scene **and not pick it up again!** To suggest that is absurd! More than that – it is disingenuous!

Instead, the murderer brought the cap along to pad his gun when he struck Nicole from behind, so the gun's handle should not leave an identifiable imprint in the skin on Nicole's head. But more importantly, he brought the cap along, and tossed it on the ground, to give the investigators the **opportunity** to plant O.J.'s hairs on it later.

O.J. didn't **"lose"** one glove at Bundy – without picking it up – and then bring the other glove to Rockingham – **by accident** – only to **"lose"** the other glove there, behind the house! The investigators must be out of their minds, to suggest something that ludicrous!

And even if O.J., allegedly, were so sloppy and absentminded – why didn't he leave a single bloody fingerprint anywhere – in spite of, allegedly, losing his glove without noticing it? And why is there no trace anywhere, of the murderer's bloody clothes, bloody shoes, and bloody murder knife?

Regardless of who killed Nicole and Ron – he got away with murder! He did, indeed! That's not something you do **by accident!** At least not if you are up against the combined resources of the LAPD, the FBI, the Los Angeles DA's office, and 200 million sets of American "private eyes"!

> The obvious reason Nicole's and Ron's murderer is not behind bars, is that this murderer is **not** an impulsive, sloppy, careless, and desperately jealous ex-husband – but **a cold blooded, clever executioner – well skilled in murder investigations!**

He had a "perfect" plan, he was well prepared, and he knew exactly what he wanted to do – in minute detail!

Nicole's and Ron's murderer knew exactly what items and evidence he **wanted** to leave behind – and exactly what he did **not** want to leave behind!

This crime was from beginning to end meticulously set up to frame O.J.

Fuhrman kept Nicole alive for close to 20-30 seconds. Nicole was also stabbed or cut several times in her head and neck. It is hard to determine precisely whether some of these injuries were inflicted before or after the major injury to her neck.

Most likely, they were inflicted **after** Nicole's neck was cut, but **before** she died. I believe those stab wounds were inflicted after Fuhrman had determined he had enough blood on the ground, and wanted to end Nicole's life as soon as possible and simultaneously, perhaps, make her murder appear to have been committed in a jealous rage.

Or perhaps the other stab and slash wounds were created to cover up the, otherwise, obvious purpose behind the major cut to Nicole's neck. What is important, however, is that the cutting of Nicole's neck was the murderer's main objective.

A clear indication that Nicole's murder was committed in such a way as to frame O.J. with deliberately planted bloody Bruno Magli shoeprints is this:

> **Nicole was obviously struck absolutely unconscious, with a hard blow from a heavy object like a gun, padded in a soft material. I will return to the details later.**

Now, if the murderer was in a jealous rage, hated Nicole, and wanted her to **suffer** – he would **not** have knocked her **unconscious before he cut her neck!** Rather, he would have confronted her. If so, Nicole would not have turned her back to the murderer until he was outside the gate and she had locked the gate behind him.

If it is any comfort to her parents, to her children, and to O.J. – **Nicole did not suffer! She was unconscious from the moment she was hit in the head, and until she died!** Let me prove that!

> OK! Nicole's right leg was forcibly lodged underneath the fence. But it was in no way "stuck"! Sharp points on the underside of the fence caused a **long,** cut up the length of the back of Nicole's leg, severely enough to cause the wound to **bleed.** That means the wound was inflicted before she died. Had Nicole been **conscious** she would have felt a fairly strong pain in her leg, and therefore never stuck her leg underneath the fence in the first place.
>
> And if she had regained consciousness, she would have pulled her leg away from underneath the fence.
>
> **The murderer** must have pulled Nicole's unconscious body backwards, causing her leg to slide underneath the fence. **Why** the murderer did this, I will explain later. At this point, we should simply understand that Nicole **herself** would not have stuck her leg underneath the fence if she was **conscious**. And she **could** not have done it if she was **un-conscious**! The murderer caused this injury to Nicole's leg – and she must have been unconscious when it occurred.

The reason Nicole didn't resist, or bend her leg to avoid the sharp points underneath the fence, was that she was deeply unconscious from the severe blow to her head, and therefore, had no idea what the murderer did to her.

Obviously, the murderer had no intention of making Nicole suffer. Not that the murderer deliberately wanted Nicole **not** to suffer. He just didn't care. He simply wanted to knock her unconscious, **by surprise**, so she shouldn't escape, resist, or scream, when he cut her neck and killed her. Whether she suffered or not, was of no concern to the murderer!

> **But since the murderer had no intention, at least, of making Nicole suffer – why did he create such a bloody mess, when Nicole already lay helplessly unconscious on the ground?**

Why didn't the murderer simply break Nicole's neck, or strangle/choke her, or whack her with the gun a couple of more times in the head, or knock her head against one of the concrete steps, to fracture her skull, after she lay unconsciously on the ground?

If so, the murderer could have walked away after 5-10 seconds – before Ron showed up. Hence, there would not have been a struggle with Ron.

> Accordingly, there would have been **no bloody mess, no bloody shoeprints, no blood drops along those shoeprints or on the rear gate, no bloody Bruno Magli shoes and bloody clothes to get rid of, no cut finger** (remember, though, that O.J. is not the murderer)**, no blood in the Bronco, no blood in O.J.'s driveway, and no bloody murder gloves at Bundy and behind O.J.'s house!**

Isn't it obvious that the murderer **deliberately** created this bloody mess, and **deliberately planted all the evidence he left behind**?

CHAPTER 26

The "Execution" Of Ron

After cutting Nicole's neck and keeping the gaping wound open until he had all the blood he wanted on the patio, Fuhrman wiped off his knife and sheathed it in his belt. Nicole was dead.

Suddenly Fuhrman heard footsteps approaching the gate from the sidewalk along Bundy Drive. It was Ron arriving.

Let me now explain something which the prosecutors have been totally reluctant to discuss even, but which is one of the great mysteries of this murder case.

– Of course, **the murderer would never have initiated the attack on Nicole, if Ron had been present!** At least, not if the murderer were O.J.! What if Ron had yelled and screamed, and then managed to escape?

– Obviously, **Ron did not arrive during the murder of Nicole, either!** If so, Ron would, likewise, have screamed for help, and also, most likely have managed to escape or defend himself.

– Nicole's blood was found underneath Ron's shoes. This indicated that he had stepped in her blood when he arrived, or when he fought with the murderer. **Hence, Ron must have arrived shortly <u>after</u> Nicole was killed!**

There was also a drop of Nicole's blood on top of Ron's shoe. This has led some to believe that Ron was present when the murderer killed Nicole. However, this drop of blood, more likely, dripped from the murderer's hand or knife or shoe, onto Ron's shoe while Ron was still standing. But Nicole was already dead then.

- With Nicole lying dead in a pool of blood – why did Ron approach so calmly and seemingly trustworthily?
- How could the murderer so easily have overpowered Ron?
- Why didn't Ron have the opportunity – or try – to scream for help, flee the scene, keep his distance, or fight off the murderer ?

There is a short walkway of about 20 feet from the sidewalk along Bundy Drive and up to the gate. Right inside the gate were the murderer and Nicole's dead body.

To get to the spot where he was killed – in the "niche" to the right (north) of, and adjacent to the patio – Ron literally had to step over Nicole's dead body!

The walkway from the sidewalk and up to the Bundy gate is so narrow, that Ron would **always** have Nicole's body – **and the murderer – in front of him,** until he eventually must have walked **over Nicole's body** and a step or two to the "north" – into the narrow niche where he was killed.

Hence, **there was no way the murderer could have surprised Ron!** And what the heck was Ron thinking, if he, indeed, walked into that niche on his own initiative?

To anyone who has not heard my theory, it must be a mystery why Ron, seemingly trustworthily, walked silently right into the murderer's open arms, **turned his back to the murderer,** and let himself be executed, without uttering a word, in spite of seeing Nicole's dead body in a pool of blood, right in front of him.

Had Ron seen O.J. or any man – **other than a police officer –** standing over Nicole's bloody body – wearing a **dark knit ski cap** on his head and **bloody leather gloves** on his hands in the middle of the summer, Ron would, of course, have understood, immediately, that **this man had killed Nicole**. Ron would have screamed for help, and kept far away from the murderer.

All due respect to the victims and their families! But don't give me the **nonsense** about **Ron – the "hero" – who fought** to save Nicole! Nicole was stone dead **before Ron arrived!** And Ron did **not** fight to be a hero! **He fought for his own life, because he was attacked.**

As narrow as the walkway is, and Ron approaching the gate from the sidewalk, he would have had the murderer in front of him, until the murderer – somehow – lured Ron into the "niche"!

What was it about the **real** murderer that made Ron act so irrationally that he walked right into the niche and got himself killed?

Everyone with an IQ above 70 should ask themselves:

Why couldn't and didn't Ron back off, or turn around and flee the scene, or scream for help, or stand his ground against the murderer – by the gate, or outside the gate?

Why didn't the prosecutors try to answer this question? As a matter of fact, they did try, but their answers made no sense.

The prosecutors suggested that both Ron and Nicole were present when the murderer attacked. The murderer quickly knocked Nicole unconscious, and then attacked Ron. If that were the case, then Ron would have had plenty of time to jump the murderer from behind and at the same time scream for help – before his neck was cut – defend himself, or even escape. The Bundy gate opened outward, so Ron could have fled east or west! Obviously, the prosecutions's theory was incorrect. Frankly, their theory was **absurd**!

Imagine Ron approaching the gate from the outside and, allegedly, seeing O.J. four feet in front of him, right inside the gate, next to Nicole's body. Ron would have been on the alert.

Unless O.J. had knelt by Nicole's body, sobbing, crying, and urging Ron to run for help, call an ambulance or the police, Ron must have sensed that something was terribly wrong with the entire situation. Under those circumstances Ron would never have fallen victim to an attack by O.J.

What was it about the murderer that made Ron walk up to

the gate, enter through the gate, step over Nicole's bloody body and into the narrow niche, turn his back to the murderer, and allow the murderer, knife in hand, to reach over Ron's shoulder and cut his neck from behind?

This entire scenario would have been so **"unique"** – for lack of a better word – that Ron could not possibly have encountered O.J. there at the murder scene!

It had to be someone special – like an LAPD officer!

According to the medical examiner, Ron's neck was cut from behind, by the perpetrator reaching over Ron's right shoulder. So, how did O.J. – **allegedly** – position himself **behind** Ron?

"Ron, would you please turn around, so I can cut your neck from behind?"

My readers can clearly see that there are serious inconsistencies in the prosecution's theory regarding the M.O. The defense tried to take advantage of this by introducing the **"two killer theory."** Ron could have been held and muffled by one man, while another man stabbed Ron and cut his throat.

Perhaps there were more than one killer at Bundy that night. Perhaps Fuhrman had an accomplice – or two. However, that does not explain how Ron was lured into the "niche." And O.J., at least, could not have trapped Ron like that! There must be a more reasonable explanation – and there is! What caused Ron – so mysteriously – to walk quietly into the murderer's open arms? I think the answer is obvious.

Ron didn't see O.J.! Ron saw the **real** murderer! He saw Detective Fuhrman! That's why Ron was not alarmed. **Why?**

As soon as Detective Fuhrman heard footsteps, he drew his gun again and took out his police badge. When Ron turned onto the walkway and approached the gate, Fuhrman pointed his gun at Ron, flashed his police badge and said in a low voice:

> *"I'm a police officer. There has been an accident. Keep your hands were I can see them, and walk over this way!"*

We have all seen such a situation many times, in TV drama's and in movies.

Ron followed the orders of a police officer – without protest – just like any normal, law abiding citizen would have done, and walked over to Detective Fuhrman!

Had Ron seen any other man than a police officer in that situation, he would have believed this person was the assailant.

Only if the murderer is a police officer, would Ron have approached without a word of protest!

As Ron got to the spot where his body was found, Detective Fuhrman might have become restless or impatient, or he simply wanted to appear and act like a "no-nonsense" police officer. So he roughed Ron up against the fence enclosing the small niche – as in preparation to search Ron for a weapon.

His dignity hurt by Detective Fuhrman's attitude and pushing, which suggested that Ron might be a suspect, Ron, naturally, reacted with the only words any witness reported hearing:

> *"Hey - hey - hey!"*

. . . so as to say:

> *"Take it easy, man! I haven't done anything . . .!"*

In a low, but deep, commanding voice Fuhrman instructed Ron, as if he intended to search Ron for a weapon.

"Hands on the fence . . . step back . . . spread your legs!"

Ron, naturally, complied with **the police officer's order.**

Leaning forward, hands on the fence, and with his legs spread, Ron was completely unsuspecting and totally defenseless.

Detective Fuhrman was standing behind him in the darkness. Fuhrman pulled his razor sharp knife from his belt and held it close behind Ron's back, where Ron could not see it.

Pretending to search Ron for a weapon, Detective Fuhrman's hands moved up Ron's body, towards his neck. Ron was unaware of any danger!

Directly behind and between Ron's shoulders Detective Fuhrman used his left hand to rotate the knife in his right hand, so that the edge of the blade would point in towards Ron's neck when Fuhrman put his right arm over Ron's shoulder.

Before Ron realized what was happening, Fuhrman attacked Ron from behind, by quickly reaching over Ron's right shoulder, stabbing the knife deeply into the left side of Ron's neck and cutting a deep, gaping wound more than 3 inches long.

Petrified, in total shock, and because his neck was paralyzed by the huge cut, Ron was unable to utter a word. Fuhrman continued to attack Ron, stabbing him repeatedly all over his body, while Ron tried in vain to defend himself. **Shortly thereafter Ron was dead.** I doubt the struggle lasted more than 60 seconds.

No question about it. A police officer, like Fuhrman, had the perfect opportunity. But more importantly:

A police officer is probably the **only** person who could have killed **both** Nicole and Ron **without any of them getting suspicious, screaming for help or escaping!**

It is quite possible that Ron managed to fight his way out of the niche, temporarily, and that the two combattants fought also on the patio, or even outside the gate. Some blood that was found outside the gate, might suggest that. But as Ron gradually lost his strength, Fuhrman forced him back into the niche, where Ron's dead body was, ultimately, found.

Unless someone comes up with a better explanation – or any reasonable explanation – as to why Ron, without ever screaming for help, would walk quietly up to the murderer, turn around, and let himself be executed from behind, right next to the spot on the ground where Nicole's body was lying dead in a pool of blood – I believe the murderer **must** be a police officer! **In my opinion, this police officer's name is Mark Fuhrman!**

L et us look at a little detail from Mr. Robert Heidstra's testimony during the civil trial, where he testified for the plaintiffs.

Robert Heidstra was Nicole's neighbor. He is the one who heard Ron say:

> **"Hey – hey – hey!"**

Heidstra explained that another man with a deeper voice responded, but Heidstra couldn't understand what the other man said, because **he spoke so fast.** What could the murderer have said, and why did he **speak so fast** that Heidstra didn't understand what he said?

O.J. isn't the murderer – but **if** he were – he might possibly have responded to Ron's, *"Hey - hey - hey,"* by saying:

> *"Shut up . . . you asshole! . . . I'll teach you to screw around with my ex-wife! . . . I'm gonna kill you!"*

– or something to that effect. That, at least, is a scenario of "jealous rage" which O.J.'s adversaries claim existed at Bundy that night. But that would certainly have been something the witness, Robert Heidstra, would have understood. Furthermore, an improvised angry or derogatory response like that, which we might have expected from the murderer, if he and Ron were arguing, would **not** have been spoken very **rapidly**.

Rather, it would have been spoken with emphasis on each word, **so that Ron would get the meaning!**

The murderer's response was therefore, probably **not** an improvised, angry or derogatory response by the murderer to scare, intimidate, or insult Ron.

I believe Detective Fuhrman is the murderer, and that he responded by instructing Ron:

> *"Hands on the fence* [hood, car, wall, gate, etc.] *... step back ... spread you legs!"*

This is a phrase Fuhrman, the police officer, knew by heart, and had used during arrests perhaps as much as **ten thousand times** during his 19 year career! It is typically a phrase police officers **"spit out"** almost as if it were one long, continuous word:

> *"Hands-on-the-fence-step-back-spread-your-legs!*

If that indeed was the case, it explains why Robert Heidstra heard the second man, the murderer, talking, **but could not understand what the murderer said** – because he spoke so **fast**!

It is remarkable how all the seemingly insignificant details of this murder mystery – as they become known, one after the other – fit my theory, make sense, and fill in all the gaps the prosecution and the plaintiffs did not have any answers for!

CHAPTER 27

More Irrefutable Proof
Of O.J.'s Innocence

This chapter will show how various clues and pieces of evidence you might never expect had anything to do with each other, may be tied together in a mosaic picture that looks nothing like the isolated images investigators, prosecutors, or counsels for the plaintiffs showed us during O.J.'s criminal and civil trials.

This will demonstrate how important it is, that the experts only present the facts, and that we don't rely on them to draw any conclusions outside the strict realm of their specialties.

In other words, let the **DNA expert** tell us whose DNA he found in the blood on swatch # 47. But don't use this DNA expert, or his results, to jump to the conclusion that O.J., or anyone else, ever set foot at Bundy on June 12, 1994!

Let **the medical examiner** describe the wounds to Ron's body. But don't allow this medical examiner to reenact in the courtroom, second for second, with a prosecutor as medium, how the life and death struggle between Ron and the murderer occurred. Not unless the medical examiner has extensive experience in such deadly fights.

Through this chapter my readers will come to understand that the Simpson case is far from solved – at least not by those who think O.J. is the killer.

Most people may think O.J. is guilty. He simply raced over to Bundy in a jealous rage and killed Nicole (and Ron) before leaving for Chicago. All the evidence in the case originated with O.J. Theories of a conspiracy and evidence tampering are just smoke screens.

Hopefully, my readers have long since realized that there are far more interesting issues and suspects in this case than *"a jealous O.J. out of control."*

A hair and fiber expert analyzed the hairs on the cap, found that some of them were similar to O.J.'s, and six of them were from an African American – other than O.J. Two hairs were from Caucasian people. One of these hairs was dyed blond, but the person's natural hair color was light brown.

That's when the hair and fiber expert should have stopped. And that's when the prosecutors should have asked themselves this question: *"What are **all** the possible ways for those hairs to have ended up on the cap?"*

Instead, they jumped directly from the hair expert's scientific results, to the conclusion that best fit their preconceived theory of O.J. being the murderer. When the experts have delivered their purely scientific results, that is the time for the investigators and prosecutors to **start** asking questions – **not to jump to conclusions.**

Together, the hair expert and the prosecutors saw that the hairs fit their theory of O.J. being the murderer. So they immediately concluded that O.J. wore that cap for disguise when murdering Nicole (and Ron). That's how O.J.'s hairs ended up on the cap. If there were other hairs on the cap they might have *"flown in with the wind, at Bundy"*!

That seemed fair – for the hair and fiber expert – because hairs and fibers are all he is an expert on. It seemed fair for the prosecutors also, because they relied, completely, on the conclusions of a medical examiner for as much as the injuries were concerned, and neither of them, hopefully, ever dressed up to murder someone with a knife. But jumping to conclusions does not solve this case.

If the hair expert tells us that some of those hairs are similar to O.J.'s, and others are not, that's all we need to know – from him! **We don't have to be experts** on hairs and fibers to take full advantage of the probative value of the cap.

Now it is important that we don't grab the first and best explanation that fits a preconceived theory of O.J. being the killer, who wore that cap. Instead we should try to come up with **a lot of different scenarios** and ask a lot of critical questions, before we eventually reach the conclusion that best ties in with **all the rest** of the evidence.

The prosecutors in the Simpson case just considered the individual pieces of evidence isolated from the rest. They looked at the cap – by itself – and concluded that O.J. wore it. They never questioned if that tied in with **the bloody shoeprints!** Or with **the way Nicole was killed!**

The prosecutors looked at the five blood drops at Bundy, isolated, and concluded that O.J. bled as he fled the murder scene. That conclusion fit the cuts on O.J.'s left hand. But the prosecutors never questioned how those blood drops tied in with the murder gloves, and the bruise on Nicole's head – or if there even was a connection.

This is where I hold an advantage over investigators, experts, and prosecutors who are **not** looking to solve a murder mystery, but instead, are **trying to create support for a conclusion they have already reached.**

Military personnel are experts on disguises (some hunters, too, by the way). I know, from my **military background**, that you don't wear a knit ski cap to disguise yourself in Los Angeles in the middle of the summer. To disguise yourself, you try to **"blend in"!** That's **"the first rule of disguise"!** Accordingly, a soldier will wear camouflage in a jungle.

A "four star general" may tell us this from the witness stand. But in trying to solve this case – by the same token as with respect to the hair and fiber expert – we don't **need** to be **"four star generals and camouflage experts,"** either, in order to understand his testimony and realize that the cap was **not** used as a disguise!

Obviously, the cap wasn't used to keep the murderer's ears warm, either – on June 12! So what was the purpose of the knit ski cap? Perhaps the cap was **not** worn by the murderer at all, but just brought along and planted to frame O.J.

Or perhaps the cap was worn by a Caucasian murderer! Whereas African-American hair is just that – African-American hair – and a dark knit cap, therefore, does not at all disguise an African American, a **Caucasion murderer might benefit much more from wearing a knit ski cap.**

Caucasians – much more so than African Americans – may be identified by their hairs: as being dark, light, blond, red, white, wavy, straight, curly, long, short, etc. – in addition to any **combination** of the same! Let us say that the murderer is a Caucasian with short, red hair, or long white hair. Such a killer may benefit from wearing a knit kap, because the advantage of preventing potential witnesses from identifying his hair, outweighs the disadvantage of a the attention drawn to the killer because of the cap.

An African American, however, does not benefit from wearing a dark knit ski cap. His hair is African American – regardless. The cap cannot disguise that.

Hence, we use the hair and fiber expert for his expertise on hairs – but we don't buy his, or the prosecutors' conclusion with respect to the cap itself. Instead, we search for the **real** truth.

The cap was found under some shrubbery, and there was no blood on the cap itself. **If the murderer wore the cap at all – on his head – and he lost it in a struggle with Ron – why was there no blood on the cap?**

That's the first questions we must ask ourselves. Perhaps the cap wasn't worn by the murderer! Perhaps it was used for a totally different purpose, and was planted afterwards – by the murderer.

Perhaps the murderer brought the cap to the murder scene and left it there, to give the investigators the **opportunity** to plant O.J.'s hairs on it later in the crime lab.

If the murderer is an LAPD homicide detective, he would know that in a "first degree" murder case like this, O.J. – if he became a suspect – would not be allowed to post bail, but would have to remain in jail until after the trial. If Fuhrman is the murderer, he would know that the investigators could pick as many of O.J.'s hairs as they wanted – from the pillow case in his jail cell – while O.J. was in court during the pre-trial stages.

Or even easier – the investigators could probably pick as

many hairs as they wanted, from O.J.'s hair brush in his bathroom at Rockingham.

Hence, perhaps the murderer – a homicide detective, like Fuhrman, brought the cap along, and purposely left it at the murder scene – as "bait" for the investigators, so they could help Fuhrman in framing O.J., by planting O.J.'s hairs on the cap – in their crime lab.

That would suit Fuhrman perfectly, because only O.J. or the investigators could have planted O.J.'s hairs on the cap. So if the investigators took this "bait" and planted O.J.'s hairs on the cap, it would, first of all, be a very powerful piece of evidence against O.J.

More importantly for Fuhrman, however, if he "set up" the investigators like that, and they took his "bait" – is the position he put the investigators in! They could hardly, later, charge Fuhrman with the murders – even if they should suspect him!

The reason is that if Fuhrman (and not O.J.) is the murderer, then **O.J.'s hairs on the cap must have been planted.** Fuhrman could not have planted O.J.'s hairs on the cap – **only the investigators could have done that** – in their crime lab – with hairs from O.J.'s hair brush, or from the pillow case in his jail cell!

Consequently, if the investigators took Fuhrman's "bait," by planting O.J.'s hairs on the cap, they could not, later, charge Fuhrman with the murders, without implicating themselves in evidence fabrication against an innocent O.J. – something that could land the investigators in prison for 20 years!

By the way, if the investigators didn't take Fuhrman's "bait," but left the cap as it was – the cap would not implicate Fuhrman anyway, since he never wore the cap. Fuhrman only bought the cap and planted it in order to frame, hopefully, both O.J. – **and the investigators!**

As you see, from Fuhrman's perspective, the cap served a double purpose. But you shall soon learn that Detective Fuhrman might have had yet another use for the cap.

We are about to solve this murder mystery now – at least for as much as O.J. is concerned.

Earlier, we have proven that O.J. must be innocent, because **the glove evidence** proved that he could not have bled at Bundy – not even if he were the murderer. Therefore, the blood swatches with his blood on them – allegedly collected at Bundy – must have been fabricated (by Detective Vannatter, as we shall later see).

Furthermore, **the glove evidence** proved that both gloves must have been deliberately deposited – by the murderer himself. And since O.J. could not possibly have deposited the Rockingham glove, because the blood on it was wet when it was found by Fuhrman – O.J. could not be the murderer.

Of course, in addition, considering O.J. as a suspect, we have the impossible timeline and the obvious planting of the cap. We also have the inconceivable task of O.J. murdering two people with a knife, at the same time, without any of them screaming for help or fleeing the scene.

And we have the absurdity of suggesting that Ron would have approached the murder scene, silently and trustworthily and allowed the murderer to attack him from behind. Unless the murderer is, and acts like, a police officer, Ron would never have behaved so "gullibly."

On the pages to follow, we are about to prove in yet another way – irrefutably – that O.J. is innocent.

I will also **illustrate** this part of my theory **at the end of this chapter**, to make it crystal clear to anyone with a minimum of common sense, that O.J. did not murder Nicole and Ron.

You shall learn about **crucial, new evidence** which – all by itself – holds the key to solving this murder mystery. Yet, this most important evidence has been completely **overlooked** by all the investigators, the prosecutors, the plaintiffs, and the experts.

Or, if they did consider this evidence, **they either did not understand it – or they deliberately withheld it** because it clearly proved that O.J. is innocent, and that **the investigators and the prosecutors, therefore, indeed, had conspired to frame him!**

As I have explained, we have proven in several different ways, that O.J. did not murder Nicole and Ron. Instead, the **real killer** not only murdered Nicole and Ron, but he framed O.J. directly, with some of the evidence. More importantly, however, the murderer also "set up" the investigators with this evidence, so that they should believe O.J. were the murderer.

The real murderer persuaded the investigators to fabricate the most incriminating evidence against O.J. In doing so, they made O.J. appear guilty. But more importantly – from the murderer's perspective – after having been "set up" and persuaded to fabricate this false evidence against O.J., the investigators could not possibly, later, charge the real murderer instead of O.J, without implicating themselves in serious evidence fabrication.

This theory of mine is not only plausible. There is also overwhelming evidence to support it. Some of this evidence, like the glove evidence and the cap, I have already discussed.

However, one thing is missing, so far – because no matter how much we prove that the investigators fabricated false evidence against O.J., some people will always say that these rogue investigators simply *"framed the guilty man"*!

That's why we still would love to find that **one, conclusive piece** of evidence, proving, irrefutably, that the **murderer** – and not rogue investigators – **deliberately** created, planted, deposited, or left behind, at least, **some** of the evidence at the murder scene – with the obvious purpose of framing O.J.

And, most importantly, we want this particular evidence to be evidence O.J. could **not possibly** have left behind.

How can we determine if such a piece of evidence – if we find it – could **not** have been left by O.J.? That sounds hard to determine.

Well, suppose we find this piece of evidence, and it becomes **absolutely clear** that this evidence was **deliberately created**. In other words, this, so far, hypothetical evidence could not have been caused or created by **accident**, forgetfulness, or sloppiness. The murderer himself, regardless of who he is, **must** have **created** or deposited this evidence – **on purpose.**

Suppose, also, that this hypothetical evidence – which the murderer deliberately created – could **only harm O.J., regardless of how we interpret it!**

Is it not obvious, then, beyond any doubt, that O.J. could not possibly have created this hypothetical piece of evidence? Not unless, of course, he wanted to get caught! But if so, it would be much simpler for him just to confess!

If such evidence exists, O.J. must be innocent!

Maybe one of the reasons why no one else has discovered this evidence, is that at first glance it doesn't seem that important. Another reason may be that it requires a rather broad background of knowledge and experience to interpret this evidence correctly. It is not sufficient simply to be a forensic pathologist, a DNA expert, a shoe expert, a hair and fiber expert, or a homicide investigator. I'll leave it at that, since you will soon learn why.

Are you anxious to find out what I have discovered, and which no one else, seemingly, have discovered?

Eventually, consult the illustrations I have provided at the end of this chapter (**but don't do it yet!**). OK. Here we go!

The medical examiner's **autopsy report** states that Nicole had a bruise, measuring about 1" x 1" on the upper right side of her head. The **skin** covering that bruise was **smooth**, not abraded and **not lacerated**. So, the plaintiffs' "expert" medical examiner, Dr. Spitz, suggested that the blow was perhaps **not too hard**. Nicole may have been "dazed" – but not totally unconscious. To support their assumption the medical examiners pointed to the fact that Nicole's brain did not show any sign of trauma or hemorrhage.

However, it is quite possible for a person to be knocked deeply unconscious, without any apparent signs of brain damage, acute or permanent. Again, the medical experts drew unsubstantiated conclusions!

Dr. Spitz suggested that the bruise in question could have come from the end of a knife's handle, held by Mr. Simpson.

I disagree – completely! I believe all the four forensic pathologists that officially worked this case "fumbled the football"!

The bruise on Nicole's head, and the minor injuries to Nicole's **left leg,** are more important, in terms of solving this murder mystery, than even the most serious **knife wounds** to any of the victims. The knife wounds, actually, could have been inflicted by **anyone.**

However, the bruise and the leg wounds, all by themselves, may hold the key to solving this murder mystery. You are about to learn why!

About to be caught with their pants down, so to speak, the medical examiners may use their credentials to blast me for the theory I am about to share with my readers. Let them! I think my theory makes a heck of a lot more sense than theirs! I let my readers be the jury!

My versatile athletic career has taught me a lot about the appearances of bruises inflicted by various hard or soft, sharp or blunt instruments (including competitors' arms, legs, and heads, hockey sticks, skies and soccer shoes).

My background as a boxer, and a few street fights I have been involved in, has taught me the effects of various blows to a person's head and what it takes to knock someone unconscious, as well as the best way to do it!

Majoring in physical education, and having studied physical therapy and athletic injuries for two years, I know a bit about anatomy, and about bruises and hemorrhages – although far less than the medical examiners, I admit.

My police background, as well as a career as a pistol marksman, has given me some experience with handguns. Let me apply some of this experience:

> According to the autopsy report, in the **deeper layers of the flesh,** directly underneath the bruise on the upper right side of Nicole's head, where Nicole's flesh touched her skull, so to speak, there was a **hemorrhage** about **two and a half times the area of the bruise:** 2" x 1.25", or **2.5 sq. inches** (compared to 1" x 1", or **1 sq. inch** for the bruise).
>
> **Every one of four expert medical examiners has overlooked the significance of this hemorrhage – as it relates to the bruise!**

According to Dr. Spitz' testimony, Nicole died **within** 30 seconds, due to the massive loss of blood from her cut neck. I agree with him on that point.

Do my readers see how extremely important **all** of this information is? Four expert **medical examiners** in a row have seen the bruise, but none of them have understood the significance of it! They don't even know what caused it, or what effect it had on Nicole! Consequently, **none of the investigators, prosecutors, or counsels for the plaintiffs have understood how Nicole was attacked.**

Therefore, they have no idea this bruise might prove that not only the knit cap, but also **the bloody shoeprints, were purposely planted by the murderer**!

Imagine the importance of such information! If the bloody shoeprints were purposely planted by the murderer, then obviously **the murderer** was trying to frame O.J.! This means, of course, that we have yet another – ultimate – proof that O.J. is innocent!

And all the talk about O.J. wearing Bruno Magli shoes means nothing!

I bet most of my readers don't see this connection, either – at least, not yet! But it will become clear, shortly.

This is where it is so important to have a broad background

and plenty of life experience. It allows us to reach a totally different conclusion with respect to the bruise, the cap, the shoeprints – and in fact a totally different conclusion with respect to the entire murder case – than anything any single medical examiner, hair and fiber expert, DNA expert, shoeprint expert, investigator, prosecutor, or counsel for either side has suggested.

> **This is one of those times when you need to concentrate –** and, indeed, **think** about what you read!

The hemorrhage on the upper right side of Nicole's head, in the deeper layer of the flesh underneath the bruise, must have been caused by a **heavy** object **crushing Nicole's flesh against her skull**, thereby damaging several capillary blood vessels or minor veins in the flesh, and simultaneously causing the bruise in her skin.

> **I take no responsibility for the following, if you should harm yourself! It is entirely up to yourself whether or not you want to try this!**

If you are young, healthy, and in good shape, you can try hitting yourself with the "little finger" side of your **clenched fist** on the upper right side of your head – approximately 4 inches above the external auditory canal (the entrance to your "ear"). That is the way Nicole was struck if we accept Dr. Spitz' theory of O.J. hitting her there, from behind, with his hand clenching the knife's handle.

If you are like me, it won't hurt much, and you can hit your head surprisingly hard, without even a trace of injury to your scalp – not to mention any hemorrhage (swelling due to bleeding) – not even if you hit so hard that you get "dizzy"!

This should give those of my readers who tried this experiment, a clear indication as to **how hard Nicole must have been struck**, in order for that blow to create a **massive hemorrhage** underneath the impact bruise – **in a matter of a few**

seconds!

If you have a ruler in your house, you can try to draw a rectangle 2 inches by 1.25 inches. Imagine a bump on your head that size! Wow! **That must have been some punch Nicole received.** Of course!

How can four expert forensic pathologists brush this aside, or skip over it, and not even **try** to establish correctly what caused that injury?

What conclusions can we draw from the appearances of this bruise and the underlying hemorrhage?

- The material of the instrument which caused the bruise must have been **firm** to cause the hemorrhage. It must also have had a fairly flat and even, smooth surface, and have had a relatively **soft texture**, or have been **padded,** in order not to cut, abrade, or lacerate the skin.

- **Only seconds** after the blow to Nicole's head, her neck was cut. To cause such a fairly large hemorrhage (250% of the area of the impact bruise) – in just a few seconds – the **force** of the impact of the blow must have been **substantial!** Consequently, the object that hit Nicole must have been **quite heavy** – most likely a fairly **large metal object**.

The blow did not just "daze" Nicole – it knocked her out, cold!

How can we know Nicole's neck was cut only seconds after the blow to her head knocked her unconscious? Well, any second a neighbor might show up unexpectedly, see the murderer ramming the knife into Nicole's neck, scream, *"bloody murder,"* and take off. Then there would be an eyewitness on the loose!

So, I hope no one suggests that the murderer knocked Nicole unconscious, and then hang around whistling *"Yankee Doodle"* for five minutes before he killed her with his knife!

And I also hope no one suggests that the blow did not knock Nicole unconscious. Had that been the case, Nicole would, of course, have yelled and screamed for help and woken up the entire neighborhood!

We all know from the 911 tapes that Nicole knew how to scream when she felt threatened! And had the murderer put his hand over her mouth while Nicole was conscious, she would have bitten him so hard that **he** would have screamed!

Obviously, the murderer wanted Nicole silenced and defenseless, so he could **cut her neck undisturbed.** He knocked her unconscious – **from behind!** She fell to the ground, he grabbed her hair and pulled her head back. Then he cut her neck!

The blow to Nicole's head was the very **first** injury to Nicole.

The murderer did not risk attacking Nicole face to face, with his fists or with the knife, before she was unconscious. Had he tried that, and Nicole had evaded the blow or the knife, she might have screamed in panic, while fighting back or escaping. Help might have arrived, and the entire murder would have been bungled.

Nicole's murderer didn't take any chances!

That is why the murderer did **not** confront Nicole in her **doorway,** where the murderer could **not** get good **"leverage"** for his blow (because the door and the door frame were in the way). In the doorway, Nicole might even have dodged the blow and managed to slam the door in the murderer's face.

So, instead, he purposely **lured** her down **to open the gate.** The murderer knew Nicole. So after saying, *"Hi!"* and opening the gate, she would **turn around** to lead the way back, up the steps. That's what the murderer had planned. That is **when,** and **where,** he had **planned** to knock her down **from behind.**

[The publisher's address is in the back of this book. If I write anything in this book, which you find lacks in logic or reason, take a note of it let me hear about it!

On the other hand, if you think my theories and explanations make more sense than what you heard from O.J.'s adversaries during the trials, contact the media, and let them hear your opinion! Chances are they won't listen to you, though]

Back to the murder of Nicole.

Nicole's neck was probably cut within 5-10 seconds after the blow to her head was struck.

According to the autopsy report, the cut totally severed both the left and the right common carotid arteries, the left internal jugular vein (except for a sliver), and cut a substantial, 1/4 inch, gash in the right internal jugular vein. According to Dr. Spitz, Nicole died within 30 seconds, from massive loss of blood.

Not after 30 seconds, but as soon as her neck was cut, the blood pressure **in her head** fell to **zero!** It happened almost as **instantly** as if you had popped a balloon!

Nicole's heart was still pumping blood to other parts of her body for another 20-30 seconds. Some of **this blood gushed out** through her severed common carotid arteries **in her neck wound**. But **that blood never reached Nicole's head! It couldn't – the connection was cut!**

At the same time, any blood pressure originally present in Nicole's head, would immediately fall to zero since there was **free "exit"** for that blood **in both "directions"** – both through the **incoming, severed arteries** (where that blood had come from), and through the **exiting veins**.

Consequently, after the cut to Nicole's neck, there would be practically speaking **no further expansion of the hemorrhage** underneath the bruise on the upper right side of her head.

Hence, for that hemorrhage – in a matter of seconds – to **expand** into the surrounding undamaged tissue – to a size **two hundred and fifty percent** of the area of the impact bruise (2.5 sq. inches vs. 1 sq. inch) – the blow to Nicole's head must have

initiated the attack on her. But more importantly, the blow must have been struck with **substantial force**, and with a **very heavy** instrument, to cause such a severe hemorrhage in such a short time.

Based on the appearance of the bruise and the underlying hemorrhage, the blow must have been struck with the "butt end" of a **heavy,** firm, but soft textured, smooth, flat object with tapered (not sharp) edges, somewhat rectangular and measuring about (1 x 1) sq. inch.

> There can be no doubt that **the murderer intentionally knocked Nicole completely unconscious with a heavy instrument – before attacking her with his knife!**

I believe my readers could follow my line of reasoning, although you may not be forensic pathologists either! Let me elaborate on this.

The "best" way to knock someone unconscious – if attacking the opponent (Nicole) from the front – is to strike the victim **from the side, directly on the chin.** Because the chin "sticks out," a blow to the chin causes **both** a quick **tilting** – and simultaneously a **rotating** – motion of the head and the brain.

Your brain is not "glued" to the inside of your skull. Instead, it is smaller than the inside of your skull, and "floats" freely in liquid. So such a quick, "tilting" motion of the skull in two different directions sends the interior of the **skull "slamming"** against the victim's **brain**. This causes the brain to **"bounce"** off the inside of the skull and sends the **brain** slamming back against the **opposite** side of the **skull** (if the blow is heavy enough)!

In common language one might say that such a blow to the chin **"rattles"** the brain. It's almost like **a multi-directional "whip lash"**! What knocks the person unconscious is the sudden shift in the position of the brain – often most effectively, in two different directions in quick succession.

This is several times more effective than to hit an opponent on top of the head, and does not require a heavy instrument. An empty, clenched fist is more than sufficient **when facing your opponent,**

so you can hit him or her sideways on the chin!

It is a **"hook"** to the chin – the same punch that, more than any other punch, sends boxers to the canvas!

Now, this is the best way to knock an opponent unconscious when **facing** the opponent. But Nicole's murderer didn't take the chance on striking her face to face, in the doorway, as I explained. Rather, Nicole's murderer planned to attack her **by surprise, from behind.**

The best way to knock an opponent unconscious if attacking your opponent from **behind**, is to hit the opponent on the neck, **just underneath the basis** of the skull, **or** on the **upper** portion of the **side of the head** – exactly where Nicole was hit! Again, let me elaborate!

To knock someone unconscious from behind often **requires the use of a heavy object.** The reason is that the back of the head is almost flush with the spine – in particular with the first and second cervical (neck) vertebrae. The back of the head does not protrude away from the central axis of the spine, like the chin. Therefore, a blow to the head from behind does **not** create a **rotating** action between the first and second vertebrae (where 90% of the rotating and tilting action of the head is created). It creates a **tilting** action **only**.

Besides, the **muscles** in the neck preventing the head from **tilting** (sideways or back or forth) are **much stronger** than the muscles preventing the head for being **rotated**. Therefore, it takes a rather **heavy blow,** from a rather **heavy object**, to knock someone unconscious **from behind**.

Hence, **a blow from behind is not at all as effective as a sideways blow to the chin.** This is reflected in movies, for instance, which mimic **real life** situations.

Hardly ever, have you seen a "movie-gangster" knock someone unconscious, from behind, with a "hook punch" to the back of the victim's head. He hits with a gun or a club – high up on the side of the head, or directly underneath the basis of the skull. On the other hand – hardly ever have you seen a gangster knock someone unconscious, from the front, with a blow to the chin – using a gun or a club. From the front, with a sideways blow to the chin, the fist is more than sufficient.

I explained why the murderer did not risk attacking Nicole face to face, in the doorway. He needed to attack her by surprise, **from behind.** Therefore, he needed to strike her with a **heavy instrument** – to make sure she was knocked unconscious.

So, one of the best ways to create the most effective result in terms of knocking someone unconscious **from behind** – by causing the brain to bounce off the inside of the skull – is to strike the blow **high up on the side** of the head – **as far away from the first and second cervical vertebrae as possible** – exactly where Nicole was struck – and preferably with a **heavy instrument**, so as to create the strongest possible force – or **"torque,"** if you prefer that expression – thereby creating the **quick, sideways tilting action** of her skull, needed to knock her deeply unconscious

Obviously, the murderer knew what he was doing, and his objective was to knock Nicole **totally unconscious**!

So far, from all of this, we can state with confidence:

The murderer definitely **intended to knock Nicole unconscious – before cutting her throat.** The intention being that Nicole should not see the knife and scream for help or resist. Most likely, the assailant was also afraid Nicole might dodge the knife attack or deflect it if she saw what was coming, and immediately scream for help.

That's why the murderer didn't confront her in her doorway, but **lured her down to the gate** where he could strike her **from behind** – after she, necessarily, had to **turn around to head back up the steps**. And because a blow from a fist is less effective when struck from behind, the murderer used a **heavy instrument**!

All these clues indicate that my theory is **"right on." The murder of Nicole was planned over a long time, by a murderer who**

was an experienced fighter, and knew exactly what he was doing!

The butt end of Fuhrman's revolver handle is **flat** and **smooth** and it, probably, has **tapered** edges. It would leave a bruise exactly like the 1" x 1" bruise on Nicole's head – without cutting her skin!

The fact that Nicole's skin was not cut or abraded in spite of the heavy impact, proves that the impact must have come from a **heavy, firm, but soft textured or padded instrument!**

Fuhrman padded the revolver handle with the knit cap, which he wasn't wearing anyway, since it was just brought along to frame O.J.

By the way, regardless of who the murderer is, he wouldn't wear the knit cap when confronting Nicole. It would have put Nicole on the alert!

Fuhrman padded the handle, because, being a detective, he knew that the bare handle might leave imprints in Nicole's skin that could have been identified as having come from the handle of a revolver.

Had investigators identified the bruise as having come from a revolver handle, the obvious question would be, of course:

*"Why did the murderer kill Nicole with a **knife**, if he had already knocked her unconscious with a **revolver**?"*

The padding didn't reduce the impact. It was the **weight** of the gun that knocked Nicole unconscious, not the **hardness** of the object that struck her.

Four medical examiners, with all their expertise, have not been able to tell us what struck Nicole. **Yet, that is essential to understanding and solving this murder mystery!**

They have suggested everything from the butt end of the **handle of the murderer's knife**, to O.J.'s **fist**, and even suggested that the bruise was caused by Nicole's head **hitting the ground**.

I think my readers agree with me that the **handle of a revolver** is not only a likely explanation, but **the only explanation.** There are other good reasons to suspect that:

> The instrument that struck Nicole, most likely, must have been "L" shaped – like a revolver!
>
> The instrument must be elongated, for the murderer to get a good grip on it. But a bat, a baton, a flashlight, a night-stick, or similar, would not have yielded a bruise about 1 inch x 1 inch, but rather, a more **narrow, elongated** bruise. And it would probably have **cut Nicole's skin.**
>
> Nicole's bruise must have come from the butt end of an instrument. This makes it likely that the instrument was "L" shaped, so the murderer could hold it in the "stem" of the "L", and strike with the butt end of the "foot" of the "L."
>
> Typically, the murderer could have held the revolver by its barrel, and struck Nicole with the butt end of the revolver handle.

A skilled fighter, Fuhrman had probably sparred many times, wearing soft/padded boxing gloves. He knew that it isn't the hardness of an instrument that knocks an opponent out, but the speed of the punch – and most of all the **weight** behind the punch.

However, what kind of a man would have the knowledge and the sense to pad the revolver handle he struck Nicole with?

> **Exactly – a homicide detective! Don't underestimate Detective Fuhrman! I will repeat that several times throughout my book!**

The investigators and the prosecutors suggested that the bruise on Nicole's head might have been caused by the end of the handle of the knife used to cut her neck a few seconds later.

No-no! They like to suggest that, because it fits their

theory of O.J. killing Nicole with a knife held in his right hand. But **they are not even close!**

The end of a knife's handle is not smooth, with a flat area somewhat larger than 1" x 1"! The end of a knife's handle is elliptic**, or pointed, or undefined/irregular.** Based on the severe impact necessary to create the sudden, fairly large hemorrhage in the deeper layers of Nicole's flesh, such a knife handle would have **cut** Nicole's skin.

Had the murderer hit Nicole with his **clenched fist only**, he must have struck the blow from slightly **above** her head. If so – since Nicole was fairly tall (5' 6") – he could not have hit her on the **upper** portion of her head, with the **knuckles** of his fist, but would have had to hit her with the soft "meaty" part of the **ulnar** ("little finger") side of his fist. Clench your fist and check it out!

Hitting Nicole with the "meaty" part of a clenched fist would hardly have caused a mark on Nicole's head, even!

Nicole hitting the ground could never have caused such a limited and well defined, rectangular bruise either, without cutting the skin – and highly unlikely on that particular spot of Nicole's head, unless she was **"diving"** – **head first** – towards the ground.

However, for Nicole to fall like that **she would have to be knocked unconscious first.**

Hence, **if** the bruise on the upper right side of Nicole's head (the bruise we have been discussing) was caused by her head hitting the ground – where was the bruise from the blow that **caused** Nicole to fall to the ground? See! Any other possible explanation hits a snag!

L et me return to the theory about the revolver. Isn't it likely that a murderer who for some reason drove to Bundy with the somewhat **precarious intention of committing murder,** by killing Nicole with a **knife**, would have **a gun** as a **"back up"** or as an **"insurance policy"** – in case he was surprised by a neighbor or a friend of Nicole's – an eyewitness who screamed for help, and tried to flee, or offered resistance which the murderer could not quickly overcome with just a knife?

Hence, the **butt end** of his **revolver handle** is probably what the murderer used to knock Nicole unconscious!

I am looking at my own revolver handle. It fits perfectly. It is smooth, flat, with tapered edges. It would leave an impact bruise about (1 x 1) sq. inch, without cutting the skin. And the impact of such a blow would definitely be heavy enough to **quickly cause the hemorrhage** in the deeper layer of Nicole's flesh, underneath the bruise.

With my own revolver I "tap" myself **carefully** on the upper right side of my head, the same spot where Nicole was struck. Because of the weight of the gun, I sense that hitting my head even just slightly harder would leave me dazed! A severe blow with a gun like this, would definitely knock me deeply unconscious!

But why wasn't Nicole's skin **cut**? Two explanations: the grip was flat and smooth, with rounded edges. In addition, perhaps, it was not made of wood, but was one of those **composite rubber** grips, that wraps around the steel frame of the gun's handle – or the grip was **padded by the murderer's knit cap!**

As a former police sergeant, I know that a heavy blow from the end of a revolver handle – even one with a composite rubber grip – **might** have left an imprint in Nicole's skin, perhaps from the grip's **logo** or from the **mid "seam"** where the two halves of the grip are joined, or from the contours of the edge of the grip – and which could identify the blow as having come from a revolver handle. If the murderer was a detective, he didn't want to leave the investigators with such a clue – pointing to himself, and away from O.J.!

Therefore, if the murderer had police background, say as a homicide detective, he, too, would know that. So to **disguise** what kind of object he used when knocking Nicole unconscious, I suggest that

the murderer "padded" the revolver handle in the knit cap!

That is why the impact didn't **cut** Nicole's skin and didn't leave an **imprint**. But the **force** of the impact was still heavy enough to **crush** her flesh against her skull, and cause a rather **severe** underlying hemorrhage **in a matter of seconds**!

It was **not** the **hardness** of the gun's handle that knocked Nicole unconscious – it was the **weight** of the gun! And no doubt about it – the murderer **wanted** to knock Nicole **completely unconscious** – and he did! **The huge hemorrhage underneath the bruise, left no doubt about the murderer's intentions!**

> If it may be any comfort to her family – Nicole was "out cold" **before** her neck was cut. **She didn't feel any pain.** That will become even more evident, when I discuss the wounds on Nicole's leg.

Based on the above conclusions, we are able to draw a lot of related conclusions, that would pass by most prosecutors and experts.

According to the prosecutors, the murderer, allegedly, wore the cap on his head, and he didn't even touch it to remove it himself – he either lost it in a struggle with Ron, or Ron pulled it off the murderer's head! That's, allegedly, why it was found at the murder scene. But why would either of these men be concerned about the cap – engaged as they were, in a deadly struggle. Can my readers picture Ron disregarding the murderer's knife, and instead pulling the cap of the murderer's head:

"Gotch'a! I have your cap! Do you give up, now?"

Besides, if Ron or the murderer removed the cap by hand, there should have been blood on the cap. Besides, this cap would have fit O.J. so snugly that he would never have **lost** it.

> Why do O.J.'s many adversaries always claim that he "lost" everything, each time they are stuck for any sensible explanation as to where different pieces of evidence came from?

"The Bronco fiber on Ron's shirt? Oh! Yeah – O.J. lost it"!

"The Bundy glove? Oh! Yeah – O.J. lost it!"

"The knit ski cap? Oh! Yeah – O.J. lost it"!

"The glove behind O.J.'s house – wet with blood, eight hours after the murders? Oh! Yeah – O.J. lost it!

Do you now see that there is something **extremely peculiar** about the murder of Nicole, and which all the investigators and counsels have missed – because they didn't bother to analyze the bruise on Nicole's head?

- Why would the murderer knock Nicole unconscious with a **lethal weapon** like a gun – **but not kill her with that gun?**
- Secondly, when the murderer already had Nicole completely unconscious and intended to kill her, why did he pull out a **different** weapon – the knife – and cut her throat?
- Why didn't he, instead, simply break Nicole's neck (rapidly rotating her head) when she was already unconscious and defenseless?
- Or, when Nicole already lay on the ground – knocked unconscious by a heavy blow from a revolver handle – why didn't the murderer "finish the job" by whacking her a few more times with the gun to fracture her skull a couple of places?

  Or why didn't he crush her skull against the concrete tiled steps or the patio? Had he done that, Nicole would have died instantly, and the murderer could have been gone before Ron even showed up!
- Nicole was already completely unconscious. That will become even more evident, when I discuss her leg wounds.

  So, obviously, she wuldn't have felt anything, regardless of how she was being killed! Consequently, **the purpose of the knife**, could not have been to **frighten** Nicole, or to cause her excessive pain. **She never even saw the knife!**
- So, why did the murderer **purposely** create the bloody mess, and all the blood evidence, when it was **gory, repulsive,**

slower, more difficult, riskier – and absolutely unnecessary!

Remember, also, at this point, when Nicole had just been knocked unconscious, **Ron had not yet showed up!** So, if the murderer, at that point, had broken Nicole's neck or crushed her skull in a flash of a second and disappeared immediately, **Ron would not have seen him.** Hence, there would have been

- no struggle with Ron, and hence,
- no lost knit cap at Bundy – and, consequently, no hair or fiber on that **non–existing** cap,
- no bloody glove at Bundy,
- no cut finger (don't forget, though, that O.J. is not the murderer – but anyway),
- no bloody shoeprints from any Bruno Magli shoes – and, consequently,
- no "five blood drops" next to those non-existing shoeprints,
- no blood on the rear gate at Bundy,
- no blood in O.J.'s driveway,
- no bloody glove behind O.J.'s house, and
- no blood in O.J.'s Bronco (regardless of who the murderer is), because there wouldn't be any blood at the murder scene!

Let me stop there!

Now, why in heavens name would the murderer take out a knife and cut Nicole's neck at this point – unless he **purposely** created the **bloody mess** so that he could leave all this blood evidence – either **pointing to O.J. directly,** or **allowing the investigators to replace it in the LAPD's crime lab?**

The murderer **must** have created all this blood **on purpose!** That means – as I have argued since 1994 – that the murderer not only planted the gloves (and the cap). The murderer **purposely planted** all the blood evidence I listed above!

That is why **he chose a knife as his murder weapon! And that is why he not only killed Nicole with the knife, but cut Nicole's neck so grotesquely.**

If O.J. were the murderer, perhaps he could have been "clever" enough to plant the glove behind his own house, so he could later say:

> *"See! Someone is trying to frame me!"*

However, when it was totally unnecessary, would he, **deliberately**, have planted bloody shoeprints from exclusive Bruno Magli shoes? Would he have dripped blood along those shoeprints, smeared blood in his Bronco, dripped blood in his driveway, risked cutting his finger on the knife during a struggle with Ron, deposited the knit ski cap, etc., etc.? One must be out of one's mind to even think such foolish thoughts!

> The prosecutors and the plaintiffs explained that O.J. killed Nicole in a jealous rage, and that he wanted to **hurt** her. **But that is totally contradicted by the fact that the murderer knocked Nicole completely unconscious before he cut her neck**.

Nicole didn't feel a thing, although she may have reacted reflexively, but unconsciously, by moving her hands after her neck was cut!

When someone, deliberately, does something which is totally **unexpected and out of the ordinary, slower, harder, messier, and more troublesome than necessary, riskier than necessary, and gory and repulsive where that is not necessary either** – there is only one explanation:

There is a **reason** for it, or a **purpose** behind it!

Obviously, Nicole's murderer wasn't acting in a **rage**. Instead, he was **cool as a cucumber**, and the way he killed Nicole – by cutting her neck – was part of a **detailed plan** to frame O.J. with the bloody shoeprints, as well as with other false blood evidence the murderer **anticipated** the investigators would tamper with or replace – once they were convinced that O.J. were guilty.

Anyone can obtain an unlicensed gun in Los Angeles in a matter of minutes. A criminal's gun is usually not registered in the criminal's name. So if O.J. had attacked Nicole with a gun in the first place, he would probably also have killed her with that gun. A criminal doesn't worry about ballistic evidence. But a "smart" police officer would!

LAPD officers also carry guns. Contrary to a criminal's gun, an LAPD officer's gun is registered. And both ballistic evidence, as well as imprints from a gun's handle on a victim's skull can assist in identifying a gun, if it had been used to kill Nicole.

The murderer being "clever" enough to "pad" the revolver handle to avoid leaving identifiable imprints on Nicole's head – or blood on his gun – and being clever enough to plan the killing of Nicole (and Ron) with a **knife – although he has a gun –** indicates, to me – although hardly to a medical examiner – that an LAPD officer might be the perpetrator.

If the murderer is an LAPD detective, he would have a gun – as insurance, and to knock Nicole unconscious – but prefer not to use it to murder Nicole (and Ron)! And he would know enough about murder investigations to be smart enough to take such precautions.

The murderer didn't care whether Nicole suffered or not. All the murderer was interested in was to create a bloody murder scene, in order to frame O.J. with bloody Bruno Magli shoeprints, and other blood evidence the investigators would be able to tamper with. And for that he needed Nicole unconscious, so he could **cut her neck almost completely while still keeeping her alive!**

This also explains why the murder of Nicole took place down by the gate. Part of the murderer's plan was – definitely – to knock Nicole unconscious before slitting her throat. Had he faced Nicole in the doorway to her condo, he could not have attacked her, by surprise, from behind. And he would not have had room to swing his hand with or without a gun or a knife, sideways against her chin. It would definitely have been possible for Nicole to avert or deflect the blow, in her doorway, and start screaming.

To make certain that Nicole was struck completely unconscious, totally by surprise, from behind, in one clean powerful blow, the murderer lured her down to the gate, where he could strike her from behind – with the handle of his revolver – as she turned around and led the way back to the steps.

Then, after she was unconscious, the murdered killed her – not with the gun, nor with his bare hands, strangling or choking her, nor by breaking her neck or crushing her skull, but by **using a totally different murder instrument**, namely the knife.

All of this is simply too peculiar and too much of a coincidence to be unplanned. The murderer knew exactly what he was doing – and why!

Now to the wounds on Nicole's right leg. They are even more **convincing!**

The wounds on Nicole's leg have been completely overlooked by all four medical examiners. Yet, as my readers will come to understand, **the wounds on Nicole's leg may hold the most important key to understanding what really happened at Bundy – and why!** First some background information:

The murderer must have known both Nicole and O.J. Otherwise he wouldn't have killed Nicole, and left one of the murder gloves behind O.J.'s house and smeared the victims' blood in O.J.'s Bronco, etc.

I believe the murderer is an LAPD officer, probably Mark Fuhrman. Detective Fuhrman knew O.J. and Nicole. He had been to Rockingham investigating a 911 call from Nicole in 1985. Fuhrman hated interracial couples strongly enough that he might have decided to kill Nicole and frame O.J. for the murder.

According to Fuhrman's own testimony, his meeting with the Simpsons *"impressed itself on his memory"*! And, of course, my readers still have *"The Fuhrman Tapes"* fresh in their memories.

There were even some speculations that Fuhrman had an intimate relationship with Nicole. Fuhrman himself bragged about that to his colleagues. He also mentioned to them – before the murders – that Nicole had a "boobs job" (breast implants), and he called himself, *"Nicole's cop."* This **suggests**, at least, that Fuhrman had an intimate relationship with Nicole.

If so, Fuhrman could have bought a pair of Bruno Magli shoes, because he knew, from Nicole, that O.J. had a preference for Italian shoes. Or he could have observed this himself, if he visited Nicole at Rockingham, when O.J. was away at football games.

Nicole was not killed with a knife because O.J. hated her and was in a jealous rage. Nicole was killed with a knife because the murderer wanted to create a pool of blood, which he could step in, thereby leaving bloody Bruno Magli shoeprints – pointing to O.J.!

The murderer needed more than just blood splatters on the ground. He needed a large puddle of blood in which he could plant **the entire soles** of both his shoes – so forensic experts should have **no problem identifying** those bloody shoeprints.

That's why a knife was used. And that's why Nicole's neck was cut so viciously, in spite of the fact that the murderer probably had a gun and had already knocked Nicole unconscious.

That's the reason why the murderer struck such a severe blow to Nicole's head, with his gun, although he didn't intend to kill her with the gun. The murderer was making absolutely certain that Nicole was knocked unconscious. The murderer wanted Nicole silenced and unresisting so he could calmly cut her neck with a clean, deep cut.

However, the murderer didn't want to kill Nicole with the gun, because then he couldn't create the bloody mess, even if he later cut her throat. Her heart wouldn't be

pumping out any blood, if he killed her with a second blow to her head!

Fuhrman had lured Nicole down to the gate. She recognized Fuhrman. They said, *"Hi!"* Fuhrman probably had a date with Nicole, or he simply told Nicole that he needed to talk to her about something important, and asked if he could come in. She agreed, opened the gate, then **turned around to her left** to lead the way up the steps.

As soon as she took a step to her left and turned around, Fuhrman struck her from behind, with his gun padded in the knit cap. Nicole's knees buckled, but before she fell, Fuhrman grabbed her around the waist and put her down gently. That's why there was **only one** bruise and severe hemmorhage from a blow to her head.

Fuhrman didn't want her to simply fall down. Had he allowed that, and Nicole had hit the concrete steps, or the concrete and steel railing, with her head, she could have fractured her skull and died instantly. If so, Fuhrman could not have created a pool of blood on the ground, because Nicole's heart would not be beating.

Besides, if Nicole had received a severe contact injury to her head, from falling down, forensic pathologists could have determined that Nicole was purposely knocked unconscious before her neck was cut. Perhaps that would have made investigators look at the use of a knife as a murder weapon in a different light. However, I don't know if Fuhrman had this in mind when he put Nicole down gently.

Let me set the scene more accurately. It is useful to refer to directions in geographical terms rather than as left or right, since left and right changes with the perspective of the person I am referring to (see illustrations at the end of this chapter, and also the front cover of this book):

There is a narrow, concrete, tiled, walkway between Bundy Drive, in front (**east** side) of Nicole's building, and the alley at the rear (**west** side) of the building. At each end of the walk-way there is a gate referred to as the **"Bundy"** gate and the **"rear"** gate. The direction of the walkway is **east-west** from Bundy Drive to the alley.

Coming from the alley, towards Bundy Drive, the walk-way ends in four steps leading down to a small "patio," about 3 ft long and 3.5 ft wide. At the end of this patio is the Bundy gate, opening outwards, hinged on its **north** side and with it's latch on its **south** side. Outside the Bundy gate there is a short 20 feet continuation of the walkway to the Bundy Drive side-walk.

Right along the **south** edge of the small patio there is a fence, from the corner of the wall at the bottom of the steps, and to the gate post for the latch. To the **north** there is an opening from the patio into a small fenced-in **"niche"** – a vegetation area with some shrubbery and some tree stubs.

The niche was just dirt ground and vegetation, while **the patio was covered with tiles.** (I say "was" because today, the whole area has been rebuilt).

The gate's latch, as seen from inside the Bundy gate, was on the right (south) side. Flush with the gate post was the fence. Hence, after opening the gate, Nicole had to turn to her **left** (north) – into the **center** of the patio – when she turned around to lead the way up the steps. Had she turned to her **right** (south) she would have turned directly into the **fence**.

When Nicole was struck from behind, she must have been somewhere in the **middle** of the small patio – in other words, fairly close to the **steps** and to the **dirt area of the niche**. A good esti-mate is probably **one foot** from the steps and equally close to the north edge of the patio and the vegetation area.

It is also worth noticing that she was **barefoot!** It is unthink-able that her bare feet could slip or slide on the dry, tiled patio.

Let us now return to the drama as it unfolded. The fact that the blow to Nicole's head clearly indicated that she was knocked deeply unconscious, but yet, she had no injuries indicating that she had

fallen down, obviously suggested that she did not fall down – she was **grabbed**, as her knees buckled, and **put down gently!**

Had Fuhrman not grabbed Nicole, she would probably have fallen, head first, against the concrete steps or the steel railing. If so, she would most likely have sustained rather severe injuries to her head or face, like for instance, a broken nose, a cut eyebrow, a cut lip, broken teeth – or perhaps even a fractured skull.

In case of a fractured skull, Nicole would have died instantly, and the murderer could not have created the blood he wanted – because Nicole's heart would have stopped beating, instantly.

Hence, immediately after knocking her unconscious, the murderer grabbed Nicole from behind, with his left arm around her waist. He held her up for a second or two, while he tossed the knit cap on the ground and holstered his gun. Then he put her down gently.

Again, when the murderer knocked Nicole unconscious, with the intention of killing her within seconds, but he still didn't allow her to fall against the concrete steps, there must be a specific reason for it. The murderer wanted Nicole unconscious – **but alive**, so her heart could pump the blood the murderer needed for his bloody shoeprints – and all the other blood evidence he intended to leave behind in order to frame O.J.! There is no other logical explanation for it!

Because Nicole's bare feet must have been just one foot or so from the steps, her head and neck ended up over the two lower steps at first. That was the direction she was leaning when she was struck.

Not risking that she might regain consciousness and scream – the murderer immediately – cut her neck. Her blood gushed out on the lower step.

However, that's not where the murderer wanted the blood!

He wanted to create a large puddle of blood on the **tiled patio,** where he could cover the underside of his entire soles with blood.

So, he quickly lifted Nicole's upper body and pulled her off the steps. But as he now lowered her upper body, he realized that her head and neck would end up over the vegetation area instead! **The patio was much too small for Nicole's body!**

Had the murderer put her down with her head inside the vegetation area, most of her blood would have disappeared into the ground, and he would not have been able to create a well defined, large puddle of blood.

Fuhrman needed Nicole's blood well onto the tiled patio – where he could use a large blood puddle almost as a red ink pad for his rubber soled Bruno Magli shoes!

Therefore, **he didn't put her down – yet.**

With his hands still around Nicole's waist and one foot on each side of her legs, Fuhrman "jerked" her body backwards.

In doing so, **Nicole's left foot and right leg was pushed underneath the fence on the south side of the patio.** (See ill.).

Sharp points underneath the bottom of the fence scraped and cut the skin on Nicole's right leg, upwards along the calf muscle, almost all the way to the back of her knee.

This injury has been completely overlooked or ignored by four expert forensic pathologists! How is that possible?

Where Nicole's leg was at its thickest, it got jammed, or it stopped because of her bent knee. Fuhrman couldn't pull her further back.

Now, Nicole's bleeding leg was jammed underneath the fence, but still, if the murderer had put her straight down – on her stomach – her hips would stretch out and as a result her head and neck would "slide" off the patio and into the vegetation area again.

So what did the murderer do?

He pulled Nicole **further back by bending her hips and knees – until her head and neck was well over the tiled patio –** and then <u>he turned her **sideways**</u> before he put her down.

On her side, Nicole's body would remain crouched and hence, entirely on the patio. **The murderer put her down on her left side, in the fetal position.**

Turning Nicole like that, **Nicole's right leg <u>rotated</u>** underneath the fence, **causing two parallel, rotating scraping marks on the upper part of her right leg.**

Even these two characteristic, transversely rotating, parallel scraping wounds on the back of Nicole's upper right leg (from where the other, longitudinal, cut wound ended) have been totally overlooked or ignored by the pathologists in this case!

I am baffled! These wounds were far more significant in terms of solving this murder mystery, than all the knife wounds combined. These wounds – if the pathologists and the investigators had bothered to study them – clearly indicated that the murderer **purposely** pulled Nicole's body backwards, onto the patio, and **then turned her body sideways**, before he put her down – **so her neck should remain onto the tiled patio!**

Nicole ended up in a "fetal" position (hip, waist, and knees bent), on her left side, facing the gate, and with her right leg jammed underneath the fence.

Most importantly, however, Nicole ended up with her head and neck well off the vegetation area and the steps, and onto the tiled patio.
That's exactly how she was found 75 minutes later!

NOTICE! It is unthinkable that Nicole could have positioned herself underneath the fence like that, and **self-inflicted** the wounds on her leg. There is no way Nicole could have **fallen** and, all by herself, gotten her leg jammed underneath the fence – not to mention suffering a scraping, bleeding wound up the length of the back of her calf muscle, and **rotating** marks in the skin of her leg, where the bleeding wound ended, near the back of her knee.

She must have been pulled underneath the fence, **after** she was knocked **unconscious,** but **before** she died! Here is further proof of that:

The wounds bled, so her heart must still have been beating when she got those wounds on her leg.

Of course, suffering such wounds must have hurt Nicole – if she were **conscious**! Hence, if she were conscious, she would never have jammed her leg underneath the fence like that.

On the other hand, if Nicole was **un-conscious**, she could never have moved her entire lower right leg from the middle of the patio to underneath the fence.

Furthermore, if Nicole had regained consciousness during her murder, she would reflexively have pulled her leg away from the fence, because of the pain, and also kicked and squirmed because of the murderer's attack.

The fact that she was found, 75 minutes after her death, in this **exact same position**, clearly proves that Nicole never regained consciousness after the initial blow to her head knocked her unconscious.

You have just read what represents the key to solving the Simpson murder mystery! We have a lot to talk about now!

The only one who could have pulled/pushed Nicole's leg underneath the fence was the murderer! So why would he do that only seconds after cutting her neck?

Did it matter if Nicole's neck bled on the steps or inside the "niche" to the north of the patio, where she would have ended up if the murderer had just laid her down, or let her fall down? Was it that important to the killer to position Nicole's neck over the tiled, patio? What if he had laid her down with her bleeding neck inside the niche? That would actually have been safer – from the murderer's standpoint – because then she couldn't be seen from the sidewalk along Bundy Drive.

To anyone else, only out to murder her, it would not have mattered.

But to this murderer it obviously mattered! Because the murderer wanted Nicole's blood on the tiled patio (where he could step in it) and not on the bottom step, or in the dirt area where Nicole's blood would simply have disappeared into the ground!

Isn't it obvious, now, that the murderer didn't choose a knife as the murder weapon and cut Nicole's neck so viciously because he was in a rage. He did it because he wanted a large puddle of blood he could step in with both his shoes, so he could leave bloody Bruno Magli shoeprints framing O.J.!

That's why the murderer needed to pull Nicole's head and neck off the step, and away from the vegetation area, and onto the smooth, tiled patio!

To manage that, **he had to pull her backwards, towards the fence, and force her leg underneath the fence.**

But even that was not enough. He also had to bend her body, and then turn her sideways, so her head and neck would remain over the patio when he put her down.

Hence, the bloody shoeprints must have been deliberately planted. Therefore, O.J. must be innocent!

The fact that Nicole's leg got lodged underneath the fence, and suffered two parallel, **"rotating"** scratch wounds, demonstrated that the murderer first pulled her hips up and jerked her backwards. That's when she got the long bleeding wound up the back of her leg.

Then in a second effort the murderer turned Nicole sideways so he could pull her head completely onto the patio, and put her body down in a sideways, fetal position. That's when the "rotating" scratch wounds occurred.

The only reason a murderer would care whether Nicole's neck wound bled over the bottom step, in the niche, or two feet further south – on the patio – must have been that he intended to create this large puddle of blood for his Bruno Magli shoes.

Actually, it would have been **safer** for a murderer, simply out to kill Nicole, if he had **not** pulled Nicole **onto the patio**, but in the opposite direction – into the niche – because then he could not have been seen from the Bundy sidewalk. Pulling Nicole out of the niche, **which was covered by shrubbery,** and onto the patio, **directly inside the open gate to the Bundy Drive sidewalk,** represented an **added risk of exposure!** Hence, this must clearly have been **a significant part of the murderer's plan.**

I am amazed that four expert medical examiners have not even bothered to pay attention to the scraping wounds on Nicole's leg – and in particular the characteristic double, parallel, rotating wounds.

For two and a half years they have argued about **single edged or double edged knives**, and **one or two assailants** and **how long time** the murders took.

And all the time, right under their noses lay the key to solving this murder mystery!

For, I assume, everyone must realize now, that if the bloody Bruno Magli shoeprints at Bundy were no accident, but were **deliberately** created by the murderer – then there can no longer be any doubt that someone created this entire bloody murder scene in order to frame O.J.!

All the stuff about a **long struggle**, **defensive wounds** on Nicole's hands etc., is just **nonsense**. Nicole was knocked unconscious before she even knew what happened. She was placed down on the patio, in the exact same position she was found in 75 minutes later. The evidence is the wounds on her leg.

Had Nicole been pulled underneath the fence **after** she was dead, the wounds would not have bled! So it must have happened before she died. But her neck was cut right after she was knocked unconscious. There was also a lot of blood on the lowest step, but that's not where Nicole ended up. This blood on the lowest step could not have run "upwards" from the patio, so Nicole's neck must have been cut over the lowest step, and then, quickly, she must have been moved off the steps, onto the patio, and underneath the fence.

This proves that the murderer cut Nicole's neck **immediately – even before he moved her.** This again, proves that Nicole's neck was cut by the murderer without a second's hesitation. He knew, in other words, exactly what he wanted to do. The deliberate cutting of Nicole's neck was part of a detailed plan.

Of course, had Nicole been conscious, or regained consciousness during the murders, the wounds on her leg would have been painful. Even though her neck would have hurt much more, she would still – reflexively – have pulled her leg away from the fence. Besides, had she regained consciousness during the murder, she would have "squirmed," and her leg would have come loose from underneath the fence, or shown a disorganized wounds pattern.

Nicole was found dead, in the exact same fetal position which the murderer must have put her in – with her leg jammed underneath the fence. She didn't move an inch. Therefore, **Nicole never suffered – not even for a fraction of a second.**

Don't be fooled by medical examiners talking about "defensive cuts" on Nicole's hands. Hopefully, I have made it crystal clear how much, or little, the expert opinions of the medical examiners are worth! The fact that their four "expert opinions" differ like north and south, east and west, just goes to underline how little they understood!

It is definitely conceivable that Nicole could have received the cuts on her hands by **reflexively** moving her hands and arms, even while she was deeply unconscious. Just think about how you toss and turn during your sleep. And even though your arm may be jammed underneath your body for a long time, and really hurt, you don't feel that pain until you wake up. Nicole never woke up!

So, perhaps Nicole's hands moved, in front of her neck.

Or perhaps her hands were just in the way and got cut, when the murderer stabbed her repeatedly in the neck just before she died.

Besides, imagine Nicole being alive and conscious just before the murderer attacked her with his knife. Would she have defended herself, so her hands got cut, but not screamed for help? Are these medical examiners "nuts"?

Anyway, those injuries to her hands were not "defensive wounds"!

Surprisingly, the most significant elements in Nicole's autopsy report were the seemingly innocent bruise on her head and the wounds on her right leg.

Three professional forensic pathologists for the prosecutors and the plaintiffs, have studied Nicole's autopsy report and the accompanying pictures. All of them have seen these two relatively minor, non-fatal injuries.

Yet, these professional experts, with all their credentials, had not the foggiest idea that they were staring at the keys to solving the Simpson murder mystery.

Instead, they orchestrated the most absurd theories and court-room demonstrations, trying to match the victims' injuries to their theories of O.J. as the perpetrator.

Understand why I have little or no respect for such "experts" – but pity O.J. and his children whose lives and futures may forever have been destroyed by such charlatans!

Let me mention one other set of evidence and circumstances supporting my theory and demonstrating how little the "experts" and the prosecutors understood of this case – unless they conspired to frame O.J.!

Literally, "lumps" of Nicole's hair was found on Ron's flannel shirt. We are talking about 30-40 hairs! Now, how could that have happened? Do my readers recall from the trial, how the prosecutors and the medical examiners claimed that Nicole was knocked out, but she was not killed immediately. Then the murderer (O.J. allegedly) fought with Ron and killed him. Finally, the murderer returned to Nicole and slit her neck. That was the prosecutors' scenario. But how could Ron have Nicole's blood underneath his shoes then, if her neck was not yet cut. And how could 30-40 of Nicole's hairs end up on Ron's shirt, if this is what happened?

The prosecutors and the "expert" medical examiners could not explain that – because they had no idea what actually had transpired. Rather than teasing you with more questions, let me tell you what happened, and how all those hairs ended up on Rons shirt. You will see that even this strange occurrance fit right in with my overall theory.

The murderer put Nicole down gently, over the lowest step. Now, immediately he wanted to cut her neck. Again I have to use an example. If it sounds disrespectful, that is quite unintentional.

I have already explained how difficult it must have been to cut Nicole's neck so completely, even with an extremely sharp knife. I compared the situation to that of cutting a raw steak or a large fish.

Now, imagine you – for some reason – intend to cut the head off a "rag doll" with long hair. If you hold the doll hanging by the hair and apply the knife, the doll will just move about. You wouldn't even make a mark in the fabric surrounding the doll's neck.

So instead, you lower it to the floor and step on the dolls legs. Then you pull the doll "taut" by its hair. Now, you can cut the neck of the doll, but still not very easily, because the neck will move back and forth with the movement of your knife.

What do you do, instead? You put the doll down and step on its upper back, very close to the neck. Then you grab the hair and pull the **neck** taut – so the neck can't move! Now your sharp knife can cut the neck rather easily.

No disrespect – it was the same with Nicole's neck. If the murderer simply grabbed her hair and lifted her head up and back, he could not have cut her neck as thoroughly as he did – because her neck would move with the movement of his knife. To be able to cut Nicoles neck the way he did, the murderer had to **fixate** (immobilize) **her neck** completely.

To do that, the murderer gathered almost all her hair between his two gloved hands. He arranged it into a "pony tail," so to speak. Then he held this pony tail up with his right hand so he could grab it with his left hand – in a taut grip all the way down near Nicole's skull. Sqeezing her hair as hard as he could, the murderer could bend Nicole's head back and lock it firmly in this position. Now, Nicole's neck would not yield to the knife and move.

Grabbing Nicole's hair so tautly, was simply necessary in order to cut her neck so completely. Naturally, grabbing Nicole's hair so hard and tautly, pulled lumps of hairs from Nicole's head. They stuck to the murderer's **left** glove. Along came Ron, and was attacked by the **police officer** the way I have explained it. From behind, the murderer, pretending he was searching Ron for weapons, placed his left hand around Ron's chest and held him in a firm grip, while the murderer's right hand attacked Ron with the knife over and across Ron's right shoulder.

Placing his open gloved left hand across Ron's chest, just as he initiated the knife attack on Ron, transferred the lumps of Nicole's hairs, from the murderer's left glove to Ron's shirt.

On the cover of my book, I wrote that solving this murder mystery, didn't take "a brain surgeon"! Everything is actually pretty obvious, if you analyze the evidence conscientiously – and you have the right theory!

The transfer of the "lumps" of Nicole's hair onto Ron's shirt, further proves that Nicole's neck was cut before Ron was attacked. That again contradicts the official theory of the prosecution. How could they **not** see this?

I think they saw it. But to present the murder of Nicole as a **well planned deliberate attack** contradicted their theory of O.J. committing these murders in a state of jealous rage. As part of a conspiracy to frame O.J. and hide the shocking truth – that a police officer had murdered Nicole and Ron – the prosecution and the medical examiners concocted their totally irrational and incorrect scenario.

On the following pages I shall briefly illustrate how Nicole – and later, Ron – were killed. The few illustrations do not cover all the details. Likewise, the texts accompanying the illustrations are only meant to give short descriptions of what happened. For details the reader should refer to the descriptions of the murders, given earlier, throughout this chapter.

Overview of the Bundy Murder scene

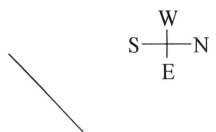

To the rear gate and the "alley"

——— To Nicole's condo

The "niche"

The "patio"

The "buzzer"

The Bundy gate

To Bundy Drive and the Bundy sidewalk

Knocking Nicole unconscious – by **surprise** – while facing her in her **doorway**, would be almost impossible. The murderer could not get behind her, and he could not get any sideways "leverage" for a blow. Even outside her door Nicole would **not have turned her back** to the murderer.

There was only one **place** and **time** the murderer could attack Nicole – by **surprise**, from **behind** – and that was **down by the Bundy gate** – **after** Nicole had opened it and she had just turned around to lead the way back up the steps. That was **where** and **when** the murderer had planned to knock Nicole **unconscious** – from behind – with his **gun,** perhaps padded in **the knit cap**.

Nicole fell forward, towards the steps. But the killer caught her by her waist and put her down gently on the bottom step. He tossed away his cap and holstered his gun. Then, immediately, he cut her neck, where she lay. That is why there was **a lot of blood also on the lower step**.

However, the killer wanted Nicole's blood on the **wider, tiled**

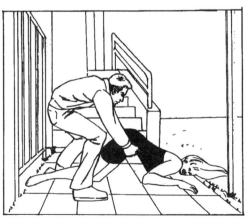

patio. There he could better step in it with his Bruno Magli shoes – **to frame O.J.** Quickly, the m u r d e r e r lifted Nicole by her waist, off the steps and onto the tiled patio. Clearly – if he just put her straight down – Nicole's head would be off the patio and into the dirt area, the "niche," to the north. There, all the blood would just disappear into the ground.

To get Nicole's blood where he could step in it, the killer rapidly **"jerked"** her body backwards. That is how her **right leg** got wedged **underneath the fence** on the opposite (south) side of the patio –

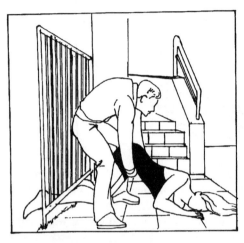

causing a **bleeding wound** up the **back** of her leg.

However, the patio was so small that if the killer put Nicole down – **on her stomach** – her body would stretch out and her head would slide back off the patio.

To keep Nicole's body crouched – so her cut neck would remain onto the tiled patio – when he put her down, the murderer turned Nicole's body sideways. Nicole's right leg turned with her body. That is how she got the "rotating" scrape marks on the back of her leg, just below the back of her knee.

In this sideways position the murderer could put Nicole down –

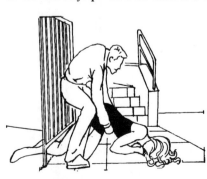

with her head still onto the tiled patio. Now, all the blood would gush out onto the patio where the murderer could better step in it, **deliberately, with the purpose of leaving behind full, bloody Bruno Magli shoe-prints, pointing to O.J**!

There is no way Nicole could have placed herself with her legs in this position. **Consciously – she wouldn't! Un-consciously – she couldn't!** The murderer placed her there, so he could get her

blood where he wanted it. This is exactly how Nicole was found, one hour and 15 minutes later. She had not moved an inch.

Photographs of Nicole's leg clearly shows that the murderer jerked her body backwards, **forcing** her right leg underneath the fence, causing a distinct, bleeding cut wound up the length of her leg, almost to behind her knee. The **rotating scrape marks** in her skin – from where the longitudinal wound ended, and towards the right – shows that, **after** he had jerked her **backwards**, the murderer turned Nicole's body **sideways**. The murderer's only reason for doing that was to be able to put her down on her left side, in a **crouched**

position, with her head onto the **tiled patio** – so Nicole's blood would gather there, and not disappear into the dirt and grass in the "niche."

Suddenly, Ron approached. The murderer had anticipated something like that. Being an LAPD detective, the killer quickly pulled his gun and flashed his police badge.

> **"There has been an accident! Keep your hands where I can see them, and walk over here!"**

Like any normal citizen would have done, Ron complied with the police officer's order! He had nothing to fear from an LAPD officer – **he thought**! That is how the murderer got Ron into the position where he could attack Ron from behind – by surprise! With Nicole at his feet, dead in a pool of blood, **only a police officer** could have fooled Ron like that!

The detective ordered Ron into the niche and roughed him up against the fence so as to search Ron for weapons, causing Ron to exclaim: *"Hey – hey – hey!"* The police officer sneared back:

> **"Hands on the fence – step back – spread your legs!"**

Ron was completely unsuspecting. Behind Ron's back where Ron could not see it, the detective holstered his gun and took out his knife again.

Pretending he were searching Ron for a weapon, the LAPD detective's deadly knife approached Ron's neck!

Before Ron realized what happened, the police officer reached over Ron's right shoulder and rammed his knife deep into Ron's neck. Unable to scream, but desperate, Ron had only one thought in mind – escape, to the sidewalk and the street! He grabbed the fence bars and then the gate post trying to pull himself out of the trap – past the LAPD detective who was stabbing him repeatedly.

Ron managed to get a few feet outside the gate before he lost his strength and the murderer dragged him back inside the niche again.

When all of Ron's strength was gone, his knees buckled, and he slumped in the murderer's arms.

The detective didn't try to hold Ron up any more, but half pushed him, half laid him down against one of the tree stumps. Later, that was where Ron was found.

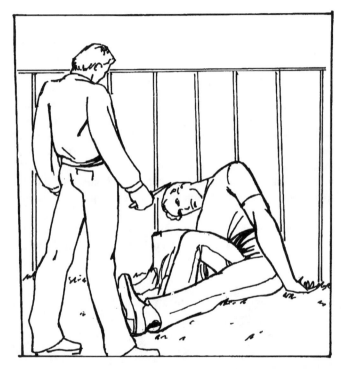

Ron's *"Hey – hey – hey!"* makes it clear that he was not ambushed. He saw the murderer!

With Nicole dead in a pool of blood, there is no way **O.J.** could have fooled Ron and lured him into the niche, so Ron could be attacked, by surprise, from behind.

Only an LAPD officer with a gun and a police badge could have trapped Ron this way!

CHAPTER 28

"Ugly Ass Shoes"

I trust most of my readers agree with me, by now, that the murder of Nicole was in every detail set up to frame O.J., and that O.J., therefore, must be innocent.

From this perspective, it doesn't even matter if O.J. ever owned a pair of Bruno Magli shoes. The shoeprints were purposely planted to frame him. I trust I've proven that, convincingly, in the previous chapter. The bloody Bruno Magli shoeprints were the cornerstone of the murderer's plan to frame O.J. And if so, ten thousand photographs of O.J. wearing Bruno Magli shoes doesn't make him one bit less innocent!

O.J. denied ever owning a pair of Bruno Magli shoes. Then someone came up with a bunch of photographs of O.J. wearing such shoes. OK. So O.J. may have lied!

Because his adversaries didn't understand the truth about the bloody shoeprints, as I have explained it above, they attacked O.J. so viciously with accusations and innuendos. In his struggle to preserve his life and protect his children from being taken away from him, he may have been **forced to lie!**

Maybe O.J. lied. But that doesn't make him a murderer!

Let me ask my readers what they would have done.

Suppose you were O.J. You may have had a pair of Bruno Magli shoes. A murderer knew that, and was trying to frame you for a murder you did not commit – and you know you are innocent. You have no idea who left the bloody Bruno Magli shoeprints. You just know that you didn't leave them!

The lynch mob, however, have already thrown the rope over the hanging three and are shouting that if you ever wore a pair of Bruno Magli shoes, they are going to stretch your neck until it leaves your children orphaned!

Tell me – honestly! What would you have done? I know what I would have done!

To save my life and my children, I would have sworn that I would never have worn those *"ugly ass shoes"*!

In my heart, I would have asked God's forgiveness for having lied, and prayed that nobody would show up with an old picture of me wearing Bruno Magli's!

O.J. was framed with the knit cap, the bloody murder scene, the bloody shoeprints, the blood drops next to them, the blood drops on the Bundy gate, the blood in the Bronco, the blood in his driveway, and the Bundy glove.

The other bloody murder glove, behind his house, was just the **"trigger"**! This theory explains so many things:

- What the cap was doing at Bundy in the first place;
- O.J.'s hairs on the cap (planted by the investigators);
- the bruise on Nicole's head;
- the position of the bruise;
- the size and shape of the bruise;
- why Nicole's skin was not cut at the bruise;
- the presence of, and the size of the hemorrhage underneath the bruise;
- the wounds on Nicole's leg and how she must have received those wounds.
- the use of a gun;
- the use of a knife – in spite of the presence of the gun;
- the vicious cutting of Nicole's neck; all the blood;
- the amount of blood on the lowest step, proving that Nicole's neck was cut there, and then moved to the position where she was found
- the conspicuous double set of bloody Bruno Magli shoeprints I return to that later).

Talking about the Bruno Magli shoes, let me bring up a few other points. There has been so much "hoopla" surrounding the photographs depicting O.J. wearing Bruno Magli shoes. I have discussed the possibility that O.J. lied about never having worn Bruno Magli shoes, simply because he was scared to death of admitting having owned such a pair of shoes. Imagine O.J. saying:

> *"Yes, I once had a pair of shoes like that, but someone stole them from me two months before the murders."*

Or:

> *"I gave the Bruno Magli shoes away last spring, but I don't remember whom I gave them to."*

No one would have believed him anyway. He would have been crucified! He would have lost his house, his money – and his children. He didn't have any choice. Public opinion – because people were so prejudiced against him – may have forced him to lie.

What is more interesting, rather, is to look at the shoes, in and of themselves. What **kind** of shoes are these Bruno Magli shoes that everyone is talking about?

First of all, this particular model – the Lorenzo model – is a **"snow shoe"! It's a "winter boot"!**

Born in a typical **"winter country,"** Norway, I know what I am talking about! The murder shoes, are in fact not **shoes** at all.

- They are typical **winter boots!**
- They cover your ankles, to prevent snow and ice from entering.
- They are warm.
- They have thick rugged rubber soles.
- The rubber soles have a rough design to give good traction and prevent you from slipping and falling on slick ice and snow – built on the same principle as the winter/snow tires for your car!
- An extra wide, protective, rubber guard runs all around the

side of the soles about one inch up on the sides of the shoes, to protect the edges of the soles, and the lower portion of the upper leather, from getting wet, due to snow, slush, and ice.

The Bruno Magli murder shoes are most definitely not a pair of shoes any "sane" person would put on in Los Angeles in the middle of the summer. In Europe where these shoes originate (Italy), they are used as warm, protective foot gear in icy and snowy conditions, in or near the Italian, Swiss, Austrian, German, and French Alps, as **"after skiing"** wear in Alpine villages; and in the colder Scandinavian countries they are worn as everyday foot wear during the long, cold winter.

I have owned many pairs of similar boots. In Scandinavia, when the spring comes, people put away these winter boots for 5-6 months, and take out their spring and summer shoes. I assume the same had been the case with O.J. if the pictures of him wearing Bruno Magli "shoes" are real.

Typically, the pictures were taken during the football season, in other words during the fall or winter.

The only reason for O.J. to wear a pair of Bruno Magli winter boots in Los Angeles in the middle of June – **if** he were the murderer – would be to wear rubber soles, to avoid slipping. But were that the case, it would have been far more natural for a man like O.J. to put on a pair of Nike's or Reebok's, or keep on the tennis shoes he already wore that day, and which Detective Lange collected at O.J.'s house the next day.

The only person I can see, who would put on a pair of Bruno Magli, Lorenzo model, snow shoes before driving to Bundy in the middle of June to murder someone, would be a murderer who was trying to frame O.J. for the murder – by leaving behind bloody shoeprints from those Bruno Magli shoes.

Do my readers see that nothing makes sense in this murder case against O.J.?

Suppose, however, as I have suggested, that Fuhrman knew O.J. had a preference for Italian shoes, and he wanted to frame O.J. by leaving bloody shoeprints from a pair of fairly rare, expensive Italian shoes, which could point to O.J.! What brand would Fuhrman pick?

Well, he couldn't pick a pair of sleek, elegant **leather soled** Italian summer shoes, because they wouldn't leave distinct sole patterns. Fuhrman – if he bought a pair, solely for the purpose of leaving distinct bloody shoeprints, framing O.J. – would purchase or aquire, and wear the Bruno Magli "Lorenzo" model!

It is a winter boot. But what is more important, it has the required rugged design, and most of all, it has a **rubber** sole.

The murderer, with his Bruno Magli "Lorenzo" model boots, stepping in the blood at Bundy, was almost as **wetting a rubber stamp in a red ink pad** – to leave your return address on an envelope!

Everything regarding the bloody Bruno Magli shoeprints was so conspicuous and "studied" that it had to be a "set-up." The coincidences were just too many.

Even if O.J. were the murderer, and he didn't think about what he were doing and what evidence he left behind, he would have had to do so many incredibly strange things!

Imagine O.J. driving to Bundy in the middle of June, wearing Bruno Magli "Lorenzo" model winter boots, Kashmere lined leather gloves, and a knit ski cap, create the bloody mess, step in it and walk away – twice, lose his ski cap and his gloves, but not pick them up again, etc., etc.! It is absolutely out of the question that he could even have thought about all of it – not to mention, do it – even if he totally didn't care! **Actually, I am a bit surprised the investigators didn't also find one of his golf clubs under the shrubbery at Bundy!** Or O.J.'s Heisman trophy on the steps!

I f O.J. were the murderer he must have sat down in the evening of June 12, 1994, and told himself:

I am going over to murder Nicole. And I am going to wear the *wackiest outfit I can think of – like thin, black, formal **"dress socks,"** in a pair of **winter boots**, with a knit **ski cap on my head**, and **leather gloves on my hands** – and kill Nicole in the most grotesque manner anyone has ever seen, and do the, apparently, most ridiculous and stupid things imaginable – like throwing away the ski cap full of my hairs, and one of the bloody gloves, next to the body of Nicole, and dump the other bloody glove behind my own house, smear Nicole's blood in my car, and cut my finger and drip my blood all the way from Bundy to my foyer! That way no one will think I did it!.*

Many have characterized the murder of Nicole as **"over-kill."** Doesn't it strike my readers that the evidence against O.J. is also a kind of "over-kill"?

From the perspective of an investigator or a prosecutor, if all the evidence against O.J. were real – it were almost too good to be true. There is a saying in the business world:

> *"If something seems too good to be true – it usually is!"*

CHAPTER 29

Nicole's Watch And More Suspicious Evidence

The amount of evidence proving that O.J. is innocent is so enormous. As soon as we dig just a little bit deeper into any piece of evidence – and not just consider it in a 10 second sound byte on the evening news, or in a five word headline in a newspaper – we discover discrepancies followed by discrepancies. Nothing is what it, at first, seems to be.

I didn't want to get too bogged down in details when I laid out my main murder theory. I concentrated on the central pieces of evidence which proved that O.J. is innocent, and on how I believe the murders were committed.

In a later chapter, titled **"The Rest Of The Evidence,"** I shall discuss most of the other familiar pieces of evidence in the case – rebutting them, or even showing that they corroborate my theory.

Throughout this case, the alarming trend was that all the pieces of evidence which might be construed to point to O.J.'s **guilt**, were such which **might** have been **fabricated, planted, or tampered with** in some way or form – and in most cases there were clear signs of that actually having been done. On the other hand, all the pieces of evidence which could **not possibly have been tampered with**, pointed to O.J.'s **innocence**.

That was directly "alarming" in itself. But the worst part of it was that the investigators and prosecutors, and later, the plaintiffs – in spite of knowing this – continued to pursue their cases against O.J. When they came across evidence which clearly was planted in an effort to frame O.J., or evidence which clearly proved that O.J. was innocent, or even evidence that pointed straight at Mark Fuhrman, the investigators, the prosecutors, and the plaintiffs either suppressed such evidence, or misrepresented it.

Most people never heard about this. You see, if a piece of evidence didn't fit the theory of the investigation and the prosecution, they just dropped it! Often, the defense, even, didn't learn about it until it was too late. When the defense did learn about it during the trials, they were often precluded from introducing it, because they could not, conclusively, prove what had happened. Besides, we all know how Judge Fujisaki ruled on the admissibility of evidence of police conspiracy and evidence tampering:

"Request denied! The police is not on trial in this case!"

And sometimes, the defense simply didn't **understand** how certain pieces of evidence actually exonerated O.J.

I have already proven, conclusively, several different ways, that O.J. could not be the murderer. And although there is no direct **physical** evidence tying Mark Fuhrman to the murders, **the circumstantial evidence against Mark Fuhrman is overwhelming.**

First of all, since O.J. could not possibly have committed these murders, there isn't any other suspect than Fuhrman, who could tie in with all the evidence. More specifically, as I proved earlier, Fuhrman must have planted the Rockingham glove. Nobody else could have done it, and as I have shown, there is plenty of circumstantial evidence to suggest that he did it. Unquestionably, that makes him, at least, part of the murder conspiracy.

Add to that Fuhrman's racism and his hatred towards interracial couples in particular, his history of violence – documented by many charges of police brutality and use of excessive force, as well as thousands of pages of Internal Affairs investigations and psychiatric reports on him, his psychopathic history, *"The Fuhrman tapes,"* as well as his role in MAW (and WASP?) and his neo-Nazi sympathies, and the fact that Fuhrman knew O.J. and Nicole – the latter, perhaps, intimately. Also take into account that the murders, as I have justified rather convincingly, must have been committed by an LAPD officer, and that the bloody, gruesome MO seems right up Fuhrman's alley.

Most of all, though, consider that Mark Fuhrman committed yet another, hitherto unpublicized, act of **perjury** during his **sworn** testimony, when he – assisted by Prosecutor Marcia Clark – **gave himself a false alibi for the time of the murders!** And when this, after the criminal trial, was exposed – although not publicized – even the new alibi Fuhrman presented us with, was not believable.

First of all, why would he present a false alibi during his testimony, if he actually used his American Express credit card to pump gas in Pomona at the time of the murders? Secondly, what's to say that **Fuhrman** is the person who used his credit card at that gas pump in Pomona. Automated gas pumps don't require a signature in conjunction with the use of a credit card. Someone else – an accomplice – could have used Fuhrman's credit card to give Fuhrman an apparent alibi.

This is so obvious, however, that during his testimony in the criminal trial, Fuhrman and Prosecutor Clark elected to concoct a different alibi, by having Fuhrman's wife corroborate that he got home at 10:30 pm – from the **non-existing barbecue** at the **non-existing Protective League seminar** at La Quinta!

When you have all this circumstantial evidence against Mark Fuhrman, and when all the physical evidence clearly demonstrated that O.J. was being framed and that the investigators were being set up, you must be "dumb and dumber" not to see that Mark Fuhrman is a much more likely suspect than O.J. – or, rather, that Fuhrman is the **only** suspect!

And then, Marcia Clark sat there, a couple of weeks before Fuhrman's testimony, knowing not only that Detective Fuhrman lacked an alibi for the time of the murders, but that he was about to present a **false alibi during his sworn testimony** – saying he was at a Protective League seminar and got home to his wife five minutes before the murders took place!

The State's lead prosecutor let it happen. During Fuhrman's obviously perjured testimony, she even smiled and joked along with Fuhrman, while knowing that he probably killed the two people she was trying to convict O.J. of having killed!

We shouldn't be concerned about the physical evidence pointing to O.J., because the murder of Nicole was deliberately planned with the intent of framing O.J., and all of that evidence was clearly fabricated. And we shouldn't be concerned about the lack of physical evidence against Fuhrman, because there was such an enormous amount of circumstantial evidence against him. Besides, Fuhrman knew how to avoid leaving any evidence pointing to himself. Fuhrman's initial attempt to create a false alibi – and the fact that even his newest, alternative, alibi (the use of his credit card in Pomona) is uncorroborated – proves he is hiding what he did between 10:30 and 11:00 pm on June 12, 1994!

How can the U.S. public and the media continue to torture O.J. and his children with the obviously false accusations against him. Don't they see that he is innocent, that he was cleverly framed by a group of racist, brutal, macho, violent, LAPD officers, and that Mark Fuhrman, and a couple of his colleagues, probably, murdered Nicole and Ron, **just for the heck of it, to prove to themselves that they could do it – and get away with it, because they were LAPD officers!**

> Imagine what O.J. and his children have suffered already. And observe how gracefully O.J. is accepting and handling this brutal fate life has dealt him! If there ever were a modern version of the *"Book of Job"* . . .!

America – regardles of how embarrassing it may feel – isn't there a time when we should say, *"Enough is enough!"*?

Obviously, the majority of the public and the media refuse to listen to reason and common sense. So let me continue to prove that O.J. was being framed, and also add to the circumstantial evidence against Mark Fuhrman.

There are, in particular, three pieces of evidence which add to my already convincing theory: Nicole's watch, a bloody finger-print on the rear gate at Bundy, and the man's, large size, jeans jacket left in Nicole's kitchen. For those who still don't believe

O.J. was framed and that Fuhrman is the murderer, maybe this will convince you!

The crystal (glass) of Nicole's watch was crushed and her watch had stopped on 10:03.

We don't know for sure, of course, if it was **"pm"** or **"am,"** but we have every reason to believe that the watch indicated 10:03 **pm**. Had Nicole's watch been crushed and stopped at 10:03 **am,** Nicole must have noticed it long before leaving the house to drive to Sydney's dance recital that afternoon. If for nothing else, Nicole must have kept an eye on her watch that particular day to make sure she and the children got to the recital on time!

Nicole would not have left the house with a crushed, stopped watch. I assume she had a second watch, so if her watch had been crushed and had stopped at 10:03 in the morning, Nicole would have worn a different watch – or no watch at all.

Initially the investigators thought the watch could be an important piece of evidence – so **the investigators photographed Nicole's watch – close up!**

By then they had already spoken with Kato Kaelin, who explained that he and O.J. had returned from McDonalds at 9:30 pm, whereafter O.J. had gone inside his house, alone. After that, nobody saw O.J. until the limo driver saw him at 10:55 pm.

Of course, initially, it suited the investigators and the prosecutors perfectly, to have Nicole's watch crushed and stopped on 10:03 (pm). That opened up the "window of opportunity" much better than if Robert Heidstra, for instance, testified that Ron, probably, was alive as late as 10:45 – or a couple of minutes earlier.

Accordingly, the investigators treated the crushed watch as an important piece of evidence – initially!

During the criminal trial, the prosecution tried desperately to move the timeline back towards ten o'clock. So why didn't they present Nicole's watch into evidence?

No, you see, later, they found out that O.J. had called Paula

Barbieri on his cellular phone at both 10:02 and 10:03 pm! There were phone records to that effect. So then he couldn't have parked his Bronco in the alley behind Nicole's condo; gathered a knife, gloves, and a cap; walked to the Bundy gate in front of Nicole's condo; rung the buzzer by the gate; waited for Nicole to come down to open the gate; and killed Nicole at that same time – 10:03 pm – when he was on the phone to Paula!

Besides, according to the prosecution, the break-up with **Paula** was supposed to be the "trigger" that created such a rage in O.J. that he decided to kill **Nicole** – understand that one, if you can! So then, after having tried, in vain, to contact Paula, O.J. must have driven home first to change into his murder outfit and grab a knife – if we accept the prosecutions theory.

Hence, the prosecution soon realized that 10:03 pm was not the time of the murders. Besides, it became more and more evident that the murders took place after 10:30 pm. Robert Heidstra's testimony was corroborated by Sydney (although she was not asked to give a statement). And 10:35-10:40 also tied in better with the thumps on Kato's wall, corroborated by Kato's telephone records – although **the thumps on Kato's wall** – unquestionably timed by Kato's telephone record to 10:40-10:42 pm – **busted the prosecution's timeline from the opposite end!** There simply was no window of opportunity for O.J. to have committed these murders.

What should honest investigators do under those circumstances? Right! They should say:

> *"Sorry! We were wrong! The watch indicates that Nicole was murdered at 10:03 – but she wasn't! Maybe someone is trying to frame O.J. and set us up. If so, O.J. must be innocent. Let's look for another suspect!"*

Again, not these investigators and prosecutors! They found a better way to deal with Nicole's watch. **They disposed of it!** That is not to say that they threw it away. What I mean by **"disposed of it,"** is that they put it aside and never mentioned it anymore, since it didn't fit their theory!

These murder investigators never ceased to astonish me! But I am even more astonished by the **media** – persistently refusing to pick up on these things.

I am also a bit surprised that the **defense** did not follow up on Nicole's watch. But there was a reason for that.

The defense were trying to push the murder timeline forward, as close as possible to 10:55 when the limo driver spotted O.J. at Rockingham, since that would give O.J. an alibi.

At first glance, it is understandable that the defense had no interest in the watch. **10:03** pm was obviously not the time of the murders. And it was not apparent to the defense that the watch could help – or hurt – them in any way. They simply didn't care about it.

However, the watch could, definitely, help the defense and hurt the prosecution, and I am a bit surprised that the defense didn't see it – just as I am upset that the prosecutors suppressed it. Do my readers see how the watch, stopped at 10:03 could help the defense? Take a few seconds to think about it – if you care – before you read on!

– First of all, as I explained, 10:03 must have been 10:03 **pm.**
– Secondly, 10:03 pm wasn't even close to the time of the murders. According to Mr. Heidstra and Sydney, 10:03 was about 32-37 minutes off. Hence, the point of time, **10:03, had nothing to do with the murders**, directly. Nor could that time simply indicate that Nicole's watch was a few minutes off! 32-37 minutes is not "a few minutes" off!
– Furthermore, it would have been a rare coincidence if Nicole's watch had stopped, and the glass had been crushed, just be cause she fell. Wrist watches are much stronger than that. Perhaps the glass might have gotten scratched. But to crush the glass and stop the watch, simply by falling to the ground from an upright position – that would have been an extremely rare coincidence! (Of course, we are used to extremely rare concidences in this case!)

- Anyway, I have earlier explained that Nicole **didn't** fall down. As the murderer struck her unconscious, he grabbed her around her waist and put her down gently. That is the reason why her face did not show any marks or wounds from her having **fallen down onto the steps**.

- Finally, just check this out yourself! **Imagine** that you are knocked unconscious and fall to the ground – totally limp! Look at your arms and your wrist, where your watch is.

  Do you see how impossible it is that the outside of your wrist would hit the ground – **first** – if you are unconscious? Your fingers and hands would point downwards as you fall, and make contact with the ground first and asorb the impact – even if your watch, too, made contact, later.

- **Besides, even if Nicole's watch had been crushed in a fall, it would not have stopped on 10:03 – because Nicole was not killed at 10:03!**

There is only one **reasonable** explanation:

> **Someone "fiddled" with Nicole's watch! Someone set Nicole's watch to 10:03 – and crushed it** – so it should remain at 10:03 – and hence – make if **appear** that Nicole were murdered at 10:03 pm!

There are **only two people** who could have done that – Nicole or the murderer! Does anyone on the surface of this planet believe Nicole set her watch back to 10:03 and crushed it, just before she was murdered, or that she, perhaps, crushed it exactly at 10:03 (pm), but continued to wear the crushed watch until she was murdered half an hour later? Of course not!

> **The murderer, who killed Nicole around 10:35-45 pm, lifted up Nicole's wrist – after Ron, too, had been murdered. The murderer set the clock to 10:03 and smashed Nicole's arm, with the watch, against the tiled patio – or he smashed the glass with his gun – to stop the watch at 10:03.**

Of course, the watch could, theoretically, have been crushed when Nicole was attacked and killed. However, her watch could **not** have been crushed when Nicole was attacked – and then **set itself back** 32-37 minutes!

That must have taken the deliberate doings of a human being. And the choice is either a **dead Nicole**, or a **live murderer**! The choice is easy! So now, we must ask ourselves:

Why would the murderer set the watch back 32-37 minutes?

Secondly, we must ask ourselves:

This murderer, who set Nicole's watch back 32-37 minutes, could he be O.J., or could he be, for instance, Mark Fuhrman?

The "trick" about setting a clock back, or forward, and then break it, to make a murder appear to have taken place sooner or later than when it really occurred, is as old as murder mystery novels! The purpose is threefold:

- Giving the murderer an alibi.
- Casting suspicion on an innocent person.
- Confusing the investigators.

Old trick – but it is still worth trying! It is the only logical explanation as to why Nicole's watch was crushed, and it had stopped on 10:03. **Crushed? Okay! – Stopped on 10:03? No way!**

Let us now consider who the murderer might be, since he could have an interest in pulling this trick.

If **Fuhrman** is the murderer, who knew that O.J. preferred Italian shoes, and who was trying to frame O.J. with bloody Bruno Magli shoeprints, as well as in any other way he could, and who also knew that O.J., normally, would be leaving for the airport around 10:45 pm to fly to Chicago, it would definitely be **in Fuhrman's interest to set Nicole's watch back to 10:03**, thereby creating a window of opportunity for O.J. to have committed the murders and gotten back to Rockingham, cleaned up, and be ready by, say 10:45.

Had Fuhrman **not** set the watch back, the entire framing of O.J. could have been for nothing – because O.J. would have had an alibi – **if he had not run late that evening!**

Now consider **O.J.** as the potential killer. If **he** wanted to reset Nicole's watch and stop it by crushing it – it would have been **disastrous** for **him** to set Nicole's watch **back**– rather than **forward**!

Trying to convince the investigators that the murders took place around 10:03 pm, or a couple of minutes later (if Nicole's watch was off a couple of minutes), would suddenly have **given O.J. opportunity** to have committed the murders.

If O.J. were the murderer who reset and crushed Nicole's watch, he **must** have set the watch **forward – towards 10:55.** That way he would have given himself a definite alibi – if the investigators had fallen for it.

The obvious conclusions are:

The murderer – and not Nicole – set Nicole's watch to 10:03 and crushed it to stop it. **O.J.** could **not possibly** have had any interest in setting the watch **back**. Quite to the contrary!

Had O.J. altered the time of the watch and crushed it to stop it, he **must** have set it **forward – not 32-37 minutes back!**

Consequently, also the watch – although not representing the time of the murders – proved that O.J. is innocent.

Furthermore, the watch episode ties right in with my overall theory, that **the murderer is trying to frame O.J.** The murderer tried to frame O.J. with his hairs (the cap), the gloves – one at Bundy and one behind O.J.'s house, the blood (the five drops next to the bloody shoeprints, the blood in the Bronco), and the bloody Bruno Magli shoeprints. With Nicole's crushed watch the murderer is **also** trying to frame O.J., **by busting O.J.'s possible timeline alibi**.

Is this the reason the prosecutors did not introduce Nicole's watch, but, in fact, supressed it? Nothing surprises me anymore!

The wounds on Nicole's leg, the blow to her head, and the manner in which her body was found, with her leg wedged underneath the fence, was irrefutable evidence, and absolute proof, that the murderer deliberately used a knife, in order to create the bloody Bruno Magli shoeprints, as well as all the other blood evidence at the crime scenes – as part of a meticulous plan to frame O.J. and "set up" the investigators to believe O.J. were the murderer!

Clearly, in spite of all the bloody mess, the murder of Nicole was not a rage killing by a jealous ex-husband, but a well planned and carefully executed murder, deliberately set up to frame an innocent man!

And Nicole's watch, deliberately set to 10:03 pm and then crushed – **by the murderer** – underscored it.

Of course, the glove evidence, all by itself, proved that O.J. was innocent. But in addition, both the obvious manner in which Nicole was attacked and killed, and the condition of her watch, must have eradicated any doubt any honest investigator or prosecutor could possibly have had about O.J.'s innocence. These three sets of evidence cried out to the world:

O.J. Simpson did not commit these murders! He was being framed. And the investigators were being "set up"!

How could the investigators, the prosecutors, and the plaintiffs claim that they did **not** understand this? No-no! They did understand it! But it is embarrassing to be set up – and fall for it!

And it is devastating to your career, if you have already acted on this set-up to fabricate false evidence against an innocent murder suspect – and then get caught. That's why the investigators and the prosecutors just marched on in their vicious efforts to convict O.J.

My readers know everything about Robert Heidstra's testimony and the *"Hey - hey - hey!"* by now. Let me also mention that Mr. Heidstra's testimony was corroborated by O.J.'s daughter, Sydney, who heard the words through her open bedroom window.

The prosecutors never called Mr. Heidstra as a witness (the defense called him). The reason was that Mr. Heidstra's testimony busted the prosecution's timeline in the criminal case – because he heard Ron's *"Hey - hey - hey!"* at 10:35-40 pm.

Note! In the criminal trial the prosecution's medical examiner never seriously contested Dr. Baden's 10-15 minute murder timeline. One of the reasons for that was that Prosecutor Clark wanted the jury to perceive Ron as a "hero" who fought long and valiantly to save his friend, Nicole! Hence, the prosecution didn't call Mr. Heidstra – the most reliable timeline witness, who actually heard the murderer and Ron argue!

Consequently, they never presented even a deposition testimony from Sydney, who also heard Ron's *"Hey - hey - hey!"* That's cheating, or forgery, or whatever name you want to give it. It is covering up the truth, when the truth hurts your case!

Later, in the course of the civil suit, the plaintiffs realized that Mr. Heidstra's testimony was reliable, for as much as the timeline was concerned. They had to call him.

So the plaintiffs "fixed" the timeline instead, by hiring **Dr. Spitz**, who said the murder of Nicole took only 30 seconds, and the murder of Ron took about 60 seconds.

Nothing wrong about that, in itself. I agree with Dr. Spitz' timeline. The murders took only a couple of minutes altogether. But in calling Mr. Heidstra as a witness, it was suspicious that they didn't subpoena a deposition testimony from Sydney, who also heard what Mr. Heidstra heard.

There is something wrong about that. The excuse, commonly referred to was that they didn't want to involve Sydney. But

Sydney knew what was going on. She watched TV – and if not, her class mates would probably have told her. The real reason the plaintiffs didn't depose Sydney was probably this:

> Sydney heard her mother talk to her best friend on the phone shortly before the murders. Allegedly, this friend was Faye Resnick.
>
> Sydney said her mother was **crying** on the phone. Faye Resnick said she and Nicole were **giggling** on the phone. Sydney knew what she heard – and it didn't fit the prosecution. Remember, one of the theories of the defense was that the murderer came from *"the world of Faye Resnick"*!
>
> So they kept Sydney out of the case.

However, there was another reason for not presenting Sydney's testimony – live or from a deposition. If Sydney heard Ron say *"Hey - hey - hey!"* – she must also have heard the murderer reply! Because Sydney was much closer to the murderer than Mr. Heidstra, and Mr. Heidstra heard the murderer reply (although Mr. Heidstra didn't make out the exact words).

Sydney **definitely** knew her father's voice! So if the murderer's voice was that of her father, she would probably have said so, because Sydney didn't even know her father was a murder suspect, when she corroborated the *"Hey - hey - hey!"*

Sydney could have exonerated her father, if she could have testified that she did not recognize the second voice as her father's. So, while the plaintiffs used Mr. Heidstra's testimony, they didn't use Sydney's.

One could, of course argue that if Sydney could have testified that the second voice was **not** her father's, then the **defense** could have called Sydney. However, at that time, O.J. was in jail. And Sydney's grandparents, who were convinced O.J. were guilty, and who later sued him, were Sydney's legal guardians. **They** refused to let Sydney testify!

To have a legal battle over whether or not to involve Sydney in the murder case, force her to testify, and perhaps even expose her to cross examination, would hurt O.J.'s case much more than Sydney's testimony could help.

And what if the court ruled, eventually, that Sydney didn't have to testify? Such a legal battle could have painted O.J. in an even worse light, and still not given him the benefit of Sydney's testimony.

It was better for O.J.'s attorneys not to try to subpoena Sydney, as long as her grandparents didn't want her to testify.

On the other hand, if Sydney's legal guardians, her grandparents – the plaintiffs – had wanted Sydney to testify – perhaps in a deposition – **they** could have let her do so with little of the public criticism that **O.J.** would have been exposed to, had **he** subpoenaed Sydney. When the Brown's didn't let Sydney testify, there is some reason to believe that Sydney's possible testimony regarding the voices she heard at the time of the murders could have helped O.J. and hurt the plaintiffs' case.

But there is more. Mr. Heidstra gave a statement to the police shortly after the murders. Although the prosecutors in the criminal trial realized that Mr. Heidstra was an important witness, they didn't call him, because his timeline actually helped the defense. The defense were the ones who ended up calling Mr. Heidstra!

Mr. Heidstra also testified that he had seen *"a white sports utility car"* speed away from the murder scene. But Robert Heidstra emphasized that he could **not identify** this white car as being a **Bronco**. Yet, as time went by, prosecutors, plaintiffs, and the media simply took it upon themselves to refer to this white sports utilty car as *"O.J.'s white Bronco speeding away from Bundy"*!

Robert Heidstra told the police that the car he saw, sped **south** on Bundy Drive – which would be **away** from Rockingham.

Of course, that would further spoil the timeline of the investigators and the prosecution. Besides, that might even cause speculations that the real murderer could have used a white Bronco – or another white sports utility car – just to cast further suspicion on O.J. had anyone seen the murderer's car at the murder scene.

This last suggestion is interesting. Shortly after the murders, reporters travelled to Sandpoint, Idaho, where Mark Fuhrman had settled down, near a **"white supremacist"** headquarter. The reporters wanted to interview Detective Fuhrman.

> While the reporters were waiting for Detective Fuhrman to show up – **Mrs. Fuhrman** left the house and drove away in a **white 4 x 4, similar to O.J.'s Bronco! Or similar to the white sports utility car Robert Heidstra reportedly saw speeding away from the murder scene shortly after the time of the murders!**

Coincidence? Well, read on! Ms. Kathleen Bell is the woman who testified that Mark Fuhrman – **way back in 1985** – had used racial slurs and advocated genocide against the African-American people. At a side-bar during Kathleen Bell's testimony, **the prosecution vehemently argued to keep out any mentioning of what kind of car Fuhrman drove!** Why this paranoia about the car Fuhrman drove when he met Ms. Bell – **nine years earlier**?

That was strange, at best, because it seemed so **totally irrelevant** to make that a big issue worth arguing. However, put in context with my claim that the prosecution knew Fuhrman was the killer, **the issue of Fuhrman's car suddenly makes sense**! And it certainly didn't cast the prosecutors in less of a suspicious light!

Prosecutor Marcia Clark didn't care about what kind of car the Fuhrman's drove **at the time Mark Fuhrman met Ms. Bell**. However, Ms. Clark did not want any mention of the fact that the Fuhrman's had at their disposal the white sports utility car reporters had seen Mrs. Fuhrman drive in Sandpoint, Idaho, **shortly after the murders** – because that could make someone suspect Fuhrman of being the killer Robert Heidstra saw speed away **south** on Bundy.

However, as Fuhrman was about to be impeached – by Ms. Bell and others – should the defense bring up the issue of the white sports utility car from Sandpoint, and Ms. Clark started to object **– at that point –** it would make that vehicle appear **even more suspect.**

So, smart as she is, Prosecutor Marcia Clark used the episode between Fuhrman and Ms. Bell in 1985, to secure the court's ruling that *"any mention of what kind of car Detective Fuhrman drove, is irrelevant and inadmissible"*!

Of course, back then, when Fuhrman met Ms. Bell, he drove a **green** car. So not only was that car irrelevant and inadmissible – it was **safe** for Prosecutor Clark to argue this issue with reference to that green car, since no one saw that green car as having anything to do with the Simpson case. That way the prosecution obtained their **strange ruling** barring any mention of what car, or cars, the Fuhrman's drove – period!

So, later, after Detective Fuhrman was impeached by Kathleen Bell, Natalie Singer, and Roderic Hodge – should anyone begin to suspect Mark Fuhrman of not only being a perjurer, but perhaps even being the killer, there would be no mention of the Fuhrman's having at their disposal a white sports utility car similar to O.J.'s – and most of all, similar to the car Mr. Heidstra had observed **speeding south on Bundy** shortly after the murders. Ms. Clark was thinking ahead! Do you see how slick this lady is!

Evidently, the conspiracy to frame O.J. and cover up the fact that Fuhrman was the murderer went way past Fuhrman himself, and the investigators. This conspiracy, obviously, went all the way to the top in the Los Angeles DA's office!

> Note also, that to get from the Bundy murder scene to Fuhrman's home you would have to go **south** on Bundy Drive! But to get to O.J.'s Rockingham estate, you would have to go **north** on Bundy Drive.
>
> No wonder, Marcia Clark and her co-conspi ... – excuse me – her co-prosecutors didn't want any mention of the the kind of cars the Fuhrman's drove!

Back to Robert Heidstra's testimony. In spite of being absolutely clear in his later testimony, that he saw the car heading **south** on Bundy – away from O.J.'s Rckingham home, and towards Fuhrman's home – and being absolutely clear that **this** was what he told the police – **the police wrote down in their report** that Mr. Heidstra had told them he saw the car heading **north** on Bundy Drive!

Again, I must ask, what kind of police, what kind of murder investigators, and what kind of prosecutors do they have there in Los Angeles?

Don't they care about the law, or about fairness, honesty, justice? Is their only goal, to put away **"somebody"** – anybody – and if possible, an African American – for life, when there has been a murder – regardless of that person's guilt or innocence?

What is "evidence"? Something you search for when you investigate a crime, and if you don't find it, you **fabricate** it?

Unless their entire law enforcement system is totally corrupt, how could Police Chief Williams and District Attorney Garcetti close their eyes to what was going on within the LAPD and the DA's office?

Even today, almost three years after the murders, amazing things are being revealed. I have alredy discussed the controversial information regarding Mark Fuhrman's alibi – his wife's attempt to corroborate his false alibi, Fuhrman's own contradictory statements about getting home at 10:30 pm, but also being in Pomona (40-50 minutes away from his home) at 10:40! And what about the mysterious phone call to the LAPD, from a woman asking if the police were *"sitting on two dead bodies in West L.A."*? I have suggested that this woman may have been Mrs. Fuhrman.

In his book, *"Murder in Brentwood,"* Mark Fuhrman is pushing a couple of interesting issues. I am thinking about the bloody fingerprint Fuhrman reported seeing on the brass handle of the rear gate at Bundy, the dark sweat suit Detectives Fuhrman and Roberts saw in O.J.'s washing machine, an empty knife box Fuhrman alleged he saw in O.J.'s bathroom, and the controversial socks in O.J.'s bedroom, which Fuhrman, today, claims he saw in O.J.'s bedroom at about 8:00 in the morning.

Fuhrman's motive for bringing up these items in his book was to make O.J. appear more guilty. But we should scrutinize this better in this chapter which deals with suppressed evidence. In that connection we should also bring up a **jeans jacket that disappeared** from the kitchen in Nicole's condo during the early hours after the murders.

Let us start with the sweat suit. Since neither the Bruno Magli shoes, nor the murder knife, have been recovered we must conclude, of course, that the murderer knew how to get rid of those items.

If you were the murderer, and you had some kind of plan for getting rid of those most incriminating pieces of evidence (the shoes, the knife, and the murder clothes) – and your plan were a pretty good one, since nobody has recovered the shoes or the knife (or, in fact, the clothes), wouldn't you keep those items **together**, so that you could make all of them disappear at the same time?

What is the use of getting rid of your shoes and the knife, perfectly, if you leave your bloody sweat suit in your washing machine?

Regarding the empty knife box in O.J.'s bathroom, the box belonged to a small "boy scout's folding knife"! O.J. had received several of these knives as promotional items from the knife company which manufactured them – to hand them out to friends. The small blade of this knife could not possibly have cut Nicole's neck! So why was Fuhrman suggesting that this knife were the murder knife, and that O.J. therefore, were the murderer?

Why didn't Geraldo Rivera and Larry King ask Mark Fuhrman such questions when he was promoting his book on their TV shows? Didn't they understand that there was something wrong with his story about the sweat suit in the washing machine – and with his story about the empty knife box in O.J.'s bathroom?

There was something equally suspicious about the bloody fingerprint Fuhrman allegedly saw on the rear gate at Bundy.

It is interesting to notice that the only person who corroborated these stories Fuhrman brings up in his book, was **Detective Brad Roberts – Mark Fuhrman's partner and "buddy"**! But neither of them informed anyone else about these pieces of evidence – in particular the extremely important bloody fingerprint on the handle of the rear gate!

Excited, we must assume, Fuhrman made a note of it. **That was, most likely, the murderer's fingerprint!** Later, Fuhrman gave his notes to Detective Phillips, who handed them to Vannatter. But at the same time, he did not bother to tell Phillips:

> *"We got this guy – there is a bloody fingerprint on the rear gate! Let me show you!"*

In terms of solving this murder case, the bloody fingerprint was ten times more valuable than the bloody glove behind O.J.'s house or the bloody shoeprints at Bundy! Had I been Detective Fuhrman, I would have been jumping up and down with exitement. Immediately, I would have put two officers by that gate (there were at least 18 of them at Bundy) just to guard that fingerprint until the fingerprint expert could collect it!

Instead, as I said, Fuhrman just handed his notes to Phillips without mentioning the fingerprint, at all! Shortly thereafter – or before – the fingerprint was gone! Phillips never saw it. The fingerprint experts never saw it. Only Detective Brad Roberts and Fuhrman saw it. Neither of them told anyone about it – and then it disappeared!

Fuhrman just stood on a street corner at Bundy for more than one hour, chatting with Detective Phillips, his supervisor (the homicide coordinator), and waiting for investigators from Robbery/ Homicide to arrive and take over the investigation. Yet, Fuhrman didn't even mention to Phillips that there was a bloody fingerprint on the handle of the rear gate!

Look into my eyes, and then go and tell Fuhrman that there is written *"stupid"* in my eyes!

In his book Detective Mark Fuhrman presents himself as *the smartest detective on the Simpson case.* He has criticism for everybody else. Yet, he failed to secure what was most likely the murderer's bloody fingerprint at the murder scene. Subsequently, the fingerprint was destroyed and disappeared – without a trace.

Wake up, America!

Anyway, upon the arrival of Detectives Lange and Vannatter from the LAPD's Robbery/Homicide Division, Fuhrman was, officially, no longer assigned to the case. Actually, he could have gone home at that point. But Fuhrman knew about Nicole's 911 calls, which he conveniently communicated to Detectives Lange and Vannatter in order to convince them that O.J., most likely, were the murderer! And Fuhrman knew how to get to Rockingham! So he drove to Rockingham together with the other three detectives, Lange, Vannatter and Phillips. Detective Roberts was not assigned to the case, either. He stayed behind at Bundy.

Later, Fuhrman returned to Bundy to get his partner, Roberts, and the two of them drove back to Rockingham – Fuhrman for the second time. The two partners checked out the Bronco and planted ... excuse me – "observed" more blood. Later the two "investigators" moved inside O.J.'s house.

- Who showed up to "find" the empty knife box in O.J.'s bathroom? Brad Roberts!
- Whom did Detective Roberts inform about the knife box? The lead investigators, Detectives Vannatter or Lange? No! Again, Officer Roberts only told his buddy, Detective Fuhrman!

Not assigned to the case at this point the two partners still hung around at Rockingham the entire day. And while every police officer in California was searching for the murder knife, neither Fuhrman, nor Roberts saw any urgency in collecting as evidence the empty knife box they allegedly found in O.J.'s bathroom! Or, was it really **empty** – when Roberts and Fuhrman "found" the box. Do we see a **"pattern"** here?

Let us take a closer look at the knife box, or, rather, the knife that allegedly had been in it. The box was for an ordinary, small folding knife of the type boy scouts use – the kind which has a couple of knife blades, a cork screw, a crown cap opener, a small screw driver, etc. This entire knife measures about 3 1/2 inches, and its longest blade is about three inches long. This was **not** the kind of knife that was used to murder Nicole, and which nearly severed her head! So why does Fuhrman make a big thing out of it in his book?

The case against O.J. gets more and more ludicrous as time goes by – even today! And do you see that Mark Fuhrman – through his book and his TV interviews – is still trying to **frame O.J.** – or at least, trying to make **O.J.** appear **guilty**, so **Fuhrman** himself can appear to be **innocent**. Otherwise, why is he spreading these stories about the bloody fingerprint, the knife box, the sweat suit, the socks, etc., which are obviously flawed and made up to make O.J. look bad? Fuhrman is trying to blame Detectives Vannatter and Lange for having bungled the case against O.J. According to Fuhrman, had Lange and Vannatter done a better job investigating, then all this additional evidence would have been secured and convinced the jury of O.J.'s guilt – meaning, of course, that Fuhrman himself were innocent.

Again, Fuhrman is clever! He knew, by 1996, that private investigators were on to him. That is why he wrote his book. It was **"damage control"**! Fuhrman needed to cast suspicion on O.J. – make O.J. look more guilty. Because if O.J. appeared **more** guilty, Fuhrman would appear **less** guilty! That was the **real purpose** of his book.

However, **"the Simpson trials"** are over. Therefore, it would be suspicious if Fuhrman, today, in his book, had come right out and said:

*There was even more evidence than you heard about in the trials, **and which proved that O.J. is guilty**. There were a bloody fingerprint at Bundy, an empty knife box in O.J.'s bathroom, and a dark, possibly bloody sweat suit in his washing machine. Besides, both Roberts and I saw the socks in O.J.'s bedroom!*

Who cares – the trials are over! So instead, **again**, Fuhrman introduced these items of "evidence" **indirectly** – by criticizing

Detectives Lange and Vannatter for not having secured this evidence. Just as Fuhrman had **expected,** Detectives Vannatter and Lange got upset – naturally! Fuhrman was there – Vannatter even left Fuhrman in charge at Rockingham, later in the morning when Vannatter went to get the search warrant for Rockingham. So, why didn't Fuhrman **himself** secure this evidence?

The answer is that all this evidence was considered at the time, and ruled to have no evidentiary value. But by bringing it up again in his book, and accusing Detectives Lange and Vannatter of negligence, Fuhrman **created a controversy**, the media got involved. Both parties were invited on national TV to talk about all the evidence against O.J. that someone missed or bungled – but which *"clearly proved"* that O.J. were guilty!

Do my readers see how smart Fuhrman is? It was exactly the same tactic he used when he introduced his new **"Pomona/pumping gas/Gold American Express card"** **alibi** – through the **"back door"**! He didn't come right out and say:

> *"I have a new alibi* (to replace my false La Quinta alibi which someone busted) *"*!

That would have been suspicious, or incriminating for Fuhrman. So, he just **hinted at it** while **appearing** to be criticizing **O.J.'s** alibi instead:

> *I know where I was at 10:40 on the night of the murders –because I was in Pomona pumping gas. But O.J. cannot tell us where he was – because he was behind his house where he lost his glove!*

Mark Fuhrman is so slick! But once we realize how he operates, it becomes easier to spot this leopard.

Why was always Officer Roberts, who wasn't even assigned to the case, the one who "found" all these things together with Fuhrman? What was he even doing at Rockingham at that time?

And what was Fuhrman doing at Rockingham? The LAPD's

Robbery/Homicide Division had long since taken over the investigation – and relieved Fuhrman of his duties in the case. Was Fuhrman just hanging around, looking out for his own interests, and at the same time maneuvering his way back into the investigation?

- Later that day, who found O.J.'s allegedly bloody sweat suit in the washing machine? Yes, Brad Roberts! Whom did he tell? Yes, Mark Fuhrman! Did Fuhrman order the sweat suit collected into evidence? No! Criminalist Fung checked out the sweat suit in the washing machine. There was no blood on it. What looked like blood, turned out to be rust marks. So why is Fuhrman bringing up such nonsense in his book?
- Later that day, Fuhrman found a pair of, allegedly, bloody socks in front of O.J.'s bed. Whom did he tell? Brad Roberts! Whom else did he tell? Well Fuhrman later said he told a detective "downstairs." But neither of them made a concurrent record of this alleged discovery.

Later, in the afternoon, the LAPD's own video cameraman videotaped O.J.'s bedroom, exactly where Fuhrman claimed he saw the socks in the morning. The socks did not show up on the video, and the cameraman testified that he did not see the socks. Then Fuhrman visited O.J.'s bedroom **again.** Ten minutes later he told Criminalist Dennis Fung that there was a pair of socks on the floor in O.J.'s bedroom, and asked Fung to collect them into evidence.

Do my readers understand what went on? Fuhrman was in O.J.'s bedroom **after** the cameraman had videotaped the room. Fuhrman found the socks in O.J.'s laundry bin and put them on the floor. Then he asked criminalist Fung to collect the socks into evidence. Fuhrman knew the pack he ran with in the LAPD, so he hoped that once the socks were brought to the LAPD's crime lab, someone there would find a way to plant Nicole's or Ron's blood on them.

That's exactly what happened. That could have nailed O.J.! There was only one little detailed that saved him. The investigators thought they were safe when they moistened Nicole's blood on her dress and smeared it onto O.J.'s sock. But you see, Nicole's dress had been washed in a laundry detergent containing EDTA. Some of this EDTA got mixed with her blood – and then transferred to O.J.'s sock. That proved where the blood came from. It did not come from Nicole – at Bundy, like Fuhrman and the investigators tried to represent. It came from Nicole's dress – in the LAPD's crime lab.

Just a detail like that – say, **if Nicole's dress had not been washed in a detergent containing EDTA** – and O.J. could have been sitting on death row today – framed by Fuhrman and the LAPD investigators, for two murders LAPD Detective Fuhrman committed. It is scary!

Luckily, the planting of Nicole's blood on O.J.'s sock was clearly exposed by the defense, because of this little detail about the EDTA, from a detergent, but also for other reasons I will discuss later. Of course, that pointed yet another finger of suspicion at Fuhrman, since he was the one who "discovered" the socks on the floor in O.J.'s bedroom. Fuhrman didn't realize that the LAPD's cameraman had videotaped that floor just minutes before Fuhrman planted O.J.'s socks there in the afternoon.

When the videotape proved that Fuhrman most likely planted those sock on the floor, Fuhrman – again – needed to do some damage control. So he wrote in his book that he had seen the socks in O.J.'s bedroom **before** the cameraman was there. And again, Fuhrman's partner, Detective Brad Roberts covered for Fuhrman by confirming that he, too, saw the socks in O.J.'s bedroom in the morning. The videotape proves that they were both lying!

Brad Roberts is beginning to look more and more like Fuhrman's possible accomplice – or at least, as a typical LAPD officer willing to protect his colleague and partner, regardless!

Apparently, Fuhrman and Roberts are the only ones investigating the murders. Naturally, Fuhrman was the one who "found" the glove, also, behind O.J.'s house.

Could Detective Roberts be Fuhrman's accomplice who made the three thumps on Kato's wall, or the accomplice who used

Fuhrman's credit card in Pomona, to create a false alibi for Fuhrman, while Fuhrman was at Bundy murdering Nicole and Ron?

Were the two officers still hanging around the crime scenes looking for, and eliminating, possible "slip-ups" like Fuhrman's bloody fingerprint on the rear gate at Bundy – and planting additional evidence against O.J., which they could not plant at the time of the murders, because they didn't have access to O.J.'s home at that time?

Besides what I have mentioned above, there is hardly anything, that I know of, tying Fuhrman's partner, Detective Brad Roberts, to the murders – except that he seemed to pop up, out of nowhere, and discover one apparent piece of evidence after the other – evidence nobody else had seen!

And each time, he only communicated it to Detective Fuhrman. Then all that evidence, which the two of them discovered alone or together, either disappeared, got bungled, somehow, or simply didn't mean anything.

– That was the case with the bloody fingerprint on the Bundy gate.
– That was the case with the knife box in O.J.'s bathroom.
– That was the case with the sweat suit in O.J.'s washing machine.
– That was the case with the blood in O.J.'s Bronco.
– That was the case with the socks in O.J.'s bedroom.
– The controversy was, certainly, no less with respect to the Rockingham glove – although Fuhrman found that evidence without the "assistance" of his partner, Officer Roberts.

The pattern was the same. Brad Roberts or Mark Fuhrman **"discovered"** the evidence – alone or together. They told each other, and looked at the evidence **together.** But they didn't tell **anyone else** about it until much, much later. By then the evidence was either **lost** or **destroyed** – or **"someone"** bungled it.

Do you remember from *"The Fuhrman Tapes"* – although it is a few chapters ago?

Fuhrman: *If I ever see the son-of-a-bitch and we're alone, I would kill him!*

McKinny: How can you get away with that?

Fuhrman: *If there's nobody except him and me, dead men tell no tales! . . . If I have the opportunity, I should kill him. And that's all there is to it.*

McKinny: Say you were **working with a partner** who saw you do that?

Fuhrman: *Can't do that.* ***You gotta have a partner that's like your brother.***

Was Detective Fuhrman committing yet another perjury during his direct testimony in the criminal trial, when he gave himself an **"alibi"** for the time of the murders? Or was he lying in February of 1997, about being in Pomona, pumping gas, at the time of the murders?

Possibly, Detective Fuhrman was desperate at the time his book came out, sensing that private investigators were on to him. I believe Fuhrman's book is an attempt to create a smoke screen, focusing attention away from himself and onto the **"incompetent investigators,"** Lange and Vannatter, who – according to Fuhrman – could have nailed O.J., but **"bungled it"**!

The more I think about the bloody fingerprint that Roberts and Fuhrman allegedly saw on the handle of the rear gate, the more suspect his story appears. We'll talk a bit about that.

Let me explain something first. Although there were 18 officers at Bundy when Fuhrman arrived, and later, many more came, these officers did not, of course, swarm all over the murder scene and trample on the evidence. Most of the officers were occupied sealing off the surrounding area, directing traffic away from Bundy, and keeping watch.

Only a couple of detectives, Brad Roberts and Fuhrman to mention two, had access to the actual murder scene – and to Nicole's condo and the rear gate, in particular.

According to his book, when Fuhrman arrived at Bundy, his partner, Detective Brad Roberts was already there. Together, the two detectives walked through the murder scene. When they reached the rear gate, **Detective Roberts**, actually, discovered the bloody fingerprint on the brass handle, and pointed it out to Fuhrman – **not vice versa**!

Had Fuhrman seen it first, and pointed it out to Roberts, one could certainly argue that if Fuhrman was the murderer – and he assumed the fingerprint was his – then he should, rather, have concealed it from his partner, and moved on – and he should have made no note of it – so he could wipe it off, secretly later.

But Fuhrman did **not** see the fingerprint **first**. Detective Roberts did! And **he** pointed it out to **Fuhrman**.

Therefore, there was no way Fuhrman could ignore or conceal the fingerprint – secretly. Instead, he had to make it appear that he was **not** concealing it. Accordingly, Detective Fuhrman made a note of the fingerprint: *"Partial, bloody fingerprint on brass handle of the rear gate. 4-5 good points."*

Ignoring the fingerprint, and then making it disappear, would certainly cast suspicion directly at Fuhrman. So he had to write the above comment in his notes – which he later handed over to his supervisor, Detective Phillips, who in turn handed the notes to Vannatter, when the latter came to take over the investigation an hour later. The note should make it appear that Fuhrman, ceretainly, was not trying to conceal the fingerprint.

As it happened, by the time the criminalists, and in particular the fingerprint expert, arrived at Bundy, the fingerprint was gone! So, what happened to it?

Only Detectives Roberts and Fuhrman saw the bloody fingerprint on the rear gate. Fuhrman was later, alone in Nicole's condo. He could easily have slipped out through the back door, wiped off the fingerprint, and then gone inside again. If my theory is correct, about Fuhrman being the murderer, then he would simply have **had to** do it. Otherwise he would have been exposed.

Let's look at the situation at Bundy at the time. Two victims lay dead in a pool of blood. There were bloody shoeprints (from the murderer?) leading towards the rear gate at Bundy. Along those bloody shoeprints there were blood drops, possibly having dripped from the murderer's hand or knife. Besides, one bloody murder glove (assumably) was found next to the victims. Consequently, there was a good possibility that the blood drops alongside the shoeprints came from the murderer himself. On the rear gate there were at least one additional blood drop. Obviously, a bloody murderer had left the murder scene through that rear gate.

Then, Detective Brad Roberts discovered a bloody fingerprint on the handle of the rear gate. He showed it to Detective Fuhrman, who was right there with him.

No doubt about it, the bloody fingerprint on the gate's handle must have been from the murderer! And if so, the murderer might as well have left **a poster with his picture, name and signature**. Hence, it is not credible at all that Detective Fuhrman did not **safeguard** the fingerprint **immediately**, and that **he did not even mention the fingerprint to the homicide coordinator, Detective Phillips**.

Disregard the fact that I am a former police sergeant. Suppose instead that I were a shoe salesman or a baker – living next door to Nicole's. I stepped outside a little after 11 pm on the night of the murders and discovered the bodies.

So, I decided to get my mobil phone in my car (parked in the alley) and call the police.

On my way to the alley, I passed the rear gate. There I saw the bloody fingerprint on the handle. What would an, assumably, complete amateur – and shoe salesman, like me – do?

I would get my mobil phone and call the police. Then – **because I am not stupid** – I would tell the police dispatcher:

> *"From what I can see, there is a bloody fingerprint on the handle of the rear gate. From the appearance of the murder scene, I conclude that it must have been deposited by the murderer. So bring a fingerprint expert over here a.s.a.p! In the meantime I will keep watch at the gate until you get here, so nobody, accidentally destroys*

this bloody fingerprint. But hurry – it's spooky here!"

Detective Fuhrman is not a shoe salesman! He is a homocide detective, with 19 years experience with the LAPD. He is the Detective with the New York Times' Bestseller list book about the Simpson case! He is the Detective who, in his book, is criticizing all the other investigators for incompetence!

What did Homicide Detective Fuhrman do, after seeing the murderer's bloody fingerprint on the handle of the rear gate?

He should be jumping up and down with exitment, embracing his partner Detective Roberts and shouting:

> *"Brad! Brad! We got this guy! This must be the murderer's fingerprint – nobody else could have left that bloody fingerprint on the handle. Think about the bloody victims and the bloody shoeprints. And apparently, the murderer lost his left glove down by the victims! This is his finger-print. It must be!*
>
> *Stay here, Brad! Don't move an inch, and don't touch the handle! I'll go and get a couple of officers to come over and guard this fingerprint. And I'll call Robbery/Homicide and tell them to bring a fingerprint expert over here immediately! Then we'll go and tell our boss, the Homicide Coordinator, Detective Phillips.*
>
> *Wow! Is this a stroke of luck, or what!"*

Alas! This (in his own eyes) "brilliant" homicide detective, Mark Fuhrman, who dishes out criticism east and west – what did he do?

–   First he shut Detective Roberts up, by telling him: *"I'll handle this. I'll go inside Nicole's condo and write a note about this fingerprint – for the detectives from Robbery/ Homicide."*

–   Fuhrman went inside Nicole's condo. There he wrote the note – to cover himself. Then he exited the rear of her condo, near the gate, walked up to the gate, wiped the fingerprint clean off the handle, and returned to Nicole's condo ten seconds later.

- Then he took off his suit jacket. In his suit jacket he concealed his own jeans jacket, which he had forgotten in Nicole's condo earlier that evening. Then he exited Nicole's condo, carrying both jackets over his arm. He went to his car, and put the jackets – not on the seat, but in the **trunk**!
- Then Fuhrman waited for Detectives Lange and Vannatter from Robbery/Homicide to arrive and take over the investigation. While he waited, for almost one full hour – together with his supervisor, Detective Ronald Phillips – at the street corner, Detective Fuhrman, allegedly, did not think about mentioning the bloody fingerprint to the homicide coordinator!

   Believe it if you will. But if so, your head can not be screwed on right!

- Of course, Fuhrman is the killer. The fingerprint was his. So he wiped it off. That's why Fuhrman could **not** tell Detective Phillips about this extraordinary discovery. Because **Detective Philips would then, of course, have posted a couple of officers at the gate immediately**. However, had he gone there to inspect the fingerprint, and point it out to the guards – it would have been gone. Detective Roberts would confirm that he discovered it and showed it to Fuhrman. Since then, only Fuhrman was back there alone. Ergo: **Fuhrman must have wiped it off.**
- For exactly the same reason, he didn't tell Detective Vannatter about the fingerprint, either. Phillips layed out the murder scene for Detective Vannatter – told him about the victims, the glove, the bloody shoeprints, etc. Then he asked Fuhrman for his notes. Fuhrman gave his notes to Phillips, who handed them over to Vannatter, who gave them to Lange, who put them on his clip board. But Fuhrman didn't mention the bloody fingerprint to any of the three

detectives. Of course, not! Because if so, Detective Vannatter would immediately have done the same as I suggested that Detective Phillips would have done – if Fuhrman had informed **him** about the fingerprint – namely safeguarded it.

– Instead, **Fuhrman gave Phillips his notes – still without mentioning the fingerprint at all.** This is so incredible that it clearly points out Detective Fuhrman as the murderer, who left this bloody fingerprint on the handle, and subsequently wiped it off – after Detective Roberts had pointed it out to Fuhrman.

– Fuhrman knew that Vannatter would not have time to read the notes until much later. So, it was safe for Fuhrman to write a note about the bloody fingerprint, and to hand his notes to Phillips who passed them on to Vannatter, as long as he didn't mention the fingerprint when the gave Phillips the notes.

It was Detective Fuhrman's clear duty to inform Phillips and Vannatter about **anything** that could be of immediate importance. What could possibly be more important than to inform the lead investigator that the murderer must have left his bloody fingerprint on the handle of the rear gate? Yet, he didn't!

– Then Fuhrman followed Detectives Lange, Vannatter and Phillips to Rockingham. By the time the fingerprint experts arrived at Bundy, the fingerprint was gone. It was not simply smudged – accidentally. It was wiped clean off the handle! The criminalists didn't even detect a trace of blood from the earlier fingerprint.

– Two and a half years later, Mark Fuhrman has the audacity to blame Detective Vannatter for the disappearance of the fingerprint – because Vannatter did not immediately read Fuhrman's three pages of notes!

How does Mark Fuhrman have the nerve! Imagine! Insinuating that the fingerprint were O.J.'s and blaming Detective Vannatter for its disappearance!

Detective Fuhrman's handling of the fingerprint leaves no doubt. He murdered Nicole and Ron! This was his fingerprint! That is why the fingerprint disappeared.

No investigator would accidentally grab that handle and thereby destroy a bloody fingerprint which most likely was deposited by the murderer. Not the criminalists, and certainly not the fingerprint expert.

But here is another point. Fuhrman (and Roberts) are the only two who knew about the fingerprint. Hence, if someone else destroyed that fingerprint, it would have been **by accident**. In other words, someone grabbing the handle of the gate – **without thinking**. But if so, they would only **smudge** the fingerprint. There should still be **blood residues**, at least, on the gate's handle, which the criminalist should have been able to detect and collect.

Do you see? **Hypothetically** – although not likely – the bloody fingerprint could have been destroyed, **unintentionally**.

But for the blood itself to disappear, someone must have wiped it clean off. That could not have happened by accident!

Consequently, one of the police officers at Bundy must have wiped off that bloody fingerprint – **on purpose**!

That means, one of the police officers at Bundy was directly involved in the murders, and had accidentally left behind that bloody fingerprint. Now, take your pick! I think the choice is pretty obvious: **Mark Fuhrman!**

Let us assume that this **was** Fuhrman's fingerprint. He wanted to remove this compromising piece of evidence. His first impuls is, of course, simply to wipe it off. Assuming nobody else had seen the fingerprint, that would be as if it were never there.

But **Roberts** was the one who discovered the fingerprint. So Fuhrman, probably, had to tell his junior partner:

"I'll handle this! I'll go inside Nicole's condo, so I can write a

note about this fingerprint."

Consequently, Detective Roberts assumed his superior, Detective Fuhrman, was handling the matter of the fingerprint. So Roberts did not mention it to anyone else.

Roberts left, and Fuhrman entered Nicole's condo. There is an exit from the rear of Nicole's condo right next to the rear gate. So, alone in Nicole's condo, Fuhrman slipped out through that exit, walked over to the gate and wiped his bloody fingerprint clean off.

Not only did Fuhrman dispose of the fingerprint – he made a note of it first and, later, handed his notes to Detective Phillips, who passed them on to Detective Vannatter, to make it appear that he was not trying to hide that fingerprint from his superiors.

But Fuhrman is just a little bit too grandiose for his own good. Someone from the LAPD **must** have removed that fingerprint – **on purpose.** And regardless of how clever he thinks he is, Fuhrman is the only likely perpetrator. Seen in context with all the other circumstantial evidence that points him out as the murderer, the removal of the fingerprint fits right in.

Conclusion: Detective Fuhrman wiped it off, to eliminate this incriminating piece of evidence.

I have already, several times, suggested that **the prosecutors** were fully aware of the fact that O.J. was innocent, and that Mark Fuhrman had murdered Nicole and Ron. Could that be the reason why Officer Brad Roberts was never called to testify?

Far less significant police witnesses were called to corroborate testimony which Detective Roberts was much better informed about. So why didn't the prosecutors call Detective Roberts to the witness stand? Could it be that Prosecutor Marcia Clark wanted to conceal the history of the bloody fingerprint, which clearly pointed to Fuhrman as the most likely murderer. If Roberts were to testify, the history of the bloody fingerprint that disappeared, would definitley be brought up. Suddenly the defense could begin to see Fuhrman as a prime murder suspect. The entire murder plot could be exposed, in which case Prosecutor Marcia Clark's **good friend**, Detective Phillip Vannatter, might be charged with evidence tampering.

My readers didn't know that the lead investigator, Phillip Vannatter, and the lead prosecutor, Marcia Clark were good friends since long before the Simpson case? They were. And Detective Vannatter is actually the one who pulled some strings to get his friend, Marcia Clark, as the lead prosecutor in this case!

Could it be that Detective Vannatter wanted to cover his back – and that he knew he could trust Marcia Clark to back him up if he fabricated false evidence against O.J., and there was any chance that this could be exposed?

Is that why Prosecutor Clark protected Detective Fuhrman in spite of all the evidence against Fuhrman. Not because she wanted to protect Fuhrman himself – but because she wanted to protect her friend, Phillip Vannatter, and his evidence fabrication from being exposed, by protecting Fuhrman from being exposed as the killer?

I love to hear Fuhrman present a different story about the fingerprint. If the fingerprint was ever there, who else than Fuhrman (or Fuhrman's partner, Brad Roberts) could have wiped that alleged, bloody fingerprint clean off the handle of the gate, by accident? It must have been done on purpose.

More things went on at Bundy in the early hours. Sgt. Riske was the first officer at the murder scene. He went inside Nicole's condo where he observed the burning candles, the ice cream, and the water in the bathtub. **Sgt. Riske also saw a large, man's size jeans jacket in the kitchen.**

Initially, investigators and prosecutors speculated that this jacket might belong to Ron Goldman, but it didn't. Besides, Ron was never inside Nicole's condo that night. He was attacked right inside the Bundy gate.

I have already suggested that Fuhrman visited Nicole just before the murders, to assure himslef that she would be alone later that night, and to set up a "date." During this earlier short visit on the night of the murders – perhaps around ten o'clock – Fuhrman was invited in. He took off his jeans jacket in the kitchen as he sat down with Nicole to have a cup of coffee. Then he forgot his jacket there.

When he returned to "investigate" he entered Nicole's condo. Suddenly, he saw his own jeans jacket. It didn't matter that Sgt. Riske had seen the jacket, too. **Fuhrman had to get rid of it.** So he re-entered Nicole's condo a little later, alone. There are reports of that. These reports stated, also, that Fuhrman was wearing his **suit jacket** when he arrived at Bundy, as well as when he **entered** Nicole's condo alone. But when he **exited** Nicole's condo a few minutes later, he had **removed his suit jacket and was carrying it over his arm.** Since then, no one has seen the large size, man's jeans jacket that Sgt. Riske and others saw in Nicole's kitchen!

Fuhrman could not simply grab his jeans jacket and walk out. So, inside Nicole's condo, Fuhrman probably removed his own suit jacket, wrapped it around the jeans jacket and carried both to his car, where he put them in the **trunk**.

That is even more suspicious. If you remove your **suit jacket** for some reason or another and put it in your car, wouldn't you put it inside your car, on the seat? Of course! But Fuhrman couldn't do that, because if Detective Phillips – who shared that car with Fuhrman – had moved Fuhrman's suit jacket, the jeans jacked, hidden inside, could have been exposed. So Fuhrman put his **suit jacket** in the trunk of the car – **together with the jack and the spare tire!** Do my readers understand what is happening here?

The murder scene was filled with police officers. Nobody could have carried that jeans jacket openly out of Nicole's condo without being spotted. The only way to do it would be to hide it inside another jacket, for instance. And here was Fuhrman wearing his suit jacket as he arrived – but exiting Nicole's condo with his suit jacket over his arm!

Let's look at another aspect of this jacket incident. Fuhrman arrived at Bundy at 2:10 am, wearing his suit jacket. Obviously, the weather was not warm enough to wear just slacks and a shirt. I believe the overnight temperature dropped to about 60 degrees.

Now from 2:10 till 3:00 am (when Fuhrman was reported exiting Nicole's condo carrying his suit jacket on his arm), it certainly hadn't gotten any warmer. It wasn't the "heat" which caused Detective Fuhrman to remove his suit jacket and put it in the **trunk** of his car. Do I have to say more?

Consider what happened to the jeans jacket, together with Fuhrman's busted alibi, *"The Fuhrman Tapes,"* the bloody fingerprint which disappeared, his failed polygraph test, his racism and his involvement in MAW and WASP, his perjury regarding the "N-word," as well as his perjury regarding the Protective League seminar, his alleged relationship with Nicole, the fact that only a police officer could have killed Ron under the circumstances, Fuhrman's "finding" the Rockingham glove, the blood on it wet almost eight hours after the murders, etc., etc.!

As a murder suspect – by a preponderance of the evidence – hasn't Mark Fuhrman passed O.J. Simpson by a mile, already?

Working on my book, I am just waiting for the moment when someone asks Fuhrman on national TV, **why he testified under oath** during the criminal trial that **he came home to his wife at 10:30 pm** – five minutes before the murders took place – when he said, in February 1997, on national TV, that **he was in Pomona,** 30-40 minutes from his home, pumping gas, at the time Kato heard the thumps on the wall, **at 10:40.**

And when Fuhrman, **predictably** responds, trying to work his way out of the jam, by saying he just got the two days, Saturday and Sunday, mixed up – after all, he gave his testimony for Prosecutor Clark almost nine months after the Protective League seminar at La Quinta . . .

– then I shall pray to my God that the TV talk show host has read my book, so he can shut up this vicious murderer and habitual perjurer, named Mark Fuhrman!

CHAPTER 30

Medical Examiner – Bought And Paid?

Our theory about a gun's handle having caused the bruise and hemorrhage on Nicole's head, how the wounds on Nicole's leg occurred, the deliberately bloody mess, and the bloody shoeprints, also explains, and tie in with, some other important evidence in this murder mystery:

How could the murderer kill Ron, so easily and quietly, right next to Nicole's bloody body?

Of course, if the murderer is a police officer, he would carry a gun – and the gun is probably what he used when initiating the attack on Nicole.

As well planned and executed as these murders were, Fuhrman had probably also anticipated that someone **might** show up during, or shortly after the murder of Nicole.

If so he would pull out his gun and his police badge, pretending he was **investigating** Nicole's death – rather than having **caused** it!

He could order Ron up against the fence, so as to search him for a weapon, and then cut Ron down from behind, before Run even knew what happened.

The bruise on Nicole's head actually explains why Ron was killed so easily – and that the killer is **not** a jealous ex-husband, but most likely a racist psycho-maniac of an LAPD officer!

Again, the murder of Nicole (and Ron) were not committed in a jealous rage, but followed a meticulously planned M.O. – from start to finish set up to frame O.J.?

The medical examiner for the plaintiffs, Dr. Werner Spitz, was completely wrong in his self assured explanation of how Nicole was killed. Dr. Spitz testified the murderer was standing behind

Nicole. Her upper body was bent forward. The murderer put his left hand across her face and bent her head backwards. Then he cut her neck from behind with the knife in his right hand.

Of course – **in the courtroom, using a complying counsel for the plaintiffs as his medium** – Dr.Spitz could demonstrate something asinine like that!

He simply **asked the counsel** for the plaintiffs to **turn** around, **bend** forward – **and stand absolutely still!**
   But Nicole would never have stood still while being attacked from behind by a man wearing a dark knit ski cap, leather gloves, and carrying a knife! Not if she was conscious!
   Next, Dr. Spitz placed his left hand over the counsel's face and bent the counsel's head back. Then he pretended that he reached over the counsel's right shoulder and cut his neck with a knife.
   That was how O.J., allegedly, should have killed Nicole! A medical examiner can do a **stupid** thing like that – with a cooperating counsel – in a courtroom! And he can suggest a **stupid** thing like that, because he has never been in a real life and death struggle with knives, or guns, or bare fists!

However, a young healthy woman being attacked from behind by a murderer doesn't stand still, bend over on command, and keep quiet, waiting for a murderer to cut her neck with a knife!

Nicole would have screamed, and fought, and bit, and kicked, and punched, and wrestled herself out of the murderer's single handed grip!
   If the murderer placed his hand over her mouth to muffle her, Nicole would have bit his fingers off! And if he moved his hand away from her mouth, she would have screamed off the top of her lungs!
   Trying to hold a man responsible for two vicious homicides based on his absurd theory, Dr. Spitz should be deeply embarrassed.

Dr. Spitz deserves to hear me state this. Because what he has done – selling his so-called "expertise" to the plaintiffs, with total disregard for the lives and future of O.J. and his children – is so despicable, that it should not be allowed to go unnoticed!

I have already explained how Nicole was killed, and why she was killed in this particular manner. However, here are a few more examples of what is wrong with Dr. Spitz' theory – besides that it was **bought and paid!**

In the dim light inside the Bundy gate, if the murderer bent Nicole's upper body forward, put a leather gloved hand over Nicole's face, and bent her head back, **Nicole's hands would have shot up and grabbed that hand faster than you can blink!**

It is a **reflexive reaction**, just as if you burn yourself on the stove and jerk your hand back, or if you get stung by a bee on your cheek and smack it so fast ...!

Or here is a better example: Imagine that you are home alone in your semi-dark house – at least, that's what you think! However, your husband (or boyfriend) had come home, quietly. In good faith, as a sign of affextion, or as a practical joke, your man have sneaked up behind you – without your knowledge. **Lovingly**, he puts his hands on your shoulders. Can you imagine, still, how you would have jumped! **I** would have whirled around screaming, and **my** hands would have shot up and grabbed the hands on my shoulders faster than you can blink!

If we should believe Dr. Spitz, the murderer must have:

- sneaked up on Nicole from behind,
- grabbed her around her waist with his right hand,
- holding the knife where Nicole could see it, of course, and
- pushed her upper body forward, with his left hand – otherwise her waist would not be bent the way Dr. Spitz demonstrated Nicole's body posture in court,
- moved his left hand up to her face,
- grabbed Nicole's face from behind, and

    – bent her head back, at least one full second or more before
    he approached her neck with his knife in his right hand.

This whole scenario would have taken, at least, **five times** as long as needed for Nicole's hands to grab the murderers hand around her waist or across her face!

Readers; slap your face lightly, and **pretend that it was some-one else who did it – by surprise!** Can you "sense" how quickly your hands would have shot up to your face to grab the perpetrator's hand or lessen the sting of the slap?

That's how quickly Nicole would have reacted to a gloved hand being placed across her face, in the semi-darkness!

Even if Nicole's hands didn't manage to wrestle the assailants hand away from her face, her hands and arms would still be up in front of her neck, protecting her neck from the murderer's knife attack. He couldn't have accessed Nicole's neck across her right shoulder.

If the murderer's hand was across her mouth, she would have bit the hand. And if the murderer's hand was **not** across her mouth, she would have yelled and screamed for help!

Furthermore, Nicole would have seen the murderer's knife as soon as the murderer put his right arm around her waist – which again, was necessary in order to bend her upper body forward! At the very instant, Nicole would have wrestled herself away from the murderer's grip and screamed for help. Nobody heard a sound!

Hence, Nicole must have been knocked unconscious before she was attacked with the knife! Of course!

However, **if Nicole was unconscious, her legs would not have supported her.** Her knees would have buckled and **she would have dropped to the ground the instant she was knocked unconscious.**

So, maybe the murderer knocked Nicole unconscious, but immediately grabbed her with his right arm around her waist, and bent her head back with his left hand.

OK! But what would happen then, as soon as the murderer

removed his right arm from Nicole's waist in order to cut her neck?

Of course, Nicole would drop to the ground like a sack of rocks! (No disrespect intended, of course).

That is why **this courtroom demonstration by the plaintiffs' self- assured medical examiner was absurd!**

Maybe that is why Dr. Spitz said Nicole was **"dazed"?**

If someone, like myself, attacked his demonstration in court and said that Nicole would have defended herself and screamed for help, Dr. Spitz would say that Nicole was **unconscious, or "dazed"!**

And if someone said that she could not have stood up like Dr. Spitz demonstrated in court, if she was **unconscious,** he could say that Nicole was **not** unconscious – only **"dazed"!**

This is how a **"clever"** medical examiner who sells his testimony to the highest bidder, but really doesn't know what he is talking about, tries to cover both his face and his butt at the same time!

I won't let Dr. Spitz get away with that! He must make up his mind! Either, Nicole was **conscious** – or she was **un-conscious!**

If she was **unconscious**, Dr. Spitz' courtroom demonstration was absurd – and if Nicole was **conscious** she would have screamed and fought back to defend herself.

Dr. Spitz can't have it both ways! You either turn off the light – or you don't turn it off. **Only in Dr. Spitz' dream world can a person be conscious and unconscious at the same time!**

Only Dr. Werner Spitz . . . turns the light *"sort of, not quite, completely, almost, nearly, absolutely off"*!

Dr. Spitz did not explain the scraping wounds on Nicole's leg, either, although these wounds held the **real key** to this murder mystery.

All the blood on the lowest step, could not have been running upwards from the patio beneath the steps. And Nicole was found dead on the patio, with her leg wedged underneath the fence. So her neck must have been cut over the lowest step, and then she must have been moved off the steps onto the patio and pulled backwards until her leg got jammed underneath the fence. It should be evident that Nicole could not unconsciously have gotten her leg lodged underneath the fence like it was.

Shouldn't that, at least, have prompted a **qualified** forensic pathologist to ask **who** placed Nicole in this position – **and why?**

In an unconscious state Nicole must have been dragged backwards to get her leg jammed underneath the fence. Why was it so important for the murderer that Nicole's neck bled over the patio, rather than over the steps or over the dirt ground in the niche?

Why didn't you explain <u>that</u>, Dr. Spitz!

Let us go back to the criminal trial! The real medical examiner, Dr. Irwin Golden, who actually performed the autopsies on Nicole's and Ron's bodies, and who is the only medical examiner who ever examined the actual bodies of Nicole and Ron – had his theory about the murders!

But his theory didn't suit the prosecutors!

So they kicked him off the team. Along came the prosecution's "hand picked" medical examiner Dr. Lakshmanan Sathyavagiswaran. He had nothing but the autopsy photos and Dr. Golden's autopsy report to aid him.

Based on this skimpy evidence, Dr. Sathyavagiswaran wrote a completely new and different autopsy report **"made to order"** and **"hand tailored"** to suit the prosecution better than Dr. Golden's theory.

Dr. Sathyavagiswaran concluded that O.J. could have attacked Ron from behind and cut and stabbed him to death with a single edged knife. The doctor spoke and demonstrated for 8 days in court. When he was done, Defense Attorney Robert Shapiro asked him **one question, only!** (In essence):

Doctor, after 8 days of examinations and demonstrations, all you are saying is that the defendant **could** *have committed the murders, using a single edged knife. But you cannot say with certainty, whether or not the defendant or anyone else actually is the assailant, or whether or not there were more than one assailant, or whether one or two knives were used – can you, Doctor?*

In fact, you haven't told us anything!

Medical Examiner Dr. Lakshmanan Sathyavagiswaran agreed – and was excused! What kind of **"evidence"** is this?

The prosecution tried to make an issue of Ron struggling with the murderer for several minutes. That's how O.J., allegedly, should have lost his left glove. That is, of course, absurd. Our discussion of the glove evidence proved that. But the prosecutors needed an explanation for the Bundy glove and the cuts on O.J.'s left finger – as well as for the Rockingham glove, of course.

The prosecution also saw that it could play well with the jurors to present Ron as a **hero** who without concern for his own safety, fought against the murderer to try to save his friend, Nicole.

That is ludicrous. If Nicole was alive, the murderer must have been attacking her, still, when Ron arrived. If so, Ron would have yelled and screamed before intervening, and not have fallen victim to a surprise attack by the murderer, **from behind.**

Nicole must have been lying dead in a pool of blood with her neck cut, when Ron arrived! There was no reason to be a **"hero"** at that moment! And if Nicole was not dead, her neck could not have been cut. So then, she should have screamed for help, while Ron fought with the murderer for several minutes. Furthermore, if Nicole's neck was not cut when Ron arrived and hence, Ron was killed first, he would not have had Nicole's blood under his shoes.

Regardless of how you look at the testimonies and theories of the investigators, the medical examiners, the "experts," the prosecutors, and the counsels for the plaintiffs in this case, **there were flaws in their theories – backwards and forwards**. For every new point or issue they brought up, their theories got more and more inconsistent and contradictory.

The only theory that does not have a single flaw in it – is our theory!

Imagine! Here was Dr. Golden who performed the actual autopsies. His theory didn't suit the prosecution's theory of O.J. being the killer. So they kicked him out, saying he was mistaken!

Enter the new medical examiner, Dr. Sathyavagiswaran! He hadn't even seen the victims' bodies. But he could surely claim that he knew more about these murders than Dr. Golden! Then he went right on using Dr. Golden's own autopsy report and photographs to come up with a totally different "autopsy report"!

But Dr. Sathyavagiswaran's new autopsy report – **hand tailored to fit the prosecution in the criminal case – didn't suit the counsels for the plaintiffs in the civil case!** So now, **they** kicked Dr. Sathyavagiswaran off the team as well, and hired their own "medical examiner"!

Enter the third medical examiner, Dr. Werner Spitz! He never saw the victims' bodies. But he was certain that both Dr. Golden and Dr. Sathyavagiswaran were mistaken! Yet, he saw nothing contradictory in using **their** reports and photos to construct his own, totally new "autopsy report" – concluding that both murders took about 90 seconds altogether, and that O.J. could have done it.

I don't object to Dr. Spitz' "timeline"! I agree with it. What I object to is the fact that four "official" medical examiners in a row could come forward and totally disagree about how Nicole and Ron were killed. And Drs. Sathyavagiswaran and Spitz, who hadn't even seen or touched the victims' bodies, were the ones who most vehemently claimed that their theories were correct – yet **their** opinions differed like north and south!

Readers! Help me here! Are we tuned in to the Comedy Channel? Or are we on the wrong planet, altogether?

With his neck cut, Ron was immediately incapacitated, and in severe shock. The fact that he might have swung around with his arms, in panic and despair, and perhaps have hit the railing, the fence, a tree, or perhaps the murderer's knife, thereby bruising and cutting his hands and arms, is in no way an indication that there ever was any kind of evenly matched struggle between Ron and the murderer. Ron didn't have a chance.

This is supported by the fact that O.J. did not have any bruises in his face or on his body. Now, we know that O.J. is not the murderer. But even Fuhrman did not have any bruises in his face, which is not surprising at all.

Had Ron hit the murderer so hard – **in the head** – that his knuckles were bruised, then the murderer's face would have been pretty beaten up. But O.J. had no injuries anywhere, except for the small cut on his left finger. Hitting the murderer on the clothed parts of his body, would not have bruised Ron's knuckles.

I wrote to O.J.'s attorneys at the beginning of the civil trial and told them that they were wrong if they claimed that the murderer struggled with Ron for 10 minutes. Of course, the motive for O.J.'s attorneys was to demonstrate that O.J. did not have time to commit the murders and get back to Rockingham by the time the limo driver saw him.

However, **they didn't need this "timeline theory"!** The evidence spoke for itself. There is no way O.J. could have killed Nicole and Ron even if the murders took place at 10:15 pm and lasted five seconds! O.J.'s attorneys could only get in trouble if they tried to establish a timeline based on

> how long it **would** have taken **O.J.** to commit two murders which **someone else committed!** (Do my readers hear how "backwards" that sounds?)

I personally guarantee that whatever struggle there was, it lasted less than ninety seconds! That's probably the only thing Geraldo Rivera and I will ever agree on in this case.

Mr. Geraldo Rivera was once an accomplished boxer. He knows

that only a well conditioned and skilled fighter could keep up an **intense** life and death struggle for more than 90 seconds. And there can be no doubt that this was an intense life and death struggle – for both Ron and the murderer. Because if the murderer won – Ron would die. And if Ron survived, the murderer would die – in the gas chamber, most likely!

Neither of the combatants could let up for a fraction of a second even. If the **murderer** let up just for a moment, **Ron would escape**. And if **Ron** let up for a moment, **the murderer would ram the knife into his body,** over and over again.

Geraldo had a few scuffles outside the ring, too. I am sure he could tell us all, when he was in shape, how quickly he would wear out an untrained opponent.

Ron and O.J. were not trained fighters. Ron may have been in good shape for an ordinary man. But he was no top athlete, and definitely not a competitive fighter.

Anyone, who has **not** fought competitively, but still argue that Ron, for as long as five or ten minutes, fought for his life against a knife wielding murderer, should get into a boxing ring and punch it out, seriously, with a **"mean"** opponent **who really hates** you and who is **trying to hurt you** as badly as he can! You will quickly get my point. And you will **never** again suggest that Ron and the murderer were engaged in a life and death struggle for more than 90 seconds! That only happens in the movies!

Besides, Ron had a gaping 3 inch long and 4 inch deep cut in his neck, and his left jugular vein was cut. And O.J. – if he were the murderer – was severely arthritic, overweight, out of shape, and about 47 years old!

I shall eat your Bruno Magli shoes if the alleged struggle between the murderer and Ron, lasted more than 90 seconds! Ron had about 30 knife wounds on his body. That is consistent with an intense struggle lasting a little under 60 seconds.

Allow me to ask, from where do the medical examiner and the prosecutors have their "fighting experience"? From the autopsy room, from the courtroom, or from the couch in front of the television set?

It is not really important to know exactly how long the struggle between Ron and the murderer lasted. The reason I bring this up, however, is to show how totally misinformed the investigators, the medical examiners, and the prosecutors can be.

That's why they could come up with their theory of O.J. being the murderer – because they have no sense of reality, with respect to what a confrontation between Ron and an armed murderer might have been like.

Enough said about the "timeline" at Bundy. This case should not be decided based on the timeline, but on the evidence itself.

Already at an early stage of the investigation, I believe, some of the investigators, at least, must have realized that O.J. was innocent, and that the murderer was one of their own colleagues. It seems so obvious!

This certainly explains why the investigators have been completely reluctant to look for an alternative suspect, other than O.J.

Admitting that a racist LAPD officer murdered Nicole and Ron and tried to frame O.J. for the murders, would cause a scandal the likes of which our country has never seen! The investigators and the prosecutors **could not** go after LAPD Detective Fuhrman – not even after they suspected that he was the murderer.

CHAPTER 31

What About *"The Mountain"* Of Evidence"?

Let us stop and see where we are now! We have proven – **"forwards and backwards"** – **several different ways** – **by examining the glove evidence** – **by analyzing the way Nicole must have been killed** – **by the overall appearance of the crime scenes and the evidence, as well as O.J.'s total lack of motive** – that O.J. could not possibly have murdered Nicole and Ron.

We have also demonstrated that there is a lot of evidence to suggest that Nicole and Ron were murdered by one or more police officers.

We have shown that there are strong reasons to believe that former LAPD Detective Mark Fuhrman is the killer, or that he is part of a murder conspiracy. To recount just a few things, off the top of my head:

- There is every reason to believe that Detective Fuhrman planted the Rockingham glove. That makes him an obvious murder suspect.
- *"The Fuhrman Tapes"* certainly suggest that he could be the killer.
- He has motive and opportunity and the MO fits him – like a glove.
- We have Detective Fuhrman's many peculiar activities during the early hours of the investigation.
- We have **the bloody fingerprint** that disappeared from the brass handle on the rear gate at Bundy. Fuhrman is, at least, a prime suspect of having wiped it off.
- We have the **jeans jacket** that disappeared from Nicole's

condo shortly after Fuhrman had been in her condo alone – on the morning after the murders.

Who else could possibly have had an interest in removing that fingerprint and the jacket? And Fuhrman is probably the only person who had the **opportunity** to do it.

– We also have his perjury, and his lies with respect to his whereabouts on the night of the murders, and in particular at the exact time of the murders.

Why would Mark Fuhrman lie about that, repeatedly, in an effort to give himself an alibi for the time of the murders, unless he is the murderer? It certainly doesn't help his cause, that his wife, apparently, was attempting to corroborate her husband's obviously false alibi, in a manner that certainly presented her as a liar, too.

I have left out countless other good points, but let me stop here.

To people who have read this first portion of my book with an open mind, it must appear that this murder mystery is already solved!

We have proven that O.J. is innocent. That in itself points a strong finger of suspicion at a police officer. Although circumstantial, and based mainly on speculations, the case against former Detective Mark Fuhrman is overwhelming! If nothing else, by the process of elimination, who else, than Mark Fuhrman, could have murdered Nicole and Ron – when O.J., clearly, didn't do it?

However, **the case is not solved** – until we have explained where the so-called *"mountain of evidence"* came from. There is no denying that hairs similar to O.J.'s were found in the knit cap, blood drops with O.J.'s DNA were, apparently, found at the murder scene, etc., etc.

Before we can declare this case "solved," we have to explain how there, apparently, could be *"a mountain of evidence"* against O.J. – if he is innocent.

We have to explain how all, or most, of this evidence could have been fabricated **by one investigator only**, or by a couple of investigators. There was no huge conspiracy – it was not necessary!

We also have to explain the **"motive"** behind the fabrication of evidence that took place. And we have to explain why nobody **"blew the whistle"** a long time ago.

Those will be the topics of the second half of my book. In some respects, you may suspect that this will be less "exiting." It is, perhaps, like watching one of those movies that starts out with "the end of the story" and then let the lead character **look back** on his life and what happened leading up to "the end."

Personally, I found it just as challenging and interesting to figure out Detective Vannatter's involvement in the conspiracy to convict O.J. – as to figure out who actually killed Nicole and Ron, and why and how they were murdered.

What made an LAPD veteran like the lead investigator, Detective Vannatter, conspire to frame O.J.? How could the lead investigator do this, unless his colleagues and the prosecutors, too, were informed and condoned it? Was there a major conspiracy after all? Or was most of it just a **"cover up"** for Detectives Vannatter and Fuhrman? Would investigators and prosecutors risk their careers to protect a man like Detective Fuhrman?

The murderer is exposed. But there are interesting questions – and answers – ahead!

CHAPTER 32

Other Theories – Other Suspects

Naturally, the prosecutors stuck to their *"O.J.-is-the-killer"*-theory. Not that I think they ever believed their own theory – that O.J. could have murdered Nicole and Ron. But they wanted to convict him for various reasons.

If O.J. wasn't the murderer, all the evidence against him must have been fabricated and planted – which it obviously was. Should that ever come out, everyone associated with the case, on the investigative and prosecutorial side, would be under heavy suspicion for having fabricated this evidence, or for having known about it and covered it up.

District Attorney Gil Garcetti, the prosecutors, and the investigators had no choice, but to keep moving ahead in their pursuit of O.J.

The defense, on the other hand, tried to come up with alternative theories for the murders. These theories were totally unfounded, but that was all right. You see, for as much as the criminal trial was concerned, O.J.'s defense attorneys didn't need an alternative murder theory. All **they** needed was to raise **reasonable doubt** regarding some of the prosecution's evidence. They did that – by a wide margin – and O.J. was, subsequently, acquitted.

O.J.'s **investigators** should be highly commended for digging up facts and evidence that raised sufficient reasonable doubt about the prosecution's evidence and witnesses, to acquit O.J.

However, with respect to the civil suit that was to follow, and not the least, O.J.'s private life after the criminal trial, it was most unfortunate that one or more of O.J.'s private investigators got so tied up in one of their alternative murder theories, that the defense failed to see and understand what I am explaining in this book.

My first book, *"If O.J. Didn't..."* – published shortly after the criminal trial – **outlines**, roughly, what I **prove** in this book:

- that O.J. is innocent, and why he could not have murdered Nicole and Ron,
- that Mark Fuhrman, probably, is the killer – and why and how he murdered Nicole and Ron, and how he got away with it,
- where all the evidence came from, and
- how and why the investigators framed O.J., protected Fuhrman, and covered it up.

At the time I wrote my first book, my main sources of information were the news media and *"Rivera Live."* Not the most reliable sources of information about the Simpson case. Accordingly, my first book contained several factual errors. Those errors did not effect the overall theme of the book, though.

Working on my first book, I contacted O.J.'s investigators and his attorneys, first of all to solicit information that could help me prove that Mark Fuhrman murdered Nicole and Ron. O.J.'s investigators were completely unwilling to contribute any information which might have helped me in that respect. I then tried to sway them to see the case **"my way"** – but to no avail. Actually, one of O.J.'s chief investigators told me:

> *"There is no way Mark Fuhrman could have come into possession of the Rockingham glove before he arrived at Bundy at 2:10 am. **He wasn't even in the vicinity"**!*

As I said, it was most unfortunate that one of O.J.'s investigators managed totally to convince O.J. that the murders of Nicole and Ron were somehow related to the "drug world" of Faye Resnick.

Not only has this private "investigation" cost O.J. a fortune. This investigation brought O.J. totally off track in his pursuit of the **real** killer, Detective Mark Fuhrman.

I won't argue that O.J.'s investigators could have nailed Fuhrman, even if they had pursued him from the outset, not only as a racist who possibly planted evidence, but as the most likely murder suspect.

What I will argue, however, is that by wasting their time and resources on all their other theories, they have made it much more difficult – perhaps impossible – to nail Fuhrman today!

I am certain O.J.'s investigators, other Simpson book authors, and O.J.'s attorneys have read my first book, *"If O.J. Didn't . . ."* Hence, I won't be surprised if we in the time to come will see several O.J. books based on the main theory of my first book, *"If O.J. Didn't . . ."* – which forms the basis also for "Solving The Simpson Murder Mystery."

The theory which started it all, came from my first book. That was the book which demonstrated that Mark Fuhrman had both **motive** and **opportunity** and that **the M.O. fit him**. My first book also raised doubt about Fuhrman's possible **alibi.** And the book explained, not only how Detective Vannatter could have fabricated **most** of the evidence, all by himself – but why, and how, his colleagues, and even the prosecutors, were likely to cover it up, if they learned about it.

L et me explain a little about one of these other murder theories, which emerged from O.J.'s investigators – **"the Faye Resnick theory."**

O.J.'s investigators may have found a lot of suspicious connections and activities surrounding Faye Resnick. Some of it also led to Nicole, perhaps. Some of it led to Ron Goldman, even. Unfortunately, these investigators, as well as O.J., failed to understand that there is, indeed, nothing "suspicious" about that at all! Let me explain.

In the celebrity society of Hollywood, with its actors, (O.J. was one), producers, Aspen ski resort vacationers, "party-goers," call girls, cocaine users, drug dealers, corrupt cops, body guards, adulterers, jealous spouses and lovers, money launderers, mafia members, suicide candidates, tax evaders, shady investors, loan sharks, celebrity lawyers, psychotherapists, etc., etc. – you could pretty much find every suspicious connection you cared to look for!

Take any individual in the celebrity Beverly Hills/Hollywood society, and I guarantee you: this individual has partied with people who are all of the above, and they know someone who either hates, or loves, or has threatened, or has slept with, or has used drugs together with, or has had shady business deals with, or been a client of – all of the above!

Of course, O.J.'s investigators could find suspicious connections between Faye Resnick and her drug supplier, tying him to someone else who knew both Nicole and Ron from Aspen, etc., etc. That person, again, might be a friend of someone whom O.J. may have had an argument with at a party. The host of the party might be a cousin of a mafia boss, etc., etc. It just goes on and on – and means **nothing!** One could write more books about such connections than needed to fill a library.

The more you dig, the more you find! Typically, the doctor delivering Madonna's baby, just happened to be the father of convicted "Hollywood Madam," Heidi Fleiss! Does that imply that the father of Madonna's child may have been a former client of Heidi Fleiss? Of course not!

Someone may find the following supernatural – but yet, it only goes to underscore how right I am about my characterization of this so-called "suspicious" Faye Resnick world:

I wrote the above – including the example of Madonna and the father of Heidi Fleiss – during my early work with this book. Later, the civil trial had started. What do you know! Defense Counsel Robert Baker, declared in his opening statement that he would show that Nicole's "partying lifestyle" included people from "Hollywood Madam" Heidi Fleiss' circle of friends!

Of course, I had to edit this "coincidence" into my book. But what it really demonstrates is that if you pick any person in the "baroque," almost unreal Hollywood society, you can establish a close connection from that person to anyone else within the "society" – including O.J., Nicole, and Faye Resnick – via a maximum of two or three other "party-goers"!

Take this, for instance: As I have already mentioned, Nicole once had oral sex with a guy named Keith Zlomsowitch. Keith, allegedly is a friend of Heidi Fleiss. Heidi's father delivered Madonna's baby. Does that mean that there may be "something" going on between O.J. and Madonna?

Again, of course not! It simply illustrates how ridiculous it is to look for **"suspicious"** connections in Beverly Hills, in an attempt to solve the murders of Nicole and Ron.

Anything you can dig up within this environment – regardless of how suspicious it may look – probably means nothing! You don't find Nicole's murderer by reading the Hollywood gossip columns!

The most popular alternative murder theory seems to be this:

Faye Resnick lived with Nicole up until a few days prior to Nicole's murder. At the time Faye was heavily into drugs.

One of Faye's drug connections wanted her killed – possibly because she owed a lot of money and didn't pay her debt. So he hired a hit man to kill Faye. But this hit man didn't know that Faye had moved from Nicole's apartment a few days earlier. He mistook Nicole for Faye, and killed Nicole instead.

At least half a dozen similar theories are circulating. My problem with these theories is this:

If Nicole's murderer didn't know Nicole, since he mistook her for Faye, then he couldn't have known that Nicole was O.J.'s ex-wife either!

So, how could he set up the murder of Nicole to look like O.J. had done it in a state of jealous rage? How can such a hit man, who didn't know Nicole better than to kill her by mistake, plant one of the murder gloves behind the house of Nicole's ex-husband?

Furthermore, it doesn't make sense that a drug dealer wanted to kill Faye, for failing to pay her debt. A drug dealer could arrange to have Faye beaten up, or have her face "fixed" – as a warning to make her pay. But he wouldn't kill her, because then he would **never** get his money!

A drug dealer might, however, have decided to kill Faye, if he realized that she **would never** pay her debt. He might have decided to kill Faye, as a warning – not to Faye, but to his other "clients" – so that they pay **their** debts on time.

But to send that message to these other clients, they must be made to understand **why** Faye (or unfortunately Nicole) was killed. Therefore, it doesn't make sense that the murder of Nicole (mistaken for Faye) were a drug hit, when the murder was set up to look like it was committed by a jealous ex-husband.

I can understand that O.J.'s investigators – as long as O.J. paid them – pursued these Faye Resnick theories. However, I am surprised that O.J. bought into these theories, so completely. Neither of these theories – how intriguing they might have appeared – tied in with any of the physical and circumstantial evidence of the actual murders of Nicole and Ron.

Accordingly, I was not surprised when Judge Fujisaki excluded the defense from even mentioning their theories regarding Faye Resnick during the civil trial.

So where was O.J. then, with respect to an alternative murder theory? Back at "square one"!

Now, that was OK for the **criminal** trial. There O.J.'s attorneys only needed to raise reasonable doubt about the **prosecution's** theory. In the **civil** trial, however, the criteria for conviction were different. The plaintiffs only needed to convince 9 out of 12 jurors that it was **more likely than not that O.J. – rather than someone else – murdered Nicole and Ron.**

Obviously, when there was a lot of evidence – fabricated or

not – against O.J., but not a single piece of physical evidence pointing to anyone else, O.J. was in trouble. He needed **another suspect!** And this other suspect better be "a good one"!

In terms of another suspect, Detective Fuhrman is not only an alternative. I believe strongly that Mark Fuhrman **is** the killer. All the evidence is consistent with my theory that Fuhrman murdered Nicole and Ron, and not only framed O.J., but set up the LAPD investigators, as well.

By concentrating so hard on Faye Resnick, O.J. lost out on his opportunity to present a credible alternative murder theory during the civil trial, and in particular – go after Fuhrman in time for the civil trial.

However, thinking ahead to the rest of his life, and to his acceptance by his peers back into society, it is **not** too late for O.J. to go after the person who has, so terribly, ravished his life.

Almost everyone I have explained my theory to, fully agrees with me. Many of them were absolutely committed in their beliefs that O.J. were guilty. Still, they were totally persuaded by the logic of my theory, and today they are convinced that O.J. is innocent – and that Mark Fuhrman, most likely, murdered Nicole and Ron.

Now back to alternative murder theories and murder suspects. Let us first look at a scenario where Fuhrman – after killing Nicole and Ron, drove to Rockingham to plant the glove.

Mark Fuhrman could have killed Nicole and Ron, then driven to Rockingham to plant the glove near the main entrance to the house. However, because the limo was parked in front of the house, Fuhrman, perhaps, changed his plan and decided to climb the fence **behind** O.J.'s house, instead. In the darkness, perhaps, he fell from the fence, against the wall, thereby causing the three thumps Kato heard – the first thump as his back hit the wall, immediately followed by one more thump from each arm as he, perhaps, swung his arms backwards to absorb the impact and protect his head, too, from hitting the wall.

Afraid that someone might have heard the noise, Fuhrman, perhaps, aborted his mission. After all, he knew he would get a second chance to plant the glove when he returned to investigate the murders the following morning.

Rather than throwing the glove back over the fence, as he left, he decided to keep it.

Because of the limo driver, Fuhrman couldn't approach the main entrance from the front of the property. Hence, his new, improvised plan might have been to climb the fence behind the house, sneak around the house, in the darkness, and from around the last corner, toss the glove over towards the main entrance, where O.J., perceivably, might have lost it.

Since Fuhrman's plan, in this scenario, was interrupted, when he fell against the wall – and he didn't readily see the consequences of tossing away the glove **behind** O.J.'s house, rather than by the entrance – Fuhrman might have decided to keep the glove, in the plastic bag, until he could plant it the following morning. So, he just escaped as quickly as possible.

Fuhrman might, however, have hung around at Rockingham long enough to open O.J.'s Bronco and smear the bloody glove inside the Bronco before he left. However, he could have done that, too, the following morning.

Here is **another alternative** – also involving Fuhrman, and consistent with everything else I have explained so far.

Fuhrman had two accomplices. I have earlier justified that, and explained how a couple of conspirators could have worked out the plan to murder Nicole and frame O.J.

There are, in particular, two good reasons to suspect that three or more conspirators were involved in the murders. First of all, the way Ron was killed – without a sound – could indicate that there might have been more than one killer.

Secondly, one of Fuhrman's motives – besides his racism – was his ego. As he indicated on *"The Fuhrman Tapes,"* Fuhrman wanted to prove that he was **clever enough, and daring enough to commit murder, and get away with it.** But he needed to prove that to someone else – not just to himself. The only ones he could safely prove this to, would be to a couple of co-conspirators.

Hence, perhaps Fuhrman murdered Nicole (and Ron), while

another conspirator used Fuhrman's credit card to fill gas in Pomona, thereby giving Fuhrman an alibi – in case he should become a murder suspect after he "found" the second glove on O.J.'s property the following morning.

In the meantime a third accomplice entered the property of Simpson's neighbor, shortly after Fuhrman had killed Nicole and Ron. His mission was **not** to plant the glove – because Fuhrman had the glove! The mission of this third accomplice was merely to "thump" the wall heavily – with the padded end of a baseball bat, a pool cue, or similar – from across the fence. The purpose was to draw attention to the area behind O.J.'s house, where Fuhrman would plant, and at the same time **"find,"** the glove the following morning.

The next morning, when the occupant of the house (Brian "Kato" Kaelin), most likely, explained about the thumps to the police – those thumps, created by Fuhrman's accomplice, at a time shortly after the murders, should cause everyone to believe the glove was lost (by O.J.) **right after** the murders – **before** he left for Chicago that night.

I detail this theory in the chapter titled *"The Thumps On Kato's Wall."* I just wanted to mention it here. There is also another variation of this last theory.

Rather than Fuhrman being the actual killer, Fuhrman's part in the murder plot might have been to plant and "find" the glove, only. If so, maybe Fuhrman, indeed, was in Pomona pumping gas at the time of the murders – thereby giving himself an alibi, since he might become a murder suspect after he "found" the glove the next morning.

In the meantime, one accomplice murdered Nicole (and Ron), while the the second accomplice waited near Rockingham, ready to thump the wall to Kato's room, as soon as the murderer called on a cellular phone and said, *"Mission accomplished."*

None of the many other alternative murder theories I have heard, changes my overall theory in this case, namely that a brutal, racist LAPD officer decided to murdered Nicole and frame

O.J. for her murder – **mainly for racist reasons,** but also **for the raw "challenge" of it!**

It is my opinion that Fuhrman played a central role in the murder plot.

Enough of alternative murder theories. Let us stick to the basic theory of Fuhrman being the murderer, and consider **what he might have done after Nicole and Ron were dead.**

CHAPTER 33

Framing O.J. – "Setting Up" The Investigators

Let me start this chapter by elaborating a bit on the notion of police investigators fabricating or planting evidence against O.J. – something I certainly have touched on earlier in my book!

Especially in larger metropolitan police departments, and in particular within the LAPD, evidence planting was so common – as Detective Fuhrman admits on his tapes – that it was hardly worth mentioning.

Understand, however, that this rampant evidence planting does not imply that police officers just randomly fabricate and plant evidence against innocent people, or even against innocent suspects.

There are exceptions, but ordinarily, only in those cases where the investigators already felt they **knew** the suspect was guilty, would they proceed to plant false evidence – in order to make sure the "guilty" suspect was convicted.

It was like **"giving Justice a helping hand"**!

It wasn't like the LAPD investigators arrived at a crime scene, saw some person walking along the street, and decided to nail him for the crime – by fabricating false evidence against him. Let me explain how the evidence planting is practiced.

Say the police were investigating the murder of a man. Several times, one of the victim's "friends" had threatened to kill the victim, and had beaten him severely on many occasions. An eyewitness said he saw the suspect beat the man to death. Circumstances in the testimony of the witness convinced the police that the witness was telling the truth.

Clearly, the investigators were convinced the suspect was guilty.

But a jury might still not convict him, because there wasn't really that much physical evidence, and the eyewitness is a known drug addict.

So then, at an early stage of the investigation, when the detectives arrested the suspect at his home, they first smeared a little bit of the victim's blood on the suspect's door knob and door frame. When they searched the suspect, they smeared a little bit of blood also on his shirt and on his door key. Then they picked up a cigarette butt from his ashtray, and some hairs from his hair brush in the bathroom – returned to the murder scene, and dropped the cigarette butt on the ground, and the hairs on the victim's shirt, where this "evidence" would later be found by other investigators or criminalists.

So then the investigators had a stronger case against the man they already **"knew"** was guilty.

Here is another example: Detectives were getting ready to raid the home of a well known drug dealer. It wasn't like they **"thought"** he was guilty, but they didn't know for sure. Rather – no question about it – the detectives knew for sure that this guy was a drug dealer. They had seen him pushing drugs outside the junior high school almost every day. And now they wanted him and all his "business" off the street.

But what if the guy – on this particular day when the police had obtained a search warrant and decided to arrest him – was clean as a baby. They found nothing on him, and nothing in his house – then what?

So to make certain they didn't come up empty, the detectives "borrowed" a couple of ounces of crack from the police evidence locker (drugs confiscated in other drug busts).

Then they raided the man's house, arrested him, and searched him. In his pocket the arresting officer "found" the crack or cocaine which he, himself, had brought along.

Perhaps this "evidence" planting wasn't necessary. Perhaps the suspect's house was full of drugs. But just in case the police didn't find any drugs during the arrest, they brought along the "evidence" as an added **"insurance,"** to make certain they did get this drug dealer off the streets.

Again, the police had no qualms about this, because they "knew" the suspect was a drug dealer, and they believed that putting him behind bars was a good and moral thing to do – regardless of how they did it!

Many ordinary, law abiding citizens may even approve of such police tactics. Consequently, have no doubt about this:

> If the police feel that their case needs it, they routinely fabricate and plant false evidence – when they have a chance to do it, and they are convinced the suspect is guilty.

Detective Mark Fuhrman knew this, and he made sure the investigators were convinced right away that O.J. were guilty. And Fuhrman also made sure – through the messy murder scene he created – that the investigators had plenty to work with in terms of creating false evidence against O.J.

But Fuhrman was smarter than that even! He created the crime scenes (Bundy, the Bronco, and Rockingham) so "cleverly" that **if** the police **"took his bait"** and used the existing evidence to create false evidence against O.J., they could do it so perfectly that, apparently, nobody could expose them.

On the other hand, if the investigators, for some reason which Fuhrman found highly unlikely, decided **not** to fabricate and plant false evidence against O.J., then the evidence Fuhrman left behind as "bait," did not implicate Fuhrman in any way, nor did it contradict the theory of O.J. being the murderer.

One example: I believe Fuhrman planted the five blood drops next to the bloody shoe prints! This evidence alone has done more to ruin O.J.'s life than all the rest of the evidence combined. These blood drops were fabricated, and there is overwhelming evidence to prove it – although nobody, so far, seems to understand how it was done. I'll return to that point, in detail, later.

As Fuhrman left the murder scene, Fuhrman planted those infamous five blood drops next to the bloody shoeprints – **using Nicole's blood.** Fuhrman dipped each of his five left fingertips in

Nicole's blood and shook the blood drops from his fingers – one at the time – as he walked away from the murder scene.

The police, of course, collected those blood drops on five so-called evidence "swatches" (small pieces of cotton fabric). Now the following could happen:

Detective Vannatter found a way to exchange those blood swatches with false swatches containing O.J.'s blood (prepared after he received O.J.'s blood reference sample in a vial). When those false blood swatches were sent to the FBI's lab or to Cellmark Diagnostics lab for DNA analyses, the results would come back, of course, that the blood was O.J.'s – without a shred of doubt! That way it would appear that O.J. had bled at the murder scene before he left for Chicago, and that he, accordingly, were guilty!

The point is that the blood they analyzed was his – but that was not the blood the criminalists collected at Bundy!

Or the following **could** have happened (although it didn't):

Detective Vannatter and his colleagues, for some reason or another, could have decided **not** to replace those five blood swatches with false O.J. blood swatches. They simply assumed it was O.J.'s blood, and sent the five swatches to the FBI's crime lab for DNA analyses. If so, the results would have come back, that it was Nicole's blood, of course!

This would not have jeopardized Detective Fuhrman in any way. The investigators would simply have concluded that O.J. had Nicole's blood all over his hands, his knife, and his clothes, and that her blood had dripped from his hand or knife as he left the murder scene.

In this case the five blood drops at Bundy would not have incriminated O.J. directly. But that evidence would not have exonerated him either. And under no circumstances would those five blood drops have implicated **Fuhrman**.

This is how **cleverly** Fuhrman **"set up"** the investigators with false evidence. He created the messiest crime scenes most investigators had ever seen. There was the **potential** for fabricating false evidence everywhere – the gloves, the cap, hairs, fibers, some of it at Bundy, some in the Bronco, some at Rockingham.

Fuhrman knew the pack he ran with. He knew the investigators **could not resist the temptation** of framing O.J. with fabricated evidence. But Fuhrman's **"ingenuity"** was that whatever evidence he laid down as "bait" – and which the investigators did **not** falsify – that evidence would still not point to anyone else, and it would not appear to have been planted!

Was Detective Fuhrman that "smart"? Absolutely! **Fuhrman graduated from the LAPD's Lincoln Heights Academy second in his class!** And remember what he said on the Fuhrman Tapes (in essence):

> *I am so good at fabricating false evidence, that nobody can ever catch me.* ***I could have murdered people and got away with it!***

What exactly did he mean by that? Well, to say what he said, Detective Fuhrman must, **at least**, have **considered** murdering people, just to prove to himself that he could get away with it, because he was so "clever" at planting false evidence – after (in his mind) having committed such "fantasy murders" – that nobody could catch him!

And he also meant, obviously, that if we, in trying to expose his (or his colleagues') evidence planting, figured out a scheme whereby Fuhrman **could** have done it – then Detective Fuhrman, most likely, would already have figured it out himself, and even "done us one better"!

Isn't it amazing that no one from the LAPD or from the district attorney's office seriously considered the possibility that Detective Fuhrman actually murdered Nicole and Ron? Not even after reading or hearing what Detective Fuhrman said on *"The*

Fuhrman Tapes"?

Detective Fuhrman knew how his colleagues in the LAPD routinely planted or fabricated evidence in criminal cases, and in particular he expected that they would do it in this high profile murder case, where there would be so much public and official pressure on the investigators to secure a conviction.

So Detective Fuhrman did leave a **"mountain of evidence"**! But it was not evidence of O.J.'s guilt. It was merely such a bloody mess and so many clues that the investigators were given the **opportunity** to build an air tight case against O.J. – if they wanted to, and if they were willing to fabricate false evidence.

> **They wanted to, all right! And they were willing to do it – because they believed O.J. were as guilty as sin, right from the moment Detective Fuhrman showed them the bloody glove behind O.J.'s house!**

But I am getting ahead of myself now. Let me slow down a bit and return to the Bundy murder scene, just after Detective Fuhrman had knocked Nicole unconscious.

As I stated earlier, Fuhrman had already tossed the knit cap over towards some shrubbery, right after he knocked Nicole unconscious with the butt end of his revolver handle. If he had padded his gun with the knit cap before he struck Nicole with it, then he tossed the cap away before he holstered his gun and took out his knife to cut Nicole's neck.

Fuhrman never intended to wear the knit cap. He only brought it along to frame O.J. The cap provided an excellent opportunity for the investigators to plant O.J.'s hairs on it. Besides it was perfect as padding for his gun.

The investigators could have picked the hairs from O.J.'s hair brush in his bathroom, a few hours after the murders. Or they could have picked them from the pillowcase in his jail cell.

Some time later they asked O.J. to volunteer some hair samples for comparison – which O.J. did. The planted hairs from the cap were, of course, similar to O.J.'s. Hence it appeared that Ron had fought with O.J., and that O.J. had lost both the left glove **and the knit cap** during the struggle. We know better!

After he had killed Nicole and Ron, Detective Fuhrman started the framing of O.J. Fuhrman removed his left glove by tugging repeatedly on each of the fingertips of the glove, using the thumb and index finger of his right hand. He tossed the glove over towards Ron's body. Then he wiped off the knife and sheathed it in his belt.

Next, Fuhrman removed the right (Rockingham) glove. **He folded it over,** and put it in the plastic bag where the cap had been, and stuck the bag back in his pocket.

Fuhrman had to fold the glove over, in order to make it fit in the plastic bag, as well as in his pocket and later inside his sock.

Fuhrman kept the bloody, wet glove, folded inside the plastic bag for almost 7 1/2 hours. Of course, when he later planted it behind O.J.'s house, the glove, after being folded over for 7 1/2 hours, would not straighten itself out, even if Fuhrman tried to do so. That's why the glove was partly folded over when it was found!

This is just another proof that the Rockingham glove was planted long after O.J. left for Chicago. But I return to that later.

Fuhrman had purposely cut Nicole's throat so as to spill a lot of blood. Before leaving he stepped in this pool of blood, thereby making his Bruno Magli shoeprints as bloody and conspicuous as possible.

Let me explain something about the bloody shoe prints and the five blood drops before I continue.

First of all, the five blood drops were **not** to the **left** of the shoeprints! The prosecutors and the media repeatedly **mis-stated** that, in order to make it **appear** that the blood drops corresponded to the cut on O.J.'s **left** finger. But that was simply not true!

The **first** blood drop (after 4-5 steps) was **way over to the left** – almost as if the murderer had held his left arm straight out to the side and let the drop fall down – way out there.

The other blood drops, however, did not appear to have fallen from a cut on the murderer's left hand, either. The second and third blood drops were found, kind of, **"between"** the bloody shoeprints (as if they had fallen right **in front of** the person who was walking away).

I think this is important. You shall soon learn why! The position of the fourth and fifth blood drops were, kind of, ambivalent, because the bloody shoeprints didn't lead that far away from the murder scene. They had faded.

Then there were the bloody shoeprints. Strangely, there were **two sets of bloody shoeprints** leading away the bodies. Both sets were made by the same pair of shoes. Apparently the murderer had begun to walk away, had stopped, turned, and gone back to the bodies, and then walked away a second time.

Nobody has been able to explain this. The prosecutors called those shoeprints turning around, *"The O.J. shuffle"!*

That was clever by the prosecutors! When they couldn't explain something based on their theory, because their theory had a flaw in it, they should have scrapped their theory, and admitted that perhaps O.J. isn't guilty anyway.

But not these prosecutors! Instead they suggested that maybe O.J. took a few cha-cha-cha's as he walked away. Everybody laughed. That was smart, because when you make people laugh, they relax and lose their concentration. By the time people in the courtroom got serious again, they had forgotten about the apparent mystery of the double set of bloody shoeprints!

The prosecutors needed some kind of explanation for the double set of shoeprints, though. So they suggested that O.J. had started to walk away, but then he realized that he had lost his glove and knit cap. So he turned around and walked back to look for those items.

However, again, the prosecutors were totally wrong! If O.J. returned to pick up the glove and the cap, why didn't he pick them up, then?

Time and time again, the prosecution's theories led to the most absurd contradictions.

This time they explained that O.J. simply didn't find the glove and the cap!

The area where Nicole and Ron were found is approximately 3 ft x 7 ft. The area is about the size of your dinner table! It should not be hard to find a glove and a cap in an area that small – even if you were blind!

Next issue: **I have always maintained that the bloody shoeprints must have been deliberately planted by the murderer, in order to frame O.J. That explains the vicious cutting of Nicole's neck!** We have already discussed that, and proven it, in connection with the wounds on Nicole's leg and the blow to her head. Let me support this assumption:

Picture yourself walking along a sidewalk. You are wearing $160 Bruno Magli shoes. A dog has left its calling card, and someone has stepped in it. There are half a dozen brown shoeprints, and some smears, along the sidewalk. What do you do – instinctively? Yes, you step around it or over it!

Further along, there is some mysterious "liquid" across the sidewalk. It could be just water. But again you take a long stride and step over it. Right?

Then you get to an almost dried out puddle, left over from yesterday's rainstorm. There is some muddy water in the middle and a wider muddy area around it – about 3-4 feet in diameter. It's "clean mud." But approaching the semi-dry puddle you take a few running steps and jump over it! You've done that haven't you? Many times, huh?

We humans simply instinctively avoid stepping in anything unknown, or dirty, smelly, wet, muddy, slippery, or whatever!

What does this have to do with the Simpson case? Well, here is the murderer, having killed Nicole first. She was lying in a pool of blood at the bottom of the steps up to the walkway leading to the rear gate. Then the murderer attacked and killed Ron, in the niche, three feet to the north of Nicole's body.

The murderer was about to leave. He had to step over

Nicole's bloody body, and there were one big puddle of blood, as well as many smaller blood spots on the ground.

What would any normal human being have done in this situation – **purely by instinct**? Right! He would instinctively have avoided stepping in the blood! He would have grabbed the railing, taken a long stride and stepped directly onto the second or third step leading up to the walkway.

Only on **purpose** would a murderer, wearing $160.00 Italian shoes step into the largest blood puddle with both his shoes, leaving almost complete, bloody shoeprints, for the next few steps, at least. It **must** have been done **deliberately** in order to plant those bloody Bruno Magli shoeprints – almost as red prints from a rubber stamp!

Just think about what you would have done, with all that blood on the concrete patio. Would you have trampled right into the largest of the blood puddles? Of course not!

But consider what happened next! Naturally the blood wore off the soles relatively quickly. The bloody shoeprints were fading.

Then for some reason or another, the murderer stopped, turned around, and went back to Nicole's body. The prosecutors and the plaintiffs said it was O.J. returning to look for his glove and his cap. I have a different explanation, as you shall soon learn.

By the time the murderer had walked back to Nicole's body, the blood under his soles had worn off and the bloody shoeprints had faded completely. Whatever reason the murderer had for going back, he presumably did what he wanted to do, and then he was ready to walk away for the second time.

Again – for the second time – the murderer stepped into the largest blood puddle next to Nicole's dead body and covered the underside of both his shoes completely with Nicole's blood, before walking away! Again, he left almost complete, bloody shoeprints for the next several

steps.

The bloody shoeprints **must** have been created **on purpose – in order to frame O.J.!**

Had there been only **one** set of bloody shoeprints, I could have conceded it might have been by accident. But not when the murderer, sort of, went back for a **"refill"**!

Suddenly both the use of a knife, and the vicious cutting of Nicole's neck make sense – in all its gore.

Come on! Wake up America!!!

There was yet another flaw in the prosecution's theory – the so-called *"O.J. shuffle"* theory!

There were **no blood drops** along the **first set** of bloody shoeprints leading away from the bodies, turning around, and returning to the victims. **The five blood drops only accompanied the second set of shoeprints**, which eventually continued towards the rear gate!

If these drops of blood had come from O.J.'s hand, because he were bleeding, and he released five drops over a distance of some 75-100 feet, why didn't that cut bleed the first time he started to walk away, or when he turned around and walked back towards the bodies? Why did that cut only bleed **one** of the times he walked away from the bodies – and in particular, the **last** time?

If anything, shouldn't we expect that a wound bled **less and less** – not **more and more**? Hence, shouldn't we expect that the murderer bled the **first** time, and not the **second** time, perhaps – but not the other way around!

Did the prosecutors claim that O.J. cut himself **after** *"the O.J. shuffle"*? I thought the prosecutors claimed that O.J. was cut in a struggle with Ron! If he wasn't, and that was the reason he didn't bleed the first time he walked away – what caused him to bleed the second time?

Furthermore, if O.J. were the murderer, and he cut himself in a struggle with Ron – why didn't he bleed on Ron's fallen body, or around the area of the victims? I know why – and soon my readers shall know it too.

There is more "funny stuff", however. Let the prosecutors or the counsels for the plaintiffs try to explain **this** with their phony theories:

> The bloody shoeprints were from a rather big man (size twelve shoes)! Yet the shoeprints were so close together that it appeared the murderer had walked away from the scene *"rather slowly"* – **with 12-18 inches between the strides, only!**

Isn't that funny, if O.J. were the murderer? Don't you think he would try to get away from the murder scene – **with long, quick strides?**

After **allegedly** having hideously murdered two people in a pool of blood, I would suggest that O.J. tried to get away from the murder scene as fast as possible, before someone showed up and screamed,

> *"Bloody murder!"*

... and people opened their windows to see what was going on!

Or I would suggest that O.J. tried to get away as fast as he could, before he bumped into one of Nicole's neighbors saying:

> *"Hi, O.J.! What's up? Have you been over to see Nicole and the kids?"*

Besides, O.J. had a plane to catch also – remember? If he were the murderer, he were already way behind "schedule"!

Here is more "funny stuff"! We humans tend to walk with our feet "in line." That makes us walk "smoothly." Had we walked with our feet, or footsteps as wide apart as when we stand up, we would have looked like ducks, wagging along!

Yet, the bloody shoeprints seemed to indicate that the murderer had been "walking like a duck" – at least a few places. Those places coincided with where the first blood drops were located. Is there any logical explanation for this? Yes! I'll get to this also, shortly.

One last point, or inconsistency. Whoever stepped in the blood puddles at Bundy could not avoid getting blood also a quarter of an inch up the along the edges of his soles. **This blood would not wear off** as he walked away from the murder scene.

However, if O.J. were the murderer, this blood should have been deposited in **curved "lumps" of blood** on the carpet floor in his Bronco. There was **nothing** of the sort on the Bronco's carpet!

Do my readers see what kind of contradictions the prosecution's and the plaintiff's theory leads to – time and time again?

Let O.J.'s adversaries present their ludicrous theories! However, that's not how **we** should approach a problem! Right? If you have a theory about the murders – and you maintain that your theory is the right one – then your theory must reconcile not only **some** of the evidence, but **absolutely every piece of evidence in the case**. And your theory must reconcile every piece of evidence – not only when it is **superficially examined**, but when it is **thoroughly scrutinized**!

My theory about Fuhrman being the murderer would have to reconcile

- the five blood drops, as well as
- *"the O.J. shuffle,"*
- the position of the five blood drops,
- the absence of blood drops along the first set of shoeprints,
- the short strides,
- the "duck walk,"
- the glove and the knit cap being left behind, and even
- the number of blood drops being exactly five – instead of zero, one, two, three, four . . . six, eight, fourteen, twenty-

three, or fifty!

In short, **a proper theory should reconcile everything.** My theory does – while the prosecution's and the plaintiffs' theories reconciled **nothing!** They just threw out **one absurd hypothesis after the other**. As soon as we tried to reconcile their hypotheses with the facts of the case, their hypotheses fell apart.

Here is what I believe happened: Detective Fuhrman had planned the murder of Nicole in minute detail, including creating a pool of blood which he could step in to leave the bloody shoeprints. He had also planned to shake drops of Nicole's blood from each of the five fingertips on his left hand, as he walked away from the murder scene. Just in case O.J. happened to have a wound somewhere on his arms or hands, this would give the investigators the **opportunity** to replace those blood drops with O.J.'s blood, in the crime lab

Fuhrman had **practiced** at home how he would release the five blood drops without shaking his hand so much that an entire spray of drops fell on the same spot. As they appeared at Bundy, the five drops were about 15-30 feet apart.

Here is how he planned to do it and had practiced it at home, perhaps using water. He dipped the fingertips of his **left** hand in water. One drop was left hanging underneath each of the **five** fingertips. He walked slowly, so he shouldn't shake his hand.

With his **right** hand's index finger he "tapped" against each of the fingers of his left hand – one at the time. That way he didn't have to shake his entire left hand, in order to release the drops. Only that finger which he tapped, would jerk a little, releasing the drop from that fingertip, only.

In preparation for the murder of Nicole, Fuhrman had gone over this so many times, that he could do it in his sleep, almost.

However, Ron's appearance at the murder scene, and the fact that Fuhrman had to kill Ron, too, had shook Fuhrman up a bit. **He lost his concentration!** So Fuhrman **forgot** about dipping his fingertips in Nicole's blood. He just stepped in the blood puddle and started walking away.

Quickly, he came to one of the spots in the walkway, where he in his mind had pictured himself, many times, as he released the second or third blood drop. He looked at his hand, and realized that he had forgotten to dip his left fingertips in Nicole's blood!

So he turned around and walked back to Nicole's body! There he bent down and stuck his five left fingertips in her blood. The viscous blood clung well to his fingertips.

Again, he methodically stepped in her blood, and walked away. That is why there were two sets of bloody shoeprints!

Then it was time to release the first drop. Had that drop been released from O.J.'s hand as he walked away, it would have fallen to the ground just a couple of inches from the nearest, left shoeprint. If you **follow my instructions,** I will now explain why the first drop of blood was so **far out to the left!**

Dip your left fingertips in some water, so that one drop hangs underneath each fingertip. (Keep in mind, that blood drops stick to your fingers much better than drops of water). Hold your left arm straight out to the side, away from your body, with a 90 degree angle at your elbow, and with your lover arm horizontally pointing straight forward. Bend your wrist downward, so your fingertips point downward too. Can you see that the thumb can be separated from the four other fingers, so that you may easily tap your left thumb with your right index finger, without disturbing the other four fingers?

But in what direction do you tap the left thumb? Exactly! You tap it straight out to the left side.

Because the blood drop clung to Fuhrman's thumb better than the water to your thumb, the blood drop underneath the tip of Fuhrman's thumb didn't fall straight down (because of its inertia), but followed the movement of his thumb, and was "flung" out to the left!

That's why the first drop ended up almost two feet away from the shoeprints! Of course, Fuhrman couldn't wipe it up. He had to leave it out there and go on!

Now continue to tap each of the other four fingers, one at the time only. Do you see that it is, kind of, awkward to do that with your left arm held out to the left? It was okay for the thumb, but not for the other fingers.

The four remaining fingers are positioned in such a way that if you tap one finger from the right side, you may accidentally tap – or jerk – the other fingers too!

To avoid that, move your left hand forward, in front of your body. Now you can easily separate one of the four fingers at the time, and snap at it **from behind** – one at the time – first the index finger, then the middle finger, then the ring finger, and finally the little finger!

That's how Fuhrman had practiced it at home. At home he had practiced with water drops. They always fell straight down. But when it was "for real" with Nicole's blood, the blood drop under the tip of his thumb clung to his thumb better than water, so the drop flew two feet out to the left.

That was why **the first** blood drop was found **way out to the left**, while **the other four** drops were found **"between"** the shoeprints.

Everything fits! My theory explains the double set of bloody shoeprints leading away from the bodies. It explains the positions of the drops. It explains why there were two set of shoeprints, but only one set of blood drops. It explains why the blood drops accompamied the second set of shoeprints and not the first. It explains *"the O.J. shuffle"* – which from here on should be renamed *"the Fuhrman shuffle"*!

Size 12 shoes indicated that the murderer is a big man. Just to mention it, Fuhrman is about 6' 4". Based on the shoe size experts have concluded that the murderer walked away from Bundy **"slowly and with very short strides"**!

How does that connect with O.J. being the murderer? If O.J. were the murderer, don't you think he would have walked away from Bundy rather quickly? As I mention, he even had a plane to catch!

The slow and deliberate shoeprints indicated that O.J. is definitely not the murderer. I think the slow and deliberate shoeprints indicated that Fuhrman was walking carefully, because he had a drop of Nicole's blood hanging underneath each of his five left fingertips – and he didn't want to lose any of those drops until it was time to release them!

Fuhrman was releasing one drop at the time at certain intervals of about 15-30 feet, to **"set up"** the investigators, so that they could replace Nicole's blood with O.J.'s blood, thereby making it appear that O.J. were bleeding from his hand as he left the murder scene. That's why Fuhrman was walking so slowly and carefully.

One more point about the appearance of the bloody shoeprints. Not only were they short paced. The left and right feet also moved apart, sideways – at those places where the blood drops occurred. Doesn't that further indicate that the murderer was carefully planting those drops and slowing down or stopping when he released a drop?

I don't know if my readers have given it some thought at all. But we humans tend to walk with our footsteps somewhat "in line," rather than apart like a duck! But in order to keep our balance when we slow down or stop, we must move our feet more apart from each other. That was exactly the case with the bloody shoeprints at Bundy. This indicated that the murderer (Fuhrman) slowed down or stopped each time he released one of the blood drops.

Finally! Assuming that O.J. were the murderer and that he were bleeding continuously from a cut on his left hand – why should this cut bleed **exactly five** drops of blood? Why not 8 drops, or 13 ... 25, 50? Why didn't the cut continue to bleed 25-50 drops of blood in his Bronco, if he was still bleeding in his driveway at Rockingham when he, allegedly, returned there?

If O.J. left those blood drops at Bundy, he must have been bleeding at the rate of one drop every 6-7 seconds, approximately. Driving from Bundy to Rockingham takes about 5 minutes or 300 seconds. It is plain arithmetic that O.J. should have bled **at least 40 drops** in his Bronco – unless someone was out to frame him!

Only 7/10 of one drop of O.J.'s blood was found in the Bronco.

That's exactly as much blood you would get from one falsely fabricated swatch with O.J.'s blood on it – if you moistened such a swatch in distilled water and smeared it inside the Bronco!

But back to the five drops at Bundy. **If** O.J. were the murderer, perhaps the bleeding stopped because he covered the cut with his right hand, or perhaps he stuck his left hand in his pocket. If so, why did he do that after the cut had released 5 drops? Why didn't he do that right away, before it released any drops at all? Or after it had released one drop, or two, or three, ... or six or seven or eight?

The point is this: If O.J. were the murderer, and those blood drops had come from a cut on O.J.'s hand, as he were leaving the murder scene, we could have expected **any number of blood drops, from zero to 45,** from the victims bodies and to, and inside, the Bronco.

However, if my theory is correct, and those blood drops were planted – as I explained that Fuhrman probably did – to "set up" the investigators to frame O.J, and Fuhrman used Nicole's blood – as so many other characteristics about these drops and their accompanying shoeprints indicated –

> then we should expect **exactly five drops of blood – one from each of the five fingertips on his left hand – no more, no less!**

Between zero and fifty – how many drops were there? **Exactly – five!**

Now think back to our conclusion based on our analysis of the glove evidence, which was that O.J. could not possibly have murdered Nicole and Ron. But even if O.J. **were** the murderer, **he could not have bled at Bundy!**

Do my readers remember that conclusion from our glove analysis? If not, you may want to go back to the chapter I titled **"The Glove Evidence."**

Also, recall that our analysis of the glove evidence, as well as our analysis of the way Ron was killed, strongly suggested that Detective Fuhrman is the murderer.

Combine those conclusions with my discussion of the five blood drops next to the bloody shoeprints, and I assume my readers are beginning to realize that the evidence in this murder mystery does not point to O.J. at all!

The evidence points overwhelmingly to a police officer like Detective Fuhrman – and to the investigators!

We shall look at one last set of evidence from Bundy – the two blood drops on the horizontal, lower rail of the rear gate at Bundy.

O.J. had a cut only on his **left** finger, but his right hand might have brushed against the cut. Hence, if O.J. were the murderer – which he isn't – he could perceivably have left **"stains"** of his own blood from **either** hand. But a blood stain transmitted from his **right** hand could only be in the form of a **"smear"** – not a **"drop"**!

Again, O.J. is not the murderer. But let us for a second, hypothetically, assume that he were the murderer.

Since the two blood stains on the gate were drops, they must have come directly from O.J.'s **left** hand, and not from his **right** hand.

The rear gate **opens away** from someone approaching the gate from inside the walkway – **and it is hinged on the right side!**

Furthermore, a witness, Robert Heidstra, heard the murderer slam the **metal** gate shut.

Consequently, **if** O.J. were the murderer, he would, of course, have grabbed and opened such a gate with his **right** hand, walked through, and still holding on to the gate, have closed it behind himself with that same **right** hand.

Therefore, even **if** O.J. were the murderer, who opened and closed that gate – his blood **drops** could not be on the gate!

Early during the civil trial, I wrote to O.J.'s attorney, Mr. Robert Baker, and suggested that he should make an exact replica of the rear gate at Bundy – mounted in a sturdy frame. Furthermore, I suggested he should bring it to the courtroom, and challenge the police witnesses, who testified under oath that they had seen these three blood drops on the rear gate at Bundy. Let them – or Mr. Petrocelli – try to demonstrate for the jury how they believed O.J. had walked through that gate and deposited the three blood drops on the gate, exactly where they, allegedly, were found – three weeks after the Bundy murder scene investigation had been concluded!

Of course, if the plaintiffs and their witnesses claimed O.J. left those blood drops on the gate, they ought to be able to demonstrate how – in their opinion – it happened! Hence, I didn't see how Judge Fujisaki could disallow such a demonstration.

I think that could have been an interesting spectacle, which really could have demonstrated how outrageous the plaintiffs' murder theory was. Besides, it would, most likely, have demonstrated how blatantly the police witnesses lied!

Mr. Baker didn't take my advice. Instead, he allowed the three police officers to "testi-lie" – uncontested – for the plaintiffs, about seeing O.J.'s blood on the rear gate at Bundy, just hours after the murders! There were a lot of things Mr. Baker did – or did not do – and which I didn't understand. However, my readers can perform **"the rear gate experiment"** themselves.

Find a door in your house, opening away from you and to the right! Walk through it – grabbing the door handle with your **left** hand, as the prosecution claimed O.J. might have grabbed the gate.

Hold on to the door with your **left** hand, while you quickly walk through, and then – still holding on to the door – slam it shut behind you, using your **left** hand! Do you see how awkward that is!

Now walk towards the same door, open it and slam it shut behind your back using your **right** hand! Do you see that this is definitely the hand you would use – and which O.J. would have used – **if he were the murderer**?

Furthermore, observe your left hand as you approach and reach for the door with your right hand! Do you see that when your right hand reaches for the door, your **left** hand, automatically, moves **back – away from the door**?

But even more inconsistent is the fact that O.J.'s blood was found at the bottom frame of the gate – at all!

Here was O.J., allegedly, bleeding one drop of blood every 6-7 seconds. Suddenly he bled three drops on the rear gate. That means he must have stood there, absolutely still, for 18-21 seconds, waiting for the three drops to trickle from a cut on his finger. Simultaneously – for those 18-21 seconds – he must have been aiming down over his left finger so that he could hit the narrow bottom rail with each of the two drops that were found there!

I find this entire scenario so utterly absurd that I can't even take it seriously! How is it possible to even suggest something that ludicrous. Those two blood drops must have been planted from a pipette, from just a few inches above the bottom metal frame of the gate.

Add to that the fact that the three drops were not collected until three weeks after the murders! They did not appear on photographs taken of the gate on the day after the murders! And finally, they contained traces of EDTA, which indicated that they were planted from O.J.'s blood vial!

Conclusion: It is no mystery at all how O.J.'s blood ended up on the rear gate. **It was planted there! It had to be!**

That is important in itself. But just as important is the conclusion we can draw from that irrefutable fact, namely that the police witnesses perjured themselves – one after the other!

How much more evidence do people need, before they understand that O.J. was framed – right from the outset?

If someone **claims** that O.J. is the murderer, I like that person to explain the following:

- Why **didn't** the murderer pick up the cap and the glove?
- Why did the murderer turn around and go back to the victims?
- Why didn't blood drip from his hand on or around the

victims, or the first time he walked away?

- Why did the murderer walk so slowly, with just 12-18 inches between the bloody shoeprints, in spite of being in the procss of leaving a murder scene, and – if O.J. were the murderer – having a plane to catch?
- What did the murderer do, to toss the first blood drop way out to the left?
- If the second and third blood drop fell from his left middle finger knuckle, why did they end up right in the middle of (between) the shoeprints, instead of a few inches to the left of them?
- Why did the murderer alternate between walking with his footsteps "in line" and wider apart "like a duck"?
- Why did he open and close the **right**-hinged gate with his **left** hand?
- Why was there **EDTA** in the two blood drops on the rear gate?
- Why did he bleed exactly **five** drops as he walked away?
- Why didn't O.J. bleed two or three drops at the spot where he **allegedly** entered his Bronco?
- Why didn't he continue to bleed another 40 drops of blood at the same rate while he **allegedly** drove his Bronco to Rockingham?
- Why were there no "lumps" of blood from the outer edges of the Bruno Magli shoes on the Bronco's carpet?

Do you see, how many problems the prosecutors and the plaintiffs failed to answer with their theory? They just assumed that O.J. were the murderer. Allegedly, O.J. killed Nicole and Ron with a knife and walked away; and if there was blood somewhere, it probably came from him. That's the scope of their theory!

There are certain objections to my theory about the blood drops at Bundy. You see, O.J.'s blood vial contained EDTA, a preservative to prevent the blood from coagulating or getting contaminated.

If the police fabricated those **five drops** – in their crime lab – using blood from O.J.'s vial, then that false blood evidence would, arguably, contain EDTA.

Those blood drops were actually never tested for EDTA. So they could, theoretically have been fabricated directly from O.J.'s blood vial. Investigators, prosecutors, the plaintiffs and the media, however, just assumed that these blood drops were tested for EDTA and that the test was negative, since the defense never claimed that there was EDTA in those blood drops. Therefore, prosecutors, investigators, the plaintiffs and the media vehemently argued that those five blood drops could **not** have been fabricated.

An obvious question from "amateurs" like you and me would be, of course: *"Why didn't the defense demand that the five blood drops be tested for EDTA."*

Such a request seems so obvious. That's why "everyone" seemed to believe that those five blood drops were tested for EDTA, but the test was negative. Dozens of times I heard O.J.'s adversaries on TV, claiming that there was no EDTA in those five blood drops. Here is the answer to our question above.

Unless you have a rather large blood sample, you cannot perform both an EDTA and a DNA test on it, because the EDTA test destroys the sample for DNA testing. By demanding that these blood drops be DNA tested, the investigators and the prosecutors precluded the defense from performing EDTA tests on them.

Besides, there are several very simple ways in which Detective Vannatter might have circumvented the EDTA in O.J.'s blood vial. And there is **"an ocean of evidence"** to suggest that he actually did it! I will return to that issue later.

If the investigators, indeed, could have fabricated those five blood drops **– which no one thinks could have been fabricated –** don't you agree that the investigators could have fabricated **every** piece of evidence against O.J., after Fuhrman had set them up?

Don't think for a moment that the glove evidence and the five blood drops were the only pieces of evidence that pointed away from O.J. and right at Fuhrman and the investigators. This case is full of such evidence. But I had to start somewhere.

Back to Bundy and Fuhrman, just after he had planted the five blood drops. Reaching his car, Fuhrman took off his bloody coverall, his shoes, and the latex gloves, and removed the knife from his belt.

He placed everything in a box in the trunk of his car, then he put on a clean pair of shoes and drove home.

Fuhrman knew he would be called to the murder scene later that night, since Brentwood was his district. His plan, then, was to bring the investigators to Rockingham. There he would plant the second glove on O.J.'s property, and claim, rather, that he "found" the glove there.

This theory must, however, explain logically, the "thumps" on Kato's wall – and it does! Simultaneously, this theory will provide, yet another, irrefutable proof that O.J. did not murder Nicole and Ron.

In light of the thumps on Kato's wall at 10:40-10:42, it may seem contradictory that my murder theory can send Fuhrman straight home from Bundy – with the murder glove. But Fuhrman had an accomplice at Rockingham, who thumped on Kato's wall five minutes after Fuhrman informed him over his cellular phone that he had killed Nicole and Ron. But bear with me till we get to the chapter titled, *"The 'Thumps' On Kato's Wall"*!

CHAPTER 34

The "Thumps" On Kato's Wall

Until today, the three thumps on the wall outside Kato's room in O.J.'s house at Rockingham, has remained a mystery. What caused those thumps? What did they imply? Were they a signal? Did someone fall against the wall back there? Did O.J. – or Fuhrman – climb the fence, and fall against the wall? Did the thumps tie in with the second murder glove that Fuhrman said he found behind O.J.'s house? If so, was the glove lost in connection with those thumps? Was the glove purposely deposited behind O.J.'s house?

Did O.J cause those thumps? Did he, or someone else walk or run into the air conditioning unit which protrudes from the wall? Would O.J. do that? If the blood on the glove was still wet when Fuhrman found it, then the glove could not have been deposited when Kato heard the three thumps on his wall the night before. But the thumps seemed to tie in with the time shortly after the murders at Bundy, and with the glove that was later found behind O.J.'s house. So what is the connection?

O.J. had lived in the house for 17 years! He certainly knew that the air conditioning unit was there! If O.J., or someone else ran into that unit by accident, why didn't they leave any blood or skin fragments on the sharp, metal vents on the sides of the unit?

Consider this: Kato testified that he was talking to a friend on the phone when he heard the thumps. Phone records show that the thumps occurred at about 10:40-10:42 pm, which was shortly after the murders were committed at Bundy. The thumps on Kato's wall were so heavy that the entire wall shook. They were so heavy that Kato honestly believed he was experiencing an earthquake! He got extremely scared – so scared, in fact, that before he ventured outside to investigate what had happened, he instructed his friend on the phone to call the police, if Kato was not back on the phone within ten minutes!

Those were not just some "taps" on the wall. This was serious stuff! So what caused it?

The air conditioning unit protruded so far out from the wall that it almost blocked the entire walkway behind the house, and it was about head high. If O.J. had run into that unit – or Fuhrman had run into it – so hard that the impact could have caused the thumps Kato described – why didn't O.J., or Fuhrman, have bloody cut marks all over his face?

O.J. was photographed, from top to toe, in his underpants, shortly after he returned from Chicago! Except for the small cuts on his finger, O.J. had no cuts or bruises on his entire body. Had O.J. caused those thumps, by running into the air conditioning unit, for instance, his face would have been a bloody mess!

And if the thumps on Kato's wall were caused by O.J. – or anybody – running into the air conditioning unit – why were there **three** heavy thumps on Kato's wall? Do the former prosecutors, or the plaintiffs suggest that O.J. enjoyed the encounter so much that he banged his head against the unit two more times – for good measure?

The speculations were many. No one seemed to know the answers.

Again, the prosecution **and the plaintiffs "cheated"** us with their **"O.J. is the murderer theory."** Their theory simply couldn't answer any of the questions above. But instead of scrapping their theory and admitting that O.J. could not be the murderer, they simply stuck to their air conditioning unit theory without further justification or explanation.

Long after the criminal trial had ended, in an effort to discredit O.J., Prosecutor Darden was spreading rumors about some traces of blood that allegedly were found on top of the unit, and which **"might"** have proven to have come from O.J. – *"if only the investigators had analyzed those traces of blood"*!

What kind of mean spirited garbage is this former prosecutor spreading? Do my readers think the investigators would have declined to analyze such traces of blood and introduce the results in court – if those alleged traces of blood really existed – not to mention if they could had come from O.J.?

Such bull-shit, by Christopher Darden, now Professor of Law, discredits Professor Darden – more than O.J. So why does he keep on saying things like that every time he appears on TV talk shows?

Unfortunately, he does this, because he knows that millions of Americans don't bother to analyze and criticize all the nonsense which O.J.'s adversaries throw at us through the media. Most people just accept what Mr. Darden and his kind tell us – because Mr. Darden was a former Simpson prosecutor, because he is a professor, because he is on TV, or simply because **a lot of people want to believe that O.J. is guilty!**

If there were blood on the air conditioning unit – which I doubt – and since the prosecutors did not introduce any such blood evidence in court, I would rather suggest that, perhaps, the criminalists analyzed that, imaginary, blood and found it to be Detective Fuhrman's!

Is that why they didn't introduce it – if it was there! Because if the blood was Fuhrman's, they were looking at a police scandal – and a cover up – of such immense proportion that the consequences scared the hell out of both the prosecutors and the police!

But don't worry. I am sure that neither O.J.'s blood, or anyone else's blood, was on the air-conditioning unit – except perhaps in Professor Darden's dreams.

The prosecution's air-conditioning unit theory is obviously flawed. But since the unit was there, the prosecution conveniently "grabbed" it, in order to "explain" the otherwise obvious inconsistency in their theory, namely that O.J. should have entered his property by climbing the fence behind his house, and lost the second murder glove there – before leaving for Chicago!

There were numerous other inconsistencies in the theory that O.J. caused those thumps. I cannot waste pages mentioning all of them. But I shall list a few more.

There was no reason for O.J. to climb the fence behind his house, in the first place. Even if he were the murderer – returning from Bundy – O.J. could simply have entered through his Rockingham Avenue gate. There was nothing suspicious about that. Even if someone had seen him, he could simply have claimed that he came from **inside** his house, to fetch something from his Bronco, and that he was on his way **back** inside his property when he was spotted.

It would have been far more suspicious if O.J. had tried to enter his own property by climbing the fence behind his house, and he had been caught tresspassing on his neighbor's property just minutes after Nicole had been murdered.

More importantly, however, O.J.'s fingers and knees were severely arthritic. It would have been excruciatingly painful for him to climb a fence like the one behind his house. Literally, he would have had to hoist his 200 lbs body up over the fence – by his three middle fingers on each hand.

If you don't have arthritis – don't even try to imagine what such a maneuver would have been like. But if you suffer from severely arthritic fingers, you know – O.J. did not climb the fence behind his house. Maybe he did it fifteen years ago – but not in 1994!

Shaking Kato's wall so it might be mistaken for an earthquake, could not have been caused by someone running into the air-conditioning unit. Besides, running into the air-conditioning unit might perceivably have accounted for the first thump – but then what?

Would the person take a step back and head-butt the unit two more times "for good measure"?

Furthermore, had anyone done that, his face would have been a bloody mess.

Nor could anyone walking along the narrow pathway have caused such heavy thumps on the wall by tripping over something and falling against the wall. The pathway is so narrow that anyone walking that pathway would have his shoulder brushing against the wall on one side and the fence on the other.

Therefore, even if a person suddenly stumbled and fell, his momentum would be parallel to the wall, and he would be too close to the wall to be able to build up any kind of sideways momentum against the wall.

Next, the fence was completely covered by shrubbery and foliage. Yet, not a leaf or twig was damaged!

Again, after Fuhrman reportedly had found the glove, the investigators walked farther behind O.J.'s house – from the spot where the glove was found, near the air-conditioning unit, and towards the place where Kato heard the thumps on his wall. The investigators testified that they experienced plenty of cob webs, indicating that nobody had been back there for months. If O.J., therefore, had walked back there, he would have been covered with cobweb. Some of that cob web would have been deposited in his house right afterwards. I never heard anyone mention cob web in O.J.'s house.

And perhaps most significantly there was absolutely no blood behind O.J.'s house. Not on the fence, not on the ground, not near the bloody glove, and not even back around the house to O.J.'s entrance door. There is only one logical inference to be drawn from this:

> Before Fuhrman walked behind the house, where he alleged he found the glove – **nobody had been there for weeks!**
>
> Obviously, O.J. did not cause the thumps on Kato's wall. Therefore, obviously, O.J. did not deposit or lose the glove behind his house, either. By the way, we knew that already, because the blood on the glove was **wet** when Fuhrman found it. Obviously, someone else – caused the thumps and deposited the glove.
>
> This is, yet another, proof that O.J. is innocent, and that someone framed him.

So what? We are just as far from solving the problem of the thumps on Kato's wall.

Before I actually tell my readers what happened, I like to say something about **the theory of the jurors in the civil trial**.

After their verdict in the civil trial, the jurors participated in dozens of interviews and press conferences asserting the correctness of their verdict, and the unity among the jurors. According to the jurors, they discussed everything, agreed on everything, and had no doubts about anything. Great!

Naturally, if they were so confident, it would be interesting to hear what they thought about the thumps on Kato's wall – severe enough to be mistaken for an earthquake – a mystery nobody else has been able to explain.

So, one of the jurors was asked about that. Here is the juror's explanation (in essence):

> *We thought long and carefully about those thumps. We couldn't know for sure. But we decided on what we found to be **the most reasonable explanation.** Mr. Simpson had walked behind his house to **change clothes** after the murders. He put the clothes in a bag. That's when he lost the glove there.*

That is what these twelve jurors found **most likely!** It is frightening to think that **under other circumstances, they could have sent a man to the gas chamber with their "wisdom"!**

They believed, in other words, that O.J. walked up his own driveway – without being spotted by the limo driver. But then, instead of pulling off his shoes, entering his foyer and changing there, in the privacy of his home, he walked behind his house to change clothes, **according to this "intelligent" jury!**

According to this jury, O.J. continued to walk around his property, to the back of the house – **bleeding profusely everywhere else, but not a single drop as he walked to the spot where he, allegedly, lost his glove!** There he took off his shoes and pants and shirt and put them in a **bag.** That's when he lost the glove – again, according to the intelligent civil jury!

If so, the glove must have fallen down less than 4 inches from the bag. Yet, O.J., allegedly, didn't see it, or find it and pick it up? Brilliant explanation!

Anyway, now O.J., allegedly, stood up – without shoes, shirt, and pants and walked back around his house again, and entered his foyer.

As O.J., according to this "intelligent" jury, walked away from the back of his house, he banged his head against the air-conditioning unit, so hard that Kato thought he experienced an earthquake!

Evidently, O.J., according to this "intelligent" jury, must have enjoyed the encounter between his head and the air-conditioning unit so much, that he purposely head-butted the unit two more times for good measure, since Kato heard **three** thumps. Is that what people in Los Angeles call "after shocks"?

Yet, the "bionic superman," O.J. did not suffer a single cut or bruise to his head! All "good" things must come to an end! O.J. couldn't continue head-butting the air-conditioning unit forever – regardless of how much he enjoyed it! He had a plane to catch, remember! So three times had to be enough. Then he walked away!

This civil jury really enlightened me!

Even this time, when O.J. crossed his lawn and entered his house without shirt, pants, and shoes, the limo driver didn't see him. But three minutes later, when O.J. came downstairs all showered and dressed up, and started to carry his luggage outside, he was immediately spotted by the limo driver.

As O.J., according to these "brilliant" jurors walked past his entrance door – on his way behind his house, to change clothes – why didn't he simply skip out of his Bruno Magli shoes, enter his foyer carrying the shoes in his hands, and tip-toe upstairs and into his bathroom – and change there!

One more question: Where did the bag come from? I am sure it wasn't waiting for O.J. behind the house!

Probably, according to the civil jurors' theory O.J. crossed his lawn, walked up to his entrance, went inside his house, picked up an empty bag, walked outside again and behind his house.

There he undressed and put his shoes, knife and dark sweat suit in the bag. Then he walked back inside his house for the second time. There he took the sweat suit out of the bag and put it in the washing machine – if we are to believe Detective Fuhrman!

However, he kept the shoes and the knife in the bag, and disposed of them some perfect place where no one has been able to locate them. In the meantime, the sweat suit remained in the washing machine – waiting for Officer Roberts and Detective Fuhrman to pick it up!

Even just **imagining** that my life, under the worst of circumstances, could be taken from me by such jurors, is frightening.

But it is even more frightening to witness a unanimous press corps hailing this prejudiced, racist, predominantly white – and **shallow** – jury as being conscientious, honest, intelligent – and *"color blind"*!

Blind? – Yes! *"Color blind"* **– No way!**

These jurors were just as ignorant and shallow as most of O.J.'s adversaries. They accepted, uncritically, the first and best explanation the plaintiffs gave them for each piece of evidence, without the slightest regards for whether or not that explanation tied in with all the other evidence!

Just like the investigators, the prosecutors, the counsels for the plaintiffs, and the media, the civil jurors never really questioned the logic of their deductions and conclusions – like I am doing in this book!

This jury's explanation for the thumps on Kato's wall, which all of them allegedly agreed on, clearly demonstrated the level of their deliberations.

Here is another, typical, example from the jurors' press conference. Again, to save them the embarrassment, I won't mention the juror's name. According to one juror – and I quote –

"This verdict was the easiest decision I have ever had to make in my life!"

She repeated that exact statement in several interviews. What this juror was saying was that to sit in judgement of O.J., consider all the evidence, reach a conclusion, and find O.J. responsible for two gruesome murders, was easier for her, than to decide which set of earrings to put on in the morning.

O.J.! I pity you who were cursed to have your fate decided by white jurors of this caliber!

Of course, this juror spoke from **emotion**, without thinking about what she was saying. But that raises a couple of other question:

Did she also speak from emotion – without thinking – when she voted with her fellow jurors to find O.J. responsible for the murders of Nicole and Ron?

And, is this juror representative of the level of deliberations that took place in that jury-room?

Let us leave these jurors in their ignorance, and instead explore what further happened – **according to my scenario.**

The last time we left Detective Fuhrman, he had just murdered Nicole and Ron, prepared the Bundy crime scene with evidence intended to frame O.J. and set up the investigators to help him do it. Then Detective Fuhrman entered his car and drove home.

Part of the murder scheme could have been for Fuhrman to use a car similar to O.J.'s white Ford Bronco. Remember that Robert Heidstra testified he saw a white sports utility car speed away from the murder scene, coming from "Dorothy" and heading south on "Bundy."

Fuhrman could have used such a car, on purpose, because he knew O.J. had a similar car. Fuhrman could even have waited for a little while before he drove away, until he saw someone (Mr. Heidstra). Then he could have sped away "leaving some rubber" as he turned the corner on Dorothy and Bundy just so that Mr. Heidstra, perhaps, would remember this white sports utility car!

Earlier, I have explained why Detective Fuhrman could have had one or more **accomplices**. For one thing, reaping someone's admiration for his "skill" and "daring," was one of

Fuhrman's motives. He could not do that, unless he had some accomplices. Besides, an accomplice could have assisted Fuhrman in creating a false alibi – for instance by **using Fuhrman's credit card to fill gas in Pomona**, at the same time as Fuhrman committed the murders at Bundy. **Fuhrman's statement on Fox News Network** could indicate something like that was part of the murder plot. However, here is the real evidence that Fuhrman had accomplices.

> Obviously, the thumps on Kato's wall tied in with the murders at Bundy and the glove behind O.J.'s house.
>
> But just as obviously, nobody walked behind O.J.'s house around the time when Kato heard the thumps. And nobody climbed the fence. I have already explained how the physical appearance of the area proved that.
>
> And just as obviously, the glove was **not** deposited at that time. Everything about the glove indicated that.
>
> In other words, someone must have thumped Kato's wall, three times – with some long object like a baseball bat – from the neighbor's property and across the fence.[By the way, that fence was just two feet from Kato's wall].

Suddenly, this makes sense! I believe Fuhrman had two accomplices. One created an alibi for Fuhrman in Pomona. The other waited near O.J.'s house at Rockingham, while Fuhrman committed the murders at Bundy.

All three had cellular phones. As soon as Fuhrman had commited the murders, and was on his way home from Bundy, he called the guy in Pomona, so he could start pumping gas, using Fuhrman's credit card.

Then he called the other guy at Rockingham, a block away from O.J.'s house and reported *"Mission accomplished"*!

The guy at Rockingham waited a few minutes – as long as it **would** have taken O.J. to drive from Bundy to Rockingham.

Fuhrman's accomplice didn't have the murder glove – Fuhrman would plant that glove later when he brought the investigators to O.J.'s house the following morning.

> But part of the plan was to **make everyone believe** that the
> glove was planted **shortly after the murders** – while O.J.
> was still at home and could, hypothetically, have done it!

One question I expect to hear now is this: Why couldn't Fuhrman's
accomplice have received the glove from Fuhrman, right after the
murders, driven up to Rockingham, parked a block away, entered
the neighbor's property – as he did – and just tossed the glove over
the fence **at the same time as he thumped on Kato's wall?**

Then Fuhrman wouldn't even have to worry about planting the
glove the following morning.

I shall explain this through a fictional dialogue suggesting
what I believe expired between the three accomplices during the
planning stages of the murder of Nicole and the framing of O.J.

Let me name Fuhrman's acomplices, **"Chuck"** and **"Billy"** –
and let me use Mark Fuhrman's first name.

Mark: *We have to do it around 10:30-10:40. No sooner, no later!*
Billy: *Why not earlier?*
Chuck: *We discussed that! If we do it earlier, and a neighbor dis-
covers the body immediately after Mark and I have left, then they
might notify O.J. before he leaves for Chicago. He would, of course,
cancel his trip, inform Arnelle and – what's this other guy's name
– Kato Kaelin? It will be impossible to plant the glove at his house.
So it has to be after 10:30.*

> *But it can't be too much later – otherwise, we might give him
> an alibi.*

Billy: *Okay. So I'll be in Pomona using Mark's credit card at an
automated gas pump, around 10:40, so Mark gets an alibi.*
Chuck: *Yes. After she's dead and Mark and I have planted the left
glove, the cap, the bloody shoeprints, and the rest of the blood at
Bundy, we drive to Rockingham. You scale the wall, Mark, and
run up to the front entrance and toss away the right glove there.
Then you disappear back over the wall and we drive home. Later*

when you're called to investigate, you pretend you "find" the glove. Isn't that good?

Mark: *Are you crazy? O.J. is still there – and the limo. O.J. knows me. What if I run into him? Besides, we have to make some kind of noise or disturbance when we plant the glove, so Kato or Arnelle will remember it. Otherwise, someone may accuse me of having planted the glove when I say I found it.*

Chuck: *Okay. So you have to make some noise up there – before O.J. leaves – make it appear that he might have lost the glove before he went to Chicago.*

. . . How about this? You enter his neighbor's property – behind O.J.'s house. You toss the glove over the fence somewhere back there. Then you thump the wall a few times, so hard that this guy, Kato, has to notice it. Then you get back in the car and we drive away.

Mark: *That's a good idea, in itself. But I can't do it. You would have to do that, Chuck. You'll wait at Rockingham, while I take care of things at Bundy.*

Chuck: *Why? I won't have the glove then!*

Mark: *Exactly! We don't have to plant the glove at that time. It is safer if we don't. Remember, I have a legitimate reason to enter his estate later that morning. I can easily plant the glove then. I'll just keep it in a plastic bag inside my sock. Nobody will even think that I could do that – not at that time.*

However, shortly after the killing, should you, perhaps, be caught trespassing, by a security guard who calls for backup, and they search you – and find the bloody glove in your pocket – we're in deep shit!

So, I'll tell you what we'll do! We all have cellular phones. I call Bill in Pomona first, as soon as it's over. Bill takes care of Pomona. Then I continue home – with the glove and everything. As soon as I'm on my way I call you, Chuck. You wait at Rockingham, a block away from O.J.'s house. You bring your Doberman, Tara. If someone confronts you, you pretend you are out walking your dog.

If you're caught trespassing, then, you just say Tara must have caught the scent of a rabbit or something, because she ran into the property of O.J.'s neighbor. She didn't come when you called her. So rather than hollering and hollering waking up the entire neighborhood, you decided to just go in and get her.

Then, if you're searched, they'll find nothing – because you're just out walking your dog. No gun, not tools, no car keys – so obviously, you're not a burglar. You are just walking your dog!

You have no bloody glove, no ID, only a sweat suit and that old baseball bat Tara loves to chew on – the one you throw and let her fetch all the time. No one can hold you for that. They just let you go. But most likely, you won't see anyone.

Before you leave your car, you call this Kato guy on your cellular phone, to make sure he is in his room – Sunday night, he probably is. If he picks up the phone, you just hang up. That happens all the time. If his phone is busy you also hang up, of course. In either case, the guy is home.

Inside the neighbour's property you walk over to the fence. Then you reach over the fence and thump his wall with the bat – hard, a couple of times – and leave.

Chuck: *What if nobody answers, and the line is not busy?*

Billy: *You call O.J.'s daughter – stupid! She lives two rooms down that wing. If she's home, you thump on her wall instead. One of them's got to be home on a Sunday night.*

Mark: *One of them will hear the thumps. There is no risk, because you were not at Bundy, and you don't have the glove – see!*

Then I isolate Kato – or Arnelle – the following morning when I come there to investigate. Whoever it is, he or she will tell me about the thumps – if you make them loud enough!

We must expect Robbery/Homicide to have taken over by then. So I'll bring the "witness" to the lead detective and ask him to listen to the same story.

In the meantime, I go outside and smear some of Nicole's blood in O.J.'s Bronco. I'll also bring a small rag dipped in her blood, and a vial of distilled water to dissolve it, and plant some drops of her blood in his driveway.

Then I pretend to check out the back of the house, and plant the glove there.

Ten minutes later, the lead detective has heard the story about the thumps. I go back inside: **"Bingo! Guess what I found?"**

Chuck: *That is really brilliant – except for one thing. What if they find the marks on the wall, from the baseball bat? Then they may suspect that the thumps were just to draw attention to the glove.*

Mark: *Good point! That's why we discuss this so thoroughly – to cover everything. We could solve this problem, though. You cut out a thick patch of rubber and nail it to the end of the bat. It will rattle the wall just as much, but it won't leave a mark. You could try it on a similar wall first, just to make sure.*

Chuck: *Okay.*

Billy: *Are you sure you can do it – alone I mean?*

Mark: *Of course! What's there to be scared of? A woman – and a nigger? Give me a break! You should have been with us in 'Nam!*

So, we're all set for Sunday, then – unless there is a last change of plans for anyone.

Back to Rockingham on the night of the murders. Right after the murders, Fuhrman called his accomplice who was waiting near O.J.'s house. The accomplice waited a few minutes. Then he called Kato. The line was busy – Kato was in his room.

Together with his dog, the accomplice entered the neighbor's property and approached the fence. He reached over the fence and rammed the rubber padded end of his bat against Kato's wall three times.

The wall and the room inside gave a "music box effect." Inside the room the effect was much greater than one can imagine. Kato thought he experienced an earthquake. Still, the rubber padding on the bat prevented any marks on the wall.

Fuhrman's accomplice left Rockingham quickly, without having been seen.

Nobody had climbed the fence, that's why there were no broken twigs or leaves around the fence. Nobody threw the glove over the fence at that time or walked behind O.J.'s house. That's why there was no blood inside the fence and no sign of disturbed leaves on the ground immediately surrounding the glove.

The bat was padded, that's why there was no mark on the wall, in spite of the heavy thumps.

So now the perpetrators had alerted Kato that someone was behind O.J.'s house around 10:40-42 pm.

In the meantime, Fuhrman came home, cleaned up, got rid of the bloody clothes, the Bruno Magli shoes and the murder knife. Then he waited for Detective Phillips to call him about the murders. Phillips called at 1:05 am. Fuhrman pretended he were asleep and that he got up. He put the plastic bag with the bloody glove inside his sock. Then he was ready to meet Phillips and drive to Bundy.

Later, Fuhrman's job was to bring the investigation to Rockingham. There Fuhrman would try to speak to Kato alone. Then he would go behind the house, plant the glove there, and pretend he "found" it at the same time.

This theory, involving three accomplices provides, perhaps, the best explanation for the Rockingham glove and the three thumps on Kato's wall. It was also the safest plan – from the perpetrators' point of view, since they didn't risk bringing the murder glove to Rockingham until the following morning – when Fuhrman could do it safely.

Once the investigators got to Rockingham, Fuhrman improvised a little. As soon as Fuhrman scaled the wall at Rockingham, he went behind O.J.'s house and planted the glove where he knew that one of his accomplices had thumped on Kato's wall earlier.

Fuhrman was fairly certain that he would get an opportunity to "find" the glove, back there, before anyone else. In particular, if Fuhrman could prevent Kato from talking to anyone else for a while, Fuhrman might get a chance to go behind O.J.'s house, by himself, and "find" the glove.

Returning from behind the house, Fuhrman also planted the blood in O.J.'s driveway. Then he opened the gate for his colleagues.

Normally, to scale the Rockingham wall and open the gate would take less than 20 seconds. Yet, Fuhrman spent several minutes alone inside O.J.'s property – out of sight of the other detectives. Nobody has offered a reasonable explanation as to what Fuhrman did during those minutes. What I have suggested above, is one possible explanation.

Let me mention one other point. Unless Detective Fuhrman already knew that his accomplice had thumped on Kato's wall – and not on Arnelle's – Fuhrman should have stayed behind and interviewed Arnelle, rather than Kato. Being O.J.'s daughter, Arnelle was a much more interesting witness than Kato – as long as Detective Fuhrman didn't know what any of them would say.

The fact that Detective Fuhrman immediately stayed behind and isolated Kato – instead of Arnelle, indicated that Fuhrman already knew that someone had thumped on **Kato's wall** the night before.

Again, we see that events and evidence that could otherwise not be explained, fit right in with my theory of Fuhrman being the murderer. If someone challenge my explanation for the three heavy thumps on Kato's wall, I like to hear what kind of explanation **they** can come up with which fits the time, the blood being wet 8 hours after the murders, all the mysterious circumstances connected to those thumps, the position and the condition of the glove, and the undisturbed surroundings behind O.J.'s house.

CHAPTER 35

Completing The "Set-Up"

Fuhrman got rid of the evidence (the knife, the latex gloves, the shoes, and the clothes). Then he showered, got dressed, and put the plastic bag with the second murder glove inside one of his socks, as he was used to doing from his days as a U.S. Marine.

All Marines routinely carry their billfolds, keys, etc. in their socks, rather than in their pockets, so their uniforms shall look sleek when they are on leave.

Let us discuss the blood drops in O.J.'s driveway. I think part of Fuhrman's plan was to plant some drops of blood also in O.J.'s driveway when he arrived later in the morning to investigate the murders.

Do you remember I said earlier that Fuhrman is **"smart"**? He graduated second in his class at the police academy, and he bragged about being **so clever at planting false evidence that nobody could catch him.**

NOTE! As a detective, Fuhrman had been working day out and day in for nineteen years, catching criminals, by discovering small, or large, mistakes that the criminals made.

Many of the criminals Fuhrman captured during his years as an LAPD detective, believed they had covered their tracks. But the police uncovered various small mistakes the criminals had overlooked.

Detective Fuhrman became an expert on fooling investigators, through the experience he received from exposing criminals who constantly tried to outsmart him.

Hundreds of times, Fuhrman must have said to himself:

"Gotcha! You shouldn't have done this!" Or *"You shouldn't have done that!"*

For every crime he solved, Fuhrman told himself:

> *"I wouldn't have made **this** mistake. I wouldn't have made **that** mistake!"*

After 19 years as an LAPD detective, Fuhrman had seen every mistake a murderer could make. He knew every pitfall there was. And he knew how to avoid them.

He found little challenge and satisfaction in **outsmarting criminals.** He knew every trick in the book. The only challenge for Fuhrman was to see if he could also **outsmart the investigators! He knew he could do it! And he did it!**

What I explain that Fuhrman did, to get away with murder – wasn't that spectacular. It was **clever**, perhaps, and rather daring! But it was at least two steps short of **ingenious!** After all, he did make a few mistakes. Besides, with rogue LAPD investigators like Detective Vannatter & Company – even I could have committed the perfect murder, if I wanted to!

Obviously, if I could think of a "clever" way for Fuhrman to plant blood in O.J.'s driveway, then Detective Fuhrman – definitely – would have thought about it, too. So don't say:

> *"Oh-no! Fuhrman couldn't have thought about that!"*

He could! He had 9 years to plan the murder of Nicole and the framing of O.J. And what finally pushed him over the edge, was the fact that he thought his plan was **so perfect** that nobody could catch him.

When I spoke to Defense attorney Robert Baker, he objected to my theory by claiming that Fuhrman could not harbor such hatred towards O.J., that he killed Nicole and framed O.J. in 1994, just because he investigated domestic abuse at Simpson's house nine years earlier. But typically, Fuhrman could.

A witness in the criminal trial, an **African American,** testified that he had been arrested by Fuhrman, but released after all charges were dropped. As he was released, Fuhrman told the man:

"Some day I'll get you – nigger!"

Years later, Fuhrman again arrested the man. Fuhrman recognized him. Again, the man was innocent and was released. But before that – just after the arrest – Fuhrman turned to the African American suspect, who sat handcuffed in the back of his car, and said:

"I told you I would get you – nigger!"

Understand from this that it was not at all strange that Detective Fuhrman could be possessed with the idea of killing Nicole and framing O.J. – for many years.

Understand also, that although Fuhrman may have begun planning the murder of Nicole many years earlier, it was not something he could just go out and do one night. It took a lot of planning. So many things had to be right. And still it was not easy to **"just do it!"**

As the plan grew more and more perfect, and Fuhrman kept thinking about the interracial couple he so despised, his devilish plan got harder and harder to resist. It became an obsession he could not overcome. But it did indeed take 9 years before he got to that point.

One of the main characteristics of Fuhrman's **"master-plan,"** was that he only planted such evidence that one could normally expect to find wherever Fuhrman laid out his "baits" for the investigators. Such were the knit cap and the five blood drops at Bundy. Fuhrman had a similar plan for the blood drops in O.J.'s driveway.

There are many ways Fuhrman could have planted that blood. The following is just one possible method.

Fuhrman could have used **animal blood**, from a rat, or a dog, or a cat, for instance. The principle is the same, so let us go with blood from a rat.

Fuhrman could buy a rat in a pet store. That way he could get a small vial of rat blood.

When Fuhrman got home after the murders he got the animal blood, either from his freezer, or from a live rat in a cage. He brought it with him to Rockingham later that morning, and planted it in O.J.'s driveway.

Again the principle was the same as with the drops of Nicole's blood at Bundy:

> If the investigators took Fuhrman's "bait" and, in the crime lab, replaced the blood from O.J.'s driveway (the rat blood) with false blood swatches prepared from O.J.'s blood vial – then O.J. would be framed also by that blood evidence.
>
> On the other hand, if the investigators did not replace the rat blood with O.J.'s blood, but simply analyzed it and found it to be rat blood – that would not be suspicious at all, and it would not incriminate Detective Fuhrman in any way.

The investigators would simply conclude that O.J.'s dog, or a stray cat, had caught and bit a rat, which subsequently managed to escape – leaving drops of rat blood in O.J.'s driveway.

They would disregard the rat blood. No one would suspect Fuhrman or anyone else of having planted rat blood in O.J.'s driveway. With or without the rat blood, O.J. would appear just as guilty!

Another method Fuhrman could have used was this: Before leaving Bundy, he soaked a small rag in Nicole's blood. The blood would be partly dry by the time Fuhrman returned to Rockingham together with the other investigators. But Fuhrman could wet the cloth with distilled water to dissolve the blood, and wring the cloth to drip some drops of Nicole's blood in O.J.'s driveway.

Fuhrman could actually have done that to plant the blood drops in O.J.'s foyer, too, while the other detectives were in a different room in the house. However, for various reasons which I will return to later, I believe someone else, most likely Detective Vannatter, was responsible for the blood in O.J.'s foyer.

My readers should understand the following **important** point:

The basic principle of Detective Fuhrman's "master plan" was his "clever" way of setting up the investigators with

such false evidence which would frame O.J. "perfectly" **if** the investigators took Fuhrman's "bait," but which would appear completely normal if the investigators did **not** take his "bait"!

After Detective Fuhrman in his planning of the murders stumbled upon this, rather simple, but extremely clever "principle" of evidence planting – figuring out ways to do it, was the easiest thing in the world! He simply said to himself:

– I want to give the investigators the chance to make it appear that O.J. bled at the murder scene!

   OK! So, whose blood can I plant there? Nicole's!

– I want to give the investigators the chance to make it appear that O.J. bled in his driveway!

   OK! So, whose blood can I use there? The blood of an animal, or Nicole's blood again, wrung from a cloth soaked in Nicole's blood, and moistened with distilled water.

– I want the investigators to be able to frame O.J. also with his hairs!

   OK! So, I'll leave a knit cap at the murder scene, and let the investigators figure out how to plant O.J.'s hairs on it.

– I want to give the investigators a chance to frame O.J. with his shoeprints.

   OK! so, I'll figure out what kind of shoes he wears, and then I will wear that brand of shoes, and leave bloody shoeprints at the murder scene.

– Finally, to get the investigators going, I will plant one bloody glove at Bundy and one at Rockingham. Then I will bring the investigators to Rockingham, and "find" the bloody glove for them!

Listen! If you are a racist psychopath who has decided to murder Nicole and frame her husband for the murder – just to prove to yourself and your racist buddies that you can do it, and get away with it – this plan isn't so spectacular.

   I admit it is clever! But out of Detective Fuhrman's reach?

Definitely not! Both Fuhrman and Vannatter are much smarter than people give them credit for.

Fuhrman checked the animal blood in his test tube by holding it up against a light, to see if it was still liquid, which it was.

Then Fuhrman waited for his partner to call him about the murders. At 1:05 am Fuhrman's partner, Detective Ronald Philips called. Fuhrman pretended he had been asleep.

The two detectives agreed to meet at the police station to pick up a police car with a homicide kit. From there they drove to Bundy. For a short while Fuhrman was in charge. But eventually Detectives Lange and Vannatter from the Robbery/Homicide Division of the LAPD arrived and took over the investigation. From that moment Fuhrman was officially no longer assigned to the case.

As soon as Vannatter and Lange arrived, Fuhrman told Vannatter that O.J. was a convicted wife beater and that he (Fuhrman) had personally investigated an incident of domestic violence at O.J.'s house – as had Detective Edwards, too, on another occasion.

Vannatter was immediately convinced that O.J. were the killer. **Although Vannatter and Lange denied it, together with Fuhrman and Phillips they decided to drive to Rockingham to arrest O.J.** At least, they expected to find him there, together with plenty of incriminating evidence.

While still at Bundy, Fuhrman removed his jacket. The defense counsels in the criminal trial suggested that Fuhrman did that to demonstrate that he didn't carry anything in his pockets – like, for instance, one of the murder gloves in a plastic bag.

That could be one reason. But I think the main reason Fuhrman removed his dress jacket in the middle of the night – and put it in the trunk of his car – was that he used his jacket to conceal that he was removing a jeans jacket from Nicole's apartment.

I discussed that earlier, and suggested that the jeans jacket was Fuhrman's, and that he had forgotten it in Nicole's apartment earlier on the night of the murders. When he came back to investigate the murders, he saw his own jacket there. So did other officers at the scene. Yet, the jacket, mysteriously, disappeared while

Fuhrman was in Nicole's apartment alone! Explain it any other way, if you can!

Anyway, in two police cars the four detectives arrived at Rockingham about 5:00 am. There Fuhrman was met by another obstacle. O.J. wasn't home. Both O.J.'s daughter Arnelle, and Kato, lived in the guest house behind the main building. Neither of them heard the detectives calling on the intercom outside the locked gate.

Unless Fuhrman got inside O.J.'s property rather soon, it might be too late for him to plant the glove. After daybreak, or when O.J.'s estate was swarming with investigators and reporters, Fuhrman could no longer risk planting the glove, because he couldn't know if someone else had already checked out – and perhaps even photographed – the place he planted the glove.

That's when Fuhrman volunteered to scale the wall and open the gate from the inside. To allow Fuhrman to do that without a search warrant, Detective Vannatter needed a pretty good reason.

So Fuhrman wandered over to O.J.'s Bronco, which the detectives had already identified via the police computer. There, around the corner, out of sight of the other detectives, Fuhrman opened the Bronco's door. Perhaps it was unlocked, or perhaps he used a "Slim-Jim" to open it. He took out his bloody glove, and smeared it inside, thereby planting Nicole's and Ron's blood in the Bronco. He also planted a small speck of blood right above the door handle.

Then he closed the car door and returned to the other detectives. Fuhrman told Detective Vannatter that he had seen blood **on** the Bronco's door.

In his affidavit for a subsequent search warrant, Vannatter stated that Fuhrman had shown him the blood **on the Bronco's door handle.** That was just one of Vannatter's lies. Vannatter may have heard that, but misunderstood it, because the speck of blood was not on the door handle – it was on the door itself, just above the door handle. Later there should be many of **Vannatter's lies** in this case!

Vannatter did not check the Bronco to confirm what Fuhrman told him. Later, Vannatter still claimed he was faced with an emergency situation. Perhaps O.J. had also been attacked, and lay bleeding to death inside his house!

The detectives thought nothing of the sort! Fuhrman planted the blood inside the Bronco, because he wanted to get inside O.J.'s estate, so he could plant the second murder glove. And Vannatter probably thought O.J. were inside cleaning the murder knife and laundering his bloody clothes at that time!

Both detectives desperately wanted to get inside O.J.'s estate, although for different reasons.

Anyway, Vannatter sent Fuhrman over the wall and Fuhrman opened the gate. The four detectives entered O.J.'s estate.

Much later, when Fuhrman was questioned about his entering O.J.'s property without a search warrant, Fuhrman testified that he knew the laws about entering someone's property without a search warrant, and the legal interpretations of **"probable cause"** as reason to enter someone's property without a prior search warrant. Proudly, Fuhrman explained that he knew these things, because he had just studied the rules three weeks before the murders!

Was Fuhrman shooting himself in the foot – again! Could it be that Fuhrman knew O.J. would be out of town on the night following the murders, and that it therefore would be necessary to enter his estate without a search warrant?

Is that why Fuhrman brushed up on those legal matters only three weeks prior to the murders, to make sure he had the right to scale the fence at Rockingham, so he could get inside and plant the glove behind O.J.'s house, before day break?

Otherwise, why would Detective Fuhrman, a nineteen year veteran of the LAPD suddenly decide to bring out his old **"Law books"** from the Police Academy, and brush up on **"probable cause"** three weeks before the murders I say he committed, and then use that exact legal information as his justification to scale the wall at Rockingham.

Isn't it funny, how so many small details seem to make sense, when we consider Fuhrman as a likely murder suspect?

I just hope Mark Fuhrman keeps on talking and bragging and giving interviews! Every time he does, he seems to trip up a little more.

CHAPTER 36

More Discrepancies

L ater, in the morning, following the murders, **Detective Vannatter left Mark Fuhrman in charge** of the investigation at Rockingham, so Vannatter himself could go downtown and write the affidavit for the subsequent search warrant. (Detective Lange had returned to Bundy to be in charge there). This period, by the way, is when Detective Fuhrman could have ordered collected into evidence all the items he and Detective Brad Roberts, allegedly, found so important! But he didn't!

Only when Mark Fuhrman decided to write a book – as damage control, because he was about to be exposed – did he think that an empty knife box for a boy scout knife, a dark bloodless (according to Criminalist Fung) sweat suit in O.J.'s washing machine, a bloody fingerprint on the rear gate, etc., was important enough that it should have been safeguarded – **but ... by someone else, of course**! Be that as it may!

In his affidavit for the subsequent search warrant, Vannatter lied, so blatantly, about his motives for entering O.J.'s estate without a search warrant, that Judge Ito characterized Detective Vannatter as having *"a reckless disregard for the truth"*!

In legal terms, that is as close as a judge can get to calling Vannatter a *"damn liar"*!

Later, in his testimony during the pretrial hearings Vannatter referred to Fuhrman, who had told Vannatter he had seen blood **in** the Bronco. But Fuhrman couldn't have seen blood **in** the Bronco, unless he had opened the Bronco's door.

Fuhrman was already under suspicion for having planted the Rockingham glove behind O.J.'s house – since **he** "found" it! O.J.'s attorneys had already begun suggesting that Fuhrman could also have smeared the bloody glove inside the Bronco – before he planted the glove behind O.J.'s house!

So now the stories of the two detectives got really interesting. They both lied, but for totally different reasons. Suddenly they had to reconcile their lies!

First of all, Fuhrman realized that it was suspicious that he had seen blood **in** the Bronco. So on his report, and later when he testified, he said that he didn't tell Vannatter that he had seen blood **in** the Bronco, but **on** the Bronco. He qualified his statement by specifying an area on **the lower portion of the Bronco's door!**

Now the ball was in Vannatter's court. Subsequently, Detective Vannatter changed **his** testimony and said that he could not remember whether Fuhrman had told him that he saw blood **in** the Bronco, or **on** the Bronco. Fuhrman might have said **on** the Bronco!

The comedy – or the tragedy, rather – continued. Fuhrman was under pressure. O.J.'s attorneys didn't believe his and Vannatter's stories. So now Fuhrman tried to explain **why** he couldn't have smeared the glove inside the Bronco, **by saying the Bronco's door was locked, so he couldn't have gotten inside.**

Unfortunately for Fuhrman, another LAPD officer who arrived shortly after Fuhrman and Vannatter & Co., testified, later, that when he came to Rockingham, he wanted to check the engine of the Bronco, to see if it was warm, indicating that the Bronco might have been driven lately.

So what did this officer do? Yes, he simply **opened the unlocked door** of the Bronco, reached inside and unlatched the hood!

It is rather interesting in itself if Fuhrman lied about the Bronco's door being locked. So, let us scrutinize his statement a bit closer.

If the door was unlocked when the second officer tried it, then the door must have been **unlocked** also when Fuhrman, allegedly **"checked"** the door. Agree!

I don't care if the door was unlocked **before** Fuhrman got to Rockingham, or if **Fuhrman unlocked** the door with a "Slim-Jim." That's irrelevant!

Fuhrman must have lied, and the door **must**, in some way,

have been **unlocked** when he grabbed the door handle – regardless of whether Fuhrman unlocked the door or not! **That** is the important point!

Fuhrman said the door was **locked**. He couldn't know that unless he had actually **tried to open the door – by pressing the knob and pulling on the door handle!**

So, with this statement – that he checked the door, and it was locked – **Fuhrman revealed that he did press the door knob and pull on the door handle!** Agree?

But regardless of **when** the door was **unlocked**, or who unlocked it, it **must have been unlocked** when Fuhrman tried to open the door (according to the testimony of the LAPD officer who later opened the Bronco's door and reached inside to pull the latch for the hood, so he could check the temperature of the Bronco's engine)!

But if you grab the door handle of a Bronco, press the knob and pull on the door handle – to check if the door is locked or unlocked – and the door is **unlocked – then the door will open!**

So, **Fuhrman must have opened the Bronco's door!**

Perhaps it is a bit complicated to follow. But if you reason through my arguments slowly, I think you will realize that this is nothing but straight forward **logic!**

Again, Fuhrman must have opened the Bronco's door! But why would he lie about it? And why would he open the Bronco's door in the first place?

There are only two answers to that last question. Fuhrman must have done one or the other:

1. To look inside, only, do something **legitimate**, and close the door again.
2. To reach inside and do something **illegitimate** – like smearing the bloody glove all around!

Since Fuhrman lied about this, he couldn't have done **the first** of the above. Because there would have been **no reason to lie about that**!

Again, the only **logical** conclusion is that Fuhrman **must** have done **the second** of the above.

The comedy/tragedy didn't end there, either! Nobody had seen the blood Fuhrman **later** referred to – on the lower portion of the Bronco's door. The simple reason was that Fuhrman lied. There was no blood there. That "blood" was created by Fuhrman's imagination, to explain how he could have seen blood in (or **on**) the Bronco without having opened the Bronco's door.

The Bronco was examined by criminalists several times. They didn't find any blood on the lower portion of the door, because **that blood was not planted until 6 weeks after the murders!** More precisely, it wasn't planted until Prosecutor Clark was in jeopardy of losing all the evidence from Rockingham, because the criminalists had not found the blood Fuhrman had referred to.

If the blood was not there – on the outside lower portion of the door – then Fuhrman had lied. Consequently, Detective Vannatter did not have "probable cause" to enter O.J.'s estate without a search warrant!

All the evidence from Rockingham was in jeopardy of being thrown out of the case because of this **technicality.** I shall return to that in a later chapter.

Millions of people, the media included, have been poking fun at O.J. for being inconclusive about his actions and his whereabouts on the night of the murders. His alleged sleeping, chipping golf balls, taking a shower, etc., prior to leaving for the airport, must have been the most repeated joke on U.S. comedy shows and talk shows for two years!

But look at the main characters on the side of the prosecution! Detectives Vannatter and Fuhrman are lying through their teeth and changing their testimonies every time they open their mouths!

Besides, O.J. had no reason to take notes of what he was doing on June 12, 1994, or remember it. Detectives Vannatter and Fuhrman, however, were **required** to keep track of their actions and observations – but didn't.

Yet, as these two "partners of deception" were pushed from one lie to the next, the media and the prosecutors just nodded approvingly and accepted their concocted stories! Are there nothing but "zombies" in the media?

B ack to the night of the murders. Eventually the detectives got access to O.J.'s house. The first person they met was Brian "Kato" Kaelin, a friend of Nicole's, then living as a permanent houseguest in a wing of O.J.'s house, referred to as the "guest house." Kato lived in the room inside the wall which Fuhrman's accomplice had thumped on with a baseball bat, a pool cue, or similar earlier that night.

Of course, if Fuhrman is the murderer, it was of great interest to him to learn whether Kato had heard the thumps or not.

But it was even more important for Fuhrman that he – **before anyone else** – could find out what Kato had heard or not heard.

The reason is obvious? Because of the thumps on Kato's wall, deliberately caused by Fuhrman's accomplice, Fuhrman had long since figured out that the best place to plant the glove was behind O.J.'s house – granted that someone had heard those thumps.

However, if one of the other detectives learned that Kato had heard those thumps on his wall, at a time corresponding to shortly after the murders, then Vannatter might, perhaps, order everyone outside – in groups of two – to search O.J.'s property, and in particular search behind O.J.'s house. If so, it might be impossible for Fuhrman to plant the glove behind O.J.'s house. Or if Fuhrman had already planted the glove – when he went over the wall to open the gate – it might, at least, be difficult for him to isolate himself from the other detectives, and be the one to find the glove, and thereby get credit for having solved the murder case.

So now, Fuhrman, the junior detective, not even assigned to the case any longer, managed to push the other detectives away from Kato, while he positioned himself alone with Kato in Kato's room.

Let me say a few words about being junior or senior detective in a case like this. The lead investigator, Detective Vannatter, is the one who should have interviewed an important witness like Kato, to learn – first hand – what Kato had to say, and based on that, possibly, have decided what investigative steps to proceed with.

Instead, as I said, Fuhrman interviewed Kato – alone. Kato had heard the thumps. He was bound to tell the other detectives eventually. So now Detective Fuhrman needed to go behind the house and, perhaps plant the glove, but at least, find the glove, before Lange and Vannatter learned about the thumps.

Fuhrman led Kato to O.J.'s living room where he sat Kato down next to Vannatter, and literally, "ordered" his senior officer to listen to what Kato had to say.

All the strange things Detective Fuhrman did appeared so unreal for someone with investigative experience, that there had to be more to this than Detective Fuhrman and Detective Vannatter have told us!

Detective Vannatter was occupied with Kato, and Fuhrman was without any particular assignment. So now Fuhrman told Vannatter he would go outside *"to take a look around."*

Fuhrman went behind the house, opened up the plastic bag with the bloody glove. Carefully he placed it on the ground.

Then, possibly, Fuhrman went over to the driveway, took out the vial with animal blood and planted some drops leading away from the gate, towards the main entrance.

As I mentioned earlier, there were other ways Fuhrman could have planted the blood drops in O.J.'s driveway. When he left the murder scene, right after the murders, he could for instance have brought with him a piece of cloth dipped in Nicole's blood. Later, at Rockingham, he could have moistened the blood on the cloth and wrung it to drip the blood drops in O.J.'s driveway.

There might even be other ways he could have planted the blood in O.J.'s driveway. There is no sense in trying to cover them all. The important thing is that planting false blood evidence in O.J.'s driveway was not very difficult at all.

The "genius" of Fuhrman, was his clever method of

planting evidence against O.J. in such a way that he really didn't plant the false evidence himself, but just "set up" the investigators so that they should later fabricate the false evidence for Fuhrman.

Besides creating the bloody shoeprints, I think what I discussed above was the main reason why Fuhrman created such a bloody murder scene. The bloodier and sloppier, the more likely the investigators could find various ways of fabricating false evidence against O.J.

Had the murder scene been fairly clean, it would be impossible for the investigators to fabricate much false evidence. Suppose the murderer, as I explained earlier, had whacked Nicole in the head with his gun a few more times, after Nicole was already unconscious – or broken her neck. Then the murderer could probably have left Bundy before Ron showed up, and there would hardly have been any evidence at Bundy, at all. In particular, there would not have been a single blood drop at Bundy, or any bloody Bruno Magli shoeprints – or a dead Ron Goldman!

However, because there seemed to be such a bloody mess all over the place, the investigators, Vannatter that is, could more confidently fabricate false blood evidence on, and in, the Bronco, in O.J.'s driveway, inside his door, next to the bloody shoeprints at Bundy, on the gloves, on O.J.'s socks etc., etc.

NOTE! I will later, in detail, explain how Detective Vannatter managed to create as many false, EDTA free O.J. blood swatches as he wanted. I will also explain how easily he could have replaced every **real** blood evidence swatch he wanted it to appear had O.J.'s blood on it, with a **false** O.J. blood swatch.

Vannatter could simply decide what blood evidence he wished had O.J.'s DNA in it. Then he could replace the blood swatches from that blood evidence, with his false O.J. swatches – easily and quickly, in the crime lab, when no one else was there.

The key to this massive evidence fabrication is Vannatter's method for circumventing the EDTA in O.J.'s blood vial.

Everyone seems to think that the EDTA made it impossible to use O.J.'s reference blood sample to plant false blood evidence in this case. Vannatter could easily overcome this apparent problem.

The evidence is overwhelming, that Detective Vannatter did this.

But my readers must wait a little longer for that. I want things in a somewhat chronological order.

After about 10 minutes, Fuhrman returned inside. Triumphantly he told the other detectives:

"Bingo! Guess what I found? We can wrap up this case now!"

One at the time, Detective Fuhrman led the other detectives outside and showed them the glove. That was when Detective Vannatter tapped the glove carefully, got fresh blood on his finger, and consequently, testified in court that the blood on the glove was *"sticky and moist."*

Already at that moment the lead investigators should have known that the glove was planted, and that someone tried to frame O.J. Remember, Vannatter had already learned that O.J. left for Chicago almost seven and a half hours earlier – and the blood was still sticky and moist! How ignorant can a lead homicide investigator from the LAPD be?

Immediately, all the detectives – except Fuhrman, of course, who knew better – believed O.J. were as guilty as sin. Now their main objective was to make sure he got convicted.

How many of them were directly involved in fabricating false evidence, how many covered it up, how many of them knew about it, but looked the other way, I don't know. It is irrelevant. Theoretically they could all have been involved, or Detective Vannatter could have done it all by himself.

CHAPTER 37

The "Point Of No Return"

For every little piece of false evidence Detective Fuhrman lured the investigators (mainly Detective Vannatter) to fabricate, Fuhrman's own chances of getting away with murder grew better and better.

In planning the murder of Nicole, Fuhrman counted on that. Fuhrman knew, or anticipated, that at some point, rather early in the investigation, he would be **"home free"** and have the investigators and the prosecutors at his mercy.

How? Well, let me explain!

I keep returning to the glove evidence. According to the glove evidence, O.J. could not have bled at Bundy, next to the bloody shoe prints – even if he were the murderer. That blood must have belonged to Nicole (or Ron)!

At some point, therefore, someone must have exchanged the blood swatches from those blood drops, with false blood swatches containing O.J.'s EDTA free blood. Although theses swatches were never tested for EDTA (as I explained earlier), I don't think Vannatter dared substitute the blood swatches from Bundy with swatches containing O.J.'s EDTA blood! He must have had a method of circumventing the EDTA in O.J.'s blood vial – just in case!

Don't ask me yet, how it was done. It seems impossible. But logic tells us it must have been done, and I will explain, convincingly, in a later chapter, how it was done. It is in fact very simple, and it didn't take a major conspiracy to do it – just one man, Vannatter!

Next, Fuhrman lured the investigators into planting O.J.'s hairs on the knit cap. The investigators reasoned:

"What the heck! O.J. is as guilty as sin, anyway, and this is

his cap. Normally his hairs would be on it, so, just in case they aren't, we might as well put some of his hairs there, to strengthen the case against him."

The same went for every new piece of evidence the investigators fabricated, like O.J.'s blood inside the Bronco, and later on the lower portion of the Bronco's door; like the blood drops on the rear gate at Bundy, which unquestionably were not there on June 13, but showed up three weeks later – **and contained EDTA**; like Nicole's blood on O.J.'s sock; like the carpet fiber from the Bronco found on Ron's shirt; etc., etc.

Fuhrman knew what evidence **he** planted. Accordingly, he also knew what evidence **the investigators must** have planted – and probably **who** planted each piece of false evidence. Some of the evidence planting, like the blood on the lower portion of the Bronco's door, must have been planted on direct orders from the prosecution – maybe even on District Attorney Gil Garcetti's order! I will return to that argument later.

As the investigation "progressed," Fuhrman knew that both the investigators and the prosecution, and perhaps even the criminalists, got deeper and deeper involved in evidence fabrication and evidence planting against O.J.

Of course, initially, they never suspected that Fuhrman, or anyone other than O.J., had murdered Nicole and Ron. But then, at some point, they **must** have realized that O.J. could not possibly be the murderer, and that Detective Mark Fuhrman, rather, not only was the killer, but that he had "set them up" so cleverly that there was no turning back!

If they suddenly changed direction and said that they now believed O.J. was innocent, and that Fuhrman had murdered Nicole and Ron – how in heavens name would they explain where all the "evidence" against O.J. had come from?

After the "investigation" passed a certain **"point of no return,"** they had no choice but to move ahead and try their best to convict O.J. At that point **it wasn't any longer a matter of convicting a murderer – it was a matter of protecting their own careers and**

their own butts.

Should it ever come out, that Detective Fuhrman was the murderer, and that he had set them up with some crucial pieces of evidence which he planted, and that the investigators – sometimes even with the approval of the prosecutors – had fabricated all the rest of the evidence against O.J., their careers would be over for good. But more importantly, they would all go to prison for a long, long time.

Detective Fuhrman, at some point, realized that they had crossed that line, and that he had the entire investigation – prosecutors included – in a "choke hold"!

That coincided with the time when someone began criticizing Detective Fuhrman for his racism, which had begun to emerge. Prosecutors and investigators tried to downplay Fuhrman's role, saying he wasn't essential to the case. Others suggested dropping him altogether. Speculations floated around that Fuhrman had planted the Rockingham glove.

Fuhrman, though, was as cocky as ever. He responded with the mysterious words, quoted in various fashions throughout the media:

> *"I **am** the investigation! The glove is everything. If I go down, the entire investigation goes down!"*

The media and the public really didn't know what he meant by this bold, defiant statement. I knew. And I am sure the investigators knew.

If they went after Detective Fuhrman and accused him of having planted the Rockingham glove – which would be synonymous with Fuhrman being the murderer – he would bring down the entire investigation team, and most likely, also the prosecutors and District Attorney Gil Garcetti.

Earlier I asked you to keep a book mark on my quotes from the Fuhrman Tapes. Look it up if you like. Do you remember, after Fuhrman and his three buddies had tortured, and almost killed four innocent Latinos (one of them actually died) and there was a major Internal Affairs investigation directed at Fuhrman? What did he say?

> *"Well, they know I did it. **They know damn well I did it!** There's nothing **they** could do, but I could. ... I mean, **we could have murdered people and got away with it!"**

I believe the lead investigator, Detective Vannatter, the prosecutors, and possibly, even Gil Garcetti, at some point confronted Detective Fuhrman with their new theory – that he was the murderer. Face to face, I think Fuhrman boldly told them, basically, the same he had told Ms. Laura Hart McKinny regarding the above mentioned brutal assault on the four latinos:

> *"**Yes, I killed Nicole and Ron!** I did it – and there is not a damn thing you can do about it!"*

Then, I think, Fuhrman continued:

> *"There is not a damn thing you can do about it ... because I know what evidence **I** left behind. Therefore, I also know what evidence **you** must have fabricated and planted – and in particular, I think I know exactly which one of you fabricated each piece of evidence, who gave the orders, who covered it up, and who just looked the other way! If you charge me, I'll squeal on all of you!*
>
> *To explain why you believe I am guilty – in spite of all the evidence against O.J. – you would have to tell the jury that **you** fabricated that evidence and tried to **frame** O.J. with it, because you thought he were guilty.*
>
> *Why should the jury believe that you aren't trying to frame me, too – the same way you tried to frame O.J.?*
>
> *There is only circumstantial evidence against me. You'll never be able to pin me to the Bruno Magli shoes, the bloody clothes, the bloody gloves, or the bloody knife!*
>
> *On the other hand, there is a lot of evidence against O.J.!*

*Therefore, if you charge me, chances are good that I will be acquitted – while you, **most certainly**, will be convicted of having fabricated false evidence against an innocent man accused of first degree murder.*

So, lay off! Or go to jail – with or without me!"

Sadly, the investigators and the prosecutors realized that Detective Fuhrman was right. He had them all by their throats! Consequently, the investigators continued to frame O.J. with more fabricated evidence, while the prosecutors reluctantly embraced Fuhrman – even after *"The Fuhrman Tapes"* surfaced.

Yes, Prosecutors Marcia Clark and Christopher Darden defended Fuhrman right up to the very end, when he was caught lying under oath in his testimony against O.J. And when Fuhrman's perjury was exposed, and he pleaded the Fifth Amendment, the prosecutors fought intensely to keep this information away from the jury.

Even then, the District Attorney's office continued to defend and protect Mark Fuhrman, saying he had little bearing on the case against O.J.

Right! – Except that Fuhrman probably murdered the two people O.J. was accused of having killed!

I guess such immaterial details didn't concern the prosecutors and District Attorney Gil Garcetti!

The public demanded an investigation of Mark Fuhrman, so the DA's office and the LAPD "whitewashed" him. One year later they declared him innocent of any wrong doing during his years with the LAPD. They even called him **"an excellent police officer"!** Former LAPD Chief Daryl Gates characterized Detective Mark Fuhrman as follows – on "Larry King Live" February, 1997:

*"In my opinion, Mark Fuhrman was **a hell of a fine police officer**"!*

Talk about conspiracy! Read the transcripts from *"The Fuhrman*

Tapes" again, and then tell me that there is no **"code of silence"** within the LAPD, and no conspiracy against O.J. Simpson. When former Police Chief Gates and former Detective Fuhrman are presented as heroes, more or less, on CNN by Larry King – we may start to wonder how far the conspiracy has spread!

Is this the reason why everyone associated with the LAPD or the DA's office, even today, seems to embrace and **protect** Fuhrman – this perjuring, racist murderer?! (Again, my opinion).

And is this the reason why California's Attorney General, on October 3, 1996, struck a plea bargain deal with this perjuring, racist psycho, saying there was nothing to suggest that Fuhrman planted evidence, or otherwise did anything wrong, except forgetting that he used the word "nigger" 8-9 years ago?

Did Mark Fuhrman tell District Attorney Gil Garcetti that if he was charged with murder, or even given one day in prison, he would tip off the media with respect to the fabrication of false evidence against O.J.? Is that why the LAPD and the district attorney washed their hands of the Fuhrman case, and handed it over to the California Attorney General's Office – to make the "whitewash" appear legitimate?

Did the Los Angeles District Attorney's Office and the California Attorney General's Office strike a deal, to let Fuhrman get off with three years probation and a $200.00 fine, so they could whisk him off to Idaho, where he cannot be subpoenaed to testify against any members of the LAPD or the L.A. District Attorney's Office?

This way Detective Mark Fuhrman has forever been swept under the rug. The LAPD and the prosecutors are finally off the hook.

The only ones left to pay the price for their horrendous crimes, are O.J., his children and his mother – and Nicole's and Ron's families.

CHAPTER 38

Detective Philip Vannatter

In my opinion, Detective Fuhrman, basically, laid the "bait", by "finding" the Rockingham glove and planting the cap, the bloody shoeprints, the five blood drops next to the shoeprints, some of the blood in the Bronco, and perhaps the blood in O.J.'s driveway.

Were it not for Detective Vannatter, I believe this evidence would **not** have been very incriminating to O.J., because true analyses of that evidence would have revealed that it didn't come from O.J.

O.J.'s real troubles started as soon as Fuhrman showed up with the Rockingham glove, and convinced Detective Vannatter that O.J. were guilty.

Let me counter one argument, repeatedly claimed by the prosecutors, by Vannatter himself, and by most of O.J.'s critics:

> **Why would Detective Vannatter – who was about to retire as soon as the Simpson case was over – jeopardize his entire career, his name and reputation, his integrity as a police officer, and his pension – and even risk going to prison for many years – by fabricating false evidence against O.J.?**

Vannatter was no party to these murders. To him it didn't make any difference who had committed them – O.J., some burglar, a jealous lover, a mafia hit man, or anybody. Detective Vannatter had no ax to grind with O.J. All Detective Vannatter wanted was to take the case wherever the evidence led him, solve the murder case, and assure a conviction of the person responsible – whoever he was.

To most people, that sounded so convincingly on *"Rivera Live."* But it didn't float! **I will put Detective Vannatter in the**

right perspective for my readers.

Detective Vannatter was characterized by the judge as having

"a reckless disregard for the truth"!

In legal terms, that is as close as a judge can come to calling Detective Vannatter *"a damn liar"*!

Vannatter was caught lying on the witness stand over and over again. **One of his lies** occurred when he – under oath – testified for Defense Attorney Robert Shapiro that O.J. was no more of a suspect than Mr. Shapiro!

Another of Vannatter's lies occurred when he told the cross examining defense attorney that he left the police head-quarters downtown, to drive to Rockingham at 2:30 pm on the day after the murders, when in fact he didn't leave until about 4:00! That was the day he brought O.J.'s blood vial to Rockingham.

Only after being confronted with the time log from Rockingham, and the log proved that Vannatter must have spent almost ninety minutes downtown, **after he received O.J.'s blood vial from the police nurse** – did Vannatter admit that he didn't leave for Rockingham until around 4:00 pm.

Next lie: When asked what he did during that hour and a half – when he had O.J.'s fresh blood vial in his possession – Detective Vannatter could not give any reasonable answer.

His only answer on the witness stand, after having been exposed as a liar, was that he *"might have had a cup of coffee in his office"*!

That lie exposed yet **another of Vannatter's lies:** Earlier, during the cross examination, the defense attorney had asked Vannatter **why** he brought the vial to O.J.'s house. Vannatter answered that he **didn't have time** to book in O.J.'s vial before he had to leave for Rockingham, because he wanted to give the vial to Criminalist Fung before Fung left Rockingham.

That was **yet another earlier lie**, of course! Chew on this! Here is Detective Vannatter just having received O.J.'s blood vial from the nurse. This in itself was highly irregular. The nurse was a sworn police officer who had drawn hundreds of blood samples before, and booked them in as well.

Why didn't the nurse book in the vial himself if Vannatter didn't have time to do it?

There was a crime lab just two blocks away, and there was even an evidence locker in the very building he found himself in. Vannatter could have taken the elevator up to the 9th floor and booked in the vial there. It would only have taken him a couple of minutes.

Vannatter's excuse for bringing O.J.'s blood vial to Rockingham was that he was rushed for time. Yet, as soon as he received O.J.'s blood vial, he had time to spend one and a half hours in his office – doing nothing but drink one cup of coffee!

The examples I have mentioned here are just short excerpts of Vannatter's dishonesty! Isn't it obvious that Detective Vannatter was lying through his teeth throughout this case? And Vannatter was the lead investigator! The obvious question when Detective Vannatter, so obviously, was lying, over and over again, is:

> **Why was Detective Vannatter lying? If you have done nothing wrong, and you have nothing to hide, you can confidently tell the truth! So what skeletons did Detective Vannatter hide in his closet?**

I shall tell you what Detective Vannatter was trying to hide by lying:

> **Detective Vannatter was trying to hide the fact that he is responsible for having fabricated almost all of the evidence against O.J.**

As for jeopardizing his pension and his career, I don't think Vannatter gave that one iota of a thought. Here is why:

Through his 27 year career with the LAPD Vannatter was so accustomed to fabricating false evidence against suspects he thought were guilty, that it never even crossed his mind that he couldn't get away with it – this one last time!

With respect to Vannatter's pension and his future – in terms of evidence fabrication – it made no difference that this was his **last** case before retiring. Had LAPD officers routinely been charged with evidence tampering, and convicted every other day, but Vannatter throughout his entire career **never even once** had tampered with evidence – then I agree that Vannnatter would probably not risk his reputation and his pension by fabricating evidence in this, his last case.

But Vannatter, like so many other LAPD investigators had probably tampered with evidence so often that there was no added risk doing it this one last time. There was no more risk of being exposed this time than, say, in his second last case, or a case a month earlier, or a year ago, or three years ago.

I never heard that there is a special two week statute of limitation on evidence tampering, so that if nobody catches you in the act, so to speak, and a couple of weeks pass, you don't have to worry about it anymore! Of course, the statute of limitation for committing the extremely serious felony of evidence fabrication is just as long as for the murder case in which you tamper with the evidence.

So, if Vannatter had ever tampered with evidence in his career, his pension and future would be just as much – or as little – in jeopardy from such earlier evidence tampering as from tampering with the evidence in the Simpson case. There was nothing special about the Simpson case just because it was Vannatter's last case before retiring.

The LAPD were notoriously infamous for planting false evidence against suspects they thought were guilty. And they were used to getting away with it – all the time! That wasn't strange at all. For one thing, there was a **"code of silence"** within the LAPD. A good LAPD officer simply didn't "rat" on his colleagues!

Besides, if a victim of false evidence fabrication wished to file a complaint and have the matter investigated, to whom would he have to address his complaint and his request for an investigation? Right! To the LAPD investigators themselves!

The LAPD had a fail-safe system for fabricating false evidence, as well as for covering it up. Hence, Detective Vannatter wasn't concerned about being accused of fabricating false evidence against O.J.

What rather concerned Vannatter was that the Simpson case was not only his **last** case, but by far his **most important** one. This was **the case Detective Vannatter would forever be remembered for**.

If he failed to secure a conviction, Detective Vannatter would forever be remembered as the detective who, in spite of overwhelming evidence, failed to nail the most celebrated murderer of the century.

On the other hand, if he nailed O.J., Vannatter's name would forever be etched in the annals of our justice system.

The choice was not very difficult. Vannatter was willing to do absolutely anything, in terms of fabricating false evidence or giving false testimony, in order to secure a conviction of O.J.

My readers may be stunned by reading this, and wonder how I dare say it. However, there is plenty of circumstancial evidence to back it up my assumptions. Besides, just like Fuhrman can refer to his Fifth Amendment privilege, I can refer to my First Amendment privilege of free speech.

As I wrote in the "Foreword," **I am simply stating my opinion and my theory** regarding how Nicole and Ron were murdered, and how O.J. was framed.

My readers themselves must draw their own conclusions regarding the guilt and innocence of the various principals in the Simpson case.

I believe, though, that you will come to understand my theory better once you read on.

CHAPTER 39

The *"Trail Of Blood"*

As soon as Detective Fuhrman revealed the Rockingham glove, Detective Vannatter who already believed O.J. were guilty, became absolutely convinced. Vannatter didn't want to go out with a failure. He needed to nail O.J.

Vannatter had already surveyed the extremely bloody murder scene. Right away he realized how he could nail O.J. with fabricated blood evidence – if he could only get a blood sample from him. That's what I shall explain about next.

By the way, Vannatter could, of course, not fabricate false blood evidence from O.J.'s blood vial, unless O.J. had a cut or a wound somewhere, preferably on one of his hands or arms.

I shall discuss this later, and show that it wasn't really a problem – how strange that may sound at this point.

Vannatter was confident that he would soon obtain a blood sample from O.J. If O.J. refused, the police would just get a court order. On the other hand, Vannatter could tell O.J. that if the police got a blood sample from him, the police would test it, and if it didn't match the blood at the crime scenes, O.J. would no longer be a suspect.

So already long before O.J. returned from Chicago, Vannatter began planning his blood evidence fabrication.

Fuhrman who set the whole thing up by creating the bloody murder scene, also **"knew"** that Vannatter would get O.J.'s blood. Since O.J. was innocent, **Fuhrman knew O.J. would be "over-anxious" to give the police his blood sample.** Let me quote from O.J.'s taped interview with Detectives Lange and Vannatter, conducted only hours after O.J. returned from Chicago:

Vannatter: *"We've got some blood on and in your car, we've got some blood at your house, and sort of a problem."*
Simpson: *"Well, take my blood test!"*

That didn't sound like a man who had something to hide, did it? O.J. let the police nurse draw a vial of blood, **8.0 ml to be exact. (1 ml = 1 milliliter = 1 cc)**

The blood in the vial contained EDTA – a chemical used to prevent the blood from coagulating, and from getting contaminated. The EDTA in the blood vials is a dry powder, present in the bottom of the vials. To indicate to lab personnel that a vial contains EDTA, it is equipped with a characteristic **purple** rubber cap.

The EDTA is not added to the blood by the nurse. The EDTA is already present inside the vials as they come from the pharmaceutical manufacturer.

When the blood enters the vial, directly through the hypodermic needle, or via a syringe, the EDTA is dissolved and mixes with the blood. From then on, wherever the blood goes, the EDTA goes right along with it. The existence of EDTA in a sample of blood can be determined through a chemical analysis.

If a blood spot does **not** contain EDTA, it can **not** have come from the EDTA blood in O.J.'s blood vial. On the other hand, if a blood sample **does** contain EDTA, it **must** have come from O.J.'s blood vial.

In other words, if Vannatter planted blood from O.J.'s blood vial, that blood would contain EDTA. The EDTA would show up in subsequent blood analyses, indicating that the blood had been planted from the vial.

It may **appear** that this was an **insurmountable problem** for Detective Vannatter. But actually, **it was the very key to the plan that had already begun to crystalize in his head!**

How could the presence of EDTA in O.J.'s blood vial actually help Vannatter's evidence fabrication against O.J.?

Well, if Vannatter knew a **secret** method of circumventing the EDTA in O.J.'s blood vial, he could pretty much do whatever he wanted in terms of blood evidence planting.

The prosecutors told the jury that if Vannatter had planted false blood from O.J.'s blood vial, that blood would have had EDTA in it, which would have shown up in blood analyses. Consequently, the people, the media, and all of O.J.'s adversaries bought that – unconditionally!

Frankly, I must have heard and seen that argument raised by former investigators, prosecutors, criminalists, medical examiners, attorneys, judges, legal analysts, talk show hosts, news anchors, reporters, authors of 'Simpson books,' and by members of the victims' families – publicly (on TV) – at least four hundred times over the last two and a half years!

The difference between myself and most other people interested in this case is that they pretty much accept what people of authority tell them, without questioning it.

I, on the other hand, didn't take anything for granted. And I didn't believe anything the investigators, the prosecutors, or the expert witnesses said, **unless I understood** in my own mind that it was correct.

The prosecutors started **their** theory with the five blood drops at Bundy:

- The blood drops were collected before O.J. returned from Chicago, so they couldn't have been planted.
- The blood didn't contain any EDTA. (That's what they implied, at least). So the blood could not have been "fabricated" in the LAPD's crime lab, either (using blood from O.J.'s blood vial).
- The blood was DNA analyzed. It was O.J.'s blood.
- Therefore, O.J. must have bled at Bundy – before he left for Chicago.
- Consequently, O.J. were guilty!

I agree that their argumentation sounded reasonable – for people who didn't like to figure out things for themselves.

However – as my readers know – we didn't start **our** theory with those five blood drops! We started with **the glove evidence!** In doing so, we reached a totally different conclusion than the prosecutors, namely that **O.J. could not possibly have bled at Bundy – even if he were the murderer!**

Do my readers remember from the chapter titled **The Glove Evidence,** that I asked you never to forget that, or start **"babbling"** about EDTA and **"stuff"**? **O.J. could not have bled at Bundy – period!** The glove evidence proved that!

Consequently, if the prosecutors argued that the blood swatches from the five blood drops at Bundy contained O.J.'s DNA, then they **must** have been fabricated.

And if the blood on those swatches didn't contain EDTA, there **must** have been a way for the investigators (Detective Vannatter in particular) to **circumvent** the EDTA in blood vials.

It didn't matter what the experts said! Let me quote Sherlock Holmes!

> *"If you **eliminate the impossible,** then **what remains** – however improbable – **must be the truth!"***

Or as Sherlock Holmes would have said if he were O.J.'s private investigator:

> *Since O.J. couldn't have bled at Bundy, the blood **must** have come from his **blood vial.** If the blood vial had EDTA in it, and the Bundy blood did not, there **must** be a way for the investigators to eliminate the EDTA!*
>
> *However improbable – that must be the truth!"*

Since O.J. could **not** have bled at Bundy, but the prosecution alleged that the blood at Bundy was O.J.'s, it could only have come from the vial. And if the blood didn't contain EDTA, there **must** be a way ... **All I had to do was to find it!**

I started out by looking at everything the investigators said and did, and which appeared, sort of, **unreliable, inconsistent,**

strange, unexplainable, out of place, unmotivated, etc.

You see, I didn't believe lead homicide investigators, with 27 years of experience in our nation's second largest police department, make many **"blunders"** – unless it is **"intentional"**!

I was not too concerned about regular **"sloppiness,"** such as a criminalist forgetting to change latex gloves between picking up two different pieces of evidence, or not wearing plastic shoe covers (for his own protection). Nor did I think about a major "boo-boo" like spreading a woolen blanket over Nicole's body, with the ensuing risk of transferring hairs and fibers all over the murder scene. That was clearly done out of respect for Nicole's body and her family's feelings.

I was more concerned about the smaller, subtle detail, where one **might think**, at first, that the "culprit" just acted out of thoughtlessness, but where one **upon closer review** might realize that the culprit had actually been in a position to **make a conscious, deliberate decision.**

Scattered throughout this chapter and the next, I shall mention some of these smaller, subtle detail that just didn't fit, and which pointed towards a well orchestrated blood evidence fabrication. I shall mark them with a bullet (•) to point them out. Some of them I may already have mentioned.

(•) The detectives at Rockingham told Kato that he had to check with them before leaving the house on the morning after the murders, because **they didn't know yet** if they wanted a written statement from him or not.

Of course, they knew! And of course, they wanted Kato's written statement. He had given the investigators important information about the thumps on the wall, just where the glove was later found, and at a time corresponding to shortly after the murders.

What Detective Vannatter **should** have told Kato was that he couldn't leave Los Angeles without checking with the police, or that he had to meet at the police station at a certain time, to give his written statement. Instead one of the detectives at Rockingham told Kato, *"... we don't know yet ..."!*

I didn't buy that! This is what I think happened after the

detective told Kato that, and Kato went back to his room.

Detective Vannatter already knew, from Kato, that he and O.J. had been to McDonalds for hamburgers the night before, so ketchup was a natural, explainable "**blood substitute**." Hence, Vannatter brought out a bottle of ketchup from O.J.'s refrigerator. Carefully he planted three drops of ketchup on the parquet floor of the foyer, just inside O.J.'s entrance door.

An hour or two later, Kato wanted to leave, so he checked with the detectives. They had no objections to Kato leaving, of course.

Kato had lived in the house for several months. He knew his way around the house. But instead of telling Kato that there was evidence in the foyer, so he had to use the side door – the detective led Kato **straight through the foyer, towards the "blood" (ketchup) drops!**

Just before Kato got to the drops, the detective grabbed Kato's arm and jerked him back – so Kato jumped! The detective pointed to the three drops of ketchup that Vannatter had planted. Then he said to Kato:

> *"**Watch out,** so you don't step on the **blood**!"*

Kato looked down, saw three red spots, and believed, of course, that he was seeing blood drops! Then the detective led Kato around the drops and opened the door for him.

What I have just recountet, is exactly what Kato testified to in the criminal trial.

The way the detective had surprised him, Kato would, of course, remember the episode, and later testify in court that he saw blood inside O.J.'s foyer about eight o'clock in the morning – **long before the police had received a vial of O.J.'s blood.**

Upon reflection, Vannatter, obviously, wanted an independent eyewitness, like Kato, to corroborate that O.J.'s blood was there, in the foyer, before he had received O.J.'s blood vial – as evidence that the blood was not planted.

Why would Vannatter be concerned about someone possibly

suspecting that the blood drops might have been planted – so he needed a "neutral" witness like Kato to confirm that the blood was there already before O.J. had returned from Chicago? Because planting blood drops in O.J.'s foyer, later – after he received O.J.'s blood vial – was exactly what Vannatter intended to do!

Later, after Vannatter had received O.J.'s blood vial, and arranged to extract 1.5 ml of O.J.'s EDTA **free** blood from that vial, he brought this EDTA **free** blood to Rockingham, wiped away the ketchup drops with a wet paper towel, and replaced them with three drops of **O.J.'s EDTA free blood**.

In the meantime the ketchup drops had been recorded. Then, after Vannatter had replaced the ketchup drops with drops of O.J.'s EDTA free blood, the **real** drops were photographed and collected on blood evidence swatches.

From then on, of course, it would appear that O.J. had bled in his foyer, before he left for Chicago on the night of the murders.

However, it should take another 7 weeks before that blood, together with the rest of the blood evidence was sent away to outside crime labs for DNA analyses.

Hence, perhaps Vannatter fabricated this blood evidence in a different manner. Perhaps he just allowed the criminalists to collect the ketchup drops – on blood evidence swatches – and bring them to the LAPD's crime lab, were they would be kept for many weeks.

Back in the LAPD's evidence room, or the serology room, Vannatter replaced the blood (ketchup) swatches from O.J.'s foyer with false blood swatches he had fabricated from O.J.'s blood vial.

Regardless of the method used, eventually Vannatter managed to fabricate false EDTA free blood swatches with O.J.'s EDTA free blood – apparently having been collected in O.J.'s foyer – before the swatches were sent out to Cellmark Diagnostics Lab or to the FBI's lab for DNA analyses. Of course the results would come back, that this was O.J.'s blood! **Vannatter had made sure it was!**

Furthermore, the blood did not contain EDTA (at least, that's what the prosecution contended), so it appeared that it could not have come from O.J.'s blood vial – in spite of the fact that Vannatter had brought the blood vial to Rockingham.

It was a "double left hook" directly on the chin of O.J.'s defense team!

Kato remembered the episode when he testified during the criminal trial. He was shown a picture of the three "blood" drops inside the door. Almost one year later, Kato could, of course, not remember if the drops he saw were 1/16 of an inch more to the left or right, than the drops on the photographs they showed him in court! Hence, when asked during his testimony, he confirmed that those were the drops he saw when he left the house early in the morning – before O.J. had returned from Chicago! Apparently, O.J. had bled inside his door on the night of the murders!

I have shown you, however, how easily Vannatter could have fabricated that blood evidence. And the way Kato, obviously, was "set up" clearly suggested that those three blood drops were fabricated.

It all hinged on whether or not Detective Vannatter knew a way to circumvent the EDTA in O.J.'s blood vial.

The way the detectives "set up" Kato proved to me that there was something "fishy" about those blood drops. I figured, that what you have just read is the way they set up Kato to make it appear to the jury that this blood could not have been planted. But it was planted! There was plenty of evidence to suggest that.

The drops were nice and circular – not the elongated splatter design one could expect if they had fallen from the hand of a tall man in motion across the room.

Furthermore, the drops were located immediately inside the door. That proved to me that they were planted; because the limo driver testified that O.J. and Kato had walked in and out through that door **three times**, carrying O.J.'s luggage and stuff like that, just before O.J. left in the limo. Besides, the limo driver, Allan Park, testified that he also walked inside O.J.'s door – out of curiosity, because he wanted to see the inside of the house of the famous O.J.

(•) It is impossible to imagine how these three men could have walked right over those blood drops – O.J. and Kato three

times each – without any of them stepping on the blood drops, even once!

Besides, if O.J. bled so profusely in his foyer, just minutes before leaving on his trip to Chicago, and just before carrying his luggage from the foyer to the limo – why were there no blood drops on his luggage, directly underneath the handles or carrying straps?

There is yet another thing that puzzles me about this so-called "trail of blood" that O.J., **allegedly**, should have left behind. We have proven, I trust, that O.J. could not have bled at Bundy, even if he were the murderer. So this "trail of blood" **must** have been planted or fabricated.

What is so interesting, however – if we consider that this trail of blood was planted or fabricated, partly by Detective Fuhrman after he had murdered Nicole and Ron, and partly by Detective Vannatter after he was convinced that O.J. were guilty – are **the particular places these blood drops were located.**

They were, allegedly, deposited at Bundy, as O.J. was walking away from the murder scene. Then in the Bronco, as he allegedly was driving back to Rockingham. Then in his driveway, as he allegedly was walking up to his door. And finally, in the foyer, right inside the door.

There, inside the door, O.J. were, allegedly, still bleeding so profusely that three blood drops fell to the floor right next to each other.

Then, however, mysteriously, the bleeding suddenly stopped. There were no blood drops leading up the stairs to O.J.'s bedroom, and no blood drops in his bedroom. The investigators claimed that there was blood residue in the sink's drain in the bathroom. However, the amount was too small to be tested. So this was just one of many such unsubstantiated allegations they "leaked" to the media.

(•) The thing that doesn't seem to make any sense is that there was **no blood leading up the stairs, and no blood in the rooms upstairs** – in particular, in O.J.'s bedroom. And there was no blood to and from the back of the house, where the glove was found.

If O.J. had an open cut on his finger, **the one time that cut should have bled more than ever, must have been in the bed-**

room, when O.J. lowered that finger almost to the floor, and bent and stretched that finger as he untied his shoe laces, and slipped his pants under his feet.

That would be the time when the cut would open up, and the blood would rush down into his hands, causing the alleged cut to bleed faster than ever.

Yet another time when the alleged cut would bleed more than normally would be when O.J. got out of the hot shower. The warm water would dissolve whatever crust might have started to form on that alleged cut. And the warm water would make O.J.'s blood rush to his skin, away from his internal organs, as a result of the body's natural, physiological temperature control.

Hence, returning to the bedroom after the shower, we should expect more blood than ever – at least if O.J. had bled so openly down in the foyer.

(•) As my readers remember, I have earlier discussed the inconsistency with respect to the rather heavy bleeding at Bundy, as well as at Rockingham – but the almost total lack of blood in the Bronco (less than 7/10 of one drop)!

(•) There were at least twice as many blood drops in O.J.'s driveway as there were at Bundy. If O.J. were the murderer, he must, in other words, have bled more and more, rather than less and less. Explain it if you can!

(•) There were some 25 or more drops of blood in the driveway, but not a single drop or trace of blood leading to or from the back of the house! Then the bleeding, allegedly, started again inside the foyer, but stopped abruptly as O.J. went upstairs!

–   Is there an explanation for this highly inconsistent bleeding pattern?
–   Is this explanation consistent with my theory that this so-called "trail of blood" was planted?

The answer to both questions is **yes!**

Let us consider that Detective Fuhrman, and later Detective Vannatter, planted and fabricated this so-called "trail of blood" leading from the victims' bodies, and into O.J.'s house! **Where** could Fuhrman, first of all, have planted blood – without exposing himself?

Remember that Fuhrman and Vannatter did not have access to O.J.'s blood – **yet.** And Fuhrman could not be absolutely sure that the investigators would swallow his "bait."

Both Fuhrman and Vannatter would have to use a "substitute" blood, temporarily, since the LAPD did not have access to O.J.'s real blood until after they received his blood vial! That is important!

Fuhrman would have to use Nicole's (or Ron's) blood as a substitute for O.J.'s blood (which he didn't have), for as far as it was conceivable that her blood could have reached.

We realize that **if this "trail of blood" had come from O.J.,** then it should have continued – in the form of blood **drops** – all the way from Bundy, **inside his Bronco**, in his driveway, **behind his house** to where the glove was found, **and back again**, inside his foyer, **up the stairs, and into his bedroom**.

However, if Fuhrman **planted part of this "trail of blood,"** by using Nicole's blood as a substitute – **hoping/trusting** that the investigators would later replace her blood with O.J.'s blood – then **Fuhrman's "trail of blood" had to stop at Bundy – or in O.J.'s driveway, if he used animal blood, or wrung a wet cloth with Nicole's blood on it in the driveway, when he returned with the other detectives later that night.**

(•) That's exactly what happened! It is striking, that this "peculiar bleeding pattern" is precisely what we could all observe!

In my opinion, that explains why O.J.'s (Nicole's) **"dripping"** blood, allegedly, was found at Bundy, near the victims, but not in the Bronco (just a smear, less than 7/10 of one drop, which could have been planted, or "replaced," weeks later).

It also explains why there was no blood leading to or from the back of O.J.'s house – **although O.J., allegedly, were still**

bleeding profusely, both in his driveway and inside his foyer!

You see, by the time Fuhrman got to Rockingham, he didn't have any dripping blood from the victims (Nicole), which he could plant there. And he did not have access to O.J.'s blood, of course. So Fuhrman's section of the "trail of blood" actually stopped at Bundy – at least right after the murders.

But Fuhrman had done what he set out to do. He had "set up" the investigators (Vannatter). They swallowed Fuhrman's "bait." They swallowed it – bait – hook – line – and fishing rod!

When Fuhrman told Vannatter he had seen blood in O.J.'s Bronco, and Fuhrman later showed the investigators the bloody glove behind O.J.'s house, **Vannatter was 110% convinced that O.J. were the murderer.**

So now Detective Vannatter took over the fabrication of the rest of "the trail of blood" – just as Fuhrman had expected!

As "substitute blood," Vannatter could use ketchup or "film blood" inside O.J.'s house. And he could use animal blood (or ketchup or film blood) in O.J.'s driveway – if Fuhrman hadn't already planted animal blood (or Nicole's blood) there.

Or Vannatter could use any number of substitutes he might know as being suitable for fabricating **temporary**, false blood evidence which could be recorded, photographed, and witnessed (Kato) while Vannatter still did not have O.J.'s real blood.

Even Vannatter – just as well as Fuhrman – could have wiped up some of Nicole's blood at Bundy on a piece of cloth, and used that as substitute blood in O.J.'s foyer and driveway. That would have been safe, because it was still plausible, with some stretch of imagination, that O.J. – if he were the murderer – had transferred Nicole's blood all the way to Rockingham.

Detective Vannatter was in a less precarious situation than Fuhrman with respect to evidence planting, because Vannatter would have the opportunity, later, to replace whatever substitute he used, with O.J.'s blood, after he received O.J.'s blood sample.

So now, I believe, Detective Vannatter – possibly encouraged by Fuhrman, who still hung around Rockingham the entire day, in spite of having been removed from the case – began fabricating false blood evidence against O.J.

Initially, Vannatter had to use a blood substitute, like ketchup, animal blood, or a cloth with Nicole's blood on it (moistened with distilled water), since he didn't have access to O.J.'s blood yet.

One can argue that Vannatter could not start planting blood evidence against O.J., since he didn't know if O.J. was cut or not. But that was the whole idea of using an appropriate "substitute blood."

If O.J. was not cut, the substitute blood would not expose Vannatter's evidence tampering, because the substitute blood was such as could normally be expected to be found at Rockingham – even if O.J. was innocent. I explain more about this in the chapter titled, "The Handcuffing Of O.J."

Vannatter's plan was to let the criminalists collect this "substitute blood" evidence. Then Vannatter would intercept it in the LAPD's crime lab, before it was packaged and sent away to outside, independent crime labs for DNA analyses.

Being the lead investigator, Vannatter could easily intercept the blood evidence and replace the "substitute blood" evidence with false, fabricated, EDTA free O.J. blood swatches, after he received a sample of O.J.'s blood.

I don't know what kind of "substitute blood" Vannatter used. But just for the sake of this argument, **let us imagine that he used something as conspicuous as ketchup.**

Don't argue that the criminalists must have seen the difference between ketchup and human blood! I just use ketchup as an example. Vannatter might as well have used animal blood or Nicole's blood. What substitute "blood" Vannatter used is irrelevant. I am just explaining the **method** at this point!

By the way, with respect to planting blood in the Bronco, Vannatter didn't have to worry about that. The Bronco would be impounded by the police. No outsiders (investigators for the defense) would be allowed to examine the Bronco until Vannatter gave permission. Hence, he could plant blood in the Bronco later. Besides, Fuhrman had already reported that there was blood in the

Bronco

With respect to the Bundy murder scene, Vannatter had already seen that there was an abundance of blood evidence there. If O.J.'s blood was not among the blood evidence at Bundy, he could surely replace some of that blood evidence with O.J.'s blood later – in the crime lab.

However, with respect to O.J.'s estate – and assuming that there wasn't any blood there originally – **Vannatter could not simply wait until he got O.J.'s blood sample,** and then begin to plant O.J.'s real blood everywhere – directly in his house, driveway and garden. He had to use a **"temporary blood substitute."**

Why? Because criminalists, police photographers, video cameramen, news reporters, as well as countless other "observers," would soon swarm all over O.J.'s estate. What if Vannatter planted blood somewhere, and photos proved, later, that there was no blood at that spot on the morning after the murders?

Vannatter had to plant a blood substitute, which could be recorded, photographed, collected, and sent to the crime lab. There, in the crime lab, Vannatter could intercept the "blood evidence" and replace it with O.J.'s blood – once he got a vial of O.J.'s blood.

(•)These facts led me to raise the following critical questions:

– If Vannatter didn't do this, because all the blood at Rockingham had indeed come from O.J. – then why did they **"set up"** Kato, so obviously?
– But more importantly, why was there **no blood on** the plush, **white carpe**t covering the stairway and the rooms upstairs – in particular on the carpet in O.J.'s bedroom? And why was there no blood on O.J.'s **luggage**, and no blood on the **ground** or on any of the **foliage** behind O.J.'s house – where the glove was found?

Those contradictions raised serious doubts in my mind about the blood having come from O.J. Were these discrepancies consistent with my theory, which suggested that the blood at Rockingham was planted and fabricated?

All of this has to do with the question of **where** Vannatter (and Fuhrman) **could** plant false blood evidence – if that's what he was doing – and **where** he **could not** plant false blood evidence!

What if Vannatter planted false "substitute blood," say **ketchup**, on the lacquered parquet floor in O.J.'s foyer? If so, the drops could be photographed and recorded. Later Vannatter could wipe away the ketchup with a wet paper towel and replace it with O.J.'s real blood. Or, he could let the criminalists collect the ketchup drops on swatches and bring them to the LAPD's crime lab. There, Vannatter could later replace the swatches with false, EDTA free O.J. blood swatches.

If the defense didn't trust this false blood evidence, they had no way of **double checking** on it by returning to O.J.'s foyer and wiping up residues from those ketchup drops (perhaps proving that this was not O.J.'s blood, after all) – **because the ketchup wasn't there any longer!**

So Vannatter, who temporarily had to use a "blood substitute," could plant this substitute blood in O.J.'s **foyer.**

Vannatter could also plant a blood substitute on the smooth cobblestones in O.J.'s **driveway,** because the blood could be completely collected from the smooth surfaces of the cobblestones in the driveway.

Furthermore, after the investigators and the criminalists had concluded their investigation, the driveway could be hosed down – if the rain hadn't already removed any remaining blood residues.

However, Vannatter could **not** plant his false "blood substitute" in the stairway or upstairs in O.J.s bedroom, because these areas were covered with plush white carpeting!

If Vannatter planted false blood substitute anywhere on the white carpet – and even if the criminalists cut out entire sections of O.J.'s carpet – there would always be some minor residues on those carpet sections, which the defense, later, could request to analyze separately for themselves.

Imagine this scandal: "Blood" drops, allegedly, were found on O.J.'s bedroom carpet. Blood swatches were prepared from the blood drops on the carpet. The blood swatches were sent to the

FBI for DNA analyses. The results proved that the blood contained O.J.'s DNA.

The defense, however, requested to perform an independent test on the "blood" residue on that carpet – and it turned out that the "blood" residue on the carpet did **not** contain O.J.'s DNA, but ketchup, or Nicole's DNA!

Do my readers see the situation Vannatter was faced with? What I have explained above was by no means a difficult problem to solve for Vannatter. But he had to consider **where** he decided to plant the temporary false "blood substitute" in the so-called "trail of blood"!

That's why there was such a peculiar inconsistency in the so-called "trail of blood"!

Judging from the appearance – and disappearance – of this "trail of blood," it seemed like O.J. had turned the periodically profuse bleeding "off and on" as if the alleged cut on his finger had a "faucet" on it!

In my opinion, the obvious explanation for the peculiar "bleeding pattern" is, rather, that **there was no "trail of blood"!** At Bundy the blood drops attributed to O.J., and which the criminalists collected at Bundy, had been planted by Fuhrman, using Nicole's blood. That's how far **"Fuhrman's trail of blood"** extended. Nor was there any "trail of blood" at Rockingham.

(•) The "blood" the criminalists collected at Rockingham was simply a totally disconnected and unrelated number of blood drops, planted where Vannatter or Fuhrman imagined O.J. could be suspected of having bled – but only at such locations where there was no chance of the defense being able to **double check remaining residues** of Vannatter's or Fuhrman's **"substitute bloods"**!

Do my readers see, just like I do, that as soon as we consider the possibility that O.J. is innocent, and that the evidence against him was fabricated, then **one peculiar thing after the other (dozens of them, in fact) – which we earlier could not explain or**

understand – suddenly make perfect sense!

Understanding this basic principle, we see that there were **only three places** (areas) in this entire, so-called "trail of blood" where Vannatter could **not** plant substitute blood.

One of these areas was on the carpet covering the stairway up to the second floor and in O.J.'s bedroom.

Had Vannatter planted, for instance, drops of Nicole's blood on the carpet, there would always be some residue from this substitute blood, which the defense might request to test later.

An other area was behind O.J.'s house. There the ground was covered with leaves. Substitute blood would have to be planted on these leaves. They would be identified, recorded, and collected. The criminalists could not wipe the blood off these leaves and onto blood evidence swatches. Had they done that, the old leaves would have broken into dust. (Note! On June 12 the leaves on the ground would be at least 7-8 months old, and dry and brittle). Any old leaves with substitute blood on them would have been collected as they were and kept in test tubes. And it would have been impossible to replace substitute blood on the leaves with real blood, in the crime lab, without destroying the leaves.

The third place where we should definitely have expected O.J.'s blood – if he, indeed, had left this "trail of blood" – was on his luggage, right underneath the handles. Strangely, also there O.J.'s blood was suspiciously absent!

Why couldn't Vannatter plant O.J.'s blood there? It was silly of me to ask! Of course, Vannatter didn't have access to the luggage – it was with O.J. in Chicago! Besides, if Vannatter plantet a blood substitute on the fabric of the luggage, also that blood substitute would leave some residue after the criminalists had collected their portion of that "blood."

(•) Hence, Vannatter could **not** plant "substitute blood" on the **leaves** behind O.J.'s house, nor in the **stairway** and in O.J.'s **bedroom** or on O.J.'s **luggage.**

Those were precisely the only places where the "trail of blood" was absent!

Everywhere else Vannatter and Fuhrman – independently of each other – **could plant a "trail of blood." That is precisely where the "trail of blood" was present!**

O.J.'s critics like to point to their so-called "mountain of evidence" and ask, how could there be **so many coincidences pointing to O.J.** – like the blood everywhere, his hairs on the cap, Bronco fibers on Ron's shirt and on the Rockingham glove, the cut on O.J.'s left finger, the victims' blood in the Bronco, the bloody shoeprints, etc. etc.

I trust my readers, long since, instead have begun asking themselves:

> (•) How can there be so **many coincidences pointing to evidence planting,** and evidence fabrication, unless all of this evidence was planted as part of a concerted effort to frame O.J.?

There are at least three times as many "mysterious coincidences" pointing to evidence fabrication and evidence planting, than coincidences pointing to O.J.'s guilt.

There is something flawed or suspicious about absolutely every single piece of evidence in this case!

People haven't seen the "big picture" earlier, because they haven't understood why and how Detective Fuhrman murdered Nicole and Ron and framed both O.J. and Vannatter. Once we understand that, all the many dozens of otherwise unexplainable details fit right in.

CHAPTER 40

O.J.'s Blood Vial
& The EDTA

I thank my readers for their patience. Finally, we have reached the discussion of O.J.'s blood vial and the EDTA.

Unquestionably, Detective Vannatter's handling of O.J.'s blood vial is one of the most important aspects of the entire Simpson case.

Except for Vannatter and a few other culprits (plus myself, of course) people have no idea what **really** happened to O.J.'s blood vial, and how it totally changed the aspect of the Simpson case.

Actually, O.J.'s blood vial could be the strongest evidence for **either side!** The problem for O.J., however, is that so far, the prosecution and the plaintiffs are the only ones who have taken advantage of it.

How is that possible? How can the **same** evidence be equally valuable to **both the opposing parties** in a criminal case? Well, let me give you one of my examples again. That will give you a chance to relax for a few minutes, before we get serious, since the example is completely **hypothetical.**

L et us say that some money was stolen from a company's safe. Apparently, the only person with access to the safe was the company's account executive, because she was the only one who had a key to the safe. Not even the president of the company had a key! Suspicion fell on the account executive. She was charged.

The account executive vehemently denied the charges and swore she was innocent. But nobody believed her, because everyone was convinced that she had the **only** key to the safe.

That made the account executive not only the prime suspect,

but the only suspect.

What people didn't know, however, was that the company's janitor one day had removed the key from the account executive's handbag for just 10 seconds, while she had stepped out of her office to get a cup of coffee.

The janitor, who had been looking for this opportunity for a long time, quickly made a **wax cast** of the key.

While on vacation in a far away state the janitor had a local locksmith there prepare a replica of the key to the safe. The locksmith knew that it was illegal for him to make the key without authorization from the legal owner of the safe the key belonged to.

But the janitor offered to pay the locksmith well, so he agreed to make the key. The locksmith asked for $1,500. After some bargaining they settled for $1,000. The janitor didn't have that much cash, so the locksmith accepted a check from the janitor.

During his lonely nightly rounds through the company building the janitor opened the safe, and stole thousands of dollars in cash on several occasions.

But here comes the account executive's **real** problem! When she first discovered that $2,000 was missing, she dared not tell the vice president, because she knew – or thought she knew – that she had the only key. She was responsible for the company's treasury. She believed she must have lost the money, somehow. She was afraid she would be fired, so she didn't tell anyone about the missing $2,000. However, she could not afford to replace it right away. She needed **time**, so she could save up $2,000 and put it **"back"** in the safe.

So then, she **altered the company books** to make it **appear that no money was missing**, while she began saving money to replace the $2,000 in one lump sum. Once she had replaced the $2,000 she would alter the books back again to cover up both transactions!

Next month, however, another $3,000 disappeared. Again, the account executive was afraid to tell the vice president, because by now she had altered the books to cover up the first $2,000! Her only choice seemed to be to alter the books again, to cover up the

$3,000, too! Which she did!

Next month, the janitor stole another $3,000.

Shortly thereafter, even before the account executive had noticed that the last $3,000 were missing, the company got **audited**! The account executive tried in vain to convince the board of executives that **she had not stolen the money – just altered the books!**

Of course, they didn't believe her!

She was fired and charged with grand theft and embezzlement. Lucky for her, one juror held out for a hung jury, and she was released.

The account executive continued to claim her innocence, but the entire town **knew** she was guilty and shunned her!

One day, the locksmith who had made the duplicate key for the janitor, read about the case in his local newspaper, which had picked up the syndicated story from a news agency. There was a picture with the article.

The picture showed the company's **new** account executive at his desk, with the safe in the background. However, next to the new account executive's desk was 3/4 of **the face of the janitor,** who just happened to lean forward and empty the wastebasket at the very instant when the picture was taken.

The locksmith immediately recognized the janitor, and put two and two together! Still in his workshop was the wax cast he had used eight months earlier when he made the false key for the janitor.

But even the locksmith had a problem! You see, he was on **parole** for assault! Furthermore, it was illegal for the locksmith to make that false key without an authorization from the legal owner of the safe. So the locksmith, if he came forward, would go back to prison to serve out his time. In addition he stood to lose his license as a locksmith, as well as being charged with conspiracy, or as an accomplice. He could even be sued by the company and held responsible for the company's loss.

I shall leave this story unfinished for a little while, as I continue! What I wanted to point out, however, was that it is possible for people to be innocent, even though all the evidence – and even the person's own actions – apparently indicate that the person is guilty.

Secondly, I wanted to point out that certain evidence may be interpreted **totally differently** – depending on the circumstances.

In the **absence** of the **wax cast and a copy of the janitor's check** to the locksmith – the **uniqueness** of the key to the safe was the strongest evidence **against** the account executive. With the – **apparently** – only key to the safe in her possession, she was the only suspect. The key was so unique that **no other key** could have opened the safe

However, in the **presence** of the **wax cast** and a copy of the **janitor's check** to the locksmith – the **uniqueness** of the key to the safe becomes the strongest evidence **in favor of** the account executive! Because what else could that wax cast have been used for, than to make a false key to the account executive's safe?

You see? Had the key to the safe been fairly **common** – perhaps fitting thousands of different locks – then the wax cast might have been for a key to any one of those other locks.

However, as it turned out, the **uniqueness of the key**, made it obvious that the wax cast must have been used to prepare a false key to this particular safe. The janitor's check made that even more obvious – and equally obvious, the janitor, who had ordered the false key had plenty of opportunity to rob the safe during his nightly rounds through the company's building.

As I said, the **uniqueness** of the key to the safe, could – under different circumstances – be, either the **worst** evidence **against** the account executive, or the **best** evidence in her favor!

Back to the Simpson case: From the perspective of the prosecutors and the plaintiffs, as well as in people's opinion – the **EDTA** in O.J.'s blood vial is the strongest evidence **against** O.J.

The reason is that people don't realize what **might** have happened – and most likely **did** happen – to O.J.'s blood vial.

That is Mark Fuhrman's best protection. Detective Vannatter plays the role of the locksmith – and Vannatter isn't talking, because he is in trouble too – just like the locksmith!

On the other hand, O.J.'s blood vial, and what happened to it, is also the strongest evidence **in favor of O.J.** – if we can unlock the **secrets** of that blood vial.

Back to our fictional story: Although the locksmith wasn't talking, a private detective suspected the janitor, because he had faith in the account executive, and **the janitor** seemed to be the **only possible** suspect – **if** the account executive was innocent.

The private detective – through his connections – obtained an unauthorized transcript of the janitor's bank statement!

The detective discovered that the janitor had made three large deposits, inconsistent with his salary – on dates corresponding to the times the account executive, according her testimony, had "discovered" that money was missing from the safe.

The detective believed he was on to something. He discovered the $1,000 check to "someone" out-of-state. More follow-up, and the detective learned that the recipient of the check was a locksmith, and a former convicted felon on parole.

Bingo! Case solved!

Again, back to the Simpson case: Also we can suspect what **really** happened to O.J.'s blood vial. And although Detective Vannatter isn't "talking," we may still come up with evidence of what he in fact did to O.J.'s blood vial. That is what this chapter is about. I believe it may open the eyes of a few of my readers who have been troubled by some of the blood evidence in this case.

> **The story of O.J.'s blood vial is much more serious than the prosecutors, the counsel for the plaintiffs, Judge Fujisaki, Detective Vannatter, the media, and most people made it out to be.**

Observing the bloody murder scene, every investigator on the Simpson case must have realized that the blood evidence would play a crucial role. Naturally, **the question of evidence tampering would come up sooner or later**. Anyone could have anticipated that. Therefore, there was absolutely **no reason to even accept** a blood sample from O.J. when he returned from Chicago.

O.J.'s blood would not be DNA analyzed for months. If the investigators wanted a preliminary blood type testing of O.J.'s blood, they might just as well have asked him or his doctor what his blood type was.

[Do you remember what I used the **bullets (•)**'s for? I said earlier that I would use them to represent something suspicious in relation to the blood evidence – like the peculiar bleeding pattern in the so-called "trail of blood", or the suspect manner in which the investigators drew Kato's attention to the so-called "blood" drops inside O.J.'s entrance door, etc., etc.]

(•) Having O.J.'s blood in a vial already on June 13, had absolutely no investigative value whatsoever. It could **only** serve one purpose – **evidence fabrication and evidence planting.**

Tactically, it was so outright stupid that **I can hardly imagine why experienced investigators could make such a blunder,** as to draw O.J.'s blood sample just hours after the murders, and at a time when most of the blood evidence had not yet been collected, and none of it had been analyzed.

The police should have waited a few days, or a week – or better still, they should have waited **8 weeks!** In other words, they should have waited until all the blood evidence had been collected, sent to the FBI's crime lab, or other crime labs, for DNA analyses – **and the results were in!**

Only then should the police have asked O.J. to volunteer some of his blood for reference and comparison. That way the LAPD could have eliminated any question regarding tampering with the blood evidence.

(•) **It is inconceivable that such a blunder was the result of**

mere stupidity. It must have been done on purpose. And the only purpose it could serve, was to provide the perfect **opportunity** for blood evidence tampering, fabrication, and planting.

I am sure my readers understand the points I am making. But now, consider what further happened to O.J.'s blood sample!

NOTE! Keep my earlier harsh criticism of Detective Vannatter's actions and his testimonies in mind!

Obviously, any investigator should know that in order to eliminate the suggestion from the defense, that blood had been planted, it was **vital** that the suspects blood sample was handled extremely carefully, and **strictly according to police instructions.** Of course, under no circumstances whatsoever must the suspect's blood sample be brought to the crime scenes! You don't have to be an investigator even, to realize that!

Police instructions require that the blood vial immediately be sealed in a special, dated blood vial envelope, to be **booked in as evidence without delay.**

In this case there was an evidence locker in the same building as the nurse's office, and there was a crime lab only two blocks away.

O.J.'s blood vial could have been booked in, minutes after it was drawn. The police nurse was a sworn police officer. He could have booked it in.

(•) Yet, neither the police nurse, nor Detective Vannatter, who was there, booked in O.J.'s blood vial!

An "excuse" frequently presented by Detective Vannatter, as to why he brought the vial to Rockingham, was that he wanted to give it to Criminalist Fung, so that Fung could book it in. The peculiar justification for this being that Fung, who was the person who assigned the particular evidence numbers to the various pieces of evidence, could book in the blood vial, and at the same time assign it a particular evidence number which corresponded to the chronological order in which the blood vial was collected – or something like that!

It is not easy to understand Vannatter when he tries to explain away what he was doing throughout this case. But I think this is what he said – or meant to say! In other words, he wanted the blood vial to have an evidence number, or a booking number, **# 17**, which indicated **what time** it was obtained, compared to the other pieces of evidence that were collected.

Again, I must appeal to my readers. **Isn't Vannatter's excuse ridiculous?** It was a lame attempt to explain why he did not book in O.J.'s blood vial right away.

O.J.'s vial was a **totally independent reference sample** that did not belong together with the actual evidence collected at the crime scenes. If the police had received O.J.'s blood sample an hour earlier, the vial might have received a different number, perhaps. Had they received it three days later, the vial would have been assigned yet a different number.

Had O.J. refused to give the police his blood sample, and the issue had gone through the Court of Appeals, they might not have received his blood sample for several months, in which case the blood vial would have received, perhaps, the very last evidence number assigned in the case. This would have had no effect on any of the other evidence in the case, or on the organization and interpretation of that evidence.

(•) Another excuse Detective Vannatter frequently presented on TV talk shows, was that he put O.J.'s blood vial in his pocket – to *"protect the chain of custody."* I am sure those of my readers who followed the Simpson saga on TV, have heard Vannatter say this many times. But what could **"protect the chain of custody"** better than if Detective Vannatter, or the nurse, had **booked in** the vial **immediately** – as Vannatters instructions required that he **should have done!**? Would O.J.'s blood vial be **less safe behind locked doors in the LAPD's crime lab, than in Vannatter's pocket** on his way to Rockingham?

How much nonsense shall we hear from Detective Vannatter? Besides, what was so important about **"the chain of custody"** for O.J.'s blood vial. Suppose the vial got lost or broken! So what? All the LAPD had to do, was to get another vial of O.J.'s blood a few days later.

There could never have been a strict priority to protect the chain of custody for O.J.'s vial. There was EDTA in the vial, which should show up if the blood from the vial was planted somewhere – the invetigators could always get more of O.J.'s blood if they neeeded to – and no one could alter O.J.'s DNA, regardless of how hard they tried, or how much of his blood they requested.

(•) Vannatter's excuse for bringing O.J.'s blood vial to to his office for 90 minutes, and on to Rockingham, was nothing but a blatant lie.

How many times Detective Vannatter lied in this case has become an impossible task to keep track of!

But there is more to this! Vannatter, allegedly, brought the vial to Rockingham, so he could give it to Criminalist Fung, immediately, so that Fung could give O.J.'s vial its **proper** – and allegedly, so **vital – evidence booking # 17.**

Vannatter gave the vial to Fung, allegedly. Did Fung mark it down with evidence number 17? No! Fung brought O.J.'s vial home with him! The vial wasn't booked in until 24 hours later!

By that time Detective Lange had already booked in O.J.'s tennis shoes with evidence number 17 – although the tennis shoes were collected later than O.J.'s blood reference sample (the vial)!

So, therefore, O.J.'s blood vial received evidence number 18, or a higher number – which, of course, contradicted the chronological order Detective Vannatter, during his later testimony, referred to as being so vital!

(•) Suddenly, Vannatter's "excuse" for bringing O.J.'s blood vial to Rockingham fell apart!

To repair Vannatter's explanation, and make it appear that Vannatter had brought O.J.'s blood vial to Rockingham so it could be given its **"chronologically correct"** evidence booking **number (#17)** – Fung ordered his assistant Ms. Andrea Mazzola to **erase** the **"#18,"** for the vial, on the official document, and write **"#17"** instead, to make it appear that O.J.'s blood vial was booked in before the tennis shoes! Otherwise Vannatter's explanation for bringing O.J.'s vial to Rockingham would appear to be sheer nonsense – which it was under any circumstances!

> Dear America: Please be real! Lead investigators, criminalists, and prosecutors don't do this kind of stuff, and lie about it so vehemently, unless they are trying to **cover up** some serious misconduct – or even criminal action!

O.J.'s defense attorneys, or we, may not understand **why** they are lying so blatantly, and altering official documents to cover it up. But there must be a reason for it! And the reason must be pretty serious! But this thing is far from over:

The special **"blood vial envelopes"** to be used for blood reference samples have an extra strong seal, which would have to be broken when the vial is removed from the envelope – thereby exposing that the envelope, indeed, had been opened.

(•) Instead of placing O.J.'s blood vial in a prescribed **new** blood vial envelope – and seal it properly – the nurse and Vannatter put O.J.'s blood vial in a **used, unsealable envelope**!

The envelope had been used – sealed and opened again earlier. Its seal was broken. Hence, it was impossible to prove whether or not Detective Vannatter, too, opened that envelope in his office, after he received O.J.'s blood vial from the nurse!

> (•) **Is anyone going to tell me that the police nurse at the second largest police department in the nation, gradually ran lower and lower on his stock of specified blood vial envelopes, and that he didn't reorder a new box of envelopes, or went and picked one up, until he had used the very last envelope in the box?**
>
> **And even then, when the box was empty, he didn't fetch another box, but instead simply resorted to using old, previously used, regular business envelopes for blood evidence in high profile murder cases!**

It is an insult to our intelligence for the police nurse and Detective Vannatter to even **think** that we could be made to believe that!

(•) Detective Vannatter who had no business even touching O.J.'s blood vial – since he was headed for Rockingham – requested that he be given the blood vial. Then he proceeded to put O.J.'s blood vial in his pocket and drove 25 miles to O.J.'s house with it!

This stinks! For the lead investigator to act like this in the most high profile murder case of the century, is so outrageous that I am stumped for words to characterize such lack of judgement.

(•) I find no possible – reasonable – explanations for this. I must state categorically that the police nurse and Detective Vannatter deliberately acted as they did, in preparation for evidence tampering and evidence fabrication.

If Philip Vannatter wants to refute my theory in a court of law – let him! I'll be there!

Lack of personnel, lack of time – it doesn't matter. If the investigators receive the suspects blood sample, just hours after a double murder – the correct handling of that blood sample takes priority over any other matter.

One of the crime scenes is the absolute last place the suspects blood vial should be taken – under any circumstances!

Bring the vial to the moon! Bring it to China! Bring it to Disneyland! Or book it in, of course!

But regardless of the circumstances – **don't bring the suspects blood vial to the crime scenes!**

(•) Still, that's exactly what Detective Vannatter did. And he did it on purpose! He wanted O.J.s blood vial, so he could plant O.J.'s blood everywhere he felt that it was needed, in order to secure a conviction of O.J.! There is no other logical explanation.

Detective Vannatter, the prosecutors, District Attorney Gil Garcetti, Judge Ito, Judge Fujisaki, the counsels for the plaintiffs, and the media, can scream and holler all they want. It doesn't make a bit of difference. Detective Vannatter took control of O.J.'s blood vial when he shouldn't have. And in spite of being right next to the crime lab and the evidence locker, he didn't book in the blood vial, as his police instructions require that he should have done.

Instead he brought O.J.'s blood vial 25 miles farther away from the crime lab – to O.J.'s house.

The only possible reason was to fabricate false blood evidence against O.J.

Give me one other plausible explanation, and I might reconsider. But I haven't heard such a plausible explanation yet.

Regardless of the circumstances, Detective Vannatter was asked by Defense Counsel Robert Baker **why he didn't seal the envelope** containing O.J.'s blood vial, **before** driving to Rockingham and giving it to Fung.

You see, somewhere along the way Vannatter obtained a sealable envelope for O.J.'s blood vial (which makes it even more suspect that the nurse didn't seal O.J.'s blood vial envelope right away – before giving it to Detective Vannatter).

Vannatter answered, **under oath,** that since he was giving the vial to Fung, so Fung could book it in – **Fung needed to see** that the envelope, indeed, contained O.J.'s blood vial!

How much "bull" do we have to hear from Vannatter's mouth before the American people realize that this man is a habitual liar who planted all the blood evidence against O.J.!

(•) Is **the LAPD's lead homicide investigator** telling us, **under oath**, that **if** he handed a <u>sealed</u> envelope to his lead criminalist, Mr. Fung, saying,

"This is O.J.'s blood vial, which I just picked up at the police nurse's office. Please book it in for me!"

– then Criminalist Fung would have had to <u>tear open</u> that envelope to make sure that his lead investigator wasn't bluffing or lying!

Perhaps Criminalist Fung knows his boss better than most of us!

Detective Vannatter, and everyone who ever laid their hands or eyes on O.J.'s blood vial have gotten themselves entangled in such a web of lies and contradictions that they simply can't escape their own testimonies.

Every time they are impeached, they must concoct new lies, creating new contradictions.

By recounting what these investigators have testified to under oath, with respect to O.J.'s blood vial – any normally intelligent person should understand that all the blood evidence against O.J. must have been fabricated from his blood vial.

Maybe we cannot **prove** how they fabricated the blood evidence against O.J. Maybe we don't even **understand** how they did it. **But they did it! Their lies prove it!**

The media keep telling us that since O.J. testified in the civil trial, that he never hit Nicole – while other witnesses claimed that was a lie – O.J. must be guilty of double murder!

Why don't the media apply the same standards to the lead investigator, Detective Philip Vannatter, who lied about almost everything he did – from his motive for driving to Rockingham on the night of the murders; on his affidavit in connection with his entering O.J.'s estate without a search warrant; and right up to his testimony in the civil trial regarding his handling of O.J.'s blood vial?

Why don't the media apply the same standards to Detective Vannatter as they apply to O.J., and conclude that Vannatter planted the blood evidence against O.J. – from O.J.'s blood vial – and if he denies it, he shouldn't be trusted, because he lied about everything – every time he opened his mouth in this case?

Detective Vannatter, the other investigators, the former Simpson prosecutors, the counsels for the plaintiffs, and the media keep arguing that the blood in O.J.'s blood vial contained EDTA – the preservative. If Detective Vannatter, or someone else, planted blood from the vial, that blood would contain EDTA.

Except for the blood drops on the rear gate at Bundy, no EDTA was found in any of the blood evidence attributed to O.J. Therefore, the prosecutors and the media argued, the blood could not have been planted. It must have come from O.J.'s body directly. So, O.J. must be guilty.

However, except for the blood on the rear gate, **none of the other blood evidence attributed to O.J. was tested for EDTA.**

> It is one of the greatest misconseptions of this case – that there was no EDTA in the blood attributed to O.J. The truth is that of all the blood evidence attributed to O.J. only the blood from the rear gate was tested for EDTA – **and that blood contained EDTA!**

The prosecution and O.J.'s adversaries in the media gave the American public the impression that there was no EDTA in the rest of the blood evidence attributed to O.J. Consequently, the majority of the people thought the five blood drops next to the bloody shoeprints at Bundy could not possibly have been planted or fabricated. Hence, that blood evidence alone – in most people's opinions – was more than enough to find O.J. guilty of double homicide.

It didn't matter, they argued, whether or not Detective Vannatter brought O.J.'s blood vial to Rockingham, since no EDTA was found in the bood evidence – except in the blood on the rear gate.

Of course, the prosecutors and the media **should, instead, have told** the American people that the investigators blocked the defense from testing the blood for EDTA, by demanding that the blood be **DNA tested instead**. Since the EDTA testing spoils the blood for DNA testing, they could only do one or the other.

To the best of my knowledge **only two** blood evidence samples were tested for EDTA: **O.J.'s blood on the rear gate**, and **Nicole's blood on O.J.'s sock.**

(•) Both items tested positive for EDTA – **proving that both**

were planted or fabricated! No wonder the investigators and the prosecutors blocked any further EDTA testing of the blood evidence!

The situation was comparable to that of a supermarket manager who checks out his apples to see if they are fresh or rotten. He cuts one apple in two. It is all brown and mushy inside, and there are worms crawling everywhere. Disgusted, but not discouraged, the manager cuts open a second apple – same thing!

Does the manager throw out the entire batch? No! Rather, **he stops checking!**

Minutes later a young mother considers buying some of the apples for her children. But first she asks the manager if the apples are good.

"Yes," the manager replies, *"we just checked them, and threw out the ones we found to be bad."*

How do my readers feel about this supermarket manager? Regardless, that's how you should feel about the investigators, prosecutors, and media, too, when it comes to their presentation of the blood evidence in the Simpson case. Like the supermarket manager they argued:

*"We checked **some** of the blood evidence for EDTA. But we haven't found any EDTA in the **rest** of the blood evidence."*

Of course not – because they didn't check the rest of the blood evidence for EDTA.

The way O.J.'s adversaries cheated and lied in this case is just out of this world. But the media is equally responsible for this travesty of justice – since the media perpetuated these lies through their support of the prosecution and the plaintiffs throughout the criminal and the civil trials, and even today.

(•) There is another suspicious little detail, worth mentioning, in connection with the issue of EDTA testing versus DNA testing.

Of course, as the investigators and the prosecutors argued, wherever they could do only one or the other, the DNA testing had to be given priority. So, when they only had five drops of blood along the bloody shoeprints, for instance – and they didn't know if all five of them came from the same person – they had to DNA test all five drops, in which case they could not EDTA test them.

This argument is "bull"! But anyway, let's accept that. However, there was another area, where there was an **abundance** of blood drops – namely in O.J.'s driveway. Actually, there were as many as 25 blood drops or more in the drive way. (Whoever planted these blood drops wanted to create a "trail of blood" all the way from O.J.'s Bronco, and up to his entrance door!).

In other words, this could have been a place where the investigators could have tested at least some of the drops for EDTA. Agree?

So how did Vannatter assure himself that even with this abundance of blood drops, none of them would be tested for EDTA?

Would you believe this? Detective Vannatter **ordered** Criminalist Fung to collect only a couple of samples of these 25 or more blood drops, and **ignore the rest**!

I mean, this case – and Vannatter's handling of it – is totally out of this world!

Back to Vannatter and O.J.'s blood vial. It didn't matter if Vannatter brought the vial to Rockingham, the prosecution argued. Because there was no EDTA in the blood evidence attributed to O.J. – except for the blood on the rear gate.

That is the issue we shall deal with now. I shall explain that even if they were right, and there was no EDTA in the blood evidence attributed to O.J., this blood evidence could still have been fabricated by Detective Vannatter and his colleagues – and there was plenty of circumstantial evidence to suggest that they did fabricate it.

Was it possible for Detective Vannatter to circumvent the EDTA in O.J.'s blood vial, and thereby extract from that vial a quantity of O.J.'s EDTA free blood?

It was possible! There is a "mountain of evidence" to suggest that Vannatter did just that! In the following I shall explain how Detective Vannatter might have managed to obtain **the EDTA**

free blood he wanted, for all purposes.

EDTA vials contain EDTA – a powdered preservative to prevent the blood from coagulating or getting contaminated. A purple rubber cap seals the vial, and at the same time indicates that the vial contains EDTA – even after the EDTA is invisible because it has been dissolved and mixed with the blood.

The EDTA is **not** applied to the blood by the nurse **after** the blood has entered the vial. The EDTA powder is **already present** in the bottom of the vials as they arrive, sterile, from the pharmaceutical manufacturer.

The subject's blood is drawn into a syringe. From the syringe it is transferred to the vial. Once inside the vial the blood gradually dissolves the EDTA and gets mixed with it. To speed up this process one may **shake the blood vial vigorously.** Actually, the person preparing an EDTA vial is **supposed to shake the vial** vigorously, according to police instructions.

Once the blood and the EDTA are mixed, the EDTA follows any portion of that blood, wherever it goes.

Nobody, to my knowledge has suggested any method to circumvent the EDTA in a blood vial, once the blood has entered that vial.

- That is why the majority of the population honestly believe that O.J. must have deposited the five blood drops next to the bloody shoeprints at Bundy.
- And that is the main reason they believe O.J. murdered Nicole and Ron.
- And that is why they are so angry with him today.

It all hinges on people's inability to understand how easily this blood could have been fabricated – and still not contain EDTA.

The prosecutors, the plaintiffs and the rest of O.J.'s adversaries say it is impossible. And most people believe them. O.J.'s defense attorneys and investigators have not been able to explain this, either.

So those who think they understand this EDTA thing, are

convinced O.J. is a murderer.

And those who don't care about the EDTA, and simply argue that the entire case against O.J. was suspect, and that all the evidence was fabricated – regardless of how it was done – they believe he is innocent.

Hopefully, when I explain how Vannatter managed to circumvent the EDTA, more people will realize that O.J. is innocent. Hopefully, they will realize that this case does not stand or fall on the five blood drops at Bundy, **and understand that more attention should be given to the evidence which, irrefutably, proves that someone was trying to frame O.J.**

Already in the procedure for preparing an EDTA vial lies the possibility of blood evidence tampering. Suppose the nurse drew 10 ml (ml = milliliter = cc) of O.J.'s blood into the syringe, but subsequently transferred just 8 ml of that blood to the EDTA vial. He would then have a syringe with 2 ml of O.J.'s EDTA free blood – which he could hand over to Detective Vannatter, who, again, could use that EDTA free blood to plant O.J.'s EDTA free blood anywhere, or to fabricate false blood evidence swatches with O.J.'s EDTA free blood on them.

I shall outline another very simple method by which Detective Vannatter could have circumvented the EDTA. The method required the cooperation of the police nurse. In that case we are talking about a small "conspiracy" between Vannatter and the police nurse.

There are strong reasons to believe that the nurse was more than willing to assist Detective Vannatter in circumventing the EDTA. I will discuss that in the next chapter. But I mention it now, anyway, just in case some of my readers doubt that the police nurse would be willing to assist Vannatter in this matter.

The LAPD was notoriously infamous for fabricating and planting false evidence. **The ultimate false evidence, obviously, must have been EDTA free blood from a suspect's EDTA vial!**

As frequently as the police fabricated false evidence, I find it most likely that the LAPD investigators had given quite a bit of thought to the problem of circumventing the EDTA in EDTA vials. Because if they solved **that** problem, they could pretty much nail any suspect involved in a bloody crime.

Accordingly, I find it highly probable that Vannatter could have had an ongoing **"EDTA-conspiracy"** with the police nurse. You know, over a 27 year career you do tend to loosen up and get more intimate with some of the colleagues you work with on a daily basis.

Perceivably, Vannatter and the nurse could have figured out the following method for circumventing the EDTA **– to be used whenever Vannatter felt that he needed to do it!**

A rriving at the police nurse's office O.J. had no idea what a proper EDTA vial look like. He would however, be able to describe it afterwards, as well as explain to his attorneys the procedures the nurse had followed.

This would make it appear to any "outsider" that correct procedures were followed, and that the EDTA, unquestionably, could not have been circumvented.

Assuming Vannatter and the nurse conspired, and that they had done this before, **this is the "secret method" I believe they used in the Simpson case:**

Alone in his office, the nurse removes the **purple EDTA rubber cap** from an EDTA vial. Then he **cleans out the EDTA powder** from the inside of the vial.

This vial will now consist of a **clear, transparent** test tube, and a **purple "EDTA rubber cap."**

This fake EDTA vial has no EDTA in it, only a purple rubber cap! For someone without professional knowledge of blood vials, this fake vial is absolutely indistinguishable from a real EDTA vial.

This fake, **EDTA free** vial may be **reused** as many times as Detective Vannatter and the nurse may choose to use it. After each use, the nurse simply cleans out the blood residue and dries the fake EDTA vial. Then it is ready to be used again.

The fake EDTA (free) vial is put back in the box with other unused, **real** EDTA vials, but in such a fashion that the nurse easily recognizes it – for instance, by placing it in the opposite direction of all the other – **real** – EDTA vials.

Back to the Simpson case: Vannatter calls the nurse in advance and informs him that the Simpson case is a case where they need **their "special," fake, EDTA free vial!** At the same time, over the phone, Vannatter gives the nurse the necessary data on O.J. and the case, so the nurse can prepare the appropriate **label** on a **real** EDTA vial! Yes, on a **real** EDTA vial!

The office of the police nurse, Monday June 13, 1994 at 2:15 pm – enter Vannatter and O.J.:

Vannatter and the nurse shake hands. The nurse secretly hands Vannatter the **pre-labelled, real – but empty – EDTA vial!** Vannatter puts it in his pocket!

Now the nurse turns to O.J. and introduces himself. The two men shake hands. Then the nurse takes out the **fake, EDTA** free vial.

In front of O.J. the nurse prepares a label for the vial. Next he asks O.J. to roll up his sleeve for the extraction of his blood. The nurse enters the needle of the syringe into O.J.'s vein and draws **8.0 ml** of O.J.'s blood into the syringe. Then he transfers the blood from the syringe to the **fake EDTA free vial!**

O.J.'s blood enters the vial. Conspicuously in front of O.J., the nurse lays down the empty syringe, puts the purple rubber cap back on the (fake) vial, and then **shakes the fake EDTA vial vigorously in front of O.J.'s eyes!**

O.J. will, of course, remember this. To any outsider, **it appears that his blood vial was correctly prepared, and that his blood was immediately mixed with the EDTA!**

But there was no EDTA in that vial!

The nurse puts the vial in the **old, used** envelope that can not be properly sealed. He hands the envelope to Detective Vannatter, who puts **also this vial** in his pocket.

O.J. is released, and drives home (or wherever), while Detetive Vannatter brings O.J.'s fake blood vial, as well as **the new unused, empty, and correctly labelled real EDTA vial** – to his office.

In his office, Vannatter opens up both vials. Then he pours 6.5 ml – of the 8.0 ml – of blood into the real EDTA vial he received from the nurse. Vannatter puts the caps back on both vials. He shakes the real EDTA vial, and places it in the open EDTA vial envelope.

Detective Vannatter now has one **official** real EDTA vial with 6.5 ml of O.J.'s blood mixed with EDTA, and – **one unofficial, fake, EDTA free vial with 1.5 ml of O.J.'s EDTA free blood!**

From this blood he can now prepare as many false **EDTA free "O.J. blood swatches"** as he wants to (at least 30, if necessary).

Now tell me! That was not so difficult to figure out, was it? At least, it was easy to understand, I assume.

There is strong evidence to suggest that Detective Vannatter did this, alone in his office, **during the ninety minutes he could not account for**, and which he, during the criminal trial, repeatedly lied about under oath.

Let me mention some of this (circumstantial) evidence, simultaneously explaining in some detail how Vannatter proceeded to manufacture the false blood swatches – and why he had to do it in a particular manner.

First Vannatter poured some of the EDTA free blood out on his desk, on a piece of plastic. He smeared it out. Then he took out two dozen new, unused blood evidence swatches and a bottle of distilled water. By the way, **all the LAPD's homicide detectives have evidence collection kits containing blood swatches and distilled water,** since the detectives themselves sometimes have to collect blood evidence at various crime scenes.

Vannatter moistened the swatches with distilled water. This is correct procedure for preparing blood evidence swatches.

The reason he did that, even though the blood was still wet, is that even wet blood is **absorbed** differently into, a wet cotton fabric swatch, than into a dry one – and blood **spreads** differently over a dry swatch than a wet one.

Forensic experts might have uncovered that Vannatter's swatches had been incorrectly prepared, had he **not** moistened them. Out at the crime scenes, the criminalists moistened **their** swatches before wiping up blood evidence. Vannatter had to do the same.

There has been a widespread tendency to underestimate Detective Vannatter. Don't make that same mistake! Vannatter did not become the LAPD's lead homicide investigator by being stupid!

Eventually, Vannatter had two dozen wet blood swatches on his desk.

Normally, blood evidence swatches should be allowed to dry overnight in separate glass test tubes, to reduce the risk of contamination. As my readers may know, bacteria grow and spread faster in wet, than dry materials.

But Vannatter could not leave them there to dry overnight and drive to Rockingham. What if someone entered his office and saw all the blood swatches while he was gone? Besides, he did not have two dozen test tubes in his office.

Accordingly, **Vannatter needed to put the wet swatches in individual paper "bindels" right away, and shove all the bindels into a larg business envelope or plastic bag which he could put in his briefcase, before driving to Rockingham.**

(•) Since the swatches were wet, however, some of them caused **wet blood transfers onto the bindel papers.**

Let me explain what **"bindels"** are. They are papers used to protect the blood swatches. The swatch is placed on the bindel paper, which is then folded in three, both vertically and horizontally, over the swatch. Then the criminalist initials the bindel. Finally the bindel is put in a **coin envelope.**

The coin envelope is not sealed, because several labs may eventually perform tests on the same swatch, and we don't want them to have to **destroy** the coin envelope to remove the bindel. We want the original coin envelope preserved, since it contains vital information about the evidence inside it.

Back to Vannatter's office. He had to put his two dozen wet swatches in bindels right away.

(•) That's why there were wet blood transfers – that should normally not have been there – on the bindel papers of some of the evidence bindels the various outside crime labs received.

And that again is what the renown criminalist, Dr. Henry Lee referred to when he stated his famous words: *"Something is wrong!"*

Furthermore, all the bindels with "mysterious" blood transfers on them, were among the bindles **allegedly** containing **O.J.'s blood – collected at Bundy!**

Someone might suggest that Vannatter could have avoided this problem, by simply replacing the swatches themselves, only – after they had dried – **and not the bindel papers.** But again, I have to remind you, that Vannatter is the LAPD's lead homicide investigator. **Vannatter is not stupid!**

Let's assume, for some reason or another, that the real blood swatches which Criminalist Andrea Mazzola collected at Bundy, were not completely dry by the time **she** put them in **her** bindel papers the next morning! Suppose **her** swatches, too, had caused some minute, **almost invisible** blood transfers onto her bindel papers. Vannatter couldn't know that.

If Vannatter then, had replaced **only the swatches**, and not the entire bindels, the forensic scientists at Cellmark's lab or FBI's lab in Washington, might have found themselves looking at

> **O.J.'s blood** on a certain blood swatch – but **Nicole's blood** in a blood transfer on the bindel paper belonging to that swatch!
>
> If so, the prosecutors could have shut their briefcases and gone home!
>
> And Vannatter and possibly other LAPD investigators would be facing a major scandal – and probably many years in prison.

What I have explained above, are the reasons why Vannatter had to put his false O.J. swatches in bindel papers **while they were still wet.**

(•) That again, explains Dr. Henry Lee's serious problem – *"Something is wrong!"*

What I have explained above, is also the reason why Vannatter had to replace not only the swatches, but the **entire bindels**, wherever he made this forgery.

(•) That again, explained why **Ms. Mazzola's initials seemed to have disappeared – mysteriously – from some of her bindels.** (Of course, Vannatter could not risk forging her handwriting).

Through this simple forgery, made possible by the very simple, and absolutely undetectable, **method of circumventing the EDTA** in O.J.'s blood vial, **Detective Vannatter could plant as much false O.J. blood evidence as he wanted – everywhere he wanted – without even stepping out of his office or the LAPD's crime lab.**

To any normally intelligent human being, it would appear impossible for anyone to have **planted** or **fabricated** the five blood drops found next to the bloody shoeprints at Bundy – whether they contained EDTA or not:

– The blood drops could not have been **planted** – because they were photographed and collected before the LAPD even

had O.J.'s blood sample.
– The blood drops could not have been **fabricated** either, because if so, they **must** have been fabricated with blood from O.J.'s blood vial – and that blood vial contained EDTA!

As I have explained earlier, the great public misconception was that the five blood drops from Bundy did not contain EDTA. That is not necessarily true, because that blood evidence was never tested for EDTA. However, this misconception made no difference, because the prosecutors and the media, as well as O.J.'s adversaries among legal analysts on TV spread this misconception every opportunity they got. So the public **believed** those five blood drops did not contain any EDTA.

This false evidence – the five blood drops that allegedly were found next to the bloody shoeprints at Bundy – was so strong that the investigators, prosecutors, and plaintiffs have even been able to **flaunt** it – to the media, as well as to O.J. and his attorneys.

Seemingly, the investigators had, at least, one piece of evidence against O.J. – a most incriminating piece of evidence – which **irrefutably** could **not possibly** have been fabricated, and which **tied O.J. to the murder scene by his own blood.**

Now, hopefully, my readers know better!

The lead investigator in the Simpson case, Detective Vannatter, ended up with 1.5 ml of O.J.'s EDTA free blood in a separate container, while the other 6.5 ml of O.J.'s blood was correctly preserved with EDTA in a real EDTA blood vial.

The method was so simple that it wasn't even funny. Until now, nobody – except the culprits themselves, and I – seem to have figured out how Vannatter did it!

Just because **they** didn't understand how Vannatter could have done it – Geraldo Rivera, Charles Grodin, almost the entire media, and 75 % of the American people, thought it could not be done. Consequently, they would have been willing to send O.J. to prison for the rest of his life, based on such falsely fabricated evidence!

I am shocked!

After all, or most, of the blood evidence had been collected, but before it had been packaged and processed to be shipped to various crime labs, Detective Vannatter went to the LAPD's serology room or evidence room one night when nobody was there. The door was locked with a card key lock. So Vannatter either went there with an accomplice who had the card key, or he borrowed one – unless he had his own card key.

Actually, there was nothing wrong or suspicious about the lead investigator wanting to take a look at the evidence in the case, to see what evidence the investigators had so far, to coordinate it and organize it, and thereby decide what further investigative actions to initiate.

Whatever, Detective Vannatter ended up, by himself, together with most of the blood evidence. Being the lead investigator, Vannatter knew exactly where each piece of blood evidence had been collected.

So Vannatter simply decided where he thought it would be **"good for the investigation"** if O.J.'s blood would be found. Then he made sure it was found there!

Let us say, Vannatter wanted a certain blood drop that was collected at Bundy, to appear to be O.J.'s! Let's assume the swatch from that blood drop was given the number **"47"**! The lead investigator, Detective Vannatter, would know that! So he simply opened up coin envelope #47, containing that blood swatch. Then he took out the bindel with the swatch in it. He picked one of his own bindels with a false, EDTA free O.J. blood swatch inside, and put it into the coin envelope.

> **Regardless of whom the blood drop #47 originally belonged to, Vannatter had made sure – from now on – it could, apparently, only have come from O.J.!**

All the talk about DNA, the probability being *"170 million to 1"* that this blood was O.J.'s, and statements like that, were totally meaningless!

Of course, the blood was O.J.'s! Detective Vannatter had made certain that it was – behind the locked door to his office and in the LAPD's crime lab!

There was no conspiracy. Vannatter could have fabricated and planted **all the blood evidence** against O.J. – all by himself – in a matter of 15 minutes!

It is not a question of **whether or not** the blood is O.J.'s. Nor is it a question of DNA analyses procedures, or of contamination in the crime labs. **It is O.J.'s blood!** The question is:

- Did Ms. Mazzola collect that blood at Bundy?
- **Or did Detective Vannatter replace the blood from Bundy, with his false EDTA free O.J. blood swatches?**

Remember all of Vannatter's lies, in his effort to hide what he was doing in his office during the one and a half hours after he received O.J.'s blood vial from the nurse. **Then consider this!**

(•) During cross examination by the defense, Ms. Mazzola was asked repeatedly if she initialed all her bindels. She confirmed it, and **reconfirmed** it.

When the bindels Ms. Mazzola prepared with the blood evidence swatches from Bundy, arrived at the outside crime labs, **her initials had disappeared from several of the bindels that allegedly contained O.J.'s blood!**

How can there be any stronger proof that Vannatter had **replaced** her bindels with his false O.J. bindels? Vannatter could not falsify Ms. Mazzola's **initials**, so he just left his bindels **without** initials.

Immediately the prosecution went to work with **"damage control"**!

The prosecutor did not **dare** recall Ms. Mazzola to the witness stand right away, for re-direct examination. Ms. Mazzola had just told the court that she initialed **all** her bindels. **What if she stood by her statement on re-direct! The scandal would be complete.**

(•) So the prosecution "cleverly" **requested a recess**. In their office, the prosecutors gave Ms. Mazzola a "work-over," basically telling her that she **had** to change her story – if she had any desire to continue as an LAPD criminalist!

The **next** day they called her back on redirect. **Now, Ms. Mazzola was no longer absolutely 100% sure, that she initialed each and every one of her bindels!**

Again, I am shocked by how the prosecutors operated in their **conspiracy** to convict O.J.!

Since the defense, of course, could not prove that Ms. Mazzola indeed had remembered to initial all her bindels, the defense were precluded from further pursuing the matter. The reason for this is something our **"justice"** system calls "foundation."

If you don't have evidence (foundation) to back up an assumption or a theory, you are not allowed to present it or argue that assumption or theory in court.

My book, however, is not a court of law. I tell the truth as I see it. In my book the principals in the Simpson case answer to me. I make the rules!

In my rule book, Ms. Mazzola's initials were missing, because someone replaced her bindels with false O.J. bindels! The person who did it is Detective Vannatter!

Detectives Fuhrman and Vannatter should have been on trial in this case – not O.J.!

Of course, Vannatter had to do a few other things to his false blood swatches before he could submit them to the crime labs. I didn't mention this during the outline I just gave my readers. If I discussed every little detail, the main procedure might get lost in such details.

However, let me mention one of these details, at least, so my readers shall not think I have forgotten them.

When the criminalists, at a crime scene collects a blood drop onto a swatch, they wet the swatch in distilled water. Then they place the wet swatch over the blood drop and let the blood dissolve and absorb into the swatch.

Of course, outdoors this wet swatch will also attract some dust and dirt. Therefore, Vannatter would have to press his false, wet swatches against the ground or floor, where he wanted it to appear that the false swatches were collected. Otherwise, if his false swatches had arrived at the FBI's crime lab clean as new – except for the blood on them – the DNA scientists might suspect that there was something wrong with those swatches, and that they were not prepared out in the field, but in an office or in a sterile crime lab.

I assume my readers realize that this was not a difficult problem to overcome. Vannatter just had to be aware of it – and do it. I am sure he took his precautions.

There is still one more significant little detail that supports my assumption regarding the fabrication of false O.J. blood swatches.

Let's assume, as I argue, that Vannatter and the police nurse had the above mentioned ongoing stand-by procedure for preparing fake EDTA vials whenever Vannatter decided that he needed one. Of course, frequently, suspects would be accompanied by their defense lawyers when their blood samples were drawn. In that case, it might be far too risky to use a clean (fake) EDTA vial, in case the lawyer should ask to look inside it.

Consequently, Detective Vannatter had to give the nurse some kind of advance notice on this problem whenever he wanted the nurse to prepare a fake EDTA vial.

Vannatter didn't know for sure if O.J. would be accompanied by his attorney, or not, when he arrived at police headquarters for interrogation around noon the day after the murders.

Hence, Vannatter had **two problems** to contend with in connection with the interrogation of O.J. (O.J.'s so-called "taped statement" to the police):

1. Vannatter had to make O.J. agree to the interrogation **without the presence of his attorney.** Hence, Vannatter could bring O.J. over to the police nurse's office directly from the interrogation room – without the presence of his attorney.

2. Vannatter had to give the police nurse a **notice a few minutes before** they arrived, so the nurse could prepare a pre-labelled **real** EDTA vial for Vannatter, and also bring out a fake EDTA vial and put it in the box together with the real vials – but in the opposite direction – as I explained.

I assume my readers understand that these two problems had to be solved. But it is equally obvious, of course, that these problems could not be dealt with until **after** Detectives Lange and Vannatter sat down with O.J. in the interrogation room. **Only then, did they know for sure, whether or not O.J. would agree to be interrogated without the presence of his attorney!**

O.J. had no idea that I had figured out all of this. And I had no idea what went on during O.J.'s taped statement to the police, other than that they sat down, started the tape recorder, and began the questioning. I have never exchanged one word with O.J. – not even over the phone. Hence, O.J. and I can not be suspected of having "concocted" the following. I just wanted to mention that.

Isn't it funny! For two years we have been told that O.J. made the statement without the presence of his attorney, because that was what he wanted to do.

(•) Surprise! During his testimony in the civil case, O.J. testified that he was **coerced** into giving his statement without the presence of his attorney. According to O.J. the tape recorder was started, then O.J. was informed of his right to have a lawyer present. O.J. said:

"Yes, I want my attorney present!"

Of course, this did not suit Vannatter's plans for fabricating false blood evidence against O.J.! An argument ensued. Detective Vannatter told O.J. that if he wanted his attorney present, then they would keep him the entire afternoon, so he might not be able to see his children that day!

Hence, **reluctantly**, O.J. agreed to give his statement without the presence of his attorney.

Of course, the detectives didn't want a recording of themselves coercing O.J. to give a statement without the presence of his attorney. That was such a serious breach of investigative procedure that it would have thrown out a confession even – if O.J. had given one! **Consequently, the tape recorder was stopped and rewound,** then started again. This is evident if one reads the transcript. The very first words on the tape – by Vannatter – starts in the middle of a sentence. (Quote from the transcript of O.J.'s taped statement):

Vannatter: *". . . my partner, Detective Lange, and we're in an interview room in Parker Center. The date is June 13, 1994, and the time is 13:35 hours.*

(•) Detective Vannatter doesn't even introduce himself, and the first "sentence" is totally **"incoherent."** Obviously, the start of this tape recording was cut.

Anyway, Detective Vannatter had overcome **the first** obstacle. He had coerced O.J. to give up his right to have his attorney present. Consequently, if Vannatter could later have O.J. agree to give his blood sample, **Vannatter could take O.J. to the nurse's office without the presence of O.J.'s attorney. Under those circumstances, it would be "safe" to use the fake EDTA vial.**

There was one additional "technicality" though, which Vannatter had to take care of in order to obtain a fake EDTA vial of O.J.'s blood:

If my theory is correct, as I have explained it so far, then Vannatter had to leave the interview shortly before it was over, and tell the nurse that O.J. would be coming down without the company of his lawyer – so the nurse could safely **bring out the fake EDTA vial**, and – more importantly – secretly prepare an additional, **real** EDTA vial for Vannatter, before Vannatter and O.J. arrived.

Let us see if Vannatter did excuse himself towards the end of the interview – a few minutes before it was over – leaving Detective Lange to finish it up! Again I quote from the transcript of O.J.'s taped statement to the police, about 3 minutes before the end of the interview:

Vannatter: *"Well, I'm going to step out, and I'm going to get a photographer to come down and photograph your hand here. And then here pretty soon we're going to take you downstairs and get some blood from you. OK? I'll be right back."*

Three-four minutes later, Vannatter returned. Did he get a photographer, **or did he only talk to the nurse?**

Lange: (to Vannatter) *"Got a photographer coming?"*
Vannatter: *"No, we're going to take him up there."*

(•) So, now Vannatter had taken care of the last obstacle. He had notified the police nurse that he was bringing O.J. to the nurse's office alone – **without O.J.'s attorney** – and that the nurse, accordingly, could prepare the fake EDTA vial.

Maybe there was nothing sinister about Vannatter's actions, getting rid of O.J.'s attorney, and making arrangement with the police nurse while O.J. was still being questioned by Detective Lange. But in context with everything else that Vannatter and the nurse did, one can, at least, say that **it certainly fit in!**

Should my book ever be given some media attention, and former Detective Vannatter be asked to comment on my accusations, I want my readers to know – and think about the following:

A sure sign that former Detective Vannatter is guilty of the actions/crimes I suggest, would be if the former detective refuses to face me publicly (for instance on TV) and answer my accusations – perhaps stating, instead that he thinks my book is not worthy of his comments. That is the typical reply – or excuse – from a guilty person! So listen for it!

CHAPTER 41

The Police Nurse

Did you think the story of O.J.'s blood vial was over? Think again! During the pre-trial hearings **the police nurse, Mr. Peratis, who drew O.J.'s blood, testified, under oath – twice – that he drew exactly 8.0 ml (milliliter) of O.J.'s blood** (1 ml = 1 cubic centimeter = 1 cc). The vial he used had easily readable volume markings for each 1/10 of a milliliter – similar to what you see for degrees on many thermometers.

Later it was revealed that 1.5 ml of O.J.'s blood was missing from O.J.'s blood vial.

It was never an argument that those 1.5 ml of missing blood could have been lost **gradually** as more and more crime lab technicians performed tests on the blood from the vial. Each of the lab technicians could, sort of, have reported a little bit inaccurately how much blood they used. And after a while many small errors could have added up to 1.5 ml.

The reason this was never an issue is that **the missing 1.5 ml of blood was recorded by the very first lab technician** who performed tests on the blood – before he even opened the vial for the first time.

This crime lab technician simply recorded – routinely, as his instructions required him to do – how much blood was in the vial when he received it, how much blood he used, and how much blood was left when he sent it back. **The vial contained 6.5 ml when he got it. But the nurse drew 8.0 ml from O.J.!**

(•) Between the time the nurse gave the vial to Detective Vannatter, and the time this first lab technician recorded that it contained only 6.5 ml, the vial had only been in Vannatter's and the LAPD's custody. Therefore, either Vannatter or someone else within the LAPD must have

removed 1.5 ml of O.J.'s blood.

What in heaven's name could Vannatter, or another LAPD investigator, use 1.5 ml of O.J.'s blood for – other than for fabricating false blood evidence???

Add this to what I have already explained in the previous chapter about:

– Detective Vannatter's countless lies,
– his suspicious activities in connection with the vial,
– the use of an old, unsealable envelope,
– the wet blood transfers on some of the bindel papers, and
– the initials that had "disappeared" from Ms. Mazzola's Bundy bindels,

and I think any unbiased person realizes that Vannatter removed 1.5 ml of O.J.'s blood and used that blood to fabricate all the false blood evidence against O.J.

The argument has been raised that the blood swatches from Bundy were kept behind a locked door – in the serology room or the evidence room at the LAPD's crime lab. Therefore, Vannatter could not have replaced them. Well, someone from the investigation did replace them, obviously. Vannatter's many lies, and his many irregular activities point him out as the prime suspect.

For the prosecutors to suggest that the lead investigator in the case were precluded from having unsupervised access to the evidence in the case, sounds even more suspicious to me than simply to say,

"Yes, Vannatter could have done it, but we don't think he did it."

If the LAPD could not trust the **lead investigator** to have unrestricted access to the evidence he was assembling in the case he was investigating – how can we trust the ones who locked up that evidence because they did not trust their lead investigator?

Obviously, Vannatter must have had the opportunity to replace the blood swatches with false O.J. swatches – and he took advantage of it.

- Again, **the glove evidence** has proven to us, that the five blood drops at Bundy could not have come from O.J. So they must have been replaced by someone within the investigation, after Ms. Mazzola collected them.
  Vannatter took possession of O.J.'s blood vial. He did not book it in, as he should have done.
- Vannatter lied about what he was doing after he got the vial. He still has not accounted for the 90 minutes he spent, alone, in his office together with O.J.'s blood vial.
- 1.5 ml (approximately 30 drops of blood), several times the blood attributed to O.J., disappeared from the vial **after** Vannatter received it from the nurse, but **before** any lab technician opened up the vial to perform tests on the blood.
- Ms. Mazzola's initials were missing from some of her bindels from Bundy – the ones which allegedly contained O.J.'s blood!
- There were "unexplainable" wet blood transfers on some of those same bindels from Bundy.

In my opinion, the evidence suggesting that someone fabricated false blood evidence against O.J., is **overwhelming.**

If someone says O.J. is guilty, because his blood was found at the crime scenes – they should take a second look at the evidence I have presented, and which proves that blood evidence against O.J. **must** have been fabricated.

The only plausible reason to reject the notion of blood evidence fabrication in this case, is the problem of the EDTA. But as my readers remember from the previous chapter, **the EDTA was no problem at all. Vannatter and the nurse could have fixed that in a heartbeat!**

So let us consider the integrity of the police nurse! In his sworn testimony during the pre-trial hearings, **the nurse testified, under oath – twice – that he drew exactly 8.0 ml of O.J.'s blood.** The defense attorney who cross examined the nurse, asked him again, how sure he was about the amount. The nurse replied that he was **absolutely certain.** To **qualify** his answer he said (in essence):

> *It could have been 7.9 ml, or it could have been closer to 8.1 ml – but it was pretty darn close to 8.0 ml!*

Of course, at that time he didn't know the defense had found out that 1.5 ml were missing, under such circumstances that the missing blood must have been deliberately and illegitimately removed.

Months later, during the trial, the defense revealed the discrepancy of the 1.5 ml of missing blood. The prosecution realized that they were in trouble.

(•) That's when the police nurse developed "instant" heart trouble and "amnesia"! He was given sick leave until after the trial and given a doctor's order not to testify in court!

Time and time again, I can hardly believe what happened in this trial, in terms of cover-ups by the LAPD and the prosecution! I would not have dreamt that something like this could have happened in Russia under the KGB, or in Germany under the GESTAPO, even!

Anyway, Judge Ito actually precluded O.J.'s defense attorneys from even mentioning that 1.5 ml of O.J.'s blood had disappeared from his vial (around the time it was in Vannatter's possession). The defense had the lab report that the vial only contained 6.5 ml. They also had the pre-trial sworn testimony by the nurse that he drew 8.0 ml. But Judge Ito ruled that the defense were not allowed to subtract 6.5 ml from 8.0 ml and tell the jury that 1.5 ml were missing or unaccounted for.

Here is the background for Judge Ito's ruling. The prosecution provided the police nurse with a doctor's order that he was too sick to testify in court. Normally, that should instead have opened up for his sworn pre-trial testimony to be presented to the jury –

end of story!

(•) But instead, two of the prosecutors and an LAPD video cameraman went home to the nurse, who allegedly was too sick to talk – at least to a jury. There in his home they taped an incredibly amateurish "interview" with the nurse. In this interview the nurse explained that he might have been wrong about the 8.0 ml of blood, which he testified to shortly after he drew it.

Instead, now, during the video taped interview, **more than a year later,** *"seriously ill, and under heavy medication"* – the nurse suddenly *"remembered"* he might have forgotten, during his pre-trial testimony, that he perhaps only drew 6.5 ml of O.J.'s blood!

Obviously, **the nurse was instructed to lie** – and did lie – **to protect his LAPD colleague, Detective Vannatter**. Based on my theory – that the nurse and Detective Vannatter may have conspired to circumvent the EDTA in O.J.'s blood vial – the taped interview with the nurse fit right in!

The entire story about the nurse and the taped interview, his illness – which was not too severe for him to give a videotaped interview, but severe enough for him not to be questioned by O.J.'s attorneys – was perhaps the most bizarre intermezzo of the entire trial.

(•) The nurse was **exactly so ill** that he could not testify in court – in person. But at the same time he was **just well enough** to give a taped interview to the prosecutors, to be played in court – so that the defense could be excluded from quoting the nurse's **earlier** sworn testimony to the jury instead!

But then again, during the taped interview he was **not well enough** to be questioned by a **defense attorney**, only well enough to be questioned by a **prosecutor**!

The nurse was **not even sworn in** before the interview started. There were **cuts in the tape**, indicating that the nurse might have given the "wrong" answer somewhere, and that the interview was interrupted so **the "wrong" answer could be erased** and the nurse could be **coached!**

In addition, the defense were not given notice of the interview, so they were not given the opportunity to watch it or ask questions.

It was nothing less than **outrageous** for Judge Ito to allow this taped interview to be played to the jury, as proof that 1.5 ml of blood were **not** missing from O.J.'s blood vial – anyway!

This was not only Judge Ito's worst decision. It is possibly the worst decision I have seen any judge make – except, of course, Judge Fujisaki who topped everybody and was in a league by himself!

Judge Ito's **legal basis** for allowing the taped interview of the nurse to be played in court, was **the nurse's illness** – precluding him from appearing in person. But why should that justify a **new** – out-of-court – interview of the nurse, when the court **already** had the nurse's **sworn testimony** from the pretrial hearings – during which testimony the nurse, obviously, was **not so ill**, and also had the events **more fresh in his memory**?

Again I have to ask what kind of justice system do we have in this country?

Obviously, the nurse cooperated and participated in this cover up, in order to protect Detective Vannatter and cover up Vannatter's blood evidence fabrication against O.J. Add to this what I have earlier explained about the nurse placing O.J.'s blood vial in an old, used, un-sealable envelope – and the reason he gave for doing that:

He had run out of new, unused blood vial envelopes!

Obviously, Detective Vannatter and the police nurse **conspired** to circumvent the EDTA in O.J.'s vial. Most likely they had done the same thing many times before.

Imagine what went on – and still goes on in this case! And imagine that if O.J. had not been as rich as he **was**, then this team of cheating, deceiving, lying, perjuring, false evidence fabricating investigators and prosecutors would have railroaded O.J. right into the San Quentin gas chamber! It is really scary!

CHAPTER 42

The Perfect "Decoy"

I am sure many of my readers wonder why Detective Vannatter brought O.J.'s blood vial to Rockingham – not to mention, why he allowed the defense to expose that.

If Detective Vannatter – as I allege – already had O.J.'s EDTA free blood in a separate vial, why would he expose himself to severe criticism and suspicion, by bringing the suspect's blood vial to the crime scene? It wasn't there, at Rockingham – but in the crime lab – Vannatter intended to plant his false blood evidence aganst O.J.

There were **two reasons** Vannatter brought O.J.'s blood vial to Rockingham. One reason was that by the time he had prepared all the false EDTA free O.J. blood swatches and bindels, in his office, he was, perhaps – as he testified to – **"rushed for time,"** and didn't have time to book in the vial before driving to Rockingham.

Of course, after preparing the false swatches, **he could have returned the real vial to the police nurse,** and asked the nurse to book it in. I am sure the police nurse, a sworn LAPD officer, had booked in hundreds of blood vials before.

However, if Vannatter had returned the vial to the nurse, that would have raised the serious question, **why Vannatter requested the vial from the nurse in the first place** – if he handed it right back to the nurse one hour later! It isn't easy to be an honest crook – or a crooked police officer! But Vannatter tried his best!

Vannatter needed **an excuse** for receiving the vial from the nurse in the first place. This excuse was that he wanted to give the vial to Criminalist Fung at Rockingham. So then, once he had the vial, he had to bring it to Rockingham.

However, I believe Vannatter brought the vial to Rockingham for a different reason.

(•) The **real reason** why Vannatter brought O.J.'s blood vial to Rockingham – in spite of having O.J.'s EDTA free blood in a separate container – was this:

The **real** vial was a perfect **"decoy"**!

Of course, Vannatter didn't bring O.J.'s blood vial to Rockingham in order to plant blood – from the vial. He couldn't – and didn't – because that blood would have had EDTA in it.

All his false blood evidence was prepared from the fake vial which did not contain EDTA.

However, by bringing O.J.'s **real** blood vial to Rockingham anyway, Vannatter managed to get everyone's attention focused on the real blood vial itself – **and on the EDTA!**

That way **people didn't understand** where the **real deception** and forgery – the real evidence fabrication – took place.

This is exactly the same trick magicians use. They will draw your attention to their **right** hand, by pretending they are hiding something in it. While you watch the **right hand**, the magician pulls a pigeon out of his **left tuxedo sleeve**! And at that exact same moment, when you realize you have been tricked, and your eyes gaze at the pigeon – the magician slides a deck of cards from his **right sleeve** and palms it in his **right hand** – in preparation for his next trick!

Rumors started that Vannatter might have planted blood from O.J.'s blood vial, since he, against all instructions, brought the vial to O.J.'s house. Defense attorneys and lab technicians went **scrambling for EDTA**. With a smile, Vannatter could **flaunt the vial,** saying:

"Of course, we didn't plant O.J.'s blood anywhere. Had we done that, it would have contained EDTA! Stop bothering us about O.J.'s blood vial!"

Again, I must remind my readers that most of the blood evidence attributed to O.J. was not tested for EDTA. But except for the blood on the rear gate at Bundy, I don't think the defense would have found EDTA in that other blood anyway – even if they had tested it. The reason for my assumption is that Vannatter, so obviously, circumvented the EDTA in O.J.'s blood vial. Therefore, Vannatter could conficently flaunt the fact that he brought O.J.'s blood vial to Rockingham. That vial was not the one he planted O.J.'s blood from.

By bringing O.J.'s real blood vial to Rockingham, Vannatter turned everyone's attention to that blood vial. No one figured out that Vannatter already had O.J.'s **EDTA free** blood in a **separate test tube**, and that he had **already** made the necessary preparations to plant O.J.'s blood in a much safer place than out at the crime scenes – namely **in the LAPD's own crime lab**.

> Bringing O.J.'s real blood vial to Rockingham, served as the perfect **decoy**!

Is Detective Vannatter that smart? Yes, I think he is. Again, he didn't become lead homicide investigator in the second largest police department in the nation – by being stupid!

I don't consider myself particularly smart, so if I could figure this out, I bet Vannatter could have figured it out, too.

I am sure Detective Vannatter had discovered, or learned from someone else, that the EDTA could be circumvented like this. It is always like that: someone develops a safe system – and immediately someone else finds a method to overcome it!

By the way, Vannatter didn't necessarily come up with this **"fake EDTA vial trick"** himself. Perhaps he didn't even think of the **"decoy trick"** himself. For more than one hundred years, thousands of rogue police officers in this country have figured out one sophisticated method after the other, regarding how to convict suspects with fabricated evidence.

Detective Vannatter could have picked up the "EDTA trick" and the "decoy trick" from anyone of thousands of police investigators he had met over the years.

CHAPTER 43

The Handcuffing Of O.J.

We have seen how Detective Vannatter "set up" Kato with the three blood drops in O.J.'s foyer, by telling Kato to check with the detectives at Rockingham, before he left the house, and then making sure Kato saw the "blood" drops, at a time when O.J. had **not yet** returned from Chicago.

To most people it later appeared that O.J. **must** have left those "blood" drops **on the night of the murders**. But based on what I have explained about Detective Vannatter, my readers probably realize that **Kato was "set up."** The way the detectives led Kato to those "blood" drops – it was almost like they were saying,

> *"Take a good look at these blood drops for us, because we need you to vouch for them later!"*

Add to that Vannatter's handling of O.J.'s blood vial, the inconsistent bleeding pattern of the so-called "trail of blood," the appearance of the drops, and how unlikely it would be that the three drops directly inside O.J.'s door – if they had come from O.J. before he left for Chicago – would have remained undisturbed in spite of the traffic in and out through that door.

It was an obvious "set-up" by Vannatter, and it tied in with everything else that man did.

Again, it involved Detective Vannatter, and added to the "ocean of evidence" which proves that the lead investigator in the Simpson case fabricated evidence against O.J. on a grand scale.

At the time when Vannatter fabricated all the blood evidence against O.J., Vannatter truly believed that O.J. had slaughtered Nicole and Ron. The mere thought of Nicole's and Ron's murderer escaping justice, must have been the investigator's worst nightmare. It was terribly wrong to fabricate the false evidence, but I could, at least, **understand** Vannatter – at that point!

What I **despise** about Detective Vannatter, however, is that he, at some point, **must** have realized that O.J. was innocent and that he, the lead investigator, was trying to convict an innocent man to life in prison – and yet, he didn't stop! He went right on throughout the trial – and even after the trial – trying to convince people that O.J. were guilty.

Although I don't condone it, of course, I can to some extent "understand" a police officer who plants evidence against a suspect he "knows" is **guilty**. But Vannatter **must** have known, at some point, that O.J. was **innocent**! Because without Vannatter's false evidence, the rest of the evidence against O.J. would, indeed, appear to be the "set-up" it obviously was. Besides, it became clear, rather soon, that Detective Fuhrman must have murdered Nicole and Ron.

After a week or two, Vannatter didn't fabricate evidence against O.J. simply in the belief that he was trying to put a dangerous criminal behind bars – for the greater good of society. Vannatter, at some point, continued to fabricate false evidence against O.J. to cover up the false evidence he had already fabricated, in order **to protect his own skin.**

That is what I despise about Detective Philip Vannatter – the **"malice"** by which he **continued** to go after O.J. with falsely fabricated evidence – after he **must** have known that O.J. was innocent!

Following is another interesting – or suspicious – little episode which seems to have eluded legal analysts, attorneys, and the media. I am referring to **the handcuffing of O.J.** upon his return to Rockingham.

Many of my readers remember that when O.J. returned from Chicago and arrived at Rockingham, **he was handcuffed for a short while – just a couple of minutes. Then the cuffs were removed.**

This episode was televised all over the world. The consensus is that the handcuffing of O.J. was an **innocent mistake**. The officer who handcuffed O.J. didn't think about what he was doing, but then he realized the mistake – or Vannatter realized it – and corrected it.

Another explanation is that Vannatter ordered the handcuffing of O.J. in order to humiliate him, but that was not the reason, either. Yet a third explanation is that Vannatter and Lange were trying to play the game of "bad cop – good cop" vis-a-vis O.J., to "soften him up," in preparation for the interrogation they were about to conduct as soon as they got O.J. to Parker Center police headquarters. I also doubt that was the reason.

I have earlier used a bullet (•) to indicate some of the suspicious things Detective Vannatter did, and which indicated that he fabricated, or made preparations to fabricate, false blood evidence against O.J. **It is time to place another bullet (•) here.**

(•) The handcuffing of O.J. was a mistake, all right. But only because I have come to realize **the true significance** of this **apparently trivial** episode. It ties right in with my theory about Vannatter's fabrication and planting of false blood evidence against O.J., and all the many other suspicious things Vannatter did in preparation for it.

I ask my readers to forgive me for taking you on a little **"detour"** in getting to the "handcuffing episode":

Already when Detectives Fuhrman, Vannatter, Lange, and Phillips, left Bundy and drove to O.J.'s estate at five o'clock in the morning, Vannatter **suspected** that O.J. had killed Nicole and Ron. Shortly thereafter, when Fuhrman reported having seen blood on the door of O.J.'s Bronco, **Vannatter was convinced – O.J. were the murderer**!

Then Fuhrman showed Vannatter the bloody glove behind O.J.'s house! That was it! Vannatter immediately decided that **he was going to nail O.J. – one way or the other!** Vannatter reasoned:

O.J. had used gloves. Maybe he wasn't injured. Maybe the

blood wasn't his. If so, O.J.'s lawyers might be able to raise doubt about his guilt. Vannatter wasn't going to let that happen. If the blood wasn't O.J.'s, **Vannatter knew some "tricks" that would make the blood appear to be O.J.'s!**

Vannatter immediately began setting up and preparing his fabrication of false blood evidence. He already knew the trick about circumventing the EDTA in blood vials. The police nurse fully understood that *dangerous murderers had to be taken off our streets* – and routinely cooperated with Vannatter when asked.

Vannatter knew he would get a blood sample from O.J. any time Vannatter wanted it. It would be futile for O.J. to refuse. It would only make him look more guilty in the eyes of a future jury. Besides, if O.J. refused, Vannatter would simply get a court order to draw O.J.'s blood.

Vanatter was reasonably certain that O.J. would agree to come to Parker Center Police Headquarters to give a taped statement. **If he refused, the police could simply arrest him.** It turned out that O.J. cooperated fully with the police. He agreed to give a statement, even without the presence of his attorney – and he volunteered his blood sample right away, even without being asked!

Be that as it may. One way or the other, Detective Vannatter would get O.J. to Parker Center as soon as he returned from Chicago. And **one way or the other, Vannatter would get O.J.'s blood sample after he got O.J. to Parker Center.**

Hence, Vannatter could begin to **prepare** the framing of O.J. the very second he saw the bloody glove behind O.J.'s house.

Vannatter's plan was to make certain that what appeared to **him** to have happened – also appeared to everyone else to have happened:

- O.J. had lost his left glove and, subsequently been cut in a struggle with Ron,
- O.J. had bled at the murder scene, and
- "the trail of blood" led directly from the victims' bodies, via

the Bronco, and to O.J.'s house.

Immediately, Vannatter planted some **"substitute blood"** in O.J.'s foyer, and in the driveway (if Fuhrman hadn't already done it).

Note! The very manner – the deliberate, confident manner – in which Vannatter prepared for and carried out the fabrication of the false blood evidence, demonstrated that **this was not the first time Vannatter had fabricated false blood evidence.**

The nurse was ready to cooperate. The trick to circumvent the EDTA by the use of a fake EDTA vial, was already set up, as a **"stand-by procedure"** whenever Vannatter requested it!

Part of the **"false blood evidence routine"** must have been to use **"substitute blood"** until he could get the suspects real blood. This "substitute blood" should preferably be something that would not expose Vannatter, in case his scheme had to be aborted. One way of avoiding suspicion, in case Vannatter could not follow through with his blood evidence fabrication, would be to **use a "substitute blood" one could otherwise expect to find, wherever Vannatter planted it.**

Detective Fuhrman used the same principle, when he planted the five blood drops alongside the bloody shoeprints – using Nicole's blood.

Accordingly, Vannatter could have **soaked a small piece of cloth in Nicole's blood** at Bundy, and concealed the cloth afterwards (actually, Fuhrman could have done that too). Then, at Rockingham he could have **moistened the cloth with distilled water** and **"wrung"** it, thereby dripping Nicole's blood in the foyer and in the driveway. Distilled water was used anyway, when soaking up blood evidence onto swatches. So this method of using a blood substitute could never be exposed.

But Vannatter could also have used "film blood" (O.J. is a movie actor) or simply ketchup (Kato and O.J. had been to McDonalds for hamburgers on the night of the murders).

There was another small problem, though – and now we are slowly getting to the handcuffing!

What if O.J. didn't have any cuts on his hands or his head (or on other parts of his body)?

In that case, Vannatter could **not** plant O.J.'s blood **anywhere!**

As a matter of fact, if Vannatter did plant O.J.'s blood to create false evidence against O.J., and O.J. didn't have any cuts or bruises – Vannatter would be in deep trouble!

However, Detective Vannatter knew how to get around this problem, too!

If O.J. didn't have a cut anywhere, the police could give him one!

When they arrived at the police station for Detectives Lange's and Vannatter's taped interview with O.J., they could tell O.J. that he had to wait a few minutes, while they set up the tape recorder.

Furthermore, they could tell him that he was a suspect, although they hadn't decided yet, whether to charge him or not. Therefore, **police procedures required** that they **handcuffed** him and kept him in a **holding cell** until they could start the interview.

Had O.J., as a result, requested the presence of his lawyer, they would still have handcuffed him and kept him in a holding cell.

Now I want those of my readers who care, and dare to try this little "experiment," to **pinch themselves** – really hard – in the skin covering **the outside middle finger knuckle** of your left hand. Use the **nail of your right thumb against the tip of your index finger.**

Most of you will, perhaps **surprisingly**, discover that **it doesn't hurt much at all** – regardless of how hard you pinch! The reason is that you have very **few "pain receptors"** at this particular spot on your finger.

If O.J. did not have any cuts on his body, Vannatter could handcuff O.J. and simultaneously give him a small nick or cut with a razor blade or with a blade from a wall paper knife, or similar, on that particular spot on his finger. I am certain O.J. wouldn't even have felt it. And he wouldn't have seen it either – behind his back.

Then, when Detective Vannatter retrieved O.J. for the interview and removed the handcuffs, the detective would "discover" the cut and ask O.J. to explain how he got that cut!

Don't get ahead of me now! Don't think I suggest that Detective Vannatter "arranged" to give O.J. the infamous cut on his left middle finger knuckle, when the police officer handcuffed him at Rockingham! That's not my point. So read on!

Anyway, giving O.J. a cut, **if necessary**, required some preparation at the police station – like clearing up O.J.'s legal status with Vannatter's superiors; arranging for the tape recorder to be absent from the interrogation room; and things like that – so that they would have **a legitimate excuse to handcuff O.J.** and take him to a holding cell for a while, and during this – nick one of his fingers.

Hence, Vannatter needed to know – in advance, and preferably as soon as possible – whether or not O.J. did have a cut somewhere (preferably on one of his hands).

That would make it clear to Vannatter, **whether or not he needed to make all these other preparations.**

However, when O.J. returned from Chicago, Detective Vannatter couldn't ask O.J. to **show** his hands. Why not?

Right! If Detective Vannatter had asked O.J. to show his hands, and O.J. did **not** have a cut anywhere, then it would have been **impossible** for Vannatter to give O.J. a cut on one of those same hands – at the police station!

Now you understand where I am heading! Evidently, Detective Vannatter had long since, begun setting up and preparing his fabrication of false blood evidence against O.J. However, **Vannatter needed to inspect O.J.'s hands**, as soon as he returned to Rockingham. But **Vannatter could not ask O.J. to show his hands!** So what did Vannatter do?

Right again! **Detective Vannatter told one of his junior officers, in advance, to handcuff O.J. as soon as he arrived at Rockingham, and at the same time take a close look at his hands, to see if he had a cut somewhere. Vannatter also told the officer not to mention this to anyone afterwards, but only report back to Vannatter himself.**

So that was exactly what happened! The officer **handcuffed** O.J., **examined** his hands at the same time, **saw** the cut, and **reported** back to Detective Vannatter. **Shortly thereafter, Detective Vannatter ordered the handcuffs removed from O.J.'s hands.**

Vannatter then knew that he did not have to make any special arrangements. O.J. already had a cut. All he needed to do was to **get rid of O.J.'s attorney, and to notify the nurse** about using a fake EDTA vial before Vannatter brought O.J. to the nurse's office to get a blood sample.

As I have already explained in an earlier chapter, that was exactly what Vannatter did.

He had to **coerce O.J. to get rid of his attorney!** And Vannatter had to **excuse himself** three minutes before the interview with O.J. was over, so he could **notify the police nurse** that they didn't have to worry about O.J.'s attorney when they fabricated the fake EDTA vial.

Why do I think that this is what was behind the **"handcuffing episode,"** and that it, therefore tied right in with Detective Vannatter's plan to fabricate false blood evidence against O.J.?

Well, Detective Vannatter was the lead investigator, the senior homicide detective at the Robbery/Homicide division of the LAPD. He **"called the shots."** Vannatter told everyone else **what to do, and what not to do,** in this murder case.

(•) No casual, ordinary LAPD officer would, **on his own initiative – while Detective Vannatter, the lead investigator, was standing right next to him –** have **dared** to handcuff O.J. in front of the entire worldwide media!

This LAPD officer who handcuffed O.J., **must have**

acted on Vannatter's direct order! He must have done **exactly what Vannatter had told him to do!** There can be absolutely no doubt about that!

Detective Vannatter was the lead homicide detective, with 27 years of experience with the second largest police department in the U.S. Would he have made such a blunder, as to order one of his junior officers to handcuff O.J. – at a time when O.J. was not yet a **suspect**, no one had read him his **"rights,"** and he had not been **charged** with any crime?!

The answer is: **Absolutely not! Of course, Detective Vannatter could never have made such a blunder – just by mistake!** Vannatter knew exactly what he – and the handcuffing officer – were doing. And now my readers know it, too!

I am not quite finished with that episode. Even the officer who handcuffed O.J. – on Vannatter's order – was an educated, sworn police officer. He knew such elementary procedures as reading a suspect his rights!

I take it for granted that when Vannatter gave the officer the order to handcuff O.J. as soon as he arrived at Rockingham, the officer **must have asked Vannatter** whether or not he should, *"read O.J. his rights."*

Since he eventually did not read O.J. his rights, we must conclude that **Vannatter actually told the officer to break the rules**, and **not** read O.J. his rights when he handcuffed him!

That makes this handcuffing episode **even more suspicious**. Today, all of this is "water under the bridge." But it would have been interesting to "cross examine" both the officer and Vannatter on this point!

Considering all the things I have explained about the framing of O.J. and about Vannatter's sinister scheme – can we possibly top this? Yes, we can!

Detective Vannatter must have been an extremely busy man during the first few days after the murders. Yet, he found the time to attend the autopsies of both Nicole and Ron.

Such autopsies take several hours each. Vannatter is no medical examiner. Wouldn't Detective Vannatter's time be better spent investigating the crime scenes, while he awaited the medical examiners preliminary report the next day? Did he have to spend hours and hours in the medical examiner's autopsy room?

Of course not! But evidently, Detective Vannatter didn't want to miss the autopsies for anything in the world. In talking to the investigator from the Department of Coroner on the morning after the murders Detective Vannatter made certain the investigator wrote on his report – with capital letters:

AUTOPSY NOTIFICATION:
PLEASE CONTACT DET(S) LANGE AND VANNATTER AT LEAST TWO HOURS PRIOR TO EXAMINATION.

So why was Detective Vannatter so eager to attend both autopsies on June 13, 1994?

(•) Would you believe that Detective Vannatter went to the Department of Coroner (the autopsies) and requested two small **unpackaged** test tubes containing Nicole's and Ron's bloods, respectively? The examining pathologist, **Dr. Golden, found this so strange that he refused to give Vannatter the blood vials without clearing it with the coroner's office first!**

Not only was Vannatter – against direct police instructions – walking around with O.J.'s blood on the day after the murders. The very next day, he was also walking around with the victim's blood in two unpackaged test tubes!

Again, Detective Vannatter concocted a story about being an **"errand boy,"** so to speak – this time for the LAPD's blood analyst, Criminalist Collin Yamauchi.

According to Vannatter, he wanted a blood type testing of Nicole's and Ron's blood. So less than 48 hours after the murders, in the most hectic phase of the investigation, he decided to spend **five hours** in the Department of Coroner to pick up the blood samples for Criminalist Yamauchi!

Is that what the LAPD use their **lead homicide investigators** for? Wouldn't you think the lead investigator could have picked up his phone and simply asked Criminalist Yamauchi to test the blood types of Nicole and Ron. Anyone could have fetched the victims' blood vials and brought them to Criminalist Yamauchi – including Mr. Yamauchi himself.

(•) The lead investigator, Vannatter, getting the victims' blood to Yamauchi, was like President Clinton running around in the White House, delivering the morning mail to the members of his staff!

There seems to be no end to Detective Vannatter's blatant efforts to fabricate false blood evidence against O.J.

Maybe I have interpreted more into some of these episodes than what was really there. But the **magnitude** of it all clearly proves what went on!

If O.J.'s adversaries and accusers, the former prosecutors and investigators, the counsels for the plaintiffs, legal analysts on TV, the media, and people in general, still claim that they don't understand what went on in this case – in terms of evidence fabrication – they are, in my opinion, not only deaf and blind – but disingenuous.

After what I have explained in this book, how can anyone in the world trust even the slightest little fragment of blood evidence in this murder case?

You know the facts now. I don't know what stronger evidence one can ask for, to prove that O.J. is innocent. If anything at all, it would have to be confessions from Detective Mark Fuhrman and Detective Philip Vannatter. Don't hold your breath, waiting for that to happen.

These two former LAPD detectives are a disgrace to all decent police officers. Again, in my opinion, **they** should have been on trial instead of O.J. – **one for murder, and the other for fabricating false evidence against an innocent man!**

CHAPTER 44

The Rest Of The Evidence

In the latest chapters I have purposely concentrated on Vannatter and the "trail of blood" evidence, pointing to the many strange or suspicious activities and circumstances that surrounded this portion of the evidence against O.J.

I have not done so because the rest of the evidence is more, or less, credible than what we have discussed with regards to O.J.'s blood vial. Every bit of evidence the prosecution presented was fabricated, planted, misinterpreted, or misunderstood. Vannatter's handling of O.J.'s blood vial, and "the trail of blood," was just a good example, and needed to be dealt with, as everything else.

One of my objectives with the discussion of the blood evidence, and the roles of Detectives Fuhrman and Vannatter, as well as Vannatter's lies and covert actions, was to explain the apparent "set up" by Mark Fuhrman, and the grand scale evidence fabrication by Detective Vannatter.

> The most important conclusion we should draw from the latest chapters is not the fact that blood evidence **was** fabricated. That seems so obvious. Rather, I wanted to explain **how** all this "trail of blood" evidence could have been planted and fabricated by **two men only** – Detectives Fuhrman and Vannatter.
>
> **Fuhrman supplied the "raw material,"** so to speak – and **Vannatter was the "manufacturer."**

How many times have you heard O.J.'s adversaries "explain" that O.J. could not have been framed, because it would have involved so many "dozens" of conspirators that it was just unimaginable! Right? You have heard that from investigators, prosecutors and legal analysts on TV, many times – haven't you?

What you should understand, however, from the discussion of "the trail of blood" and Vannatters handling of O.J.'s blood vial, is this:

- **Fuhrman and Vannatter did not conspire at all!** They had their **two completely different agendas** and motives for framing O.J. – and what they did, they did completely independently of each other.
- Fuhrman framed O.J. with some evidence directly. But more importantly – **Fuhrman "set up" Vannatter** and provided Vannatter with the **"raw material"** (the blood, the cap, the gloves, the blood in the Bronco, etc.).
- Once Fuhrman had convinced Vannatter that O.J. were guilty, Vannatter took over – **completely on his own**! He and Fuhrman never discussed evidence fabrication. That is how perfect Fuhrman had planned everything.
- Vannatter, on the other hand, didn't conspire with anyone else either – at first. He created his part of the "trail of blood," all by himself. He didn't need help from anyone else – except perhaps from the nurse, to create the fake blood vial.
- **Others** did not get involved until **after** Vannatter had planted most of the blood evidence against O.J. But even then, there was never any kind of major conspiracy to frame O.J. Others simply got sucked in, one by one, as they contributed their parts in the effort to convict O.J.

O.J.'s adversaries, many against their better knowledge, **parodied** how they claimed the defence's suggested evidence fabrication must have taken place. Mocking O.J.'s supporters, they suggested that framing O.J. would have to be some sort of **"conspiracy town hall meeting"** where 30 or 40 central figures from the investigation and the prosecution came together and discussed the matter – before voting unanimously to frame O.J. with false evidence and cover it up. That is just a ridiculous way of trying to explain why, in their opinion, O.J. were not framed. But he was!

Fuhrman killed Nicole and Ron. He convinced the lead

investigator that O.J. had done it. **Exit Fuhrman!**

At that point, Vannatter took over the baton. He, too, ran **his** leg of the relay **alone – at least the first part of it**! He fabricated most of the blood evidence against O.J. – all by himself.

So now, everyone else involved with the investigation or the prosecution, was convinced that O.J. were guilty. By themselves, one after the other, they contributed their parts – to the extent that it was necessary or desirable.

One detective or criminalist smeared some more blood in the Bronco. Another planted some Bronco fibers on Ron's shirt. Some smeared Nicole's blood from her dress onto O.J.'s socks. Gradually the case against O.J. grew stronger and stronger because of this false evidence.

Each individual who participated in this evidence fabrication, did not know about the other culprits. It was never anything like a roll call one morning, where the Captain handed out the day's "evidence fabrication assignments" to a dozen police officers! Rather, by themselves, each one – or a couple of them together – did his and her little shares, individually, over the 6-7 weeks following the murders.

Take the Bronco fiber on Ron's shirt, for instance. Vannatter discussed that, perhaps, with one of his or criminalists:

Vannatter: *"Listen, we both know O.J. is obviously guilty. Think of all the evidence we have against him – blood and hairs and gloves, and shoeprints and everything. But I still wish we had something that could tie his **Bronco** directly to the murder scene – just to make the picture complete.*

Now, you have that roll of carpet from the Bronco and Ron's clothes over there at the crime lab – they are kept in open card board boxes, arent they? Wouldn't it be perfect, if we found a carpet fiber from the Bronco – on Ron's shirt!"
Criminalist: *"I know what you mean!"*

This criminalist, if he "accidentally" transferred a carpet fiber onto Ron's shirt, didn't think he did anything real bad. He felt sure that

O.J. were guilty – because of all the other evidence. So he was just **"giving justice a helping hand."** This case wouldn't rest on one little carpet fibre.

One man, only, had the "big picture" – namely **the lead investigator**, Detective Vannatter. That is why there was never any major conspiracy, although the entire case against O.J. was fabricated.

Had all the culprits gathered at the outset, however, and Vannatter, **then**, had handed out all the evidence fabrication **"assignments,"**someone would surely have protested. Because then, they would all have seen that there really wasn't any evidence against O.J. – just the murderer's attempt to frame him.

This is why none of them sounded the alarm. You see, each of them thought **all the rest** of the evidence was **ligitimate**! The little piece of evidence each of them fabricated, was seen as just a small detail, to make the case "perfect."

Fuhrman's initial "set up," followed by Vannatter's sinister framing of O.J. with false blood evidence, created this case.

Later, when the two detectives, independently of each other, had convinced "everybody", including all the investigators, the criminalists, and the prosecutors, that O.J. simply **had** to be guilty – several of them were more than willing to follow up with less significant, but still important evidence fabrication.

A nyway, it is time to address the other so-called "evidence" in this case. Some of it I have touched on earlier in chapter 3 (**The Inconsistent Evidence**).

1. The knit ski cap:

I have earlier explained how **Detective Fuhrman purposely left the knit cap at the murder scene**, trusting that the investigators would find a way to plant O.J.'s hairs on it – which they, indeed, did.

Perhaps, to look for illegal drugs, allegedly, an investigator searched O.J.'s jail cell while O.J. was in court. On O.J.'s pillowcase he found plenty of hair fragments and picked two dozen or so. Or perhaps the investigators picked some of O.J.'s hairs from his hair brush in his bathroom one day.

Back in the crime lab the investigator placed several of O.J.'s hairs inside the cap. He also placed one of O.J.'s hairs on Ron's shirt, and another hair on one of the murder gloves.

Later the cap was examined by someone else, who "found" the hairs and examined them. Then they asked O.J. to volunteer some samples of his hair for comparison, which O.J. did. Of course, the hairs from the cap, the shirt, and the glove were similar to O.J.'s hairs.

Had the investigators not resorted to such criminal behavior, the cap would not have compromised O.J. But regardless of that, the cap would never, under any circumstances, have compromised Fuhrman either, since Fuhrman only brought the cap to frame O.J. and never wore the cap himself.

The interesting thing, though, was that the criminalists also found, I believe, **six** other African-American hair fragments on the cap, and **these hairs did not belong to O.J.!** They also found two blond hairs, one of the hairs showed signs of having been bleached or colored. Suspiciously, these hair fragments belonged to strangers who have never been identified. Apparently, these unidentified hair fragments did not belong to anyone associated with O.J. or the case. So how could this be O.J.'s cap?

If this was O.J.'s ski cap, we would expect **his** hairs to be on it. But we wouldn't expect to find hairs from "other people" on the cap. And if we found hairs from other people on it, we would have expected those hairs to have come from someone in O.J.'s household, and not from total strangers!

The explanation could be rather simple. Detective Fuhrman bought this cap in a store, just to frame O.J. with it. He "knew" the investigators would find a way to plant O.J.'s hairs on that cap.

However, before Fuhrman bought it, several other customers had tried on the cap in the store. They left those other unidentified hair fragments inside the cap.

Because Fuhrman never wore the cap, he never washed it either. Hence, the hairs from other customers, remained on the cap. Had this been O.J.'s **ski cap**, he would, most likely, have had it for years, and washed it many times, in which case hairs from other customers would have been washed away.

Furthermore, no one reported that they had sold O.J. such a cap – not recently, not ever.

The prosecutors could not come up with any reasonable explanation for the unidentified hairs. Their best, and only, explanation was that the unidentified hairs on the cap *"flew in with the wind"*! Sure enough, there were TV cameras in the courtroom. But did the prosecutors believe the cameras were from the Comedy Channel?

According to the prosecutors, we should believe that eight , unidentified hairs came flying through the air at Bundy. Like guided missiles from outer space they caught the cap on radar, zeroed in on it, and landed – every one of them – on the cap, but nowhere else! And just before the hairs landed, the cap – mysteriously – opened up to allow the hairs to land **inside!**

Again, the prosecution's theory seemed "all right" at first:

The cap is O.J.'s and he lost it when he murdered Ron. That's why the cap was found at Bundy, and that's why O.J.'s hairs were on it.

However, as soon as we started to scrutinize the prosecution's theory – not a single thing seemed to fit.

I won't repeat my detailed discussion of O.J.'s total lack of motive for wearing such a cap. It couldn't be for disguise, and it certainly couldn't be to keep his ears warm in the middle of the summer. Prosecutors Clark and Darden, or counsel for the plaintiffs, Mr. Petrocelli – please tell me why **you** think O.J. wore the cap!

Warm leather gloves, a knit ski cap, and rugged Bruno Magli winter boots!

Maybe the murderer didn't intend to kill Nicole. Maybe he was on his way to Alaska to go skiing – an just got lost on his way, and ended up at 875 South Bundy Drive instead!

So much about the knit ski cap!

2. The blood on the Bundy Gate:

A week or so after the murders, it must have dawned on the investigators that O.J. did not murder Nicole and Ron. But by then, Detective Vannatter had already planted most of the blood evidence. Vannatter had cleverly circumvented the EDTA in the blood evidence he fabricated. But even so – if O.J. was innocent, and Fuhrman was the murderer – Vannatter was in deep trouble! There was no turning back now.

Vannatter needed more evidence to convict O.J., thereby covering up the fact that most of the evidence against O.J. was fabricated. So, someone planted two additional drops of O.J.'s blood on the bottom rail of the **rear** gate at Bundy.

Whoever planted those blood drops wanted them to appear to have come from O.J.'s hand as he left through the gate. If so, it **might** have been a **smear**, or it might have been a drop. However, they couldn't plant blood spots up around waist level or higher, because it was unthinkable that such a blood spot could have been missed by the investigators during the early days of the investigation.

The new blood spots would have to be planted on the bottom rail of the gate, where they arguably might have been overlooked. But that meant the blood must have **dripped**. They couldn't suggest that O.J. had crawled through the gate and **smeared** the blood there!

So whoever planted the blood on the bottom rail of the gate, had to plant **drops**, not smears. But the only liquid blood belonging to O.J. was in his vial. The choice was clear: **Drops from the vial,** or no blood at all.

Of course, if the blood drops came from the vial, they should contain EDTA. The inverse is also true, namely that if the blood contained EDTA, it **must** have come from the vial.

Do I need to say more? Yes, of course, the two blood drops on the bottom rail of the rear gate contained EDTA.

But there is more evidence that the blood was planted. Police witnesses testified during **the criminal trial** that they had only seen **one** blood spot on the gate, on June 13. Reports – from those who wrote reports – confirmed this. Then, three weeks later there were **two** additional drops, on the bottom rail of the gate.

Furthermore, photographs taken on June 13, proved that there was only one blood spot on the rear gate. Three weeks later there were three blood spots there.

EDTA or no EDTA – the two drops must have been planted after June 13!

The above is the plain and simple **physical** explanation for the blood drops on the gate. But there could be a more sophisticated explanation, too. I don't rule out the possibility that Detective Vannatter **purposely** arranged for the two blood drops to be planted on the rear gate – **even though he knew they contained EDTA**!

Why would Vannatter do an apparently "dumb" thing like that – if that is what he did? The forgery was bound to be exposed. Apparently, planting the EDTA blood on the rear gate could only hurt the prosecution.

I have said it before, and I repeat it: Detective Vannatter is **much smarter** than he is given credit for. **If** he arranged for the blood to be planted on the gate, **he knew exactly what he was doing.** So why might he have planted it – when it contained EDTA? Let me explain.

Two-three days or so after the murders, Vannatter had already replaced the five blood swatches Ms. Mazzola prepared from the blood drops next to the bloody shoeprints at Bundy. That was Vannatter's most urgent and critical evidence fabrication – which should irrefutably tie O.J. to the murder scene by means of his own blood. **Then, suddenly, diaster struck Vannatter!** (Again, this is my theory).

Proud and happy the LAPD's blood analyst, Criminalist Colin

Yamauchi approached the lead investigator, Detective Vannatter.

Yamauchi: *I thought you like to know – I tested two of the seven swatches Ms. Mazzola prepared at Bundy, from the blood drops next to the shoeprints. The blood type was consistent with **Nicole's**. I guess her blood must have dripped from the murderer as he walked away.*

Vannatter: *I thought there vere only five swatches from those blood drops?*

Yamauchi: *No, Andrea (Mazzola) made **two extra ones**, so I could blood type a couple of them for you.*

Vannatter had, of course, thrown away the real blood swatches he had replaced – the ones containing Nicole's blood. Vannatter became nervous, thinking that he, perhaps, had been framing an innocent man with false evidence **he could no longer reverse.**

What if his false blood swatches were analyzed by the FBI and found to contain O.J.'s DNA, while Yamauchi's blood typing report proved that the blood could **not** be O.J.'s, but, most likely, was Nicole's?

At that time, Vannatter began to realize that Fuhrman had set him up. He saw his entire career and pension go down the drain. He got extremely nervous.

Vannatter had to level with Criminalist Yamauchi. He persuaded Yamauchi to throw away his "private" test results, and perform a new blood typing test on one of the false swatches Vannatter's had used to replace the swatches Ms. Mazzola had prepared at Bundy!

As a result, one or two of the blood swatches from those blood drops at Bundy **"disappeared."** Yes! They did! No one seemed to know what had happened to them, but apparently, the number of blood swatches the criminalists ended up with, did not correspond with the number of blood swatches Ms. Mazzola had prepared at Bundy! Explain **that** one – any other way!

The "explanation" later given by the investigators and the prosecutors – to account for this apparent "mystery" – was that the criminalists at Bundy (Ms. Mazzola) did not keep track of how many swatches she prepared. Again, Ms. Mazzola was forced to take the blame, in order to cover up her superior's evidence fabrication.

The entire murder case against O.J. was just so **incredible** that it was – yes, **unbelievable!**

B ut we were discussing the two blood drops on the bottom rail of the rear gate at Bundy. Vannatter sensed that also the **defense,** began speculating that the blood evidence against O.J. was fabricated. Obviously, **if** O.J. was innocent, all the blood evidence **must** have been fabricated – **even the five blood drops along the shoeprints**.

Should the defense, seriously, begin to consider that possibility, they might perhaps stumble upon Vannatter's method of circumventing the EDTA in O.J.'s blood vial. That would have been disastrous, not only for the case against O.J., but for Vannatter himself. Because, if the defense realized that there must exist a method for circumventing the EDTA – then the flood gate was really opened up!

Consequently, Vannatter had to **divert the attention** away from any such ideas.

Vannatter had to convince the defense, first of all, but also everybody else, that **if** blood evidence had been planted in this case – then it would definitely contain **EDTA.**

If everyone was convinced of that, then Vannatter's method of circumventing the EDTA would not be exposed.

So, to throw the defense off track, and to get everybody's attention back on the EDTA, Vannatter, perhaps, simply **"gave"** the defense the two blood drops on the rear gate at Bundy!

The two drops could not have come from O.J. – they must have been planted. The photographs proved that. So, the two drops on the bottom rail of the gate were far too conspicuous to have been planted, primarily, to frame O.J. directly.

The drops would, of course, be found to contain EDTA. The

defense would get very upset, and argue that the drops must have been planted.

However, Vannatter reasoned that when weighed against the rest of the "mountain of evidence" the two drops on the gate didn't amount to much anyway. Preventing the defense from understanding how he had circumvented the EDTA in much of the other blood evidence, was far more important.

Vannatter, literally, made the defense **"shoot themselves in the foot"**! Upset, the defense argued:

> *"A-ha! See, the EDTA in the blood on the gate proves that the LAPD investigators planted false blood evidence against O.J. They **must** have planted that blood from O.J.'s blood vial – because there is EDTA in it!"*

This might have been exactly what Vannatter wanted them to think: If blood had been planted, it must have come from O.J.'s blood vial, and therefore, it must contain EDTA.

And consequently, if blood did **not** contain EDTA, it could **not** have come from O.J.'s blood vial, and therefore, it could **not** have been planted!

The two blood drops Vannatter arranged to be planted on the rear gate – although **somewhat** damaging to the prosecution – served to authenticate, apparently, the five much more important blood drops that **allegedly** were found alongside the bloody shoeprints, but which Vannatter had **actually fabricated** with blood from his fake EDTA vial.

Detective Vannatter "traded" some insignificant blood spots on the rear gate, against something immensely more important – his secret method of circumventing the EDTA in O.J.'s blood vial, and the apparent authenticity of the five blood drops alongside the bloody shoeprints.

That's a pretty good trade-off – considering that, at this point, Vannatter's own future was at stake, too!

In doing so, Vannatter lost **"the battle"** of the blood on the gate, but won **"the war"** of his blood evidence fabrication in general, including the five blood drops next to the bloody shoeprints, and much of the rest of the blood evidence.

The immaterial blood on the gate may have been another of Detective Vannatter's **"decoys"**! It may have been a "bait" **given** to the defense by Detective Vannatter, to limit their search for false blood evidence – to a search for EDTA.

It was "damage control" – all the way!

Don't tell me that I am so much smarter than Detective Vannatter, and that he, therefore, could not have figured this out!

Actually, there exists "semi-official" **CIA terminology** for this particular kind of **"damage control"** – indicating that the Simpson case was not the first case in which the authorities had used such tactics. It also indicated that the conspiracy against O.J. Simpson originated much higher up than with Detctive Philip Vannatter.

The CIA terminology for admitting to some limited wrong-doing in order to cover up some more serious wrong-doing, is **"limited hang-out"**!

Talking about CIA cover-up tactics, let me return to Fuhrman's and Vannatter's tactic of using, temporarily, a substitute blood that could readily be expected to be found whereever they planted it – so that **if** their evidence fabrication got bungled, there would be an **acceptable** explanation for the substitute blood they planted. Fuhrman used Nicole's blood at Bundy, and Vannatter, I suggested, could have used Nicole's blood too, or ketchup, film blood, or animal blood, for instance, at Rockingham.

The **CIA** even have a term for this kind of evidence fabrication or cover-up. They call it **"plausible denial."** In other words, if the CIA get caught in their evidence fabrication or in their cover-ups, they have a **plausible** way of **denying** any wrong-doing!

So don't come here and tell me that Detectives Fuhrman and Vannatter did not know what they were doing!

I am not through with those blood drops on the Bundy gate, though. As my readers understand, there is so much wrong with every little facet of the prosecution's case. Of course, when the prosecution presented us with one of their limited hypothesis, and we just accepted that hypothesis without thinking more about it – the hypothesis seemed to make sense.

As for the blood on the gate, the prosecution told us:

Three drops of O.J.'s blood were found on the gate. Obviously the blood must have come from the cut on O.J.'s hand, as he left through that gate.

At first, that sounded very plausible!

Again, Detective Fuhrman, in planning the murder of Nicole, in carrying it out, and in "setting up" the investigators and framing O.J., didn't make many mistakes. His plan was **near perfect**, and from his point of view his execution deserved an **"A-"** on his scorecard.

Detective Vannatter, smart as he was, could not compete with Fuhrman. For one thing, he allowed Fuhrman to set him up! Vannatter made a few other mistakes, too. The blood on the gate was smart in itself – as damage control. But if those three drops on the gate were intended to frame O.J. directly, then Vannatter had overlooked one more thing.

I assume my readers still remember my discussion of these three blood drops in an earlier chapter where I explained that they could not have come from O.J., because O.J.'s cut was on his **left** hand, but the gate opened away from the murderer, and swung to the **right** when it was being opened.

And it was equally "strange" how O.J. – **allegedly** – could have stood by the gate for, perhaps, twenty seconds, to wait for two drops to trickle from a cut on his finger, and simultaneously "aim" down over his finger, so that both those drops could hit the bottom rail of the gate – neither of them missing, and hitting the ground instead!

However, as I suggested, maybe Vannatter **wanted** the defense to prove that those drops were planted.

One last point: In spite of photographs, earlier testimonies during the **criminal trial,** and other evidence that the blood drops on the rear gate were planted, **three police officers testified under oath in the civil case,** that they had seen all three blood drops on the gate in the early morning on June 13. That was impossible! **They had to be lying! The EDTA in two of those drops proved that they were lying! And so did the photographs. Didn't Judge Fujisaki understand even that much?**

This goes to show, that police officers will go to any length to protect their colleagues, even when it is obvious that they are being disingenuous. I bet these officers would have sworn that the sun is green, if Vannatter, the prosecutors, or the counsels for the plaintiffs had asked them to do it!

Again, the prosecution's theory seemed "all right" at first:

O.J. was bleeding as he opened the gate – that's why his blood was on the gate.

However, as soon as we start to scrutinize the prosecution's theory – not a single thing seems to fit. Their theory was flawed from top to bottom, and from left to right!

So much about the blood on the Bundy gate!

3. The blood IN or ON the Bronco:

I have briefly mentioned this blood in connection with Detectives Fuhrman and Vannatter. Here are more details. But let me first make a reservation.

There is such an enormous amount of information in this case. Facts and speculations are being thrown at us from all angles and sources. No one seems to bother about checking the accuracy of their information. Even the former prosecutors and investigators – like Darden and Vannatter – are spreading lies or misinformation through TV talk shows as well as through their books.

As best I could reconstruct the history of the blood on the lower portion of the Bronco's door, this is what happened:

The four detectives, Lange, Vannatter, Fuhrman, and Phillips came to Rockingham without a search warrant. Nobody answered when they buzzed the intercom at the gate. They couldn't get in.

Fuhrman was the driving force in their efforts to get inside. He needed to plant the murder glove behind O.J.'s house a.s.a.p.

So Fuhrman walked over to O.J.'s Bronco, which they had already identified. The Bronco was parked around the corner, out of sight for the other detectives. Fuhrman opened the Bronco's door (perhaps the door was unlocked, or perhaps Fuhrman used a "Slim-Jim"). He smeared the bloody murder glove inside, thus planting Nicole's and Ron's blood in O.J.'s Bronco. Then he closed the door.

Fuhrman walked back to the others, and told Vannatter that there was blood **in** the Bronco. Vannatter didn't bother to check Fuhrman's information, because he was just as eager as Fuhrman to get inside O.J.'s house. For all Vannatter knew, O.J. could be cleaning the blood off the murder knife at that time.

Hence, Vannatter sent Fuhrman over the wall. He opened the gate from the inside, and everyone entered.

Later, in his testimony before the grand jury, Vannatter stated that Fuhrman had seen blood **in** the Bronco. Therefore, according to Vannatter, someone might be bleeding to death inside O.J.'s house! He claimed he faced an emergency situation, and entered O.J.'s house without a search warrant. Believe it if you want to!

The defense argued during the pretrial hearings that Fuhrman could not have seen the faint blood smears that were later found **inside** the Bronco, unless he had opened the door. But if he had opened the door, he might, perhaps, have smeared the bloody glove inside the Bronco at the same time – before he planted it behind O.J.'s house!

It was clear where the defense were heading. So Fuhrman vehemently denied that he had opened the door. He even justified his answer by saying that he checked the door and it was **locked!** Furthermore, he said he had told Vannatter that he had seen blood, **not in** the Bronco, but **on** the Bronco.

However, Vannatter's testimony said **in** the Bronco. Later, Vannatter was cross examined on this. He changed his story, too, in order to make it correspond with Fuhrman's new explanation. Vannatter testified that he could not remember if Fuhrman had said **in** or **on** the Bronco.

So Fuhrman was asked to specify where he had seen the blood. He described the blood as being on the outside lower portion of the Bronco's door. Funny thing – the criminalists had examined the Bronco twice, without finding any blood where Fuhrman said he saw it.

It didn't make things any better for Fuhrman and the prosecution that another officer contradicted Fuhrman's testimony on an important point. This officer claimed that he arrived at Rockingham shortly after the four detectives. He wanted to check the temperature of the Bronco's engine, to see if it had been driven recently. The Bronco was not locked! He simply opened the door, reached inside, and pulled the latch which opened the hood.

If Fuhrman lied, then the detectives had entered O.J.'s property illegally. All the evidence from Rockingham would have been illegally obtained. It might be thrown out by the judge because of this "technicality."

At this time the prosecution was convinced that O.J. were guilty. The prosecutors were desperate. Imagine losing this case on a technicality like that!

It was then Prosecutor Marcia Clark had a chat with Criminalist Dennis Fung. Fung had already examined the Bronco twice without finding the blood spots Fuhrman had referred to. Marcia Clark asked Fung to go back one last time and see if he could find the blood spots. In particular, Ms. Clark instructed Fung exactly where to look.

Reluctantly, Fung returned to the Bronco **for the third time** – and what do you know? Suddenly he saw the blood smears he had not seen on his two earlier examinations of the Bronco.

Fuhrman is in the clear – Vannatter is in the clear – the prosecution is in the clear!

Is Prosecutor Marcia Clark psychic? If not, I assume this was what is called **"women's intuition"**: Marcia Clark suddenly got the "psychic" idea, that if she sent Fung back to the Bronco for the **third** time and instructed him exactly where to look, he would find the blood spots he and his colleagues had not uncovered for six weeks – just in time to prove that Detective Fuhrman hadn't lied.

Is anyone going to tell me that Prosecutor Marcia Clark had not **"arranged"** for someone from the LAPD to plant the blood where Fung found it – or that she didn't know that someone else had arranged for it to be planted exactly where she told Fung to look?

Even police witnesses testified that some blood spots that were found in the Bronco had not been present on the day after the murders. As rampant as the blood evidence planting was in the Simpson case, it is astounding that Judge Fujisaki (civil trail) simply took it upon himself to decide what blood evidence Simpson' attorneys would be allowed to argue had been planted, and what blood evidence they would not be allowed to argue had been planted!

I thought it was up to the **jury** to evaluate the evidence and decide what evidence **they** trusted and what evidence they did not trust. **With a judge like Fujisaki, who needs a jury?!**

The judge allowed the defense to argue that some of the blood in the Bronco, the blood on the gate, and the blood on one of O.J.'s socks might have been planted, but the defense were not allowed to argue that the five blood drops at Bundy, O.J.'s blood at Rockingham, and some of the blood in the Bronco had been planted.

Let me explain the logic – or lack of logic, rather – in Judge Fujisaki's ruling:

> While the Bronco was in the custody of the LAPD, some blood was recovered from the Bronco shortly after the murders and some more was recovered a couple of weeks later. The criminalists who collected the blood on both occasions swore that the blood they collected the second time, was not present the first time they examined the Bronco.
>
> Obviously, someone from the LAPD planted blood in the Bronco between the first and the second examination. It can't be harder to understand than that.

Yet, Judge Fujisaki ruled that while someone, obviously must have planted some blood in the Bronco between the two examinations, it was absolutely **inconceivable** (again, according to this "smart" judge) that anyone could have planted blood in the Bronco **prior** to the first examination!

What are the requirements for becoming a judge in the Santa Monica Court District of California, if Judge Fujisaki can't even put two and two together?

According to the prosecution, they found microscopic traces of O.J.'s blood inside the Bronco. All in all it was less than 7/10 of one drop! We know already that O.J. could not have bled at Bundy, and therefore, probably not in his Bronco either – not even if he were the murderer.

But set that aside. Let us **hypothetically** assume that O.J. were the murderer, and that he had cut his finger during the murders, and therefore, bled at Bundy, in his Bronco, and at Rockingham!

Wouldn't you think that **if** O.J., allegedly, bled at least 5 drops of blood as he walked away from Bundy and three drops as he passed through the rear gate, and he were still bleeding rather profusely in his driveway leading up to his house, and inside his foyer – then he would bleed more than 7/10 of one drop of blood inside his Bronco, driving 2 1/2 miles from Bundy to Rockingham?

Of course, we **know** that his blood in the Bronco, as well as that of the victims, must have been planted. What I explained above, further proves it.

7/10 of one drop of blood is exactly as much blood you would get from one of Vannatter's false blood swatches, if you moistened it and smeared it inside the Bronco!

So much about the blood IN or ON the Bronco!

4. Carpet fibers on Ron's shirt and on the knit cap:

The investigators were supposed to exercise full control over the Bronco, the victim's clothes, the knit cap, O.J.'s hair samples, and all the other so-called evidence. However, several witnesses testified that there was absolutely no control with respect to who entered the Bronco. It was even **broken into** while it was in the custody of the LAPD.

The security was not much better inside the LAPD's crime lab. A section of the Bronco's carpet, the gloves, and the knit cap, were all kept unsealed and unpackaged inside the same large open cardboard box!

It was the easiest thing in the world for an investigator to pluck some fibers from the Bronco's carpet, in the crime lab, and put the fibers on Ron's shirt and on the cap. Later they could let someone else, conveniently, **"discover"** the carpet fibers on the shirt and the cap.

Isn't it funny that a carpet fiber from the Bronco's carpet was found on the cap? How did it fly up to the cap on the murderer's head?

No-no! The prosecution must have reasoned that O.J. didn't wear the cap. It was on the floor of the Bronco – that is why a carpet fiber got on it.

That makes sense? You fetch a knit cap in order to disguise yourself so no one shall recognize you as you leave your house and drive two miles to the murder scene. But you don't wear the cap on your way to the murder scene! Instead you place it on the floor in your car.

However, when you have already reached the murder scene, so you don't need the disguise anymore, because you don't expect to encounter anyone other than your victim or her neighbors, who would recognize you regardless of the cap – **then** you put on your so-called "disguise"! Brilliant!

If O.J. were the murderer, and the cap was his disguise, we would expect he should have worn it in his Bronco, on his way to Bundy, but removed it as soon as he got there. Otherwise he would probably scare the heck out of Nicole, so that he could not attack her by surprise.

Instead, according to the prosecution's theory, O.J. did the exact opposite! He didn't wear the disguise when he needed it – driving to Bundy. The cap was on the Bronco's floor! But at Bundy, where the disguise would only complicate matters, he put it on!

One last point regarding the so-called **Bronco** carpet fibers. The prosecutors and the plaintiffs – as well as the media – tried to make a big point out of the fact that this particular carpet was only used in a smaller number of all Ford Bronco's. Still, it was used in thousands of Bronco's, though.

What the prosecutors and the plaintiffs – as well as the media– failed to inform us about, however, was the fact that although this particular carpet was not used in every **Bronco**, it was commonly used in the **Ford Taurus** model. What is even more interesting is that Ford Taurus is a rather common police car in Los Angeles. Eventually, as many as 28 different Ford Taurus police cars stopped over at Bundy during the investigation. Several of the LAPD officers at Bundy on the night of the murders, might have arrived in Ford Taurus's. Perceivably, they might have brought with them fibers from their cars, fibers which could have been mistaken for fibers from a Ford Bronco.

Most likely, though, the "Bronco fibers" were planted by the investigators in the LAPD's crime lab.

So much about Bronco carpet fibers!

5. Nicole's blood on O.J.'s socks:

I could go on, for ever, like this. Not one single piece of evidence against O.J. was **trustworthy.**

> **There was something suspicious, or inconsistent, or contradictory, or even ridiculous, about every single piece of evidence in this case.**

Take O.J.'s socks for instance. Here is the story about the socks:

June 13, an LAPD cameraman was sent to Rockingham to videotape O.J.'s home. He videotaped "everything," and especially any object that he considered out of its normal place. In one room he videotaped a glove, only because it appeared not to belong there. Naturally, he would have videotaped a pair of used, black dress socks lying on a light colored carpet, in an otherwise meticulously neat room.

The cameraman also videotaped everything in O.J.'s bedroom. He stood on the exact spot on the light colored carpet where Criminalist Fung later said he found O.J.'s used black socks. Had the socks been there, the cameraman would have seen them and, hence, he would have videotaped them. But he didn't

His video camera recorded the exact time on the videotape, so we know that he videotaped O.J.'s bedroom at 4:13 pm.

Criminalist Fung recorded, and later testified, that some 20 minutes after the cameraman had left, Fung was shown the socks by Detective Fuhrman, and told to collect them into evidence.

Obviously, unless the LAPD used a **blind** cameraman, **the socks must have been planted – by Fuhrman – after the cameraman left.**

Typically, in their books, Lange and Vannatter try to cover up this embarrassing case of evidence planting by saying that Criminalist Fung collected the socks some time **between noon and 3 o'clock**. That's why the socks did not appear on the video tape.

However, Fung himself testified that he collected the socks after the cameraman had videotaped O.J.'s bedroom. Furthermore, Fungs evidence collection sheet supported his testimony.

To top it off, the time log from Rockingham showed that Fung was not even at Rockingham between noon and 3 o'clock!

This is how the lead investigator tries to mislead the American public in an effort to cover up the fact that he fabricated almost all the evidence in the Simpson case – except the evidence Fuhrman planted.

Talking about Mark Fuhrman – he is not much better. In his book, Fuhrman "informs" us that he saw those socks already at 8:00 in the morning. Therefore, he argues, the socks were not planted after the cameraman had left. However, Fuhrman too is lying, because the socks were not present when the cameraman videotaped O.J.'s bedroom. But 20 minutes later when Fung collected the socks, they were, obviously, there.

Typically, between the cameraman's visit to O.J.'s bedroom – which Fuhrman didn't know about at the time – and Fung's visit, to collect the socks – only Fuhrman visited O.J.'s bedroom! Hence, Fuhrman must have planted the socks in O.J.'s bedroom! Surprised? Hardly!

How can one investigator after the other – Lange, Vannatter, Fuhrman – and we may as well add prosecutors Darden and Clark to the list – write such obvious lies? They all do it to cover up their misconducts or criminal conducts in the Simpson case.

But how, can they write such lies when it is so obvious that they are lying. They do it, because their books are not a criminal trial. Their books are their fights for the public's opinion of the case. And 99% of the public, who are convinced that O.J. is the murderer, simply don't know enough about this case to realize that they are lying and spreading misinformation about O.J. and the case.

That is why I am writing this book – to counter their blatant lies and cover-ups and expose how they conspired to frame O.J. **Even I may make a few mistakes here and there**. But, at least, I admit it – and it is not intentional!

Some of my readers may object to my conclusion regarding the socks, arguing that the investigators wouldn't have sent a cameraman to record that there were no socks on O.J.'s bedroom carpet, and then have planted the socks on that very same carpet 20 minutes later.

True! But the investigators didn't send the cameraman! He wasn't there to videotape for the investigators. He was sent by a totally different branch of the LAPD, and for a totally different purpose. He was videotaping to protect the LAPD against a possible law suit, should objects disappear from O.J.'s home while the LAPD were there investigating. The investigators hardly knew that the cameraman was there, or what he was videotaping.

Anyway, the socks were collected and sent to the LAPD's crime lab. They were examined **twice**, and reports were written that **there was no evidence of blood on the socks.** Weeks passed, then the socks were examined again, by someone else. This time one of the socks had plenty of blood on it!

Between the two first, and the third examination, the socks had only been in the custody of the LAPD. Is anyone going to tell me that the blood on the sock was not planted by the LAPD investigators?

Later the socks were sent to the FBI's crime lab in Washington DC, for DNA analyses. Before the DNA analyses were performed, someone within the LAPD informed the media that the blood on one of the socks contained Nicole's DNA. Later it turned out that this information was correct.

When the blood on the sock was not DNA tested yet, how in heavens name could someone within the LAPD know that the blood on the sock contained Nicole's DNA, unless that person had planted Nicole's blood on the sock – or knew someone who had done it?

But there is much more to this story! At some point the defense got the socks for examination. Criminalist Herbert MacDonell, examined the socks for the defense. Later he testified that the blood on the sock appeared to have been pressed onto (rubbed into) the sock while it was lying flat on a hard surface, like a table.

MacDonell found it most unlikely that the blood could have come – as the prosecution argued – from Nicole's hand grabbing O.J.'s ankle as she was falling, or lying on the ground.

The reason MacDonell gave was that the wet blood had been pressed through from the fabric on **one side** of the sock, to the corresponding area on the **inside** of the fabric on **the other side** of the sock.

Of course, this could not have occurred if O.J.'s leg had been inside the sock, keeping the two opposite sides of fabric apart from each other.

Pretty obvious for someone with an unbiased mind! Dr. McDonell's opinion was supported by other experts. Furthermore, the blood on the sock contained **EDTA** – the preservative. This further suggested that the blood on the sock had not come from Nicole's body directly, but had been planted – possibly from the test tube with Nicole's blood that Vannatter picked up at the coroner's office, but more likely, from the blood on Nicole's own dress, which was also kept in the LAPD's crime lab.

The pair of socks was one of the most alarming and important pieces of evidence in the case – proving beyond any doubt that the LAPD investigators planted false evidence against O.J.

Prosecutor Marcia Clark should have blasted the investigators for having fabricated this scandalous piece of false evidence! Instead, she protected the rogue investigators and tried to cover up the embarrassment.

Prosecutor Marcia Clark knows some tricks of her own! So she deliberately saved, what she thought was a "smart" question, for her **rebuttal closing arguments.** Those were the last remarks the jury heard from the attorneys before they started their deliberations. Hence, the defense were **precluded from countering** Ms. Clark's remarks about the socks, and Marcia Clark could let the following question "hang in the air":

> *"Assuming the defense is right, and the socks didn't have any blood on them to start with – why would the detectives bother to plant a pair of sock that didn't have any blood on them? The insinuation from the defense is ludicrous!"*

I shall answer for the defense!

The detectives wanted to plant Nicole's blood on O.J.'s sock, arguing that Nicole had grabbed O.J.'s ankle as she fell, or lay on the ground.

That would indeed have been a powerful piece of (**false**) evidence – had they succeeded!

However, Nicole's wet blood was not available to the investigators at Rockingham in the afternoon of June 13. **Her blood would be available to the investigators (Vannatter) later on, though – in the LAPD's crime lab!**

So this evidence fabrication had to be a **"two stage rocket."** **First,** they had to provide (plant) the socks, and bring them to the LAPD's crime lab. **Secondly,** they had to figure out a way, in the lab, to plant Nicole's blood on one of the socks.

There was testimony indicating that Detective Fuhrman had been up in O.J.'s bedroom – alone – shortly after the video cameraman left, but before Criminalist Fung was told to collect the socks. This strongly suggested that Fuhrman removed those socks from O.J.'s laundry bin and planted them on the bedroom floor.

The socks were definitely planted. And Nicole's blood was definitely planted on the socks – **after** they were collected and brought to the LAPD's crime lab!

Think about it! Have you heard about **this procedure before**?

Someone planted a piece of evidence, although that piece of evidence in itself, initially, was not compromising to O.J. at all. The person who planted the evidence, however, trusted that the detectives or the criminalists would be **tempted** to plant blood, fiber, or hair on that piece of evidence later – and find a way to do it – after the evidence had been collected and brought to the LAPD's crime lab!

Here again, a neutral piece of evidence had obviously been planted to frame O.J. Again, the prime suspect is Detective Fuhrman. The procedure, or the principle, was the same as I suggested Fuhrman used at Bundy, in connection with the five blood drops, and with the cap.

He planted a piece of evidence against O.J. Not because the evidence was in any way incriminating to O.J. – **in its pristine state** – but because Fuhrman trusted that the criminalists or the investigators would find a way of changing or modifying that **neutral** piece of evidence in the LAPD's crime lab – in order **to make it incriminating to O.J.!**

The method, or the principle, was so characteristic in both cases – so similar! And Detective Fuhrman was the probable culprit in both incidents – both at Bundy and in O.J.'s bedroom!

Was Fuhrman still trying to set up the investigators with neutral evidence, whenever he saw the opportunity to do it, so that the investigators and the criminalists should be tempted to

"modify" that evidence against O.J., back in their crime lab?

Criminalist Fung collected the socks and booked them into evidence. In the now infamous opinion of Detective Fuhrman, it was (in essence),

> *the duty of all good police officers to falsify evidence –*
> *if necessary – in order to convict a suspect they thought were*
> *guilty.*

Maybe the criminalist at the crime lab wasn't *"a good LAPD officer."* **Maybe, instead, he was honest!** Detective Fuhrman couldn't know for sure. Of course, he (or Vannatter) couldn't tell Fung to include a "notice" with the socks, reading:

> *"Don't examine these socks until we have had time to plant*
> *Nicole's blood on them!"*

So Fuhrman just planted the socks, clean as they were, and let Fung collect them and get them booked in as evidence. **Later,** Fuhrman hoped, someone in the crime lab would figure out a way to plant Nicole's or O.J.'s blood on them.

If they later didn't get an opportunity to plant Nicole's or O.J.'s blood on the socks anyway, there would be no reason to raise any eyebrows. They could simply explain that they saw the socks in O.J.'s bedroom, collected them and examined them. If there was no blood on the socks – so be it!

Unfortunately for Detectives Fuhrman and Vannatter – but luckily for O.J. – someone did examine the socks – twice! And fortunately, they were honest – at least until the pressure from their rogue colleagues got to them. So they recorded the results of their examinations and concluded:

"No blood apparent"!

Either, the conspirators didn't know that the socks had been examined. Or they didn't care – because **they hoped the defense**

would not find out about the two first examinations, or because **the power of such a false evidence would be so immense – if they got away with it – that they were blinded by the prospect.**

So the LAPD sent the socks to an independent lab for DNA analyses – **but not until a _"good LAPD officer"_ had planted Nicole's blood on one of the socks, in order to strengthen and continue the conspiracy to frame O.J.**

There can't be any doubt that this is what happened.

- The LAPD cameraman proved it!
- The videotape proved it!
- Photographs taken in O.J.'s bedroom proved it!
- The "time frame" proved it!
- Criminalist Fung's collection sheet proved it!
- The two first examinations of the socks proved it!
- The way the blood was pressed onto the sock proved it!
- The transfer of blood from one side to the other proved it!
- The experts' testimonies proved it!
- The fact that someone from the LAPD "knew" – before the test results were in – that the blood on the sock contained Nicole's DNA, proved it!
- And finally – and conclusively – the EDTA in Nicole's blood on the sock proved it!

Besides, this "method" of evidence planting was exactly the same as Detective Fuhrman had used in connection with the blood drops and the knit cap at Bundy. The "method" carried Fuhrman's stamp on it!

Even today, long after the criminal trial, I hear former prosecutors on TV constantly trying to misinform the public about everything in this case, in an effort to cover up the massive fabrication of false evidence against O.J.

One such misinformation is that the EDTA in Nicole's blood could have come from residues of laundry detergent in the fabric of the sock.

Obviously, the former prosecutors and investigators are deeply embarrassed when they are confronted in public with all the false evidence they presented against O.J. Otherwise they would not have resorted to such **obvious lies** in their desperate efforts to save face.

The fact is that there is no way to escape the scandalous socks! **The fabric of the sock was tested separately for EDTA, just to see if the EDTA in Nicole's blood could have come from laundry detergent resudue in the sock. But there was no EDTA in the fabric itself – only in Nicole's blood!**

The next lie former prosecutors and investigators were spreading on TV talk shows, in order to lessen the embarrassment of the socks, was an argument that **there was not enough EDTA** in the blood on the sock.

There was, arguably a higher concentration of EDTA in Nicole's blood vial which Detective Vannatter had picked up at the coroner's office on June 14, 1994.

EDTA is normally present in the human organism, but in very small amounts. That could explain why there was EDTA in the blood on the sock – but not enough EDTA, according to the prosecutors, for that blood to have been planted from Nicole's blood vial.

The former prosecutors, investigators, and others who present such garbage on national television failed to inform the audience that even though there may have been a higher concentration of EDTA in the blood vial, than in the blood on the sock,

the concentration of EDTA in Nicole's blood on O.J.'s sock was about **one thousand times higher** than what is normally found in the human body, and **such a concentration would have killed Nicole** long before any murderer could have gotten to her!

Evidently, the civil jurors – who according to the media, were so intelligent – did not understand that they were being misled by the counsels and the expert witnesses for the plaintiffs.

When the media could characterize those jurors as being intelligent – obviously, the media did not understand much either!

I trust my readers are more intelligent than either of the above, so let me explain what really happened to O.J.'s socks. Actually, it does not require much intelligence to understand it – so don't get too cocky, just because you understand what I am about to explain:

EDTA is an **anti-coagulant**, as I have explained before. It prevents the blood from coagulating. Therefore, with the concentration of EDTA found in Nicole's blood on the sock, Nicole would have bled to death in her sleep, long before June 12, 1994 – if the blood on O.J.'s sock had come from Nicole's body directly.

My readers should be aware of the fact that we humans don't just bleed through **cuts in our skin**. Almost continuously small blood vessels burst inside our body, in our intestines, in our sinuses, in our muscles, etc. We never notice it, because we don't see these bleedings – and they stop by themselves, because the blood coagulates and allow these minor, internal wounds to heal.

However, if the concentration of EDTA – **the anti-coagulant** – in Nicole's blood, **in her body,** had been even close to the concentration of EDTA in Nicole's blood **on O.J.'s sock** – then dozens of minor, bursted blood vessels in her body would never have healed. Instead they would have continued to bleed forever, so Nicole would, simply, have bled to death in her sleep one night!

However, former prosecutors and investigators, as well as reporters, and others, critical of O.J. can freely spew their lies and misinformation on national TV, because most people don't understand that they are being lied to, and the TV talk show hosts are either ignorant, or so bias that they decline to invite other panelists who can correct them!

The latest lie in "the socks mini-series" came during the civil trial, when lab Director Robin Cotton of Cellmark Diagnostics lab testified for the plaintiffs. She claimed that the **contamination** of the blood on the **sock** was **less** than the contamination of the blood in the **vial** Vannatter got from the coroner's office on June 14, 1994. Therefore, Nicole's blood on the sock, most likely, did not come from that vial, in spite of the presence of the EDTA in the blood on the sock. Therefore, Nicole's blood could not have been planted on the sock – at least **not from the EDTA vial**.

Ms. Cotton explained that the blood in a victim's body, often gets more contaminated than parts of the victim's blood found on, for instance, the victim's clothing. The reason is that the blood in the victim's body is kept warm for quite some time. Besides, it is kept wet (liquid). Those are perfect conditions for bacterial growth. And bacteria are everywhere – not the least, inside our body.

On the other hand, a blood spot on the victim's clothing will quickly dry up. And bacterial growth is rather slow in dry materials.

I have no problem with Ms. Cotton's explanation. But it was a smoke screen! Who said Nicole's blood on the socks must have been planted from her **blood vial** – if it was planted?

What if Nicole's blood had come from her dress? Her dress was present in the crime lab. It was dry, and the blood on it would therefore, arguably, be less contaminated. Someone could have moistened a blood spot on Nicole's dress with distilled water, and then rubbed the spot on the dress against O.J.'s sock – or vice versa.

Later during the civil trial, an **expert witness** for the plaintiffs confirmed my theory. He testified that **the concentration of EDTA in Nicole's blood on O.J.'s sock was exactly the same as the concentration of EDTA in Nicole's blood on her dress!**

I couldn't believe my ears! The plaintiffs were actually proving that Nicole's blood on O.J.'s sock was planted – and they even explained how it was done. **Yet, the defense did not realize it and pick up on it. I was stunned!** The plaintiffs' argument was this:

The blood on Nicole's dress had come from **Nicole's body** – directly. Since the concentration of EDTA in Nicole's blood on O.J.'s sock, was **the same** as the concentration of EDTA in Nicole's blood on her dress – Nicole's blood on O.J.'s sock could **also** have come from **Nicole's body** – directly!

Even today I am stunned by the plaintiffs making that argument. The fact that the concentration of EDTA in Nicole's blood on O.J.'s sock was about **one thousand times higher** than what is normally found in the human body – an absolute **lethal** concentration – proved that Nicole's blood on O.J.'s sock **must** have been planted. The plaintiffs just proved **how** it was done!

According to the plaintiffs' witness, the LAPD had prepared swatches from Nicole's blood on her dress – for reference analyses. Analyzing the blood on these swatches they found that the concentration of EDTA was the same as that in the blood on O.J.'s sock. Apparently, that should prove that Nicole's blood on O.J.'s sock had **also** come from **Nicole's body** directly. **But that was a ridiculous conclusion!**

Instead, here is the obvious – proven – explanation! Nicole's blood was not originally found on O.J.'s sock. Earlier reports indicated that: *"No blood apparent"*! Remember?

Weeks later the LAPD criminalists were preparing blood swatches from Nicole's blood on her dress. The proper way to do that (as you know by now) was to wet the swatches in distilled water, and perhaps even wet the blood stains on the dress.

Because the dress may have been washed in a laundry detergent containing EDTA, some EDTA from the detergent was probably left in the dress fabric. This EDTA got dissolved into the wet blood – either on the night of the murders, or when the dress was moistened in the LAPD's crime lab.

That's how EDTA ended up on these blood swatches – from the detergent in the dress fabric – in a concentration approximately one thousand times higher than what is normally present in human blood.

But then, suddenly, some smart-ass in the LAPD's crime lab probably said:

*"Let's rub off some of this blood, **also on O.J.'s sock,***

> *suggesting that Nicole might have grabbed O.J.'s ankle, as she lay on the ground. . . . After all, the bastard is guilty as hell!"*

The other criminalists agreed:

> *"Brilliant! Perfect! The blood on the dress came directly from Nicole. There is probably just her normal bodily concentration of EDTA in that blood. So if we do this, it will look like the blood we plant on O.J.'s sock must also have come from Nicole's body directly. That should nail this monster! Let's do it. Let's not allow this murderer to escape justice!"*

The criminalists thought, of course, that they were doing society a service. Fortunately for O.J., Nicole's dress must have been washed in laundry detergent containing EDTA, and **not have been rinsed too well.** And fortunately, the LAPD's own video cameraman proved that the socks were planted in O.J.'s bedroom. Otherwise, the good intentions of these rogue LAPD criminalists could have sent Sydney's and Justin's father to the gas chamber!

So much about the socks from O.J.'s bedroom!

6. Blue-black fiber from clothing:

The prosecutors in the criminal trial and the counsels for the plaintiffs in the civil trial have tried to link a blue-black fabric fiber, found at Bundy, to a jogging suit O.J. allegedly should have worn on the night of the murders.

This is so far-fetched that it goes way past absurdity. The counsels were playing to jurors and to an audience unable to understand and evaluate such information critically. Perhaps the counsels even considered that some of this misinformation would reach the unsequestered civil jury. Let me try to put some sense into the story of this "celebrated" blue-black fabric fiber.

The sidewalk at Bundy Drive may appear clean, just like the air in your house may appear clean. Luckily, we don't see the dirt that surrounds us. Otherwise, we would be scared to breathe. If you filter the air you breathe in a few minutes, or you vacuumed with a new filter just a few square feet of your living room carpet, or kitchen floor, took out the filters, and looked at them under a microscope, you would be shocked!

You would see a "jungle" of living, crawling, eating, reproducing organisms you never even heard of, surviving as predators and scavengers more scary than even Steven Spielberg could have dreamt up. There would be microorganisms, bacteria, mites, thousands of fragments from dead skin cells, thousands of fragments from organic as well as synthetic fibers, plain dirt, and dead cells from both humans, animals, and plants.

A criminalist doing the same thing from the walkway at Bundy could find anything he wanted to find. It is simply a matter of what he decided to look for. The investigators heard Kato say that O.J. might have worn a dark blue or black outfit, so they looked for a dark blue or black fiber in their microscope. Had Kato said that O.J. wore a yellow tuxedo, I am sure they would have found a yellow fabric fiber!

It's like shopping at MACY's, in miniature. If you want a gray suit, you look around and find a gray suit. If your wife wants a red dress, she looks around a little more, and finds a red dress. If your son wants a stuffed animal, or your daughter wants a makeup set, they'll find that too.

A good sweep of the murder scene when viewed under a criminalist's microscope would reveal something similar. If you look for a blue fiber, you'll find a blue fiber, if you look for a pink fiber, you'll find that. If you look for a piece of skin, you'll find that. If you want Afro hair, blond hair, Asian hair, red hair, dog hair, synthetic hair – it is all there, probably. If you want a live "animal" I am sure the criminalists could find an entire zoo for you – anything from harmless bacteria to scary mites, ants, beatles, worms, and all sorts of insects.

A murderer who, concealed by the darkness, sneaks over to Bundy late at night to kill Nicole, is not likely to wear a pink suit! With 95% certainty we could predict that he would wear a dark blue or black outfit. Hence, to say,

> *"We found a blue-black fabric fiber at Bundy, and O.J.*
> ***may*** *have worn a dark blue or black jogging suit during the*
> *filming of an exercise video many weeks ago – so he*
> *probably killed Nicole and Ron,"*

is almost as silly as saying,

> *"We are sure the murderer wore pants, and O.J. owns several*
> *pairs of pants, so he probably killed Nicole and Ron."*

The investigators have had that blue-black fabric fiber for two and a half years. If that fabric fiber had anything to do with O.J., then they should have identified the fiber two years ago. They had no problem identifying a fiber as having come from a carpet used in Ford Broncos (and other models). Nor did they have any problem identifying shoeprints as having come from size 12, Bruno Magli shoes.

If the investigators had **wanted** to, they could have identified that fiber a long time ago, saying – with absolute certainty – that the fiber belonged, for instance, to a particular suit made by Hagar's or Docker's, or to a particular warm-up suit made by Nike's – or to the particular jogging suit they allege that O.J. wore.

The contention was that this blue-black fiber belonged to a jogging suit O.J. allegedly wore during the filming of an exercise video. So now they demanded that O.J. come up with this particular jogging suit – which O.J. denies that he kept after the filming.

According to the investigators – and 2 1/2 years later, according to the plaintiffs – they were waiting for O.J. to produce a jogging suit he doesn't have, so they could compare it to this infamous blue-black fiber. What kind of nonsense is that?

Regardless of what O.J. says about this issue, what the investigators should have done, was to ask the video producer, who provided the jogging suit in question, what kind of suit O.J. wore during the filming of the exercise video, and where they bought it.

The fact of the matter is, namely, that **the producer purchased**

this particular jogging suit for O.J to wear during the filming.

Next, the investigators should have purchased an identical jogging suit, compared the Bundy fiber to fibers from the identical jogging suit, to see if they matched. The investigators didn't need to worry about O.J. at this point, or whether or not he received this jogging suit after the filming, or whether he borrowed it, gave it back, never received it, or whatever.

Let us first of all determine whether the blue-black Bundy fiber even belongs to such a jogging suit.

Then – if it does – we can start considering whether or not O.J. ever had such a jogging suit, except during the filming of the exercise video.

And if the fiber **does not** match the jogging suit O.J. wore during the filming, then the investigators can forever put this blue-black fiber aside.

To me this seems like such an obvious, logical investigative route to follow. I think the investigators for the plaintiffs purposely **avoided eliminating or including** this fiber – although they could easily have done it – because they were afraid it would **not** match the jogging suit O.J. wore during the filming.

By **not** identifying the fiber as having come from the jogging suit – or not – they let people – and the jurors – **assume** that the fiber **would** match a jogging suit O.J., allegedly, should have worn **– if he would only come up with it!**

Hence, the plaintiffs could keep on insinuating that O.J. had disposed of this alleged jogging suit because he didn't want it matched against the blue-black fiber collected at Bundy.

When the investigators, and the counsels for the plaintiffs, still, 2 1/2 years after the murders, have not identified this blue-black fiber – they should instead shut up about it.

Since they, with all their resources and expertise, haven't tied this fiber to the particular jogging suit O.J. wore during the filming of the exercise video, my readers, at least, should know that this fiber probably belonged to someone else's piece of clothing. Therefore, as things stand today, **this fiber points to O.J.'s innocence.**

As a matter of fact it does! The woman in charge of providing the outfit O.J. wore during the filming of the exercise video, testified for Judge Ito, outside the presence of the jury. She said that the outfit she provided for O.J. was not blue black – it was solid black. Besides, the blue-black fiber was a synthetic fiber, while the fabric of O.J.'s outfit was cotton.

Hence, Judge Ito didn't even allow this woman to testify, since the blue-black fiber the prosecutors (and later the plaintiffs) made so much fuzz about – had nothing to do with O.J.

In spite of this, the blue-black fiber is tossed around even today, three years after the murders, as alleged evidence of O.J.'s guilt, and as an insinuation that he disposed of his outfit from the exercise video to cover up the fact that he killed Nicole and Ron.

How deceitful can O.J.'s adversaries, the prosecutors and investigators in this case, and the plaintiffs, possibly get?

Let me give you a comparable example :

Suppose the investigators had found a key underneath Nicole's body! This key could not be identified as belonging to O.J. – and the key could not be identified as belonging to Nicole or any other person associated with the murder case, either. There is a fair possibility then, that the key belonged to the murderer. He might have lost it.

Since the key couldn't be identified as belonging to O.J., the key becomes a strong piece of evidence that O.J. is **not** the murderer.

I trust my readers see the absurdity in the prosecutors or plaintiffs arguing:

*"We found a key at Bundy. We have **not identified** it, so it **might belong** to O.J. Therefore, the key proves that O.J. is guilty"*!

The blue-black fabric fiber falls into that exact same category. If the investigators find evidence they believe may have come from the **murderer**, and they cannot tie this evidence to O.J., then that evidence speaks **for** O.J. – **not against** him!

This entire blue-black fiber story is one big hoax! It is my argument that the investigators knew they couldn't tie this fiber to O.J. Therefore, they **deliberately declined** to identify it conclusively.

It served the prosecutors, and the plaintiffs, better to leave it hanging in the air, as an **insinuation** they didn't have **to substantiate** – rather than to identify the fiber and finding out that it did not come from O.J.'s jogging suit!

You see – after both the prosecutors and the plaintiffs had argued for two years that the fiber came from the **murderer** – identifying the fiber could tend to exonerate O.J. rather than incriminate him!

Who knows? Perhaps, one day, somebody ties this fiber to O.J. But they haven't done it yet!

So much about the blue-black fiber!

My discussion of the blue-black fabric fiber may seem like much ado about nothing.

The fiber, by itself – yes! But it was worth discussing, anyway. You see, most people think criminal investigators collect and examine every bit of potential evidence in connection with a crime, then interpret that evidence objectively, and eventually present the prosecutors and the jurors with an unbiased representation of what, in their opinion, took place at the crime scenes.

I am sorry if I destroy anyone's illusions about the LAPD, or crime investigations in general. But unfortunately, this is **not** how criminal investigations are conducted. **Had investigations been conducted in this manner, we would not have solved many crimes!**

Instead – **as quickly as possible** – the investigators try to limit the number of suspects to **one prime suspect!**

Simultaneously, the investigators try to come up with one

single, most probable **motive** and **MO** (the investigators' theory regarding why and how the crime was committed **by their prime suspect**).

This may surprise my readers. But except for the very early stages of a criminal investigation, the investigators don't investigate to **find out what happened!** They have already made up their minds about what happened, who committed the crime, how, and why!

Once they reach that stage, very quickly, they pool all their resources in an effort to try **to find evidence against their prime suspect!** The major part of the investigation is about proving that their preconceived theory is correct!

They don't look for evidence pointing to anyone else than their prime suspect!

Only if they are unable to find sufficient evidence against their prime suspect – and they really become convinced that their prime suspect is innocent – do they start looking for evidence pointing to someone else.

Should the investigators run into such a dead end street, however, they often perceive this as a **personal failure**. Some investigators have trouble admitting that they were wrong initially, apologize to the prime suspect, face the media's criticism, and go back to square one, looking for the **real** perpetrator.

Investigators who can not handle situations like that, psychologically, sometimes fabricate false evidence against their prime suspect, to cover up the fact that they were mistaken. We saw that in the DuPage case which I related earlier.

My readers should understand that such rogue investigators don't necessarily fabricate false evidence in an effort to convict their suspect and send an innocent man to his execution.

Initially, their motive for fabricating false evidence may simply be to make their suspect appear **"a little bit more guilty"** – so the public and the media shall better understand why the investigators, wrongfully, suspected this innocent person.

However, as it so often happens, one lie leads to another, a false testimony by one officer is refuted, the officer looks bad, so a second officer steps in to corroborate his colleague's perjured testimony. One piece of fabricated evidence comes under scrutiny, so the investigators fabricate another piece of evidence to support the first piece of false evidence and prevent it from being exposed.

Before they know it, the investigators' life and future is on the line. To save their own careers the investigators must seek, by all means, to convict their initial prime suspect.

That's probably what happened in DuPage. Especially in high profile murder cases where there is a lot of pressure on the investigators, there is also a temptation to **enhance** the evidence.

There is a saying, that if the police don't solve a murder case **within the first 72 hours** of their investigation, they will, most likely, **never solve it**.

This is why Detective Fuhrman could frame O.J. and set up the investigators so easily.

It is time to say something collectively about all the physical evidence in this case. Had ...

– both gloves been found at Bundy, or
– neither of the gloves been found at all, or
– the left (Bundy) glove been found turned "inside out," or
– the left middle finger of the glove had a cut, and
– no carpet fibers been found at all, or
– several Bronco carpet fibers been found leading to Bundy,
– the knit cap not been found at all, or
– only O.J.'s hairs been found on the knit cap, and
– many drops of O.J.'s blood been found in the Bronco, or
– O.J.'s blood not been found in the Bronco at all, and
– the gloves been found together with the bloody clothes, the bloody shoes, and the bloody knife, and
– the five blood drops next to the bloody shoe prints at Bundy been found to be Nicole's blood, and
– O.J.'s bloody fingerprints been found somewhere at Bundy,

... then **maybe** I could have **started, at least,** to believe **some** of this ludicrous murder case theory the prosecution concocted against O.J. But the way everything presented itself, it was just too absurd.

When will O.J.'s adversaries stop lying about this case? Not only did O.J. lack any sort of a motive. None of the various pieces of evidence fit the prosecution's theory.

Isolated, many pieces of evidence might be construed to point to O.J. For instance the five blood drops next to the bloody shoeprints might point to O.J. **when viewed all by themselves.** O.J., allegedly, had lost the left glove and cut his finger in a struggle with Ron – so he bled as he left the murder scene.

However, as soon as we start to put this evidence into a wider context, it falls apart. **For instance**:

- How could O.J. have lost that glove in a struggle with Ron?
- Why were no blood drops not found next to the first set of bloody shoeprints – or why was O.J.'s blood not found **at the actual murder scene or on the victims**?
- Why were the shoeprints so close together?
- Why were there exactly 5 blood drops?
- Why were four of the blood drops found "between" the bloody shoeprints, and not to the left of them?
- Why was there not even one full drop of O.J.'s blood in the Bronco, if his blood dripped freely both at Bundy and minutes later in his own driveway?

Every piece of evidence, when put into a wider context, becomes thoroughly flawed!

Every piece of evidence bears signs of having been manipulated or tampered with. Much of the evidence simply **must** have been fabricated.

The only pieces of evidence that exist against O.J. are such pieces of evidence that **could** have been fabricated, and in many instances **obviously were fabricated**. Any possible potential piece of evidence that **could not** have been fabricated, like for instance O.J.'s fingerprints, the bloody clothes, the murder knife, and such, are conspicuously absent!

Even the evidence which the prosecution **did** present, proves that O.J. is innocent, like the appearances of each of the gloves. The blood on the Rockingham glove being "sticky and moist" more than 7 hours after O.J. had left for Chicago, and the Bundy (left) glove having no cut on the middle finger, having Ron's blood on it, and being not even the least bit turned "inside out."

All of the evidence either points to Fuhrman, or another police officer, being the murderer, or is consistent with such a theory. Besides, there is an "ocean of evidence" to suggest that the lead investigator, Detective Vannatter, fabricated all the blood evidence against O.J.

Investigators and prosecutors alike lied repeatedly in court. The prosecution's key witness, Detective Mark Fuhrman, committed perjury, and had to be whisked away secretly! After the civil trial it has become evident that **Mark Fuhrman even committed perjury with respect to his alibi for the time of the murders!**

I mean, this case is so incredible that it is hard to grasp even half of all the covert actions the investigators and the prosecutors got themselves involved in.

Had one, or a few, threads from the knit cap been found in Ron's clenched fist, and had the Bundy glove been found, turned inside out, in Ron's clenched fist, as if he had wrestled it away from the murderer – then, perhaps, the cap or the glove wasn't left intentionally. However, are O.J.'s adversaries telling me and my readers – and expecting us to believe it – that O.J., sheerly by mistake or sloppiness,

- **accidentally** dropped one glove at Bundy, and
- **accidentally** forgot to pick it up again, in spite of the fact that the glove must have been deliberately removed by the murderer, and
- **accidentally** forgot to remove the other glove together with the first one, and
- **accidentally** lost that other glove, too, behind O.J.'s house

at Rockingham, because he

- **accidentally** stumbled and fell, and that he
- **accidentally** didn't spill a trace of blood on the ground when he lost this glove, in spite of the allegation that O.J.'s finger was dripping blood everywhere else, and that he
- **accidentally** forgot to pick up that glove too, and that he
- **accidentally** lost his knit ski cap at Bundy, and
- **accidentally** forgot to pick it up, and
- **accidentally** stepped in the largest blood puddle at Bundy, so as to
- **accidentally** leave behind the most conspicuous bloody shoeprints, and
- **accidentally** shook five blood drops from his hand as he left Bundy, but
- **accidentally** left only microscopic smears of his blood in the Bronco on its, alleged, trip from Bundy to Rockingham, in spite of the fact that he, a few minutes later,
- **accidentally** bled rather freely in his driveway and inside his house, but again,
- **accidentally** didn't leave any traces of blood going upstairs to his bedroom, or while changing clothes in his bedroom.

If this is the LAPD's characteristics of Nicole's and Ron's murderer, I am surprised that he didn't **"accidentally"** lose his pants at Bundy, or **"accidentally"** get lost on his way home!

And I am even more surprised that the LAPD were unable to nail this murderer, if he were such an "idiot"!

Are we to believe that such a sloppy and absentminded "idiot" simultaneously didn't leave a single fingerprint anywhere, in spite of, allegedly, losing his left glove without noticing it?

Are we to believe that this "idiot" drove – in the city of Los Angeles – back and forth between Rockingham and Bundy, in a shiny white Bronco, without being seen by a single witness?

Are we to believe that this "idiot" – who seemed to lose everything he wore or carried – still managed to get rid of his bloody clothes, his bloody shoes, and his bloody murder knife, so effectively that the entire LAPD, the Chicago PD, the FBI, and the rest of the nation have been unable to uncover these items – and probably never will?

> The fact of the matter is that **if we <u>didn't</u> have the bloody gloves and the bloody shoeprints – O.J. would have been in more trouble.**
> Those two (or three) items **prove**, as I have demonstrated in this book, that O.J. – and the investigators – were being **framed and set up**.

The autopsy report on Nicole proved that the bloody shoe-prints **must** have been deliberately fabricated in order to frame O.J. I assume my readers remember that from my discussion of the scraping wounds on Nicole's leg, and the bruise and the hemorrhage on Nicole's head, which all indicated that the murderer must purposely have created the large puddle of blood on the tiled patio, instead of inside the dirt area or on the steps – in order to create the bloody Bruno Magli shoeprints.

The appearance of the Bundy glove proved that O.J. could not have left the blood drops next to the bloody shoeprints. So those blood drops must have been deliberately fabricated also.

The fact that those blood drops were collected before Vannatter received O.J.'s blood vial, proves that not only were those blood drops planted by the murderer at Bundy, but they were replaced, later, in the LAPD's crime lab – probably by Vannatter – with blood from O.J.'s reference blood vial.

Again, the "sticky and moist" blood on the Rockingham glove proved that O.J. could not have dropped it behind his house. So someone else must be responsible for the murders.

> However, **imagine that the bloody shoeprints and the bloody gloves didn't exist!**

We couldn't prove then, that the five blood drops were fabricated. Instead, they could perceivably have come from the cut on O.J.'s finger, since we wouldn't have realized that his left hand must have been protected by the Bundy glove until after both Nicole and Ron were dead.

Again, if the gloves didn't exist, the investigators, prosecutors, and plaintiffs wouldn't have to worry about the tight timeline at Rockingham, caused by the thumps on Kato's wall. The reason being, of course, that without the glove behind O.J.'s house at Rockingham, nobody would have tied those thumps on Kato's wall to the murders at Bundy.

Likewise with the bloody shoeprints. If the bloody shoeprints didn't exist, then the autopsy report which I have demonstrated clearly points to an MO intended to frame O.J. – **with those bloody shoeprints** – would instead, perhaps, point to jealous rage.

The presence of the bloody shoeprints, together with the autopsy report, and the fact that Nicole must have been dragged backwards until her head and neck was on the patio, clearly demonstrate that creating a blood source for the bloody shoeprints must have been one of the main purposes behind the manner in which Nicole was slaughtered.

Do you see? **O.J. would actually be in more trouble if the bloody Bruno Magli shoeprints and the bloody gloves never existed.** Had that been the case, it would appear less likely that O.J. was being framed – both by the murderer, and by the investigators.

Yet, those particular pieces of evidence were considered by most people to be the strongest pieces of evidence the prosecution and the plaintiffs had against O.J. That, kind of, shows us how **"backwards"** this case really is.

The prosecution's strongest evidence against O.J. is actually proving O.J.'s innocence, rather than his guilt!

CHAPTER 45

A Jig-Saw Puzzle

In this chapter I shall try to explain why people – the investigators, the prosecutors, and the media included – so totally misjudged this case. Why have so many intelligent people totally misunderstood what really happened? As I write this, an anecdote from my native country, Norway, comes to mind. I relate it with a clear sense of **self-irony.**

Back in the twenties, then Crown Prince Olav, later the beloved, late King Olav the Fifth of Norway, attended the Norwegian equivalent to West Point.

Of course, it represented a problem of etiquette, how to correct or discipline a **future king** – especially during the first weeks of boot camp, and in particular during closed drill, which certainly was not one of Crown Prince Olav's favorite activities! Frequently, *"Cadet 01 Olav"* was marching **"out of step."**

One drill sergeant solved the problem eloquently when he shouted: *"Everyone, but Olav, is 'out of step'!"*

Following the media's coverage of the continued "Simpson Saga," I sometimes feel like everyone, but myself, is out of step! Then I think about Crown Prince Olav, and wonder if, perhaps, **I am the one who is out of step.**

Of course, had I believed that, this book would never have been written. But **sometimes I do feel like the only sane person in a mental institution**. I think I share that feeling with a lot of frustrated people who have bothered to dig a little deeper into this case, than the ones who just scanned the newspaper headlines or listened to O.J.'s adversaries "analyze" the case and the court proceeding on TV talk shows like *"Rivera Live."*

Watching talk show panelists "analyze" the Simpson case on TV, I wouldn't be surprised if many of my readers, at times also felt like they had been transferred to one of their State's mental institution!

Anyway, let me now try to explain why so many people could be fooled by the Simpson case.

Solving a murder case is in many ways like solving a jig-saw puzzle. It is amazing how many similarities there are.

There are simple jig-saw puzzles – and simple murder cases.

For instance, a man enters a bar and asks someone's girlfriend for a dance. They hit it off on the dance floor. The girl's boyfriend gets jealous. He goes home to fetches his shotgun, returns to the bar and shoots his rival. The assailant is quickly subdued by half a dozen patrons, until the police arrest him.

The motive is clear. The murder weapon has the murderer's fingerprints on it, there were 20 eyewitnesses who never took their eyes off the assailant until the police arrested him.

This is like one of those toddler's jig-saw puzzles, where there are only four or five pieces, and each piece fits into its own separate slot!

Then there are more difficult jig-saw puzzles – and more difficult murder cases.

You know, the jig-saw puzzles with one hundred pieces, or so, where the puzzle forms a nice picture, or **"motive,"** eventually. That's like solving a murder mystery where there were no eyewitnesses – and the murder weapon had to be recovered from the bottom of a nearby lake. However, the suspect appeared rather early, and the **motive** was obvious right from the start. Eventually, the police pieced everything together – and the suspect, perhaps, confessed even.

Let's now skip to the really difficult puzzle – and later compare it to the Simpson case.

I assume my readers are familiar with those huge boxes of several thousand small jig-saw pieces that look almost identical, except for their color.

How do we solve those kinds of puzzles? How does that compare to the Simpson case? And why did the Simpson case throw almost everybody off?

First of all we look at the **motive!** We look at the picture on the cover of the box. So now we know what we are trying to create.

However, in the Simpson case, the investigators didn't have a motive. Detective Fuhrman, in my opinion, had purposely misled us in terms of the motive.

Fuhrman killed Nicole for racist reasons. He wanted to kill O.J., too, for the same reason. But to throw us off, Fuhrman only killed Nicole – and Nicole was white. Therefore, it didn't look like a **racist motive**. Then, instead, he **framed** O.J.

The murder of Nicole looked like a murder committed by a jealous and possessive ex-husband out of control! **The investigators never saw the real picture!**

In terms of a jig-saw puzzle, it was like the creators had not only omitted the picture of the completed puzzle. **They had purposely put the wrong picture on the cover of the box!**

Anyway, let us proceed with the puzzle. First we turn all the pieces, color side up. Then we look at the wrong picture on the cover of the box, and start to organize the pieces – the pieces of evidence – incorrectly, of course!

The **incorrect picture** shows a landscape. There is blue sky, green, grassy slopes, a yellow house in the foreground. The creators of the puzzle purposely selected that **false** picture for the cover of the box – **to throw us off** – because the real puzzle has a lot of light blue and green pieces, and some yellow pieces, too.

That's exactly how Fuhrman, too, misled everyone. He presented us with a false motive to start with. He used a knife, and cut Nicole viciously to make the murder appear like the act of jealous ex-husband in a violent rage. Then Fuhrman created a lot of **false pieces** of evidence that **fit this false motive** – like the gloves, the blood in the Bronco, and the Bruno Magli shoeprints (and Nicole's broken watch).

Of course, when the picture – the motive – is deliberately misleading, we are bound to make a lot of mistakes in our interpretation of the puzzle pieces – our interpretation of the evidence. Let us assume that **the real motive** of the puzzle is:

a **photograph** of someone's **living room,** with a large **poster** covering most of the **wall in the background**!

The motive of **the poster** is an elevated view of a grassy country side with a calm lake reflecting the blue, partly cloudy sky above it.

The yellow pieces do not constitute a house, but **a yellow sofa in the living room!**

Do my readers see the problems we would have in solving this jigsaw puzzle – because we would have been **totally misled by the deliberately false motive** on the cover of the box?

We would, of course, initially, have concluded that the blue and the light gray pieces represented the "sky with some clouds," and that they, therefore, belonged on the **top** of the picture. However, the blue, or light gray pieces belonged in the **middle** of the puzzle – because although they depicted "sky," they were just a **reflection** of the sky – in the lake – in the poster – on the **middle** of the wall – in the living room – on the photograph!

Back to the Simpson case again. When someone – the murderer – purposely, and cleverly, fooled the investigators into suspecting a totally incorrect **motive**, then the pieces of evidence which they thought supported that motive, was readily **incorrectly** interpreted, and put in the wrong place in the murder puzzle.

Evidence the investigators thought pointed to a motive of **jealousy,** was interpreted that way, while it in fact turned out to be deliberately fabricated by the murderer – whose motive was **racism, sexism, and "machoism".**

What looked like real sky and clouds, turned out to be part of a poster on the wall in a living room. A yellow sofa was mistaken for a yellow house, because we **expected** to see a house.

Similarly, a glove which was interpreted to have been lost by O.J., behind his house, turned out to prove, rather, that he couldn't be the murderer. Bloody Bruno Magli shoeprints which were interpreted as having been left by O.J., proved, instead – **based on the injuries to Nicole's head and right leg** – that the entire murder scene was a **"set-up"**!

Not only did Fuhrman create a near perfect, false jealousy

motive, pointing to O.J. He also made sure that there was nothing that pointed to the real motive of racism – by killing Nicole, who was white – but **not O.J.**, who is an African American!

Next Fuhrman supported this false motive with false evidence. Even this false evidence was extremely cleverly fabricated! Some of it pointed straight at O.J. That framed O.J. directly, but it also set up the investigators, so they believed O.J. were guilty.

Other, "secondary, neutral" evidence was simply created by the murderer – not to frame O.J. directly, but to give the investigators the **opportunity** to frame him. Convinced that O.J. were guilty, the investigators used this secondary, neutral evidence to fabricate "real" – but false – evidence against O.J. which the murderer himself could not possibly have had access to, and therefore could not have deposited.

It was like the creators of the jig-saw puzzle, who created an image of a sky – but as a **reflection** in a lake – in a poster – in a living room – so that we should put those blue pieces on the top of the puzzle, instead of in the middle, as a reflection in the lake, where they belonged.

Fuhrman made it appear that he could not have framed O.J. After all, Fuhrman did not have access to O.J.'s house, or to his blood, or his hair.

At the same time, by setting up the investigators to complete the framing of O.J., and by supplying them with the materials to do it, **Fuhrman made it appear that the investigators could not have fabricated the false evidence either** (for instance the five blood drops at Bundy or the knit cap). Those pieces were already present before the investigators entered the murder scene.

The only "solution" most people saw, was that O.J., indeed, had murdered Nicole and Ron – and that he, indeed, had left behind all the evidence it **appeared** that he had left behind!

On the Fuhrman tapes, Detective Fuhrman is heard saying that he was so clever at fabricating false evidence that nobody could catch him.

He was so clever that he could even commit murder and

get away with it. Perhaps that was precisely what he did!

It was exactly as if Fuhrman had sat down and created the toughest jig-saw puzzle you could think of – where nothing was what it seemed to be.

Defense Attorney Robert Baker didn't understand that Fuhrman had switched the picture on the cover of the jig-saw puzzle's box! Nor did the investigators, at first.

How could Mr. Baker convince the jurors that blue pieces did not belong on the top of the picture – where everyone else believed they belonged – when nobody, not even Mr. Baker, knew what the motive was supposed to look like? How could he convince the jurors that what everyone believed to be a yellow house in a pretty valley, was instead a yellow sofa in someone's living room?

How could Defense Counsel Robert Baker convince the jury that the "mountain of evidence" was fabricated, when he didn't even know what the murderer's motive was?

Most people, and certainly the media, looked at the evidence which **apparently** pointed to O.J. – and could not solve the murder mystery. They may still think O.J. is guilty, but there are so many flaws in their theory, and in the evidence, that they will never convince those who still have the ability to put two and two together.

I, on the other hand, said to myself:

"There is something wrong with all this evidence."

I realized that the evidence could never be reconciled with O.J. being the murderer. So I asked myself:

"If not O.J. – then who? What if Fuhrman is the killer? How do the pieces of the puzzle fit then?"

Actually, it wasn't such a wild guess, after all. There were a lot of indications that Fuhrman not only planted the Rockingham glove, but actually murdered Nicole and Ron.

Suddenly, everything fit. All the pieces of the puzzle found their natural places. The key to solving the murder mystery was to come up with the right **motive – the right theory!** Then, putting the pieces together was rather easy.

Coming up with the right theory – seeing the whole picture – was what the investigators failed to do, what the prosecutors failed to do, what the plaintiffs failed to do, what the media failed to do, and what O.J.'s attorneys, even, failed to do. That's why O.J.'s attorneys lost the civil trial. And that's why O.J. is still the villain in the eyes of most people.

Perhaps I confused my readers more than I enlightened them with this comparison to a jig-saw puzzle. I hope not. And I hope my book will open people's eyes, and perhaps, become a turning point in the public's perception of both O.J. and this murder case.

CHAPTER 46

"The Thief And The Prosecutor"

It baffles me that people like Geraldo Rivera can see so clearly what is happening in America today, when it comes to racist white police officers murdering blacks for no apparent reason – at an almost epidemic rate.

Mr. Rivera also sees clearly how such murders by white police officers are followed by cover-ups, tampering with evidence, false testimonies etc., etc. by **all** their colleagues (without exception) in order to set such murderous cops free to do it all over again – and simultaneously send the message to other rogue cops everywhere, that it is "open season" for them too.

And yet, Mr. Rivera cannot possibly get it through his skull that an LAPD investigator, like Detective Vannatter, could conceivably drip a few drops of blood from O.J.'s blood vial onto some small pieces of cotton fabric, borrow a card key – or together with a colleague who had a key – enter the serology room or the evidence room, one night after everyone else had left, and exchange some of the real blood evidence swatches (which perceivably contained Nicole's blood) with his own false O.J. swatches!

> Rogue police officers **murdering innocent African Americans on an epidemic scale – no problem!**
> Rogue police officers **replacing a few, small pieces of cotton fabric – no way!**

It is like Mr. Rivera and his likes, are saying:

"Yes, we realize that this Ahmed Ali Hassan from the Middle

East is a drug pin, a bank robber, a murderer, a torturer, a rapist, a hijacker, and a terrorist bomber! – But I, honestly, don't think he is the one who snatched two brownies from the cookie jar in the lunch room! That seemed so mean spirited!

The point many people are missing is this:

The real murderer "set up" the investigators!

I have to repeat this, until people begin to understand it. The real murderer is an LAPD detective himself, so he knew exactly how to do it! And he also knew how his colleagues would react as soon as he had convinced them that O.J. were guilty by planting the two gloves, and the blood in O.J.'s Bronco!

Vannatter **immediately** believed O.J. were the murderer. Vannatter just wanted to **"give justice a helping hand."** He thought he was doing society a service! Vannatter saw how he could nail O.J. with blood from his vial. He began setting it up right away – and completed it after a few days.

From that moment he was **"hooked"!** The real murderer had "hooked" both O.J. – and Vannatter! Eventually, Vannatter realized that – but by then it was **too late.** Vannatter had already fabricated and planted blood evidence which made it appear that O.J. had bled at Bundy.

Not even the murderer – could have planted O.J.'s blood at Bundy. If O.J. were innocent, then that blood evidence **must** have been **"fabricated"** or planted in the LAPD's crime lab.

Only one man could have fabricated that blood evidence, namely Vannatter, who against every rule in the book, had requested O.J.'s blood vial from the police nurse, received it in an unsealed, illegitimate envelope, brought it to his office, where he kept it by himself for one and a half hours, lied about it on the witness stand, had it booked in later with 1.5 ml of O.J.'s blood missing from the vial, etc., etc.

Forget the EDTA! Vannatter – **as well as you and I** – know how to eliminate the EDTA so it would not show up in any EDTA test!

If O.J. was innocent, but the blood evidence still indicated that he had bled at Bundy – that blood **must** have been fabricated!

The only one who **could** – and **must** – have done that was the lead investigator, Detective Vannatter.

If someone could prove that O.J. was innocent – **Vannatter would go to prison for a long, long time!** That's the key to understanding what happened later.

Vannatter's only hope, was to continue to fabricate so much additional false evidence against O.J., that "nobody" would doubt he were guilty.

That set up the exact same situation within the LAPD's Robbery/Homicide Division, as the situations Mr. Rivera so eloquently call our attention to almost every week – in connection with police officers who **murder** African-American men, and then go free because their colleagues cover for them.

In such police murder cases, the perpetrator's colleagues fabricate or plant false evidence which makes the victim appear like a dangerous criminal, for instance, so the murder shall appear to have been justified. If necessary they remove incriminating evidence, concoct corresponding false reports and testimonies, etc., etc.

If necessary they will sacrifice **any outsider** – in order to protect one of their own! This phenomenon does not only apply to **a few rogue cops**. It applies to **everyone** who ever wants to work in a U.S. police department for the rest of his, or her, life.

We saw it with the Rodney King beating. There were 25-30 police officers there. Every single one of them – even black officers – lied about the beating afterwards, to protect their rogue colleagues! **25 out of 25! That is 100%!**

Every police officer is not a murderer or a criminal. There are just **a bunch of rotten apples** out there. Some of them may even get involved in a criminal act with the best of intentions – like Vannatter!

He wanted to make certain he got whom he believed was a vicious double murderer, off the streets for good!

However, regardless of the circumstances – once a police officer gets in trouble – **every one of his colleagues will step in and do whatever is necessary to protect him – even if the rogue officer has committed murder!**

That's why Vannatter, once he had started, could, and had to, continue to plant all the evidence against O.J. He **had to** in order to save his own, and his family's future. And he **could** because all his colleagues were willing to help, and none of them dared turn in Vannatter or anyone else.

There is indeed **"a code of silence"** – in the LAPD, as in all other U.S. police departments. **Nobody breaks that code!**

Let me ask – with special address to Mr. Geraldo Rivera:

Knowing that every other cop in the LAPD would destroy him if he did – do you think that anyone within the LAPD would dare to ruin the future of several of his colleagues, just to save an African American, O.J., from going to prison?

Get real, Geraldo! Maybe some LAPD officers had taken a dip in O.J.'s swimming pool, or received O.J.'s autograph.

OK! So what? Do you think that made any difference in this situation? Imagine an LAPD officer saying:

"I am sorry, but I have to tell the truth and ruin Vannatter's future – because I took a dip in O.J.'s swimming pool last summer"!

The situation was not much different for the prosecutors. They knew, rather early, what was going on. But they weren't going to turn on Vannatter, either. How were they ever going to win such a case – investigated by Vannatter's own subordinate colleagues?

They would only make fools of themselves! I have to say it again: **Get real, Geraldo!**

Of course, they talked about this among themselves – both

within the LAPD, and in the district attorney's office. So for every day that went by, they committed **the crime of cover-up**, all over again, by not coming out with the truth. Therefore, rather quickly, they all got sucked into this. Very soon, it was too late to get out. They just had to play along!

Rather early, the prosecutors must have known that O.J. was innocent! Otherwise they must indeed have been less than intelligent. All the **trustworthy** evidence of the case proved or indicated that O.J. was innocent, that investigators had fabricated and planted false evidence, that only a murderer with police authority could have killed Ron so quietly, that Detective Fuhrman was a racist who must have planted the Rockingham glove, and that Fuhrman, therefore, probably, was the murderer.

It is deplorable, that the prosecution's main objective was to win – regardless of their methods – rather than to make sure the guilty person was convicted and the innocent was set free. But from watching them during the trial, I understand. That's the way they were. That's the way their brains functioned.

The prosecutors must have known, long before the trial started, that **so much** of the evidence against O.J. was fabricated – that there was every reason to believe that **all** of it was fabricated. Let me explain:

If the prosecutors were made aware that there was a trace of EDTA in the blood drops on the Bundy gate, they might think there was an acceptable explanation for that. But the EDTA in the blood on the gate should have made them **suspicious.**

Now, if they **also** learned later that Nicole's blood – **containing EDTA** – was found on O.J.'s sock, but they already had **an earlier lab report** stating that **there was no blood on the socks** – then the prosecutors should have suspected that someone was **"fiddling"** with the evidence, to make O.J. look more guilty.

The prosecutors might still look at all the other evidence, and believe that the two possible discrepancies were isolated incidents.

However, during the course of the investigation, one piece of evidence after the other became suspect:

- It was inconceivable that O.J. could have dripped two drops of blood from his **left** hand, on the narrow bottom rail of the rear gate at Bundy, and hit the "target" with both drops!
- However, this was even more incredible, as the gate was hinged on the **right** side and swung **away** from the murderer and over to the **right!**
- Why were there **no blood drops alongside the first set of bloody shoeprints** at Bundy (the so-called *"O.J. shuffle"*) if O.J., allegedly, cut his finger in a struggle with Ron? Did the murderer cut himself **after** the *"O.J. shuffle"*?
- Some blood evidence was not present on the day after the murders, but showed up weeks later!
- EDTA was found in blood evidence!
- Vannatter acted in the most suspicious manner; he couldn't explain his actions, and he lied repeatedly, and in particular, about his whereabouts while in the possession of O.J.'s blood vial!
- O.J.'s blood vial turned up in the lab with 1.5 ml of blood missing and unaccounted for!
- Unexplainable blood transfers showed up on those very blood swatch bindels one might suspect Detective Vannatter had fabricated from the 1.5 ml of blood that were missing from O.J.'s blood vial!
- Ms. Mazzola's initials had disappeared from those very same blood evidence bindels!
- Both these discrepancies were exactly the kind of discrepancies one might have expected, if Vannatter had fabricated those blood swatches with blood from O.J.'s vial.
- Hairs nobody could identify showed up on the cap!
- The trail of blood **only** showed up at those places where it might have been planted without O.J.'s own forensic experts being able to go back and double check the original source

of that blood! (The floor in O.J.'s foyer was washed.
The Bundy crime scene was hosed down as soon as the criminalists had collected their blood evidence samples. The rest rained away.)

– The lead investigator was caught lying time and time again!
– The key witness (Fuhrman) was exposed as a racist who, later, was caught perjuring himself.
– Detective Fuhrman lied about his departure from La Quinta, which gave him his so-called "alibi" for the time of the murders. In fact, Fuhrman didn't have an alibi – and Prosecutor Marcia Clark must have known that!
– The blood on the murder glove, which Fuhrman alleged that he "found" behind O.J.'s house, was "sticky and moist" almost 8 hours after the murders, and more than 7 hours after O.J. left for Chicago. Etc., etc.

Let me stop there! You know I could have continued for at least a couple of more pages! The prosecutors **must** have realized, long before the trial started, that **all** the evidence against O.J. probably was fabricated. Yet, they argued, persistently, that every piece of evidence should be considered absolutely trustworthy – unless the defense could prove, irrefutably, that it had been fabricated, as well as prove how it was fabricated, and who had done it.

How could the defense prove that? I guess they would have had to ask Detective Vannatter and Robbery/Homicide to investigate themselves!

To illustrate how the prosecutors treated this case, let me give my readers yet another of my examples, which, has given the title to this chapter, _"The Thief And The Prosecutor"_:

One evening Prosecutor Marcia Clark is approached in downtown Los Angeles by an obviously suspicious looking male, in his thirties. The man wants to sell her a **watch.** Actually, looking for a present for a good friend's birthday, Ms. Clark shows some interest, although she is suspicious. Trying to establish some rapport, the man introduces himself as

"Charlie."

"Charlie" immediately pulls out three watches! Being a prosecutor, Marcia Clark doesn't want to purchase **stolen goods**! So she asks the man if the watches are **his**, which he confirms. He hands Ms. Clark one of the watches.

Marcia Clark turns it over. Inscribed on the back it says: *"To our son, **Peter**, on Graduation day, June 8, 1993"*!

Somewhat disappointed Marcia hands back *"**Peter**"*'s graduation watch to **Charlie**! *"This is not your watch!"* she says. The man hands Marcia Clark the second watch. *"This one is mine – honest to God!"* he says.

Again, Marcia Clark turns the watch over. There is an inscription on the back of this watch, too. It reads: *"To Steven. Love, Diana"*!

Disgusted, Ms. Clark hands back the second watch, too. *"You **stole** these watches?!"* she says in a tone of voice which makes it unclear whether she is **asking** the man, or **accusing** him.

Chagrined, Charlie replies: *"Well, let's say that they weren't mine, at least... But listen ... This last watch is definitely mine! You can have it for 15 bucks."*

Gullibly, Ms. Clark reaches for the watch Charlie hands her. She turns it over. **There is no inscription on the back!**

"See! There is no inscription on it – because it's mine!" Charlie says.

Prosecutor Marcia Clark reaches for her purse. *"Good!"* she says. *"I'll buy it!"*

As it relates to the Simpson case, I assume my readers have long since figured out that **Chrlie represents Detective Vannatter** and the investigators. **The three stolen watches represent the corrupted evidence they "sold" to the prosecutors**. And **Prosecutor Marcia Clark?** Yes – she is herself!

CHAPTER 47

Dr. Ameli – Nicole – Fuhrman – Lange

Quite a few people who have involved themselves in trying to solve the Simpson murder mystery, have come to the conclusion that O.J. must be innocent. Whether O.J. is guilty or not, someone, obviously, is trying to frame him with false or fabricated evidence. But at the same time there doesn't seem to be any direct, concrete evidence pointing to anyone else.

Hence, many people are more or less searching in the dark, everywhere, for theories, solutions, suspicious activities, and connections, in their efforts to explain what might have happened. To nobody's surprise, many such suspicious connections between O.J. and Nicole, Ron Goldman and Faye Resnick, Detective Fuhrman, the LAPD, and others, lead both to and from the fast paced entertainment/Hollywood/celebrity society.

If there indeed is an LAPD conspiracy to cover up the fact that Detectives Fuhrman and Vannatter, as well as others within the LAPD may have been criminally involved in the Simpson case – although for different reasons and based on different motives – there may be a relevant connection between the persons and the events I shall discuss, later, in this chapter.

However, there is such a web of connections – good and bad – in the movie/entertainment/Hollywood milieu that we could probably find something apparently suspicious going on between any two or more randomly picked people in this environment. Such suspicious connections are ambiguous at best.

The fact that **Mr.** Black was at a party where **Drug Lord** White was present, doesn't mean that **Mrs.** Black has a drug problem because she was cut off in traffic by an unknown motorist the day after the party!

That is the kind of loose gossip and speculations that pop up from all directions and angles in the Simpson case.

I want my readers, therefore, to read this chapter with due skepticism. My theory, suggestion, and conclusion may be as ludicrous as those of any others. But the following incidents, apparently, occurred, so let me show that they could, at least, tie in with my overall theory. But don't judge my overall theory, based on this chapter! Let me set the stage first (some, but not all, of the bare facts are taken from the book, *"Killing time,"* by Donald Freed and Raymond P. Briggs; Macmillan, 1996):

1. There are certain indications that Mark Fuhrman had an on-going intimate relationship with Nicole. I have touched on that earlier. He might still have hated her, despised her, and wanted to kill her.

2. Detective Fuhrman had ties to neo-nazi groups. Neo-nazi groups had threatened O.J. and Nicole, both by phone and letter in 1993-94, with reference to their interracial relationship. Both Nicole and O.J. had told Kato Kaelin about this.

3. A clinical psychologist, Dr. Jennifer Ameli, counselled both Nicole and Ron during the weeks prior to their murders.

4. According to Dr. Ameli's statements on TV talk shows, after O.J.'s acquittal in the criminal trial, Nicole's motive for seeking Dr. Ameli's services, was that Nicole feared O.J. Other sources say that Nicole was referred to Dr. Ameli by her divorce counsel. Allegedly, Nicole was trying to overturn her and O.J.'s prenuptial agreement. Provisions called for the cancellation of this agreement if O.J. had abused Nicole physically after 1989. Allegedly, Nicole's divorce counsel wanted Dr. Ameli to establish such abuse, through consultations and conversations with Nicole.

5. On several occasions in 1994-95, Dr. Ameli herself was harassed and threatened, and her offices were repeatedly broken into during the investigation of the Simpson case and during the early stages of the criminal trial.

   During one of these incidents, someone called Dr. Ameli

and asked to purchase her files on Nicole and Ron, which she refused to sell, of course. Shortly thereafter her office was broken into and some of her files were stolen.

During another incident she was attacked from behind, and threatened not to reveal anything in regards to the Simpson case. Dr. Ameli did not see the face of the perpetrator, but she described him as being **tall**. (Note that Fuhrman is about 6 feet 4 inches).

6. Dr. Ameli reported all the incidents to the police, and the police investigated the threats and the burglaries.

7. According to Dr. Ameli, during the investigation, also the police removed files from her office – without permission.

8. The police investigators were insulting and victimizing towards Dr. Ameli. In short, they treated her badly. They even accused her of passing on privileged client information to the media.

9. LAPD Detective Tom Lange, who was one of the two lead investigators in the Simpson case, also headed the investigation of Dr. Ameli's complaints.

10. Other threats and harassments, as well as burglaries, followed. Three burglaries were reported between September 1994 and April 1995. That was the time the prosecution prepared the Simpson case, and up until, and including, the time of Detective Fuhrman's testimony.

11. Eventually Dr. Ameli had her home searched for electronic listening devices. Several such devices were found.

12. Naturally, both the investigators and the prosecutors, knew about Dr. Ameli's connection to the Simpson case, but neither of them ever asked her to testify.

My hypothesis may be as good, or bad, as anyone else's. The whole thing may mean nothing! However, what I mentioned above seems like so many coincidences put together, that those coincidences might be related in some form or fashion. My hypothesis, may be incorrect. But I feel an obligation, at least, to demonstrate that these incidents may be reconciled by my overall theory in the Simpson case.

Can we make some sense out of these events? Can these seemingly unrelated facts tie in with our **main theory** of

- Detective Fuhrman being the murderer,
- Detective Vannatter and other LAPD investigators framing O.J. with fabricated evidence, and
- both the investigators and prosecutors knowing, at an early stage of the investigation, that Fuhrman is the murderer – but both being afraid to expose that horrible truth?

The facts and circumstances surrounding Dr. Ameli, represent no proof that our theory is correct. On the other hand, **if** our theory is correct, we can certainly see how the events surrounding Dr. Ameli **might** make sense.

Let us assume that Detective Fuhrman had an ongoing relationship with Nicole, but still hated her, and was planning to kill her. Fuhrman was a member of a neo-nazi organization which might have been behind the threats against O.J. and Nicole.

Already several years earlier Fuhrman had decided to kill Nicole and frame O.J. for the murder. Fuhrman's ongoing relationship with Nicole served three purposes.

- The relationship in itself.
- Gathering information about Nicole and O.J., useful both for the purpose of killing Nicole, and for the purpose of framing O.J.
- Feeding Nicole information which might cause her to take actions that eventually would make O.J. a stronger suspect.

Fuhrman joined the neo-nazi group and the group got involved in Fuhrman's plan to kill Nicole and frame O.J. One of Fuhrman's ideas was to scare Nicole into believing that **O.J.** were trying to kill her. If Nicole expressed her fear of O.J. to other people, O.J. would become a **stronger suspect** after Fuhrman had killed her.

Being a police officer, who had investigated one of Nicole's many 911 calls at Rockingham, and having Nicole's confidence, Fuhrman might have told Nicole that *"based on my experience from domestic violence cases I have investigated, O.J. could be plotting to kill you."*

There is really nothing to suggest that. Nicole was suffering from pneumonia just 3-4 weeks prior to her death. O.J. was the one she turned to. And O.J. visited her and cared for her every single day of her illness!

Fuhrman however, could perceivably have told Nicole that this is **exactly** how some murderers behave just before killing their ex-wives, in order to make it appear that they are caring and loving, instead of hateful. That, surely, would scare Nicole.

Fuhrman, plotting to kill Nicole with a knife, could have told Nicole that many men kill their wives and ex-wives with a knife or a pair of scissors. It doesn't matter if this is untrue. Fuhrman's purpose was to scare Nicole, make her fear O.J., and make her tell Kato, for instance, that she thought O.J. might one day kill her with a knife or a pair of scissors!

If Fuhrman had planned this, it certainly worked out perfectly, since Kato, later, testified that Nicole had told him – out of the blue – that she feared O.J. might one day kill her with a pair of scissors!

What made Nicole tell Kato something like that – unless someone had planted the idea in Nicole's head?

Now, let us bring Dr. Ameli into the picture. Independent of Fuhrman's trying to influence and scare Nicole, she was referred to Dr. Ameli via her divorce attorney. Naturally, trying to work out a better divorce agreement, Nicole was not going to tell Dr. Ameli that she had an affair with Detective Fuhrman!

Nicole did tell Dr. Ameli that she was afraid of O.J. and that he had beaten her. That might have been part of Nicole's plan and effort to have the prenuptial agreement overturned.

Then Nicole was killed.

During the investigation Fuhrman learned that Nicole had been seeing Dr. Ameli. Dr. Ameli is a psychologist. People tend to relate their personal secrets to psychologists and psychiatrists.

Fuhrman feared that Nicole might have told the psychologist

about her affair with Fuhrman. Perhaps Fuhrman had scared Nicole by telling her that O.J.'s caring for her during her illness might be a sign of immediate danger, and telling her about divorced men murdering their ex-wives with knives or scissors. Maybe Nicole had related this to Dr. Ameli.

If Fuhrman had said something like that, in order to scare Nicole, and make her talk to others about her fear of O.J. – and since it was utter nonsense, it could – if it became known that Fuhrman had implied these things – cast suspicion on Fuhrman himself. Did he indeed "set up" O.J.?

Fuhrman could have instructed Nicole **not** to mention that he was seeing her, nor that **he** had told her these things – saying that if she told anyone, O.J. might hear about it and get even more angry. So Nicole didn't mention Fuhrman to anyone. She only said she feared O.J. – for no apparent reason.

Eventually, the Simpson investigators learned about Nicole's connection to Dr. Ameli. They may have learned about it from her divorce attorney, or from Nicole's receipts from Dr. Ameli, or from cancelled checks from Nicole to Dr. Ameli. Anyway, they eventually learned about it.

At this time, when the harassment and the threats of Dr. Ameli and the burglaries started, the police knew that O.J. was innocent and that Detective Fuhrman was the murderer. Should this come out, it was perhaps even more dangerous to the investigators, and later on also to the prosecutors, as they became involved in the cover-up.

All of them became very concerned about what information Nicole might have given Dr. Ameli. Had Nicole given Dr. Ameli information about Fuhrman, which might make Fuhrman a suspect, and eventually lead to his indictment, then the investigators who had fabricated most of the false evidence against O.J., could be indicted too – for having fabricated that false evidence. They might be facing long prison terms.

And later, when the prosecutors got involved in the cover-up and the protection of Detective Fuhrman, they too, were in jeopardy from whatever information they feared Dr. Ameli might have received from Nicole, and might be hiding in her file cabinets!

That may explain why the co-lead investigator in the extremely high profile Simpson murder case, **Detective Tom Lange,** was also assigned to the somewhat **"trivial"** Ameli case!

According to Dr. Ameli – Detective Lange, and the other investigators she got involved with, were insulting and victimizing. And the police themselves removed files from Dr. Ameli's office.

Obviously, someone, even the police, seemed to take a special interest in Dr. Ameli's client files on Nicole and Ron. Why?

Dr. Ameli, obviously believed O.J. had threatened Nicole. Normally she would have been a wonderful witness for the prosecution. So why did the investigators treat her so badly? Did the police fear that Dr. Ameli had received information from Nicole, which pointed to **Fuhrman**?

Did two groups with similar motives – Fuhrman and his neo-nazi group, and the LAPD's investigator group – both try to get hold of Dr. Ameli's files, **to make sure nothing leaked out that could tie Fuhrman to the murders?**

The neo-nazi group were afraid they might be tied to the murders via Fuhrman, and the LAPD's investigator group were afraid they might be tied to evidence tampering – if Fuhrman was tied to the murders.

If so, that could explain why someone called Dr. Ameli and asked to purchase Dr. Ameli's files on Nicole and Ron.

When she refused to sell them, her office was broken into. Maybe the person(s) interested in the files, tried to steal them when they couldn't buy them.

They didn't find what they were looking for. So then, a "tall man," like Fuhrman, threatened Dr. Ameli not to reveal any information she might have about the Simpson case.

In the meantime, Dr. Ameli had reported the threats and the burglaries to the police. The investigators in the Simpson case were afraid Dr. Ameli could expose Fuhrman, thereby exposing their own evidence fabrication. So they made sure Simpson investigator, Detective Tom Lange, took hand of the Ameli case, too, thereby, hopefully, finding out if Dr. Ameli had heard anything from Nicole about Detective Fuhrman. And if so, Detective Lange could suppress the information.

Vitally interested in securing whatever information Dr. Ameli might possibly have about Fuhrman, Detective Lange and his investigators took the opportunity to remove some of Dr. Ameli's files, while investigating the burglary.

But they, too, came up empty handed. Hence, we had two groups that for different reasons were equally eager to find out if Nicole had told Dr. Ameli anything that could tie Detective Fuhrman to the murders.

They tried to buy Dr. Ameli's information. When that didn't work, the neo-nazi group tried to steal it. The police simply used their authority as investigators, and removed the files they wanted.

When neither group found what they were looking for, they harassed and threatened Dr, Ameli. But still they weren't sure if she knew "something."

The neo-nazi group couldn't break into Dr. Ameli's offices any more, looking for additional files or information. It was too risky, since the police were investigatiiong the break-ins. Instead, they installed listening devices in Dr. Ameli's home, to hear if she would mention, in ordinary conversation, anything Nicole might have told her.

The police, on the other hand, had no fear of breaking into Dr. Ameli's office again and again, because if someone reported the break-ins, the police themselves were the ones to show up and investigate. So, perhaps the police were the ones who broke into Dr. Ameli's office three more times between September 1994 and April 1995. If this is what happened, no wonder the police never caught the perpetrators!

Of course, there might be other explanations for the repeated threats, harassment, and burglaries Dr. Ameli fell victim to during the investigation of the Simpson case, and the early part of the trial.

It is, however, hard to find any other explanation which can reconcile why someone would take such an extreme interest in

Dr. Ameli's relationship to Nicole, clearly demonstrating that **"information" was all they were after.**

And it is even harder to find any other explanation which can reconcile why the LAPD's lead investigator in the Simpson case, was **also** investigating the **"trivial"** Ameli case.

Furthermore, why did the police seem more interested in Dr. Ameli's files, than in the burglars and assailants?

Dr. Ameli had information that Nicole was scared of O.J., and Nicole had been consulting Dr. Ameli just a few days prior to her murder.

Why then, did the police and the prosecutors seem more interested in keeping Dr. Ameli out of the Simpson trial, than including her as a witness.

And finally, why didn't the police ever catch the assailants or the burglars, in spite of so many repeat incidents, and the top priority they seemingly gave this trivial case by assigning their lead homicide investigator to it?

By all means, if someone comes up with a better explanation, I shall be listening.

CHAPTER 48

"Kato" – The Dog!

As long as I have just finished one set of **"ludicrous speculations"** in the previous chapter – which I admit – why not talk about Nicole's dog, the Akita, at the same time – and get it over with! Then we can get serious again!

Nicole's dog, *"Kato,"* is by some attributed with determining the time of the murders. Several people reported hearing Kato bark loudly around the time it is estimated that the murders took place.

Later Kato's barking changed to wailing, which lasted for a long time. Eventually, Kato left the murder scene through the East (Bundy Drive) gate and down Bundy Drive. Kato's pads were bloody and he left bloody pad prints as he walked away from the murder scene.

I have a rather interesting hypothesis regarding Kato, his wailing and his leaving the murder scene. Dog experts, and dog psychologists must determine whether my hypothesis is sound or not. By any standard, my theory is not very significant, even though it may be correct. But Kato – the dog – has become part of this case, too. So, I should discuss him.

Dogs are by nature what we refer to as **"pack animals"** just like wolves and hyenas. Man has domesticated his dogs, but deep inside, in a crisis situation a dog, still, has the **instincts** of a pack animal.

This pack instinct is stronger the closer a breed is to its wild cousins, the wolves. In that respect, I guess a poodle does not carry much pack instinct. On the other hand, one cannot come much closer to a wolf, than the Akita's

The main feature of this "pack" instinct is that the members of the pack recognize a **leader of the pack,** which the other members of the pack respect and follow. The "leader of the pack" is almost always the strongest and most agile and intelligent member of the pack. The entire pack benefits from following such a leader. It is nature's way of securing the survival of the pack – and the species.

When the leader gets too old or too weak to lead the pack, he is either challenged and replaced by a stronger dog in the pack, or dies, perhaps, from wounds suffered in a struggle with other wild animals.

What is important, however, is that pack animals don't hold any "grudges" against the new leader for replacing the old one, whether it occurs by natural death, by accident, or through a challenge and subsequent life and death struggle.

If one old leader is challenged and eventually overpowered, ousted, or even killed, the rest of the pack don't "blame" their new leader, turn their backs, and walk away. Quite to the contrary, the rest of the pack immediately show loyalty to the new leader of the pack.

This is the law of nature for wild dogs, wolves, hyenas and other pack animals. It gives each individual in the pack its best chance of survival.

By virtue of living as individual members of a human family, our domesticated dogs are somewhat different. But the pack instinct is still in them, at least in the breeds closest related to the wolves, like the Akita's and similar breeds.

A family dog, like Nicole's Kato, quickly accepted that each member of the human family is the dog's leader. But even within this hierarchy, Kato would recognize that Nicole was the **real** leader of "Kato's pack," since she was the adult, and the one who represented the highest degree of authority at Bundy. Also O.J. was recognized by Kato as one of its leaders, but not to the same degree as Nicole, since O.J. was not at Bundy every day.

Notice, however, that also in the wild, the leader of a pack of dog's may wander off on its own for days, but still return with its authority intact. So O.J. was definitely the **"second in command,"** for as much as Kato was concerned. We could even consider O.J. as Kato's real leader whenever he he was around.

Under O.J. and Nicole in rank, came Sydney and Justin, who were also considered by Kato as his leaders, when Nicole and O.J. were not present.

When Nicole was killed, we could expect Kato to bark intensely. However, **if O.J. – hypothetically – were the murderer,** we would **not** expect Kato to remain for very long by Nicole's side after she was dead, but instead listen to his instincts and follow the member of the pack whom Kato now immediately recognized as its new leader – namely O.J.!

Dogs, by nature, look for a new leader as soon as the old leader of the pack dies. It is essential to their survival! Pack animals don't enter into a state of ritual mourning, like humans do, when their old leader dies. Instinctively the dogs know who their new leader is and immediately follow him.

Dogs are not human. Instead they are driven by the law of nature – their nature. Hence, dogs don't grieve, pass moral judgement on the killer of their old leader, hold grudges, or "take sides." They let the leading rivals battle it out, and then the rest of the pack loyally follow the victor.

By the very law of nature that drives them, they appreciate in a way that the old leader is dead. Because by virtue of killing the old leader, the **new leader has proven** that he is the one better suited to lead the pack.

According to this hypothesis, I believe that Kato, a pack animal by nature, with natural wild dog instincts, would, as soon as Nicole was dead, recognize O.J. as his new leader – **if O.J. had been there and he had killed Nicole!**

Kato would have followed O.J. – if O.J. had been there!

However, if the assailant was someone other than O.J. – a total stranger – Kato would find himself without a leader, in this time of crisis. As soon as Nicole was dead, Kato would not know where to turn.

Kato did not recognize the murderer – and O.J. was not there to take over!

Typically, in this situation Kato would remain with Nicole and wail for a long time. Finally Kato would resign to the fact that neither O.J., nor Sydney or Justin was there to take charge. So Kato would just drift off, aimlessly, without anyone to lead him. That was how some neighbors found him an hour after the murders.

The fact that Kato did **not** follow the murderer going west through the **rear gate**, suggests strongly, that **O.J. is not the killer**. Deprived of its former "leader of the pack," **Kato would probably have followed O.J. if he had been present** – regardless of whether O.J. had killed Nicole a few minutes earlier.

At least, if O.J. were the killer who left the bloody shoeprints and the blood drops next to them, Kato would have followed those bloody shoeprints, once he **did** leave Bundy.

However, if the murderer is not one of Kato's natural leaders, then Kato would stay with Nicole's body, and eventually leave in the direction he normally takes when he goes for a walk.

The prosecutors in the criminal trial suggested that Kato, the dog, was "telling" us something with his wailing. They might have been right. Perhaps Kato **was** telling us something – whether he knew it or not. **Kato might have been telling us that O.J. is not the murderer!**

CHAPTER 49

Allan Park – Rosa Lopez – Mark Fuhrman

Ms. Rosa Lopez was the house maid of O.J.'s neighbor. She was a brave woman who deserved much credit for her testimony about observing O.J's Bronco outside his Rockingham home at the time when the murders took place at Bundy. Instead, Ms. Lopez was viciously attacked during cross examination by Prosecutor Christopher Darden, in an unspeakably unfair manner.

Mainly because of a **language barrier** and **cultural differences** this mild mannered, honest and dependable Salvadoran woman was made out to be a liar by the prosecutor, who tricked her into contradictions regarding totally irrelevant matters.

In his cross examination of Ms. Lopez, Prosecutor Christopher Darden showed his mean spirit, and exposed what I have always maintained, namely that the prosecutors weren't concerned about the truth; all that counted was to **win** at any cost, regardless of who was left bleeding on the battlefield – Ms. Rosa Lopez, O.J., his mother, or Nicole's and O.J.'s children.

On several talk shows after the criminal trial was over, Mr. Darden has expressed openly that his, and the entire prosecutions objective was not to play **"fair"** – but to win, any which way they could. No wonder the prosecution presented evidence they must have known was tampered with or fabricated.

They put Fuhrman on the witness stand even though they knew he was a racist. They knew he perjured himself; yet they tried to protect him. Probably, they even knew that he had murdered Nicole and Ron, and was lying about his whereabouts at the time of the murders. Still, they embraced Mark Fuhrman until the very end – and even after the trial!

However, let me get back to Ms. Lopez and Prosecutor Darden.

Unsuccessful in refuting Ms. Lopez' critical testimony regarding the Bronco, Prosecutor Darden changed tactic. Instead he cross examined her about **totally irrelevant matters**, regarding the dates, and the times of the nights, she had spoken to her employer on long distance calls from England many months earlier; and what dates her airline tickets were issued! Who bothers to remember such silly things?

Let me ask my readers: When you order an airline ticket over the phone, and receive the ticket in the mail about a week later, do you check to see what date the ticket was **issued**? I sure don't. All I care about is to check that the date and time of my **flight** is correct. And if you had spoken to your employer on a long distance call to Europe six months ago, you might still remember what you spoke about. But would you remember the exact date and what time of the night the conversation took place? Hardly!

Such were the questions Prosecutor Darden grilled Ms. Lopez about. Ms. Lopez got confused, she became understandably irritable when she was made out to be a liar, because she could not remember what she had said from one day to the next regarding those phone calls or the issuing date on her airline ticket.

In my eyes, Prosecutor Christopher Darden lost all his credibility and integrity during his encounter with Ms. Rosa Lopez. Prosecutor Darden must have felt he had a "field day" with Ms. Lopez on the witness stand. Instead, in the long run, Christopher Darden turned out to be the loser!

Ms. Lopez was steadfast about her observations of O.J.'s Bronco outside his house during the entire period when the murders at Bundy were committed. She never wavered.

Only Ms. Lopez testified that she saw the Bronco at Rockingham that night. However, it is certainly worth noticing that no witness ever testified that he or she positively observed that the Bronco was **not** there, either.

The prosecution could never establish that the Bronco was not parked at Rockingham when the murders took place at Bundy. Every witness who was asked about the Bronco, testified that they weren't looking for the Bronco, so it might very well have been there.

When assessing the credibility of Ms. Lopez' testimony, however, several points are worth noticing. It is true that Ms. Lopez was the only witness who positively claimed to have seen the Bronco parked at Rockingham during the critical time period. But not even in retrospect, reflecting back on that crucial night, did one single witness come forward to testify that he or she had seen a shiny white Bronco between Rockingham and Bundy!

Back and forth that's a five miles drive through Los Angeles. It is so totally unlikely that O.J.'s Bronco could have made that trip without being observed by a single witness, that this fact absolutely corroborated Ms. Lopez' testimony.

Prosecutor Marcia Clark made an issue of the fact that the limo driver, Mr. Allan Park, when he came to pick up O.J. to drive him to the airport, could not remember seeing the Bronco. That was not remarkable at all, because the limo driver wasn't looking for the Bronco, so it might have been there, even if he didn't see it.

What is more remarkable though, is the fact that the Bronco, unquestionably, was parked outside O.J.'s estate later, without the limo driver noticing the Bronco arriving.

If O.J. had been driving the Bronco to and from Bundy, and the Bronco were **not** parked outside Rockingham when the limo driver arrived, then O.J. **must** have arrived in the Bronco while the limo driver was there! Agree?

The driver testified that he had repeatedly called on the intercom outside the gate, without any response from the house. The house looked dark, except for some lights upstairs. The driver was concerned, because **he thought O.J. was not home,** and therefore, might miss his flight to Chicago.

But the natural thing for the limo driver to do under those circumstances – as he perceived them – would be to look up and down the street, constantly, to see if O.J. might be coming home.

So when the limo driver didn't see or hear any Bronco arriving, we can undoubtedly assume that it never left Rockingham that night.

By the way, O.J.'s neighborhood was very quiet and of course almost completely dark around 10:30 pm on a Sunday night.

The authors of the book, *"Killing Time,"* (Macmillan, USA; 1996), Donald Freed and Raymond P. Briggs, Ph.D., performed serious, reliable, accurate, high tech experiments in and around O.J.'s Rockingham estate, under the exact same conditions that existed on the night of the murders.

Their experiments revealed that the area, in fact, was so quiet and undisturbed that they could easily pick up the sounds of **insect wings** in the area! And it was almost completely dark.

They let a 4 x 4, Ford Bronco, similar to O.J.'s, approach the place where the Bronco was parked on the night of the murders. The headlights of the car lit up the entire neighborhood and were visible for more than three hundred feet as the car approached. Whether the test vehicle arrived from Ashford Street or along Rockingham Avenue the headlights were so prominent that the limo driver must have seen the Bronco arriving on the night of the murders, unless the Bronco was already parked when the driver arrived.

Besides, the Bronco's big engine roared like a brass band when the Bronco arrived.

In the opinion of the authors of *"Killing Time"* there was no way O.J. could have arrived in his Bronco – after the limo driver – without the driver observing it – not even if he weren't looking for the Bronco.

The ultimate rebuttal of Mr. Park's testimony about not seeing the Bronco lies in the fact that **he didn't even see the Bronco when he left Rockingham.** Regardless of whether the Bronco was parked outside Rockingham the entire time when Mr. Park was there, or O.J. arrived in the Bronco while the limo driver was waiting for him, the Bronco must unquestionably have been parked outside O.J.'s estate when the limo driver left Rockingham to take O.J. to the airport.

Allan Park was asked if he saw the Bronco parked outside O.J.'s estate when he **left** Rockingham. He didn't see it! But it must have been there at **that** time. That makes Mr. Park's testimony about not seeing the Bronco when he arrived, either –

totally worthless. Obviously, Mr. Park was not very observant!

Of course, we could also consider the possibility that the Bronco was absent both when the limo driver arrived and when he left. But if so, someone else must have been using the Bronco at the time of the murders, and returned it after the limo driver and O.J. had left. But if so, then O.J. could not be the murderer – at least not if we accept the prosecutions claim that his Bronco was the "murder car."

Let me give you an example to demonstrate how absurd it was for Prosecutor Clark to have Allan Park vouch for the alleged absence of the Bronco – since he didn't even see the Bronco when he left!

I don't know if Marcia Clark has a son or not, but **for the sake of my example**, let's assume she does.

Prosecutor Marcia Clark's son asks her if he may go to the refrigerator and take a sip of orange juice. Marcia Clarks says, **"Sure!"**

Twenty minutes later her son asks if he may go and take another sip. It's a hot summer day, so Marcia Clark, again says, *"Sure."*

Her son returns to the living room. Marcia Clark is thinking about her shopping list. Since her son just returned from the refrigerator, she asks him:

"Do we have any more eggs?"

Of course, her son wasn't looking for any eggs, so he answers:

"I didn't see any."

Ms. Clark doesn't feel like getting up from her chair to inspect the refrigerator herself, so **unfairly annoyed** with her son, she says:

"Are you blind? You've just been to the fridge, and you didn't see if we have any more eggs?"

Now her **son** gets a bit annoyed, too, as he replies:

> *"No, I didn't see any – **because I wasn't looking for the stupid eggs!**"*

Marcia Clark realizes that her son had reason to be upset, so she pleads with him:

> *"I am sorry! Would you please take a look for me? I am trying to figure out what we need at the supermarket."*

Her son is a nice fellow, after all, so he goes to the refrigerator for his mother and calls back:

> *"We have 4 eggs left."*

"Thanks," Marcia Clark says, as she writes, ***"1 doz. eggs,"*** on her shopping list.

Then she ponders. Her pen drops to the floor. She looks stupefied, as she mumbles to herself:

> *"Hmm, that's strange! The kid didn't see the four eggs the first two times he opened the refrigerator. But now they are there. They must have walked by themselves from the supermarket and straight into my refrigerator!"*

I trust my readers see the direct comparison to Prosecutor Marcia Clark's attempt to make the limo driver vouch for the absence of O.J.'s Bronco. Allan Park didn't see the Bronco when he arrived. **He didn't see it when he left, either.** Unquestionably, the Bronco was parked on Rockingham when the police came there to investigate. Of course, that didn't prove that O.J. arrived in the Bronco while the limo driver was there! It simply meant that the limo driver wasn't very observant – or that he wasn't looking for the Bronco, and therefore, he didn't see it!

This was the kind of "evidence" the prosecution presented

throughout the entire trial: – Allan Park – Detective Vannatter – Dr. Sathyavagiswaran – Andrea Mazzola – Dennis Fung – Police Nurse Peratis – and Detective Fuhrman!

Doesn't that tell us something about the quality and reliability of the entire case against O.J.?

Back to Ms. Rosa Lopez. The limo driver's unreliable testimony regarding the Bronco strengthened the credibility of Ms. Lopez' testimony. The Bronco never left Rockingham! Hence, O.J. could not have murdered Nicole and Ron!

On behalf of our nation I felt so bad vis-a-vis Ms. Lopez for the way Prosecutor Darden treated her, that I am glad I can rehabilitate her through my book. She was credible and trustworthy, and she deserved better!

I have heard many people who followed the trail, express this exact same feeling in regards to Ms. Lopez. Prosecutor Christopher Darden wasn't after the truth – he was only concerned about **winning!** How appropriate that **he** eventually lost the case!

The conclusion we can draw from all of this is that, regardless of the blood in the Bronco, the Bronco never left Rockingham on the night of the murders, so O.J. could not have been over at Bundy. Instead, the blood in the Bronco must have been planted, probably by Detective Fuhrman, as I have explained with my theory.

It is amazing how every new piece of information in this case seems to corroborate our theory, and contradict the prosecution's theory. I have earlier suggested that the prosecution, whenever they could, deliberately kept out any evidence or testimony pointing to O.J.'s innocence. Here is more.

When a police officer, on the morning after the murders, learned what Ms. Lopez had to say, he wasn't interested, and never asked her for a statement. Also the **prosecution** knew about Ms. Lopez, but in their so-called *"search for the truth"* they never bothered to call her as a witness – naturally!

Outside Rockingham, on the morning after the murders, Ms. Lopez spoke to a police officer about her observations of the Bronco.

At that time her recollection from the night before must have been quite good and accurate.

It is certainly suspicious that the police officer who spoke with Ms. Lopez on that occasion, and heard what she had to say about the Bronco – **was identified in court as being Detective Mark Fuhrman!**

Of course, if Rosa Lopez could provide O.J. and his Bronco with an alibi – that would mess up Fuhrman's plans for framing O.J. for the murders I suspect Mark Fuhrman himself committed.

This certainly explains why Detective Fuhrman pretended to make a note of Ms. Lopez' name and phone number, and **told her that she did not have to report her information to anyone else.** Fuhrman told her that he would pass the information on to the investigators, and if they thought her information was of any help in the investigation, the police would contact her.

That was, of course, just something Detective Fuhrman said to Ms. Lopez, in order **to shut her up**, because he didn't want anyone to hear Ms. Lopez' information about the Bronco, in which he had smeared the bloody glove.

Hence, instead of making out a report on his conversation with Ms. Lopez, Detective Fuhrman simply pretended it never occurred. He threw away his note with her name and phone number, and kept her important information regarding the Bronco away from the investigators.

Isn't it remarkable, once we are able to free ourselves from the notion that O.J. killed Nicole and Ron, and instead consider that Detective Fuhrman is the murderer – then every piece of evidence, or information, or mysterious little episode, that earlier, sort of, didn't fit, falls right into place in this murder mystery. Detective Fuhrman's actions in regards to Ms. Lopez certainly tie in with our theory.

CHAPTER 50

O.J.'s Statement To The Police

Typical of a man who had nothing to hide, and therefore, did not fear any question from the investigators, O.J. agreed to give a taped statement to Detectives Lange and Vannatter, just half an hour or so after he had returned from Chicago.

Had O.J. been guilty it would have been wise of him to have his attorney present. Even innocent people can benefit from the assistance of an attorney when they are being interrogated by the police in a murder case. But O.J. accepted to talk to the investigators without the presence of his attorney. I say, because he is innocent.

On the much talked about taped statement, O.J. admits that he might have cut his finger before leaving for Chicago. He also talks about possibly bleeding when he went to get his mobile phone in the Bronco. According to many, this was damaging evidence that O.J. were bleeding before he left for Chicago, and that all the blood evidence attributed to him were real.

However, if one listens to the tape carefully, it becomes evident that O.J. does not remember specifically that he bled while searching for the mobile phone in his Bronco. It is more like he just assumed he must have cut his finger somewhere, when rushing around and getting ready to go to Chicago. Quote:

"I bleed all the time. I play golf and stuff. There is always something, nicks and stuff here and there. It was no big deal."

O.J. also explained that he had received the cut on his finger while in his hotel room in Chicago. Over the phone he had just heard from the police that Nicole had been killed. A little later, he entered the bathroom. There, in despair, he broke a glass he was holding and cut himself when he swiped the pieces into the bathroom sink. Blood stains on the sink and on a towel confirmed that.

In spite of O.J.'s statement about possibly having cut himself at his house, and bleeding when searching for the mobile phone, his defense attorneys tried to establish that O.J. did **not** cut himself **before leaving for Chicago**. Nobody testified that they had seen a cut on his hands or fingers, or a band aid, on the night he went to Chicago.

Kato didn't see any, the limo driver didn't see any, the baggage handler didn't see any, the stewardess didn't see any, the passenger next to him didn't see any.

In fact, the passenger next to O.J. testified that he kept staring at O.J.'s fingers, looking for a Superbowl ring (which O.J. didn't have, though) and which the passenger could have used as an introduction piece to strike up a conversation with O.J. And, of course, O.J. didn't leave any blood spots anywhere, which any of these people reported seeing.

Nor did O.J. leave any blood spots on the luggage he was carrying out of his house and into the limo at Rockingham, and out of the limo at the airport.

I assume the investigators checked the areas underneath the handles of O.J.'s various pieces of luggage, since that would have been the most obvious place to search for blood, if O.J. did have a cut on his finger before he left for Chicago.

When you carry luggage, your hand is held down and low, increasing the blood pressure to your hands. Also, you strain your fingers around the luggage handles. In doing so, a cut on your finger knuckle will point straight down – and open up. The piece of luggage moves with the movements of your hand, and is always directly under your knuckles, collecting whatever blood might be dripping from a cut on one of your knuckles.

If O.J. bled – as profusely as the prosecutors and the counsels for the plaintiffs claim he bled, and in particular just inside his door as he was leaving – **the one place his blood should have been found, was on top of his luggage, directly underneath the carrying straps or handles!**

I can think of few other situation when a fresh cut on a finger knuckle would bleed more profusely than when carrying luggage. Since O.J.'s blood was not found on his luggage, it is almost inconceivable that he could have bled both in his driveway and directly inside his door, just a few minutes, or seconds, even, earlier.

Furthermore, the fabric of a piece of luggage would absorb the blood, and make it absolutely impossible for O.J. to wash it away completely – in his Chicago hotel room – if his blood had been on his luggage.

The defense argued that the blood at Rockingham and Bundy was planted, and that O.J. cut himself in Chicago only. The prosecution made mocking remarks about that, since O.J. admitted in his statement to the police that he bled before he left for Chicago.

It appeared that **O.J. was stuck with both his answers.** Today, evidently, most people believe O.J. cut himself before going to Chicago, and that he left the blood drops both at Rockingham and Bundy.

We on the other hand know that O.J. didn't bleed at Bundy. Even if he were the murderer – he could not have been cut in a struggle with Ron, and he could not have had an old cut that opened up during an alleged struggle with Ron, either (see **"The Glove Evidence"**). The five blood drops at Bundy **must** have been fabricated.

The obvious **"set-up"** of Kato by the detectives at Rockingham indicated that the blood in O.J.'s foyer was also fabricated. This assumption was strengthened by the appearance of those drops, as well as by the fact that nobody ever stepped in them, and finally by the fact that O.J.'s blood was only "found" where it could have been safely planted without anyone from the defense being able to secure their own test samples of that blood – directly from residues of the blood spots!

Every place where O.J.'s blood could **not** have been planted without the perpetrators running the risk of being exposed – **there was no blood!** This was the case behind O.J.'s house, where the glove was found, as well as up the stairway and in O.J.'s bedroom. Especially in the bedroom, we would expect to find blood, if O.J.'s blood were found in the foyer. But there was no blood in the bedroom.

I have suggested what the reason is for this inconsistency. The plush carpeting would have enabled the defense to double check the primary source of a blood drop in the bedroom – directly from the carpet. That's why the culprits, while waiting for O.J.'s real blood, planted **a temporary blood substitute** many other places, but were smart enough not to plant it on any absorbent material, like a plush carpet.

Is it possible to reconcile O.J.'s "admitting" he might have bled at his house before going to Chicago, with the suggestion that the blood at Rockingham (and Bundy) was planted or fabricated? I think so. **I believe O.J. did not bleed at Rockingham – even if he told the police that he bled there!** Yes – I mean what I am saying!

June 13, Detective Vannatter knew he would soon be getting O.J.'s EDTA free blood, ready to be planted, or to be made into false blood swatches, which, again, would make it appear that O.J. had bled "everywhere." Vannatter had already planted "substitute blood" in the driveway and in O.J.'s foyer, and he had set up Kato regarding the blood drops in the foyer. Vannatter also knew – from the handcuffing episode – that O.J. had a small cut on his left middle finger knuckle. It was "straight ahead" for Vannatter at this point!

So now Detectives Vannatter tried to **bluff** O.J., and make him admit that he bled before he left for Chicago. That would make the framing perfect!

<u>Vannatter:</u> *We have found your blood both inside and outside your house, so you must have been bleeding yesterday. And we found one murder glove at Bundy, and one behind your*

house. We know you did it – and you know it, too! Why don't you make it easy on yourself, and confess?

I am sure my readers, as well as I, have often cut ourselves **without noticing it.** Later we see blood on a tablecloth, on a towel, or on our shirt. We realize that we must have cut ourselves and search our hands. We find a small cut, where the bleeding may already have stopped.

O.J. must surely have experienced the same many times, during football practices at least, or when playing golf or otherwise just rushing around. He reasoned:

If my blood, according to the police, is in my house and outside, I must have cut myself – although I never noticed it. It could have been when I searched for the mobile phone in the Bronco – or perhaps when I was just rushing around, trying to get ready for my trip.

So, **trusting** Detective Vannatter on his word, that blood was everywhere around his house, **that** is what O.J. answered. Now it seems that O.J. is stuck with his answer.

As I sit by my PC writing this book, I look at my hands. I have one abrasion, and three different cuts, all of which are large enough that they might have deposited drops of blood somewhere. But I have no idea when I got them! And I have no idea whether I spilled some blood anywhere! And the wounds don't hurt at all.

Now if the police had arrested me as I was attending a movie this afternoon, told me my blood was all over my apartment, pointed to the three nicks on my hands, and asked me to explain the blood in my apartment, then – just like O.J. – I might have admitted that *"I cut myself all the time, but it is no big deal"*! I would have suggested that I might have cut myself when vacuum cleaning this morning, or when repairing the ceiling fan in my bedroom, or when washing my car, or, perhaps, when I worked out in the boxing gym last night.

Should I be stuck with my answers, if it later turned out that **there was no blood** in my apartment to start with – only strong indications that the police had planted that blood later?

I can't see any contradiction in O.J. retracting his earlier statement to Detectives Lange and Vannatter, saying:

> *"The police told me I had bled both inside and outside my house. So I concluded that I must have cut myself before I left for Chicago. But I sure didn't notice any blood – **otherwise I would have cleaned it up, of course!***
>
> *If it turns out that the detectives might have been bluffing, and that they might have planted that blood the next day, then, obviously – as I thought – I did **not** cut myself before going to Chicago!"*

Most likely, Detectives Lange and Vannatter will criticize my explanation, saying that there is nothing on the taped interview indicating that O.J. was **coerced** into explaining about the cut and his bleeding at Rockingham.

Of course not! The detectives would be **stupid** if they **recorded themselves coercing O.J.**! But there is something called **"off the record,"** you know!

Vannatter: *Let's sit over here O.J. and talk a little before we start the tape. Let me tell you what we got – just so you don't think we're trying to trick you or anything.*

      OK. Nicole ... and Ron Goldman, were killed last night. There is a lot of blood everywhere ... also inside and out-side your house! ... I see you have a cut on your finger ... It seems like the blood at your house might have come from that cut ... Were you bleeding last night?

Simpson: *No, I cut it in Chicago. I broke a glass when I heard Nicole had been killed.*

Vannatter: *But the blood around your house ... you must have cut yourself before Chicago ... Maybe you just opened it up again in Chicago?*

Simpson: *I don't know ... I bleed all the time ... nicks and stuff ...*

from playing golf and stuff ...

Vannatter: *Tell us about it ... you know ... the blood must have come from somewhere ...*

So now O.J. starts to tell about his cut, assuming he cut himself before going to Chicago. He thinks about the blood which allegedly – **according to Vannatter** – is inside and outside his house. O.J. senses where the detectives are heading. But he certainly didn't have anything to do with the murders of Nicole and Ron.

O.J. wants to make sure the detectives don't think he were over at Bundy and cut himself there, and that he is trying to hide that.

Simpson: *It's no big deal ... I cut myself all the time ... I could have cut myself last night while rushing, trying to get ready to go to the airport ... or perhaps when I searched for my mobile phone in the Bronco ...*

Vannatter: *So that's when it must have happened .. when you were rushing last night ... in your house?*

Simpson: *Yes, it must have ...*

Vannatter: *OK ... Let's talk about something else ... Or ... why don't we start the tape now ... if that's OK with you?*

Simpson: *No problem!*

Do you see how an experienced interrogator like Vannatter can actually instill in O.J.'s mind that he cut himself at his house the night before!

Even though O.J. initially said he cut himself in Chicago, Vannatter can lead O.J. to conclude that he **must** have cut himself at his house, **too!**

Through a set of logically interrelated questions and answers Vannatter can convince O.J. that his blood, dripping from that cut, were present both inside and outside his house! Vannatter even makes O.J. believe he might have been bleeding on his way to or from the Bronco when he went to get his mobile phone.

Through several hypothetical questions, Vannatter leads O.J.

to the conclusion that he had a cut the night before, and that he bled from that cut at Rockingham – although **not one of half a dozen witnesses who saw Simpson that night, recalls seeing any such cut or any blood.**

Not even the witness who testified that he **stared** at O.J.'s fingers, onboard the airplane, in search of a possible Superbowl ring, saw any cut or a band-aid. And there was no blood on top of any of his pieces of luggage.

> **That says it all. There was no cut on any of O.J.'s fingers before he left for Chicago! There couldn't have been. Therefore, all the blood evidence that allegedly contained O.J.'s DNA, must have been fabricated. Hence, O.J. must be innocent!**

Let us scrutinize some more the blood O.J., allegedly, deposited at Rockingham before leaving in the limo. If we are to trust the investigators, that the blood at Rockingham had come from O.J.'s finger we have the following situation:

An alleged cut on O.J.'s finger is bleeding so profusely, that three drops run down his finger and drip to the floor right inside his entrance door – in a couple of seconds. Next, rushed for time, O.J. must have walked to his Bronco rather quickly, to get his mobil phone. So, in the few seconds it took him to walk back and forth between his entrance and the Bronco, he allegedly dripped more than 25 drops of blood in his driveway!

Obviously – if we are to believe this asinine allegation from the investigators – the cut on O.J.'s finger weren't **"dripping"** drops of blood. Blood must have been **pouring out** of that alleged cut! Yet, not one, of half a dozen witnesses close to O.J. at the time, saw any cut or any blood!

And reaching inside his Bronco, searching for his mobil phone, the alleged cut suddenly didn't bleed anymore? How dumb do the investigators expect the public to be?

There were no drops of O.J.'s blood in the Bronco, just a faint **smear**, less than 7/10 of one drop! Just as much blood as we could expect if someone moistened one of Detective Vannatter's fake O.J. blood swatches and smeared it inside the Bronco!

If there is any logic to the investigators' allegations, this profusely bleeding cut would have caused the blood to be smeared all over O.J.'s hand and fingers, since his hand wasn't kept immobile and pointing straight down all the time. After all, he opened and closed his entrance door, as well as the Bronco's door. Reached inside the Bronco, or for the light switch in his foyer, as well as for the control panel for the alarm, bent down to pick up his luggage, handed it to the limo driver etc. etc.

If O.J. had dripped more than 25 drops of blood from this alleged cut, just walking quickly to and from his Bronco, his entire hand should have been a bloody mess. Yet, nobody, not even O.J., noticed any blood – anywhere! And nobody saw a band-aid!

Together with everything else I have explained about this so-called "trail of blood," there can be no doubt – the blood, allegedly found at Rockingham, must have been planted by the investigators. Anyone suggesting that this blood came from O.J.'s finger on the night of the murders, better see a psychiatrist!

B ack to O.J.'s statement to Lange and Vannatter. Later, when the real questioning starts, O.J. has already been convinced by a set of logical conclusions – **based on Vannatter's faulty premises** – that he bled at his house!

This is how experienced investigators build a case against a suspect, where they really didn't have much to go on in the beginning. **"Off the record"** they bluff or confuse the suspect, until the suspect admits to what the investigators want him to say. **Then**, they start the **taped** statement!

On the tape Vannatter asks about a lot of other things first, to make O.J. relax and not think about the blood. Simultaneously, Vannatter manages to establish a friendly rapport with O.J., while leading him into the trap.

Suddenly the investigators change subject. As I quote from the taped interview, my readers should bear in mind the **"off the record"** conversation I constructed above. Then you may understand why O.J. might have **"admitted"** that he bled at Rockingham before going to Chicago, although no one on a long list of witnesses saw any cut or blood or a band-aid.

Quote from Simpson's statement to the LAPD (approximately 15 minutes into the statement):

Vannatter: O.J., what is your office phone number?
Simpson: *(Number deleted)*
Vannatter: And that's area code 310?
Simpson: *Yes.*

Suddenly, Vannatter changes to a completely different subject!

Vannatter: How did you get the injury on your hand?
Simpson: *I don't know. The first time ... when I was in Chicago and all ... but at the house ... I was just running around.*

To me it sounds as if O.J. doesn't quite agree with what Vannatter has led him to believe – off the record.

O.J. wants to say that **the first time** he cut his finger was in Chicago – which, of course means that he couldn't have cut his finger at his home – before going to Chicago.

But then he remembers the conversation I stipulated took place **"off the record"** **before** the taped statement. So O.J. gets confused, and his answer turns into an **incoherent** sentence as soon as he tries to bring the blood around his house into the picture.

My readers should try to pretend that **you** are asking O.J. **how** he got the cut on his finger. Pretend also that you know nothing about O.J.'s explanation regarding the cut, or where and when he got them! Now, read O.J.'s answer again!

Isn't it pretty obvious from O.J.'s answer that he is responding to something he and Vannatter have **already discussed**? Otherwise, his answer makes absolutely no sense!

Try this experiment! Let us change Vannatter's question a little bit, to indicate that he had **already** discussed the cut with O.J. Then you will see that O.J.'s answer, although still incoherent, appears to be much more **responsive.**

Vannatter: (our experiment only) Tell us – **again** – O.J., how you got the injury to your hand!

Simpson: *I don't know. The first time ... when I was in Chicago and all ... but at the house ... I was just running around.*

Do you see? O.J. **assumes** that Vannatter and Lange **already know** what he is referring to, both with respect to Chicago and the house. So he leaves out all the details. That indicates that they had discussed the cut before they started the tape – **off the record** – just like I suggested.

It appears that the detectives want O.J. to admit that he cut his finger **both** in Chicago **and** at his house – **as if they had already discussed it with him!** I continue to quote from the same passage:

Vannatter: How did you do it in Chicago?

Simpson: *I broke a glass. One of you guys had just called me, and I was in the bathroom, and I just, kind of, went bonkers for a little while.*

Here O.J. is telling the truth. Therefore, although his answer is fairly long, it is still **coherent and easy to understand**.

Let me take a few minutes to arrest certain people on a point they frequently bring up in a derogatory way. O.J.'s adversaries argue that O.J.'s last answer indicated that he was on the phone when he broke the glass in the bathroom – but there was no phone in the bathroom! Therefore, they argue – he is lying about the cut!

This is a classical example of how the police skew the evidence to make O.J. appear guilty. You see, there are **no punctuation marks on an audiotape.** The listeners have to **"imagine"** the **punctuation marks** themselves. This may result in different interpretations of the same statement.

My readers are accustomed to my "examples" by now. Some of you, perhaps, hate them. Anyway, I am going to give you another example, to demonstrate how important correct punctuation may be:

A convict was on the scaffold, awaiting his execution. His last appeal had not been answered by the governor yet. The warden E-mailed the governor one final letter, asking **if he should proceed with the execution – or wait for the governor's review of the convict's last appeal.**

Minutes later, the governor's E-mail reply appeared on the warden's computer screen. His secretary read it to a dispatcher, who quickly wrote down the governor's reply, ran out to the scaffold with it, and handed it to the warden. The warden read:

"Dear Warden:
No!
Don't *wait for my review of his appeal!"*

Seven seconds later the convict was dead!

The warden returned to his office. There, on the computer screen he read:

"Dear Warden:
No – don't!!!
Wait for my review of his appeal!!!"

Back to O.J.'s statement: When the police made a transcript from O.J.'s audiotaped statement to Lange and Vannatter, they took full advantage of **"clever" punctuation**, in order to make it appear that O.J. were lying.

Look back at the last exchange between Vannatter and O.J.!

Vannatter: How did you do it in Chicago?
Simpson: *I broke a glass. One of you guys had just called me,*

> *and I was in the bathroom, and I just, kind of, went bonkers*
> *for a little while.*

It appears that O.J. had broken a glass – first of all.

Then, because of clever punctuation by the police, O.J. is – apparently – explaining that he was talking to the police from the bathroom, and that he broke the glass while he was still on the phone, in the bathroom. Construed in this manner, it appeared that O.J. might be lying – because **there was no phone in the bathroom!**

Now, let **me** punctuate O.J.'s answer – **correctly**!

<u>Vannatter:</u> How did you do it in Chicago?
<u>Simpson:</u> *I broke a glass – one of you guys had just called me.*
And I was in the bathroom, and I just, kind of, went bonkers
for a little while.

What O.J. is saying is this:

> *"I broke a glass!"*

Then he **interjects** the reason why he broke the glass:

> *"– one of you guys had just called me."*

O.J. refers to the call he **received** from the police – **earlier** in the morning – informing him that Nicole had been killed.

> *"– one of you guys **had just called** me."*

does not indicate that he was still on the phone with the police officer when he broke the glass. Had that been the case, the correct way of expressing that would have been to say:

> *"I **was talking to** one of you guys on the phone.*

"... had just called ..." clearly indicated that the conversation had **ended before** he went to the bathroom, where he **eventually** broke the glass.

After this **interjection** about the phone conversation – where O.J. explains **why** he **later** broke the glass – O.J.'s mind is still on the situation when he broke the glass, so he continues this line of thought by saying:

> *"And I was in the bathroom, and I just, kind of, went bonkers for a little while."*

Do my readers see how a clever police officer or prosecutor, when preparing a transcript of O.J.'s statement, can totally change the meaning of the statement, by switching around a few commas and periods here and there?

The police knew there was no telephone in the bathroom – so don't tell me that this was just a "slip of the pen," so to speak! It was deliberate! And that makes it a forgery – or even, a crime!

Detective Lange proceeds to remind O.J. about the other incident which they **already** discussed – in connection with the blood at O.J.'s house.

Lange: Is that how you cut it?

O.J. does not deny that he might have bled at his house, so obviously, **he is not trying to hide anything** from the investigators. He simply can't seem to get **their** "logic" to coincide with **his own** "logic" and recollection.

His answer seems to indicate that. So O.J.'s next answer gets **incoherent again.** In addition, O.J.'s next answer is clearly **a response to something that has already been discussed** between him and the investigators. The shortness of his answer indicates that O.J. is simply **confirming** something he believes Lange **already** knows.

Lange: Is that how you cut it?

Simpson: *M-mm, it was cut before, but I think I just opened it again. I am not sure.*

What is incoherent about this answer? Well, if O.J. **knew that his finger was cut before** – and he had already explained, a few seconds earlier, that he **definitely** cut it in Chicago – then he **must** have **known** that he *"just opened it again"* in Chicago.

So how can he say, *"I think I just opened it again,"* and add to that answer, *"I'm not sure"*?

To me it is pretty obvious that Lange and Vannatter coached O.J. before they started the tape recorder, and coerced him to **"understand"** that he **must** have bled at his house, although O.J. doesn't seem to have any recollection of having bled before going to Chicago.

A few seconds later O.J. seems to confirm that this is what probably happened during his statement.

Lange: So, do you recall bleeding at all?

Simpson: *Yeah, I mean, I know I was bleeding, but it was no big deal. I bleed all the time. I play golf and stuff, so there is always something, nicks and stuff here and there.*

This last answer clearly suggests that although O.J. is willing to concede that he might have bled at his home – since that is what the investigators had told him – he has absolutely no precise recollection of any such bleeding **in particular.**

Lange: So, did you do anything? When did you put the band-aid on it?

Simpson: *Actually, I asked the girl this morning for it.*

This exchange is interesting in itself. Clearly, when O.J. cut his finger in Chicago, he put a band-aid on the cut. Neat as he is, O.J., obviously, didn't want to smear his blood on his clothes or any-where else.

So why didn't he put a band-aid on his finger **also before** he went to Chicago?

Because he didn't have any cut on his finger before he went to Chicago!

At least he didn't know of any cut, or see any cut, while he was still at his house. Evidently, when O.J. "admits" on the tape that he cut himself while rushing around at his house, his admission of that must be a result of the detectives **coercing** him to believe that he had bled at his house. Otherwise, as neat as O.J. is, he would have wiped up the blood, and put a band-aid on the wound.

In particular, if O.J. had just committed double homicide – and cut his finger during a life and death struggle with one of his victims – and he realized that he had cut himself – wouldn't he have wiped up the blood drops and put a band-aid on the cut? Give me a break!

Under such circumstances, how could O.J. possibly get into the following exchange with Detective Lange, unless he was coached and coerced – **before the tape recorder was started** – to believe that his blood had been found at his house.

Lange: So, do you recall bleeding at all?
Simpson: *Yeah, I mean, I know I was bleeding, but it was no big deal. I bleed all the time. I play golf and stuff, so there is always something, nicks and stuff here and there.*

When asked by Lange if he **recalled** bleeding, O.J. first says **"Yeah."** But, obviously, he immediately realizes that this is not correct. He didn't **"recall"**! So he corrects this in the same sentence saying,

*"I mean, I **know** I was bleeding, but it was no big deal. I bleed all the time. I play golf and stuff, so there is always something, nicks and stuff here and there."*

Time and time again, the investigators try to get O.J. to admit that he saw, or recalled, that he was bleeding at his house before going to Chicago.

O.J. is cooperating fully with the investigators. He does not try to deny that he might have bled at his house. But the closest they get O.J. to concede that he bled at his house, is that O.J. says he *"knows"* he **must** have been bleeding – because that is, probably, what the investigators convinced him of, **before they started the tape recorder.**

However, O.J. does not **recall** specifically where he bled, like for instance, in his foyer, where the police, allegedly discovered three blood drops. Sure enough, O.J. says that he saw some blood on the kitchen counter and grabbed a napkin to wipe it up.

I don't believe it. I think O.J. was coerced into **"believing"** that he saw blood on the kitchen counter.

He might have seen ketchup or Taco sauce somewhere, and again – neat as he is – he immediately grabbed a paper towel and wiped it up.

However, **if O.J., really thought that the spots he wiped up were blood – his blood – he would of course search his hand to see where the blood might have come from!** In particular if he had just committed double homicide with a knife, and then believed he saw blood on his kitchen counter! Had he then, had any bleeding cut on his hands or fingers, he would of course have put a band-aid on it.

As my conclusion I suggest that O.J. was telling the truth about receiving the cut on his finger in the hotel room in Chicago. But everything else he might have said about bleeding around his house the night before, or having had the cut before he got to Chicago, was simply the result of ideas and conclusions the detectives persuaded him to believe, because they lied to him initially – off the record – by telling him they had found his blood in his Bronco, in his foyer, and in his driveway.

Detectives Lange and Vannatter may try to deny that they spoke to O.J. – off the record – **before** they started the recording, to coerce O.J. to admit that he bled at Rockingham before going to

Chicago.

If you ask them, they will probably protest vehemently, saying they would never coerce a suspect – off the record – before interrogating him.

However, do my readers remember from an earlier chapter, how O.J. testified that, at first, he requested to have his attorney present? What happened? Detectives Lange and Vannatter coerced and, actually, **threatened** O.J. – saying that if he insisted on having his attorney present during the interrogation, they would keep him for the rest of the afternoon, so he wouldn't be able to see his children that day!

Then, after O.J. accepted to be interrogated without the presence of his attorney, the detectives rewound the tape, and started the recording anew, to cover up the fact that they had coerced and threatened O.J. just minutes earlier.

Of course, Lange and Vannatter can deny that this happened, and claim that O.J. is lying – and that I am lying! By now, we are used to their denials of the obvious facts in this case. But the tape itself speaks clearly of what must have transpired.

Clearly, something was erased from the start of the tape, indicating that O.J. is telling the truth in this matter. The opening of the recorded statement is totally incoherent.

As I quote from the transcript, my readers can, again, judge for themselves, whether or not they believe that **"something"** was erased from the start of the tape, whereafter the tape recorder was restarted.

These are the very first recognizable words on that tape!

Vannatter: . . . *my partner, Detective Lange, and we're in an interview room in Parker Center. The date is June 13, 1994, and the time is 13:35 ...*

What kind of a start is that, on an important, official interrogation of the prime suspect in a grizzly, high profile, double homicide case?

Detective Vannatter didn't even introduce himself!

Obviously, something transpired between O.J. and the detectives – **both off and on the record** – before Vannatter rewound the tape and started the recording over again, thereby covering up what was said. Clearly, O.J. must have been telling the truth, when he testified about this.

I am a bit surprised that O.J.'s defense attorneys did not put on an expert witness, a speech analyst and psychologist, to analyze the taped statement like I have done above, and introduce it as evidence of O.J.'s innocence.

Instead, they let the plaintiffs introduce the tape as evidence that O.J. cut himself on the night of the murders – before going to Chicago! Again and again, I was baffled by the defense in the civil case – not only by what they did present, but also by what they did not present.

Of course, as an outsider without access to the courtroom, I probably missed much of the anti-defense atmosphere Judge Fujisaki created. He did his best to destroy Mr. Baker's defense of O.J., by cutting off the defense even before they got started.

I have probably been grossly unfair to Defense Attorney Robert Baker in my book. It must have been an extremely frustrating situation for Mr. Baker. My readers should view my criticism of Mr. Baker in light of Judge Fujisaki's administration of the trial. The judge simply didn't allow Mr. Baker to defend O.J.

I am fairly certain that the full extent of Judge Fujisaki's bias against O.J. and Mr. Baker escaped the public, simply because the judge shut the doors to his "star chamber" courtroom and only allowed a few, hand-picked, equally biased, news reporters to convey to the American people how he administered **"his justice."**

Judge Fujisaki wasn't administering **"justice."** He was administering a **"legal lynching"** of **"just another African American"**!

Many critics of O.J. have asked why the prosecutors did not introduce the taped statement in court during the criminal trial. Of course, had the tape been damaging to O.J., the prosecution would have introduced it faster than you can shout, *"guilty"*! But there was nothing on the taped interview that was damaging to O.J. Quite to the contrary, the tape contained O.J.'s absolute denial, as well as an attitude of cooperation with the police which was consistent with his innocence.

What I have explained above shows clearly that what many thought were devastating to O.J. (his explanation regarding the cut), was in fact not inconsistent with his innocence at all. **And since the rest of the tape was favorable to O.J., the prosecution elected not to play it to the jury!**

That was a constant theme by the prosecution, throughout the entire criminal case.:

> **Anything favorable to O.J. – audio tapes, video tapes, physical evidence, test results, witnesses, and testimonies – were deliberately kept away from the jury, if the prosecutors were able to do so.**
>
> The prosecution's case wasn't a *"search for the truth,"* as the prosecutors wanted us to believe.
>
> **From day one, the prosecution's case was one of lies and perjury, deception, fabrication and planting of false evidence, cover ups, and hiding the truth!**

Furthermore, as I have just explained, the tape showed clear signs of **"off the record"coercion**, as well as **"clever" editing** of the official transcript. Had the prosecutors in the criminal trial introduced the tape, things could have become rather embarrassing, since Judge Ito was fairly liberal in allowing in evidence. Maybe that was the main reason the prosecution did not introduce Lange's and Vannatter's taped interrogation of O.J.

The plaintiffs however, could introduce the taped interrogation without any risk. Judge Fujisaki would protect them, and make ceretain O.J.'s attorneys were not allowed to suggest that there was anything suspect regarding the tape or its transcript.

S easoned investigators, prosecutors, and district attorneys have criticized Detectives Lange and Vannatter on TV, for bungling the recorded interrogation of O.J. on June 13.

They criticized the detectives for not following up some of

O.J.'s answers with more aggressive questions, and most of all, for letting this opportunity to question the suspect without the presence of his lawyer, slip away, by concluding the interrogation after only **32 minutes**.

One former district attorney (and Simpson book author) have commented on TV that he would have grilled O.J. for at least two-three hours – perhaps four! Every prosecutor seems to agree that this would have been the right thing to do.

Maybe they are right. Maybe Vannatter made a big mistake. But if so, **I like to ask why?**

By now, my readers know me well enough to realize that I want to find the reasons **behind** people's actions or decisions – especially when they **deliberately** do something strange or unexpected.

OK. So **why** would Detective Vannatter interrogate O.J. for only 32 minutes, when he was given this extraordinary opportunity to grill him without the presence of O.J.'s attorney, for several hours, perhaps?

> It was like you and your spouse receiving two tickets to the Opera, and then leave after the first act, so you can go home and do your laundry before the eleven o'clock news!

What was more important than to interrogate the prime suspect without the presence of his lawyer?

Could it be that **Vannatter had to get a blood sample from O.J. as soon as possible**, so he could get the blood evidence fabrication rolling?

I don't know. This is just one more of those peculiar events Detective Vannatter has never explained.

However, if Detective Vannatter concluded the interrogation of O.J. long before anyone else would have done it, the reason, most likely, is that he had something more important to do!

So what did he do next – that was so important? He took

O.J. to the nurse's office, got O.J.'s blood vial, and brought it to his own office, alone!

Rather than interrogating O.J. for another hour or so, Detective Vannatter should soon spend 90 minutes, alone in his office – with O.J.'s blood vial in his possession!

Why was this more important to Detective Vannatter, than interrogating O.J.? You tell me! Or perhaps Detective Vannatter can tell us!

When cross-examined about what he did during those 90 minutes, all Vannatter could answer – **on the spot** – was that he might have gone to his office to drink **one** cup of coffee!

Later, Detective Vannatter has, of course figured out several other explanations as to what he was doing with O.J.'s blood vial during those critical 90 minutes . . .

– when I believe he was fabricating false, EDTA free blood swatches from the blood in O.J.'s blood vial.

I'll let my readers draw their own conclusions.

CHAPTER 51

A Question Of Trust

Let me return to the knit cap for a minute. As with all the so-called evidence in this case, the knit cap fell right into place in this murder mystery. The cap served a definite purpose if we accept my theory that Detective Fuhrman murdered Nicole and Ron.

If we don't accept my theory, but the prosecution's, then the knit cap becomes yet another mysterious piece of evidence that doesn't fit, and which the prosecutors can not explain.

Or do you believe the prosecution's theory that a black man like O.J. would put on a dark knit ski cap, at 10:30 pm, in Los Angeles, in the middle of the summer – to look less conspicuous and avoid attracting attention to himself if he should be spotted? I mean, how do the prosecutors come up with all their absurd ideas and theories – time and time again?

I sense that critics of O.J. – and of my theory – are aching to argue that we cannot assume the LAPD fabricated **all** the evidence, just because they unquestionably fabricated **some** of it – like O.J.'s hairs in the knit cap.

Why shouldn't we? Let me explain this!

There was, irrefutably, plenty of evidence fabrication by the LAPD in this case. I shall list some of it again, shortly.

Notice that I do **not** include here the evidence the **murderer** himself planted or fabricated in his effort to frame O.J. – like the planting of the gloves, the planting of the knit cap, the planting of the bloody shoeprints, the five drops of Nicole's blood next to the bloody shoeprints at Bundy, the original blood in the Bronco, etc.

Although planted or fabricated (by the murderer), those

were pieces of evidence that were already present when the investigators arrived.

I shall only list such evidence which the **investigators** must have fabricated. I make this distinction in order for my readers to understand that possibly **all** the evidence against O.J. was fabricated – some of it by the murderer, but most of it in a **well planned, organized, comprehensive scheme,** initiated by Detective Vannatter.

Here are just **some** of the obviously fabricated pieces of evidence:

- The hairs on the cap, that allegedly were similar to O.J.'s. The cap was an obvious "set-up."
- The Bronco fibers allegedly found on Ron's shirt and on the knit cap. It's inconceivable that those fibers could have ended up there by accident.
- The blood drops on the rear gate at Bundy. They weren't there on the day after the murders, and they contained EDTA.
- The socks in O.J.'s bedroom.
- The blood on those socks. The story of the socks is well documented in another chapter.
- The blood in the Bronco which wasn't there on the day after the murders, but appeared later.
- The three blood drops in O.J.'s foyer, which nobody stepped in.

Add to this list, the obvious blood evidence fabrication scheme initiated by Detective Vannatter, in a conspiracy with the police nurse. I am sure my readers remember my discussion of Vannatter and O.J.'s blood vial, as well as the evidence which suggested that Vannatter circumvented the EDTA and fabricated false blood swatches from O.J.'s blood vial. For instance:

- 1.5 ml of blood missing from O.J.'s vial.
- The nurse's retraction of his earlier sworn testimony regarding the amount of blood he drew, and the

circumstances surrounding his videotaped "statement."

- Vannatter's many lies related to his handling of O.J.'s vial.
- The handcuffing of O.J.
- The mysterious blood transfers onto some of the blood bindels, referred to by Dr. Henry Lee – *"Something is wrong."*
- Ms. Mazzola's initials, which mysteriously disappeared from some of her bindels.
- Vannatter also requesting and receiving two vials of the victims' bloods, less than 48 hours after the murders.
- Nicole's blood on O.J.'s socks. The concentration of EDTA in that blood being "lethal," but also being almost identical to the EDTA concentration in blood swatches prepared from Nicole's blood on her dress – indicating that Nicole's blood on O.J.'s sock must have been transferred from her dress, by the investigators.

Look at this **"enormous"** list of fabricated evidence or suspect or covert activities, cover ups, and lies! And this is just a short excerpt!

I don't believe some casual, subordinate, LAPD investigator would say to himself:

> *"I am going to help my superiors and the prosecutors convict O.J. So I am going to access the Bronco without authorization and pluck some fibers from its carpet. Then I am going to enter the crime lab and put those fibers on the knit cap and on Ron's shirt, when the criminalists are not looking."*

That is absurd in itself! But furthermore, how could this subordinate investigator possibly think that such an effort on his behalf would make any difference, whatsoever, in this case, considering the so-called "mountain of evidence" of much greater importance.

Even if this hypothetical subordinate investigator conceived such a ridiculous idea, how could he possibly think it could aid the investigation?

Every **individual**, subordinate investigator (detective or criminalist), regardless of what idea of evidence fabrication he might have come up with, **must** have realized that it was a "dead lame" idea – to do something like that **on his own!**

What I am suggesting is that for evidence fabrication to have any meaning or effect, it had to be **organized** and carried out on a **much larger scale**. Whoever initiated any evidence fabrication in this case, must have been able to see the **"big picture."** He had to see the combined effect of **all** the evidence fabrication.

Each little evidence fabrication initiative, by itself, could only hurt the investigation. Only if all the fabrication of false evidence was initiated and carried out in a well planned effort to frame O.J. – could such evidence fabrication succeed.

I see, in other words, **a central coordinator** who could organize and direct the massive evidence fabrication which obviously took place – judging from the long lists above.

This organizer and coordinator must have been the lead investigator, Detective Vannatter.

Much of the evidence fabrication Detective Vannatter carried out personally, like most of the false blood evidence that was replaced in the LAPD's crime lab. But Vannatter didn't personally run around plucking Bronco fibers in the LAPD's car impound, planting blood on the rear gate at Bundy, and things like that. Most likely this other evidence fabrication, was carried out by his subordinates, **but on Vannatter's orders.**

It was not like Vannatter told just "anybody":

"Hey, Detective Patterson – take this blood vial, and plant a few drops on the rear gate at Bundy for me!"

It was much more **"subtle"** than that. Vannatter was a 27 year veteran, and the LAPD's lead homicide investigator. He knew his men! He knew whom he could trust, who had planted evidence before, and was willing to do it again. Vannatter knew the sentiment of each investigator towards O.J. and towards the case in itself.

Vannatter knew exactly whom he could ask to plant or fabricate evidence – where and when. The following is **an example** of how the two blood drops on the rear gate at Bundy **might** have come about.

<u>Vannatter:</u> *Hey,* [investigator] *Charlie – how is your part of the investigation going?*

<u>Charlie:</u> *Good. We're almost finished over at Bundy.*

<u>Vannatter:</u> *I know how you feel about O.J. Can you suggest something we could do to really nail this guy?*

<u>Charlie:</u> *He-he! Like **"giving justice a helping hand,"** you mean?*

<u>Vannatter:</u> *Yeah – something like that. We both know the bastard did it!*

<u>Charlie:</u> *I told you last night how I feel about this case. So you tell me – what you want me to do – and I'll do it!*

<u>Vannatter:</u> *Well, you're going over to Bundy this afternoon, aren't you? Maybe you could take this vial, and **"lose"** a couple of drops on the rear gate?*

<u>Charlie:</u> *Sure! Maybe I should **"lose"** them on the bottom of the gate then – where we, sort of, might have overlooked them earlier?*

Later Vannatter talked to other of his investigators. Soon one was back from O.J.'s bathroom with hairs from his hair brush, another smeared some of O.J.'s blood in the Bronco, and returned with some fibers from the Bronco's carpet.

Someone planted the socks in O.J.'s bedroom. Before the socks, together with much of the other evidence, was packaged and sent to outside forensic labs, someone else planted some of Nicole's blood on one of the socks – just in case, like for "good measure." He moistened some of the blood on Nicole's dress, and rubbed it into the sock.

My point with this is to explain why, and how, Detective

Vannatter must have had a finger in all of the planting and fabrication of false evidence. It simply wouldn't have made sense for any of his subordinate investigators to plant single pieces of evidence individually.

Their individual efforts in this respect would not appear to them as having any significant impact on the outcome of the case. It could only hurt the case if it was exposed.

Furthermore, individual, subordinate investigators wouldn't dare do something like that – possibly jeopardizing the entire investigation – unless they had the support and backing of the lead investigator, Detective Vannatter.

The matter of O.J.'s blood vial strongly suggested that Vannatter was heavily involved in evidence fabrication on his own. It is therefore, in my opinion, pretty obvious that **absolutely all the planting and fabrication of evidence in the case was orchestrated by Detective Vannatter!**

Had there only been a few sporadic, unorganized, incidents of evidence tampering against O.J., one might have attributed this to various, perhaps, over-eager, rookie investigators. And if we suspected that a particular piece of evidence **might** have been fabricated, **but we couldn't prove it** – we would tend to **assume that there was, perhaps, nothing suspect** about that particular piece of evidence.

However, assume that there is every reason to suspect that false evidence had been manufactured **on a grand scale and in an organized fashion,** and we **now** discover several **other** pieces of evidence which we suspect are also fabricated – although we cannot prove it, **then we are definitely justified in assuming that also these other suspect pieces of evidence have indeed been fabricated – just like the rest of the obviously false evidence in the case!**

The police obtained samples of O.J.'s hairs for comparison purposes. I believe they received over 100 hair samples from O.J.'s head. Several of the hair fragments on the cap matched the samples taken from O.J. The question, however, is whether or not these hair fragments, allegedly found on the cap, had been planted by the police, using hairs collected from O.J.'s hair brush or from his pillowcase in his jail cell – or perhaps, using some of the very hair samples they received from O.J.!

As with most evidence, it would be impossible for the police to prove that they did **not** fabricate the hair evidence.

However, it would be just as impossible for the defense to prove that the police **did** fabricate the hair evidence – or any of the other evidence, even though the defense might have suspected it. So whom were the jurors supposed to trust and believe?

It is generally accepted as a **legal principle** that the police do not have to prove that the evidence they present in a criminal case in **not** fabricated. If the defense suspect foul play, the burden of proof is on them – at least when it comes to falsifying evidence. **We simply assume that the police play fair!**

However, if the defense, by a stroke of luck, or through good investigative work, could prove, **beyond any doubt whatsoever,** that even **just one small piece** of evidence was falsely fabricated by the police – out goes **all** the rest of the evidence as well! It ought to, at least!!!

Unfortunately, that was not the case during the Simpson murder trial and civil trial. Both the judges, the prosecutors, and the counsels for the plaintiffs **must** have realized that some of the evidence, unquestionably, was fabricated and planted against O.J. But rather than admitting this, and dropping the case against him, Prosecutor Marcia Clark fought back, arrogantly arguing:

> *"So what? Let the defense throw out this particular piece of evidence, which they say they can prove is fabricated – and let us even disregard Detective Fuhrman who found the glove behind O.J.'s house! There is still "a mountain of evidence" against the defendant!"*

Rarely have I heard anything so ridiculous! Again, I have to turn to one of my examples to demonstrate how absurd the prosecution's argument was.

Young Christopher Darden is caught cheating on question 37 on his math SAT – because the inspector sneaks up on Master Darden while he is copying the answer to **question 37** from his classmate's answer sheet. Naturally, Master Darden has **cheated** and, therefore, **disqualified himself from the entire SAT!**

It isn't a question of **how much** he cheated! **He cheated! Get out! Period!**

However, following **Prosecutor** Darden's rules and logic, young **Master** Darden should have been allowed to continue his SAT and argue successfully to the school board as follows:

> *"The inspector only caught me cheating on question 37. He didn't catch me copying the answers to any of the other questions. So, I should get full credit for the **rest** of my SAT"!*

Wow! Do my readers agree with him? I hope not!

The police have an **enormous advantage** over the defendant, in as much as the court generally accepts that the police play by the rules and don't cheat or lie. The police have our trust. Therefore, the police **normally** don't have to prove that they **did not** fabricate every piece of evidence. We assume they didn't.

However, **if the police break that trust,** by trying to boost their case through the fabrication of false evidence, **and we catch them doing it – even just once – then they have turned the table on themselves 180 degrees!**

Now suddenly, the police are no longer worthy of our trust, and should be required to prove that every single piece of evidence which they want to present, could not possibly have been fabricated.

This is how most just, fair, and moral people **should** think! And that might be yet another sound reason why the criminal jury acquitted O.J. after only four hours of deliberations.

The police could not be trusted! Obviously they cheated. And when the prosecution tried to cover it up, the prosecution could not be trusted either.

When the police obviously lied, and obviously fabricated **some** of the evidence, trying to deceive the jurors – should the jurors then trust **"the rest"** of the evidence, simply because they couldn't figure out how the police might have fabricated **that** evidence, too?

Of course not! How could the jury convict a man to life in prison, on the words of people who cheated and lied, and tried to deceive the jurors? How could those same jurors trust such police investigators and prosecutors. The criminal jury's decision was not difficult to make. Nor did it take the jurors long to reach it!

It is astonishing that the jurors in the civil trial did not see it the same way. In reality, the civil jurors must have argued:

> *We admit that we **understand** how **some** of the evidence against O.J. Simpson was fabricated by the investigators.*
> (Otherwise they must have been both dumb, deaf, and blind!)
> *However, there is still a lot of other evidence against Mr. Simpson, which **we do not understand** how the investigators could have fabricated.*
> *So – **based on our ignorance** – we have to declare Mr. Simpson responsible for the deaths of Nicole Brown Simpson and Ronald L. Goldman.*

In post trial interviews most of the jurors have claimed that they considered **all** the evidence and deliberated conscientiously.

After the last African-American juror was dismissed by Judge Fujisaki, the judge admonished the jurors to start their jury deliberations over again **from scratch** – even re-electing a jury foreman.

From that moment on, the jury reached their verdict in less than eleven hours!

Considering that the trial itself took five months, how could this jury possibly claim that they conscientiously evaluated **all** the evidence?

The civil jurors were not conscientious, educated, and **intelligent!** They were **ignorant – and prejudiced!**

They didn't **understand** how O.J. was framed. And because **they** did not understand **how** the police fabricated the evidence against O.J. – they claimed it could **not** have been **done.**

In principle, there is no difference between reaching a verdict after **four** hours of deliberations or **eleven** hours of deliberations. Both juries must have had their minds made up long before they even entered the jury deliberation room.

What is worth noticing, though, is that the media viciously accused the predominantly African-American jury in the criminal trial for lacking in intelligence and education, and handing down a racially motivated verdict.

The predominantly white jury in the civil trial, however, was hailed by the same media as well educated, intelligent, and conscientious, and were commended for not allowing race to play any part in their verdict.

How on earth do the media know so much about what these two juries based their verdict on?

If the jurors became convinced, during the trials, that the investigators fabricated much of the evidence against the defendant – and the jurors, therefore, had reasonable doubt already as they entered the jury deliberation room – it should not even have taken five minutes to reach a verdict of *"Not guilty"*!

Because the investigators so obviously fabricated false evidence against O.J., I am surprised the verdict in the criminal trial even took as long as four hours.

The "not guilty" verdict in the criminal trial did not reflect jury nullification or a racist statement. It was the only possible verdict any responsible juror could reach.

To set an innocent defendant free, has no adverse repercussions for this defendant. Accordingly, once the jurors were convinced that O.J. was innocent, or had reasonable doubt regarding his guilt, there was no reason to continue the deliberations beyond that point.

The civil jurors, however, were in a totally different situation. Yet, they deliberated for less than eleven hours (over a couple of days) before reaching their verdict against O.J. That smells much more of jury nullification and a racist – or political – statement, than the criminal jury's verdict.

Why? Because a verdict **against** O.J. in the civil trial had far reaching repercussions – way beyond what a *"Not guilty"* verdict had in the criminal trial.

The civil jury had to consider that a verdict **against** O.J. would be devastating both to O.J. himself, and to his children. It would possibly ruin O.J. But if so, it would also have a huge impact on the future of his children – both psychologically, socially, and financially.

Against such a back drop I find it preposterous that the civil jurors rushed through their deliberations in less than eleven hours! How could they possibly have covered, and deliberated over, a murder case it had taken five months and close to 150 witnesses to present?

Had the civil jury found O.J. "not responsible" for the deaths of Nicole and Ron, they would simply have declared that there is not enough trustworthy evidence against O.J. to hold him responsible. End of story. To reach such a verdict shouldn't, necessarily, take very long.

It was, however, nothing less than **a travesty of justice** for the jury in this complicated case, to rush to a verdict **against** O.J. in less than eleven hours and simply say:

> *The guy probably did it! Let's forget about 150 testimonies and **an ocean of contested evidence**! The heck with Mr. Simpson and his family! The guy may be broke already! So what? Let's smack him with $8.5 million in compensatory damages and $25 million in punitive damages, anyway!*

What more can I say? Perhaps what O.J. said: *"This is far from over!"*

CHAPTER 52

A "Politically Correct" Conspiracy

If the district attorney's office charges a suspect with a crime, the prosecutors should – as an absolute prerequisite – be able to present a reasonable theory, as to **how** the accused **might**, at least, **have committed the crime**. Let me give you an example, perhaps my last!

A factory building was on fire. The smoldering fire was extinguished, but the co-owner of the factory, Mr. Smith, who was sleeping on a couch in his office, still succumbed from smoke inhalation.

Investigators concluded that the fire started on the second floor, in the room directly outside Mr. Smith's office. However, there was no sign of forced entry through any of the doors or windows. They were all secured from the inside with locks or latches that could not be opened or closed from the outside. (I know this sounds unlikely, but let us for the sake of argument, assume that this was the case).

In a bar, a few hours before the fire started, Mr. Smith had a hefty argument with his nephew and sole heir, Mr. Hall. Witnesses testified that Mr. Smith had thrown a drink in Mr. Hall's face, where-after Mr. Hall had yelled at Mr. Smith:

"I don't give a shit about the factory. I'm going to burn it down!"

Upon Mr. Smith's death, legally, Mr. Hall acquired sole ownership of the factory, which was fully insured for 3 million dollars!

Mr. Hall had motive: He was angry with Mr. Smith, and he

gained sole ownership of the factory upon Mr. Smith's death.
Mr. Hall had opportunity: He lived only two blocks away, and could have walked over to the factory and set the fire.

Mr. Hall had no alibi: He maintained that he was home alone, sleeping, when the fire started. Naturally, Mr. Hall's fingerprints were all over the factory, which he had visited many times.

However, unless the prosecution could explain how Mr. Hall could have entered the factory to set the fire, and exited again, without leaving behind at least one unlatched door or window – or a hole in the wall – there is no way they could charge Mr. Hall with arson – not to mention expect a conviction.

The prosecutor could not simply tell the court:

"We don't know how the defendant managed to set the fire, but we are certain he did it!"

It is an absolute prerequisite that the prosecution present a **reasonable theory**, at least, as to how the defendant **might** have committed the crime he is accused of. That brings us back to the Simpson case.

The prosecutors failed miserably in their attempt to explain how O.J. **just might have killed Ron,** in particular. It is true that O.J., as well as anyone, might have rung the buzzer by the Bundy gate, and knocked Nicole unconscious and slashed her throat as soon as she came down to open the gate.

However, the prosecutors should not even be allowed to **suggest** that O.J., or anyone, could have done that with Ron watching just a few feet away – or arriving only seconds later – and that O.J. then, immediately, could have turned against Ron and killed him too, **without Ron being on the alert, being able to defend himself, being able to scream for help, or being able to escape.**

Remember that a witness, Robert Heidstra, testified that he heard Ron say: *"Hey - hey - hey!"*

This proves that Ron must have realized what he was up against, and he must have been facing the murderer initially. In other words, **Ron did not fall victim to a surprise attack from an assailant he didn't see until it was too late.**

If we try to believe the prosecution, Ron had just watched O.J. (wielding a bloody knife and wearing leather gloves and a dark knit cap in Los Angeles in the middle of June) attack and kill Nicole – or Ron had every reason to believe that had happened.

Ron **must** have realized that his own life was in serious jeopardy. Ron must, therefore, have defended himself and resisted any attempt by the murderer to turn him around and get behind his back.

Within the confined area where the murders took place, it would have been easy for Ron to position himself with his back against a wall or a fence, perhaps even in a corner, so that he could better defend himself, and **scream for help** while he tried to keep the murderer away – kicking and punching.

If Ron – as both the prosecutors and the plaintiffs argued – **heroically**, and hence, **deliberately**, engaged in a struggle with the murderer, in an effort to protect Nicole – it would have been practically speaking **impossible** for the murderer to position himself **behind** Ron. But that is how these same prosecutors and plaintiffs argued that the attack on Ron was initiated. He was stabbed in the neck from behind – by surprise!

The prosecutors' and the plaintiffs' theories are full of such contradictions. If we follow their theories, **Ron must have had more than ample opportunity to scream for help and alarm the entire neighborhood.** Since he didn't, we can with 100% certainty conclude: **This was not the way the murders were committed – at least not the murder of Ron.**

However, this is the way the prosecution, as well as the counsels for the plaintiffs in the civil trial – and their **"expert"** witnesses – portrayed it.

As I stated above, the prosecutors failed miserably in terms of presenting any credible theory as to how O.J. could have murdered two people simultaneously, in the same small area – and especially **how O.J. could have turned Ron around and cut his throat**

from behind, without Ron resisting or screaming for help first.

Like in my example with Mr. Hall and Mr. Smith, the prosecutors in the Simpson trial simply made a giant leap of logic, saying:

> *"We know O.J. did it, so we don't have to explain how"*!

Set aside the rush to judgement – Mark Fuhrman and his perjury – Vannatter's handling of O.J.'s blood vial – the blood missing from O.J.'s vial – Vannatter's obvious lies – mysterious blood transfers and missing initials on blood evidence bindels – the obvious planting of false evidence – the impossible time frame – the absence of the murderer's bloody clothes and shoes – the absence of the murder knife – the absence of O.J.'s fingerprints – the more than one dozen serious inconsistencies in regards to the bloody shoeprints and the five blood drops at Bundy – the absurdity of the two blood drops on the bottom rail of the rear gate – the obvious planting of Nicole's blood on O.J.'s sock – the manner in which the murderer must have pulled Nicole's unconscious body away from the steps and the dirt area, and onto the tiled, concrete patio, to let her bleed to death there – etc., etc.! Disregard all of that!

The prosecution's and the plaintiffs' case against O.J. was still preposterous, because it lacked the most fundamental element of all, namely a credible explanation as to how O.J., under any circumstances, could have committed the murders – without Ron escaping or screaming for help.

Besides, what would O.J.'s **motive** be? The **"pleasure"** of spending the rest of his life in prison with the "satisfaction" of knowing that he had disposed of his children's mother?

What we have is a murder case

- without a motive,
- without opportunity,
- without a recognized M.O.,
- without any witnesses,

- without a murder weapon, and
- without any fingerprints!

What we **do** have, however, is also a suspect who

- wrestled with his ex-wife – one time – 5 1/2 years before the murders, and
- cut his finger when he broke a glass – in despair – upon learning that the mother of his children had been killed.

That's all. Everything else is flawed and corrupted.

As I have explained earlier, Ron could not even have been present when Nicole was attacked. Therefore, most likely, the murder of Nicole was completed before Ron arrived.

The only person who could have made Ron, when he arrived, step over Nicole's bloody body and into the niche where he was to be murdered, and who could have positioned himself behind Ron, and who could have put a knife to his neck, while Nicole's dead body was lying there in a pool of blood – without Ron protesting, resisting, or getting suspicious – **is a police officer.**

I understand that **the LAPD and the prosecutors have trouble accepting it. But that is the ugly and bitter truth!**

It is true that certain pieces of "evidence" pointed to O.J. But there is also an "ocean of evidence" to suggest that all of it was planted or fabricated. And, **if we consider O.J. as a suspect,** it is **impossible** to explain **several dozens** of other pieces of evidence in this murder mystery, like:

- The impossible timeline.
- The absence of witnesses observing O.J.'s Bronco between Rockingham and Bundy. (I don't consider Robert Heidstra, who simply saw a white sports utility car speed south – which is **away from Rockingham**, incidentally)
- The moist blood on the Rockingham glove, and the absence of insects and debris on that glove.

- How Ron was killed.
- The absence of O.J.'s fingerprints.
- The absence of the bloody clothes, the bloody shoes, and the bloody knife.
- The 1.5 ml of blood missing from O.J.'s blood vial.
- Detective Furman's and Detective Vannatter's lies.
- The fact that the gloves did not fit O.J.
- The purpose of the knit ski cap.
- Mark Fuhrman's perjury also with respect to his "alibi" for the time of the murders. Etc., etc.

Consider on the other hand that Nicole and Ron were murdered by a police officer – possibly Detective Mark Fuhrman! Consider that Fuhrman set up Detective Vannatter to believe O.J. were guilty, and that Fuhrman provided the investigators with crime scenes full of opportunity for evidence tampering and evidence fabrication, and that Vannatter got irreversibly **hooked** when he swallowed Fuhrman's "bait" and fabricated the first false blood swatches against O.J.

That is, in my opinion, **not only a** possible explanation that can tie together all the various pieces of evidence, all the inconsistencies and contradictions, all the evidence fabrication and the cover ups, all the lies and the suspicious activities of several investigators, criminalists and prosecutors. **It is the only possible explanation!**

I would not be surprised if one day we should learn that both the lead investigator, Detective Vannatter, the prosecutors, and District Attorney Gil Garcetti had reached this same conclusion at an early stage of the investigation.

I believe they did! But they also realized that the city of Los Angeles – in the wake of the Rodney King riot – could not survive another such, even greater, scandal, namely that

a racist white police officer had deliberately murdered Nicole (because she had married an African-American man), and that the police officer had proceeded to frame Nicole's ex-husband, the former football star, O.J. Simpson, for the murder.

If this horrible truth came out, it could trigger a riot so severe that with the recent Los Angeles riot in mind, it was frightening even to think about it. The entire city could have been destroyed, hundreds of innocent people killed.

It is certainly conceivable that the district attorney might have suggested to **sacrifice one man only**, namely O.J., in order to save the lives of hundreds, and prevent billions of dollars worth of destruction.

If this was the case, it ties up yet another couple of **"loose ends"** in this murder mystery:

- Why was the murder trial moved from Santa Monica to Downtown Los Angeles?
- Why didn't the DA seek the death penalty?
- Why was the jury even given the option of **"second degree murder"**?

The murder of Nicole, at least, was as premeditated, cold blooded, ruthless, and grotesque, as any murder you can think of. The prosecution even suggested that she had been **tortured!**

How could the district attorney defend that this could have been **"second degree murder"**? If the district attorney believed O.J. were guilty, I fail to see how he could have had a more obvious capital murder case. In the Menendez murder case the district attorney sought the death penalty. Why did he compromise in the Simpson case?

Furthermore, if the district attorney believed O.J. were guilty, why should he decide to move the trial from the predominantly white Santa Monica Court District, where Nicole lived and was murdered, to the predominantly black downtown Los Angeles, where a conviction, in the wake of the Rodney King case, was much less likely?

Of course, District Attorney Gil Garcetti could be telling the truth, when he said that the old court house building in Santa

Monica was not suited to handle the security that the Simpson case required. That still didn't answer the question of life in prison versus the death penalty.

Those were yet other small pieces of the prosecution's case that didn't seem to make any sense.

By the way, the Santa Monica court house was, obviously, more than adequate to handle the Simpson civil trial.

On the other hand, **assuming that Detective Mark Fuhrman is the murderer, and that the investigators, as well as the prosecutors, knew it rather early**, even those small pieces of the puzzle fit my theory.

After a week or so, when things settled a bit, and the investigators had time to gather their thoughts, someone **must** have put two and two together, like I have done in this book.

Once they began to suspect Detective Fuhrman of not only having planted the Rockingham glove, but of actually having murdered Nicole and Ron, **it was too late.**

Detective Fuhrman had already set them up, and implicated them in fabricating and planting most of the false evidence against O.J.!

There was no way the investigators could turn in Detective Fuhrman at that point. Sure, they could still probably have proven Fuhrman guilty of double homicide. But what about their own fabrication and planting of false evidence against O.J.?

How in the world were they going to explain that O.J.'s blood and hairs and Bronco fibers were found all over the crime scenes – if Detective Fuhrman was the murderer?!

The investigators couldn't simply admit that they had fabricated all the false evidence in a capital murder case. Their careers would be over. They might be sentenced to life in prison.

Some of the evidence planting even appeared to have been done with the approval of the prosecutors. If the investigators were charged with evidence planting, they were sure to drag the DA's office down with them!

Detective Fuhrman had everyone by their throats! He still has! If the district attorney touches him, he can squeal on all of them. The point is that Fuhrman – if he is the murderer – knows exactly what evidence he planted or left behind. Therefore, he also knows what evidence the investigators must have manufactured – and in particular, who manufactured each piece of false evidence!

As I see it, this "problem" is the only reasonable explanation why Detective Fuhrman got off with probation and a $200 fine for committing perjury in the murder trial against O.J.

Obviously, Mark Fuhrman has an edge on the criminal justice system in Los Angeles. That edge, I believe, is that he knows who planted all the evidence against O.J. – because Fuhrman murdered Nicole and Ron!

The D.A.'s office, on the other hand, do not hold a reciprocal grip on Mark Fuhrman. Because if they decided to indict Fuhrman for the murders of Nicole and Ron, there is no way they could even hope to achieve a conviction. Several years after the murders, and with all the evidence fabricated against O.J., how can the DA's office possibly pursue Mark Fuhrman. He holds all the aces.

Let us again, look at the suprise move by District Attorney Gil Garcetti – to ask for life in prison, versus the death penalty:

The maximum punishment for fabricating false evidence against an innocent suspect in a first degree murder case is **equivolent to the punishment** this innocent suspect either received – **or might have received** – due to the falsely fabricated evidence.

Suppose now, the district attorney as well as his prosecutors and the LAPD investigators knew that Fuhrman was the murderer, and that they were about to charge an innocent man based on false evidence and perjured testimony. Should that ever be revealed, the perpetrators (the district attorney, his prosecutors and the investigators) would qualify for the death penalty – **if Garcetti asked for the death penalty in the case against O.J.!**

Maybe District Attorney Gil Garcetti was protecting himself and his prosecutors against the death penalty, and even threw in the possibility of second degree murder **as an added insurance for themselves** – in case the obviously psychopatic Mark Fuhrman suddenly confessed to someone that he had murdered Nicole and Ron – and set up the investigators!

We see a motive behind the ridiculous *"life in prison"* and *"second degree murder"* decision by the district attorney! He wasnt't avoiding the death penalty – for O.J. Simpson's sake! He was avoiding the death penalty for his own sake – in case the real truth behind the Simpson case should ever be exposed!

I credit Donald Freed and Raymond P. Briggs, the authors of *"Killing Time"* (page 250); and ultimately Bill Boyarsky, *"Simpson Case Catches Up To DA's Race,"* (*Los Angeles Times,* February 25, 1996), for providing me with the background information for the following episode. It simply gets too complicated trying to write this episode in quotes with correct references, since everyone seems to be quoting everyone else in this case. Besides, I want **my own observations** tied in with the facts as referred to in *"Killing Time"* and in Bill Boyarsky's article in *Los Angeles Times.*

Credit to the above mentioned, but this is the episode, **the way I interpret it:**

As I have mentioned in this chapter (as well as in the chapter titled, **"Did The Prosecutors Know?"**), in my opinion, both the investigators and the prosecutors **must** have known, **rather early**, that O.J. was innocent, and that **Fuhrman had murdered Nicole and Ron**, and set up everybody so perfectly that there was no way out!

I have explained how Detective Vannatter fabricated the false blood evidence against O.J. and how everyone got sucked into this conspiracy. The only way for someone to avoid getting sucked into the conspiracy, once he learned about it, was if that person said, **right away – without a second's hesitation:**

"I will not be part of this. You are framing an innocent man. I will take my charges to the highest authority this very second!"

If a person paused to considered the consequences or his career, hesitated, and waited a few days, consulted his colleagues, and such, he had already become part of the coverup!

I have estimated that about one week, at the latest, after the murders, Detective Vannatter must have realized that Fuhrman had set him up and that there was no way for Vannatter to retreat. Prosecutor Marcia Clark must have known it too.

As I have mentioned already, I even believe District Attorney Gil Garcetti knew it at that time, and that they confronted Fuhrman, who had them all in a choke-hold. At that time, all of them faced the following alternatives:

- Sacrifice Detective Vannatter, Prosecutor Marcia Clark, and whoever else in the LAPD or in the DA's office who had assisted Vannatter or Clark in fabricating false evidence against O.J., or known about it, but covered it up – perhaps even Gil Garcetti, if he knew what went on and hadn't put a stop to it.
- Or sacrifice the African-American *"wife beater,"* O.J. Simpson.

I believe Marcia Clark informed Gil Garcetti, and Garcetti, although he may not have liked it, decided to sacrifice O.J., and support his prosecutors and the investigators – all the way. There was no middle alternative.

In late June, 1994, **two weeks after the murders, Prosecutor Clark presented her first draft of the Simpson case to the rest of the prosecution team** – plus District Attorney Gill Garcetti and Assistant District Attorney **Peter Bozanich.**

Assistant District Attorney Peter Bozanich was District Attorney Gil Garcetti's highest assistant at the time of the murders.

I didn't learn about this until I read *"Killing Time."* But I may have been "right on" all along!

It didn't take a rocket scientist or a brain surgeon to figure out that Fuhrman had set up the investigators. As I have said so many times throughout this book, the glove was the key to this murder mystery. It is just a matter of putting two and two together:

- Fuhrman must have planted the Rockingham glove.
- Whoever planted the Rockingham glove, is the murderer – or part of a murder conspiracy.
- Hence, Fuhrman is the murderer, or part of a murder conspiracy.
- Therefore, if the blood from Bundy is attributed to O.J., that blood evidence must have been fabricated.

Peter Bozanich might have realized something along those lines, at least. So when Marcia Clark, in her presentation, reached the Rockingham glove, Bozanich, allegedly, said (*"Killing Time,"* page 250), quote:

> *There is something wrong with the glove ... What is it doing there? That doesn't make any sense. How did the glove get there?* [Why was there no blood near the glove?]

Obviously, Peter Bozanich was not part of the coverup! He was not even part of the prosecution team, but attended the meeting in the capacity of being Garcetti's highest ranking assistant DA.

As an intelligent human being, perhaps he saw that O.J. was being framed. So he raised the obvious questions everyone else should have raised at that meeting – if not much earlier:

> *"The evidence makes no sense! What is going on here...???"*

Everyone else at that meeting was already part of the coverup and part of the plan to continue to frame O.J., rather than cause a major scandal. They had already taken that first, crucial step. After that, there was no escape for any of them. They had to go all the way.

Assistant District Attorney Peter Bozanich was not part of the Simpson case, as I said. So he showed no sign of being willing to accept Prosecutor Clark's and District Attorney Garcetti's obviously flawed theory.

First, of course, Garcetti tried to talk some "sense" into his assistant. But Bozanich was not swayed. Quite to the contrary, he confronted District Attorney Garcetti, warning him urgently that there was something wrong with the glove! There it was again – the glove evidence!

Garcetti, Clark, Vannatter and the rest of the bunch were way past **"the point of no return,"** however. And since **Peter Bozanich wouldn't join them in their scheme to frame O.J. – they had to get rid of him.**

> **So already by July 1994, a few weeks after the murders District Attorney Gil Garcetti's highest assistant, District Attorney Peter Bozanich, was demoted and transferred to "Siberia"!**

Isn't it pretty obvious what is going on? And isn't it pretty obvious that a major scandal of national proportions is brewing here?

> **That is what the media should focus on in the Simpson case!**

I believe the lead investigator, Vannatter, confided in the lead prosecutor, his personal friend, Marcia Clark, who again confided in District Attorney Gil Garcetti. Garcetti was not happy with the surprising turn of events. But **he was running for political office,** and could not afford another scandal or failure. He had two options:

First option: The district attorney could go after Detective Fuhrman, admitting that a psychopathic, racist, white LAPD officer had murdered Nicole (and Ron), and tried to frame Nicole's black ex-husband for the murders – and that the LAPD investigators had swallowed the murderer's "bait" and proceeded to manufacture all the false evidence against O.J.

However, charging Fuhrman with murder was one thing. Because of the evidence the investigators had planted against O.J., Fuhrman, most likely, would be acquitted!

Thereby, District Attorney Gil Garcetti's own career would be over. The DA's office would destroy, completely, whatever little credibility the LAPD had left after "Rodney King," and a vicious murderer would go free because of the corruption and the incompetence of the "system."

But more importantly, as a result, the district attorney would probably have ignited the most horrendous riot in this country since the Civil War. Los Angeles would have been been levelled, hundreds of people killed.

Second option: The district attorney could ignore Detective Fuhrman, save his own political career, save the LAPD, save the city of Los Angeles and hundreds of innocent lives – **but in the process sacrifice one man only, namely O.J. Simpson!**

The district attorney reasoned: *"O.J. is a convicted wife beater. Because of his fame, he had gotten off with a warning, but O.J. probably deserved some time behind bars anyway."*

The district attorney was in a dilemma. He had to consider the law, and the rights of O.J. But he also had to weigh that against the lives of, perhaps, hundreds of innocent people who might be killed if Los Angeles exploded in an other riot.

Most of all, however, District Attorney Gil Garcetti considered his own political future!

How should he handle this critical situation? Obviously, the rights of O.J. figured the **least** in his decision.

After the meeting in which he decided to get rid of Assistant District Attorney Peter Bozanich, I believe District Attorney Gil Garcetti may have summoned the mayor and Police Chief Williams to a secret meeting.

District Attorney: *I have called you here to discuss an extremely* *serious matter ...*

The district attorney explained the situation – and the two available options – as he saw them.

District Attorney: *... There you have it. What do we do about it? We cannot ignore the recent riot. No question about it, Fuhrman deserves the worst we can throw at him. But is he worth the lives of hundreds of innocent people and the destruction of Los Angeles – not to forget the total collapse of the LAPD?*

Chief of Police: *If this meeting decides to go after Fuhrman, and ask for yet another federal investigation of the LAPD, I won't stand in the way. Sometimes, however, reason has to outweigh the law.*

Mayor: *We could ask the governor to call in the National Guard to keep order. I know it is drastic. Perhaps it will only escalate a conflict. But we have to consider the rights of O.J., too. These murders, from what I understand, definitely qualify for the **death penalty**. Should O.J. be executed, I would be a murderer myself. I couldn't do that.*

District Attorney: *What if we agree that I ask for **life in prison** instead of the death penalty?*

Chief of Police: *That could be an acceptable compromise.*

Mayor: *It is still a man's entire life taken away from him. And what about his and Nicole's children? They would grow up without their father, stigmatized by his conviction. I don't like this!*

District Attorney: *I could move the trial from Santa Monica to downtown L.A. O.J. could probably get a hung jury there. If so, we try him again, once, then let him off.*

Mayor: *There is no guarantee of that. You know, if your prosecutors pursue this case halfheartedly, someone might understand what is going on here, Then **we** could be in trouble too!*

Chief of Police: *I agree. May I suggest a possible **compromise**?*

First of all, we go after O.J. as hard as we can. But we don't seek the death penalty, and we give him a fair chance downtown. Here is my compromise:

Sometime during the trial, perhaps during closing arguments, the prosecutor gives the jury the option of second degree murder! At that point it may simply appear that the prosecution is desperately doing everything in their power to secure any kind of guilty verdict, regardless.

A second degree murder conviction could be a welcome compromise for the jury, too. O.J. could be out again in 6-10 years, even if he is convicted.

Mayor: *Considering the alternative, I think I could live with such a compromise.*

District Attorney: *OK. I shall talk to my prosecutors and the lead investigators. After what they've already done, they don't have any choice but to go along and do their best to convict O.J. – in order to save their own butts.*

Chief of Police: *Yes – and keep their mouths shut!*

CHAPTER 53

Verifying Our Theory

Any theory is just that – a **"theory"**! Formulating a theory is to observe certain events and, based on those events, try to come up with a broader principle.

Let us imagine that we are in the middle of a **crossword puzzle.** We have completed the **"obvious"** and have begun to put some less certain sections together.

Solving a crossword puzzle is to come up with **"mini-theories"** (or small sections of the puzzle), all the time, and to test them out by combining them with other parts of the puzzle, and see if they "fit."

I am sure my readers know how you can often work your way from one word to the next ... and the next ... That is not necessarily a guarantee that your **mini-theory** is correct, though. Because suddenly you could be looking at some **"sure"** words – which combine to give you a **"Q"** immediately preceding an **"N"**! You have to bring out your eraser and start over. There is no such word in the English language!

The real proof that your **mini-theories** are correct, comes when **one** section (one mini-theory) of the puzzle suddenly ties in perfectly with **another** section **that it was not connected to when you started it!**

Solving the Simpson murder mystery is in many ways like solving a crossword puzzle. We have a lot of facts (evidence). This evidence may be interpreted in different ways. We have to find the interpretation that fits **all** the evidence – and **not just some of it.**

In a crossword puzzle, it doesn't help much to jot down a few words here and there, based on what suddenly comes to our mind. We have to solve all the pieces of the puzzle, and see that all of them fit! And if one little "mini-theory" of the puzzle leads us into a **contradiction**, or an "impossible" word, we have to scrap that mini-theory and start over.

It is the same with the Simpson case. It doesn't help us any to say the left glove at Bundy suggests that O.J. lost it and subsequently cut his left hand and, therefore, bled at Bundy, in his driveway, and in his foyer. **It is a fascinating idea!**

However, if that cut did **not** bleed at the immediate murder scene – nor on the two victims – and it did **not** bleed the **first** time O.J., **allegedly**, walked away from the murder scene – but started to bleed the **second** time – and allegedly bled, five drops along the walkway at Bundy and three on the rear gate – but then only bled about a 1/2 drop (or a "smear") in the Bronco he allegedly drove from Bundy to Rockingham in – but then mysteriously picked up again, and bled some 25 drops in his driveway at Rockingham – but **nothing** behind his house where the second glove was found – but three drops in a small area in his foyer – but, again, not a single drop in the stairway or on the second floor – and there is no blood in his bedroom – and nobody who saw O.J. that night, discovered any cut or blood or a band-aid on his finger – and there was no blood on his luggage which he carried from his foyer to the limo – and the gloves didn't fit O.J. – and the evidence indicated that he could not have lost the glove at Bundy, even if he were the murderer – and the blood on the Rockingham glove was moist more than 7 hours after O.J. had left for Chicago – and a lot of things like that – then this **"fascinating" mini-theory** we started out with must be **incorrect!**

When that is the case, we cannot simply ignore all the rest of the facts, and stick to this **mini-theory**, because *"we like it so well"*!

Instead we have to come up with another, **different**, mini-theory which will fit not just **some** of the evidence, but **all** the evidence – **even if it excludes O.J.!**

If a mini-theory (a section) of your crossword puzzle creates a word with **"... QN..."** in it, you must have the guts to **scrap** that mini theory. You can't say:

> *"I like the other words so well, that I'll keep them – regardless" of the 'QN'!*

This is the **major "boo-boo"** everyone seems to make in trying to **"solve"** the Simpson murder mystery. They *"fall in love with"* their **mini-theories**, instead of trying to solve the **entire** murder mystery! And in doing so, they make O.J. look bad over and over again, because their mini theories are flawed. They fall in love with the Bundy glove – with O.J.'s cut – with the drops of blood that allegedly contained his DNA – and with the bloody Bruno Magli shoeprints. Therefore, they don't care that

there is "QN - QN - QN ..." written all over this so-called "evidence"!

Although **some** of the evidence seems to fit O.J., there are many other important and significant pieces of evidence that **directly contradicts** the assumption that O.J. is the killer. When that is the case, people must have the guts to scrap their theory that O.J. is the murderer, and instead search for **other theories** that can reconcile **all** the evidence, and not just some of it!

After they first drafted their theory that O.J. were guilty, the investigators and prosecutors never reconsidered this theory – not even when the evidence proved that he could not possibly be the murderer.

Let us, however, concentrate on our own theory! Of course, there is no sense in pursuing a theory which we know is incorrect – "right off the bat," so to speak. We should not even consider a theory unless it reconciles **all** the evidence which is "on the table" when we start theorizing. We "shape" our theory around **all** the evidence we have. Hence, obviously, our theory **should** fit all the evidence we have **at the outset.**

The **real** test of our theory comes when we measure it against the facts and evidence that were **unavailable or unknown** to us when we drafted our theory! Again, let me explain this with an example from the Simpson case:

My theory of Detective Fuhrman being the murderer – who had set up the investigators with some initial evidence – reconciled that evidence, as well the many "mini-theories" regarding how Ron was killed, how Fuhrman planted both gloves, why the blood on the Rockingham glove was wet when he found it, how Fuhrman could have aquired a pair of Bruno Magli shoes, solely for the purpose of framing O.J., etc., etc. In short, that theory reconciled all the evidence I knew about at the time I drafted my theory.

Suddenly I learned about the unidentified hairs on the knit cap, which I didn't know about, and therefore, hadn't considered when I drafted my theory. If my theory should withstand scrutiny, it must also reconcile the hairs on the cap.

The prosecution could not explain how those hairs ended up on the cap, if the cap, allegedly, were O.J.'s. Their only explanation was that *"the hairs flew in with the wind, at Bundy"*!

Obviously the cap did not fit their theory. Rather than **scrapping their theory** of O.J. being the murderer, they simply **disregarded the unidentified hairs** on the cap!

Scientifically, that was so terrible that it would have **made an honest forensic scientist puke!** What they should have done was to **scrap their theory,** and try to come up with a different one that could reconcile also the unidentified hairs on the cap – **as well as the presence of the cap in the first place!**

I also, initially, overlooked the cap when I drafted my basic theory. The reason was that the prosecutors disregarded it, so there wasn't much talk about it – except that O.J.'s hairs were said to be on it. However, long after I drafted my theory, I learned about those unidentified hairs on the cap.

I have already explained how the cap evidence is consistent with my theory of Fuhrman purchasing the cap solely for the purpose of framing O.J., by **giving his colleagues the opportunity to plant O.J.'s hairs on it** in the crime lab, thus tying O.J. to the murder scene also by means of his hairs.

The unidentified hairs on the cap could have come from other customers having tried on the cap in the store before Fuhrman bought it. Assuming the cap was O.J.'s, however, does not reconcile those unidentified hairs.

In other words, the cap fit **my** theory, but it didn't fit the **prosecution's** theory.

The best proof of the validity of a theory is **not** just that it fits the facts and evidence available when the theory is formulated. It must! Otherwise you wouldn't formulate this theory.

It would be ridiculous, and a waste of time, to formulate a theory which you know is contradicted by some of the facts and evidence already from the start.

The best proof of the validity of a theory is that a **lot** of **new** facts and evidence surface **after** we have already formulated our basic theory – and that **all** of these **new** facts and pieces of evidence are **totally reconciled** by our **initial**, basic theory.

That's why I am so confident that my theory is correct and that an LAPD officer – probably Mark Fuhrman – murdered Nicole and Ron. You see, I didn't start out with all the facts when I first drafted my theory. Initially, this is what I said to myself:

- The appearance of the Bundy glove proves that both gloves must have been deliberately removed and planted by the murderer – **after** both victims were dead. Therefore, O.J. could not have bled at Bundy, even if he were the murderer.
- The Rockingham glove could not have been planted by O.J., because the blood on it was moist when Fuhrman found it. Hence, O.J. could not possibly be the murderer!
- The Rockingham glove must have been planted only a short while before Fuhrman found it. Consequently, Fuhrman, most likely, must have planted it.
- But Fuhrman could not have found the Rockingham glove at Bundy when he arrived there about 2:10 am. If he brought the Rockingham glove to O.J.'s house and planted it there, he must have **brought it with him when he came to Bundy at 2:10 am** – because **he** had already **murdered** Nicole and Ron earlier that night.

Those were the facts, evidence, and deductions I started with. Based on that I formulated my initial, rather tentative, theory, that

O.J. is innocent – that Fuhrman is the murderer – and that Fuhrman not only tried to **frame O.J. directly** with some of the evidence, but that he also **"set up" the investigators** to complete the framing.

Then I began to check out all the rest of the evidence – as it became available – to see if it, too, fit this basic theory.

As my readers have learned throughout this book, **everything** – even the apparently most devastating evidence against O.J., or the obviously fabricated evidence, as well as facts, circumstances, and evidence the investigators, the prosecutors, and the plaintiffs could not explain – **fit our theory that O.J. is innocent, and that Mark Fuhrman murdered Nicole and Ron!**

Let me repeat just some of the **new** factors that fell right into place in my theory as I began scrutinizing the Simpson case:

- The use of a knife as murder weapon, the vicious slashing of Nicole's throat – and the bloody shoeprints.
- *"The O.J. shuffle,"* the double set of bloody shoeprints.
- The five blood drops at Bundy.
- The position of the five drops in relation to the shoeprints.
- The two blood drops on the rear gate at Bundy, and the EDTA in those drops.
- The short distance between the shoeprints.
- The knit ski cap, and the unidentified hairs on it.
- The obviously planted Bronco fiber on the knit cap, and on Ron's shirt.
- The way Nicole must have been pulled back, onto the patio, before she died – the bruise on her head, and the wounds on her leg.
- The way Ron must have been killed.
- The *"Hey - hey - hey!"* and the subsequent *"fast"* words Mr. Heidstra could not understand.
- The fact that Ron did not scream for help or in pain, escape, or defend himself, before it was too late.
- Fuhrman taking command at Rockingham.
- Fuhrman lying about the blood on the Bronco door.

- The blood in the Bronco that showed up several weeks after the murders.
- Fuhrman interviewing Kato.
- The thumps on Kato's wall.
- The detectives "setting up" Kato.
- O.J.'s blood not present behind his house, in his bedroom, or on his luggage.
- The hosing down of the Bundy crime scene shortly after the investigators had collected **their** samples of the blood evidence there, and before the **defense** could collect their own **control** samples.
- The handcuffing of O.J.
- Vannatter taking charge of O.J.'s blood vial.
- The old, un-sealable, blood vial envelope.
- Vannatter's lies about the time he spent downtown after receiving O.J.'s blood vial.
- The 1.5 ml of blood missing from O.J.'s vial.
- The concocted "testimony" given by the police nurse in a videotaped interview.
- The wet blood transfers on some of the blood evidence bindels (Dr. Lee: *"Something is wrong"*).
- Ms. Mazzola's initials disappearing from some of her bindels.
- The history of O.J.'s socks, and Nicole's blood on one of the sock.
- Fuhrman concealing from the investigators Rosa Lopez' information about the Bronco .
- The absence of the bloody clothes, the bloody shoes, and the bloody knife.
- The absence of O.J.'s bloody fingerprints at any of the crime scenes.
- Nicole's watch – set at 10:03 and crushed.
- The jeans jacket that disappeared from Nicole's condo – right after Detective **Fuhrman** had been there **alone**.
- The bloody fingerprint Detectives Fuhrman and Roberts saw on the handle of the rear gate, and which subsequently disappeared – also after **Fuhrman** had been in the vicinity **alone**.

> – Fuhrman not informing his superiors about the bloody fingerprint.

Having read most of my book, you know that the above list is far from complete. I could have gone on ... and on ... For instance:

> – *"The Fuhrman Tapes."*
> – Fuhrman's psychiatric reports and evaluations.
> – Thousands of pages of internal affairs investigations directed against Fuhrman for violence, excessive force, brutality, racism, fabrication of false evidence, etc., etc.
> – Fuhrman bragging about his intimate relationship with Nicole.
> – O.J.'s total lack of motive.
> – The impossible timeframe which could not possibly be reconciled with O.J. being the killer.
> – The bloody and gruesome MO which does not point to O.J. at all, but based on Fuhrman's psyche, his prior behavior and his earlier actions is right up **his** "alley."
> – The LAPD's and Prosecutors Marcia Clark's countless attempts to "whitewash" Fuhrman, cover for him, and hide his possible involvement in the case, as well as support his unquestionably false alibi.
> – Etc., etc., ... etc.!

It is scientifically – i.e. mathematically, statistically, and logically – **impossible** to come up with a basic theory (as I did) concluding that an LAPD detective, likely Detective Fuhrman, murdered Nicole and Ron, planted some evidence to frame O.J. directly, and some other evidence to set up the investigators to complete the framing – and then have **all** of the above pieces of evidence, facts, and circumstances fit this basic theory – **after** it was initially drafted – **unless the theory was correct to start with!**

And, of course: **the gloves didn't fit** – O.J. that is!

**How about former LAPD detective Mark Fuhrman trying
on those gloves on national TV!**

There was no doubt about it – in my mind – that LAPD Detective
Mark Fuhrman had murdered Nicole and Ron! I was so convinced
by all the evidence in the case, that I started to write this book –
based on all the evidence you have just read.

However – there was one huge **"but"** I could not explain!

If Fuhrman was the murderer, how could he testify during the
criminal trial – under oath, for Prosecutor Marcia Clark – and
say that he left **a Protective League seminar** (*"a police officers' function"*) at La Quinta, at 8:00 pm on the night of the
murders, to drive home, and that he got home to his wife at
10:30 pm and went to bed a little after 11:00?

If this "alibi" for the time of the murder did not hold up –
why did Marcia Clark allow Fuhrman to present it? She must
have checked out Fuhrman's "story"! When she allowed him
to present this "alibi," she indirectly vouched for it! So, apparently, Detective Fuhrman had a solid alibi!

Besides, if there was something wrong with Fuhrman's
La Quinta "story," why hadn't O.J.'s excellent defense team
uncovered it?

Was I mistaken?

Still, all the other evidence fit my **"Mark Fuhrman theory"** so
perfectly that I just **"knew"** there had to be something "fishy" about
his **"La Quinta alibi."**

I could not pin-point it. After all I was thousands of miles from
California at that time, and did not have the resources to start a
private investigation of Mark Fuhrman – or of the LAPD and the
Los Angeles DA's office!

However, I wrote, already at that time, in my first book,
"If O.J. Didn't . . ." – (quote):

"Alibis may be manufactured! So even if Detective

Fuhrman arguably spoke in front of 1,500 people at an out-of-state churchgoers' convention, between 10:30 and 11 o'clock on the night of June 12, 1994, his alibi ought to be rechecked, together with whoever supported it." [End of quote].

There was, simply, **so much evidence against Mark Fuhrman** that I decided to write this 700 page book about it – in spite of the fact that Fuhrman seemed to have a perfect alibi! My readers may object now, and ask me:

Isn't that exactly what I just criticized the investigators and the prosecutors for: Clinging to a theory when there is **"QN"** written all over it!

No! That was not what I was doing. Fuhrman's "alibi" did not represent a **"QN"** in my theory. As I wrote – **alibis may be manufactured!** Fuhrman didn't necessarily **have** a perfect alibi. He just had an alibi I had not yet cracked!

Anyway – what happened? Well, you know what happened. The one single, little thing that was not yet reconciled with my theory – **Fuhrman's alleged alibi, concocted with, and vouched for by, Prosecutor Marcia Clark** – came crashing to bits and pieces during 1996-97!

- There **was** no Protective League seminar in La Quinta Sunday night, June 12, 1994!
- There **was** no barbecue starting at 8:00 pm!
- Fuhrman did **not** come home at 10:30 pm and go to bed with his wife at a little past 11 o'clock!
- Fuhrman could **not** even have been home by 11 o'clock, be cause – according to Fuhrman's latest "alibi story" – he was pumping gas in Pomona at 10:45, using his Gold American Express credit card!

Of course, Fuhrman's "Gold American Express alibi" doesn't even compete with O.J.'s *"chipping golf balls, sleeping, and taking a shower"*! Fuhrman's new "alibi" is worthless. **Anyone** could have used his credit card in Pomona, to make it **appear** that Fuhrman was there!

But Fuhrman's *"Gold American Express card"* **alibi** is flawed for several dozen other reasons – namely all the evidence which ties him to the Bundy murder scene at the time he now claims he were in Pomona!

I "knew" Fuhrman's La Quinta "alibi" was a lie! It had to be. Sure enough – eventually, the truth came out! The last piece of the puzzle fit.

There is no way O.J. could have killed Nicole and Ron! **O.J. must have been framed**, initially by the murderer, and later by the LAPD investigators – and, apparently, even by the prosecutors!

As my readers know, I am **not** the only "Simpson book author" to claim that. However, what all the other authors have failed to do, so far, is to answer the all important questions:

- **If O.J. did not murder Nicole and Ron – then who murdered them – and why – and how?**
- **If O.J. is innocent – how could his blood, apparently, be found at the murder scene?**

Besides proving O.J. innocent, those questions are exactly what I have answered in this book. That's why I titled my book:

"Solving The Simpson Murder Mystery"

I hope and trust my readers agree with me, that the book you are about to finish puts all the pieces together and explains what really (might have) happened, from beginning to end.

"Solving The Simpson Murder Mystery" proves – irrefutably – that **O.J. did not kill Nicole and Ron**.

More importantly, however, *"Solving The Simpson Murder Mystery"* is the first book which logically explains how all the evidence, not only could have been, but probably was, fabricated.

However, the real significance is that

> **"Solving The Simpson Murder Mystery" is the first book which logically and analytically explains how all the evidence in the case actually points to an LAPD officer – namely former LAPD Detective Mark Fuhrman!**

My readers should respect, however – **as I do** – that . . .

> **. . . unless Mark Fuhrman confesses to the murders of Nicole and Ron, or unless he is found guilty of the murders by a court of law – Mark Fuhrman should be considered innocent of this horrible crime.**

That is the all important principle of our criminal justice system – and of our Constitution – which so many failed to respect in the case against O.J. Simpson:

> **"Innocent – until proven guilty"!**

Don't confuse this important principle with the verdict in the civil trial. **The civil trial was not about guilt or innocence.** O.J. Simpson was forever found **"Not guilty"** of the murders – by the unanimous jury in the criminal trial. Nothing can ever change that!

The civil trail was nothing but a farce. It did not even **resemble** a proper trial.

It was not about guilt or innocence. It was about **money, greed, anger, misguided vengeance – and empathy** with the grieving families of the victims.

It was about finding **"sombody"** responsible – **so the 75% of Americans who believed O.J. were guilty could go on with their lives and sleep better at night!**

In the civil trial the **"system"** required that O.J. – a former football player, of all things – should **solve a murder case the police themselves had failed to solve**, and that O.J. should present the jurors with **"the murderer's head on a silver platter"**!

The "system" required that O.J. prove someone else – rather than himself – committed this crime!

O.J. was an excellent running back, once. And he has a lot of other qualities, too. But I do not think "homicide detective" is one of them. What kind of legal "system" do we have in this country, which requires that a former football player solve murder cases the police have given up on – or forfeit his fortune!

When O.J. didn't – and of course, he couldn't (not in judge Fujisaki's court room) – O.J. was to be declared **"statutorily" responsible** for two murders he did not commit!

This civil trial had nothing to do with justice, at all! It was, as I said earlier, nothing but

"a legal, modern day version of a white mob lynching an innocent black man suspected of having killed a white woman."

Those who refuse to believe that, take a minute to consider the following question:

All circumstances the same, do you believe O.J. Simpson would have been walking the streets of Los Angeles – or that he would have been resting 6 feet under the turf – if Mark Fuhrman had murdered Nicole and Ron one hundred years ago, instead of on June 12, 1994?

Just think about it! Then you should recognize that this innocent black man – O.J. Simpson – was lynched by the white jury in Judge Fujisaki's "star chamber" courtroom.

CHAPTER 54

Some Closing Thoughts

What I have expressed throughout this book is not necessarily proven facts. Nobody knows all the facts of this case. I have looked at the evidence and the actions of the various participants in the Simpson drama, and tried to come up with a theory that can embody, not only a select few facts and pieces of evidence, but **everything** that happened, both openly and covertly.

The Simpson case is a controversial murder mystery, and may forever remain unsolved. The reason is that there is so much conflicting evidence.

- On the one hand, O.J. was accused of having abused Nicole physically, of being violent, jealous and possessive. A man who could not let go – after his divorce from Nicole. If he were guilty, that should be his motive.
- On the other hand, it seem so utterly irrational that O.J. had so much going for him; and apparently he wasn't jealous, or angry with Nicole, in spite of learning from Nicole herself that she entertained numerous lovers. How could a man like that, throw away his wonderful life, just for the urge to kill the mother of his children – and in such a gruesome manner?

Contradictions!

- There was O.J.'s cut on his left middle finger, which could explain why his blood allegedly were found everywhere.
- On the other hand, there is strong evidence to suggest that he could not have lost the Bundy glove – even if he were the murderer. Therefore, he could not have cut himself at Bundy. And since his blood was not found inside the Bundy glove,

he could not have had a cut before he got to Bundy, either –
even if he were the murderer!

None of half a dozen witnesses who observed O.J.'s left
hand before and during his trip to Chicago, saw any cut on
his finger, or any blood on his finger, on his luggage, on a
napkin aboard the airplane, or any blood any other place.

So the blood at Bundy could not have come from O.J.
– regardless of what the DNA tells us.

Contradictions!

– There was the other blood evidence. Both O.J.'s and the
  victims bloods were found in the Bronco, as well as in a
  trail of blood, all the way from the victim's bodies to inside
  his foyer.
– On the other hand, this trail was compromised by the most
  peculiar interruptions, and O.J.'s blood did not appear some
  places where we should have expected it the most, namely
  near the glove behind his house, in his bedroom, and on his
  luggage. Furthermore, some of the blood evidence showed
  up "late"! And some of it contained EDTA!

Contradictions!

– There was the cap, with (similar to) O.J.'s hairs in it, tying
  him to the murder scene.
– On the other hand, there were several unidentified hairs on
  that same cap, indicating that the cap belonged to someone
  else and that O.J.'s hairs were planted on it.

  If the cap was not planted, why should O.J. wear a knit
  ski cap? To keep his ears warm? Or to disguise himself by
  trying to "blend in"?

Contradictions!

– There was O.J.'s lack of alibi. Apparently, he could not prove

what he was doing at the time of the murders.
- On the other hand, there was the prosecution's and the plaintiffs' impossible "time line."

Contradictions!

- We had *"a mountain of evidence"* **against** O.J.
- However, we had **another** mountain of evidence, too. It was *"a mountain of fabricated evidence"!*

Contradictions!

- Why would the LAPD try to frame O.J. if there was already a mountain of evidence against him? Did they try to **frame a guilty man?**
- Or were they trying to frame an **innocent** man?

Contradictions!

- There were the two gloves – one by the victims, and the other behind O.J.'s house – strongly incriminating O.J.
- But then we have the question: Could O.J. be that stupid – allegedly losing one glove at Bundy, and then throw away the other glove behind his own house before leaving for Chicago? And why was the blood on the Rockingham glove wet more than 7 hours after O.J. had left for Chicago? And most importantly, **the gloves didn't fit!**

Contradictions!

- The crime scenes pointed to O.J., **allegedly**, being so sloppy and careless that he lost, dropped, or accidentally left behind, everything – all over the place.
- Yet, the investigators haven't found one fingerprint tying O.J. to the murders, and nobody has been able to recover the bloody clothes, the bloody shoes, and the bloody knife!

Contradictions!

I am not going to write my book over again, so I shall stop here. If one word could describe this murder mystery, it is the word

CONTRADICTIONS!

For every point of view, and every argument, there seems to be an opposing point of view and a counter-argument. Those among us who have not made an effort to learn **all the facts** as they have been presented from both sides, have instead had their opinions in the Simpson case shaped by the advocates they have been listening to.

It is said that the "Simpson divide" follows racial lines. That is, unquestionably, true. But there is another less noticeable line of separation between those who believe O.J. is guilty, and those who believe he is innocent.

There is a somewhat obscure line between,

- on one side, those who seem to **know a lot** about this case, and who are **still eager to learn** all they can about it, and
- on the other side, those who **do not know much** about the case, but have made up their minds anyway, and are **not interested in learning more** about the case than whatever little they already know.

From communicating with people, especially over the Internet, I have the distinct impression, that **the more people know** about the Simpson case, and, **in particular,** the more **interested** they seem to be, still, in terms of learning everything about it – **the more likely they are to believe that O.J. is innocent.**

It is probably true that about 75% of all whites believe O.J. is guilty, and, perhaps, 60% of all blacks believe he is innocent and that he was framed. The difference in perception is still **not racially motivated.** It only appears that way!

If you analyzed the white group (or any group of people) separately – by **testing them, objectively, with respect to their level of knowledge about the Simpson case**, as well as their interest level in terms of wanting to learn as much as possible about the case – I am confident that you would find that the less people know about the case – really know about it – and the less interested they are in getting to know everything there is to know about the case – the more likely they are to believe that O.J. is guilty.

What also, really, determines people's perceptions of the Simpson case, are their **life experiences** and backgrounds. When most blacks believe O.J. is innocent, it is not because **O.J.** is black and **they** are black. Rather it is because most blacks have **experienced** – personally, or through some close relative or friend – Mark Fuhrman's kind of racism and police misconduct, which created the Simpson case.

Therefore, 60% of all blacks understand and recognize that there are people as demented as Detective Mark Fuhrman – who would love to *"gather all blacks and burn them to death in one big fire"*! Not too long ago there were millions of such people in the South. Therefore, blacks understand that a man like Detective Fuhrman, could conceivably have murdered Nicole and framed O.J.– not because of **their** racism, but because of **his**!

Most blacks, therefore, understand that the police – in spite of what they claim – indeed do, routinely, fabricate false evidence in order to frame black suspects. Blacks understand that the police routinely do lie, they do commit perjury, they do cover it up – even if their colleagues have committed murder!

And most blacks believe that the authorities, too, like DA's offices and judges, cover up to protect **their image** from the embarrassing truth.

Blacks believe this because they **know it** and have **experienced it**. Whites deny it because of **ignorance or embarrassment**, and because they have **not** experienced it.

Five hundred years ago, when Ferdinand Magellan first sailed around the world, proving that the world was not **flat**, after all – most pople did not believe him. Many thought he had just sailed down the coast of Africa and returned a year later.

Magellan knew he was right, and that the world is round, because he had **experienced it**! His opponents had **not** experienced what Magellan had experienced – so they doubted him and continued to claim that the earth were flat. They claimed Magellan lied! According to Magellan's adversaries – the authorities and many respected scholars of his time – **he could not have sailed east for a year** and returned from the **west,** because then he would have fallen off the end of the world!

It was the same with Christopher Columbus thirty years earlier. The authorities told Columbus that he was **"crazy"** if he believed he could sail **west** and reach India. They described for him how he would sail off the end of the world one dark night and fall right into the flames of hell.

So Columbus showed them a globus! He explained that the Earth was a sphere, so if he sailed in the same direction long enough, he would reach India – and eventually, if he continued west, return to where he came from . . . to which his adversaries brought up **a very good point**:

> Bartholomeu Diaz of Portugal had already sailed around the **southern tip of Africa**. If the Earth was a globe, then Diaz must have sailed upside down at some point. If so, he would have fallen off the earth!

Don't laugh! I think that was a very good point – **back in 1492**!

Diaz, Columbus and Magellan should have taught us that when **one** group of people **believe** something (like the framing of O.J., or the fact that the earth is a sphere) – **because they have experienced it**, while **another** group of people **disbelieve** it – because they have **not** experienced it – we should **believe the ones with the experience**!

If a police officer beats you up – you know the police is capable of doing that – or of planting evidence and framing people, or testi-lying, covering up, or whatever.

The fact that a **white** person across town has **never** been beaten up by the police, or experienced other forms of police misconduct, does not **dis-prove** the fact that the police do such things against our **black** citizens!

When blacks believe O.J. is innocent, they simply recognize what they **know exists** and what they **know happens**, because they have **experienced** it themselves, or know some close friend, neighbor, or relative who has experienced it. In spite of civil rights, human rights, and democracy, the slave ships aren't really that far away, after all.

Most whites have never experienced what blacks go through every day. They simply **don't understand** how the Simpson case could happen – the way blacks believe it happened. Actually – and it is frightening – **white people are starting to hail the neo-Nazi, Mark Fuhrman, as a "hero" today!**

But this is not really an expression of racism. It is merely an expression of **ignorance**! Just like many children have to burn themselves before they realize that the stove is dangerously hot – people have to experience racism and police corruption, too, before they realize that it exists.

Blacks experience that – every day – either personally, or through relatives, friends or neighbors. Whites don't – so whites simply don't believe it happens – in 1997!

Whites' experiences with the police is, frequently, the local, jovial officer who helps them recover their cat from the tree in their garden, or helps them recover their silverware after their house has been burglarized.

Blacks' experiences with the police, on the other hand, are, frequently, a brother being beaten up by five white police officers, or a black suspect being shot through a car window during a routine traffic stop – whereafter the police plant crack and a gun in the victim's car to justify the murder!

The difference in perception of the Simpson case, between blacks and whites is **not based on race – it is based on life experience.**

Take a predominantly **white** neighborhood, where crimes go hand in hand with police brutality, misconduct and corruption – and the police routinely harass and beat up young white men – and

I think you will find that these young white men's perception of the Simpson case is quite similar to that of blacks in general.

I am white! I am middle aged! I am fairly well educated! I am a former (military) police sergeant (MP). I should be right in the center of the **anti-O.J.** community.

> However, **I cannot sit back and keep my mouth shut about this case, just because most ordinary people have been brain washed by the media and don't understand what went on in this case!**

I don't expect to sell many copies of my book, because I doubt the media will promote it. Besides, most people don't **want** to read anything that contradicts their conviction of O.J. being guilty.

Instead, I actually hope some of the people I attack in my book, have the guts to sue me! Perhaps then, we who believe O.J. is innocent, will have a forum for raising the issues I bring up in this book.

My book may perhaps not change many people's opinions directly, since the ones who are likely to read it, are the ones who already know so much about the Simpson case that they are convinced he is innocent.

It is my hope, however, that the arguments, theories, and explanations I have presented in my book, will cause some of O.J.'s adversaries to stop and think before they again, uncritically, declare him a murderer.

I cannot count the number of times I have heard talk show hosts, reporters, and legal analysts on TV, proclaim:

> *"O.J.'s blood was found at the crime scene. That blood, at least, could not have been fabricated, because it was collected before the police received O.J.'s blood, and it did not contain EDTA!"*

So far, O.J.'s supporters have been stumped for answers, each time his critics proclaimed the above. It has become

"the argument to stop all arguments."

It seems to work – all the time. The five blood drops at Bundy, have become the favorite statement from all of O.J.'s adversaries. They fire it off – and then there is, sort of, nothing more to discuss.

Hopefully, my book has forever rebutted this argument. The blood drops at Bundy could very well have been fabricated, and there is **"an ocean of evidence" against Detective Vannatter** to suggest that they were!

Towards the end of the civil case another argument seemed to take over as equally powerful, namely **the photographs of O.J. wearing Bruno Magli shoes.** Hopefully, my book has explained how

Nicole must have been knocked unconscious and had **her neck pulled onto the tiled patio by the murderer, for the sole purpose of creating a puddle of blood from which he could create those bloody Bruno Magli shoeprints** – as well as all the other blood evidence – in order to frame O.J.

In other words, there is strong – even irrefutable – evidence that **the bloody Bruno Magli shoeprints were deliberately created. Only a murderer with a motive to frame O.J. could have done that.**

Hence, even if the media presented us with **one thousand photographs of O.J. wearing Bruno Magli shoes,** it would only underscore the fact that **the murderer knew what he was doing, when he set out to frame O.J. also with those bloody shoeprints.**

Actually, the more photographs the plaintiffs provided, depicting O.J. wearing Bruno Magli shoes – and in particular the photo which was **published eight months before the murders** – the more likely it appears, that also the murderer knew that leaving bloody Bruno Magli shoeprints at the murder scene, was a near perfect method of framing O.J. for the murders.

The purpose of my book is threefold:

1. I believe O.J. is innocent, beyond a shadow of a doubt. I wanted to prove it for O.J.'s sake, of course. But O.J. can handle the fate life dishes out for him! So, more importantly, I wanted to prove to **Sydney and Justin**, as well as to their friends, that **Sydney's and Justin's father is no murderer**!

2. Another objective was to give a reasonable explanation for **all** the evidence in the case – even the evidence nobody else has been able to explain.

3. My third and final objective was to come up with a comprehensive theory which could incorporate all the **facts**, all the significant **actions** of the various participants, and all the significant **evidence** – whether it be fabricated or not, and explain:

   – who might have murdered Nicole and Ron, since O.J. didn't
   – what the murderer's motives might have been, and
   – how the murderer might have carried out his vicious plan, in a manner consistent with all the bits and pieces of this murder mystery.

Although I may not have all the correct answers, either, I think my book meets these goals. It is anyone's prerogative to disagree with my theory about the Simpson murder mystery. But let me say to those who still think O.J. killed Nicole and Ron:

Just as I respect your right to disagree with me, and argue that O.J. is a murderer – you should respect those who sincerely believe O.J. is innocent, and who argue that he is the victim of a terrible injustice.

O.J. was found **not guilty**. Several people, besides myself, have proven – irrefutably and scientifically – that O.J. could not possibly have killed Nicole and Ron. Someone – the real murderer, and the investigators – tried to frame him.

Perhaps, because some are **unable to reason logically**, and instead are **governed by emotions**, they still believe O.J. murdered Nicole and Ron. They will never be able to prove it. And they should at least **consider** the **possibility** that he is innocent.

They should, therefore, try to put themselves in his place, and imagine what terrible injustice they are doing to him **– and to his children** – if they are wrong, and he indeed is innocent!

After having read my book, how can anyone even question O.J.'s innocence?

To the **plaintiffs** in the civil suit, I have this to say: A unanimous jury of whites, blacks and hispanics, of all ages, and of both genders found O.J. *"Not guilty."* Obviously, you, the plaintiffs, did not respect the jury's decision. So you sued O.J. for the wrongful death of Nicole and Ron.

A prejudiced judge, Hiroshi Fujisaki skewed the trial so terribly against O.J. that it was disgraceful to watch the way this judge made a mockery of the American justice system.

A prejudiced jury without a single black juror – incited by the biased media – found O.J. responsible for the deaths of Nicole and Ron, in spite of the overwhelming evidence that O.J. was framed – as my book clearly proves.

But if you, the plaintiffs, so obviously **did not respect** the court's decision and the jury's *"Not guilty"* verdict in the criminal trial, how could you take your case back to this same "justice" system, to be decided, again, by a prejudiced and unfair judge and jury – and **expect me to respect you?**

Is **your form of justice** a jury which are right, when they agree with you – but wrong when they disagree with you?

What kind of justice is that, which you advocate? What kind of democracy and what kind of society would we be living in if everyone acted like you do?

Is this the kind of respect for law and justice that you think our schools and parents should teach our children? Is that the kind of parents you were to Ron and Nicole? And is that the kind of parents you, the Browns, would have been to Sydney and Justin, had you prevailed in the custody case?

To the Goldman's: You repeatedly stated that **your law suit was not about money.** If so, you should have demonstrated that, by asking for **"symbolic"** damages in the amount of $1.00 (one dollar) only! If so, nobody would suspect **greed** to be part of your motive!

To the Brown's: You admitted that **your** law suit **was** about money! But you said you were suing O.J. on behalf of Nicole's and O.J.'s children, to secure the children's financial future.

If that was your motive, why did you run up legal expenses in the millions, and drain O.J.'s and his children's (and your own) financial resources with the civil suit?

By supporting your co-plaintiffs, the Goldmans, in their and your civil suits of O.J., thereby assisting the Goldmans in obtaining a verdict against O.J. – you were instrumental in securing that verdict against O.J., which may put 21 million dollars of O.J.'s – and his children's – present and future resources into the pockets of the Goldmans!

Those 21 million dollars would otherwise have gone to secure your grandchildren's future – Sydney's and Justin's health, education and security. How can you then claim that you sued O.J. on behalf of Sydney and Justin – to secure **their** financial future?

What you have done is to rob O.J.'s children of 21 million dollars! Are you sure you sued O.J. to try to secure **Sydney's and Justin's** financial future – and not **your own**?

By the time this tragedy is over, you have with your actions made certain that there won't be any money left over for the children – regardless of who prevails in this outrageous, and totally misguided vendetta you were pursuing against the father of your grandchildren!

There is no doubt in my mind that Sydney and Justin are wholeheartedly convinced that their father could not possibly have murdered their mother. As Sydney and Justin grow older and understand better what went on in this case – and the more you try to convince them otherwise – the more they will begin to disrespect you – and, perhaps, later, despise you.

Do you believe that Sidney and Justin could ever have felt comfortable growing up in the home of people whom they believe wrongfully held their father responsible for having killed their own mother, and branded him a murderer?

How could anyone, including yourself, suggest that you should be granted custody of Sydney and Justin?

Continuing to appeal the family court's decision to grant custody of Sydney and Justin to their father, whom they expressively wanted to live with, is an attempt to commit **"legal kidnapping"** of O.J.'s children, just like you and your co-plaintiffs, Judge Fujisaki, the civil jury, and the media committed a **"legal lynching"** of O.J. himself.

I hope the evidence I have presented in this book will convince the appellate court to overturn the verdict in the civil trial – and, if so, discourage the plaintiffs from ever suing O.J. again. However, I am realistic enough to realize that the appellate court may be reluctant to send the Simpson case back to court for a third – or actually a fourth – round.

Even O.J.'s fiercest critics among the legal analysts on TV – many of them judges, prosecutors, and lawyers – agreed that Judge Fujisaki made several horrendous rulings which– **normally** – would warrant the verdict to be overturned on appeal. But they all suspected that the appellate court would not dare to overturn the verdict in the civil trial, because, although the verdict is **judicially** incorrect – it is also **politically** incorrect, to overturn it. And California appellate court judges are political figures.

If the appellate court judges don't overturn the verdict in the civil case, they will probably hide behind what they call "harmless error." In short, "harmless error" means that the appellate court can disregard an otherwise reversible error, or even several reversible errors, made by Judge Fujisaki, if they concur that there were so much other evidence against O.J. that the reversible errors would not have changed the jury's verdict anyway.

The above mentioned legal analysts most frequently mention the DNA results that link O.J.'s blood to the murder scene with a probability of 170 million to 1, and the Bruno Magli shoeprints.

You have read my theory about Mark Fuhrman being the murderer, and why the murderer, so obviously, must be a police officer; the overwhelming evidence proving that Detective Vannatter fabricated most of the blood evidence against O.J.; how easy it was for Vannatter to circumvent the EDTA in O.J.'s blood vial; and how the bloody shoeprints must, obviously, have been purposely fabricated.

Judge Fujisaki, ruled that the defense were not allowed to argue that the police planted evidence against O.J. The judge ruled that the defense were not allowed to argue that Detective Vannatter could have fabricated false blood evidence against O.J. Therfore, the defense were not given the opportunity to argue, or explain, **how** Vannatter could have circumvented the EDTA in O.J.'s blood vial. Hence, the defense were precluded from attacking the *"170 million to 1"* argument. (This just mentioned as an example).

The judge ruled that the defense were not allowed to subpoena Mark Fuhrman as a witness, unless they could prove that he planted evidence!

How could the defense prove that Mark Fuhrman planted the Rockingham glove, if they weren't even allowed to call him as a witness, or present his taped testimony from the criminal trial and/ or play *"The Fuhrman Tapes"*?

And who is Judge Fujisaki to say that if Fuhrman's testimony from the criminal trial had been admitted, the defense would not have been able to expose Fuhrman's false alibi, presented under oath and vouched for by the lead prosecutor, Marcia Clark?!

Can the appellate court predict how this serious – additional – case of perjury by Detective Fuhrman, might have effected the continuation of the civil trial and the jury's verdict?

How can an appellate court judge predict how a responsible

juror might have voted, had all of this evidence been admitted – as it should have been?

In addition, Judge Fujisaki made several other horrendous rulings, such as allowing the plaintiffs to introduce the extremely damaging allegation of O.J. supposedly having taken, and failed a polygraph test; admitting hearsay evidence, "state of mind" evidence, and so-called "diary evidence," that should never have been admitted.

Just as the trial ended, a major investigation of the FBI's crime lab, by the Justice Department's Inspector General, disclosed that the criminalists and scientists at the FBI's crime lab, who analyzed and prepared much of the physical evidence against O.J., were highly incompetent and biased against defendants, and that the FBI's criminalists frequently skewed their test results and their testimonies in favor of the prosecution.

In particular, some of the central FBI criminalists and witnesses who testified against O.J. in the criminal trial, as well as in the civil trial, were singled out in the Inspector General's report.

Besides, Judge Fujisaki skewed the jury selection process so terribly, that O.J. eventually ended up with a **"jury of his peers"** – **without a single African-American juror!**

In addition, one juror had lied on her juror questionnaire, positively denying that her daughter worked for the Los Angeles DA's office as personal secretary for one of the district attorneys who had prosecuted O.J. in the criminal trial! It is unthinkable that the DA's office, which worked closely with, and assisted, the plaintiffs in the civil trial, did not know about this juror's close ties to the Los Angeles DA's office.

The U.S. Supreme Court has ruled that a reversible error in **jury selection** can never be deemed a so-called "harmless error."

There is, in other words, no way an unbiased appellate court judge can honestly deny O.J.'s appeal.

Still, most legal analysts predicted that the California appellate court judges would deny O.J.'s appeals – simply based on what best suits their own, personal political futures and careers.

If so, they will prove to the world that O.J., in the civil

process, did not get a fair trial. If so, that would forever remain a dark and smelly stain on the records of the California Justice system, and never bring **"closure to the Simpson case."**

Of course, as I write this, I do not know what decision the appellate court will reach. Hopefully it will overturn the verdict in the civil trial. If so, my respect to them for having the courage to do the right thing in spite of strong pressure from the opinion to "whitewash" obviously incorrect decisions by a biased civil court judge.

What is ahead for O.J? And what is ahead for the plaintiffs? I hope O.J. finds a legal way to avoid the damages the civil jury awarded the plaintiffs. The appeals process itself may take many years. The process will cost O.J. But it will also cost the plaintiffs. I hope, in the meantime, that they will not receive a penny of the money the jury awarded them.

By the time the appeals process has been brought to an end, I assume O.J. will have found a way to avoid paying the plaintiffs anything. Another possible scenario is that he does succeed in his appeals, and the verdict is overturned.

If that should happen, it is questionable whether the plaintiffs are willing to engage in another legal battle – realizing that even if they win again, they, most likely, won't ever see a penny of any money the jury might award them.

I am convinced that O.J. is innocent. The overwhelming evidence I have presented in this book, proves that – beyond any doubt whatsoever. Consequently, I feel little, besides disdain, for the plaintiffs' vicious and wrongful persecution an innocent man, branding him a murderer and trying to steel from him both his hard earn assets and his children who love their father, and need him, more than anyone else, at this time in their lives.

Perhaps, therefore, it is **"a just irony"** that the damages awarded the plaintiffs in this travesty of justice, are likely to cause more harm to the plaintiffs than to O.J. How is that possible?

Well, O.J. displays every sign of being **calm, collected, and at peace with himself** throughout this ordeal. He seems to go on with his life. He knows he is innocent. **He knows that millions of**

people who have bothered to really study this murder case, agree that he could not have killed Nicole and Ron. But he also realizes that millions of other, misguided people, believe he is a murderer. There is nothing he can do about that. So he isn't even trying!

It doesn't effect O.J. any longer that Geraldo Rivera, Charles Grodin, Larry King, Mr. Petrocelli, Fred Goldman, the Brown family, and millions of others believe he killed Nicole and Ron – as long as O.J. in his heart knows that he didn't do it. O.J. does not care what Geraldo Rivera thinks! What is far more important to O.J., is that he knows – that God knows, Nicole knows, and his children know – that he is not a murderer!

Therefore, I think O.J. is at peace with himself, in a way. His finances are in fairly good order. He has been conscientious enough, through the years, to set aside much of his earnings in pension funds – intended to provide his family with financial security, should he someday not be there for them. He can provide well for his children and they and O.J. can live handsomely off those funds. The plaintiffs can never touch his pension funds.

Possibly, if O.J. starts to withdraw money from the pension funds, the Goldmans can step in and intercept 25% of whatever O.J. withdraws.

However, these pension funds were probably established by O.J. for the future welfare and security of his children. I don't know the law well enough to state the following with any certainty. But I would suggest that O.J. could gradually transfer portions of these pension funds to his children, for whom they were intended. Sydney and Justin, certainly, have not done anything wrong, so perhaps they, instead of O.J., could withdraw from these funds, as need be – and even "support" their father – without the Goldmans being able to intercept any of it.

I assume portions of the funds, at least, could be legally transferred to O.J.'s children, for whom, I assume, these funds were established in the first place! Perhaps, that is why the Browns still contest the family court's decision to grant O.J. custody of his children?

With such a travesty of a verdict which the jury came up with in the civil trial – why should O.J. go out of his way to earn money into the pockets of the plaintiffs? What I would suggest is that he and his children live comfortably off the pension funds, and that whatever work O.J. does in the future, he does it as unpaid, promotional and charity work for those companies and institutions which demonstrate that they believe in his innocence.

I would also suggest that O.J. bring his children with him and take up residency in a foreign country which does not recognize U.S. court decisions, for as much as it pertains to civil suits of the kind O.J. was subjected to.

Perhaps then, he can continue to work, wherever he wants to, but have as part of any contract he enters into, that his future earnings be paid to his bank account in such a foreign country. Or better still, perhaps – whatever work O.J. do in the future, he makes it part of any work agreement or contract, that his salary or fee shall be paid to **a foundation for his children**. That should do it!

There is nothing worse for people **obsessed with money**, than to have millions of it – **but only on paper** – and for ever being unable to access that money! **Actually, it can drive some people crazy!**

For those reasons I think the plaintiffs' totally unjust persecution of O.J., and the equally unjust verdict, may turn into a **curse** that could come back and haunt the plaintiffs.

I don't want that to happen. I sympathize with O.J. But **I also empathize with the plaintiffs who lost their children**. I strongly disagreed with their decision to sue O.J. But I don't wish anything bad to happen to anyone. That is the reason I warn the plaintiffs that if they don't let go of their vengeance, and free themselves of their hatred towards O.J. – they may be hurting themselves more than they understand today.

I don't expect the plaintiffs to take **my** word for this. But someone they trust, someone who cares about them, should explain to them, what I am trying to warn them about.

Rather than pursuing a pot of gold they can never lay their hands on, and which, therefore, may only frustrate them,

I suggest, in their own best interest, that they do as follows:

- The Goldmans should declare the verdict in the civil trial a moral victory. (Although I don't see it as such).
- They should proclaim that their civil suit was never about money – only about finding O.J. responsible for the murder of Ron and Nicole. Nor would they want to take anything away from Sidney and Justin, who are, unquestionably, the two victims most hurt by this tragedy.
- To prove their good intentions the Goldmans should, therefore, declare, that they forego all the damages they were awarded by the civil jury.

  With a book deal worth nearly half a million dollar, I think they have made more than enough money off Ron's and Nicole's deaths already!

If the Goldmans do what I have suggested, they could forever claim the civil verdict a victory, and feel that they got some sort of "closure" – because that would be the end of this case.

However, if they continue to persecute O.J., and pursue some imaginary 21 million dollars – of which they may never see as much as a snippet, there will never be any closure for the Goldmans – only expenses, disappointments, headaches and heartaches!

And when the Goldmans or their attorneys, accompanied by a sheriff's deputy, enters Sydney's and Justin's home and begin to remove their father's memorabilia, the furniture, or the pictures from the walls – I believe they will lose far more than what they hope to gain! In their own tragedy they seem to forget that there are two other victims here, who rarely make the headlines. Should Sydney and Justin suddenly become victims – **also of the Goldmans** – public opinions could shift overnight. Our country is fiercely protective of, and concerned with the safety, security, and welfare of, our children. The Goldmans should keep that in mind!

It is rather interesting to compare the manner in which Bill Cosby dealt with the loss of his son (almost the same age as

Fred Goldman's son, Ron). Mr. Cosby, I am sure felt the senseless loss of his son to a random murderer just as deeply and tragically as Fred Goldman felt the loss of his son. Yet, as tragic as the loss of his son was, Mr. Cosby was back at work two weeks later, telling the American people that *"life must go on"*!

Mr. Cosby even had the strength and decency to call up another parent, a mother who had lost her child to a senseless murderer the same day that Mr. Cosby's son was killed. The day after his own son was murdered, Mr. Cosby **apologized** to the grieving mother, because the murder of **her** child was not given the media attention that was given to **Mr. Cosby's family** and his murdered son! That shows compassion. And we haven't heard Mr. Cosby utter one single word about the guilt or innocence of the man accused of murdering Bill Cosby's son..

Reconciliation is always a better healer than hate and vengeance! Considering the positive effect a reconciliation, undoubtedly, would have on Sydney's and Justin's future, I hope the Browns and the Goldman's – as well as the rest of the nation – will come to their senses.

I thank my readers for sharing their time with me. If anyone of you would like to send me your comments on the Simpson case or on my book – by fax or E-mail – I appreciate that – even if you disagree with me and didn't like my book.

My address is:

Christopher Springer
c/o Springer USA, Inc.
Las Vegas, NV 89128
Fax #: 702– 360–4240
E–mail: ChrSprngr@aol.com